AMERICAN FOREIGN RELATIONS 1971

A DOCUMENTARY RECORD

COUNCIL ON FOREIGN RELATIONS BOOKS

Founded in 1921, the Council on Foreign Relations, Inc. is a non-profit and non-partisan organization of individuals devoted to the promotion of a better and wider understanding of international affairs through the free interchange of ideas. The membership of the Council, which numbers about 1,600, is made up of men and women throughout the United States elected by the Board of Directors on the basis of an estimate of their special interest, experience and involvement in international affairs and their standing in their own communities. The Council does not take any position on questions of foreign policy, and no person is authorized to speak for the Council on such matters. The Council has no affiliation with and receives no funding from any part of the United States government.

The Council conducts a meetings program to provide its members an opportunity to talk with invited guests who have special experience, expertise or involvement in international affairs, and conducts a studies program of research directed to political, economic and strategic problems related to United States foreign policy. Since 1922 the Council has published the quarterly journal, *Foreign Affairs*. From time to time the Council also publishes books and monographs which in the judgment of the Committee on Studies of the Council's Board of Directors are responsible treatments of significant international topics worthy of presentation to the public. The individual authors of articles in *Foreign Affairs* and of Council books and monographs are solely responsible for all statements of fact and expressions of opinion contained in them.

AMERICAN FOREIGN RELATIONS
1971
A DOCUMENTARY RECORD

Continuing the Series
DOCUMENTS ON AMERICAN FOREIGN RELATIONS

Edited by RICHARD P. STEBBINS
and ELAINE P. ADAM

A Council on Foreign Relations Book
Published by
New York University Press ● *New York* ● *1976*

PREFACE

This volume presents a documentary record of American foreign relations during 1971, a year of growing détente with the Communist powers and accelerating disengagement in Southeast Asia, but also of continuing tension in the Middle East, a war in the Asian Subcontinent, and an unprecedented upheaval in international monetary affairs. In the tradition of the *Documents on American Foreign Relations* series, initiated by the World Peace Foundation in 1939 and carried forward since 1952 by the Council on Foreign Relations, the volume also seeks to fill the gap created by the discontinuance after 1967 of the official Department of State series, *American Foreign Policy: Current Documents*. In addition, the present publication incorporates much of the background information and critical commentary provided hitherto in the annual volumes of *The United States in World Affairs*, the parallel Council on Foreign Relations series inaugurated in 1931.

As in earlier volumes, the present collection features documents of official American origin but includes material from other sources whenever relevant to the broad purposes of the series. Questions directly involving the United States have been treated in greatest detail; for other matters it has frequently appeared sufficient to indicate the essentials of the American position as set forth by qualified spokesmen. Documents have been selected solely on the basis of relevance, and the inclusion of a given document signifies neither approval nor disapproval of its contents. Editorial treatment has been limited mainly to the correction of obvious stenographic and typographical errors, the insertion within square brackets of needed supplementary details, and the elucidation of any remaining obscurities by means of explanatory footnotes. Sources referred to by abbreviated titles are fully identified in the Appendix, which lists the publications found most useful in the preparation of the volume.

Most users of this collection will be aware of the additional enlightenment to be derived from the perusal of the annual foreign policy reports made public by President Nixon and Secretary of State Rogers for the period from 1969 until early 1973. Cited in the present volume as "Nixon Report" and "Rogers Report," these documents provide a wealth of accurate and detailed information and can be unreservedly recommended to any reader endowed with normal critical faculties. Also valuable, for its "inside" knowledge as well as its freedom from official bias, is the account of some central aspects of Nixon-era diplomacy presented by Marvin and Bernard Kalb in their 1974 volume, *Kissinger*.

The editors wish to note their special indebtedness to Grace Darling Griffin, Publications Promotion Director, and Robert W. Valkenier, Editor, of the Council on Foreign Relations; and to Donald Wasson, Librarian, Janet Rigney, Assistant Librarian, Janis Kreslins, and others of the Council's excellent library staff. They are likewise indebted to the press and public relations offices of the Department of State, the United Nations, and various foreign embassies which have made their published materials available, and to *The New York Times* for permission to reprint texts or excerpts of material from its pages. The editors themselves are responsible for the choice of documents, for the manner in which they are presented, and for the form and content of the editorial commentaries and other editorial matter.

R.P.S.
E.P.A.

CONTENTS

I. WORLD AFFAIRS
THROUGH AMERICAN EYES   1

A. **Essentials of World Policy**   3

   (1) United States Foreign Policy for the 1970's—Building
for Peace: Radio Address by President Richard M.
Nixon on Transmitting His Annual Foreign Affairs Report to the Congress, February 25, 1971 (Complete
Text)   3

B. **National Security Policy**   12

   (2) United States National Security Policies: Posture Statement Presented by Secretary of Defense Melvin R. Laird
to the House Committee on Armed Services, March 9,
1971 (Excerpt)   12

C. **Government Organization for the Conduct of Foreign
Affairs**   19

   (3) The National Security Council System: Excerpt from
President Nixon's Second Annual Report to the Congress on United States Foreign Policy, February 25,
1971   19

   (4) Reorganization of the Department of State: Announcement by Secretary of State William P. Rogers, July 6,
1971 (Complete Text)   22

   (5) Establishment of the Council on International
Economic Policy: White House Announcement, January
19, 1971 (Complete Text)   25

D. **War Powers of the President**   26

   (6) The Zablocki Resolution Before the House of Representatives   27
      (a) Concerning the War Powers of the President and
Congress: Report of the Committee, on Foreign
Affairs of the House of Representatives, July 27,
1971 (Excerpt)   28

(b) Joint Resolution Concerning the War Powers of the Congress and the President, Passed by the House of Representatives August 2, 1971 (Complete Text)   30

(7) The Javits Bill Before the Senate   32
(a) Statement by Senator Jacob K. Javits to the Senate, February 10, 1971 (Excerpts)   32
(b) A Bill to Make Rules Respecting Military Hostilities in the Absence of a Declaration of War, Introduced February 10, 1971 (Complete Text)   34

(8) Congress, the President, and the War Powers: Statement by Secretary of State Rogers Before the Senate Committee on Foreign Relations, May 14, 1971 (Excerpts)   35

E. Current Progress and Problems   41

(9) America's Position in the World: Remarks by President Nixon to News Media Executives Attending a Background Briefing on Domestic Policy Initiatives, Kansas City, Missouri, July 6, 1971 (Complete Text)   41

(10) Accomplishments and Disappointments in 1971: News Conference Statement by Secretary of State Rogers, December 23, 1971 (Excerpts)   53

II. ARMS CONTROL
AND U.S.-SOVIET RELATIONS   59

A. Fundamentals of United States-Soviet Relations   60

(11) The Soviet Union: President Nixon's Second Annual Report to the Congress on United States Foreign Policy, Transmitted February 25, 1971 (Excerpt)   60

B. Progress in Multilateral Arms Control   65

1. Achievements and Current Agenda   66
(12) Work of the Conference of the Committee on Disarmament (CCD): Message from President Nixon to the Conference, February 23, 1971 (Complete Text)   67

2. The Seabed Arms Control Treaty   69
(13) Signature of the Treaty in Washington, February 11, 1971   69

(a) Remarks by Secretary of State Rogers (Complete Text)   69

(b) Remarks by President Nixon (Complete Text)   70

(14) Request for Advice and Consent to Ratification: Message from President Nixon to the Senate, July 21, 1971 (Complete Text)   71

3. **The Geneva Protocol of 1925**   72

(15) Importance of United States Ratification: Statement by Secretary of State Rogers Before the Senate Committee on Foreign Relations, March 5, 1971 (Complete Text)   74

(16) Senatorial Reservations: Letter from Senator J. William Fulbright, Chairman of the Committee on Foreign Relations, to President Nixon, April 15, 1971 (Complete Text)   80

4. **Prohibition of Bacteriological (Biological) Weapons**   83

(17) Completion of the Draft Convention: Statement by George H. Bush, United States Representative to the United Nations, to the First (Political and Security) Committee of the General Assembly, November 11, 1971 (Excerpt)   84

(18) Commendation of the Draft Convention: United Nations General Assembly Resolution 2826 (XXVI), Adopted December 16, 1971 (Complete Text)   88

(19) Convention on the Prohibition of the Development, Production and Stockpiling of Bacteriological (Biological) and Toxin Weapons and on Their Destruction: Annex to United Nations General Assembly Resolution 2826 (XXVI) of December 16, 1971 (Complete Text)   90

5. **Unresolved Disarmament Questions**   95

(20) The Disarmament Agenda: Continuation of the Statement by Ambassador Bush to the First Committee of the General Assembly, November 11, 1971 (Excerpt)   96

C. **The Strategic Arms Limitation Talks (SALT)**   101

1. **Fourth Session of United States-Soviet Talks, Vienna, March 15-May 28, 1971**   102

(21) Breaking the Deadlock: Radio-Television Statement by President Nixon, May 20, 1971 (Complete Text)   103

(22) United States-Soviet Communiqué, Vienna, May 28, 1971 (Complete Text) 104

2. Fifth Session of United States-Soviet Talks, Helsinki, July 8-September 24, 1971 **105**

(23) United States-Soviet Communiqué, Helsinki, September 24, 1971 (Complete Text) 105

(24) The Immediate Outlook: Comments by President Nixon at a Briefing for Media Executives in Portland, Oregon, September 25, 1971 (Excerpt) 106

3. Sixth Session of United States-Soviet Talks, Vienna, November 15, 1971-February 4, 1972 **108**

(25) Prospects for Agreement: News Conference Statement by President Nixon, November 12, 1971 (Excerpt) 108

D. United States-Soviet Agreements to Reduce Risk of Nuclear War, September 30, 1971 **109**

(26) A Dividend from SALT: White House Announcement, September 24, 1971 (Complete Text) 109

(27) Agreement on Measures to Reduce the Risk of Outbreak of Nuclear War Between the United States of America and the Union of Soviet Socialist Republics, Signed in Washington September 30, 1971 (Complete Text) 110

(28) Agreement Between the United States of America and the Union of Soviet Socialist Republics on Measures to Improve the U.S.A.-U.S.S.R. Direct Communications Link, Signed in Washington September 30, 1971 (Excerpt) 113

E. President Nixon's Projected Visit to the U.S.S.R. **115**

(29) Announcement of the Visit: President Nixon's News Conference, October 12, 1971 (Excerpts) 115

(30) Implications of the War in the Subcontinent: News Conference Statement by Secretary of State Rogers, December 23, 1971 (Excerpt) 122

F. The Status of Jews in the Soviet Union **124**

(31) Support of Congressional Resolution on Soviet Jewry: Statement by Richard T. Davies, Deputy Assistant Secretary of State for European Affairs, Before the Sub-

committee on Europe of the House Committee on Foreign Affairs, November 9, 1971 (Excerpts)   125

III. THE ATLANTIC ALLIANCE AND DÉTENTE IN EUROPE   135

A. The Issues   136

(32) "The United States, Our NATO Allies, and the Soviet Union in an Era of Changing Foreign Relations": Address by U. Alexis Johnson, Under Secretary of State for Political Affairs, Before the Seventeenth Annual Conference of the Cincinnati World Affairs Council, Cincinnati, Ohio, February 19, 1971 (Complete Text)   137

B. Reduction of Forces in Europe: Mutual or Unilateral?   148

   1. Defeat of the Mansfield Amendment   150

(33) Address by Senator Mike Mansfield to the Senate, with Proposed Amendment, May 11, 1971 (Excerpts)   150

(34) Statement by President Nixon, Issued at Key Biscayne, Florida, May 15, 1971 (Complete Text)   154

   2. Proposals for Mutual and Balanced Force Reduction (M.B.F.R.)   155

(35) United States-Soviet Contacts: Statement by Charles W. Bray III, Director, Office of Press Relations, Department of State, May 17, 1971 (Complete Text)   155

C. The Position of NATO   155

(36) Communiqué of the NATO Defense Planning Committee, Brussels, May 28, 1971 (Complete Text)   156

(37) Ministerial Session of the North Atlantic Council, Lisbon, June 3-4, 1971: Final Communiqué (Complete Text)   158

D. Quadripartite Agreement on Berlin, Signed in Berlin September 3, 1971   162

(38) Statement by Secretary of State Rogers, Washington, September 3, 1971 (Complete Text)   164

(39) Quadripartite Agreement on Berlin Between the United States of America and Other Governments, Signed at

Berlin September 3, 1971 (Excerpt)   166

**E. Further Discussion of Force Reduction, October-November
      1971**   **170**

  (40) High-level Meeting of the North Atlantic Council, Brus-
        sels, October 5-6, 1971: Statement by NATO Secre-
        tary-General J.M.A.H. Luns (Complete Text)   170

  (41) Mansfield Amendment to the Department of Defense
        Appropriation Bill   172
        (a) Report of the Senate Committee on Appropria-
            tions, November 18, 1971 (Excerpt)   172
        (b) Letter from President Nixon to Senator John C.
            Stennis, Chairman of the Senate Committee on
            Armed Services, November 23, 1971 (Complete
            Text)   172

**F. Force Reduction and European Security Before the North
      Atlantic Council, December 1971**   **173**

  (42) Ministerial Session of the North Atlantic Council, Brus-
        sels, December 9-10, 1971: Final Communiqué (Com-
        plete Text)   174

G. Presidential Meetings With Allied Leaders, December 1971 **180**

  (43) Meeting with President Georges Pompidou of France in
        the Azores, December 13-14, 1971: Joint Statement
        (Complete Text)   181

  (44) Meeting with Prime Minister Edward Heath of the
        United Kingdom in Bermuda, December 20-21, 1971:
        Joint Statement (Complete Text)   182

  (45) Meeting with Chancellor Willy Brandt of the Federal
        Republic of Germany, Key Biscayne, Florida, December
        28-29, 1971: Joint Statement (Complete Text)   183

H. Relations with Greece and Portugal   **184**

  1. Greece   **184**
  (46) United States Policy Toward Greece: Statement by
        Rodger P. Davies, Deputy Assistant Secretary of State
        for Near Eastern and South Asian Affairs, Before the
        Subcommittee on Europe of the House Committee on
        Foreign Affairs, July 12, 1971 (Complete Text)   184

   2. **Portugal**   **188**
  (47) Agreements with Portugal: Department of State An-
        nouncement, December 9, 1971 (Complete Text)   188

              IV. AMERICAN POLICY IN ASIA:
         THE MIDDLE EAST AND SOUTHERN ASIA   **191**

A. **The Arab-Israeli Conflict**   **192**

   1. **Implementation of Security Council Resolution 242
        (1967)**   **192**
  (48) Report on the Jarring Mission: Communications from
        the Secretary-General of the United Nations to the
        Security Council, February-March 1971   194
        (a) Report Dated February 1, 1971 (Complete Text)   194
        (b) Report Dated March 5, 1971 (Complete Text)   195

  (49) The Position of the United States: News Conference
        Statement by Secretary of State Rogers, March 16,
        1971 (Excerpts)   199

   2. **Search for an Interim Agreement on the Suez Canal,
        February-August 1971**   **203**
  (50) News Conference Statement by Secretary Rogers on
        Completion of his Middle East Trip, Rome, May 8,
        1971 (Excerpts)   204

  (51) Statement by Joseph J. Sisco, Assistant Secretary of
        State for Near Eastern and South Asian Affairs, Tel
        Aviv, August 5, 1971 (Complete Text)   207

  (52) Address by Secretary of State Rogers to the United
        Nations General Assembly, October 4, 1971 (Excerpt)   208

   3. **The Status of Jerusalem**   **211**
  (53) Action in the United Nations Security Council, Septem-
        ber 25, 1971   212
        (a) Security Council Resolution 298 (1971), Adopted
             September 25, 1971 (Complete Text)   212
        (b) Statement by Ambassador Bush to the Security
             Council, September 25, 1971 (Complete Text)   213

   4. **Reactivation of the Jarring Mission**   **215**
  (54) Action by the General Assembly, December 13, 1971   216
        (a) Call for a Resumption of Negotiations: Statement
             by Ambassador Bush to the General Assembly,
             December 13, 1971 (Complete Text)   216

(b) Shortcomings of the Pending Resolution: Statement by Ambassador Christopher H Phillips, Deputy United States Representative, to the General Assembly, December 13, 1971 (Complete Text)   218
(c) "The Situation in the Middle East": General Assembly Resolution 2799 (XXVI), Adopted December 13, 1971 (Complete Text)   220

B. The Central Treaty Organization (CENTO)   222

(55) Eighteenth Session of the CENTO Council of Ministers, Ankara, April 30-May 1, 1971: Final Communiqué (Complete Text)   222

C. The Indo-Pakistan Conflict Before the United Nations, October-December 1971   224

1. Origins of the Crisis   225
(56) Conditions in South Asia: Address by Secretary of State Rogers to the General Assembly, October 4, 1971 (Excerpt)   226

2. Action in the Security Council, December 4-6, 1971   227
(57) Request for a Security Council Meeting: Statement by Secretary of State Rogers, December 4, 1971 (Complete Text)   228

(58) Proposals to End Hostilities: Statement by Ambassador Bush to the Security Council, December 4, 1971, with United States Draft Resolution Vetoed by the U.S.S.R. December 5, 1971 (Complete Text)   229

(59) Referral to the General Assembly   233
(a) Statement by Ambassador Bush to the Security Council, December 6, 1971 (Excerpt)   233
(b) Security Council Resolution 303 (1971), Adopted December 6, 1971 (Complete Text)   235

3. Action in the General Assembly, December 7, 1971   235
(60) Urgency of a Cease-fire: Statement by Ambassador Bush to the General Assembly, December 7, 1971 (Complete Text)   236

(61) Call for a Cease-fire and Withdrawal: General Assembly Resolution 2793 (XXVI), Adopted December 7, 1971 (Complete Text)   237

4. Action in the Security Council, December 12-21, 1971   239
(62) Renewed Call for a Cease-fire: Statement by Ambassa-

dor Bush to the Security Council, December 12, 1971, with Draft United States Resolution Vetoed by the U.S.S.R. December 13, 1971 (Complete Text)   240

(63) Demanding Observance of the Cease-fire: Security Council Resolution 307 (1971), Adopted December 21, 1971 (Complete Text)   246

  5. **Aftermath of the Conflict**   **247**
(64) Policy Toward India and Pakistan: News Conference Statement by Secretary of State Rogers, December 23, 1971 (Excerpt)   248

D. The Indian Ocean   **249**

(65) United States National Security Policy and the Indian Ocean: Statement by Ronald I. Spiers, Director, Bureau of Politico-Military Affairs, Department of State, Before the Subcommittee on National Security Policy and Scientific Developments of the House Committee on Foreign Affairs, July 28, 1971 (Complete Text)   250

(66) "Declaration of the Indian Ocean as a Zone of Peace": United Nations General Assembly Resolution 2832 (XXVI), Adopted December 16, 1971 (Complete Text)   257

**V. AMERICAN POLICY IN ASIA:
THE WAR IN INDOCHINA**   261

A. Military Operations in Laos   **263**

(67) South Vietnamese Attack on Enemy Sanctuaries in Laos: Statement by Robert J. McCloskey, Department of State Press Spokesman, February 8, 1971 (Complete Text)   265

(68) Significance of the Laos Incursion: News Conference Statement by President Nixon, February 17, 1971 (Excerpt)   267

(69) Air Operations and Refugees in Laos: Statement by William H. Sullivan, Deputy Assistant Secretary of State for East Asian and Pacific Affairs, Before the Subcommittee on Refugees and Escapees of the Senate Committee on the Judiciary, April 22, 1971 (Excerpts)   271

(70) Position on Foreign Forces in Laos: Department of State Statement, August 9, 1971 (Complete Text)   276

B. The Progress of "Vietnamization"   278

(71) Report on the Situation in Southeast Asia: Radio-
Television Address by President Nixon, April 7, 1971
(Complete Text)   279

(72) Need for a Residual Force in Vietnam: Statement by
President Nixon at a Panel Discussion at the Annual
Convention of the American Society of Newspaper
Editors, April 16, 1971 (Excerpt)   285

(73) Conference of Troop-contributing Nations, Washington,
April 23, 1971: Final Communiqué (Complete Text)   287

C. Peace Negotiations in Paris, May-November 1971   292

  1. **The Two-sided (Four-party) Talks**   292
(74) New "Vietcong" Peace Proposal, July 1, 1971   295
    (a) Seven-point Proposal Presented by the Representa-
tive of the Provisional Revolutionary Government
of the Republic of South Vietnam (P.R.G.) at a
Plenary Session on July 1, 1971 (Complete Text)   295
    (b) Comment by Ambassador David K.E. Bruce, Head
of the United States Delegation, at a Plenary
Session on July 8, 1971 (Complete Text)   298

  2. **Secret United States-North Vietnamese Contacts**   300
(75) Nine-point Proposal Presented by Representatives of the
Democratic Republic of Vietnam, June 26, 1971 (Com-
plete Text)   304

(76) Eight-point Proposal Transmitted by the United States
to the Representatives of the Democratic Republic of
Vietnam, October 11, 1971   306
    (a) Covering Note (Complete Text)   306
    (b) Text of the United States Proposal (Complete Text) 307

(77) Postponement of Further Private Meetings, October 25-
November 19, 1971   309
    (a) Democratic Republic of Vietnam Note, October 25,
1971 (Complete Text)   309
    (b) United States Note, November 3, 1971 (Complete
Text)   309
    (c) Democratic Republic of Vietnam Note, November
17, 1971 (Complete Text)   309
    (d) United States Note, November 19, 1971 (Complete
Text)   310

D. Political Developments in South Vietnam 311

(78) The South Vietnamese Presidential Election of October 3, 1971: News Conference Observations by President Nixon, September 16, 1971 (Excerpt) 312

E. Policy on Troop Withdrawals 315

(79) An Act to Amend the Military Selective Service Act of 1967: Public Law 92-129, Approved September 28, 1971 (Excerpt) 316

(80) Troop Withdrawals from Vietnam: News Conference Announcement by President Nixon, November 12, 1971 (Complete Text) 317

(81) The Military Procurement Authorization Act of 1971: Public Law 92-156, Approved November 17, 1971 318
    (a) Title VI of the Act: Termination of Hostilities in Indochina (Complete Text) 318
    (b) Statement by President Nixon on Signature of the Act, November 17, 1971 (Complete Text) 319

VI. AMERICAN POLICY IN ASIA: EAST ASIA AND THE PACIFIC 321

A. Progress Under the Nixon Doctrine 322

(82) "The Nixon Doctrine: A Progress Report": Address by Marshall Green, Assistant Secretary of State for East Asian and Pacific Affairs, Before the Far East-America Council, New York, January 19, 1971 (Complete Text) 323

B. SEATO and ANZUS 329

(83) Sixteenth Meeting of the Council of the South-East Asia Treaty Organization (SEATO), London, April 27-28, 1971: Final Communiqué (Complete Text) 330

(84) Twenty-first Meeting of the ANZUS Council, New York, October 2, 1971: Final Communiqué (Complete Text) 335

C. The People's Republic of China 337

1. "Breaking the Ice," March-June 1971   **338**

(85) United States Policy Toward China: News Conference Statements by President Nixon, March 4, 1971 (Excerpts)   339

(86) Easing of United States Passport Restrictions: Announcement by Charles W. Bray III, Department of State Press Officer, March 15, 1971 (Complete Text)   340

(87) Further Easing of Trade and Travel Restrictions: Statement by President Nixon, April 14, 1971 (Complete Text)   341

(88) Appraisal of Current Prospects: News Conference Statement by President Nixon, April 29, 1971 (Excerpts)   342

(89) A Further Appraisal: News Conference Statement by President Nixon, June 1, 1971 (Excerpt)   345

(90) Lifting of United States Trade Controls: Statement by Ronald L. Ziegler, Press Secretary to the President, June 10, 1971 (Complete Text)   346

2. President Nixon's Proposed Visit   **347**

(91) Announcement of the Proposed Visit: Radio-Television Statement by President Nixon, July 15, 1971 (Complete Text)   348

(92) Expectations for the Trip: News Conference Statements by President Nixon, August-September 1971   349
    (a) Statement of August 4, 1971 (Excerpt)   349
    (b) Statement of September 16, 1971 (Excerpt)   351

(93) Preparations for the Visit, October-November 1971   353
    (a) The Second Kissinger Mission: Announcement Issued Simultaneously in Washington and Peking, October 27, 1971 (Complete Text)   353
    (b) Fixing the Date: Joint Statement by the Two Governments, November 29, 1971 (Complete Text)   353
    (c) Some Further Details: Announcement by White House Press Secretary Ziegler, November 30, 1971 (Excerpt)   353

(94) Purpose of the Visit: News Conference Statement by Dr. Henry A. Kissinger, Assistant to the President for National Security Affairs, November 30, 1971 (Excerpt)   354

D. The United States and Japan   **356**

1. **The Okinawa Reversion Agreement**   357

(95) Agreement Between the United States of America and Japan Concerning the Ryukyu Islands and the Daito Islands, Signed at Washington and Tokyo June 17, 1971 (Excerpt)   358

(96) Request for Advice and Consent to Ratification: Message from President Nixon to the Senate, September 21, 1971 (Complete Text)   364

2. **A "New Era" in United States-Japanese Relations**   367

(97) "Trends in United States-Japan Relations": Address by U. Alexis Johnson, Under Secretary of State for Political Affairs, Before the International Business Outlook Conference, Los Angeles, October 18, 1971 (Complete Text)   368

E. **The United States and the Republic of Korea**   375

(98) Agreement on Troop Reduction and Modernizaton: Joint Statement Issued in Washington and Seoul, February 6, 1971 (Complete Text)   376

(99) Progress of the Republic of Korea: Statement by Assistant Secretary of State Green Before the House Committee on Foreign Affairs, May 4, 1971 (Excerpt)   377

(100) Postponement of Debate in the United Nations: Statement by Ambassador W. Tapley Bennett, Jr., Alternate United States Representative, to the General Assembly, September 25, 1971 (Complete Text)   378

VII. THE UNITED STATES AND AFRICA   379

A. **Basic Policy Considerations**   379

(101) "Africa": President Nixon's Second Annual Report to the Congress on United States Foreign Policy, February 25, 1971 (Excerpt)   380

(102) "A Look at African Issues at the United Nations": Address by David D. Newsom, Assistant Secretary of State for African Affairs, Before the Atlanta Press Club, Atlanta, September 21, 1971 (Complete Text)   386

B. **The Question of Namibia (South West Africa)**   394

(103) Namibia Before the International Court of Justice: Oral

Statement Presented Before the Court by John R. Stevenson, Legal Adviser of the Department of State, The Hague, March 9, 1971 (Excerpts) 396

(104) "Legal Consequences for States of the Continued Presence of South Africa in Namibia (South West Africa) Notwithstanding Security Council Resolution 276 (1970)": Advisory Opinion of the International Court of Justice, June 21, 1971 (Excerpt) 403

(105) Support of the Advisory Opinion: Statement to the United Nations Security Council by Ambassador Bennett, Deputy United States Representative, October 20, 1971 (Complete Text) 406

(106) Endorsement of the Advisory Opinion: Security Council Resolution 301 (1971), Adopted October 20, 1971 (Complete Text) 408

C. The Question of Southern Rhodesia 412

(107) The United States Position on Southern Rhodesia: Statement by Assistant Secretary of State Newsom Before the Subcommittee on Africa of the Senate Committee on Foreign Relations, July 7, 1971 (Complete Text) 416

(108) Congressional Abrogation of the Embargo on Imports of Rhodesian Chrome: The Byrd Amendment 424
(a) Chrome and the National Stockpile: Conference Report on the Military Procurement Authorization Bill, November 5, 1971 (Excerpt) 424
(b) The Military Procurement Authorization Act of 1971: Public Law 92-156, Approved November 17, 1971 (Excerpts) 426

(109) Reaction of the United Nations General Assembly 427
(a) Statement by Ambassador William E. Schaufele, Jr. to the Fourth Committee of the General Assembly (Trusteeship and Non-Self-Governing Territories), November 11, 1971 (Complete Text) 427
(b) "Question of Southern Rhodesia": General Assembly Resolution 2765 (XXVI), Adopted November 16, 1971 (Complete Text) 428

D. Defense of American Policy 429

(110) United States Policy Toward Africa: News Conference

Statement by Secretary of State Rogers, December 23, 1971 (Excerpt) 431

VIII. INTER-AMERICAN AFFAIRS 433

A. The Organization of American States (O.A.S.) 434

1. Third Special Session of the General Assembly, Washington, January 25-February 2, 1971 435

(111) Convention to Prevent and Punish the Acts of Terrorism Taking the Form of Crimes Against Persons and Related Extortion That Are of International Significance, Approved by the General Assembly of the Organization of American States on February 2, 1971 (Complete Text) 437

2. Fourteenth Meeting of Consultation of Ministers of Foreign Affairs, Washington, January 30-31, 1971 441

(112) Seizure by Ecuador of United States Fishing Vessels: Statement by Under Secretary of State John N. Irwin II to the Meeting of Foreign Ministers, January 30, 1971 (Complete Text) 443

3. First Regular Session of the General Assembly, San José, Costa Rica, April 14-24, 1971 447

(113) "A More Balanced and Reinvigorated Partnership of the Americas": Statement by Secretary of State Rogers to the General Assembly, April 15, 1971 (Complete Text) 447

B. Treaty for the Prohibition of Nuclear Weapons in Latin America (Treaty of Tlatelolco) of February 14, 1967 456

(114) Proclamation by President Nixon on Ratification of Additional Protocol II to the Treaty for the Prohibition of Nuclear Weapons in Latin America, June 11, 1971 (Complete Text) 459

C. Repercussions of the United States' "New Economic Policy" 462

(115) "United States Policy Toward Latin America: Where We Stand Today": Address by Charles A. Meyer, Assistant Secretary of State for Inter-American Affairs, Before the Inter American Press Association, Chicago, October 25, 1971 (Complete Text) 463

(116) Economic Cooperation with Latin America: News Con-

ference Statement by Secretary of State Rogers, December 23, 1971 (Excerpt)   472

D. Relations With Particular Countries   **473**

   1. Cuba   **474**
(117) United States Policy Toward Cuba: Statement by Robert A. Hurwitch, Deputy Assistant Secretary of State for Inter-American Affairs, Before the Senate Committee on Foreign Relations, September 16, 1971 (Complete Text)   474

   2. Chile   **481**
(118) United States Policy Toward Chile: Statement by Assistant Secretary of State Meyer Before the Subcommittee on Inter-American Affairs of the House Committee on Foreign Affairs, October 15, 1971 (Complete Text)   482

   3. Panama   **486**
(119) Panama Canal Treaty Negotiations: Statement by Ambassador John C. Mundt, Special Representative of the United States for Panama Treaty Negotiations, Before the Subcommittee on the Panama Canal of the House Committee on Merchant Marine and Fisheries, November 29, 1971 (Complete Text)   487

IX. THE UNITED NATIONS
AND INTERNATIONAL COOPERATION   **495**

A. Review of United Nations Affairs in 1971   **496**

(120) United States Participation in the United Nations, 1971: Message from President Nixon to the Congress Transmitting the 26th Annual Report on United Nations Participation, September 8, 1972 (Complete Text)   497

(121) "The Decline in Congressional Support for the United Nations": President Nixon's Third Annual Report to the Congress on United States Foreign Policy, February 9, 1972 (Excerpt)   499

B. The Representation of China in the United Nations   **500**

(122) The Position of the United States: Policy Statement by Secretary of State Rogers, August 2, 1971 (Complete Text)   504

(123) Draft Resolutions Before the General Assembly   506
    (a) The "Albanian" Resolution (Complete Text)   506
    (b) The "Important Question" Resolution (Complete Text)   507
    (c) The "Dual Representation" Resolution (Complete Text)   507

(124) Address by Secretary of State Rogers to the General Assembly, October 4, 1971 (Excerpt)   508

(125) "Restoration of the Lawful Rights of the People's Republic of China in the United Nations": General Assembly Resolution 2758 (XXVI), Adopted October 25, 1971 (Complete Text)   512

(126) Implications of the Assembly's Action: News Conference Statement by Secretary of State Rogers, October 26, 1971 (Excerpt)   512

(127) Seating of Delegates from the People's Republic of China: Statement by Ambassador Bush to the General Assembly, November 15, 1971 (Complete Text)   513

(128) United States Support for the United Nations: News Conference Statement by Secretary of State Rogers, December 1, 1971 (Excerpt)   514

C. United Nations Organization and Finances   515

    1. United Nations Financial Problems   515
(129) Abstention on the 1972 Budget: Statement by Congressman Edward J. Derwinski to the General Assembly, December 22, 1971 (Complete Text)   517

    2. Security of Missions to the United Nations   522
(130) Shooting Incident at the Soviet Mission: Statement by Ambassador Bush, October 21, 1971 (Complete Text)   523

(131) "Security of Missions Accredited to the United Nations and Safety of Their Personnel and Establishment of the Committee on Relations with the Host Country": General Assembly Resolution 2819 (XXVI), Adopted December 15, 1971 (Complete Text)   524

    3. Enlargement of the Economic and Social Council (ECOSOC)   526
(132) "Enlargement of the Economic and Social Council": General Assembly Resolution 2847 (XXVI), Adopted December 20, 1971 (Complete Text)   527

4. **Appointment of a New Secretary-General** **529**

(133) Recommendation of the Security Council: Security Council Resolution 306 (1971), Adopted at a Private Meeting on December 21, 1971 (Complete Text) 529

(134) "Appointment of the Secretary-General of the United Nations": General Assembly Resolution 2903 (XXVI), Adopted December 22, 1971 (Complete Text) 530

(135) Statement by Ambassador Bush to the General Assembly, December 22, 1971 (Complete Text) 530

D. New Dimensions of Diplomacy **531**

(136) "New Dimensions of Diplomacy": President Nixon's Third Annual Report to the Congress on United States Foreign Policy, February 9, 1972 (Excerpt) 532

(137) Draft Articles on the Territorial Sea, Straits, and Fisheries, Submitted by the United States to Subcommittee II of the United Nations Committee on the Peaceful Uses of the Sea-bed and the Ocean Floor Beyond the Limits of National Jurisdiction, Geneva, August 3, 1971 (Complete Text) 543

(138) Convention for the Suppression of Unlawful Acts Against the Safety of Civil Aircraft, Done at Montreal September 23, 1971 (Complete Text) 548

(139) Convention on International Liability for Damage Caused by Space Objects, Approved by the United Nations General Assembly November 29, 1971 (Complete Text) 555

(140) Agreement on Establishment of the International Telecommunications Satellite Organization "Intelsat": Department of State Announcement, August 18, 1971 (Complete Text) 564

X. INTERNATIONAL ECONOMIC AND FINANCIAL AFFAIRS **567**

A. The Organization for Economic Cooperation and Development (O.E.C.D.) **569**

(141) Tenth Meeting at Ministerial Level of the O.E.C.D. Council, Paris, June 7-8, 1971 569
(a) Opening Statement by Secretary of State Rogers,

June 7, 1971 (Complete Text)   569
   (b) Final Communiqué, June 8, 1971 (Complete Text)   573

B. The United States' "New Economic Policy"   576

(142) "The Challenge of Peace": Radio-Television Address by President Nixon Outlining a New Economic Policy for the United States, August 15, 1971 (Complete Text)   577

(143) Imposition of Supplemental Duty for Balance-of-Payments Purposes: Proclamation by the President, August 15, 1971 (Excerpts)   583

(144) Explanation to GATT: Statement by Nathaniel Samuels, Deputy Under Secretary of State for Economic Affairs, Before the Council of the General Agreement on Tariffs and Trade, Geneva, August 24, 1971 (Complete Text)   584

(145) International Aspects of the New Economic Program: News Conference Statement by President Nixon, September 16, 1971 (Excerpt)   590

C. The International Bank for Reconstruction and Development (I.B.R.D.) and the International Monetary Fund (I.M.F.)   591

(146) Remarks by President Nixon at a White House Reception for Officials Attending the Annual Meetings of the Boards of Governors of the International Monetary Fund and the International Bank for Reconstruction and Development, September 29, 1971 (Complete Text)   592

(147) Statement to the Annual Meeting of the Boards of Governors by Secretary of the Treasury John B. Connally, September 30, 1971 (Complete Text)   596

(148) Resolution on the International Monetary System, Adopted by the Board of Governors of the International Monetary Fund, October 1, 1971 (Complete Text)   603

D. The Azores Meeting and the Smithsonian Agreement   604

(149) Significance of the Nixon-Pompidou Agreement: Remarks by Secretary of the Treasury Connally, Andrews Air Force Base, Maryland, December 14, 1971 (Complete Text)   606

(150) Meeting of the "Group of Ten" at the Smithsonian Institution, Washington, December 17-18, 1971 ... 607
    (a) Final Communiqué, December 18, 1971 (Complete Text) ... 607
    (b) Remarks by President Nixon During an Informal Visit After the Meeting, December 18, 1971 (Complete Text) ... 609

(151) Termination of the Import Surcharge, December 20, 1971 ... 610
    (a) Termination of Additional Duty for Balance-of-Payments Purposes: Proclamation by the President, December 20, 1971 (Complete Text) ... 610
    (b) Remarks by the President in Bermuda, December 20, 1971 (Complete Text) ... 611

E. The International Wheat Agreement, 1971 ... **612**

(152) Message from President Nixon to the Senate Requesting Its Advice and Consent to Ratification, June 2, 1971 (Complete Text) ... 613

F. Foreign Aid and Economic Development ... **615**

(153) Proposals for Foreign Aid Reform: Message from President Nixon to the Congress, April 21, 1971 (Excerpts) ... 617

(154) Rejection of the Foreign Aid Bill by the Senate, October 29, 1971 ... 629
    (a) Views of President Nixon: Statement by White House Press Secretary Ziegler, October 30, 1971 (Complete Text) ... 629
    (b) News Conference Statement by Secretary of State Rogers, November 2, 1971 (Excerpt) ... 630

(155) Generalized Trade Preferences for Developing Countries: Statement by Secretary of State Rogers, Hamilton, Bermuda, December 20, 1971 (Excerpts) ... 631

APPENDIX: PRINCIPAL SOURCES ... **635**

INDEX ... **639**

I.
WORLD AFFAIRS
THROUGH
AMERICAN EYES

["The Watershed Year" was the term employed by President Nixon to characterize the foreign policy developments of 1971 in the comprehensive foreign affairs report that he submitted to Congress early in 1972. It was, the President stated, a year in which the foundations laid and the cumulative effect of actions taken during 1969 and 1970, the first two years of his administration, made possible such historic foreign policy changes as the opening of a dialogue with the People's Republic of China, the beginning of a "new relationship" with the Soviet Union, the laying of a foundation for "a healthier and more sustainable relationship with our European allies and Japan," and "the creation of a new environment for the world's monetary and trade activities."[1]

The present volume offers documentary coverage not only of such positive developments as the planning of the presidential visits to China and the Soviet Union, but also of the year's more negative aspects, among which must be counted the continuance of the war in Indochina and the failure of American efforts to bring about a diplomatic solution of problems in that area; an ominous stalemate in relations between the Arab states and Israel; the war between India and Pakistan that accompanied the emergence of Bangladesh; the expulsion of the Republic of China from the United Nations; and the strains between the United States and its allies that followed the enunciation of Washington's "New Economic Policy" on August 15, 1971, but were later alleviated in some measure by agreement on a general realignment of exchange rates and on the opening of broad-scale trade negotiations.

As in previous years, the nation's military involvement in Indochina continued to exert a powerful influence on all aspects of American foreign policy and, together with high crime rates and persistent malfunctioning in the domestic economy, stood high among the preoccupations of both government and public. The national malaise engendered by the Vietnam experience persisted, in spite of a gradual withdrawal of American ground forces from that country and a re-

[1] Nixon Report, 1972, pp. 2-3.

duction of the American military presence elsewhere in Asia in line with the so-called Nixon Doctrine put forward in 1969. The deteriorating relationship between the government and its critics was vividly illustrated by such episodes as the mass arrests of "May Day" demonstrators in the national capital; the unauthorized publication of the so-called Pentagon Papers, an elaborate, top-secret official record of the war in Vietnam; and the illegal activities of the White House "plumbers," a special investigative unit set up in reaction to this and other security leaks.

The breadth of the desire to limit and reduce American participation in world affairs was evidenced not only by continuing agitation against the war in Indochina, but also by repeated attempts in Congress to curb the war-making powers of the President, impose a reduction of American military forces in Europe, and set a deadline for military withdrawal from Indochina; by the Senate's unprecedented rejection of the annual foreign aid bill; and by various legislative actions that appeared to reflect a lessening of American support for the United Nations. Although these tendencies were in many cases resisted by the Nixon administration, its own foreign policy actions were characterized in some instances by a degree of abruptness that was equated by some observers with indifference to the interests and opinions of friendly nations. Notable examples were the announcement on July 15, 1971, of President Nixon's intended visit to the People's Republic of China and, on August 15, 1971, the sudden suspension of the convertibility of the dollar and the imposition of a surcharge on existing import duties that remained in effect until other American requirements in the economic area had been satisfied by the so-called Smithsonian Agreements of December 18, 1971.

The majority of these developments will be more fully documented in the specialized chapters that follow. The documents presented in this introductory chapter serve mainly to set forth the broad outlines of American foreign and military policy as enunciated by such authorities as President Nixon, Secretary of State William P. Rogers, and Secretary of Defense Melvin R. Laird. The increasingly important diplomatic role of Dr. Henry A. Kissinger is only partially reflected in the documentary records of 1971; it was only in the following year that the President's Assistant for National Security Affairs was to emerge as the most authoritative "on-the-record" spokesman of the Nixon administration's foreign policy.

Also included in the present chapter are documents relating to the organization of the government for the conduct of foreign affairs and to congressional proposals to limit the war powers of the President. Though no war-powers legislation was actually adopted during the 1971 session of Congress, discussion of this issue between spokesmen of the legislative and executive branches helped set the scene for the war-powers legislation that would be enacted over President Nixon's veto in 1973.]

A. Essentials of World Policy.

[Following the practice initiated in 1970, President Nixon submitted to Congress on February 25, 1971, a comprehensive foreign policy report, entitled *United States Foreign Policy for the 1970's: Building for Peace,*[2] which combined interpretation of recent foreign policy developments with detailed analysis of current problems. The following summary of this 160-page document (Document 1) was broadcast by the President on the date of its public release.]

(1) "United States Foreign Policy for the 1970's–Building for Peace": Radio Address by President Richard M. Nixon on Transmitting His Annual Foreign Affairs Report to the Congress, February 25, 1971.[3]

(Complete Text)

Good morning, my fellow Americans:

Over the past 10 years, Presidents of the United States have come before the American people in times of crisis to talk about war or the threat of war.

Today I am able to talk to you in a more hopeful and positive vein—about how we are moving this Nation and the world toward a lasting peace.

We have brought ourselves to a time of transition, from war toward peace, and this is a good time to gain some perspective on where we are and where we are headed.

Today I am sending to the Congress my second annual comprehensive report on the conduct of our foreign affairs. It discusses not only what we have done, but why we have done it, and how we intend to proceed in the future.

I do not intend to summarize all that is in my detailed report on foreign policy at this time. Instead, I would like to focus on three key points:

—how we are getting out of the war this Nation has been in for the past 6 years;

—how we have created a new and different foreign policy approach for the United States in a greatly changed world; and

2 Nixon Report, 1971.
3 *Presidential Documents*, Mar. 1, 1971, pp. 298-304.

—how we are applying that approach in working with others to build a lasting peace.

The most immediate and anguishing problem that faced this administration 2 years ago was the war in Vietnam.

We have come a long way since then.

Two years ago, when this administration took office, there were almost 550,000 Americans in Vietnam. Within 60 days we will have brought home 260,000 men, and this spring I will announce a new schedule of withdrawals.[4]

Two years ago, our casualties each month were five times as high as they are today.

Two years ago, the additional demands of the Vietnam war cost us approximately 22 billion dollars per year. That cost has been cut in half.

Much of the progress in Vietnam was due to the success of the allied operations against the enemy sanctuaries in Cambodia last spring.[5]

The clear proof is in this figure: American casualties after Cambodia have been half the rate they were before Cambodia. Our decision to clean out the sanctuaries in Cambodia saved thousands of American lives. And it enabled us to continue withdrawing our men on schedule.

Just as last year's cutoff of supplies through Cambodia has saved lives and insured our withdrawal program this year, the purpose of this year's disruption of the Ho Chi Minh Trail in Laos[6] is to save lives and insure the success of our withdrawal program next year.

The disruption of the Communist supply line through Laos is being accomplished by South Vietnamese troops, with no U.S. ground troops or advisers. Their army is doing the fighting, with our air support, and the intensity of the fighting is evidence of the importance of that supply line to the enemy.

Consider this combination of events that many people thought was impossible only 2 years ago:

We have kept our commitments as we have taken out our troops. South Vietnam now has an excellent opportunity not only to survive but to build a strong, free society.

Thanks to the disruption of so much of the enemy's supplies, Americans are leaving South Vietnam in safety; we would much prefer to leave South Vietnam in peace. Negotiation remains the best and quickest way to end the war in a way that will not only end U.S. involvement and casualties, but will mean an end to the fighting between North and South Vietnamese.

---

[4] See Document 71.
[5] Cf. *Documents, 1970*, pp. 156-63.
[6] Cf. Documents 67-68.

On October 7 [1970], we made a proposal[7] that could open the door to that kind of peace; we proposed:

—An immediate standstill ceasefire throughout Indochina to stop the fighting.

—An Indochina Peace Conference.

—The withdrawal of all outside forces.

—A political settlement fair to both sides.

—The immediate release of all prisoners of war.

I reaffirm that proposal today. It is supported by every government in Indochina except one—the Government of North Vietnam.

I once again urge Hanoi to join us in this search for peace.

If North Vietnam wishes to negotiate with the United States, they will have to recognize that time is running out. With the exception of the prisoner-of-war issue, if North Vietnam continues to refuse to discuss our peace proposals, they will soon find they have no choice but to negotiate only with the South Vietnamese.

Our eventual goal is a total withdrawal of all outside forces. But as long as North Vietnam continues to hold a single American prisoner, we shall have forces in South Vietnam. The American prisoners of war will not be forgotten by their Government.

I am keeping my pledge to end America's involvement in this war. But the main point I want to discuss with you today—and the main theme of my report to the Congress—is the future not the past. It matters very much how we end this war.

To end a war is simple.

But to end a war in a way that will not bring on another war is far from simple.

In Southeast Asia today, aggression is failing—thanks to the determination of the South Vietnamese people and to the courage and sacrifice of America's fighting men.

That brings us to a point that we have been at several times before in this century: aggression turned back, a war ending.

We are at a critical moment in history: What America does—or fails to do—will determine whether peace and freedom can be won in the coming generation.

That is why the way in which we end this conflict is so crucial to our efforts to build a lasting peace in coming decades.

The right way out of Vietnam is crucial to our changing role in the world and to peace in the world.[8]

To understand the nature of the new American role we must consider the great historical changes that have taken place.

---

[7] *Documents, 1970*, pp. 196-201; cf. Chapter V at note 67.

[8] See further Documents 71-81.

For 25 years after World War II, the United States was not only the leader of the non-Communist world, it was the primary supporter and defender of this free world as well.

—But today our allies and friends have gained new strength and self-confidence. They are now able to participate much more fully not only in their own defense, but in adding their moral and spiritual strength to the creation of a stable world order.

—Today our adversaries no longer present a solidly united front; we can now differentiate in our dealings with them.

—Today neither the United States nor the Soviet Union has a clear-cut nuclear advantage; the time is therefore ripe to come to an agreement on the control of arms.

The world has changed. Our foreign policy must change with it.

We have learned in recent years the dangers of overinvolvement. The other danger—a grave risk we are equally determined to avoid—is under-involvement. After a long and unpopular war, there is temptation to turn inward—to withdraw from the world, to back away from our commitments. That deceptively smooth road of the new isolationism is surely the road to war.

Our foreign policy today steers a steady course between the past danger of overinvolvement and the new temptation of under-involvement.

That policy, which I first enunciated in Guam 19 months ago,[9] represents our basic approach to the world:

We will maintain our commitments, but we will make sure our own troop levels or any financial support to other nations is appropriate to current threats and needs.

We shall provide a shield if a nuclear power threatens the freedom of a nation allied with us or of a nation whose survival we consider vital to our security.

But we will look to threatened countries and their neighbors to assume primary responsibility for their own defense, and we will provide support where our interests call for that support and where it can make a difference.

These principles are not limited to security matters.

We shall pursue economic policies at home and abroad that encourage trade wherever possible and that strengthen political ties between nations. As we actively seek to help other nations expand their economies, we can legitimately expect them to work with us in averting economic problems of our own.

As we continue to send economic aid to developing nations, we will expect countries on the receiving end to mobilize their resources; we will look to other developed nations to do more in furnishing assis-

[9] *Documents, 1968-69*, pp. 329-34.

tance; and we will channel our aid increasingly through groups of nations banded together for mutual support.

This new sharing of responsibility requires not less American leadership than in the past, but rather a new, more subtle, form of leadership. No single nation can build a peace alone; peace can only be built by the willing hands—and minds—of all. In the modern world, leadership cannot be "do-it-yourself"—the path of leadership is in providing the help, the motive, the inspiration to do it together.

In carrying out what is referred to as the Nixon Doctrine, we recognize that we cannot transfer burdens too swiftly. We must strike a balance between doing too much and preventing self-reliance, and suddenly doing too little and undermining self-confidence. We intend to give our friends the time and the means to adjust, materially and psychologically, to a new form of American participation in the world.

How have we applied our new foreign policy during the past year? And what is our future agenda as we work with others to build a stable world order?

In Western Europe, we have shifted from predominance to partnership with our allies. Our ties with Western Europe are central to the structure of peace because its nations are rich in tradition and experience, strong economically, vigorous in diplomacy and culture; they are in a position to take a major part in building a world of peace.

Our ties were strengthened on my second trip to Europe this summer[10] and reflected in our close consultation on arms control negotiations. At our suggestion, the NATO alliance made a thorough review of its military strategy and posture. As a result, we have reached new agreement on a strong defense and the need to share the burden more fairly.[11]

In Eastern Europe, our exchange of state visits with Romania,[12] and my meeting last fall with Marshal [Josip Broz] Tito in Yugoslavia,[13] are examples of our search for wider reconciliation with the nations that used to be considered behind an Iron Curtain.

Looking ahead in Europe:
—We shall cooperate in our political and economic relations across the Atlantic as the Common Market grows;
—We and our allies will make the improvements necessary to carry out our common defense strategy;
—Together we stand ready to reduce forces in Western Europe in exchange for mutual reductions in Eastern Europe.[14]

The problems of Africa are great but so is her potential. The United

10 Cf. *Documents, 1970*, pp. 90-92.
11 Cf. same, pp. 99-103.
12 Aug. 2-3, 1969. *Public Papers, 1969*, pp. 603-13.
13 Sept. 30–Oct. 1, 1970. *Public Papers, 1970*, pp. 787-97.
14 See further Documents 32-45.

States will support her people's efforts to build a continent that provides social justice and economic expansion.[15]

Turning to our own hemisphere, in Latin America, there was too much tendency in the past to take our closest friends and neighbors for granted. Recently, we have paid new respect to their proud traditions. Our trade, credit, and economic policies have been reexamined and reformed, to respond to their concerns and their ideas, as well as to our own interests.

Our new Latin American policy is designed to help them help themselves; our new attitude will not only aid their progress but add to their dignity.

Great changes are brewing throughout the American hemisphere. We can have no greater goal than to help provide the means for necessary change to be accomplished in peace, and for all change to be in the direction of greater self-reliance.[16]

Turning to the Far East, a new Asia is emerging. The old enmities of World War II are dead or dying. Asian states are stronger and are joining together in vigorous regional groupings.

Here the doctrine that took shape last year is taking hold today, helping to spur self-reliance and cooperation between states. In Japan, South Korea, Thailand, and the Philippines, we have consolidated bases and reduced American forces. We have relaxed trade and travel restrictions to underline our readiness for greater contact with Communist China.

Looking ahead in that area:
- —While continuing to help our friends help themselves, we must begin to consider how regional associations can work together with the major powers in the area for a durable peace.
- —We will work to build a strong partnership with Japan that will accommodate our mutual interests.
- —We will search for constructive discussions with Communist China while maintaining our defense commitment to Taiwan. When the Government of the People's Republic of China is ready to engage in talks, it will find us receptive to agreements that further the legitimate national interests of China and its neighbors.

In Asia, we can see tomorrow's world in microcosm. An economically powerful democratic free nation, Japan, is seeking new markets; a potentially powerful Communist nation, China, will one day seek new outlets and new relations; a Communist competitor, the Soviet Union, has interests there as well; and the independent non-Communist nations of Southeast Asia are already working together in regional association. These great forces are bound to interact in the not too distant future.

[15] See further Documents 101-110.
[16] See further Documents 111-119.

In the way they work together and in the way we cooperate with their relationship, is the key to permanent peace in that area—the Far East, the scene of such a painful legacy of the recent past, can become an example of peace and stability in the future.[17]

In the Middle East, the United States took the initiative to stop the fighting and start the process of peace.

Along the Suez Canal a year ago, there was daily combat on the ground and in the air. Diplomacy was at an impasse. The danger of local conflict was magnified by growing Soviet involvement and the possibility of great powers being drawn into confrontation.

America took the lead in arranging a cease-fire and getting negotiations started.[18] We are seeing to it that the balance of power, so necessary to discourage a new outbreak of fighting, is not upset. Working behind the scenes, when a crisis arose in Jordan, the United States played a key role in seeing that order was restored and an invasion was abandoned.[19]

We recognize that centuries of suspicion and decades of hostility cannot be ended overnight. There are great obstacles in the way of a permanent, peaceful settlement, and painful compromise is required by all concerned.

We are encouraged by the willingness of each of the parties to begin to look at the larger interest of peace and stability throughout the Middle East. There is still the risk of war but now—for the first time in years—the parties are actively calculating the risks of peace.

The policy of the United States will continue to be to promote peace talks—not to try to impose a peace from the outside, but to support the peace efforts of the parties in the region themselves.

One way to support these efforts is for the United States to discourage any outside power from trying to exploit the situation for its own advantage.

Another way for us to help turn a tenuous truce into a permanent settlement is this: The United States is fully prepared to play a responsible and cooperative role in keeping the peace arrived at through negotiation between the parties.

We know what our vital interests are in the Middle East. Those interests include friendly and constructive relations with all nations in the area. Other nations know that we are ready to protect those vital interests. And one good reason why other nations take us at our word in the Middle East is because the United States has kept its word in Southeast Asia.[20]

---

[17] See further Documents 82-100.
[18] Cf. *Documents, 1970*, pp. 131-35.
[19] Cf. *The United States in World Affairs, 1970*, p. 110.
[20] See further Documents 48-54.

We now come to a matter that affects every nation—the relations between the world's two great superpowers.

Over the past two years in some fields the Soviet Union and the United States have moved ahead together. We have taken the first step toward cooperation in outer space.[21] We have both ratified the treaty limiting the spread of nuclear weapons.[22] Just 2 weeks ago, we signed a treaty to prohibit nuclear weapons from the seabeds.[23]

These are hopeful signs, but certain other Soviet actions are reason for concern. There is need for much more cooperation in reducing tensions in the Middle East and in ending harassment of Berlin. We must also discourage the temptation to raise new challenges in sensitive areas such as the Caribbean.

In the long run, the most significant result of negotiations between the superpowers in the past year could be in the field of arms control.

The Strategic Arms Limitation Talks with the Soviet Union[24] have produced the most searching examination of the nature of strategic competition ever conducted between our two nations. Each side has had the chance to explain at length the concerns caused by the posture of the other side. The talks have been conducted in a serious way without the old lapses into propaganda.

If both sides continue in this way, there is reason to hope that specific agreements will be reached to curb the arms race.

Taking a first step in limiting the capacity of mankind to destroy itself would mark a turning point in the history of the postwar world; it would add to the security of both the Soviet Union and the United States, and it would add to the world's peace of mind.

In all our relations with the Soviets, we shall make the most progress by recognizing that in many cases our national interests are not the same; it serves no purpose to pretend they are; our differences are not matters of mood, they are matters of substance. But in many other cases, our separate national interests can best be pursued by a sober consideration of the world interest.[25]

The United States will deal, as it must, from strength: We will not reduce our defenses below the level I consider essential to our national security.[26]

A strong America is essential to the cause of peace today. Until we have the kind of agreements we can rely on, we shall remain strong.

But America's power will always be used for building a peace, never for breaking it—only for defending freedom, never for destroying it.

[21] Cf. note 12 to Document 11.
[22] See note 16 to Chapter II.
[23] Cf. Document 13.
[24] Cf. *Documents, 1970*, pp. 59-65.
[25] See further Documents 11-31.
[26] See further Document 2.

America's strength will be, as it must be, second to none; but the strength that this nation is proudest of is the strength of our determination to create a peaceful world.

We all know how every town or city develops a sense of community when its citizens come together to meet a common need.

The common needs of the world today, about which there can be no disagreement or conflict of national interest, are plain to see.

We know that we must act as one world in restoring the world's environment, before pollution of the seas and skies overwhelms every nation. We know we must stop the flow of narcotics; we must counter the outbreaks of hijacking and kidnaping; we must share the great discoveries about the oceans and outer space.

The United States is justly proud of the lead it has taken in working within the United Nations, and within the NATO alliance, to come to grips with these problems and with these opportunities.[27]

Our work here is a beginning, not only in coping with the new challenges of technology and modern life, but of developing a worldwide "sense of community" that will ease tension, reduce suspicion, and thereby promote the process of peace.

That process can only flourish in a climate of mutual respect.

We can have that mutual respect with our friends, without dominating them or without letting them down.

We can have that mutual respect with our adversaries, without compromising our principles or weakening our resolve.

And we can have that mutual respect among ourselves, without stifling dissent or losing our capacity for action.

Our goal is something Americans have not enjoyed in this century—a full generation of peace. A full generation of peace depends not only on the policy of one party, or of one nation, or one alliance, or one bloc of nations.

Peace for the next generation depends on our ability to make certain that each nation has a share in its shaping, and that every nation has a stake in its lasting.

This is the hard way, requiring patience, restraint, understanding, and—when necessary—bold, decisive action. But history has taught us that the old diplomacy of imposing a peace by the fiat of great powers simply does not work.

I believe that the new diplomacy of partnership, of mutual respect, of dealing with strength and determination will work.

I believe that the right degree of American involvement—not too much and not too little—will evoke the right response from our other partners on this globe in building for our children the kind of world they deserve—a world of opportunity in a world without war.

---

[27] See further Documents 136-140.

B. National Security Policy

[A comprehensive discussion of American national security policies was included in President Nixon's annual foreign policy report to the Congress, submitted February 25, 1971.[28] Much of the same ground was covered in even greater detail in the annual "Posture Statement" presented by the Secretary of Defense to the responsible committees of the Congress. The introductory portion of the 1971 "Posture Statement," as presented to the Committee on Armed Services of the House of Representatives on March 9, 1971, is printed below (Document 2).]

(2) United States National Security Policies: Posture Statement Presented by Secretary of Defense Melvin R. Laird to the House Committee on Armed Services, March 9, 1971.[29]

(Excerpt)

Secretary LAIRD. Mr. Chairman [F. Edward Hébert], members of the committee, Chairman Moorer[30] and I are privileged today to present to this committee the first comprehensive 5-year defense program of the Nixon administration, and to discuss with you the associated fiscal year 1972 budget.

Admiral Moorer will present the most comprehensive threat briefing that I believe has ever been presented to this committee. It includes comparisons of the capabilities of our forces and the Warsaw Pact forces.

Because of the associated discussion of the 1972 budget in connection with this 5-year defense report, I have asked the Comptroller of the Department of Defense—Assistant Secretary of Defense Bob Moot, to be with me here today in case there are any technical questions regarding the financial tables and financial presentations which are a part of this 5-year defense program.

Mr. Chairman, this 5-year defense program is keyed to the twin objectives set forth by President Nixon for the last third of the 20th century: achievement for the first time in this century of a generation of peace; and in the process, enhancement of the quality of life for all Americans, while helping to improve it for all peoples of the world.

This 1972 Defense Report to Congress and the American people contains a 5-year defense program which spells out a new national security

---

[28] Nixon Report, 1971, pp. 111-130.
[29] U.S. House of Representatives, Committee on Armed Services, 92d Cong., 1st sess.; *Military Posture: Hearings on H.R. 3818 and H.R. 8687* (Washington: G.P.O., 1971), pp. 2320-25.
[30] Admiral Thomas H. Moorer, Chairman of the Joint Chiefs of Staff.

strategy of realistic deterrence. This new strategy is designed to prevent wars by furthering the President's goal of building a viable structure of peace based on adequate strength, true partnership, and meaningful negotiations.

The strategy of realistic deterrence seeks to further the goal of peace by deterrence of armed conflict at all levels. I have always tried to be a realist in fulfilling my responsibilities, whether as a Member of Congress or as Secretary of Defense. I believe the strategy we are advancing is realistic for three reasons:

First, it is based on a sober and clear view of the multiple threats to peace which exist in today's world. It neither exaggerates nor underestimates those threats.

Second, it provides for the maintenance of a strong free world military capability as the essential foundation of deterrence. It rejects the view that peace is well served if our military power is unilaterally weakened.

Third, it takes account of the strategic, fiscal, manpower, and political realities while steering a prudent middle course between two policy extremes—world policeman or new isolationism.

The strategy of realistic deterrence is new. Those who would dismiss it as a mere continuation of past policies in new packaging would be quite mistaken. Past policy was responsive and reactive.

Our new strategy is positive and active. Past policy focused on containment and accommodation. The new strategy emphasizes measured, meaningful involvement, and vigorous negotiation from a position of strength.

The strategy of realistic deterrence will provide through sufficient strength and full partnership the indispensable and realistic basis for effective free world negotiation. Most importantly, it is designed not to manage crises but to prevent wars.

The fiscal year 1971 program and budget, which was sent to Congress last year,[31] was the foundation for the transition from an era of confrontation to an era of meaningful negotiation. The fiscal year 1972 program will move us closer to this goal.

It was clear at the outset of the Nixon administration that, in order to set the stage and create the conditions for meaningful negotiation and peaceful relations, we had to move the country away from war and toward peace, away from a wartime economy and toward a peacetime economy, away from lopsided national priorities and toward a major reordering of those priorities, away from arms competition and toward arms limitation.

On the basis of the record of the past 2 years, it is my view that we have made significant—in some cases unprecedented—progress toward

---

[31] Cf. *Documents, 1970*, pp. 26-32.

the major interim goals we have set for ourselves.

In the war to peace transition: By continuing negotiations in Paris, by progress in Vietnamization, by reducing U.S. combat activities, casualties, and air sortie levels in Southeast Asia, and by an orderly, substantial, and continuing troop redeployment program.

In reordering national priorities: By shifting the Defense portion of the Federal budget and gross national product to its lowest level in 20 years and by spending more on human needs than on Defense needs.

In our Defense budget: By providing for the first time in this century the full peace dividend before the conclusion of a war. Defense costs in this budget already are back at pre-Vietnam levels in constant dollars.

In implementing the Nixon doctrine: By withdrawing more than 300,000 American troops from Asia while increasing significantly security assistance levels to our friends and allies.

In NATO: By helping foster a new spirit of meaningful burden sharing and a new awareness of the strategic, fiscal, manpower, and political realities we face in common.

In moving toward zero draft: By obtaining congressional approval for long-needed draft reform[32] to eliminate many inequities, and by cutting draft calls almost in half from 1968 to 1970 in pursuing our goal of zero draft by July 1, 1973.

In our program for human goals: By relating it to our objective of an all-volunteer force, by seeking to instill a new order of professionalism and dignity in military life, by seeking to remedy remaining shortcomings in such areas as housing and education and by continuing to lead the way toward full equal opportunity.

In taking new initiatives with regard to prisoners of war: By an unprecedented exchange offer at the Paris peace table,[33] by search and rescue missions when possible, and by focusing public attention at home and abroad on their plight.

In chemical warfare and biological research, and in defoliation: By promulgating a major new policy renouncing any use of biological and toxin weapons and renouncing first use of lethal and incapacitating chemical weapons,[34] by ending crop destruction operations in Vietnam and by restricting limited defoliation still needed for troop safety to the same regulation applied to herbicide use in the United States.

In major improvements of defense management: By adopting many of the Blue Ribbon Panel recommendations,[35] by emphasizing a new

---

[32] Selective Service Amendment Act of 1969 (Public Law 91-125, Nov. 26, 1969).
[33] Cf. *The United States in World Affairs, 1970*, p. 156.
[34] *Documents, 1970*, pp. 75-76.
[35] The Blue Ribbon Defense Panel, *Report to the President and the Secretary of Defense on the Department of Defense*, July 1, 1970 (Washington: G.P.O., 1971).

fly-before-buy policy and by increased decentralization in procurement actions.

Mr. Chairman, we are proud of the significant progress we have been able to make in establishing new directions and a steady momentum toward major goals of the American people. As I reported last year in discussing our fiscal year 1971 transitional program, the challenges here at home which we faced upon assuming office in many ways equaled, and in some ways surpassed, the growing challenges abroad.

I will not repeat in detail what I said last year, but it is important, I believe, to repeat a concluding comment I made in last year's Defense report:[36]

Transition to a new equilibrium will take time. We made a beginning in 1969 and are continuing the transition into calendar year 1970. We consider our fiscal year 1971 budget another building block in that transition.

I readily acknowledged that not all of the challenges we encountered upon assuming office had been met with the submission of the fiscal year 1971 budget. I would repeat that comment today with regard to the budget and program contained in this report. We still have a long way to go in all aspects of defense responsibility. We have never claimed to be instant problem solvers. But we have completed our year of transition with respect to basic defense planning both with regard to strategy and management. We have completed our basic reviews and have made our fundamental decisions on what needs to be done. The new strategy and defense program presented in this report embody the major elements of the decisions that have flowed from our assessments of the past 2 years. The strategy and the program, of course, cannot succeed without the understanding and support of Congress and the American people.

This report describes the major changes which have been made and which will be made in such areas as defense strategy, the defense budget, research and development, command and control, intelligence, procurement and, most importantly, the need to revamp our concepts about the recruitment and use of military manpower—both in Active, National Guard, and Reserve Forces.

I would like briefly to outline for you some of the major points in the defense report. We focus on two fundamental aspects of defense planning:

In section I—Effective implementation of the strategy of realistic deterrence.

In section II—Better management of human, material, and economic·

36 *Documents, 1970*, p. 32.

resources in the Department of Defense.

Our 5-year defense plan projects a capability to attain our goal with an efficient and modernized force that, in peacetime, would require no more than 7 percent of the gross national product and be made up of no more than 2.5 million men and women who are volunteers. This is discussed in the chapter on "Strategy Overview," which states, in essence, that a realistic military strategy cannot be an end in itself but must be inseparably linked with a broader national strategy of deterrence and "meaningfully related to our pressing requirements in the domestic field."

As I discussed in the chapter on "Concepts for Defense Planning," we intend to use a total force approach in which all appropriate resources for deterrence, United States and free world, will be available. Through the application of all resources across the full spectrum of possible conflict and the full spectrum of capabilities of our friends and allies, we will maintain sufficient U.S. strength and will mesh this strength with other nations in a new order of partnership.

For the U.S. forces, the total force concept will mean increased importance for our National Guard and Reserves. In this chapter, I analyze the progress and problems of Vietnamization, and discuss its relation to the total force concept in its broadest applications, utilizing both military and nonmilitary resources. Looking to the future, we must continue to focus on the intimate relations of the military, economic, political, and diplomatic facets of the Indochina situation as we move to terminate U.S. involvement in the fighting. This report does not address the day-to-day military situation in Indochina, or anywhere else. It seeks instead to explain the basic concepts that underlie our strategy for the future. To be realistic about it, there will continue to be ups and downs, gains and losses, temporary setbacks. The important thing is for the citizens of our Nation to keep in sight the fixed goal of a generation of peace and to insure, as best we can, that the policies we establish and the strategy we follow lead in that direction.

The chapter on "The Threats to Free World Security" provides an update of the threats to the free world at all levels of conflict. The continued momentum of the Soviet Union in strategic missiles, aircraft, naval forces, and research and development are evaluated. Chinese weapons progress is also discussed. This threat assessment is related to the need for assuring that the United States maintains its technological leadership in order to assure the safety and survival of the American people. To maintain technological leadership, we must reverse the recent downward trend in R. & D. [Research and Development] funding, which this budget does, and we must also move forward with new technological initiatives to guarantee that we have flexibility and timely options to meet possible threats of the future.

The fourth and final chapter in section I, "Force Planning Under the

New Strategy," provides a discussion of the specific programs being recommended as the basic minimum capabilities deemed necessary and appropriate for the years ahead. We have completed our transition to what we describe as baseline planning, and are now building for the future. Of course, much will depend on the outcome of the strategic arms limitation talks. Because of uncertainty associated with SALT, we must maintain present capabilities, while preserving or creating options to adjust those capabilities upward or downward as may be required.

Mr. Chairman, no one hopes more for success at SALT than the Department of Defense because of the burdens and responsibilities we would face should SALT fail. The details of the President's decision on the fiscal year 1972 Safeguard program[37] are contained in this section. Safeguard continues to be a vital factor in the SALT negotiations.

The chapters in section II are focused on the need for better management of human, material, and economic resources in the Department of Defense.

Chapter 1: "Organization and Management" focuses on our management concept, which is based on participatory decisionmaking, defined decentralization, and delegation of authority under specific guidance. I propose in this chapter the creation of an additional Deputy Secretary of Defense in order to enhance high-level civilian management and to cope with the severe time demands now placed upon the single Deputy Secretary of Defense, David Packard. I also recommend creation of two additional positions for Assistant Secretary of Defense.

We will continue, of course, to make management improvements in the Department of Defense, including a modification of the unified command structure which we are recommending to the President. We will continue to draw as appropriate on the recommendations of the. Blue Ribbon Defense Panel, which was so ably headed by Gilbert Fitzhugh.

Our examination into the intelligence activities of the Department of Defense will continue, and further changes may be anticipated, including the creation of a long-range planning group reporting directly to the Secretary of Defense. We have taken steps also to strengthen civilian control over investigative and related counterintelligence activities.

The continued progress we expect under the human goals principles of the Department of Defense are reported in the chapter on "Manpower Objectives." Of particular importance, of course, is our program to achieve zero draft calls by mid-1973 and to accomplish further improvements of the Selective Service System which would complement

---

37 For the origins of the Safeguard antiballistic missile program see *Documents, 1968-69*, pp. 83-87.

last year's reduced draft calls and national random selection system.[38] Many inequities in the draft have been eliminated in the past 2 years, but so long as we need the draft it must be made more equitable. One gross inequity today is the fact that the young men who attend college are given deferments which are denied to other young men who do not attend college. This is unfair and should be changed.

Once men and women are in the Armed Forces and are serving their country in uniform, we owe them respect and dignity for their service, and we owe them and their families fair play in the areas of pay, housing, and educational opportunities.

Let me candidly tell you that we face some formidable problems in the manpower area that are not going to be solved overnight. In addition to complex recruiting and retention problems, we share with the rest of American society the agonizing problems related to race relations and drug abuse. We in the Department of Defense are determined to continue leading the way, as best we can, in seeking solutions to these difficult problems.

A final chapter in "The Defense Budget and the Economy" surveys the impact of cuts in defense personnel and expenditures over the past 2 years in response to our changing national priorities.

The impact of the massive cuts that have been made during the last 2 years in employment and expenditures related to national defense is assessed. These cuts have resulted in a considerable amount of turbulence, which results from our shift from a wartime to a peacetime economy.

This year the rate of defense reductions is declining and we are going to do everything we can to keep to a minimum this turbulence, as it relates to our civilian employees, defense industry employees, and our military people and their families. In short, the defense budget has been heavily affected in our national reallocation of resources. The period of defense dominance in national resource allocation is over. Our fiscal year 1972 budget, in constant dollars, will be below the prewar year of fiscal year 1964. This fact cannot be ignored as we plan to implement during the next 5 years our new strategy of realistic deterrence.

In current dollars, the fiscal year 1972 Defense budget transmitted to the Congress by the President[39] totals $79.2 billion in total obligational authority and $76 billion in outlays, including amounts proposed for future pay increases. This is $3.9 billion in TOA and $1.5 billion in outlays above the respective amounts for TOA and outlays we now expect in fiscal year 1971.

---

[38] For details cf. President Nixon's message on draft reform, sent to Congress on Jan. 28, 1971 (*Public Papers, 1971*, pp. 75-77), and his statement on signing the draft extension and military pay bill (Public Law 92-129) on Sept. 28, 1971, (same, pp. 1008-9).

[39] For the President's annual message on the budget for fiscal year 1972, transmitted to Congress on Jan. 29, 1971, see *Public Papers, 1971*, pp. 80-95.

In summary, Mr. Chairman, I would repeat that we have not solved all the hard problems before us nor can I tell you that hard decisions do not lie ahead. As with the fiscal 1971 transitional budget, there is some risk attached to our fiscal year 1972 Defense budget for it continues the downward trend in overall Defense Department purchasing power at a time when the threats we face around the world continue to increase, not diminish. Should events dictate, I will not hesitate to recommend any action that may be required to insure the continued safety and security of the American people.

As Secretary of Defense, I seek your understanding and your support for our new strategy and want to assure you that I will continue to work with this committee and other committees of the Congress to advance the goals we share in common in seeking to serve the best interest of the American people.

*   *   *

C. Governmental Organization for the Conduct of Foreign Affairs.

[The advent of the Nixon administration occasioned far-reaching changes in the organization of the Federal Government for the conduct of foreign policy, particularly through the strengthening of the National Security Council system under the leadership of Dr. Henry A. Kissinger, the President's Assistant for National Security Affairs. The following documents present an authoritative account of the organization of the National Security Council system as it existed early in 1971 (Document 3); the reorganization during 1971 of the upper echelons of the Department of State under Secretary of State William P. Rogers (Document 4); and the establishment, earlier in 1971, of the Council on International Economic Policy as an instrument of coordination in the international economic area (Document 5).]

(3) *The National Security Council System: Excerpt from President Nixon's Second Annual Report to the Congress on United States Foreign Policy, February 25, 1971.*[40]

*   *   *

PART VI: THE NATIONAL SECURITY COUNCIL SYSTEM

"The NSC system is meant to help us address the fundamental issues, clarify our basic purposes, examine all alternatives, and plan

---

[40] Nixon Report, 1971, pp. 225-29; text from *Presidential Documents*, Mar. 1, 1971, pp. 375-76.

intelligent actions. It is meant to promote the thoroughness and deliberation which are essential for an effective American foreign policy."

U.S. Foreign Policy for the 1970's, A Report to Congress, February 18, 1970[41]

Upon my inauguration, I reestablished the National Security Council as the principal forum for consideration of foreign policy issues and, created a system of supporting committees to serve it. Chaired by the President and comprising the Vice President, the Secretaries of State and Defense, the Director of the Office of Emergency Preparedness and others at my invitation, the Council provides a focus at the highest level of our government for full and frank discussions of national security issues. Of course, I also consult the Secretaries of State and Defense and other senior advisors individually to obtain their views on national security issues.

Too often in the past our foreign policy machinery was the captive of events. Day-to-day tactical considerations occupied our time and determined our actions. Policy emerged from a narrow rather than conceptual perspective. The National Security Council system helps us concentrate on purposes and develop policy in the context of our long-range goals.

The Process

Creativity, systematic planning, and thorough analysis are given special emphasis. It is every concerned agency's obligation to contribute information and analysis and to present and argue its position. Only in this way can I be certain that the full range of views and reasonable options has been explored.

The system helps us to bring together all the knowledge available and to bring to bear the best analytical thought of which we are capable:

—Analysis and decision must rest on the broadest possible *factual base*. There must be a common appreciation of the facts and of their relevance.

—Coherent policy needs a *conceptual framework*. Where do we want to go in the long run? What are our purposes? Our analysis must bring out all reasonable interpretations of the facts, and treat the facts in the framework of longer-range trends and our objectives.

—I have made sure that my *choice* is not limited to ratifying or rejecting bureaucratic compromises which submerge differences to accommodate varying interests within the government. I insist that

[41] Nixon Report, 1970, p. 23.

the facts, issues, and conceptual framework for decision be presented together with alternative courses of action, their pros and cons, and costs and consequences.

The Structure

The NSC system is designed to marshal all the resources and expertise of the departments and agencies of the government. The National Security Council is the apex of the system. It is here that the final refinement of studies conducted at lower levels provides a common framework for thorough deliberation. The Council's discussions assist me by illuminating the issues and focusing the range of realistic choice before I make my decision.

The supporting interagency groups of the system do the preparatory work before consideration of major issues by the Council:

— *The Interdepartmental Groups*, each chaired by an Assistant Secretary of State, are the system's basic sub-groups for policy analysis. They are organized on a geographic or functional basis, and include membership from all appropriate agencies. They do the basic studies and develop the range of choices. In some instances ad hoc groups, each chaired by a representative of the appropriate agency at the Assistant Secretary level, are established to deal with specific policy issues.

— *The Vietnam Special Studies Working Group* is a specialized group for assembling and analyzing factual data on the Vietnam countryside, the economic situation, and other factors affecting Vietnamization. It has investigated specific topics which bear on our negotiating efforts, such as the security implications of alternative ceasefire proposals.

— *The Verification Panel*, a senior group at the Under Secretary level, performs the basic technical analysis to help develop choices and proposals for strategic arms limitation, approaches to mutual and balanced force reductions in Europe, and other major arms control subjects.

— *The Defense Program Review Committee*, also at the Under Secretary level, deals with the major issues of defense policy, posture, and budgetary support. It integrates our consideration of the strategic, international political and economic implications of defense programs. And it relates our defense programs and resource requirements to overall national priorities and the federal budget.

We made changes in the NSC system this past year in the light of experience, primarily to provide a higher-level focus and integration below the National Security Council itself. Two principal groups were raised from the Assistant Secretary to the Under Secretary level. Because the responsibilities of officials at the Under Secretary level transcend specific geographic or functional areas, they are able to view issues in broad perspective; they can draw more fully upon the complete resources of their respective agencies to assure that the entire spectrum of arguments and alternatives is exposed.

> —*The Senior Review Group* directs and reviews the policy studies prepared by the Interdepartmental Groups and Working Groups. It sees to it that these studies present the facts, the issues, the arguments and the range of choice, before the studies are considered by the President and the National Security Council.
>
> —*The Washington Special Actions Group* develops options for implementation of decisions during crises. In 1970, the WSAG had to deal with such situations as Cambodia, the Middle East and Jordan. In each case, it laid the groundwork for reasoned decisions to prevent crises from expanding and threatening our interests and the peace.

The success of any policy depends largely on effective implementation by the responsible departments and agencies. The *Under Secretaries Committee*, chaired by the Under Secretary of State, links the process of policy formulation to the operations of the government. Through interagency review and coordination it helps to ensure that decisions are carried out consistently with policy and uniformly throughout the foreign affairs community. It also recommends to me alternative operational steps to implement broad policy decisions; it develops the details, for example, of our positions in certain important negotiations within the guidelines laid down by the National Security Council.

*   *   *

(4) Reorganization of the Department of State: Announcement by Secretary of State William P. Rogers, July 6, 1971.[42]

(Complete Text)

Secretary Rogers announced on July 6 a reorganization of the Department's top echelon—the "Seventh Floor"—involving changes in the responsibilities of the Under Secretary and other key senior officials.

At the same time, the Secretary announced the introduction of a new management system on the Seventh Floor and at the level of Assistant

[42] Department of State Press Release 154, July 6, 1971; text from *Bulletin*, July 26, 1971, pp. 103-4.

Secretaries which makes use of Policy Analysis and Resource Allocation (PARA) and other modern management concepts. The Secretary also announced further extensive changes in the system for recruitment and administration of Foreign Service personnel.

These changes are among the key parts of a unique program of management and personnel reform drawn up by task forces of the Department's own employees at the Secretary's direction during 1970[43] and outlined in a 180-day progress report by Deputy Under Secretary for Administration William B. Macomber, Jr.[44] The reform program consists of nearly 500 individual recommendations. According to the report, 75 percent of these have been put into effect since the beginning of the year.

Secretary Rogers, in making the announcement, said: "The efforts we are making in-house speak very well for the vitality and dynamism of the Department and the Foreign Service. I continue to believe that if we can leave behind us an improved and modernized system for dealing with this country's future foreign policy problems, this could well be a more lasting and significant contribution to the public interest than success in handling many of the more transitory matters which necessarily occupy our attention."

The report emphasizes that the reforms do not constitute a drastic reorganization of the Department but are practical measures designed to change attitudes and practices so that the existing structure will work more effectively.

The most important of the management reforms are designed to give the Seventh Floor more systematic procedures for establishing, implementing, and evaluating our foreign policy. A new system of Policy Analysis and Resource Allocation is being installed to support the Secretary with a systematic process for better identifying issues, interests, and priorities for all U.S. Government activities abroad, matching resources and policies, and periodically reviewing real and potential issues. It will be an important instrument to support the Secretary and Deputy Secretary in managing the Department and coordinating the foreign affairs activities of the Government. In the Department's regional and functional bureaus, it will support the Assistant Secretaries in coordinating interdepartmental activities in their fields.

Complementing this PARA system, a new management evaluation group has been formed to provide the Secretary and senior officials of the Department with periodic independent appraisals of the effectiveness of ongoing policies and programs, organization, administration, and personnel. Ambassador Thomas W. McElhiney, a senior career Foreign Service officer, has been designated Inspector General and will head this expanded inspection and evaluation effort.

[43] Cf. *Documents, 1970*, pp. 33-39.
[44] *Bulletin*, July 26, 1971, 104-9.

The reorganization of the Seventh Floor also involves changes in the titles and roles of some of the Seventh Floor principals. The Department plans to propose to Congress that the Under Secretary's title be changed to Deputy Secretary to reflect not only his position as the Secretary's ranking deputy for the management of the Department but also that of principal coordinator in behalf of the Secretary of the overseas activities of all U.S. Government agencies.

No change will be made in the title or role of the Under Secretary for Political Affairs, who will remain the third-ranking officer in the Department.

With congressional approval, the Deputy Under Secretary for Economic Affairs will be raised to Under Secretary for Economic Affairs and will have responsibility for coordinating foreign economic activities within the Department and for representing the Department in major interagency bodies dealing with development and economic policy.

The Deputy Under Secretary for Administration is to be designated Deputy Under Secretary for Management and charged with exercising the Deputy Secretary's responsibilities for day-to-day supervision of the new management system.[45]

These senior officials, together with the Counselor and the Coordinator for Security Assistance, a proposed new post, will work as a coordinated management team, supported by common staffs under the guidance of the Secretary and the Deputy Secretary. Beside aiding the processes of coordination and decisionmaking, this "participative" or "team" approach to management will insure close linkage between the formulation of substantive policies and the use of resources.

As a key part of the total modernization program, a number of major reforms in personnel administration have been adopted to use talent more effectively, develop skilled specialists and managers, and bring a broader range of aptitudes to the work of the Department. The first of a series of reforms planned for the promotion system will give greater importance to the achievement of specific goals in measuring officers' performance. While retaining the principle of career competition for Foreign Service officers, the reforms also will reduce somewhat in the middle ranks the pressures that the task forces believed have worked against creativity and initiative.

The first appointments were made in June to the Foreign Affairs Specialist Corps, a new Foreign Service personnel category that provides greater recognition and career incentive to specialists. Among the other reforms outlined in the 180-day report is a "Mustang" Program, which enables the Department to tap potential sources of talent internally by regularly identifying promising clerical and staff support

---

[45] The new system was placed in effect by the Foreign Relations Authorization Act of 1972 (Public Law 92-352, July 13, 1972).

employees for advancement to officer-level positions through special training and assignments.

The report discusses a number of reforms intended to stimulate creativity and openness within the Department. Included are new arrangements to subject policies to adversary challenge at varying levels and to make use of ad hoc groups for problem-solving, crossing jurisdictional lines freely. Finally, the Department has further extended the right of employees to dissent on policy and operations.

Striving for a freer exchange of ideas and information with outside institutions as the task forces recommended, the Department has increased its use of external research and engaged in specific programs to broaden its contacts with the rest of Government, private institutions, and the universities through personnel exchanges.

(5) *Establishment of the Council on International Economic Policy: White House Announcement, January 19, 1971.*[46]

(Complete Text)

The President today established the Council on International Economic Policy, and announced the appointment of Peter G. Peterson as Executive Director of the Council and Assistant to the President for International Economic Affairs. The Council includes as members the Secretaries of State, Treasury, Agriculture, Commerce, Labor; the Director of OMB [Office of Management and Budget] ; Chairman of the Council of Economic Advisers; the Assistant to the President for National Security Affairs; the Executive Director of the Domestic Council; and the Special Representative for Trade Negotiations. The President will be Chairman of the Council.

The Council is being formed to provide a clear, top-level focus on international economic issues and to achieve consistency between international and domestic economic policy. Peterson will be responsible for developing the agenda for the Council, and for assuring timely consideration of international economic policies.

Peterson, 46, is currently chairman of the board and chief executive officer of Bell and Howell Company. He joined the company in 1958 as executive vice president, became president in 1961, and chairman in 1968. He is a graduate of Northwestern University (1947, B.S., summa cum laude) and the University of Chicago (1951, M.B.A. with honors). Peterson is a director of the First National Bank of Chicago and the Illinois Bell Telephone Company, a trustee of the Brookings Institution, the University of Chicago, and National Educational Television.

---

46 Text from *Presidential Documents*, Jan. 25, 1971, pp. 79-80; for related material see same, pp. 78-79 and 80.

In the Executive Office of the President, the Council of Economic Advisers, the National Security Council, and the Office of Management and Budget are involved in various aspects of foreign economic affairs. More than 60 other units and coordinating bodies throughout the executive branch have responsibility for certain limited portions of foreign economic affairs. Presently, no single high-level body holds the responsibility for the development of international economic policy and its relations to domestic economic policy. The Council will have this responsibility.

The Executive Director of the Council will report directly to the President, and will be responsible, in collaboration with the members of the Council, for development of the overall direction of the Council's work. Where the Council's responsibility overlaps with that of the National Security Council, as in the case of foreign aid, which has implications for both national security policy and economic policy, the Council on International Economic Policy will operate within the general framework of national security policy developed by the NSC.

Peterson presently resides with his wife, four sons, and a daughter in Winnetka, Ill. He was born in Kearney, Nebr.

D. War Powers of the President.

[Attempts to clarify and redefine the constitutional authority of the President and Congress in the field of foreign affairs, particularly as regards the power to commit the armed forces to foreign combat, were a leading preoccupation of the legislative branch throughout the early 1970s. Inspired primarily by disagreement with the policies of successive Presidents in Southeast Asia, such efforts were also part of a broader movement aimed at checking or reversing the gradual increase in presidential power over foreign affairs that had been evident since World War II. In addition to congressional initiatives directed specifically toward limiting the American engagement in Indochina and/or requiring a reduction of American military forces in Europe, proposals to restrict the President's war-making powers without regard to geographical limitations gave rise as early as 1969 to the adoption by the Senate of the so-called "National Commitments Resolution" aimed at discouraging the use (or promised use) of the armed forces on foreign territory in the absence of affirmative action by the Congress.[47] American participation in military operations in Cambodia during 1970 prompted new initiatives in both houses of Congress. A resolution relating to the war powers of Congress and the President was actually approved by the House of Representatives on November 16, 1970, but

[47] Senate Resolution 85, 91st Cong., adopted June 25, 1969; text in *Documents, 1968-69*, pp. 50-51.

was not acted upon by the Senate, where a separate war-powers bill introduced by Senator Jacob K. Javits (Republican, New York) likewise failed to come up for action.

Efforts to enact a war-powers bill were renewed on the opening of the 92nd Congress in January 1971. In the House, a slightly modified war-powers resolution was reintroduced by Representative Clement J. Zablocki (Democrat, Wisconsin) and, following unanimous approval by the Foreign Affairs Committee, was passed by the House by a voice vote under suspension of the rules on August 2, 1971 (Document 6). In the Senate, Mr. Javits reintroduced on February 10, 1971, with the cosponsorship of three other senators, a revised version of his previous war-powers bill (Document 7); and four further war-powers bills were introduced by other senators. More far-reaching than the House resolution, all but one of the Senate bills required advance congressional authorization for the commitment of the armed forces to hostilities by the President, except in certain designated emergencies in which the forces could be committed without such authorization for a period not exceeding 30 days.

Hearings on these bills before the Senate Foreign Relations Committee were held intermittently from March to October, and a detailed statement of the administration's arguments against the proposed legislation was put forward by Secretary of State Rogers in an appearance before the committee on May 14, 1971 (Document 8). Following the conclusion of committee hearings, a synthesis of the various pending bills was drafted by their sponsors and introduced in the Senate on December 6, 1971 as the proposed War Powers Act of 1971.[48] No further action was taken during the 1971 session of Congress, and the bill is accordingly not included in the present collection. It was, however, approved by the Foreign Relations Committee on February 9, 1972, and passed by the Senate on April 13, 1972, although it failed of passage by the House.

As the result of persistent differences between House and Senate, no war-powers legislation was actually enacted by the Congress until November 7, 1973, when both houses voted to override a presidential veto of a war-powers resolution limiting the President's authority to introduce the armed forces into hostilities without congressional sanction to a period of 60 days, subject to a 30-day extension in specified circumstances.[49]]

(6) The Zablocki Resolution Before the House of Representatives.

[48] S. 2956, 92d Cong., 1st sess.; text in U.S. Senate, Committee on Foreign Relations, 92d Cong., 1st sess., *War Powers Legislation: Hearings . . . on S. 731, S.J. Res. 18 and S.J. Res. 59*, pp. iii-v, and in *A.F.R., 1972*, no. 3.
[49] Public Law 93-148, Nov. 7, 1973.

(a) Concerning the War Powers of the President and Congress: Report of the Committee on Foreign Affairs of the House of Representatives, July 27, 1971.[50]

(Excerpt)

The Committee on Foreign Affairs to whom was referred the resolution (H.J. Res. 1) concerning the war powers of Congress and the President, having considered the same, report favorably thereon without amendment and recommend that the joint resolution do pass.

COMMITTEE ACTION

In the 91st Congress, the House passed a resolution (H.J. Res. 1355) relating to the war powers of Congress and the President which had been referred by the Foreign Affairs Committee. It was approved under suspension of the rules on November 16, 1970, by a vote of 288 to 39.

When the Senate failed to act on the House-passed resolution before the end of the 91st Congress, it died with adjournment.

Upon the opening of the 92d Congress the chairman of the Foreign Affairs Subcommittee which had drafted the resolution[51] following extensive hearings reintroduced it with a slight modification as House Joint Resolution 1.

Additional hearings were held by the subcommittee on June 1 and 2 when testimony was taken from Members of Congress and representatives of the executive branch.[52] On June 8 the subcommittee voted to approve the proposal as introduced. Subsequently, the full committee on July 21 voted unanimously to report the bill without amendment.

THE SINGLE MODIFICATION

As noted, House Joint Resolution 1 is identical in every respect to the war powers resolution passed in the 91st Congress—with but one modification.

The original resolution contained the phrase "whenever feasible" in section 2 as:

It is the sense of Congress that, whenever feasible, the President

---

[50] U.S. House of Representatives, 92d Cong., 1st sess., House Report 92-383, July 27, 1971.

[51] Representative Clement J. Zablocki (Democrat, Wisconsin).

[52] A statement to the subcommittee by John R. Stevenson, Legal Adviser of the State Department, appears in *Bulletin,* June 28, 1971, pp. 833-36. The arguments presented are similar to those advanced by the Secretary of State in Document 8.

should seek appropriate consultation with the Congress before involving the Armed Forces * * *.

In reintroducing the proposal in the 92d Congress the subcommittee chairman, after consultation with cosponsors, eliminated the phrase from the section. The reasons were: (1) The phrase apparently had been the controversial part of the resolution during its consideration in the House in 1970, with some Members basing their opposition on the inclusion of those words; (2) elimination of the phrase has no basically significant effect on the meaning of the resolution. The entire section remains a "sense of Congress" provision and thus advisory, rather than mandatory, on the President.

BACKGROUND

The Cambodian incursion of May 1970[53] undoubtedly provided the immediate impetus for a number of bills and resolutions on the war powers. Many Members of Congress, including those who supported the action, were disturbed by the lack of prior consultation with Congress and the near crisis in relations between the executive and legislative branches which the incident occasioned.

The issue is basically a constitutional one. It concerns the "twilight zone" of concurrent authority which the Founding Fathers gave the Congress and the President over the war powers of the National Government.

The term "war powers" may be taken to mean the authority inherent in national sovereignties to declare, conduct, and conclude armed hostilities with other states. In the U.S. Constitution the war powers which are expressly reserved to the Congress are found in article 1, section 8, of the Constitution:

1. The Congress shall have power * * *

*   *   *

11. To declare war, grant letters of marque and reprisal, and make rules concerning captures on land and water;

12. To raise and support armies, but no appropriation of money to that use shall be for a longer term than 2 years;

13. To provide and maintain a Navy;

14. To make rules for the government and regulation of the land and naval forces;

---

53 *The United States in World Affairs, 1970*, pp. 135-42.

15. To provide for calling forth the militia to execute the laws of the Union, suppress insurrections and repel invasions;

16. To provide for organizing, arming, and disciplining the militia and for governing such part of them as may be employed in the service of the United States;

*   *   *

18. To make all laws which shall be necessary and proper for carrying into execution the foregoing powers vested by this constitution in the Government of the United States, or in any department or officer thereof.

The war powers of the President are expressed in article II, section 2: "1. The President shall be Commander in Chief of the Army and Navy of the United States, and of the militia of the several States, when called into the actual service of the United States * * *."

The interpretation and application of this constitutional grant have varied widely through our Nation's history. Testimony received during the hearings confirmed the view of many Members of Congress and outside observers that the constitutional "balance" of authority over warmaking had swung heavily to the President in modern times, and that Congress is now required to reassert its own prerogatives and responsibilities.

In shaping legislation to that purpose, the intention was not to reflect criticism on activities of Presidents, past or present, or to take punitive action. Rather, the focus of concern was the appropriate scope and substance of congressional and Presidential authority in the exercise of the power of war in order that the Congress might fulfill its responsibilities under the Constitution while permitting the President to exercise his.

The objective, throughout the consideration of war powers legislation, was to define arrangements which would allow the President and Congress to work together in mutual respect and maximum harmony toward their ultimate, shared goal of maintaining the peace and security of the Nation.

The success of this effort to maintain an environment of cooperation and understanding between the two branches of Government was demonstrated, at least in part, by the willingness of representatives of the executive branch to provide consultation and advice during the period in which the legislation was being formed.

*   *   *

(b) Joint Resolution Concerning the War Powers of the Congress

and the President, Passed by the House of Representatives August 2, 1971.[54]

(Complete Text)

Resolved by the Senate and House of Representatives of the United States of America in Congress assembled, That the Congress reaffirms its powers under the Constitution to declare war. The Congress recognizes that the President in certain extraordinary and emergency circumstances has the authority to defend the United States and its citizens without specific prior authorization by the Congress.

SEC. 2. It is the sense of Congress that the President should seek appropriate consultation with the Congress before involving the Armed Forces of the United States in armed conflict, and should continue such consultation periodically during such armed conflict.

SEC. 3. In any case in which the President without specific prior authorization by the Congress—

(1) commits United States military forces to armed conflict:

(2) commits military forces equipped for combat to the territory, airspace, or waters of a foreign nation, except for deployments which relate solely to supply, repair, or training of United States forces, or for humanitarian or other peaceful purposes; or

(3) substantially enlarges military forces already located in a foreign nation;

the President shall submit promptly to the Speaker of the House of Representatives and to the President of the Senate a report, in writing, setting forth—

(A) the circumstances necessitating his action;

(B) the constitutional, legislative, and treaty provisions under the authority of which he took such action, together with his reasons for not seeking specific prior congressional authorization;

(C) the estimated scope of activities; and

(D) such other information as the President may deem useful to the Congress in the fulfillment of its constitutional responsibilities with respect to committing the Nation to war and to the use of United States Armed Forces abroad.

SEC. 4. Nothing in this joint resolution is intended to alter the constitutional authority of the Congress or of the President, or the provisions of existing treaties.

Passed the House of Representatives August 2, 1971.

Attest:

W. PAT JENNINGS.

Clerk.

---

[54] House Joint Resolution 1, 92d Cong., 1st sess; text from *War Powers Legislation: Hearings* (cited in note 48), p. 862. The resolution was passed by voice vote under suspension of the rules.

(7) The Javits Bill Before the Senate.

(a) Statement by Senator Jacob K. Javits to the Senate, February 10, 1971.[55]

(Excerpts)

S. 731–INTRODUCTION OF A BILL
TO REGULATE UNDECLARED WAR

Mr. JAVITS. Mr. President, the most compelling lesson of the 1960's for the United States is our need to devise procedures to prevent future undeclared wars as in Vietnam. I believe that an effective statutory remedy is both possible and essential. The guidelines for such legislation can be derived from within the Constitution.

Today, on behalf of myself and Senators MATHIAS, PELL, and SPONG,[56] I am introducing a bill "to make rules respecting military hostilities in the absence of a declaration of war." This bill is a serious effort to meet an important legislative need. After much thought and research, I am convinced that this approach grows directly out of the Constitution itself.

The bill deals with the initiation of hostilities in the absence of a congressional declaration of war. It makes full provision for the need for "emergency" action by specifying four categories, based on historical precedents, in which the President as Commander in Chief can initiate combat hostilities in the absence of a declaration of war.

History has demonstrated that there are situations in which military hostilities must be initiated by the Armed Forces in the absence of a declaration of war. Such cases arise in circumstances which require combat actions but which are not sufficiently serious—or in which contemporary conditions make it undesirable—to enact a declaration of war. Moreover, it has long been recognized that there are circumstances in which there is not sufficient time—or room for movement—for a congressional declaration of war before military hostilities must be undertaken.

*   *   *

I regard my bill as giving ample play to the need of the Commander in Chief to have discretionary as well as emergency authority. At the same

---

[55] *Congressional Record* (Daily Edition), Feb. 10, 1971, pp. S 1204-5.
[56] Charles McC. Mathias, Jr. (Republican, Maryland); Claiborne Pell (Democrat, Rhode Island); William B. Spong, Jr. (Democrat, Virginia).

time, the bill immediately establishes a role for Congress right from the beginning: First, by requiring the President to report fully and promptly to the Congress as to the circumstances of and the authority for the action he has initiated; second, by requiring the President to terminate in 30 days whatever actions he has initiated under one of the four specified categories, in the absence of a declaration of war, "except as provided in legislation enacted by the Congress to sustain such hostilities beyond 30 days."

The bill further provides that hostilities initiated by the President can be terminated by joint resolution of the Congress in less than the 30 days otherwise allowed. In addition, there is a detailed section which would prevent a filibuster from blocking congressional action.

The period of 30 days is, of course, essentially an arbitrary one. But I think it is just about the right period of time—and it can be shortened or lengthened in particular instances as the Congress might decide. On balance, I feel that a period of 30 days strikes a fair balance between the desirability of full deliberative action by Congress—without impairing the capacity for sudden, or emergency, action by the Commander in Chief, and the requirement of brevity to prevent the Nation from being involved beyond the point of recall before the Congress might otherwise act.

I also wish to make it clear that my bill anticipates full prior consultations between the President and the Congress with respect to developing or deepening crises which might be leading toward the outbreak of armed hostilities. There are many drawbacks in the contemporary world to a declaration of war—because of the far-reaching domestic and international implications of a declaration of war, whether enacted before or after the initiation of combat hostilities.

In developing situations which are not of a sudden nature, I believe that it would be good practice for the administration to consult with the Congress and seek a joint resolution outlining the policy which the United States intends to pursue. I would like to see this become normal practice. I am referring here to serious situations which might involve the use or threat of the use of armed force. I am not suggesting that the President should be obliged to seek a resolution from Congress to endorse all of the policies or actions he initiates—only those which move toward the exercise of the war powers.

I ask unanimous consent that the text of my bill be printed in the RECORD at this point in my remarks.

The PRESIDING OFFICER. The bill will be received and appropriately referred; and, without objection, the bill will be printed in the RECORD.

The bill (S. 731) to make rules respecting military hostilities in the absence of a declaration of war, introduced by Mr. Javits (for himself and other Senators), was received, read twice by its title, referred to the

Committee on Foreign Relations, and ordered to be printed in the RECORD, as follows:

(b) A Bill to Make Rules Respecting Military Hostilities in the Absence of a Declaration of War, Introduced February 10, 1971.[57]

(Complete Text)

Be it enacted by the Senate and House of Representatives of the United States of America in Congress assembled, That use of the Armed Forces of the United States in military hostilities in the absence of a declaration of war be governed by the following rules, to be executed by the President as Commander-in-Chief:

A. The Armed Forces of the United States, under the President as Commander-in-Chief, may act

1. to repel a sudden attack against the United States, its territories, and possessions.

2. to repel an attack against the Armed Forces of the United States on the high seas or lawfully stationed on foreign territory;

3. to protect the lives and property, as may be required, of United States nationals abroad; and

4. to comply with a national commitment resulting exclusively from affirmative action taken by the executive and legislative branches of the United States Government through means of a treaty, convention, or other legislative instrumentality specifically intended to give effect to such a commitment, where immediate military hostilities by the Armed Forces of the United States are required.

B. The initiation of military hostilities under circumstances described in paragraph A, in the absence of a declaration of war, shall be reported promptly to the Congress by the President as Commander in Chief, together with a full account of the circumstances under which such military hostilities were initiated.

C. Such military hostilities, in the absence of a declaration of war, shall not be sustained beyond thirty days from the date of their initiation except as provided in legislation enacted by the Congress to sustain such hostilities beyond thirty days.

D. Authorization to sustain military hostilities in the absence of a declaration of war, as specified in paragraph (A) of this section may be terminated prior to the thirty-day period specified in paragraph (C) of this section by joint resolution of Congress.

SEC. 2. (A) Any bill or resolution, authorizing continuance of military hostilities under paragraph C (section 1) of this Act, or of termina-

---

[57] S. 731, 92d Cong., 1st sess.; text from *Congressional Record* (Daily Edition), Feb. 10, 1971, p. S 1205.

tion under paragraph D (section 1) shall, if sponsored or cosponsored by one-third of the Members of the House of Congress in which it originates, be considered reported to the floor of such House no later than one day following its introduction, unless the Members of such House otherwise determine by yeas and nays; and any such bill or resolution referred to a committee after having passed one House of Congress shall be considered reported from such committee within one day after it is referred to such committee, unless the Members of the House referring it to committee shall otherwise determine by yeas and nays.

(B) Any bill or resolution reported pursuant to subsection (A) of section 2 shall immediately become the pending business of the House to which it is reported, and shall be voted upon within three days after such report, unless such House shall otherwise determine by yeas and nays.

SEC. 3. This Act shall not apply to military hostilities already undertaken before the effective date of this Act.

(8) Congress, the President, and the War Powers: Statement by Secretary of State Rogers Before the Senate Committee on Foreign Relations, May 14, 1971. [58]

(Excerpts)

I. INTRODUCTION

It is, as always, my privilege to appear before this committee. I am grateful to you, Mr. Chairman [Senator J. W. Fulbright], and to members of the committee for the opportunity to testify on the serious questions under consideration.

The committee has helped stimulate an important examination of the war powers of the President and Congress under our Constitution. This administration, of course, fully respects Congress' right to exercise its constitutional role in decisions involving the use of military force and in the formulation of our Nation's foreign policy. We realize that under our constitutional system decisions in this vital area should reflect a common perspective among the Legislature, the Executive, and the electorate so that each may play its proper role. We also recognize that this common perspective can only be built through cooperation and consultation between the legislative and executive branches. Generally speaking, the constitutional process so wisely conceived by the

[58] Department of State Press Release 109, May 14, 1971; text in *Bulletin*, June 7, 1971, pp. 721-33. The statement appears also in *War Powers Legislation: Hearings* (cited in note 48), pp. 485-502.

Founding Fathers has worked well throughout our history. Any attempt to change it should be approached carefully and should be subjected to long and full consideration of all aspects of the problem.

The issue before us involves the constitutional authority to commit forces to armed combat and related questions. These questions have been the subject of considerable debate and scholarly attention.[59] Unfortunately, they are often approached polemically, with one side arguing the President's constitutional authority as Commander in Chief and the other side asserting Congress' constitutional power to declare war—the implication being that these powers are somehow incompatible. The contrary is true. The framers of the Constitution intended that there be a proper balance between the roles of the President and Congress in decisions to use force in the conduct of foreign policy.

In discussing these issues with you today, I wish first to review the historical background of the war powers question, beginning with the Constitution itself and tracing the practice of the Nation throughout our history. I would then like to place the war powers issue in the modern context and discuss with you the factors which I see bearing on the issue of the exercise of Presidential and congressional powers now and in the foreseeable future. Finally, from this perspective, I will describe what I believe the national interest requires in terms of a proper balance between the President and the Congress.

First, let me stress that cooperation between the executive and legislative branches is the heart of the political process as conceived by the framers of the Constitution. In the absence of such cooperation, no legislation which seeks to define constitutional powers more rigidly can be effective. Conversely, given such cooperation, such legislation is unnecessary. Obviously there is need for, and great value in, congressional participation in the formulation of foreign policy and in decisions regarding the use of force. But at the same time there is a clear need in terms of national survival for preserving the constitutional power of the President to act in emergency situations.

*   *   *

IV. THE PROPER BALANCE BETWEEN CONGRESS AND THE PRESIDENT

Thus far I have discussed what has happened to the war powers over the course of our history and described the modern context in which those powers must be exercised. The most difficult question is still before us: What should we seek for the future—what is the proper balance between the Congress and the President?

59 Footnote in original omitted.

It seems to me that we must start from the recognition that the exercise of the war powers under the Constitution is essentially a political process. It requires cooperation and mutual trust between the President and Congress and wise judgment on the part of both if the Nation's interests are to be well served.

Your committee now has before it several bills[60] which attempt to define and codify the war powers of the President and Congress in a way that I believe would not serve the Nation's long-term interests. I believe that the objectives of the sponsors of these bills, including Senator Javits, Senator Taft, and Senator Eagleton, and most recently Senator Stennis,[61] are the same as the objectives of this administration. We both want to avoid involving the Nation in wars, but if hostilities are forced upon us, we want to make certain that United States involvement is quickly and effectively undertaken and is fully in accordance with our constitutional processes. So the difference is not in our objectives but in how to achieve those objectives.

I am opposed to the legislation before you as a way to achieve these objectives because (1) it attempts to fix in detail, and to freeze, the allocation of the war power between the President and Congress—a step which the framers in their wisdom quite deliberately decided against—and (2) it attempts in a number of respects to narrow the power given the President by the Constitution.

Regarding the first point, these bills reflect an approach which is not consistent with our constitutional tradition. The framers of the Constitution invested the executive and legislative branches with war powers appropriate to their respective roles and capabilities, without attempting to specify precisely who would do what in what circumstances and in what time period or how far one branch could go without the other. This was left to the political process, which is characteristic of the constitutional system of separation of powers. Our constitutional system is founded on an assumption of cooperation rather than conflict, and this is vitally necessary in matters of war and peace. The effective operation of that system requires that both branches work together from a common perspective rather than seeking to forge shackles based on the assumption of divergent perspectives.

As for the second aspect, although the bills recognize to a significant extent the President's full range of constitutional authority, they do tend to limit the President in some questionable ways. It appears, for example, that two of the bills[62] do not cover situations like that of the Cuban missile crisis. In failing to recognize the need for immediate

---

60 Footnote in original omitted.
61 Senators Jacob K. Javits (Republican, New York), Robert Taft, Jr. (Republican, Ohio), Thomas F. Eagleton (Democrat, Missouri), and John Stennis (Democrat, Mississippi).
62 Footnote in original omitted.

action and the propriety of a Presidential response to such situations, the bills are unduly restrictive. It is inconceivable, for example, that the President could have carried out the delicate diplomatic negotiations with the Soviets which led to the removal of the missiles from Cuba if there had been a full-scale congressional debate prior to his deciding on a course of military and diplomatic action.

Some of the bills would also seek to restrict the President's authority to deploy forces abroad short of hostilities. This raises a serious constitutional issue of interference with the President's authority under the Constitution as Commander in Chief. Moreover, requiring prior congressional authorization for deployment of forces can deprive the President of a valuable instrument of diplomacy which is used most often to calm a crisis rather than inflame it. For example, such a restriction could seriously limit the ability of the President to make a demonstration of force to back up the exercise of our rights and responsibilities in Berlin or to deploy elements of the 6th Fleet in the Mediterranean in connection with the Middle East situation.

At least two of the bills would require that action initiated by the President within his specified authority be terminated after 30 days unless Congress enacts sustaining legislation,[63] and three of the bills would permit Congress to terminate Presidential action in less than 30 days.[64] The bills would provide for expedited action on such legislation but would not and could not insure definitive congressional action within the 30-day period. This raises another constitutional issue; that is, whether the President's authority under the Constitution—for example, to protect the Nation against sudden attack—could be limited or terminated by congressional action or inaction. The 30-day limitation also raises practical problems regarding the conduct of our forces. Once our forces are committed to hostilities, it might prove impossible to terminate those hostilities and provide for the safety of our forces within an arbitrary time period. To the extent the legislation would impinge in these ways upon the President's authority as Commander in Chief and Chief Executive, it is of doubtful constitutionality.

There is another consideration. To circumscribe Presidential ability to act in emergency situations—or even to appear to weaken it—would run the grave risk of miscalculation by a potential enemy regarding the ability of the United States to act in a crisis. This might embolden such a nation to provoke crises or take other actions which undermine international peace and security.

I do not believe we have sufficient foresight to provide wisely for all contingencies that may arise in the future. I am sure the Founding Fathers acted on that premise, and we should be most reluctant to

[63] Footnote in original omitted.
[64] Footnote in original omitted.

reverse that judgment. Moreover, I firmly believe that Congress' ability to exercise its constitutional powers does not depend on restricting in advance the necessary flexibility which the Constitution has given the President.

At the same time, I want to make clear that I do not interpret "flexibility" as a euphemism for unchecked Executive power. Some have argued that Congress' power to declare war should be interpreted as a purely symbolic act with little real substance in a world in which declared wars have become infrequent despite the existence of real hostilities.[65] In my judgment, it would be improper to do so. Congress' power to declare war retains real meaning in the modern context. While the form in which the power is exercised may change, nevertheless the constitutional imperative remains: If the Nation is to be taken into war or to embark on actions which run serious risk of war, the critical decisions must be made only after the most searching examination and on the basis of a national consensus and they must be truly representative of the will of the people. For this reason, we must insure that such decisions reflect the effective exercise by the Congress and the President of their respective constitutional responsibilities.

V. CONCLUSION

What needs to be done to insure that the constitutional framework of shared responsibility for the exercise of the war powers works in the Nation's best interests?

First, we are prepared to explore with you ways of helping Congress reinforce its own information capability on issues involving war and peace. For example, I would be prepared to instruct each of our geographic Assistant Secretaries to provide your committee on a regular basis with a full briefing on developments in his respective area, if you believed this would be helpful. Regular and continuing briefings would enable the committee to keep abreast of developing crisis situations. This would be in addition to the numerous official and informal contacts which regularly take place between members of the two branches.

Second, there needs to be effective consultation between Congress and the President, and we have tried to follow this policy. It is not only Congress that is weakened by a lack of consultation. Our Nation's foreign policy is itself weakened when it does not reflect continuing interaction and consultation between the two branches.

Third, the Congress must effectively exercise the powers which it has under the Constitution in the war powers area. In its 1969 report on the National Commitments Resolution,[66] your committee recognized

---

[65] Footnote in original omitted.
[66] Cf. note 47.

that "no constitutional amendment or legislative enactment is required" for Congress to assert its constitutional authority. "If Congress makes clear that it intends to exercise these powers," the report states in referring to Congress' war powers, "it is most unlikely that the executive will fail to respect that intention."[67] I agree with that conclusion.

Fourth, there is the need to act speedily, and sometimes without prior publicity, in crisis situations. We should try to find better institutional methods to keep these requirements from becoming an obstacle to Congress' exercising its full and proper role. Suggestions have come from a number of quarters for the establishment of a joint congressional committee which could act as a consultative body with the President in times of emergencies. If, after study, you believe this idea has merit, we would be prepared to discuss it with the committee and determine how best we could cooperate.

Fifth, there is, in my view, the clear need to preserve the President's ability to act in emergencies in accordance with his constitutional responsibilities. This ability to act in emergencies, by its very nature, cannot be defined precisely in advance. Let me emphasize that I am not suggesting a Presidential *carte blanche*. As I indicated at the beginning of my statement, I believe the framers of the Constitution intended decisions regarding the initiation of hostilities to be made jointly by the Congress and the President, except in emergency situations. I believe that constitutional design remains valid today.

In conclusion, I would like to refer to the suggestion which the distinguished Senator from Mississippi, Senator Stennis, made last Tuesday [May 11] that the war powers question requires thorough consideration and full study. He said, "I think this matter should be pending for a year or more. It must be understood in every facet and the people must understand fully the question that is involved."[68] I believe that is wise advice. This is a basic question affecting our constitutional structure and the security of our Nation. It is most important that such a matter be considered deliberately and calmly, in an atmosphere free from the emotion and the passions that have been generated by the Viet-Nam conflict.

We in the executive branch are prepared to continue the discussion of the war powers question with you. Our sole objective is to insure that the Nation's interests are best served in this vital area.

My own view is that the constitutional framework of shared war powers is wise and serves the interests of the Nation well in the modern world. The recognition of the necessity for cooperation between the President and Congress in this area and for the participation of both in decisionmaking could not be clearer than it is today. What is required is

---

[67] Footnote in original omitted.
[68] *Congressional Record* (Daily Edition), May 11, 1971, p. S 6616.

the judicious and constructive exercise by each branch of its constitutional powers rather than seeking to draw arbitrary lines between them.

E. Current Progress and Problems.

[The documentary record of American foreign policy in 1971 includes, as always, a quantity of speeches, press briefings, and miscellaneous pronouncements by the President, the Secretary of State, and subordinate officials on virtually every aspect of current foreign relations. Many of these statements are included in the specialized chapters that follow. Of the two selected for inclusion here, President Nixon's briefing of news media executives in Kansas City on July 6, 1971 (Document 9) is of interest as a comprehensive survey of the interaction of domestic and international concerns at a time when the presidential visit to mainland China was under consideration and when the conditions that were to prompt the enunciation of the "New Economic Policy" on August 15, 1971, were already building up. The excerpt from Secretary of State Rogers' year-end news conference (Document 10) offers a preliminary assessment of foreign policy gains and losses during the year as a whole.]

(9) America's Position in the World: Remarks by President Nixon to News Media Executives Attending a Background Briefing on Domestic Policy Initiatives, Kansas City, Missouri, July 6, 1971.[69]

(Complete Text)

Ladies and gentlemen, from reading the agenda, I think you have had a pretty full plate on the domestic issues. I gather from looking at the people here at the head table that you have been briefed.

I heard the answer to the last question on the economy. I understand there were other questions on that, and on the health program, also on our environment, on our revenue sharing, reorganization programs, on our crime programs, particularly with regard to the control of dangerous drugs, and also programs that may be in related fields that Mr. MacGregor[70] may have covered.

I think perhaps for this kind of meeting, what I could best do is to put all of these domestic programs into a broader context, to indicate

---

[69] *Presidential Documents*, July 12, 1971, pp. 1034-40.
[70] Clark MacGregor, Counsel to the President for Congressional Relations.

the relationship between these programs and the problems that America has in the world.

Sometimes that seems very, very hard to do. I realize that it is quite the approach these days to suggest that we either ought to look at our foreign policy and put that as priority number one, in other words, the security of America must come first, or we must put our priority on domestic problems, and turn away from the problems in the world.

The answer to that is that we must do both. It would not be any good to have clean air and water if we were not around to enjoy it. On the other side of the coin, we are not going to play an effective role in the world unless we have a healthy environment, economically and every other way.

For a few moments, I would like to discuss the world position we find ourselves in today, and indicate why I believe these domestic programs, a program of reform which goes far beyond any program of reform which has been submitted to the American people in over 40 years; why that program is so essential at this particular time; why it is that America now cannot be satisfied domestically, we cannot rest on our laurels; why we have to make a critical examination of everything we are doing in this country to see whether we are doing it with the most efficiency possible.

Now, in terms of our world situation, the tendency is—and this has been the case for the last 5 to 6 years—for us to obscure our vision, almost totally, of the world because of Vietnam. That is understandable. We are always concerned about the war in which we are currently involved. That was true at the time of Korea. It is now true of Vietnam.

The difficulty is that as we obscure our vision with Vietnam, we do not see very significant changes that have occurred in the world over the past 25 years, the period since World War II, and changes that have occurred even more dramatically, perhaps, over the past 5 to 10 years, and ones that may be in the offing. So I would like to take Vietnam very briefly.

I have nothing new to say on Vietnam. It seems to me, however, that since so much has been written and said in recent weeks about how we got in, it might be well to reiterate what we are doing to get out.

On Vietnam, what we find is that 300,000 Americans have left Vietnam since this administration came in. A division a month are coming home each month at this time. As far as casualties are concerned, it is interesting to note that the casualties in the month of June were less on a monthly basis than the weekly casualties we were having a year ago. When we came into office, they were 15 times as great per month or week or day, take the index, whatever it is. One is too many, but that does indicate the winding down of the war.

As far as the ending of the war is concerned, as far as American involvement, we find that we are proceeding on two tracks. We are actively pursuing the negotiating channel. We also, regardless of what happens on the negotiating front, are pursuing our program of Vietnamization in which all Americans will be withdrawn from Vietnam consistent with two objectives: first, of course, the release of our prisoners of war; and secondly, in a way that will contribute to a permanent and lasting peace, we hope, in Southeast Asia and in the Pacific, rather than in a way that might increase the danger of another war.

I will simply conclude this section by saying this: Vietnam is an issue which, of course, concerns us. It is an issue, however, to which we have an answer. The American involvement is being ended. It will be ended certainly. The question is only a matter of time and only a matter of how. So consequently, it seems to me that a group of editors, opinion makers like yourselves, should, and I think will, appreciate the opportunity to look beyond Vietnam.[71]

For example, a year from now, what is the world going to look like as Vietnam moves from our vision, or at least recedes from it, and what will America's role in the world be at that time?

As I came into the room, I noticed Martin Hayden. I shook hands with him. I perhaps can put my remarks on the world scene in context by pointing out that he first came to see me when I was a freshman Congressman. It was 24 years ago. I was thinking how much had happened in those 24 years. Many of you, a few of you, are old enough to remember what America was 24 years ago.

We were number one in the world militarily, with no one who even challenged us because we had a monopoly on atomic weapons. We also at that point were number one economically by all odds. In fact, the United States of America was producing more than 50 percent of all the world's goods.

That was just 25 years ago. Now, 25 years having passed, let's look at the situation today and what it may be five years from now or ten years from now. I will not try to limit myself to five or ten years except to say that in the next decade we are going to see changes that may be even greater than what have occurred in the last 25 years, and very great ones have occurred in that respect.

First, instead of just America being number one in the world from an economic standpoint, the preeminent world power, and instead of there being just two superpowers, when we think in economic terms and economic potentialities, there are five great power centers in the world today. Let's look at them very briefly.

There is, of course, the United States of America. There is, second, Western Europe—Western Europe with Britain in the Common Market.[72] That means 300 million of the most advanced people in the

---

[71] See further Documents 71-81.
[72] Cf. note 2 to Chapter X.

world, with all the productivity and all the capacity that those people will have and, of course, with the clout that they will have when they act together, as they certainly will. That is a new factor in the world scene that will come, and come very soon, as we all know.

Then in the Pacific, looking also at free world countries, we have a resurgent Japan. I met with steel leaders of industry and unions this morning. I pointed out what happened to Japan in terms of their business. Twenty years ago Japan produced 5 million tons of steel; this year 100 million; 2 years from now Japan will produce more steel than the United States of America.

That is what has happened. It has happened in the case of Japan, in the case of Germany, our two major enemies in World War II, partly as a result of our help in getting them on their feet, and partly because of their own energy and ability.

Now we have three power centers—the United States, Western Europe, and Japan, noting that both Western Europe and Japan are very potent competitors of the United States; friends, yes; allies, yes; but competing and competing very hard with us throughout the world for economic leadership.

Now we turn to the other two superpowers, economic superpowers I will say for the moment. The Soviet Union, of course, first comes to mind. Looking at the Soviet Union, we are entering a period which only time will tell may be successful in terms of creating a very new relationship or a very different relationship than we have had previously.

I referred to the need for an era of negotiation rather than confrontation when I made my inaugural speech.[73] We have been negotiating. We have made some progress in the negotiations. The important thing is, we are negotiating rather than confronting in many areas of the world, where confrontation could lead to explosion. Whether it is on limitation of nuclear arms, the issue of Europe, or negotiations on the Mideast, the negotiations are going on.[74]

I am not suggesting that these negotiations are going to lead to instant peace and instant relationships with the Soviet Union such as we presently have with our friends in Asia who may be allied with us, or who may have systems of government that are more closely aligned to ours. What we have to recognize is that even as we limit arms, if we do reach an agreement in that field, and even if we find ways to avoid confrontation in other areas, and perhaps work out a negotiated settlement for mutual force reductions in Europe, and the problem of Berlin and all the others that come to mind, we must recognize that the Soviet Union will continue to be a very potent, powerful, aggressive competitor of the United States of America. And, ironically—and this is also true of

[73] *Documents, 1968-69*, p. 41.
[74] Cf. Documents 11-28.

Mainland China, as I will point out in a moment—as we have more and more success on the negotiation front, as for example the Soviet Union, like the United States, may be able if we have a limitation in nuclear arms, if we are able to turn our eyes more toward our economic development and our economic problems, it simply means that the competition changes and becomes much more challenging in the economic area than it has been previously.

So what we find, in other words, is that the success, and we do want success, of a policy of negotiation rather than confrontation will lead to infinitely more economic competition from the Soviet Union.

Mainland China is, of course, a very different situation. First in terms of its economic capacity at the present time, a pretty good indication of where it is is that Japan, with 100 million people, produces more than Mainland China with 800 million people. But that should not mislead us, and it gives us and should give none of the potential competitors in the world markets, Mainland China, any sense of satisfaction that it will always be that way, because when we see the Chinese as people—and I have seen them all over the world, and some of you have, too, whether in Hong Kong or Thailand or Singapore or Bangkok, any of the great cities, Manila, where Chinese are there—they are creative, they are productive, they are one of the most capable people in the world, and 800 million Chinese are going to be, inevitably, an enormous economic power, with all that means in terms of what they could be in other areas if they move in that direction.

That is the reason why I felt that it was essential that this administration take the first steps toward ending the isolation of Mainland China from the world community. We had to take those steps because the Soviet Union could not, because of differences that they have that at the present time seem to be irreconcilable. We were the only other power that could take those steps.

Let me be very, shall I say, limited in what I would discuss on this particular issue, because we should not consider that more has happened than has happened. What we have done is simply open the door—open the door for travel, open the door for trade.

Now the question is whether there will be other doors opened on their part. But at least the doors must be opened and the goal of U.S. policy must be, in the long term, ending the isolation of Mainland China and a normalization of our relations with Mainland China because, looking down the road—and let's just look ahead 15 to 20 years—the United States could have a perfectly effective agreement with the Soviet Union for limitation of arms; the danger of any confrontation there might have been almost totally removed.

But Mainland China, outside the world community, completely isolated, with its leader not in communication with world leaders, would be a danger to the whole world that would be unacceptable,

unacceptable to us and unacceptable to others, as well.

So, consequently, this step must be taken now. Others must be taken, very precisely, very deliberately, as there is reciprocation on the other side.[75]

But now let's see how this all fits into the economic program I mentioned a moment ago, and the economic challenge. The very success of our policy of ending the isolation of Mainland China will mean an immense escalation of their economic challenge, not only to us, but to others in the world.

I again come back to the fundamental point: 800 million Chinese, open to the world, with all the communication and the interchange of ideas that inevitably will occur as a result of that opening, will become an economic force in the world of enormous potential.

So, in sum, what do we see? What we see as we look ahead 5, 10, and perhaps 15 years, we see five great economic superpowers: the United States, Western Europe, the Soviet Union, Mainland China, and, of course, Japan.

Now, I do [not] suggest, in mentioning these five, that Latin America is not important, that Africa is not important, that South Asia is not important. All nations are important and all peoples in underdeveloped or less developed countries will play their role. But these are the five that will determine the economic future, and because economic power will be the key to other kinds of power, the future of the world in other ways in the last third of this century.

Now let's see what this means to the United States. It means that the United States, as compared with that position we found ourselves in immediately after World War II, has a challenge such as we did not even dream of. Then we were talking about the dollar gap; then we were talking about the necessity of, putting it in terms of a poker game, that the United States had all the chips and we had to spread a few of the chips around so that others could play.

We did it. $100 billion for Western Europe to rebuild them, and billions of others to other countries, and it was the correct policy as it turned out. Now as we see the world in which we are about to move, the United States is no longer in the position of complete preeminence or predominance. That is not a bad thing. As a matter of fact, it could be a constructive thing. The United States is still the strongest nation in the world, the richest nation in the world, but now we face a situation where four other potential economic powers have the capacity, have the kind of people—if not the kind of government, at least the kind of people—who can challenge us on every front.

That brings us back home, and it brings us back home for a hard look at what America needs to do if we are going to run this race economi-

75 See further Documents 85-94.

cally and run it effectively and maintain the position of world leadership, a position that can only be maintained if the United States retains its preeminent position in the economic field.

I could sum up briefly this way: First in personal terms we need a healthy people. Mr. Richardson[76] has, of course, directed his comments to the need for programs that will make us a more healthy people in a very physical sense. We need a healthy environment and Mr. Ruckelshaus[77] has directed his remarks to programs that will make the environment in this country more healthy.

We also need a healthy economy, and Mr. Stein[78] has been talking about the economy. I think it is only relevant to mention that in terms of the economy that we have a situation here that at the moment, again, obscures our vision because of temporary problems which will change once the problems move along. For example, when we consider the problems of unemployment, it must be noted that if the 1,200,000 who have been let out of defense plants and out of the Armed Forces since this administration came in were still in the Armed Forces and Vietnam and defense plants, unemployment would be less than 5 percent today. But the cost would be too high. What we want is high employment, full employment to the extent that we can get full employment, but without the cost of war. We can have it. That is what our policy is directed to achieve.

When we speak of a healthy economy, we are also speaking, as Mr. Stein mentioned—I heard his answer to the last question—of an economy in which the fires of inflation have been cooled. We are moving on that. We have made some progress, not enough, but we have made some.

At this particular point, it is essential that whether it is in having to make the hard decision to veto a public works bill which would not speak to the problem of unemployment now, but would enormously escalate the problem of inflation a year or 2 or 3 or 4 years from now, or whether it is in speaking to the leaders of labor and management and calling upon them to be responsive and responsible in their wage-price decisions in seeing that they are not inflationary, the United States, of course, if it is going to have a healthy economy, must move in those particular areas, as well as in others.

Also, when we speak in terms of our health, we must speak in terms of how we accomplish some of these goals. Let me now speak quite directly about a problem that I know has been the subject of many editorials, editorials of newspapers and, of course, on television and radio, to the extent that you are permitted to do so.

[76] Elliot L. Richardson, Secretary of Health, Education and Welfare.
[77] William D. Ruckelshaus, Administrator of the Environmental Protection Agency.
[78] Herbert Stein, member of the Council of Economic Advisers.

First, it has become rather common practice to berate the American system. Now, without being a bit jingoistic, and being totally objective, let's examine this system of ours, examine it in terms of the problems that I have just mentioned. Health: It would be very easy at the time that we are looking at the problems of the distribution of health care to throw the baby out with the bath water and to fail to recognize that at the present time while we have enormous problems which need to be dealt with, of distributing health care fairly so that everybody who needs medical care can get it, we must handle that problem without destroying what we also enjoy, the best medical care in the world in terms of quality. That is why our medical program and our health program is not one that throws out the present medical care system. It builds on it. It reforms it. It corrects it.

Let's look at the environment for a moment. Here one is tempted, as he goes into a place like Los Angeles, and I will be there in a few hours, and you see the smog, that yellow ugly smog hanging over the city or when you go down the Potomac and see the filth in that river, one is tempted to say: Wouldn't it be great if we didn't have automobiles? Wouldn't it be great if we didn't have all these factories? Wouldn't it be great if we could go back to the way it was in the beginning?

The answer is: not at all. I have been and you have been to countries who do not have the problems of the environment created by an industrial society. Those countries and those peoples, of course, would very much like to have those problems if that was the cost of raising their standard of living.

That is why Mr. Ruckelshaus, and this administration, has emphasized, and will continue to emphasize an attack on the problem of the environment, but recognizing that the genius that created the industrial might of the United States, that created the problems in the environment, can be put to the task of cleaning it up. This we will do, and this we believe we can accomplish, consistent with maintaining our system.

In terms of our economy, when we talk about how we can change it and how we can deal, for example, with problems like the wage-price escalation, it, of course, has not gone unnoticed that many at this time tend to throw up their hands and conclude that the only answer to the problem is to go to wage and price controls. Some nibble at it at the edges and say, well, we ought to have a wage-price board, or others go all the way and say, why not wage and price controls? When you talk to management, however, they want wage controls. When you talk to labor, they want price controls. When you talk to Government, they recognize, as we recognize that you cannot have wage controls without price controls and any of us, as I was—I was in the OPA [Office of Price Administration] for a few months in 1942 before I went in the service—you cannot have wage and price controls without rationing.

It would help us on the unemployment problem. I just checked and found we had 47,000 in the OPA in World War II enforcing all the regulations in wage and price controls over the country. It was not working because it will not and cannot in peacetime.

So, despite the fact that a majority of the American people, when asked, "Do you believe there should be wage and price controls?" they say yes, if they had them for a while, they would say no with a vengeance; one, because they do not work in peacetime in controlling the problem, and two, because the cost in terms of snuffing out the dynamism and strength of the American economy would be a cost much too high to pay.

When we are talking about the system we must take the necessary steps to correct the problems that are wrong about it, but recognize that it is a system that has nevertheless produced today more jobs, higher wages, and greater opportunity than any system in the world. Before lightly changing it or reforming it in a way that changes its character, let us also have this in mind.[79]

I look, for example, at the Soviet Union, and those of you who have traveled in the Soviet Union several times, as I have—my first trip in 1959, and my last in 1967—have noted the significant change that has occurred there. There we find that they have moved more and more to a system of rewards rather than every man according to his ability, and receiving according to his needs, because the other will not work.

At a time when we find them moving—and, may I say, others who are trying the total socialistic approach—moving our way, we could make no greater mistake than to move their way.

What are the economic miracles in the world today? Japan: a different system from ours in terms of government, but relying very, very heavily on private enterprise and private incentives. Germany: a different system from ours in terms of government, but again, private enterprise oriented, private incentives.

Here is the United States of America. At this particular time, as we look around the world, we should not turn away from what is really the great source of our strength.

Now, I have mentioned the personal health that is very important, the health of our environment, the health of our economy, and I should also touch upon the health of government. Government in this country needs some major surgery. It is too fat. It has in many cases too many useless limbs; some need to be chopped off. Certainly it needs to be reduced in size. Most of all, of course, it needs an infusion of leadership and responsibility at local and State levels which is going to be essential if you are going to have improvement of government in this country.

That is why revenue sharing and government reorganizaton are very

[79] See further Document 142.

high on our agenda. There is not much sex appeal in these programs unless you talk to mayors or Governors or county officials who say, please give us the money or we cannot pay our payrolls.

But on the other hand, they are enormously important because the United States cannot go into this last third of a century with competition, when we are going to have to be at our best, with an unhealthy government structure. We have to thin it down and get it ready for the race. It is not ready for the race. That is why at the present time we are strongly advocating these changes.

There is one other kind of health that the Nation needs. I don't want to sound here like a moralist or a preacher, although I have great respect for preachers and moralists. This Nation needs moral health. By moral health, I use the term in a very broad sense.

Don Rumsfeld,[80] I know, has addressed himself to the problem of drugs and, I assume, of law enforcement. I have stated categorically, and I state it again here today, that in this administration, the era of permissiveness in law enforcement has come to an end. We are going to continue to support strong laws dealing with criminal elements, to support law enforcement officials up and down this land, and continue to have a program that will reduce the rising crime and eventually reverse it.

One of our most substantial achievements has been that in cities over 100,000, that in 61 of them the crime rate went down in the last quarter, and in the city of Washington, it went down for the first time in almost 20 years. This kind of progress is, of course, significant, but more needs to be made.

Let me now address myself to the narrow, but in a sense, decisive issue of drug control. I will not elaborate on what Don Rumsfeld said, except to say that we are dealing very effectively with the problem at its source. Our arrangement with the Government of Turkey: to the great credit of the Turkish Prime Minister, we have stopped that source to a great extent, and it will be totally stopped by next year.[81] We are dealing with it in law enforcement and better education.

But the fundamental problem of drugs goes beyond that. You can stop the source of supply in one country and if there is enough demand they will go some place else. You can have the strongest laws possible, and if there is enough demand and use, you will have to add more officials.

What we really need is to get at the fundamental cause and the fundamental cause has to do, as all of you know, with basically a problem in our society. We must recognize that the problem is no longer a black problem, it is no longer a ghetto problem; it never was, as

[80] Donald Rumsfeld, Counsellor to the President.
[81] See further Document 136 at note 102.

a matter of fact, although it was predominant. It has moved to the suburbs and the upper-middle class and upper class. It is particularly a problem among younger people. It is not just limited to veterans. It goes far beyond that. All these things we know.

The real problem, fundamentally, gets down to why; why do people take them? There we find the fundamental challenge of our time, a challenge that opinion leaders have to meet. If individuals have something to live for, if individuals have something to believe in, then the tendency to throw up their hands, to retreat, to give up on life, is substantially reduced.

But as a society comes to the point where there is negativism, defeatism, a sense of alienation, it is inevitable that younger people will give up. They will turn to drugs, to any other kind of activity that is, of course, disruptive of a society.

I address myself at this point to this particular question for a reason that I think is quite relevant in view of the announcement that I made on July 3.[82] I said then that the United States was entering its bicentennial era, because 5 years from July 4th of this year we will celebrate the 200th anniversary of the United States of America.

We wonder what kind of a nation we are going to be then. Well, I will flatly predict that 5 years from now we will still be the richest nation in the world. If we want to be—and this will depend upon the American people—we need to be. We will still be the strongest nation in the world. But the critical question is whether the United States will be a healthy nation, a healthy nation not simply with a healthy government and a healthy economy and a healthy environment and a healthy physical system insofar as we personally are concerned, but healthy in terms of its moral strength.

On that, there is a question. That question is raised often in your editorial columns that I have noted, because I read many of them. It should be raised. But I would only suggest that part of the reason for raising it is that again we tend to allow the problems of the moment to obscure our vision of the future. We tend to allow our faults—and we have many—to obscure the many virtues of our society.

I will not list them. Let us simply say that world leadership—oh, I know all the criticisms: the United States can't be trusted with power; the United States should recede from the world scene and take care of its own problems and leave world leadership to somebody else, because we engage in immorality in the conduct of our foreign policy. Let's take a look.

We have been in four wars in this century, and four times young Americans have gone abroad. We have done so without any idea of conquest or domination. We have lost hundreds of thousands of lives

[82] *Public Papers, 1971*, pp. 793-98.

and we have not gotten a thing out of any of it, and we have helped each of our enemies, after each of the wars, get on his feet again.

We made our mistakes. We make them now, for example, as we made them in previous wars. Let me say this: Think for a moment. What other nation in the world would you like to have in the position of pre-eminent power? What other nation in the world that has what it takes would have the attitude that the United States has, as far as its foreign policy is concerned?

Here is a nation that did not seek the pre-eminent world position. It came to us because of what had happened in World War II. But here is a nation that has helped its former enemies, that is generous now to those who might be its opponents, a nation that, it seems to me, is one that the world is very fortunate, in a way, to have in a position of world leadership.

In terms of our domestic policies, I think we can truly say we have some problems. They are quite significant, and we like to look at those problems; not only look at them, but we must work on them, and constantly see that America is revitalized and reinvigorated.

But as we look at those problems, the enormous strengths of this country can only be appreciated once you have seen other countries, great as they are and as much as they have to offer, and come back to see what we have in America. I am not speaking of wealth. I am speaking of freedom. I am speaking of opportunity. I am speaking of concern; concern that people have not only for people here, but for people in other places.

When we presented the program on July 3d, some of you who may have heard it will note it was in the Archives Building. I am often asked, as I am sure many of you are who are in Washington, what is your favorite building? My usual answer is the Lincoln Memorial, particularly at night, with the light shining on the statue of Lincoln. But I would say that in terms of the most impressive building; impressive because it has the appearance of the ages there, it has to be the Archives, more impressive than the Capitol, the Lincoln Memorial, or the Jefferson Memorial or the White House itself.

The great marble columns give you the feeling of the past and what the Nation stands for, and you know that the building is one that holds the Constitution, the Bill of Rights, the Declaration of Independence, the great documents that started the Nation at the beginning.

Sometimes when I see those pillars I think of seeing them on the Acropolis in Greece. I think of seeing them also in the Forum in Rome, great, stark pillars—and I have walked in both at night, as I have walked down by the Archives at night from time to time.

I think of what happened to Greece and to Rome, and you see what is left—only the pillars. What has happened, of course, is that great civilizations of the past, as they have become wealthy, as they have lost their will to live, to improve, they then have become subject to the decadence that eventually destroys the civilization.

The United States is now reaching that period. I am convinced, however, that we have the vitality, I believe we have the courage, I believe we have the strength out through this heartland and across this Nation that will see to it that America not only is rich and strong, but that it is healthy in terms of moral and spiritual strength. I am convinced it is there. I am convinced, as I talk to crowds of people. I am convinced as I see a group of young people, 500 of them, going off to Europe, as I saw yesterday, from 50 States.

But also I know that people need to be reassured. The people who can reassure them are opinion leaders, editors, television, radio commentators, teachers, even perhaps Presidents and politicians. At the present time, I will simply say in raising these problems, I don't raise them in any sense of defeatism; I don't raise them in the usual sense of pointing out that the United States is a country torn by division, alienation, that this is truly an ugly country; because I don't believe that.

I honestly believe that the United States, in its pre-eminent position in world leadership, has in its hands the future of peace in the world this last third of a century. I honestly believe that the United States has the destiny to play a great role, but I also know we cannot play it unless this is a healthy land, with a healthy government, a healthy citizenry, a healthy economy, and above all, the moral and spiritual health that can only come from the hearts of people and their minds, and that will only come as people are reassured from time to time, as we discuss our faults and as we correct our faults, reassured. Keep them in balance.

Don't let the problems of the moment obscure the great and good things that are going on in this country. It is that that I would suggest to the editors and other opinion makers here: that from time to time, maybe once a month, that message might come through.

(10) Accomplishments and Disappointments in 1971: News Conference Statement by Secretary of State Rogers, December 23, 1971.[83]

(Excerpts)

Q. Mr. Secretary, globally speaking, what do you regard during the past year as the main gains and setbacks in foreign affairs?

A. Well, I have, in anticipation of that question, a checklist which I

---

[83] Department of State Press Release 303, Dec. 23, 1971; text from *Bulletin*, Jan. 17, 1972, pp. 49-51 and 58. For further excerpts from the same news conference see Documents 30, 64, 110, and 116.

would like to refer to, because I think it is important to look back over the year to see what has been accomplished and where there are disappointments.

First, I think I would put the continued troop withdrawals in Viet-Nam, the success of our Vietnamization program, and the sharp reduction in the American casualties at the top of that list. I think that all Americans can take considerable gratification in the knowledge that the Vietnamization program is working, and I think it is recognized throughout the world that it is working.[84]

Second, in the Middle East the cease-fire has held. Difficult but constructive dialogue has been undertaken, and we will continue our efforts to maintain this cease-fire and, hopefully, to bring about a successful conclusion.[85]

Third—and these are not necessarily in the order of importance—a reduction of our troop strength in Korea. We have reduced our troop strength there, as you know, to a considerable extent—approximately 20,000 troops.[86]

Four, we have made progress in the SALT [Strategic Arms Limitation Talks] talks.[87] Two agreements have been announced and signed,[88] and intensive negotiations are continuing; and we have every reason to hope that there will be further progress made in those talks in the not too distant future.

Of course, very high on the list has to be the arrangements that were made for the President's trip to the People's Republic of China[89]—and for the fact that the People's Republic of China has become a member of the United Nations and is taking a much more active part in international affairs, and it is a move that I'm sure you know we supported in the United Nations.[90]

I must hasten to add, and it's difficult to decide which of these are more important, but certainly the great strides that have been made in adjusting the international monetary system are achievements of momentous proportions and they will have a very long-term impact on the conduct of our foreign affairs.[91]

The Berlin agreement has been negotiated. This has been a flashpoint in international relations ever since World War II, and I think all Americans and all people throughout the world can be gratified, pleased, that this agreement has been successfully concluded. As you know, it has to

---

[84] Cf. Documents 71-81.
[85] Cf. Documents 48-54.
[86] Cf. Document 98.
[87] Cf. Documents 21-25.
[88] Cf. Documents 26-28.
[89] Cf. Documents 91-94.
[90] Cf. Documents 122-28.
[91] Cf. Documents 149-50.

wait now for the signing of the final protocol, but for all practical purposes, I believe that we can say that this agreement has been concluded.[92]

One thing that is not noticed very much, because it has been so successful over the years, is the continued vigor of NATO: the support that NATO is getting from our allies and the support that we have been able to give to NATO, the fact that we were able to successfully defeat the amendments of Senator [Mike] Mansfield to reduce our troop strength in NATO.[93] As you know, our allies have agreed to contribute a billion dollars more in defense budgets in the year 1972.[94]

Certainly one of the achievements that we can all be proud of, and it's a historic achievement, was the Okinawa Reversion Agreement.[95] It didn't, I think, get the attention that it deserved, but it was a momentous event. It will, I think, serve as a very important foundation for future relations between the United States and Japan for many years to come.

We have completed an international Hijacking Convention that I think will serve international interests very well in the years to come.[96]

Now, of course there have been some disappointments.

I suppose a major disappointment was the tragic event in the subcontinent.[97] Fortunately, as we approach the Christmas season, I think we can be pleased that that war has ended. It certainly was a tragic series of events. But nonetheless there is peace in the area for the moment, and we hope that it will remain peaceful.

I might, with your permission, list a few things that I think we will consider as prospects for 1972.

First, of course, would be in Viet-Nam. We are going to continue the withdrawal of troops as announced by the President, and he will make further announcements. We still have hopes that there could be some peaceful settlement reached by negotiation, but in any event we are going to continue the Vietnamization program which, as I have said before, we believe has been so successful.

We will continue the SALT talks. We are going to have intensive negotiations, and as I have indicated, we have hopeful prospects for success.

I need not mention the importance of the visits by the President to Peking[98] and Moscow.[99] They are part of a program by President

---

[92] Cf. Documents 38-39.
[93] Cf. Documents 33-34 and 41.
[94] Cf. Document 42.
[95] Cf. Documents 95-96.
[96] See note 110 to Chapter IX.
[97] Cf. Documents 56-64.
[98] Cf. Documents 91-94.
[99] Cf. Documents 29-30.

Nixon which I believe is the most comprehensive program any President has ever undertaken in the interests of peace. Obviously there are uncertainties about those visits. We want to make certain that the accomplishments are not exaggerated in advance. On the other hand, we think they are tremendously important for foreign affairs and for the future of the world and for peace generally.

We will continue our adjusting of the international monetary system and continue to press for removal of trade barriers which we believe have been unfair to American interests, and we believe that there will be progress in those negotiations so that some of the trade barriers can be removed.

You know we are committed to multilateral discussions about a European security conference when the protocol dealing with Berlin has been concluded.[100] We look forward eventually, after careful preparation has been made, to a European security conference, but a great deal of work here is necessary before that time arrives. We would expect that sometime, possibly in the fall of next year after the protocol has been signed, we can engage in multilateral talks in preparation for a European security conference.

Of course, we will make the final turnover of Okinawa to Japan in 1972. The exact date hasn't been determined, but it will be sometime probably in the middle of 1972.[101]

We will have very important humanitarian problems in the world, and particularly in the subcontinent, and those will involve the interests of the American people and the American Government.

And finally, we are going to continue a major drive to prevent drug traffic from increasing. We are going to do everything that we can possibly do as a nation to curb this practice which has such horrendous results for human beings.[102]

So, Mr. Gulick,[103] I think, as I say, we can be pleased at successes in 1971.

There have been some failures, disappointments. But on the whole, it has been a year, I think, of very substantial accomplishments. And the world is a more peaceful place today than it was at the beginning of the year.

*   *   *

I would just like to say, as I said at the beginning, I think it has been a good year in terms of foreign affairs. And I would not want the year to

[100] Cf. Document 42.
[101] Cf. notes to Documents 95-96.
[102] Document 136.
[103] Lewis Gulick of the Associated Press.

end without expressing my appreciation to everyone in the State Department, and particularly the Foreign Service, for the outstanding work that they have done. In many of these cases, tremendous amounts of work have been done with great dedication and success. And although Foreign Service officers don't get as much credit as they deserve, partly because of the nature of their job, I think it is important for us, particularly at the end of this year, to compliment them for the work they have done and say that I don't believe there is any—I am sure that there is no Foreign Ministry anywhere in the world that is more capable or more dedicated.

And I would like to also say that I am very pleased about the press corps. [Laughter.] I am serious about that. I appreciate very much the coverage that we have gotten. I have no complaints. I think it is very fair. And I will say this on the record: Merry Christmas and Happy New Year.

The press: Merry Christmas to you.

II.
ARMS CONTROL AND
U.S.-SOVIET RELATIONS

[The gradual improvement in relations between the United States and the U.S.S.R. accelerated markedly during 1971 as progress toward the resolution of longstanding issues paved the way for President Nixon's unprecedented visit to the Soviet Union in May 1972. The cautiously hopeful spirit in which the American administration awaited evidence of Moscow's intentions in the early weeks of 1971 is well reflected in an excerpt from the President's annual report on American foreign policy, in which he reviewed the major problems of U.S.-Soviet relations with special reference to the critical areas of arms control, Europe, and the Middle East (Document 11).

Subsequent progress in two of these areas—arms control and Europe—was deemed in Washington to warrant the further steps toward *rapprochement* involved in a presidential visit. In the arms control field, the signature of the seabed disarmament treaty negotiated in 1970 (Document 13) was followed by agreement on a second multilateral treaty prohibiting the development, production, and stockpiling of bacteriological (biological) and toxin weapons (Document 19). In addition, American and Soviet delegates to the ongoing Strategic Arms Limitation Talks (SALT) negotiated two bilateral agreements aimed at reducing the risk of nuclear conflict between the two parties (Documents 27 and 28). In European affairs, meanwhile, the U.S.S.R. joined the Western occupying powers in signing a special protocol designed to ease the situation in Berlin (Document 39). While continuing its advocacy of a Conference on Security and Cooperation in Europe, Moscow also displayed some interest in Western proposals looking toward a mutual and balanced reduction of military forces in Europe (cf. Chapter III).

The optimism inspired by these developments, and by the announcement of President Nixon's intended visit (Document 29), was qualified by lack of progress toward a Middle East settlement and, still more, by the repercussions of the war between India and Pakistan, which found the two major powers pursuing radically divergent policies (cf. Chapter IV). American authorities nevertheless correctly estimated that this temporary rift would not impair the prospects for the presidential visit

(Document 30). A potentially more lasting check on the development of the American-Soviet relationship arose from public and congressional concern in the United States about the status of Jews in the U.S.S.R., a preoccupation that occasioned various incidents during the year and evoked a significant expression of administration views (Document 31).]

A. Fundamentals of United States-Soviet Relations.

(11) The Soviet Union: President Nixon's Second Annual Report to the Congress on United States Foreign Policy, Transmitted February 25, 1971. [1]

(Excerpt)

PART III: THE SOVIET UNION

"The great central issue of our time—the question of whether the world as a whole is to live at peace—has not been resolved.

"This central issue turns in large part on the relations among the great nuclear powers. Their strength imposes on them special responsibilities of restraint and wisdom. The issue of war and peace cannot be solved unless we in the United States and the Soviet Union demonstrate both the will and the capacity to put our relationship on a basis consistent with the aspirations of mankind."

> Address to the United Nations
> General Assembly
> October 23, 1970

In my Inaugural Address, and again at the United Nations last October, I urged the Soviet leaders to join with us in building a new and constructive relationship. [2]

I emphasized four factors that provide a basis for such a development:

—Neither of us wants a nuclear exchange.

[1] Nixon Report, 1971, pp. 156-63; text from *Presidential Documents*, Mar. 1, 1971, pp. 354-56.
[2] *Documents, 1968-69*, pp. 41-42; same, *1970*, p. 291.

—We both should welcome the opportunity to reduce the burden of armaments.

—We are both major industrial powers, and yet have very little trade or commercial contact with one another. Both would clearly benefit if our relationship permitted an increase in trade.

—Both are deeply involved, at home and abroad, with the need for creative economic and social change. Both our interests—and the broader world interest—would be served if our competition could be channeled more into our performances in that field.

Thus, our two nations have substantial mutual incentives to find ways of working together. We are realistic enough to recognize, however, that we also have very real differences that can continue to divide us:

We view the world and approach international affairs differently. Ideology continues to shape many aspects of Soviet policy. It dictates an attitude of constant pressure toward the external world. The Soviet Government too frequently claims that the rationale for its internal and external policies is based on universalist doctrines. In certain fundamental aspects the Soviet outlook on world affairs is incompatible with a stable international system.

The internal order of the USSR, as such, is not an object of our policy, although we do not hide our rejection of many of its features. Our relations with the USSR, as with other countries, are determined by its international behavior. Consequently, the fruitfulness of the relationship depends significantly upon the degree to which its international behavior does not reflect militant doctrinal considerations.

As the two most powerful nations in the world, we conduct global policies that bring our interests into contention across a broad range of issues. Historically, international adversaries have demonstrated a compulsion to seek every gain, however marginal, at the expense of their competitors. In this classical conception, the accumulation of gains over a period of time could alter the balance of power. This may have been realistic in the past; at least it was the essence of international affairs.

But it is folly for the great nuclear powers to conduct their policies in this manner. For if they succeed, it can only result in confrontation and potential catastrophe.

The nature of nuclear power requires that both the Soviet Union and we be willing to practice self-restraint in the pursuit of national interests. We have acted on this principle in our conduct of the SALT [Strategic Arms Limitation Talks] negotiations, in our diplomatic initiatives in the Middle East, and in our proposals to improve the situation in Berlin. We are prepared to apply it to all legitimate Soviet interests.

Such a policy of restraint, however, requires reciprocity—concretely expressed in actions.

By virtue of its size and geography, the USSR has traditionally had important security interests in Europe and East Asia. Her undoubted status as a global power obviously creates interests in other areas where Russia has not traditionally been a factor. But the natural expansion of Soviet influence in the world must not distort itself into ambitions for exclusive or predominant positions. For such a course ignores the interests of others, including ourselves. It must and will be resisted. It can, therefore, lead only to confrontation.

We often approach negotiations with differing premises. We do not suggest that the starting point—or, indeed, the culmination—of our negotiations with the USSR be the acceptance of our views and positions. Nor do we expect to resolve issues by cajoling the Soviet leaders into solutions damaging to their national interests. We cannot be expected, however, to accept the Soviet definition of every issue, to agree automatically to the Soviet order of priorities, or to accept every aggrandizement of Soviet positions abroad as a "new reality" no longer open to challenge. The principle of mutual accommodation, if it is to have any meaning, must be that both of us seek compromises, mutual concessions, and new solutions to old problems.

The relationship between the two great nuclear powers in this decade must rise above tactical considerations. We must be prepared to face issues seriously, concretely, and in a spirit of mutual respect. Durable solutions will be those which both sides have an interest in maintaining.

We are engaged in a strategic and military competition. We both possess the capability to develop our military power and project it massively into distant areas. The last two decades witnessed the transformation of the Soviet Union from a Eurasian power to an intercontinental one. The USSR now possesses military capabilities far beyond those at the command of previous Soviet leaders.

In earlier periods our strategic superiority gave us a margin of safety. Now, however, the enormous increase in Soviet capabilities has added a new and critical dimension to our relationship. The growth of Soviet power in the last several years could tempt Soviet leaders into bolder challenges. It could lead them to underestimate the risks of certain policies. We, of course, continue to weigh carefully Soviet statements of intentions. But the existing military balance does not permit us to judge the significance of Soviet actions only by what they say—or even what we believe—are their intentions. We must measure their actions, at least in part, against their capabilities.

It is of the utmost importance that the new strategic balance of the 1970's and our interest in strategic stability not be misunderstood. Confrontation may arise from a mistaken perception of the posture of an adversary. Such a mistake can lead to a failure to appreciate the risks and consequences of probing for advantages or testing the limits of toleration. We believe that this was involved to some degree in the events which led up to the Middle East crisis last year.[3]

It may also have been a factor in Soviet naval actions in the Caribbean in the fall of 1970. There the Soviet Union took new steps which could have afforded it the ability to again operate offensive weapons systems from this Hemisphere. That would have been contrary to the understanding between us. Only after a period of discussion did we reaffirm our understanding and amplify it to make clear that the agreement included activities related to sea-based systems.[4]

In our relations with the USSR there should be no misconceptions of the role we will play in international affairs. This country is not withdrawing into isolation. With the Soviet Union, we want a relationship in which the interests of both are respected. When interests conflict, we prefer negotiation and restraint as the methods to adjust differences. But, when challenged, the United States will defend its interests and those of its allies. And, together with our allies, we will maintain the power to do so effectively.

A New American-Soviet Relationship

Mutual restraint, accommodation of interests, and the changed strategic situation open broad opportunities to the Soviet Union and the United States. It is our hope that the Soviet Union will recognize, as we do, that our futures are best served by serious negotiation of the issues which divide us. We have taken the initiative in establishing an agenda on which agreement could profoundly alter the substance of our relationship:

—*SALT*. Given the available resources, neither of us will concede a significant strategic advantage to the other. Yet the temptation to attempt to achieve such advantage is ever present, and modern technology makes such an attempt feasible. With our current strategic capabilities, we have a unique opportunity to design a stable and mutually acceptable strategic relationship.

We did not expect agreements to emerge quickly, for the most vital of interests are engaged. A resolution will not be achieved by agreement on generalities. We have put forward precise and serious proposals that would create no unilateral advantages and would cope with the major concerns of both sides.

We do not yet know what conclusions the Soviet Union will draw from the facts of the situation. If its leaders share our assessment,

---

3 Cf. *The United States in World Affairs, 1970*, p. 110.
4 See further the President's comments of Jan. 4, 1971, in *Public Papers, 1971*, pp. 17-18.

we can unquestionably bring competition in strategic weapons under control.[5]

—*Europe*. With our allies, we have entered into negotiations with the USSR to improve the Berlin situation. Arrangements which, in fact, bring an end to the twenty-four years of tension over Berlin, would enable us to move beyond the vestiges of the postwar period that have dominated our relationship for so long. A broader era of negotiations in Europe then becomes possible.[6]

Progress toward this goal also could be obtained through a successful agreement on mutual reduction of military forces, especially in Central Europe where confrontation could be most dangerous.[7]

—*The Middle East* is heavy with the danger that local and regional conflict may engulf the Great Powers in confrontation.[8]

We recognize that the USSR has acquired important interests and influence in the area, and that a lasting settlement cannot be achieved unless the Soviet Union sees it to be in its interest.

We continue to believe that it is in the Soviet interest to support a reasonable settlement. The USSR is not, however, contributing to that end by providing increasingly large and dangerous numbers of weapons to the Arab states, or by building military positions for its own purposes. We are prepared to seek agreement with the USSR and the other major powers to limit arms shipments to the Middle East.

We have not tried to lay down a rigid order of priorities within this agenda. It is a fact of international politics, however, that major issues are related. The successful resolution of one such issue cannot help but improve the prospects for solving other problems. Similarly, aggressive action in one area is bound to exert a disturbing influence in other areas.

An assessment of U.S.-Soviet relations at this point in my Administration has to be mixed. There have been some encouraging developments and we welcome them. We are engaged in a serious dialogue in SALT. We have both signed the treaty to prohibit nuclear weapons from the seabeds.[9] We have both ratified the treaty on nonproliferation of nuclear weapons.[10] We have entered negotiations on the issue of Berlin.[11] We have taken the first step toward practical cooperation in outer space.[12]

---

[5] See further Documents 21-28.
[6] See further Documents 38-39.
[7] See further Documents 35-37 and 40-42.
[8] See further Documents 48-54.
[9] Cf. Document 13.
[10] Cf. note 16 below.
[11] Cf. Documents 38-39.
[12] American and Soviet scientific representatives reached agreement on Oct. 28, 1970, with regard to the question of providing for compatibility of rendezvous

On the other hand, certain Soviet actions in the Middle East, Berlin, and Cuba are not encouraging. Taken against a background of intensive and unrestrained anti-American propaganda, these actions inevitably suggest that intransigence remains a cardinal feature of the Soviet system.

Yet these events may have provided a basis for future progress in our relations. Properly understood, they illustrate the altogether incommensurate risks inherent in a policy of confrontation, and the marginal benefits achievable by it.

Against this background it is an appropriate moment to take stock of our relations, and to weigh the decisions necessary for further progress.

The Soviet leaders will be reviewing their own policies and programs in connection with the 24th Congress of their Party.[13] This report sets forth my own assessment of our relations with the USSR, and the principles by which we propose to govern our relations in the future. I have outlined the factors that make for common interests and suggested an agenda of outstanding opportunities:

—a more stable military relationship for the next decade.
—a peaceful settlement of the Middle East conflict.
—an agreed framework for security in Europe.

We are under no illusion that these are easy tasks. But, as I said in my address to the United Nations:

In the world today we are at a crossroads. We can follow the old way, playing the traditional game of international relations, but at ever-increasing risk. Everyone will lose. No one will gain. Or we can take a new road.

I invite the leaders of the Soviet Union to join us in taking that new road. . . .[14]

B. Progress in Multilateral Arms Control.

[Multilateral disarmament efforts continued during 1971 to center in the work of the 25-member Conference of the Committee on Dis-

---

and docking systems of manned spacecraft and space stations of the two countries. Further discussions on Jan. 18-21, 1971, led among other things to an agreement to exchange lunar surface samples obtained by the two countries. For details see *Bulletin*, Feb. 15, 1971, pp. 202-3.

[13] Meeting in Moscow on Mar. 30–Apr. 9, 1971, the 24th Congress of the Communist Party of the Soviet Union approved a Ninth Five-Year Plan for 1971-75 and reinstalled the party leadership headed by General Secretary Leonid I. Brezhnev.

[14] *Documents, 1970*, p. 294.

armament (CCD), meeting at Geneva under the cochairmanship of the United States and the U.S.S.R. and reporting to the General Assembly and the Disarmament Commission of the United Nations. To the past achievements attributable to the efforts of this group—notably the conclusion and entry into force of the 1963 Treaty Banning Nuclear Weapon Tests in the Atmosphere, in Outer Space and Under Water[15] and the 1968 Treaty on the Non-Proliferation of Nuclear Weapons[16]— two more were added during 1971: the signature of the 1970 Treaty on the Prohibition of the Emplacement of Nuclear Weapons and Other Weapons of Mass Destruction on the Seabed and the Ocean Floor and in the Subsoil Thereof (Document 13);[17] and the completion of the draft Convention on the Prohibition of the Development, Production and Stockpiling of Bacteriological (Biological) and Toxin Weapons and on Their Destruction (Documents 17-19).[18]

Two further projects of the CCD, the development of a similar ban on chemical weapons and of a treaty banning nuclear weapon tests in all environments, continued to be blocked primarily by disagreements between the United States and certain other members of the committee, including the U.S.S.R., regarding the need for on-site inspection to monitor compliance (cf. Document 20). The U.S. position with regard to chemical warfare issues was further complicated by a disagreement between the administration and the Senate Foreign Relations Committee with respect to ratification of the 1925 Geneva Protocol for the Prohibition of the Use in War of Asphyxiating, Poisonous or Other Gases, and of Bacteriological Methods of Warfare (cf. Documents 15-16).]

1. Achievements and Current Agenda.

[The Conference of the Committee on Disarmament (CCD) held its annual session in Geneva from February 23 to May 13 and from June 29 to September 30, 1971, the principal accomplishment of the session being the elaboration of the final text of the draft Convention on the Prohibition of Bacteriological (Biological) and Toxin Weapons (Document 19).[19] A message from President Nixon, presented to the confer-

[15] Done at Moscow Aug. 5, 1963, and entered into force Oct. 10, 1963 (TIAS 5433; 14 UST 1313); text in *Documents, 1963*, pp. 130-32.
[16] Done at Washington, London, and Moscow July 1, 1968, and entered into force Mar. 5, 1970 (TIAS 6839; 21 UST 483); text in *Documents, 1968-69*, pp. 62-68.
[17] Done at Washington, London, and Moscow Feb. 11, 1971, and entered into force May 18, 1972 (TIAS 7337; 23 UST 701); text in *Documents, 1970*, pp. 69-73. For further documentation cf. Documents 13-14 below.
[18] Opened for signature in Washington, London, and Moscow Apr. 10, 1972, and entered into force Mar. 26, 1975 (TIAS 8062); text in Document 19 below.
[19] The official report of the CCD on its 1971 session (U.N. document CCD/356, Oct. 1, 1971) is reprinted in *Documents on Disarmament, 1971*, pp. 610-33.

ence on its opening day (Document 12), offered a review of past achievements and current tasks as seen from an American point of view. An appraisal of the accomplishments of the session, and of issues still awaiting solution, was later presented by U.S. Representative George H. Bush to the First (Political and Security) Committee of the United Nations General Assembly (Documents 17 and 20).]

(12) Work of the Conference of the Committee on Disarmament (CCD): Message from President Nixon to the Conference, February 23, 1971.[20]

(Complete Text)

Today the Conference of the Committee on Disarmament begins a new session of work in the vital fields of arms control and disarmament.

On this occasion, once again I want to convey my thoughts to you directly because of my conviction that few areas of endeavor go so deeply to the heart of the concerns and the aspirations of all nations as the search for restraints on armaments. Sound limitations on armaments can enhance international stability and increase the security of all countries; they can reduce the economic burden of armaments; and they can lay the groundwork for productive international cooperation in other areas.

The achievements of this Committee during the past decade have been significant, including, notably, the negotiation of the Nonproliferation Treaty and, most recently, a seabed arms control treaty which was overwhelmingly commended by the U.N. General Assembly[21] and signed earlier this month by a substantial number of states.[22]

The tasks before the Committee are very important to world security. As in the past, genuine progress can best be made through patient and careful work toward mutually beneficial measures. Opportunities for such progress can and must be realized.

I believe that an opportunity for progress exists in the field of chemical and biological weapons. Despite differences of approach, there appears to be a fundamental area of agreement and common interest in the CCD regarding this problem. All members desire the greatest possible advance in achieving effective restraints on these weapons. All members are aware that such progress will enhance their own security and international security in general.

---

[20] Text from *Bulletin*, Mar. 15, 1971, pp. 310-11. The message was read before the opening session of the conference by the U.S. Representative, Gerard C. Smith.

[21] *Documents, 1970*, p. 74.

[22] Cf. Document 13.

An agreement prohibiting the development, production, and stock-piling of biological weapons would serve these objectives. Because of the rapid transmission of contagious diseases, particularly with modern means of communications, any use of biological weapons—by any state in any conflict anywhere in the world—could endanger the people of every country. Additional restraints on biological weapons would thus contribute to the security of all peoples.

A prohibition against the possession of biological weapons could also have far-reaching benefits of another character. It could encourage international cooperation in the peaceful application of biological re-search, a field which may lead to immeasurable advances in the health and well-being of peoples everywhere.

With respect to chemical weapons the objective situation is different. Unless countries can have assurance that other parties to an agreement will no longer possess chemical weapons, there will not be a basis for a sound and reliable arms control measure. It is this basic fact that deter-mines the approach of the United States.

The common task with respect to chemical weapons now is to find solutions to the difficult problems of verification. We are determined to pursue this task. And in any biological weapons convention, we will support an unambiguous commitment engaging all parties to undertake further negotiations regarding limitations on chemical weapons.[23]

Important efforts are being made to move ahead in other areas of arms limitation. The need for constraints on nuclear arms is universally recognized. Negotiations to achieve limitations are continuing through the bilateral strategic arms talks.[24] It is our earnest hope that these crucial talks will result in positive and substantial arms limitations.

The General Assembly has requested this Committee to continue as a matter of urgency its deliberations on a treaty banning underground nuclear weapon tests.[25] It also called attention to the need to improve worldwide seismological capabilities in order to facilitate such a ban.[26] The United States will continue to support these efforts, particularly those designed to achieve a greater understanding of the verification issue.

At the same time, I hope that increasing attention will be given to the question of arms limitation with respect to conventional weapons. When such a vast proportion of all expenditures on armaments is being devoted to these weapons, all states, in all stages of development, share a common interest in exploring the possible paths toward sound agree-ments consistent with their security interests.

The seabed treaty demonstrated, as have other arms control agree-

---

[23] See further Documents 17-19.
[24] See Documents 21-25.
[25] General Assembly Resolution 2663 (XXV) B, Dec. 7, 1970; *Documents, 1970*, pp. 82-83.
[26] General Assembly Resolution 2663 (XXV) A, Dec. 7, 1970.

ments negotiated during the past decade, that steadfastness in the pursuit of common goals can lead to tangible results. When we have worked toward measures in the interests of all, we have succeeded in resolving differences and overcoming obstacles that seemed great. Let us continue to do so.

2. The Seabed Arms Control Treaty.

[Completed by the Conference of the Committee on Disarmament (CCD) in the summer of 1970 and commended by the U.N. General Assembly in a resolution of December 7, 1970,[27] the Treaty on the Prohibition of the Emplacement of Nuclear Weapons and Other Weapons of Mass Destruction on the Seabed and the Ocean Floor and in the Subsoil Thereof[28] was opened for signature at Washington, London, and Moscow on February 11, 1971. Briefly, parties to the treaty undertake "not to emplant or emplace on the seabed and the ocean floor and in the subsoil thereof ... any nuclear weapons or any other types of weapons of mass destruction as well as structures, launching installations or any other facilities specifically designed for storing, testing or using such weapons." Coastal states are exempted from this undertaking as regards a coastal (seabed) zone not exceeding twelve miles in breadth.

Sixty-two states signed the treaty in Washington on February 11, 1971, at a ceremony addressed by, among others, Secretary of State Rogers and President Nixon (Document 13); and a number of other states acceded to the treaty in Washington, London, or Moscow. Following receipt of an official report on the treaty from Secretary of State Rogers,[29] President Nixon requested Senate advice and consent to ratification in a message transmitted July 21, 1971 (Document 14). The treaty was approved by an 83 to 0 vote of the Senate on February 15, 1972, was ratified by the President on April 26, 1972, and entered into force with the deposit of ratifications by the United States, the United Kingdom, and the U.S.S.R. on May 18, 1972.]

(13) Signature of the Treaty in Washington, February 11, 1971.

(a) Remarks by Secretary of State Rogers.[30]

(Complete Text)

Mr. President, Your Excellencies, distinguished guests, ladies and

---

[27] *Documents, 1970*, p. 74.
[28] See note 17 above.
[29] S. Ex. H, 92d Cong., 1st sess.; text in *Bulletin*, Aug. 16, 1971, pp. 185-87.
[30] *Bulletin*, Mar. 8, 1971, p. 288.

gentlemen: First of all, I wish to extend to you a warm welcome on this important occasion.

We are here today to sign the Treaty on the Prohibition of the Emplacement of Nuclear Weapons and Other Weapons of Mass Destruction on the Seabed and the Ocean Floor and in the Subsoil Thereof. This treaty was worked out with great care, at the Conference of the Committee on Disarmament in Geneva and at the United Nations General Assembly. Many countries have played an active role in its shaping. It is a true product of international negotiation at its best.

We are very pleased that so many countries are today signing this treaty in London, Moscow, and Washington. It is another significant contribution to the growing fabric of multilateral arms control agreements. We earnestly hope that it will soon enter into force.

I shall be signing the treaty for the United States with Ambassador James F. Leonard [head of the U.S. Delegation to the Conference of the Committee on Disarmanent], who played a major role in the negotiation of this treaty.

(b) Remarks by President Nixon.[31]

—————— (Complete Text)

Mr. Secretary, your Excellencies, ladies and gentlemen:

It has been very properly pointed out that the seabed is man's last frontier on earth, and that frontier can either be a source of peril or promise.

By the signing of this treaty, we have pledged to seek its promise and to remove its peril. And as has been pointed out[32] by the Ambassador from the United Kingdom [Lord Cromer] and the Ambassador from the U.S.S.R. [Anatoly F. Dobrynin], while this is a modest step among many in the field of control of armaments, it is an indication of progress that has been made and continues to be made toward the goal that we all seek: the control of instruments of mass destruction, so that we can reduce the danger of war.

Certainly, speaking for the United States of America, I pledge that as we sign this treaty in an era of negotiation, that we consider it only one step toward a greater goal: the control of nuclear weapons on earth and the reduction of that danger that hangs over all the nations of the world as long as those weapons are not controlled.

And as our representatives go back to Vienna in just a few weeks,[33] we certainly hope that they will make progress. I can assure all of those gathered here that we seek, as does the Soviet Union and other nations,

---

[31] *Presidential Documents*, Feb. 15, 1971, pp. 211-12.
[32] Cf. *Bulletin*, Mar. 8, 1971, pp. 288-89.
[33] Cf. Document 22.

we seek an agreement there which will reduce the danger of nuclear war which hangs over the world and reduce it by controlling the nuclear arms, both as far as the Soviet Union is concerned and the United States.

And so on this occasion I reiterate that while the Ambassador from Great Britain quite properly said this was a modest step, it is an important step when we consider it in all of the aspects of the progress that has been made beginning in the sixties, now continuing in this decade.

We hope that we will be meeting perhaps in the future, perhaps in this room, perhaps in some other room in some other capital, for the final great step in the control of nuclear arms, the control of nuclear arms on earth.

(14) Request for Advice and Consent to Ratification: Message from President Nixon to the Senate, July 21, 1971. [34]

(Complete Text)

To the Senate of the United States:

I am transmitting herewith, for the advice and consent of the Senate to ratification, the Treaty on the Prohibition of the Emplacement of Nuclear Weapons and Other Weapons of Mass Destruction on the Seabed and the Ocean Floor and in the Subsoil Thereof, opened for signature at Washington, London and Moscow on February 11, 1971.

This Treaty is the product of intensive negotiations during the past two years at the Conference of the Committee on Disarmament at Geneva and at the United Nations. On December 7, 1970, 104 members of the United Nations voted to commend the Treaty and urged that it be opened for signature and ratification at the earliest possible date. [35]

In broadest outline this Treaty prohibits the emplacement of nuclear weapons and other weapons of mass destruction on the seabed beyond the outer limits of a 12-mile coastal "seabed zone" defined in the Treaty. The provisions of the Treaty are described in detail in the accompanying report of the Secretary of State. [36]

The seabed is man's last frontier on earth, and that frontier should be a source of promise. This Treaty represents a practical and timely step toward helping protect this new environment. It is a significant addition to the structure of multilateral arms control agreements such as the

---

[34] *Presidential Documents*, July 26, 1971, p. 1070.
[35] *Documents, 1970*, p. 74.
[36] See note 29.

Limited Test Ban Treaty,[37] the Antarctic Treaty,[38] the Outer Space Treaty,[39] and the Non-Proliferation Treaty,[40] contributing to international security.

I consider this Treaty to be in the interest of the United States and the entire world community and recommend that the Senate give its advice and consent to ratification.

RICHARD NIXON

The White House
July 21, 1971

3. The Geneva Protocol of 1925.

[International efforts to outlaw the use of chemical and bacteriological methods of warfare trace their origin to the so-called Geneva Protocol of 1925, technically known as the Protocol for the Prohitibiton of the Use in War of Asphyxiating, Poisonous or Other Gases, and of Bacteriological Methods of Warfare, signed at Geneva on June 17, 1925.[41] Parties to this protocol declared that they accepted a prohibition on the use in war of "asphyxiating, poisonous or other gases, and of all analogous liquids, materials or devices"; that they agreed "to extend this prohibition to the use of bacteriological methods of warfare"; and that they agreed "to be bound as between themselves according to the terms of this declaration." As of 1971, 96 states had become parties to the protocol, although over 30 of them, including the People's Republic of China, France, the U.S.S.R., and the United Kingdom, had attached reservations to their adherence. The United States, although it had largely inspired the protocol and had been an original signatory, had not become a party, since the Senate, whose advice and consent to ratification had been requested in 1926, had failed to take action and had returned the protocol to the President without approval in 1947.

Despite its failure to ratify, the United States during the late 1960s and the beginning of the 1970s repeatedly expressed support for the principles and objectives of the Geneva Protocol, joined in efforts by

[37] Cf. note 15 above.
[38] Signed at Washington Dec. 1, 1959, and entered into force June 23, 1961 (TIAS 4780; 12 UST 794); text in *Documents, 1959*, pp. 528-35.
[39] Done at Washington, London, and Moscow Jan. 27, 1967, and entered into force Oct. 10, 1967 (TIAS 6347; 18 UST 2410); text in *Documents, 1967*, pp. 392-96.
[40] Cf. note 16 above.
[41] Text in League of Nations, *Treaty Series*, vol. 94 (1929), no. 2138, pp. 65-74 and in *Documents on Disarmament, 1969*, pp. 764-65; partial text in *Documents, 1968-69*, p. 107n. Following ratification by the United States, the official U.S. text was issued in 1975 as TIAS 8061.

the Conference of the Committee on Disarmament (CCD) to elaborate more detailed prohibitions on chemical and bacteriological warfare, and moved to implement various provisions of the protocol on a unilateral basis.[42] In addition, President Nixon on August 19, 1970, resubmitted the Geneva Protocol to the Senate with a renewed request for its advice and consent to ratification[43] —subject, however, to certain "understandings" and "a proposed reservation" set forth in a separate report by the Secretary of State. The proposed reservation, designed to permit retaliatory use by the United States of chemical (but not biological) weapons and agents in the event of nonobservance of the prohibitions by an enemy state or any of its allies, read as follows: "That the said Protocol shall cease to be binding on the Government of the United States with respect to the use in war of asphyxiating, poisonous or other gases, and of all analogous liquids, materials, or devices, in regard to an enemy State if such State or any of its allies fails to respect the prohibitions laid down in the Protocol." The "understandings," designed to clarify the terminology of the protocol and the scope of the relevant prohibitions, read as follows: (1) "The United States considers that the term 'bacteriological methods of warfare' as used in the Protocol encompasses all biological methods of warfare and the use in warfare of toxins however produced." (2) "It is the United States' understanding of the Protocol that it does not prohibit the use in war of riot-control agents and chemical herbicides. Smoke, flame, and napalm are also not covered by the Protocol."[44]

These interpretations were further elaborated by Secretary of State Rogers when the Senate Foreign Relations Committee opened hearings on the Geneva Protocol on March 5, 1971 (Document 15). Members of the committee evinced some skepticism with regard to the proposed exclusion of "riot-control agents and chemical herbicides," the past use of which by American forces in Vietnam had provoked widespread controversy. Their doubts were reinforced by testimony from other witnesses who failed to agree with the administration view that it was in the American interest to retain the option to use "tear gas and herbicides" in future wars. The Chairman of the Foreign Relations Committee, Senator J. William Fulbright (Democrat, Arkansas), accordingly suggested in a letter to President Nixon on April 15, 1971, that this interpretation be reexamined (Document 16). Since no response was received from the President, no further action was taken during the lifetime of the 92nd Congress in 1971-72.[45]

It remained for President Ford to authorize a reexamination of the

---

[42] *Documents, 1968-69*, pp. 106-9; same, *1970*, pp. 75-76.
[43] *Documents, 1970*, pp. 76-77
[44] Report of the Secretary of State on S. Ex. J, 91st Cong., 2d sess, Aug. 11, 1970, in *Documents on Disarmament, 1970*, pp. 400-402.
[45] Senate Foreign Relations Committee History, p. 39.

U.S. position that would permit the Senate to take affirmative action. As a result of "a thorough and comprehensive review of the military, legal, and political issues relating to the Protocol," President Nixon's successor stated, "we have defined a new policy to govern any future use in war of riot control agents and chemical herbicides. While re-affirming the current U.S. understanding of the scope of the Protocol as not extending to riot control agents and chemical herbicides, I have decided that the United States shall renounce as a matter of national policy:

"(1) first use of herbicides in war except use, under regulations applicable to their domestic use, for control of vegetation within U.S. bases and installations or around their immediate defensive perimeters.

"(2) first use of riot control agents in war except in defensive military modes to save lives, such as, use of riot control agents in riot situations, to reduce civilian casualties, for rescue missions, and to protect rear area convoys."[45a]

In light of this clarification, made known December 10, 1974, and the subsequent unanimous recommendation of the Foreign Relations Committee, the Senate on December 16, 1974, voted 90 to 0 to approve the Geneva Protocol with the reservation originally recommended by Secretary Rogers. The protocol, with this reservation, was then ratified by President Ford on January 22, 1975 and entered into force for the United States with the deposit of its instrument of ratification on April 10, 1975.]

(15) Importance of United States Ratification: Statement by Secretary of State Rogers Before the Senate Committee on Foreign Relations, March 5, 1971.[46]

(Complete Text)

I am pleased to appear before the committee today to begin the testimony in support of the President's request that the Senate give its advice and consent to ratification of the Geneva Protocol of 1925.

This administration has made the problems of chemical and biological warfare one of its special concerns. Shortly after taking office in early 1969, President Nixon ordered an intensive interagency review of our policy in the field of chemical and biological warfare. Annual reviews of

---

[45a] Ford statement, Jan. 22, 1975, in *Presidential Documents,* Jan. 27, 1975, p. 74; for background cf. *Bulletin,* Jan. 20, 1975, pp. 93-95.
[46] Same, Mar. 29, 1971, pp. 455-59.

our programs and policies in the area of chemical warfare and the biological research programs are a continuing aspect of this administration's activities on the subject. On November 25, 1969, the President announced the first of a series of major policy decisions.[47] Our decision to resubmit the Geneva Protocol to the Senate was one of those key decisions.

The President also announced that the United States would reaffirm its often repeated renunciation of the first use of lethal chemical weapons, and he extended this renunciation to the first use of incapacitating chemicals.

Further, the President stated that the United States was renouncing the use of lethal biological agents and weapons and all other methods of biological warfare. He indicated that the United States will confine its biological research to defensive measures, such as immunization and protective measures.

In February of 1970, the President announced that the above decisions on the nonuse of biological agents and weapons would also apply to toxins; that is, biologically produced chemical substances.[48] As you know, on December 18, 1970, the Department of Defense announced its detailed disposal plans for existing stocks of biological agents and toxins not required for defensive research purposes. On January 27 this year, the President announced that following destruction of the stocks the biological facilities at Pine Bluff Arsenal would be taken over by the Food and Drug Administration for a major new health project to investigate the effects of a variety of chemical substances such as pesticides and food additives.

These decisions, together with the President's decision to resubmit the protocol to the Senate,[49] are truly significant steps of reason and restraint.

Also as a result of the review of chemical warfare and the biological research program in 1970, the administration made a number of decisions in this area which bear on your deliberations on the protocol. They include the following:

—To continue support for the United Kingdom draft arms control convention banning the development, production, and stockpiling of biological agents and toxins.[50]

—To continue our own efforts to achieve effective control of development, production, and stockpiling of chemical weapons and means of warfare through international agreement.

---

[47] *Documents, 1968-69,* pp. 106-9.
[48] Same, *1970,* pp. 75-76.
[49] Same, pp. 76-77.
[50] Extract in same, *1968-69,* p. 108n.

—To initiate a new review of the use of riot control agents and chemical herbicides in the Viet-Nam conflict so that the additional data obtained from the field can be used for an examination of the implications and consequences for U.S. policy of their future use in war.

—To continue provision of riot control agents to military forces to a level to be determined by relevant military and economic considerations, with the agents carefully controlled.

With respect to chemical herbicides, the administration's decisions included:

—The immediate termination of all use of chemical herbicides in Viet-Nam for crop destruction purposes and a phaseout of the use of chemical herbicides for purposes of defoliation. During the phaseout, our herbicide operations will be limited to defoliation operations in remote, unpopulated areas or to the perimeter defense of fire bases and installations in a manner currently authorized in the United States and which does not involve the use of fixed-wing aircraft.

—The preparation of disposition plans for the stocks of agent "Orange" presently in Viet-Nam.

As a result of these decisions we are now considering the question of advice and consent to ratification of the protocol in a situation vastly changed from what it was several years ago. We believe U.S. ratification of the protocol would be an important step in advancing the President's new policy in this area. Ratification would also:

—Strengthen the legal prohibitions against the use in war of chemical weapons and of biological weapons and toxins;

—Constitute a positive and constructive movement toward arms control and a direct response to United Nations General Assembly resolutions urging all members to become parties to the protocol;[51]

—Reinforce past U.S. policy statements on no first use of these agents and confirm past U.S. votes in the General Assembly in favor of strict adherence to the principles and objectives of the protocol; and

—Enhance the U.S. position in developing initiatives for future arms control measures in the chemical and biological warfare area.

PROHIBITION ON FIRST USE

Let me now turn to the protocol itself, its scope and its importance. The United States and 29 of the other states which participated in the Geneva Conference of 1925 were original signers of the protocol. There

[51] E.g., *Documents, 1968-69,* p. 121; same, *1970*, p. 78.

are now 96 parties to the protocol. Since January 1970, 12 countries, including Japan and Brazil, have become parties. All our NATO allies are parties. The Soviet Union and all but one of its Warsaw Pact allies are parties, as is Communist China.

France, the United Kingdom, the Soviet Union, Communist China, and 30 other countries which have become parties have entered similar but not identical reservations which made clear that the effect of the protocol was to prohibit only the *first use* of the weapons covered, leaving unaffected the right of retaliatory use of such weapons. Accordingly, the protocol is considered for those parties, and more generally, as a prohibition on the first use of chemical and biological weapons. As you know the Geneva Protocol does not prohibit research, development, testing, manufacture, and stockpiling of chemical or biological agents.

When President Nixon formally resubmitted the protocol to the Senate on August 19 of last year, he recommended that the United States ratification be subject to a reservation making clear our right to retaliate with *chemical* weapons should any enemy state or its allies use either *chemical* or *biological* weapons against us.[52]

Our proposal to ratify without assertion of a right of retaliation in the area of biological weapons and toxins even in the event of a first strike against us with biological weapons or toxins offers a constructive United States initiative in accord with the President's policy decisions.

INTERPRETATION OF THE PROTOCOL

The protocol is not free from ambiguity, with some differences in viewpoint still unresolved after 45 years.

As I indicated in my report to the President on the protocol, the United States considers the term "bacteriological methods of warfare" as used in the protocol to embrace all biological methods of warfare and the use in warfare of toxins however produced. This broad interpretation, though not clear from the language of the protocol, is generally accepted by the international community.

I also noted in my report that it is the United States understanding of the protocol that it does not prohibit the use in war of chemical herbicides and riot control agents. This interpretation, as you know, is one upon which there are differences of opinion in the international community.

On December 16, 1969, the General Assembly of the United Nations passed a resolution to the effect that the use in war of all chemicals is contrary to the protocol.[53] Although not specifically stated, the intent

---

[52] Cf. above at note 44.
[53] *Documents, 1968-69*, pp. 119-20.

was to include riot control agents and chemical herbicides. We took the position that the General Assembly was not the proper forum for resolving this question of treaty interpretation and, in addition, made clear we disagreed with this interpretation.[54]

The resolution was adopted by a vote of 80 to 3, with 36 abstentions. Participating in the General Assembly vote were 80 of the 84 states at that time parties to the protocol. Twenty-nine of them were among the 36 who abstained on the resolution; and two of them, Australia and Portugal, joined the United States in voting against it. This split vote among the parties to the protocol reflected not only the divergency of views on whether or not the protocol covers the use of riot control agents and herbicides but also whether the General Assembly is an appropriate or competent body to interpret international law as embodied in a treaty.

Since then Japan, which like the United States was one of the original signatories in 1925, has ratified the protocol. In the debates in the Diet, the Japanese Government made clear its view that the use in war of riot control agents was *not* prohibited. Japan did not formally transmit its view to other parties. We propose to follow the same procedure.

We have chosen to handle our understanding in this way because we believe this to be a question of setting forth our views on a disputed issue. We do not believe that a formal reservation would be appropriate. A reservation is used by a country ratifying or acceding to a treaty when that country does not wish to undertake all of the obligations set forth in that treaty. Because we do not believe that the protocol imposes any obligations concerning the use of riot control agents and chemical herbicides, it would be both unnecessary and inappropriate for the United States to enter a reservation on this point.

Occasionally a country transmits to the depositary government, along with its instrument of ratification or accession, a formal statement explaining its interpretation. It does this to insure that all states party to a treaty will be aware of its interpretation of the obligations it is undertaking. We are not proposing that this procedure be followed in this case for two reasons: First, as a result of our public statements at the United Nations and elsewhere, as well as the position set out in the documents transmitted to the Senate along with the protocol, the international community is already well aware of our interpretation. Second, if we did enter a formal interpretation, other states parties might feel obliged to take exception to our statement in order to preserve their own understanding of the protocol. We believe it is well understood that a difference of opinion exists among the parties on this point. We do not believe an exchange of conflicting formal positions at this time would contribute to a resolution of this issue.

[54] Same, pp. 115-18.

I would also note that *no* party to the protocol thus far has made a formal interpretation or formal reservation with respect to riot control agents or herbicides. For these reasons I hope this committee, and the Senate as a whole, will also accept this approach.

I would like to emphasize in connection with riot control agents that the key words of the protocol—the phrase "asphyxiating, poisonous or other gases"—are far from clear in resolving whether the protocol was intended to apply to "all other" or "similar other" gases. The equally authentic French language text uses the words *gaz similaires*.

It is our view that the protocol was not intended to cover the use in war of riot control agents. The United States Representative [Hugh Gibson] to the Preparatory Commission for the Geneva Disarmament Conference in 1930 stated that:

> I think there would be considerable hesitation on the part of many governments to bind themselves to refrain from the use in war, against any enemy, of agencies which they have adopted for peacetime use against their own population, agencies adopted on the ground that, while causing temporary inconvenience, they cause no real suffering or permanent disability, and are thereby more clearly humane than the use of weapons to which they were formerly obliged to resort in time of emergency.

The preparatory commission report itself noted it was "unable to express a definite opinion of the question of interpretation" on whether the protocol should cover tear gas. This issue remains unresolved today among the parties.

It is difficult to see how it can be argued, however, that the words "other gases" plus the phrase "all analogous liquids, materials or devices"—all of which were taken from the Treaty of Versailles of 1919—were intended to cover the use in war of chemical herbicides. Chemical herbicides were, of course, not in general use until the late 1940's. And most significantly, the negotiating history does not suggest any intention to cover the general class of antiplant, as opposed to antipersonnel, chemicals.

Our position on both riot control agents and chemical herbicides is, of course, without prejudice to the position the United States might take in any future international agreements dealing with chemical agents. Such agreements would have to be negotiated on the basis of all considerations which the parties might consider relevant at the time.

IMPORTANCE OF U.S. RATIFICATION

The failure of the United States to ratify the protocol has obscured the leading role this country has played since World War I in urging the international community not to resort to chemical or biological warfare.

Widespread acceptance of the obligations of the protocol through formal ratification or adherence has been accepted as an important goal by all members of the United Nations. Our ratification would also constitute an important step in our efforts to seek further disarmament measures relating to development, production, and stockpiling of biological warfare and chemical warfare agents.

We would hope to achieve at the Geneva Disarmament Conference, first, acceptance of the draft U.K. convention banning all biological means of warfare and, second, development of more effective controls over production and stockpiling of chemical weapons.[55] However, until we have become a party to the protocol, our ability to guide and influence the development of these further measures—measures which we consider important to our own security and to further progress in the arms control field—will be seriously undermined.

The ratification of the Geneva Protocol will have no adverse effect on our national security. The security of the United States and its allies is dependent not on our use of biological agents or our first use of lethal or incapacitating chemical agents but rather on our ability to deter the use of these weapons against us. Therefore, ratification is very much in the interests of the United States. As I have indicated, the protocol is a vital part of existing restraints on the use of chemical and biological weapons and a key step in the effort to develop more effective international arms control measures in this area.

I believe it is of critical importance to our efforts in this area that the United States now become a party to the protocol. Accordingly, I urge the Senate to give its advice and consent to ratification with the reservation proposed by the President.

(16) Senatorial Reservations: Letter from Senator J. William Fulbright, Chairman of the Committee on Foreign Relations, to President Nixon, April 15, 1971.[56]

(Complete Text)

Dear Mr. President:

The Committee on Foreign Relations has recently completed hearings on the Geneva Protocol of 1925 which you submitted to the Senate on August 19, 1970.[57] At its last business meeting the Committee dis-

---

[55] Cf. Documents 17-20.
[56] *Documents on Disarmament, 1971*, pp. 215-18.
[57] U.S. Senate, 92d Cong., 1st sess., *Geneva Protocol of 1925: Hearings* on Executive J, 91st Cong., 2d sess. (Washington: G.P.O., 1972).

cussed the testimony which had been heard and reviewed the possible courses of action open to it. The Members decided that before the Committee gave further consideration to the Protocol I should privately communicate to you certain views which many of us now hold concerning United States adherence to the Protocol.

At the outset let me express the Committee's strong approval of the initiatives which you have already taken in revising U.S. policy with regard to chemical and biological weapons. Your decisions to renounce altogether biological and toxin warfare, as well as the first use of lethal and incapacitating chemical weapons,[58] were a major contribution toward a more secure future for mankind. All of us appreciate the difficulties which confronted you in taking these steps and in deciding to resubmit the Geneva Protocol to the Senate.

There is no question of the Committee's strong support for the objectives of the Geneva Protocol. Indeed it is because we attach such great importance to the Protocol that many of us are reluctant to proceed further toward its ratification on the basis of the understandings and interpretations which have been attached to it by the Secretary of State.[59]

I believe it accurate to say that when our hearing began few of the Members had firm views on the question of tear gas and herbicides. Having heard a number of expert witnesses on all aspects of the Protocol many Members now consider that it would be in the interest of the United States to ratify the Protocol without restrictive understandings, or, if that is not possible at this time, to postpone further action on the Protocol until it is.

The Secretary of State's position on tear gas and herbicides appears to rest primarily on the grounds that the Protocol was not intended to prohibit their use. Having heard the legal testimony on both sides of this issue, many Committee Members conclude that an adequate legal argument can be made either for or against that interpretation. Given the Protocol's acknowledged ambiguity, we tend to agree with the view expressed in testimony by Mr. George Bunn, former General Counsel of the Arms Control and Disarmament Agency, who said that "any future interpretation of the Protocol should depend less on the negotiating history than on a realistic appraisal of the pros and cons—military, diplomatic and arms control—of the use of these agents in the future."

In this connection, we note that the use of herbicides in Vietnam is now being discontinued. It would appear that their actual utility in Vietnam has been marginal and that the crop destruction program may well have been counter-productive. Furthermore, the more we learn about the impact of the herbicide warfare on the ecology of Vietnam,

[58] Cf. note 42 above.
[59] Cf. above at note 44.

the more disturbing are its implications for the future. As Dr. Arthur W. Galston, an eminent biologist from Yale, reminded the Committee, "If man makes conditions unsuitable for vegetation on this earth, he thereby makes conditions unsuitable for his own existence."

Testimony on the question of tear gas also raised considerable doubt in the minds of many Members as to the desirability of its future use in war by the United States. Dr. Matthew Meselson of Harvard, who testified before the Committee and who has made a careful study of the military use of tear gas, presented the following conclusions:

1. The military value of riot gas is very low.
2. Our overriding security interest in the area of chemical and biological weapons is to prevent the proliferation and use of biological and lethal chemical weapons.
3. Our use of riot gas in war runs directly counter to this fundamental interest.

Dr. Meselson's view coincides closely with that expressed by another highly qualified witness, Dr. Donald G. Brennan of the Hudson Institute, a military strategist who last testified before the Committee in support of the Safeguard Anti-Ballistic Missile System. After a skeptical critique of many of the familiar arguments against tear gas and herbicides, Dr. Brennan concluded that the military cost of giving up tear gas and herbicides appeared relatively low and that the United States position could therefore properly "be dominated by 'decent respect for the opinions of mankind' and accept the interpretation that the Protocol embraces harassing agents and herbicides."

The latter point leads to another consideration which troubles many Members of the Committee. This is the fact that the overwhelming majority of the nations in the world already agree, as evidenced by an 80-3 vote in the U.N. General Assembly, that tear gas and herbicides should be prohibited under the Geneva Protocol.[60] If, at this late date the United States adheres to the Protocol but in so doing places its weight behind a restrictive interpretation, this cannot help but weaken the effect of the Protocol. The Committee finds it difficult to believe there would be any positive moral force to our becoming a party to the Protocol only on condition that we reserve the right to keep on doing as we wish despite the fact that most other nations believe it undesirable. Furthermore, I sense a reluctance on the part of Committee members to give advice and consent to an international agreement in the face of a virtual certainty that our interpretation will be challenged or rejected. It will not suffice, as the Secretary of State suggested, to ratify now, and work out the problems later.

---

[60] Cf. above at note 53.

We believe that these arguments are, of themselves, sufficiently compelling to warrant the Committee's request that you give further consideration to the tear gas and herbicide question. In addition, as you know, there are now several studies in progress on the use of tear gas and herbicides in Vietnam, including one requested by you as a basis for examining the implications and consequences for U.S. policy of their future use in war. It seems to us that all of these studies, but in particular the latter, should be available before any final action is taken with regard to ratification of the Protocol.

Although we would agree that the Protocol should long ago have been ratified by the United States, it is perhaps unfortunate that it comes before the Senate at a time when the United States is at war and actively employing chemical weapons which most nations consider to be prohibited by the Protocol. Possibly by the time the results of these additional studies are available the war in Indochina will be ended, or at least the level of conflict there will have been reduced to a point where our further use of either tear gas or herbicides will be unnecessary. This alone would make it easier for all concerned to make a dispassionate assessment of the issues involved.

As a practical matter I have considerable doubt that the Protocol could now receive the advice and consent of the Senate on the terms laid down by the Secretary of State, i.e., that you might not ratify the Protocol if the proposed understandings are modified by action of the Senate. At present the prospects for the Protocol are clouded by strongly held views on both sides and I personally would not wish to see it risked a second time under such circumstances. The Committee asks therefore that the question of the interpretation of the Protocol be reexamined considering whether the need to hold open the option to use tear gas and herbicides is indeed so great that it outweighs the long-term advantages to the United States of strengthening existing barriers against chemical warfare by means of ratification of the Protocol without restrictive interpretations. If the Administration were to take the longer and broader view of our own interests, I cannot imagine any serious opposition to that decision, either here at home or abroad. On the contrary, I personally believe that were you to take this initiative your action would be regarded as truly courageous and possessed of real moral force.

Sincerely yours,

J. W. FULBRIGHT
Chairman

4. Prohibition of Bacteriological (Biological) Weapons.

[Serious discussion of the desirability of amplifying and strengthening the prohibitions against chemical and biological warfare contained in the Geneva Protocol of 1925[61] was initiated in the Conference of the Committee on Disarmament (CCD) in 1968 following completion of the Nuclear Nonproliferation Treaty. In 1969, the United Kingdom submitted to the CCD a revised Draft Convention for the Prohibition of Biological Methods of Warfare,[62] while the U.S.S.R. and its allies submitted to the U.N. General Assembly a Draft Convention on the Prohibition of the Development, Production, and Stockpiling of Chemical and Bacteriological (Biological) Weapons and on the Destruction of Such Weapons.[63] The United States, while expressing support for the principles and objectives of the British draft, found the Soviet proposal deficient in that it failed to provide for adequate inspection and, by linking the relatively simple issue of a biological warfare convention with the technically more complicated questions involved in a chemical warfare ban, threatened to delay agreement in both areas.

This difference of approach, which persisted through 1970, was overcome during the spring 1971 session of the CCD when the U.S.S.R. and allied states agreed to separate the two issues and tabled a draft convention dealing only with biological weapons and toxins, leaving the matter of a ban on chemical weapons for later consideration. An agreed United States–Soviet text of a convention prohibiting bacteriological (biological) weapons was then worked out and, after further changes, approved by the CCD and forwarded to the General Assembly (cf. Document 17). In a resolution adopted December 16, 1971, the General Assembly in turn commended the draft convention and requested that it be opened for signature and ratification at the earliest possible date (Document 18). The convention (Document 19) was in fact opened for signature in Washington, London, and Moscow on April 10, 1972, and was transmitted by President Nixon to the Senate for its advice and consent to ratification on August 10, 1972.[64] Approved by the Senate on December 16, 1974, the convention was ratified by President Ford on January 22, 1975, and entered into force on March 26, 1975 with the deposit of instruments of ratification by the U.S.S.R., the United Kingdom, and the United States.]

(17) Completion of the Draft Convention: Statement by George H. Bush, United States Representative to the United Nations, to the

---

[61] Cf. above at note 41.
[62] Text in *Documents on Disarmament, 1969*, pp. 431-33; extract in *Documents, 1968-69*, p. 108n.
[63] Text in *Documents on Disarmament, 1969*, pp. 455-57.
[64] *Public Papers, 1972*, pp. 770-771.

First (Political and Security) Committee of the General Assembly, November 11, 1971.[65]

(Excerpt)

The consideration that we are beginning today of the disarmament items on our agenda is one of the most important functions of this body. The General Assembly's annual review and assessment of the challenges we face and the accomplishments we have achieved in the arms control and disarmament field, together with the overall guidance set forth in its resolutions, has provided a major stimulus toward progress in this area.

Last year in this committee there was extensive discussion regarding the question of possible prohibitions on chemical and biological weapons. That debate culminated in the adoption by the General Assembly of Resolution 2662, which took note of the various proposals that had been made for progress in this area, commended the basic approach set forth in the joint memorandum of the Group of 12, and requested the Conference of the Committee on Disarmament (CCD) to continue its consideration of the problem of chemical and biological methods of warfare with a view to prohibiting urgently the development, production, and stockpiling of those weapons.[66]

Mr. Chairman, I believe that all members of the United Nations can take satisfaction in the work accomplished by the CCD during the past year toward the realization of this objective. The draft Convention on the Prohibition of the Development, Production and Stockpiling of Bacteriological (Biological) and Toxin Weapons and on Their Destruction[67] is a solid achievement. It is an achievement that can eliminate the threat of the use of disease as a method of warfare. It is an agreement that is in the interest of all governments and of all mankind.

I would like to make a number of comments on this draft convention—on the contributions which it embodies, on some of its specific provisions, and on its general significance.

This convention is the first concrete result of some 3 years of international discussion and negotiation on the question of chemical and biological weapons. Incorporated in its provisions are a wide range of ideas, suggestions, and compromises reflecting the views of the many delegations that participated in its preparation.

---

[65] USUN Press Release 182, Nov. 11, 1971; text from *Bulletin*, Jan. 24, 1972, pp. 102-4. For the continuation of Ambassador Bush's statement see Document 20.
[66] *Documents, 1970*, pp. 77-80.
[67] Document 19.

A proposal for a concrete agreement dealing with biological methods of warfare was first put forward by the United Kingdom in 1968. Important provisions in the present convention are derived from the draft that was tabled by the United Kingdom at the CCD in 1969,[68] and again in revised form in 1970.[69] Other provisions are based on the draft presented in March of this year by the delegations of Bulgaria, Czechoslovakia, Hungary, Mongolia, Poland, Romania, and the U.S.S.R.[70] The prohibition of the production and stockpiling of toxins, which are among the most lethal substances that could be used for warfare, was suggested by my own country.[71] The broad definition of toxins which appears in article I was included at the suggestion of Sweden.[72]

During the course of the negotiations at Geneva this year the Representatives of Brazil, Burma, Egypt, Ethiopia, India, Mexico, Morocco, Nigeria, Pakistan, Sweden, and Yugoslavia presented a paper[73] containing a number of concrete suggestions that are reflected in the present text. These concerned in particular changes in the preamble designed to emphasize the link between the prohibitions of chemical and biological weapons and a strengthening of the undertaking on further negotiations regarding chemical weapons. Other proposals reflected in the language of the draft and in the statements that were made regarding its interpretation were put forward by the delegations of Argentina, Canada, Egypt, Italy, Morocco, the Netherlands, and the United Kingdom.

This brief summary is by no means a complete account of all the contributions that were made to the formulation of this convention. It illustrates, however, that this important multilateral instrument has been forged with the significant help and through the participation of many countries. It is the result of hard work, of compromise and accommodation among many points of view, and of thoughtful and painstaking negotiations.

Mr. Chairman, the provisions of this convention and a number of statements made at Geneva regarding its interpretation have been summarized in the Report of the Conference of the Committee on Disarmament to the General Assembly.[74] At this time, I would like only to highlight a few points of particular importance.

As the CCD report has noted, it was the desire of all participants in these negotiations that nothing should be done in formulating a new agreement which might in any way cast doubt on the validity of the

[68] Cf. note 62 above.
[69] *Documents on Disarmament, 1970*, pp. 428-31.
[70] Same, *1971*, pp. 190-94.
[71] Same, *1970*, pp. 272-73.
[72] Same, *1971*, pp. 395-99.
[73] Same, pp. 500-501.
[74] Same, pp. 610-33.

Geneva Protocol of 1925.[75] The protocol is in fact fully safeguarded by the provisions and by the nature of the present draft. Article VIII specifically provides that nothing in the convention should be interpreted as limiting or detracting from the obligations assumed by states under the Geneva Protocol. The preamble contains clauses whereby the parties not only note the important significance of the Geneva Protocol but also reaffirm their adherence to, call on all states to comply strictly with, and recall that the General Assembly has condemned actions contrary to, the protocol's principles and objectives. Moreover, as a practical matter, the elimination of biological agents and toxins from the arsenals of states will exclude completely the possibility of their being used as weapons.

Another matter of the highest importance to committee members was that this convention should insure that work was continued on an urgent basis on effective measures for the prohibition of the development, production, and stockpiling of chemical weapons. Accordingly, article IX of the convention reaffirms the recognized objective of effective prohibition of chemical weapons and sets forth a firm undertaking regarding continued negotiations in this area. The importance and urgency of eliminating weapons using chemical or biological agents and the fact that this agreement represents the first possible step toward the achievement of agreement on chemical weapons are recognized in the preamble.

In our view, the present convention thus fully complies with the approach recommended by the General Assembly in the resolution that it adopted last year.

Mr. Chairman, in February President Nixon indicated in a letter to the CCD[76] that an agreement prohibiting the development, production, and stockpiling of biological weapons and toxins would enhance the security of all countries and international security in general. He stated, and I quote:

Because of the rapid transmission of contagious diseases, particularly with modern means of communications, any use of biological weapons—by any state in any conflict anywhere in the world—could endanger the people of every country. Additional restraints on biological weapons would thus contribute to the security of all peoples.

A prohibition against the possession of biological weapons could also have far-reaching benefits of another character. It could encourage international cooperation in the peaceful application of biological research, a field which may lead to immeasurable advances in the health and well-being of peoples everywhere.

[75] Cf. above at note 41.
[76] Document 12.

It is thus a matter of particular satisfaction to the United States that article X of the present convention sets forth in some detail provisions designed to facilitate international cooperation regarding peaceful application in the field of bacteriology and biology.

Mr. Chairman, in accordance with his decisions regarding United States programs in this field[77] and in accordance with the spirit of the convention now before us, President Nixon announced on October 18 that the former Army Biological Defense Research Center at Fort Detrick, Maryland, is being converted into a leading center for cancer research. I would like to quote from the President's statement on that occasion:[78]

This facility, which once was so top secret, which was closed not only to Americans, but, of course, to anybody from foreign lands, now is open to all people in the world. Wherever scientists or doctors may be, whether in Europe or Latin America or Africa or Asia, they can come here. They are welcome to come here to see what we have done, just as we hope they will welcome us, so that we can see what they have done.

Mr. Chairman, this convention, which provides for the elimination from the arsenals of states of an entire class of weapons, is a true measure of disarmament. There exists already, I believe, a broad measure of consensus in favor of this agreement. I would therefore urge this Assembly to encourage prompt and widespread support for the draft convention and to request that it be opened for signature and ratification at the earliest possible date.[79]

*   *   *

(18) Commendation of the Draft Convention: United Nations General Assembly Resolution 2826 (XXVI), Adopted December 16, 1971.[80]

(Complete Text)

The General Assembly,

Recalling its resolution 2662 (XXV) of 7 December 1970,[81]

Convinced of the importance and urgency of eliminating from the

[77] Cf. note 42 above.
[78] Public Papers, 1971, p. 1051.
[79] Cf. Document 18.
[80] Text from U.N. General Assembly, Official Records: 26th Session, Supplement No. 29 (A/8429), p. 30; adopted by a vote of 110 (U.S.)-0-1 (France), with 21 absences (including China).
[81] Documents, 1970, pp. 77-80.

arsenals of States, through effective measures, such dangerous weapons of mass destruction as those using chemical or bacteriological (biological) agents,

Having considered the report of the Conference of the Committee on Disarmament dated 6 October 1971,[82] and being appreciative of its work on the draft Convention on the Prohibition of the Development, Production and Stockpiling of Bacteriological (Biological) and Toxin Weapons and on Their Destruction, annexed to the report,

Recognizing the important significance of the Protocol for the Prohibition of the Use in War of Asphyxiating, Poisonous or Other Gases, and of Bacteriological Methods of Warfare, signed at Geneva on 17 June 1925,[83] and conscious also of the contribution which the said Protocol has already made, and continues to make, to mitigating the horrors of war,

Noting that the Convention on the Prohibition of the Development, Production and Stockpiling of Bacteriological (Biological) and Toxin Weapons and on Their Destruction provides for the parties to reaffirm their adherence to the principles and objectives of that Protocol and to call upon all States to comply strictly with them,

Further noting that nothing in the Convention shall be interpreted as in any way limiting or detracting from the obligations assumed by any State under the Geneva Protocol,

Determined, for the sake of all mankind, to exclude completely the possibility of bacteriological (biological) agents and toxins being used as weapons,

Recognizing that an agreement on the prohibition of bacteriological (biological) and toxin weapons represents a first possible step towards the achievement of agreement on effective measures also for the prohibition of the development, production and stockpiling of chemical weapons,

Noting that the Convention contains an affirmation of the recognized objective of effective prohibition of chemical weapons and, to this end, an undertaking to continue negotiations in good faith with a view to reaching early agreement on effective measures for the prohibition of their development, production and stockpiling and for their destruction, and on appropriate measures concerning equipment and means of delivery specifically designed for the production or use of chemical agents for weapons purposes,

Convinced that the implementation of measures in the field of disarmament should release substantial additional resources, which should promote economic and social development, particularly in the developing countries,

---

[82] *Documents on Disarmament, 1971*, pp. 610-33.
[83] Cf. above at note 41.

Convinced that the Convention will contribute to the realization of the purposes and principles of the Charter of the United Nations,

1. *Commends* the Convention on the Prohibition of the Development, Production and Stockpiling of Bacteriological (Biological) and Toxin Weapons and on Their Destruction, the text of which is annexed to the present resolution;[84]

2. *Requests* the depositary Governments to open the Convention for signature and ratification at the earliest possible date;

3. *Expresses the hope* for the widest possible adherence to the Convention.

(19) Convention on the Prohibition of the Development, Production and Stockpiling of Bacteriological (Biological) and Toxin Weapons and on Their Destruction: Annex to United Nations General Assembly Resolution 2826 (XXVI) of December 16, 1971.[85]

(Complete Text)

The States Parties to this Convention,

Determined to act with a view to achieving effective progress towards general and complete disarmament, including the prohibition and elimination of all types of weapons of mass destruction, and convinced that the prohibition of the development, production and stockpiling of chemical and bacteriological (biological) weapons and their elimination, through effective measures, will facilitate the achievement of general and complete disarmament under strict and effective international control,

Recognizing the important significance of the Protocol for the Prohibition of the Use in War of Asphyxiating, Poisonous or Other Gases, and of Bacteriological Methods of Warfare, signed at Geneva on 17 June 1925,[86] and conscious also of the contribution which the said Protocol has already made, and continues to make, to mitigating the horrors of war,

Reaffirming their adherence to the principles and objectives of that Protocol and calling upon all States to comply strictly with them,

Recalling that the General Assembly of the United Nations has repeatedly condemned all actions contrary to the principles and objectives of the Geneva Protocol of 17 June 1925,

Desiring to contribute to the strengthening of confidence between

---

[84] Document 19.
[85] U.N. General Assembly, *Official Records: 26th Session, Supplement No. 29* (A/8429), pp. 30-32. The official U.S. text was issued in 1975 as TIAS 8062.
[86] Cf. above at note 41.

peoples and the general improvement of the international atmosphere,

Desiring also to contribute to the realization of the purposes and principles of the Charter of the United Nations,

Convinced of the importance and urgency of eliminating from the arsenals of States, through effective measures, such dangerous weapons of mass destruction as those using chemical or bacteriological (biological) agents.

Recognizing that an agreement on the prohibition of bacteriological (biological) and toxin weapons represents a first possible step towards the achievement of agreement on effective measures also for the prohibition of the development, production and stockpiling of chemical weapons, and determined to continue negotiations to that end,

Determined, for the sake of all mankind, to exclude completely the possibility of bacteriological (biological) agents and toxins being used as weapons,

Convinced that such use would be repugnant to the conscience of mankind, and that no effort should be spared to minimize this risk,

Have agreed as follows:

ARTICLE I

Each State Party to this Convention undertakes never in any circumstances to develop, produce, stockpile or otherwise acquire or retain:

(1) Microbial or other biological agents, or toxins whatever their origin or method of production, of types and in quantities that have no justification for prophylactic, protective or other peaceful purposes;

(2) Weapons, equipment or means of delivery designed to use such agents or toxins for hostile purposes or in armed conflict.

ARTICLE II

Each State Party to this Convention undertakes to destroy, or to divert to peaceful purposes, as soon as possible but not later than nine months after the entry into force of the Convention, all agents, toxins, weapons, equipment and means of delivery specified in article I of the Convention, which are in its possession or under its jurisdiction or control. In implementing the provisions of this article all necessary safety precautions shall be observed to protect populations and the environment.

ARTICLE III

Each State Party to this Convention undertakes not to transfer to any recipient whatsoever, directly or indirectly, and not in any way to assist, encourage or induce any State, group of States or international organizations to manufacture or otherwise acquire any of the agents, toxins, weapons, equipment or means of delivery specified in article I of the Convention.

ARTICLE IV

Each State Party to this Convention shall, in accordance with its constitutional processes, take any necessary measures to prohibit and prevent the development, production, stockpiling, acquisition or retention of the agents, toxins, weapons, equipment and means of delivery specified in article I of the Convention, within the territory of such State, under its jurisdiction or under its control anywhere.

ARTICLE V

The States Parties to this Convention undertake to consult one another and to co-operate in solving any problems which may arise in relation to the objective of, or in the application of the provisions of, the Convention. Consultation and co-operation pursuant to this article may also be undertaken through appropriate international procedures within the framework of the United Nations and in accordance with its Charter.

ARTICLE VI

1. Any State Party to this Convention which finds that any other State Party is acting in breach of obligations deriving from the provisions of the Convention may lodge a complaint with the Security Council of the United Nations. Such a complaint should include all possible evidence confirming its validity, as well as a request for its consideration by the Security Council.

2. Each State Party to this Convention undertakes to co-operate in carrying out any investigation which the Security Council may initiate, in accordance with the provisions of the Charter of the United Nations, on the basis of the complaint received by the Council. The Security Council shall inform the States Parties to the Convention of the results of the investigation.

ARTICLE VII

Each State Party to this Convention undertakes to provide or support assistance, in accordance with the United Nations Charter, to any Party to the Convention which so requests, if the Security Council decides that such Party has been exposed to danger as a result of violation of the Convention.

ARTICLE VIII

Nothing in this Convention shall be interpreted as in any way limiting or detracting from the obligations assumed by any State under the Protocol for the Prohibition of the Use in War of Asphyxiating, Poisonous or Other Gases, and of Bacteriological Methods of Warfare, signed at Geneva on 17 June 1925.

ARTICLE IX

Each State Party to this Convention affirms the recognized objective of effective prohibition of chemical weapons and, to this end, undertakes to continue negotiations in good faith with a view to reaching early agreement on effective measures for the prohibition of their development, production and stockpiling and for their destruction, and on appropriate measures concerning equipment and means of delivery specifically designed for the production or use of chemical agents for weapons purposes.

ARTICLE X

1. The States Parties to this Convention undertake to facilitate, and have the right to participate in, the fullest possible exchange of equipment, materials and scientific and technological information for the use of bacteriological (biological) agents and toxins for peaceful purposes. Parties to the Convention in a position to do so shall also co-operate in contributing individually or together with other States or international organizations to the further development and application of scientific discoveries in the field of bacteriology (biology) for the prevention of disease, or for other peaceful purposes.

2. This Convention shall be implemented in a manner designed to avoid hampering the economic or technological development of States Parties to the Convention or international co-operation in the field of peaceful bacteriological (biological) activities, including the international exchange of bacteriological (biological) agents and toxins and equipment for the processing, use or production of bacteriological (biological) agents and toxins for peaceful purposes in accordance with the provisions of the Convention.

ARTICLE XI

Any State Party may propose amendments to this Convention. Amendments shall enter into force for each State Party accepting the amendments upon their acceptance by a majority of the States Parties to the Convention and thereafter for each remaining State Party on the date of acceptance by it.

ARTICLE XII

Five years after the entry into force of this Convention, or earlier if it' is requested by a majority of Parties to the Convention by submitting a proposal to this effect to the Depositary Governments, a conference of States Parties to the Convention shall be held at Geneva, Switzerland, to review the operation of the Convention, with a view to assuring that the purposes of the preamble and the provisions of the Convention, including the provisions concerning negotiations on chemical weapons, are being realized. Such review shall take into account any new scientific and technological developments relevant to the Convention.

ARTICLE XIII

1. This Convention shall be of unlimited duration.
2. Each State Party to this Convention shall in exercising its national sovereignty have the right to withdraw from the Convention if it decides that extraordinary events, related to the subject-matter of the Convention, have jeopardized the supreme interests of its country. It shall give notice of such withdrawal to all other States Parties to the Convention and to the United Nations Security Council three months in advance. Such notice shall include a statement of the extraordinary events it regards as having jeopardized its supreme interests.

ARTICLE XIV

1. This Convention shall be open to all States for signature. Any State which does not sign the Convention before its entry into force in accordance with paragraph 3 of this article may accede to it at any time.
2. This Convention shall be subject to ratification by signatory States. Instruments of ratification and instruments of accession shall be deposited with the Governments of the Union of Soviet Socialist Republics, the United Kingdom of Great Britain and Northern Ireland and the United States of America, which are hereby designated the Depositary Governments.

3. This Convention shall enter into force after the deposit of instruments of ratification by twenty-two Governments, including the Governments designated as Depositaries of the Convention.

4. For States whose instruments of ratification or accession are deposited subsequent to the entry into force of this Convention, it shall enter into force on the date of the deposit of their instruments of ratification or accession.

5. The Depositary Governments shall promptly inform all signatory and acceding States of the date of each signature, the date of deposit of each instrument of ratification or of accession and the date of the entry into force of this Convention, and of the receipt of other notices.

6. This Convention shall be registered by the Depositary Governments pursuant to Article 102 of the Charter of the United Nations.

ARTICLE XV

This Convention, the Chinese, English, French, Russian and Spanish texts of which are equally authentic, shall be deposited in the archives of the Depositary Governments. Duly certified copies of the Convention shall be transmitted by the Depositary Governments to the Governments of the signatory and acceding States.

IN WITNESS WHEREOF the undersigned, duly authorized, have signed this Convention.

Done in triplicate, at . . . ., this . . . . . . day of . . . . , ...[87]

5. Unresolved Disarmament Questions.

[The completion of the Convention on the Prohibition of Bacteriological (Biological) and Toxin Weapons[88] fulfilled but a part of the declared objectives of the signatory states, which assumed the obligation in Article IX of the convention to continue good-faith negotiations with a view to early agreement on measures for the prohibition of chemical weapons as well. Still other unresolved disarmament issues were mentioned by Ambassador Bush in his presentation to the First Committee of the General Assembly (Document 20), among them questions relating to a ban on nuclear weapon tests, restraints on conventional weapons, and measures for the implementation of existing treaties; the bilateral United States–Soviet negotiations on the limitation of strategic armaments and related measures; and regional arms

---

[87] The convention was opened for signature at Washington, London, and Moscow on Apr. 10, 1972. For its ratification and entry into force, cf. above at note 64.

[88] Document 19.

control measures in such areas as Europe and Latin America. In addition to voting its approval of the Bacteriological Weapons Convention,[89] the General Assembly in a series of resolutions adopted December 16, 1971, reaffirmed the United Nations commitment to general and complete disarmament;[90] urged priority consideration of measures to prohibit chemical weapons,[91] prompt agreement on cessation of all nuclear weapon tests,[92] and adherence by all nuclear weapon states to the relevant protocol of the Treaty for the Prohibition of Nuclear Weapons in Latin America;[93] and declared the Indian Ocean to be a "zone of peace" from which military installations and activities of outside powers should be barred.[94] In view of reservations expressed by the U.S. and other delegations, a Soviet proposal to convene a World Disarmament Conference was not brought to a vote.[95] The Assembly did, however, express general support for the idea and called for its inclusion in the agenda of the 1972 session.[96]]

(20) The Disarmament Agenda: Continuation of the Statement by Ambassador Bush to the First Committee of the General Assembly, November 11, 1971.[97]

(Excerpt)

*   *   *

Mr. Chairman, I should like to turn now to a consideration of the challenging task that remains before us and to the important work that has already been accomplished with respect to further prohibitions regarding chemical weapons. At the CCD this year considerable attention was devoted to this issue. Many delegations contributed through working papers and through the participation of their leading experts on this subject in an informal meeting in July[98] to a better under-

---

[89] Document 18.
[90] Resolution 2825 (XXVI); texts of this and the following resolutions in General Assembly, *Official Records: 26th Session, Supplement 29* (A/8429).
[91] Resolution 2827 (XXVI).
[92] Resolution 2828 (XXVI).
[93] Resolution 2830 (XXVI); cf. Document 114.
[94] Resolution 2832 (XXVI); text in Document 66.
[95] Cf. statement of U.S. Representative Christopher H. Phillips to the General Assembly, Nov. 26, 1971, in *Bulletin*, Jan. 24, 1972, pp. 109-11.
[96] Resolution 2833 (XXVI). For the action of the 1972 General Assembly cf. *A.F.R., 1972*, Chapter II at note 155.
[97] USUN Press Release 182; text from *Bulletin*, Jan. 24, 1972, pp. 104-7. For the earlier portion of Ambassador Bush's statement see Document 17.
[98] *Documents on Disarmament, 1971*, p. 616.

standing of the central problems of the workability of a chemical weapons verification system. We believe that during the past 2 years a serious start has been made on exploration of possible approaches to this problem. The task still before us, as we see it, is to sort out and to examine those elements of verification that might be amenable to development as effective tools for insuring compliance with prohibitions on chemical weapons. Further progress will require study of all promising suggestions. In this regard I should like to note that a memorandum proposing elements as a basis for negotiation was presented to the CCD by a group of 12 delegations.[99] We hope that this document will contribute to continued efforts to achieve sound and reliable arms control measures in this field. For our part, we are determined to pursue this task. We will listen with care to suggestions during the debate in this committee which will, we hope, request that the CCD continue its work on this important issue.[100]

In accordance with the Resolution 2663, adopted by the General Assembly last year,[101] the CCD also continued its work on the question of a ban on nuclear weapons tests. As requested by that resolution, a special report on this issue was prepared and has been included as part III of the CCD report to the General Assembly.[102]

Set forth in considerable detail here are proposals and views of committee members regarding the nature of a possible comprehensive test ban agreement, on the concept of a threshold agreement or partial measures, and on interim measures or restraints; also included are suggestions regarding verification of a prohibition on underground nuclear weapons tests as well as regarding international cooperation in the exchange of seismic data, the improvement of worldwide seismological capabilities, and further study of detection and identification of underground nuclear tests. I am sure that all members of this body will wish to give this report very careful study.

I can assure you that my own government will continue to examine all serious possibilities for effective controls over a prohibition on underground testing. As many delegations are aware, the United States has devoted considerable effort to the study of the seismic detection, location, and identification of earthquakes and underground explosions. We have made our findings broadly available to other countries in the hope that this would contribute to a better understanding of the verification issues. The United States continues to support an adequately verified comprehensive ban on the testing of nuclear weapons.

---

99 U.N. document CCD/352, Sept. 28, 1971; text in *Documents on Disarmament, 1971*, pp. 566-68.
100 Cf. above at note 92.
101 Partial text in *Documents, 1970*, pp. 82-83.
102 *Documents on Disarmament, 1971*, pp. 625-33.

In order to be effective, we believe, verification of such a measure should include on-site inspections.

Turning now, Mr. Chairman, to another aspect of the arms race, and indeed in terms of total expenditures on armaments by far the most important aspect, I would like to comment briefly on the need to explore possible restraints on conventional weapons. As the U.S. delegation pointed out at the CCD this summer,[103] the intensive discussion of ways to control weapons of mass destruction during the past 25 years has not only resulted in a number of concrete agreements but has also helped to forge the tools for meaningful discussion on this problem. A body of common objectives and concepts, and a shared vocabulary, have been developed. As yet, we have no comparable tools for dealing with the subject of conventional arms control. We therefore urge that the international community begin now to try to reach a better understanding of which steps in this field might be possible and sensible and which might not be. Of course, in making this suggestion we need not, and should not, derogate from the priority of other issues. An effort to come to grips with the problem of conventional weapons should proceed concurrently with work in other fields.

I would emphasize that a discussion would in no way bind any of the participants to any particular approach. It would, however, initiate the process through which we must pass if we are to ascertain how restraints on conventional weapons can contribute to the security of all countries.

We make this suggestion with the full realization that the question of possible limitations on conventional weapons is not a popular topic. We are aware that there is widespread reluctance to even consider this matter. We are firmly convinced, however, that if the effectiveness of our work in the arms control field is to match the solemnity of our declarations, we must come to grips with the question of possible restraints on those armaments to which such a major portion of expenditures on weapons are devoted.

In this regard, Mr. Chairman, my delegation welcomes the publication of the Secretary General's study on "The Economic and Social Consequences of the Arms Race and of Military Expenditures,"[104] which has been prepared, pursuant to the General Assembly resolution adopted on this subject last year,[105] by a number of distinguished international experts. We are studying this document with great attention.

In his report to the General Assembly this year, the Secretary General pointed out that "during the Disarmament Decade, it is not only im-

---

[103] Statement by U.S. Representative James F. Leonard, Aug. 26, 1971, in *Documents on Disarmament, 1971*, pp. 528-37.
[104] U.N. document A/8469/Add. 1, Nov. 12, 1971.
[105] Resolution 2667 (XXV), Dec. 7, 1970.

portant that intensive and uninterrupted work proceed in the field of disarmament; it is also important that all existing treaties should be strengthened." The Secretary General added that "the strengthening of these treaties and their becoming accepted standards of international law will not only ensure that they will be observed and have continuing validity, but will also serve to make additional agreements more readily attainable and acceptable."[106] The United States is in firm agreement with this view, and we are pleased that during the past year significant progress has been made in this area.

The Treaty on the Prohibition of the Emplacement of Nuclear Weapons and Other Weapons of Mass Destruction on the Seabed and Ocean Floor and in the Subsoil Thereof, which was commended by the United Nations General Assembly last year,[107] was opened for signature in February.[108] It has already been signed by some 80 countries.

My own government has submitted this treaty to the Senate for its advice and consent to ratification.[109] We hope that it will enter into force at an early date.

The dedicated efforts of representatives of many countries have brought us closer to a realization of the objectives of the Nonproliferation Treaty (NPT).[110] Significant progress has been made during the past year by the IAEA [International Atomic Energy Agency] in elaborating a safeguards system in accordance with article III of that treaty.

Last year, the General Assembly adopted a resolution dealing with the establishment, within the framework of the IAEA, of an international service for nuclear explosions for peaceful purposes under appropriate international control.[111] The Agency has achieved a significant progress in this field, as reflected in paragraphs 94 and 95 of the Agency's annual report.[112] We continue to support further study of this matter within the framework of the IAEA, which we believe should be the international body responsible for international activities in this regard.

Mr. Chairman, the United States is deeply conscious of its responsibilities under article VI of the NPT. We have sought to meet those responsibilities through a variety of efforts in the arms control field and, in particular, through our negotiations with the Soviet Union re-

[106] U.N. General Assembly, *Official Records: 26th Session, Supplement No. 1A* (A/8401/Add. 1), p. 26.
[107] *Documents, 1970*, p. 74.
[108] Document 13.
[109] Document 14.
[110] Cf. note 16 above.
[111] Resolution 2665 (XXV), Dec. 7, 1970.
[112] International Atomic Energy Agency, *Annual Report, 1 July 1970–30 June 1971* (Vienna, July 1971).

garding limitations on strategic armaments. These negotiations have been pursued with determination and steadfastness. While much hard work and intensive negotiations remain before us, the past year witnessed important and promising developments.

In May, a joint U.S.-U.S.S.R. statement[113] announced that the two governments concerned had agreed "to concentrate this year on working out an agreement for the limitation of the deployment of anti-ballistic missile systems (ABM's)" and that they had also agreed that "together with concluding an agreement to limit ABM's, they will agree on certain measures with respect to the limitation of offensive strategic weapons." It was announced that the two sides were taking this course in the conviction that it would create more favorable conditions for further negotiations to limit all strategic arms and that these negotiations would be actively pursued.

In September, agreements between the United States and Soviet Union were signed on measures to reduce the risk of outbreak of nuclear war and on measures to improve the U.S.A.-U.S.S.R. direct communications link.[114] Secretary Rogers stated at the signing ceremony in Washington that these agreements represented "realistic and concrete steps forward, taken in the spirit of the United Nations Charter, which declares the determination of its members to 'save succeeding generations from the scourge of war.' " He emphasized as well that "these agreements are in the interest of all nations" and that they "are proof of the advantages of a sober and realistic approach in dealing with arms control."[115]

Mr. Chairman, during the past year specific steps have also been taken toward negotiations on regional arms control issues. The task of achieving a mutual and balanced reduction of forces in Europe is now being given the most serious consideration. Exploratory talks to that end were proposed in the NATO declaration at Reykjavik in 1968 and at Rome in 1970.[116] Indications of readiness on the part of the U.S.S.R. to consider reductions in armed forces and armaments in central Europe were welcomed in June in the NATO communique issued at Lisbon.[117]

In another part of the world, the United States has been gratified with the further progress that has been made with respect to the Treaty for the Prohibition of Nuclear Weapons in Latin America (Treaty of Tlatelolco).[118]

Mr. Chairman, sound and durable restraints on armaments are pos-

---

[113] Document 21.
[114] Documents 27-28.
[115] *Bulletin*, Oct. 18, 1971, pp. 399-400.
[116] *Documents, 1968-69*, pp. 133-34; same, *1970*, pp. 38-90.
[117] Document 37.
[118] Cf. Document 114.

sible only when all participants perceive that such limitations are in their own interest. This mutuality of interest can only be reached through a reconciliation of divergent views, through compromise, and through practical accommodation. I would hope that our debate on these issues this year will help to promote a better understanding of our common interests in moving through negotiation toward arms limitations that will provide greater security for all than can be achieved by arms alone.

C. The Strategic Arms Limitation Talks (SALT).

[More central to American concern than the multilateral disarmament efforts under United Nations auspices were the bilateral conversations initiated with the U.S.S.R. under a joint agreement, originally announced July 1, 1968, "to enter in the nearest future into discussions on the limitation and the reduction of both offensive strategic nuclear weapons delivery systems and systems of defense against ballistic missiles." Postponed for over a year in consequence of the invasion and occupation of Czechoslovakia by member states of the Warsaw Pact in August 1968, the Strategic Arms Limitation Talks (SALT) had been formally convened in November 1969 under somewhat broader terms of reference that called for "negotiation on curbing the strategic armaments race."[119]

The ostensible aim of both parties in the SALT talks was the reaching of agreements that would help curb the strategic arms race by limiting both offensive and defensive strategic weapon systems—on the offensive side, primarily intercontinental ballistic missiles (ICBMs), submarine-launched ballistic missiles (SLBMs), and strategic bomber aircraft; on the defensive side, antiballistic missile (ABM) defense systems such as the U.S.S.R. had begun to deploy in the mid-1960s and the United States a few years later. Of particular concern in Washington was the need to find an appropriate response to the growth of the Soviet long-range missile armory, which had been in process of expansion and improvement ever since the mid-1960s and had already overcome the numerical superiority previously enjoyed by the United States. According to President Nixon's figures, by the end of 1970 the U.S.S.R. already possessed no fewer than 1,440 ICBMs to the United States' 1,054, and 350 SLBMs to the United States' 656. Although the United States still held a marked superiority in manned bombers, it remained uncertain of Moscow's long-range intentions and looked to SALT as one possible approach to the objective of maintaining a degree of

[119] *Documents on Disarmament, 1968*, p. 460; same, *1969*, p. 499.

stability in the strategic balance between the two superpowers.[120]

The opening session in the SALT talks had been held in Helsinki on November 17–December 22, 1969, and further sessions took place during 1970 in Vienna on April 16–August 14 and again in Helsinki on November 2–December 18.[121] While the agreed statements of the two parties indicated that each had gained in comprehension of the other's point of view, it was evident that the talks thus far had been essentially exploratory in character and that no major agreements of substance were immediately in prospect. Reviewing the progress made thus far in his annual foreign policy report for 1971, President Nixon alluded to a number of points of difference and particularly stressed the U.S. view that an acceptable agreement must cover both offensive and defensive weapons, rather than being limited to one or the other as the Soviets apparently preferred. In particular, Mr. Nixon wrote, "The strategic balance would be endangered if we limited defensive forces alone and left the offensive threat to our strategic forces unconstrained. . . ."[122]

Two further sessions of SALT talks—the fourth and fifth—were held in 1971, and a sixth was commenced late in the year and completed early in 1972. The fourth SALT session, held in Vienna on March 15–May 28, 1971, was crowned by a "breakthrough" agreement which for the first time established agreed priorities as between the limitation of defensive and offensive weapon systems (Documents 21-22). The fifth session, held in Helsinki on July 8–September 24 (Document 23), brought further agreement on two peripheral accords, designed to lessen the risk of nuclear war between the two powers, which were signed in Washington on September 30 (Documents 26-28). These agreements, in turn, prepared the way for the announcement of President Nixon's projected visit to the U.S.S.R. (Document 29) and created favorable auguries for the sixth SALT session, which opened in Vienna on November 15 (Document 24).]

1. Fourth Session of United States–Soviet Talks, Vienna, March 15–May 28, 1971.

[The breaking of a negotiating deadlock through an agreement on priorities was the principal SALT development of the spring, and one that helped prepare the way for the signature just a year later, on the occasion of President Nixon's visit to the U.S.S.R., of a bilateral Treaty on the Limitation of Antiballistic Missile Systems plus an Interim Agreement on Certain Measures With Respect to the Limitation of

---

[120] Nixon Report, 1971, pp. 168-77.
[121] *Documents, 1968-69*, pp. 126-27; same, *1970*, pp. 62-63 and 65-66.
[122] Nixon Report, 1971, pp. 191-95; quoted passage on p. 194.

Strategic Offensive Arms. The basic significance of the 1971 agreement, negotiated mainly in Washington and announced by the two governments on May 20, 1971 (Document 21), was later described by President Nixon in the following terms: [123]

> This parallel effort [by the two sides] gradually became deadlocked over two major issues. First, should both offensive and defensive limitations be included from the outset? The Soviet Union proposed that the deadlock be resolved by limiting ABM systems only. The United States thought it essential to maintain a link between offensive and defensive limits; we believed that an initial agreement that permitted unrestrained growth in offensive forces would defeat the basic purpose of SALT.
>
> Second, what offensive forces should be defined as 'strategic'? The Soviet Union wanted to include all nuclear delivery systems capable of reaching Soviet territory. The United States maintained that major intercontinental systems should have priority in negotiating limitations.
>
> By late 1970 these two issues had blocked further progress. I decided to take the initiative in direct contacts with the Soviet leaders to find a solution. The result of our exchanges was an agreement on May 20, 1971, that we would concentrate the negotiations on a permanent treaty limiting ABM systems, while working out an Interim Agreement freezing only certain strategic offensive systems and leaving aside other systems for consideration in a further agreement."]

(21) Breaking the Deadlock: Radio-Television Statement by President Nixon, May 20, 1971. [124]

(Complete Text)

Good afternoon, ladies and gentlemen:

As you know, the Soviet-American talks on limiting nuclear arms have been deadlocked for over a year. As a result of negotiations involving the highest level of both governments, I am announcing today a significant development in breaking the deadlock.

The statement that I shall now read is being issued simultaneously in

---

[123] Nixon Report, 1973, p. 199; see also Kissinger statement, June 15, 1972, in *Documents on Disarmament, 1972*, pp. 300-301. The Moscow treaty and interim agreement, both of which were signed May 26, 1972, and entered into force Oct. 3, 1972 (TIAS 7503 and 7504; 23 UST 3435 and 3462), appear in *A.F.R., 1972*, nos. 13 and 14.

[124] *Presidential Documents*, May 24, 1971, pp. 783-84.

Moscow and Washington; Washington, 12 o'clock [noon]; Moscow, 7 p.m.

The Governments of the United States and the Soviet Union, after reviewing the course of their talks on the limitation of strategic armaments, have agreed to concentrate this year on working out an agreement for the limitation of the deployment of anti-ballistic missile systems (ABMs). They have also agreed that, together with concluding an agreement to limit ABMs, they will agree on certain measures with respect to the limitation of offensive strategic weapons.

The two sides are taking this course in the conviction that it will create more favorable conditions for further negotiations to limit all strategic arms. These negotiations will be actively pursued.

This agreement is a major step in breaking the stalemate on nuclear arms talks. Intensive negotiations, however, will be required to translate this understanding into a concrete agreement.

This statement that I have just read expresses the commitment of the Soviet and American Governments at the highest levels to achieve that goal. If we succeed, this joint statement that has been issued today may well be remembered as the beginning of a new era in which all nations will devote more of their energies and their resources not to the weapons of war but to the works of peace.

(22) United States-Soviet Communiqué, Vienna, May 28, 1971.[125]

(Complete Text)

The US–USSR negotiations on limiting strategic armaments continued in Vienna from March 15 to May 28, 1971.

The US delegation was headed by the Director of the U.S. Arms Control and Disarmament Agency, Gerard [C.] Smith. Members of the delegation J. Graham Parsons, Paul Nitze, Harold Brown, and Royal Allison participated in the negotiations.

The USSR delegation was headed by the Deputy Minister of Foreign Affairs of the USSR, V. S. Semenov. Members of the delegation N. N. Alekseev, P.S. Pleshakov, A.N. Shchukin, K.A. Trusov, O.A. Grinevsky, and R.M. Timerbaev participated in the negotiations.

The delegations were accompanied by advisors and experts.

In the course of the Vienna phase of the negotiations, the delegations continued consideration of questions dealing with the limitation of strategic armaments. At the final stage, there was an exchange of views

[125] *Documents on Disarmament, 1971*, p. 305.

on matters stemming from the announcement on May 20 on the under-standing between the Governments of the US and the USSR regarding further development of the negotiations.[126] It has been agreed to pro-ceed after a brief recess with the negotiations in accordance with the above understanding.

The negotiations between the US and the USSR delegations will be resumed on July 8, 1971, in Helsinki, Finland.[127]

The US and the USSR delegations express their sincere appreciation to the Government of Austria for the hospitality accorded and for assistance in creating favorable conditions for holding the negotiations in Vienna.

2. Fifth Session of United States–Soviet Talks, Helsinki, July 8–September 24, 1971.

[In addition to further examination of strategic arms limitation issues as shaped by the agreement of May 20 (Document 21), the fifth session of SALT talks in Helsinki saw the completion of the two bilateral agreements to limit the risk of nuclear war which were to be signed in Washington on September 30, 1970 (Documents 26-28).

The official communiqué of the Helsinki session (Document 23) is here followed by a comment from President Nixon on the outlook for further progress (Document 24).]

(23) United States-Soviet Communiqué, Helsinki, September 24, 1971.[128]

(Complete Text)

The US–USSR negotiations on limiting strategic armaments con-tinued in Helsinki from July 8 to September 24, 1971.

The US delegation was headed by the Director of the U.S. Arms Control and Disarmament Agency, Gerard [C.] Smith. Members of the delegation Philip J. Farley, J. Graham Parsons, Paul Nitze, Harold Brown, and Royal Allison participated in the negotiations.

The USSR delegation was headed by Deputy Minister of Foreign Affairs of the USSR, V.S. Semenov. Members of the delegation P.S. Pleshakov, A.N. Shchukin, K.A. Trusov, and R.M. Timerbaev partici-pated in the negotiations.

---

126 Document 21.
127 See Document 23.
128 *Bulletin*, Oct. 18, 1971, pp. 403-4.

The delegations were accompanied by advisors and experts.

In accordance with the May 20, 1971, understanding of the Governments of the US and the USSR,[129] the delegations have engaged in detailed consideration of issues relating to an agreement on the limitation of anti-ballistic missile (ABM) systems, and have given consideration to issues involved in agreeing on certain measures with respect to the limitation of strategic offensive arms. Some other related questions were also discussed.[130]

Certain areas of common ground with respect to such limitations have been developed during this phase of the negotiations, and a clearer understanding was achieved concerning issues to be resolved.

The two sides express their appreciation to the Government of Finland for creating favorable conditions for holding the negotiations. They are grateful for the traditional Finnish hospitality which was extended to them.

Agreement was reached that negotiations between the US and the USSR delegations will be resumed on November 15, 1971, in Vienna.[131]

(24) The Immediate Outlook: Comments by President Nixon at a Briefing for Media Executives in Portland, Oregon, September 25, 1971.[132]

(Excerpt)

*   *   *

DEFENSE CAPABILITIES

Q. Mr. President, in view of the report on comparative missile capabilities on the reduction of our armed forces, both as to Army and fleets, do you care to comment, sir, on our present or future defensive capability at this time?

THE PRESIDENT. This is Ferd Mendenhall?[133]

Q. Yes.

THE PRESIDENT. I thought so, There are no old men, incidentally, either. [Laughter] I have known Ferd Mendenhall for 20 years, too.

---

[129] Document 21.
[130] Cf. Documents 26-28.
[131] See Document 25.
[132] *Presidential Documents*, Oct. 4, 1971, p. 1343.
[133] Ferdinand Mendenhall, editor, *Valley News and Green Sheet*, Van Nuys, Calif.

Let's look at that relative balance between the Soviet Union and the United States. There is a tendency to point out that because the Soviet Union has been moving ahead during the past 10 years, at a time when the United States has been somewhat limited to the numbers, as far at least as the number of missiles are concerned, that we had back in 1962, that because of that fact that the United States has become already inferior.

Now, I would answer your question by saying, first, that what the Soviet Union needs to have a sufficient military establishment to carry out its foreign policy is different from what the United States needs. The Soviet Union is primarily a land power, and it needs, therefore, a different mix than we have.

The United States is a combination of a land and a sea power. Consequently, whereas the United States must have, in order to have an effective foreign policy to meet our needs around the world, superiority on the sea, what the United States may need in terms of divisions on land may be much less as compared with what the Soviet Union would have to have.

So when somebody says the Soviet Union has three, or four, or five times as many divisions as the United States has, that doesn't mean that what they have makes them, therefore, automatically superior.

I would say at this point that in terms of strategic missiles, there is basically a balance between the United States and the Soviet Union and that neither power at this time is going to be able to gain a clear enough superiority that either would launch a preemptive attack upon the other.[134]

That is the reason why the possibilities of success in the SALT talks, the strategic arms limitation talks, are, in my opinion, good. I think an announcement was made this morning that a significant step has already been taken with regard to accidental war and a more improved hot line.[135] That took a lot of negotiating, but it is important and it will be signed next week in Washington when Mr. Gromyko[136] is here.

That also is an indication that progress is being made on limitations of offensive and defensive weapons, which I announced on May 20th—and at the same time it was announced in Moscow—would be the goal for this year.[137]

Now, whether we achieve it by the end of this year, no one can say at this point.[138] We have made progress. And I believe the goal will be achieved. I believe that we will reach an agreement and the reason we will reach an agreement is this fundamental point that I make: Neither

134 Cf. above at notes 120-22.
135 Document 26.
136 Andrei A. Gromyko, Minister of Foreign Affairs of the Soviet Union.
137 Document 21.
138 See further Document 25.

power at this time could if it wanted to, gain that superiority which would enable it to, frankly, blackmail the other one.

*   *   *

3. Sixth Session of United States–Soviet Talks, Vienna, November 15, 1971–February 4, 1972.

[No official communiqué on the sixth round of SALT talks was issued until their adjournment on February 4, 1972.[139] The outlook for the session was briefly characterized by President Nixon at his news conference on November 12, 1971 (Document 25).]

(25) Prospects for Agreement: News Conference Statement by President Nixon, November 12, 1971.[140]

(Excerpt)

*   *   *

SALT PROSPECTS

Q. Mr. President, you met this afternoon with our SALT negotiating team which is returning to Vienna. Earlier this year you expressed the hope that some kind of agreement could be made. Do you foresee some kind of a SALT agreement before the end of the year?

THE PRESIDENT. We have made significant progress in the arms limitation talks. The progress, for example, with regard to the hot line and the progress with regard to accidental war is quite significant.[141] Also, we have made significant progress in the discussions on the limitations on defensive weapons and we are beginning now to move into the discussions on offensive weapons.

Whether we are able to reach an agreement by the end of the year, I think, is highly improbable at this point. I say highly improbable—not impossible. It depends on what happens.

Our goal is—and I discussed this at great length with Mr. Gromyko when he was here—our goal is, of course, at the highest level to urge our negotiators to try to find a common basis for agreement. But it must be a joint agreement. We cannot limit defensive weapons first and then

---

139 Text in *Bulletin*, Feb. 28, 1972, p. 278.
140 *Presidential Documents*, Nov. 15, 1971, p. 1514.
141 Documents 27-28.

limit offensive weapons. Both must go together. It will happen.

I would say this: I believe we are going to reach an agreement. I believe we will make considerable progress toward reaching that agreement before the end of the year. I think reaching the agreement before the end of the year is probably not likely at this time, but great progress will be made and I think by the end of the year we will be able to see then that our goal can be achieved.[142]

* * *

D. United States–Soviet Agreements to Reduce Risk of Nuclear War, September 30, 1971.

[Bilateral discussions on means of reducing the risk of outbreak of accidental nuclear war between the United States and the U.S.S.R. were initiated early in the Strategic Arms Limitation Talks (SALT) and carried on in parallel with the main SALT negotiations. Two special technical groups were assigned responsibility for, respectively, (1) arrangements for exchanging information to reduce ambiguities and prevent misunderstandings in the event of a nuclear incident, and (2) means of improving the Washington–Moscow direct communications link or "hot line," originally agreed upon in 1963,[143] with special reference to ways of increasing its reliability and survivability. Major substantive issues were resolved by the two groups in the spring of 1971, and the relevant international agreements were perfected during the Helsinki round of SALT talks (SALT V) during the summer. Following the announcement of approval by the respective governments (Document 26), the two agreements (Documents 27-28) were signed in Washington by Secretary of State Rogers and Soviet Foreign Minister Andrei A. Gromyko on September 30, 1971, and entered into force on signature.]

(26) A Dividend From SALT: White House Announcement, September 24, 1971.[144]

(Complete Text)

The President has approved two agreements that have been negotiated by the United States and Soviet SALT (Strategic Arms Limitation Talks) delegations.

---

[142] Cf. above at note 123.
[143] Documents, 1963, pp. 115-16.
[144] Presidential Documents, Sept. 27, 1971, pp. 1318-19.

The first agreement concerns measures to reduce the risk of outbreak of nuclear war between the United States and USSR.

The second agreement—which will serve in part to implement the first one—provides for the improvement and modernization of the Washington-Moscow Direct Communications Link, or "Hot Line," which was established in 1963.

The agreement on reducing the risk of nuclear war[145] covers three main areas:

—a pledge by both sides to take the steps each considers necessary to guard against accidental or unauthorized use of nuclear weapons.

—arrangements for rapid communication should a danger of nuclear war arise from such nuclear incidents or from detection of unidentified objects on early warning systems.

—advance notification of certain planned missile launches.

The agreement on the Direct Communications Link[146] will provide for improvements which will take advantage of technological developments since the link was established in 1963. Specifically, two satellite circuits will be established, one by each side, as well as multiple terminals to increase reliability of the link. The Soviet Union will provide a circuit through a satellite system of its own and the United States will arrange for a channel through Intelsat [International Telecommunications Satellite Consortium].

Secretary Rogers and Foreign Minister Gromyko plan to sign these agreements in Washington on September 30, 1971.

(27) Agreement on Measures to Reduce the Risk of Outbreak of Nuclear War Between the United States of America and the Union of Soviet Socialist Republics, Signed in Washington September 30, 1971.[147]

(Complete Text)

The United States of America and the Union of Soviet Socialist Republics, hereinafter referred to as the Parties:

Taking into account the devastating consequences that nuclear war would have for all mankind, and recognizing the need to exert every effort to avert the risk of outbreak of such a war, including measures to guard against accidental or unauthorized use of nuclear weapons,

---

[145] Document 27.
[146] Document 28.
[147] TIAS 7186; 22 UST 1590.

Believing that agreement on measures for reducing the risk of outbreak of nuclear war serves the interests of strengthening international peace and security, and is in no way contrary to the interests of any other country,

Bearing in mind that continued efforts are also needed in the future to seek ways of reducing the risk of outbreak of nuclear war,

Have agreed as follows:

ARTICLE 1

Each Party undertakes to maintain and to improve, as it deems necessary, its existing organizational and technical arrangements to guard against the accidental or unauthorized use of nuclear weapons under its control.

ARTICLE 2

The Parties undertake to notify each other immediately in the event of an accidental, unauthorized or any other unexplained incident involving a possible detonation of a nuclear weapon which could create a risk of outbreak of nuclear war. In the event of such an incident, the Party whose nuclear weapon is involved will immediately make every effort to take necessary measures to render harmless or destroy such weapon without its causing damage.

ARTICLE 3

The Parties undertake to notify each other immediately in the event of detection by missile warning systems of unidentified objects, or in the event of signs of interference with these systems or with related communications facilities, if such occurrences could create a risk of outbreak of nuclear war between the two countries.

ARTICLE 4

Each Party undertakes to notify the other Party in advance of any planned missile launches if such launches will extend beyond its national territory in the direction of the other Party.

ARTICLE 5

Each Party, in other situations involving unexplained nuclear incidents, undertakes to act in such a manner as to reduce the possibility of its actions being misinterpreted by the other Party. In any such situation, each Party may inform the other Party or request information when, in its view, this is warranted by the interests of averting the risk of outbreak of nuclear war.

ARTICLE 6

For transmission of urgent information, notifications and requests for information in situations requiring prompt clarification, the Parties shall make primary use of the Direct Communications Link between the Governments of the United States of America and the Union of Soviet Socialist Republics.

For transmission of other information, notifications and requests for information, the Parties, at their own discretion, may use any communications facilities, including diplomatic channels, depending on the degree of urgency.

ARTICLE 7

The Parties undertake to hold consultations, as mutually agreed, to consider questions relating to implementation of the provisions of this Agreement, as well as to discuss possible amendments thereto aimed at further implementation of the purposes of this Agreement.

ARTICLE 8

This Agreement shall be of unlimited duration.

ARTICLE 9

This Agreement shall enter into force upon signature.

Done at Washington on September 30, 1971, in two copies, each in the English and Russian languages, both texts being equally authentic.

FOR THE UNITED STATES   FOR THE UNION OF SOVIET
OF AMERICA: SOCIALIST REPUBLICS:

(*Signed*) William P. Rogers   (*Signed*) A. Gromyko

(28) Agreement Between the United States of America and the Union of Soviet Socialist Republics on Measures to Improve the U.S.A.-U.S.S.R. Direct Communications Link, Signed in Washington September 30, 1971.[148]

(Excerpt)

The United States of America and the Union of Soviet Socialist Republics, hereinafter referred to as the Parties,

Noting the positive experience gained in the process of operating the existing Direct Communications Link between the United States of America and the Union of Soviet Socialist Republics, which was established for use in time of emergency pursuant to the Memorandum of Understanding Regarding the Establishment of a Direct Communications Link, signed on June 20, 1963,[149]

Having examined, in a spirit of mutual understanding, matters relating to the improvement and modernization of the Direct Communications Link,

Have agreed as follows:

ARTICLE 1

1. For the purpose of increasing the reliability of the Direct Communications Link, there shall be established and put into operation the following:

(a) two additional circuits between the United States of America and the Union of Soviet Socialist Republics each using a satellite communications system, with each Party selecting a satellite communications system of its own choice,

(b) a system of terminals (more than one) in the territory of each Party for the Direct Communications Link, with the locations and number of terminals in the United States of America to be determined by the United States side, and the locations and number of terminals in the Union of Soviet Socialist Republics to be determined by the Soviet side.

2. Matters relating to the implementation of the aforementioned improvements of the Direct Communications Link are set forth in the

---

[148] TIAS 7187; 22 UST 1598. Printed here is the full text of the agreement minus the Annex (cf. note 150, below).
[149] *Documents, 1963*, pp. 115-16.

Annex which is attached hereto and forms an integral part hereof.[150]

ARTICLE 2

Each Party confirms its intention to take all possible measures to assure the continuous and reliable operation of the communications circuits and the system of terminals of the Direct Communications Link for which it is responsible in accordance with this Agreement and the Annex hereto, as well as to communicate to the head of its Government any messages received via the Direct Communications Link from the head of Government of the other Party.

ARTICLE 3

The Memorandum of Understanding Between the United States of America and the Union of Soviet Socialist Republics Regarding the Establishment of a Direct Communications Link, signed on June 20, 1963, with the Annex thereto, shall remain in force, except to the extent that its provisions are modified by this Agreement and Annex hereto.

ARTICLE 4

The undertakings of the Parties hereunder shall be carried out in accordance with their respective Constitutional processes.

ARTICLE 5

This Agreement, including the Annex hereto, shall enter into force upon signature.

Done at Washington on September 30, 1971, in two copies, each in the English and Russian languages, both texts being equally authentic.

FOR THE UNITED STATES   FOR THE UNION OF SOVIET
OF AMERICA: SOCIALIST REPUBLICS:

(*Signed*) William P. Rogers   (*Signed*) A. Gromyko

---

[150] The Annex (22 UST 1601-6) provides among other things for the establishment of two additional circuits using two satellite communications systems, one circuit via the Intelsat system to be established by the United States and one via the Molniya II system to be established by the Soviet Union. Each party under-

E. President Nixon's Projected Visit to the U.S.S.R.

[The announcement on July 15, 1971, of the President's intended visit to the People's Republic of China (Document 91) occasioned widespread speculation as to whether a visit to the U.S.S.R. might also be contemplated, possibly before the trip to Peking. Asked about this possibility at his news conference on August 4, 1971, the President replied that while a Moscow summit meeting in advance of the China trip would be inappropriate, he had discussed the matter with Soviet Foreign Minister Gromyko and found that the Soviet leaders shared his view "that a meeting at the highest level should take place and would be useful only when there was something substantive to discuss that could not be handled in other channels." Noting recent progress in regard to Berlin and SALT and the continuance of discussions on the Middle East, the President stated that there would be a summit meeting when and if it became evident to both sides that "the final breakthrough in any of these areas can take place only at the highest level."[151]

The subsequent completion of the quadripartite agreement on Berlin (Documents 38-39) and the signature of the Washington agreements to reduce the risk of nuclear war (Documents 26-28) signaled a further improvement in the U.S.-Soviet relationship and—with the progress of the U.S.-Chinese relationship—formed part of the background of President Nixon's announcement on October 12, 1971, that he would in fact be meeting with the Soviet leaders in Moscow in the latter part of May 1972 (Document 29). Although the subsequent crisis in U.S.-Soviet relations over the December 1971 war between India and Pakistan raised some doubt about the timeliness of the visit, Secretary of State Rogers at his year-end news conference expressed confidence that the prospects for a successful visit had not been impaired (Document 30).]

(29) Announcement of the Visit: President Nixon's News Conference, October 12, 1971.[152]

(Excerpts)

THE PRESIDENT. Be seated, please.

Ladies and gentlemen, I have an announcement which is embargoed

takes to provide and operate in its territory at least one earth station for the satellite communications circuit established by the other party, and to establish a system of terminals in its territory for the exchange of messages with the other party.
[151] *Public Papers, 1971*, p. 250.
[152] *Presidential Documents*, Oct. 18, 1971, pp. 1390-93.

till 12 noon Washington time and 7 o'clock Moscow time. In order for you to have the chance to file before the 12 o'clock deadline, I have asked Mr. [Norman] Kempster [of United Press International], who has the right to end the conference, to break it off at 5 minutes till 12. Between that time and the time that I read this announcement, of course, I will take questions on this announcement or any other subject that you would like to have covered.

The announcement is as follows:

THE PRESIDENT'S MEETING WITH SOVIET LEADERS

The leaders of the United States and the Soviet Union, in their exchanges during the past year, have agreed that a meeting between them would be desirable once sufficient progress had been made in negotiations at lower levels.

In light of the recent advances in bilateral and multilateral negotiations involving the two countries, it has been agreed that such a meeting will take place in Moscow in the latter part of May, 1972.

President Nixon and the Soviet leaders will review all major issues, with a view towards further improving their bilateral relations and enhancing the prospects of world peace.

We will go to your questions.

QUESTIONS

THE TRIPS TO CHINA AND THE SOVIET UNION

Q. Mr. President, what relationship does this have to your visit to China?

THE PRESIDENT. The two are independent trips. We are going to Peking for the purpose of discussing matters of bilateral concern there and I will be going to the Soviet Union for the purpose of discussing matters that involve the United States and the Soviet Union. Neither trip is being taken for the purpose of exploiting what differences may exist between the two nations.

Neither is being taken at the expense of any other nation.

The trips are being taken for the purpose of better relations between the United States and the Soviet Union and better relations between the United States and the People's Republic of China. And any speculation to the effect that one has been planned for the purpose of affecting the other would be entirely inaccurate.

Q. Mr. President, why announce a trip of this nature so far in advance?

THE PRESIDENT. It is vitally important, both in the case of this trip and the trip to the People's Republic of China—which, as you know, we announced far in advance, the date yet to be selected.[153] Mr. Kissinger will work out that date on his trip, which will take place within the next 2 or 3 weeks.[154]

But it is vitally important that the meeting accomplish something. It is, therefore, important that the preparation for the meeting be adequate in every respect. And in the discussion that I had with Mr. Gromyko when he was here[155] and at discussions prior to that time that were had at other levels with regard to the setting up of this trip, it was felt that May of 1972 would be the time when progress on a number of fronts in which we are presently involved with the Soviet Union, would have reached the point that a meeting at the highest level could be effective.

Q. Mr. President, do you expect to be able to sign an agreement on strategic arms when you go to Moscow next May?

THE PRESIDENT. As you will recall, we, at the highest level in May, indicated that our goal would be to try to achieve an agreement on strategic arms this year.[156] We are making progress toward that goal. We will continue to move toward achieving that goal, either at the end of this year or as soon thereafter as we possibly can.

If the goal can be achieved before May of 1972, we will achieve it and that, incidentally, is also the view of the Soviet Union.

I will not speculate as to failing to achieve that goal. If it is not achieved, certainly that would be one of the subjects that would come up.

Q. Mr. President, what would you expect other items on the agenda to be in addition to anything that is concluded at the SALT talks?

THE PRESIDENT. I have already indicated that we will review all major issues. Now, to indicate what the issues will be is quite premature. For example, the question that has just been raised with regard to the SALT talks is one that may be behind us at that point.

Both governments are working toward that end. And then the question would be, what do we do in arms control going beyond simply the limitations of strategic weapons at this point and the same would be true of the Mideast, which is a possible subject. The same is true in a number of other areas where presently the Soviet Union and the United States are having negotiations.

The fact that we are going to have a meeting in May does not mean that the negotiating tracks that we are engaged on with the Soviet

---

153 Cf. Document 91.
154 Cf. Document 93a.
155 The Soviet Foreign Minister met with the President at the White House on Sept. 29, 1971.
156 Cf. Document 21.

Union, in a number of areas, are now closed or that we are going to slow down.

We are going to go forward in all the other areas so that in May we can deal with unfinished business.

Q. Mr. President, would this include Cuba?

THE PRESIDENT. The questions as to whether peripheral areas—and I mean by "peripheral areas," areas that do not directly involve the Soviet Union and the United States—would be involved would depend upon the situation at that time.

For example, Cuba is one possibility. The question of Southeast Asia is another. As far as Southeast Asia is concerned, I would emphasize there, again, however, that, completely without regard to this meeting, and completely without regard to the meeting that will take place with the Chinese leaders at an earlier date, we are proceeding both on the negotiating track and on the Vietnamization track to end American involvement in Vietnam. We trust that we will have accomplished that goal, or at least have made significant progress toward accomplishing that goal, by the time this meeting takes place.

Q. Can you tell us the mechanics, sir? How did the meeting come about? Did their Ambassador come here? Was it hot-lined? And can you tell us, sir, when the ball started rolling toward this meeting?

THE PRESIDENT. The ball started rolling toward this meeting, I think in my first press conference when, you recall, the inevitable question came up, "Are we going to have a summit with the Soviet Union?"

I pointed out then that I did not believe a summit would serve a useful purpose unless something was to come out of it.[157] I do not believe in having summit meetings simply for the purpose of having a meeting. I think that tends to create euphoria. It raises high hopes that are then dashed, as was the case with Glassboro.[158] We are not making that mistake.

Both in our meeting with the Chinese which is being very carefully planned, as evidenced by Dr. Kissinger's visit to help prepare the agenda and the final arrangements, and in our meeting with the Soviet Union, we have agreed to summit meetings only on the basis that we would have an agenda in which there was a possibility of making significant progress, and also on which items would be on the agenda on which progress could best be made, and in some instances might only be made, by decisions at the highest level.

Now, I stated that, or at least made that point in several press conferences, including my first one. In the spring of last year there was

---

[157] News conference statement, Feb. 6, 1969, in *Public Papers, 1969*, p. 67.
[158] President Johnson conferred with Soviet Prime Minister Aleksei N. Kosygin at Glassboro, N.J., on June 23 and 25, 1967; cf. *Documents, 1967*, pp. 52-59.

some discussion with the Soviet Union at lower levels with regard to the possibility of a summit. There was further discussion of the possibility of a summit when I met with Mr. Gromyko in the fall of last year when he was here to the United Nations.

Those discussions have continued on and off, not at my level, but at other levels, until Mr. Gromyko arrived for his visit with me on this occasion. On this occasion he brought a formal invitation.

Let me say on the Soviet side that they agreed basically with my principle, which is also theirs, that a summit meeting should be held only when both sides are prepared to discuss matters of substance, and it is because both of us have been waiting for the time that we felt there were matters on which major progress could be made that the summit meeting is being held at this time, rather than at an earlier time.

I should also point out the very significant areas in which we have made progress in Soviet-American relations, both on our part and on their part. We have felt unless we were able to make progress in this era of negotiation rather than confrontation and other areas, that a meeting at the summit might mean simply an impasse; but when we look back over the record of the last 2 years, 2½ years, significant progress has been made.

We have had a treaty with regard to the seabeds.[159] We have had one with regard to biological weapons.[160] We have had an agreement coming out of the SALT talks with regard to the hot line and accidental war[161] and, of course, most important of all—and I think this is the item that, for both us and for them, led us to conclude that now was the time for a summit meeting—we have had an agreement on Berlin.[162] The Berlin negotiations, of course, are not completely wrapped up; but on the part of the Soviet Union and the United States and, of course, the other two powers involved, this agreement had historic significance.

In view of the progress that we have made, Mr. Gromyko, speaking for his Government, I, speaking for ours, agreed on the occasion of his visit that this was the time for a summit meeting.

Q. Mr. President, this then was the reason you announced you would go to Peking before May? You had this May date in mind at that time?

THE PRESIDENT. No, Mr. Theis,[163] when we announced that we would be going to Peking, we did not have an understanding with the Soviet Union that we were going to have a visit to the Soviet Union. However, I should point out that as far as the announcement with regard to the Soviet summit is concerned, that the Government of the

---

159 Cf. note 17 above.
160 Cf. note 18 above.
161 Cf. Documents 26-28.
162 Cf. Documents 38-39.
163 J. William Theis, Hearst Newspapers.

People's Republic of China was informed that this announcement would be made today, and is aware of the date of the Soviet visit that I have mentioned, the latter part of May.

I should also point out that the Government in Peking is aware of the fact that we will be working toward agreement on a date with them, which will be prior to the meeting with the Soviet leaders.

Q. Mr. President?

THE PRESIDENT. Mr. Horner.[164]

Q. Mr. President, with which Soviet leader do you expect to have your most significant talks, Kosygin, Brezhnev, Podgorny,[165] or with all three of them or any two of them?

THE PRESIDENT. Generally speaking, in the Soviet system, the talks that take place will, of course, cover all three, but the Chairman, in this case Mr. Brezhnev, is the man with whom I would expect to have very significant talks. I would expect certainly to have significant talks also with Kosygin and perhaps Mr. Podgorny.

But in the Soviet system, as I pointed out—the same is also true of the People's Republic system—in any Communist system, the Chairman of the Communist Party is the man who is the major center of power.

Q. Mr. President, at the time that the Red China trip was announced, sir, I believe we were told that it was going to be before May 1 because you didn't want to get it involved in domestic political politics. I wonder how this differs, since this is after May 1, as far as domestic political politics is concerned?

THE PRESIDENT. We have this just as close to May 1 as we possibly could. This was the best date that the Soviet Union and we could agree upon, and it will come, as I said, in the latter part of May.

We both deliberately agreed that it should not come—which would generally have been their first choice, because June or July is a better time to go to Moscow than May, I understand—we agreed for the reasons that we have mentioned that it should be in May.

Q. Mr. President, you said that it is your goal to end the American involvement in South Vietnam or at least make significant progress towards that by the time you meet in Moscow. Is it your goal that you can end at least the American ground combat involvement by that time?

THE PRESIDENT. I will have another announcement on Vietnam in November.[166] That announcement will speak to that question and other announcements after that will also speak to that question.

I will not speculate further on that. The American presence in Viet-

[164] Garnett D. Horner, *The Washington Star.*
[165] Aleksei N. Kosygin, Chairman of the Council of Ministers; Leonid I. Brezhnev, General Secretary of the Communist Party of the Soviet Union; Nikolai V. Podgorny, Chairman of the Presidium of the Supreme Soviet.
[166] Cf. Document 80.

nam, both in terms of our residual forces, the ground combat forces to which you refer, and the use of our air power, will be maintained to meet the objectives that I have oftentimes spelled out, including among others, the return of our POWs, and the ability of the South Vietnamese to take over the responsibility themselves. But I would strongly urge the members of the press not to speculate as to what I am going to say in November.

*   *   *

EXPECTATIONS FOR THE VISITS

Q. Mr. President, to clarify your expectations on the Moscow visit, it would be equally your expectation to have significant talks with Chairman Mao [Tse-tung] in Peking rather than meetings with Chou En-lai or ceremonial meetings with the Chairman?[167]

THE PRESIDENT. The question as to what kind of meetings will take place in Peking will be worked out by Dr. Kissinger when he is there. There will, of course, be meetings with Chou En-lai. I would assume that there would be meetings with the Chairman. However, in each system, the Soviet system and the Chinese system, the question as to which individual should cover which subject varies and, of course, I will be prepared to meet with whatever leader in the Soviet Union or whatever leader in the People's Republic of China has the responsibility for the particular subjects that we have in mind.

For example, take the Soviet. It may well be that Chairman Brezhnev may have the responsibility in certain political or foreign policy areas. It might be that Prime Minister Kosygin would have responsibility in trade areas. I am not trying to say what they have decided, but we are prepared, and both governments know that we are prepared, for me to meet with the head of government or the chairman of the party, or any other that they designate who has responsibility.

I should also point out that the Secretary of State will accompany me to both Moscow and Peking; Dr. Kissinger will accompany me, and it will be a small working group. And meetings will take place not only between the President and various leaders on their side, but between the Secretary of State and their people designated by them on their side.

We expect to have a very busy, working visit, not a ceremonial visit. Ceremony, I should indicate, will be at an absolute minimum in both the Soviet Union and in the People's Republic.

167 Mao Tse-tung held the position of Chairman of the Central Committee of the Chinese Communist Party; Chou En-lai was Chairman of the State Council (Premier).

I emphasize again, the purpose of both visits is not simply cosmetics. We are not taking a trip for the sake of taking a trip. The purpose of these visits is at the very highest level to attempt to make progress in negotiating in areas where there are very significant differences—differences between us and the People's Republic, differences between us and the Soviet Union.

I should emphasize, too, that in pointing out the progress we have made with the Soviet Union, that Mr. Gromyko and I agreed that we still have very great differences. We do not expect all those differences to be resolved, but there is one thing in which we agree at this point and that is that the interests of neither country would be served by war.

If there is another world war, if there is a war between the superpowers, there will be no winners. There will be only losers.

Also, I think we can both agree that neither major power can get a decisive advantage over the other, an advantage which would enable it to launch a preemptive strike or an advantage because it was able to launch a preemptive strike which might enable it to engage in international blackmail.

It is because we have reached the point that the competition in terms of escalating arms race cannot gain an advantage, and both of us emphasized this in our meeting, it is for that reason that now the time has come to negotiate our differences, negotiate with regard to our differences, recognizing that they are still very deep, recognizing that, however, there is no alternative to negotiation at this point.

*   *   *

(30) Implications of the War in the Subcontinent: News Conference Statement by Secretary of State Rogers, December 23, 1971.[168]

(Excerpt)

*   *   *

RELATIONS WITH THE SOVIET UNION

Q. Mr. Secretary, I wonder if I could return to your prospects and disappointments and other things.[169] *You didn't mention specifically our relations with the Soviet Union. What effect do you think the war*

---

[168] Department of State Press Release 303, Dec. 23, 1971; text from *Bulletin*, Jan. 17, 1972, pp. 52-53. For other excerpts from this press conference cf. note 83 to Document 10.
[169] Document 10.

in the subcontinent[170] *has had on that specific relationship, and do you think whatever alteration has happened will be a permanent one, and will it, finally, jeopardize the President's trip to Moscow, do you think?*

A. Mr. Anderson [James P. Anderson, Westinghouse Broadcasting Co.], I didn't want to leave the impression that I did not think that the relations between the Soviet Union and the United States were important. In fact, I covered that by pointing out that the President was going to take this trip to Moscow, and I thought that spoke for itself.

The fact is that our relations with the Soviet Union have improved during the year. I don't think there is any question about that. We have had several successful negotiations with them, and we are in active discussions with them on a number of issues. I think it has been a good development, and I certainly did not intend to leave that out of my summary of things that I think are accomplishments. I think it is underscored by the fact that the President is going to Moscow.

Now, the second part of your question is do I think that the events in the subcontinent have impaired those prospects—are those events going to damage the prospects for a succcessful trip or for improved relations with the Soviet Union? My answer to that is: No, I don't think so. It will obviously have to be taken into consideration, because the Soviet Union's activities and its support, and its vetoes in the United Nations in opposition to the views of 104 other nations, will have to be considered as factors. But that is not to say that it will impair the prospects of a successful visit and certainly in no way jeopardize the visit itself.

Mr. Kalb [Marvin Kalb, CBS News].

Q. Mr. Secretary, the Russians seem to be concerned about a growing cooperation or even collusion between American and Chinese policy. And I wonder if you feel in light of the events on the subcontinent that there is now a danger of the United States becoming, even against its wishes, involved in the longstanding dispute between Moscow and Peking.

A. I don't think so. It is quite apparent, Mr. Kalb, that when you attempt to improve your relations with countries that have hostilities, or at least are having difficulties—I am speaking about the Soviet Union and the People's Republic of China—there may well arise in the minds of some the thought that maybe this is in opposition to the other. Now, the President has made it as clear as we possibly can that that is not the purpose.[171] We are going to do what we can to improve our relations

---

[170] Cf. Documents 56-64.
[171] Cf. Document 29.

with both the Soviet Union and Communist China. That is why he is making the visits to both Peking and Moscow. And that is what we have told our friends and allies in private talks and publicly. So I don't believe that will be the case.

On the other hand, I think it is quite understandable that concerns of that kind may arise from time to time.

*   *   *

F. The Status of Jews in the Soviet Union.

[International concern about the disabilities suffered by Jewish citizens of the U.S.S.R., particularly as regards denial of the right to emigrate to Israel, was accentuated by the trial and sentencing in Leningrad in December 1970 of 11 Soviet nationals, the majority of them Jews, who were accused of treason and other offenses in connection with an alleged attempt to hijack a Soviet aircraft as a means of escaping the country. The sentencing of two of the accused to death, and of the others to harsh prison terms, occasioned a worldwide protest that was followed on December 30, 1970, by the commutation of the two death sentences and a reduction of the penalties imposed on some of the other defendants. Although trials of persons associated with Jewish activist groups in the U.S.S.R. continued during the greater part of 1971, restrictions on Jewish emigration were considerably relaxed and an estimated 15,000 Soviet Jews were able to enter Israel during the year, compared with 10,330 during the entire preceding decade. Most Jewish scientists, however, were still refused permission to emigrate. The intensity of feeling on this issue within the United States was expressed at various national, state, and local political levels as well as in protest demonstrations and, in some instances, in harassment of Soviet personnel. The firing of four shots into the headquarters of the Soviet Mission to the United Nations on October 20, 1971, an action widely ascribed to Jewish extremists, caused severe diplomatic repercussions in spite of its prompt condemnation by American authorities (cf. Documents 130-31). The American administration's abhorrence of such actions, as well as its support for a formal expression of congressional sentiment on the issues involved, is reflected in the following statement by a representative of the Department of State (Document 31).]

(31) Support of Congressional Resolution on Soviet Jewry: Statement by Richard T. Davies, Deputy Assistant Secretary of State for European Affairs, Before the Subcommittee on Europe of the House Committee on Foreign Affairs, November 9, 1971.[172]

(Excerpts)

Mr. Chairman [Representative Benjamin S. Rosenthal] : I am grateful for the opportunity today to present to you and the members of your committee the views of the Department of State on the situation of Jews in the Soviet Union. Let me voice at the outset the concern of Secretary Rogers and all of us in the Department of State over this problem. We have always supported the right of peoples everywhere to free emigration, to religious freedom, and to the preservation of their cultural heritage and identity. We sympathize with Jews and others in the Soviet Union who have sought through legal means to exercise these rights which are proclaimed in the Universal Declaration of Human Rights[173] and generally recognized in the community of nations.

President Nixon has given official recognition to the designation by the United Nations of 1971 as the International Year for Action to Combat Racism and Racial Discrimination.[174] He has called upon all Americans to join in observing the year "through deeds and words which promote a spirit of brotherhood and of mutual respect among all people."[175] It is in this spirit that I am making this statement.

Mr. Chairman, my purpose here today is threefold: (1) to describe the situation of Jews in the Soviet Union as we see it; (2) to discuss what is being done in the effort to improve that situation; and (3) to offer our conclusions about the right way and the wrong way to go about that effort. Upon conclusion of my remarks, I will be glad to answer any questions you or your colleagues may wish to pose.

THE JEWISH CONDITION IN THE U.S.S.R.

Restrictions against Jewish religious and cultural life in the Soviet Union have been amply catalogued in recent years and need no elaboration here: grossly inadequate religious facilities, pressures against

---

172 *Bulletin*, Dec. 6, 1971, pp. 661-67.
173 *Documents, 1948*, pp. 430-38.
174 General Assembly Resolution 2544 (XXIV), Dec. 11, 1969.
175 Proclamation No. 4022, Dec. 7, 1970, in *Bulletin*, Dec. 28, 1970, p. 774.

synagogue attendance, lack of Yiddish or Hebrew language teaching, tokenism in the publishing and staging of Yiddish works, quota restrictions on university entrance, exclusion from careers considered sensitive or from important political jobs—these are well-documented facts. Soviet Jews are deprived of the cultural ingredients needed to preserve their cultural and religious identity over the long term. And "anti-Zionism" has reached campaign proportions from time to time in connection with chronic tensions in the Middle East.

All Soviet citizens, not just Jews, suffer from the Soviet Government's policy of militant atheism and its refusal to consider emigration as a right rather than a rare privilege, as well as from other restrictions. But the limitations on Jews have in many important respects been more stringent. This is chiefly because Jews appear to be suspect in a special way—many of them have kin abroad in Israel, the United States, and Western Europe, and "Jewishness" in the Soviet Union has come to be regarded by a certain segment of Soviet officialdom as a more alien phenomenon than the fact of association with other major religious or national cultures in the U.S.S.R.

At the same time, there can be no comparison with the terrible era of the Nazi holocaust or Stalin's blood purge of Jewish intellectuals. With respect to the majority, claims that Soviet Jews as a community are living in a state of terror seem to be overdrawn. Jews continue to be eminent in the Soviet economic, journalistic, scientific, medical, and cultural worlds in numbers far out of proportion to their percentage of the population. They are still the best educated Soviet minority. There is little evidence that the regime's "anti-Zionist" propaganda has spilled over into outright and widespread antisemitism or deliberate and sustained efforts to fan a "pogrom" mentality in Soviet society at large. The line has at least officially been drawn between "loyal" Jews at home and "Zionists" abroad. The party has generally avoided outright antisemitism; for example, the U.S.S.R.'s chief antisemite in the literary field, Ivan Shevtsov, was disavowed by *Pravda* in July 1970. It even appears that Soviet Jews have derived a peculiar kind of backhanded benefit—at least on a token basis—from the regime's sensitivity to charges of antisemitism, for some Yiddish materials have been published, supplies of matzoth are reportedly more available, at least in large cities, and several Yiddish dramatic and variety troupes continue to tour.

The rebirth of Jewish consciousness and pride, especially among Jewish youth, has been dramatic since 1967. Jews have been in the forefront of a nascent civil rights movement that only a decade ago would have been both unthinkable and impermissible in the U.S.S.R. Under unprecedented pressure from sit-ins, petitioning, and even hunger strikes at home, and from public opinion abroad, the Kremlin has allowed an increase in emigration of Jews to Israel. The volume of emigration—more than 7,000 in 1971 thus far, according to press reports—is small in absolute terms but relatively large in comparison with that of any other Soviet group. It surpasses the total of Jewish emigration for any preceding year. A small number of outspoken Jewish activists have been dealt with arbitrarily and usually harshly. A number have been sentenced to terms in forced-labor camps. Individual applicants for emigration are sometimes harassed. We deplore this. But we should note that other Soviet civil rights activists and minority group militants have been subjected to similar reprisals of a severity similar to or greater than that which has been given Jewish militants.

In sum, Soviet Jews remain disadvantaged compared to most other major religious and ethnic groups, but their position has not perceptibly worsened in recent years. What has changed is the new mood of militancy and expectancy among Soviet Jews and the corresponding echo evoked among Jews and men and women of good will outside the U.S.S.R. by the expression of this new mood. Before, Jews practiced their religion and maintained their culture quietly, and at times furtively, or succumbed to pressures for assimilation. For some, assimilation was welcome; for others, it was a regretted necessity. Assimilated or not, they encountered subtle and at times not so subtle forms of discrimination and were subject to recurrent repressions simply because they were Jews.

But now thousands publicly demonstrate pride in their heritage, and large numbers have the hope that they, too, like Jews elsewhere, will not only be able to persevere as Jews but also to occupy a place of honor in the world. Thousands of predominantly young Soviet Jews now jam the streets on Jewish holidays outside Moscow's Central Synagogue and dance the hora to the accompaniment of Israeli pop songs played on tape recorders. The "Jews of silence"—to use Elie Wiesel's apt phrase—have found their voices, so that along with the discouraging aspects of their situation there are also definite grounds for hope. Those in the Soviet Union who are most determined to assert their Jewishness now tend to concentrate almost exclusively on the single issue of emigration to Israel. There are undoubtedly a much larger number of Jews in the U.S.S.R. who, if not assimilated, are at least reconciled to remaining in the Russian milieu and who would welcome greater opportunities for cultural expression.

WHAT CAN BE DONE TO HELP?

We proceed from the assumption that the Soviets are sensitive about their treatment of Jews and care about responsible public opinion abroad. We believe that the Soviets are particularly touchy about the opinion of foreign leftists and Communist parties and of prominent moral and community leaders in the West as well as in the nonaligned countries. That tangible progress can be made is shown by the statement on September 24 of Secretary General U Thant, who stated that more than 400 out of 800 Soviet Jews whose cases he had raised with Moscow had succeeded in reaching Israel. There are many other examples, not all of which have been equally publicized.

With this in mind, the United States Government has made clear where it stands on this issue.

On January 11, President Nixon joined leaders of the American Jewish community in urging "freedom of emigration as explicitly provided in Article 13 of the Universal Declaration of Human Rights" as well as "cultural and religious freedom at home and abroad.[176]

Secretary of State Rogers, in a statement to the Youth Mobilization for Soviet Jewry in October 1970, declared:

> This Government has repeatedly expressed in public and in private its opposition to antihumanitarian policies wherever they exist in the world. We believe that free movement is one of the basic human rights of all persons. We have expressed sympathy and support on many occasions for persons in the Soviet Union who wish to emigrate, often to rejoin their families elsewhere, but who are denied permission to do so. We shall continue to make these views known and to take every practical measure which could help to overcome the hardships suffered by such persons.

The Department of State's press spokesmen have publicly spelled out in more detail our views on the problem of Soviet Jewry; for example, in a statement on February 24, 1971:

> The policy of the United States Government, in accordance with the principles upon which this country was founded and in consonance with the Universal Declaration of Human Rights, supports the right of peoples everywhere to free emigration and to religious freedom.... Americans of all faiths and their Government are deeply concerned by the difficulties placed in the path of citizens of the Soviet Union, including its Jewish citizens, who have applied through legal channels for emigration and who seek to preserve their cultural heritage.

World public opinion was clearly a factor in the commutation of the death sentences passed on Jews convicted of treason in Leningrad in December 1970 for seeking to leave the U.S.S.R. allegedly by plotting to commandeer an aircraft, and in general has restrained the Soviet

[176] *Public Papers, 1971*, p. 28.

authorities from broadening the use of quasi-legal punishment against Jewish activists in the U.S.S.R.

In this connection, the Department's press spokesman, in a statement on May 27, expressed deep concern about the Soviet policy of trying people in secret and spoke for Americans of every political persuasion and religious belief in deploring the persecution of persons for actions which in most other countries would not even be offenses.

Meanwhile, the United Nations offers the best regular forum for focusing world attention on the situation of Soviet Jews, and United States officials there have repeatedly spoken out on the issue. For example, on March 17, 1970, Mrs. Rita Hauser, United States Representative on the U.N. Human Rights Commission, stated:

> We do not comprehend any policy which serves to preclude emigration of Soviet Jews who have families or cultural ties elsewhere. We also would hope that the conditions necessary for continued national identity of the Jews in the Soviet Union will prevail, for we are certain that the Jews of that country will add as much to Russian life as the Jews have added to the life of my country. Their distinct cultural and religious identity enhances life; suppression of this identity will diminish the spirit of all Soviet citizens.

At the United Nations General Assembly on December 9 and 10, 1970, U.S. Representative Dr. Helen G. Edmonds denounced the harassment of Jews wishing to leave the Soviet Union and declared:

> Last year before this committee we pointed out that, despite the guarantee of the Soviet Union's constitution and laws, Jews are not treated as citizens on an equal level with all other Soviet citizens.
>
> In this atmosphere, it is not surprising that large numbers of Jews are seeking to leave the Soviet Union. Their hopes are supported by article XIII of the Universal Declaration of Human Rights which says that "Everyone has the right to leave any country." However, the Soviet government is allowing few . . . Jews to emigrate.

Later, Mrs. Hauser reiterated the concern of the United States Government at a meeting of the U.N. Human Rights Commission on February 26, 1971:

> It is disturbing to note that any interest a Jew may evidence in Israel makes him suspect to the Soviet authorites; indeed . . . it was stated that any Soviet Jew who wishes to migrate to Israel is automatically an "enemy of the Soviet people."

*   *   *

We hope the Soviet Government will appreciate the keen interest felt in the United States, by Jews and non-Jews alike, that the large Jewish minority group in the Soviet Union be assured the right to be free of discrimination and to practice its religion freely and fully.

On November 3, 1971, less than a week ago, Arthur A. Fletcher, United States Representative to the 26th United Nations General Assembly, called upon the Soviet Union to accord its Jews the right to emigrate and to permit those who remain freely to pursue their cultural and religious interests.

The Department also has made use of private diplomatic channels to underscore the importance we attach to the right of free emigration and the reuniting of families. For example, our official representation list of Soviet residents, including many Jews, who have been refused permission to emigrate to join close relatives in the United States has regularly been presented to Soviet officials at a high level. This practice was inaugurated by the then Vice President, now President Nixon, when he visited the U.S.S.R. in 1959. Most recently, the list was handed to Soviet Foreign Minister Gromyko on September 24, 1971, during his meeting with Secretary Rogers in New York, as well as to Soviet Deputy Foreign Minister [V. V.] Kuznetsov by Ambassador Jacob Beam in Moscow on February 19, 1971, and to Foreign Minister Gromyko by Secretary Rogers in October 1970 in New York. This year's list contained the names of some 150 Soviet Jews as well as of other relatives of American citizens. Since the Soviet authorities remain extremely reluctant to permit Soviet citizens to emigrate or travel abroad, we are obliged to concentrate our interventions in behalf of persons attempting to join relatives in the United States. We cannot be of direct assistance in cases of persons seeking emigration to other countries.

The results of our representations in support of the right of families to reunite have not been as successful as we would like, but a small amount of emigration to the United States—averaging about 250 persons yearly—has taken place. We intend to continue this practice. This year, through October 31, our Embassy in Moscow has already issued 251 immigrant visas. Of this number, at least 134 were issued to Jews. This is a small number, but a good sign. In 1970 only 78 Soviet Jews were permitted by the Soviet authorities to leave the U.S.S.R. for the United States on immigrant visas, according to our visa records.

At current levels, existing immigration and refugee machinery is well able to handle Soviet Jews who obtain Soviet exit permits to join close relatives in the United States. But what would happen if, through an unexpected policy change, the Soviet authorities suddenly lifted their stringent restrictions and allowed a much larger exodus of Soviet Jews to come to the United States?

With this possibility in mind, on September 30 Attorney General

John Mitchell sent a letter to Congressman Emanuel Celler, chairman of the House Judiciary Committee, in which he said:

> The mounting evidence that Soviet Jews have unsuccessfully sought permission to emigrate from the Soviet Union has compelled a Departmental reexamination of the Attorney General's parole authority with respect to refugees. . . .
> Accordingly, I can assure you that I would exercise my discretion if the situation demanded and parole Soviet Jews who are able to leave the Soviet Union.

On October 6, Congressman Edward I. Koch, a major sponsor of special legislation to provide nonquota visas for Soviet Jews, issued a statement in which he said that he would not now press for passage of his bill inasmuch as he considered the Attorney General's letter to Representative Celler an unequivocal statement that has the same effect as passage of the Koch bill would have had, with the added advantage that use of the Attorney General's parole power places no limitation on the number of Soviet Jewish refugees who can be admitted to this country.

The Department of State supports this finding of the Attorney General. We consider his statement on parole to be preferable to and more meaningful than the establishment of a specified number of nonquota visas for Soviet Jews.

Mr. Chairman, we in the Department of State are very much aware that a number of bills have been submitted for congressional action by the many Representatives who seek to do what they can for Soviet Jewry. The Department believes that a congressional resolution on the subject would be appropriate. Toward this end, on May 14, 1971, David Abshire, Assistant Secretary of State for Congressional Relations, wrote to Chairman Thomas E. Morgan of the House Committee on Foreign Affairs, advising him of our support for Representative [Frank] Annunzio's bill, House Concurrent Resolution 8, with minor modifications. In singling out that bill, Mr. Abshire had no intention of slighting the many other excellent bills which have been introduced. But we feel that House Concurrent Resolution 8, with our suggested modification, is an excellent vehicle through which to convey the concern of the Congress over this issue.[177]

177 The operative portion of H. Con. Res. 8, 92d Cong., with the suggested modifications, reads: "That it is the sense of the Congress that persecution of any persons because of their religion or nationality by the Soviet Union be condemned, and that the Soviet Union in the name of decency and humanity allow Jews, members of other religious and minority groups, and all other Soviet citizens freedom to emigrate and to travel abroad, and allow the free exercise of religion and the pursuit of culture by Jews and all others within its borders" (*Bulletin*, Dec. 6, 1971, p. 667). The resolution was not adopted during the 92d Congress.

LAWLESSNESS AND THE PROBLEM OF SOVIET JEWRY

The influence of those abroad, including that of American public opinion and of the United States Government, can only be sadly and substantially diminished when a few American citizens break the law and resort to vigilante tactics against Soviet—or any other—diplomatic officials and commercial personnel and their wives and children in the United States. Acts of violence and disruption such as those that have occurred in this country advance no one's cause. As President Nixon has stated, they are morally wrong and injure that very cause.

We are convinced that the Soviet Government cannot be compelled to improve the lot of Soviet Jewry simply because Soviet housewives are spat upon in the New York streets or because fanatics shoot rifles into the playrooms of defenseless children. This kind of sick and mindless fanaticism plays gratuitously into the hands of those in the Soviet Union who oppose any easing of current Soviet policies toward Jews. Few Americans approve of violence; even fewer condone violence directed against the representatives of foreign governments to whom the United States is host. Virtually no one approves the harassment of women and children. Such acts only distract attention from the plight of Soviet Jewry and focus it instead on our own problems with violence and lawlessness.

Extremist disruption by a few misled individuals has provided an enormous windfall for Soviet propagandists, who could not in their most avid daydreams desire anything better. They use acts of this sort in order to discredit the much larger number of responsible Americans seeking to assist Soviet Jews by peaceful, lawful means. The Soviets have tried to alienate world public opinion from the cause of Soviet Jewry by playing up the bombings, the illegal harassment, the threats of bodily injury, the bullying of women and children by extremists. The force of world public opinion is the most important single ally that Soviet Jews have in their struggle for fair play and legal rights. Violence can only lessen the cohesiveness of world public opinion on this problem.

During the past year, the Jewish community and prominent Israeli figures, as well as non-Jewish leaders, have overwhelmingly condemned the adoption of these repugnant tactics by a few fanatics. Notably, President Nixon, in his message to American Jewish leaders on January 11, 1971, deplored these cases of lawlessness and violence and declared:

This Administration, in cooperation with local authorities, will use every means at its disposal to prevent such acts and to bring to justice those who perpetrate them.[178]

178 *Public Papers, 1971*, pp. 28-29.

Israeli Premier Golda Meir, on November 27, 1970, had said:

There is nothing in common between the just struggle for the rights of Jews in the Soviet Union and irresponsible acts such as have taken place recently in New York. If there is any connection, it is only that anyone who commits an act of sabotage against a Soviet institution sabotages the responsible and organized efforts of Jews the world over for the sake of Soviet Jewry. This has never been our way and I denounce it. It can only do harm to our just struggle. I think it would be unjust if anyone identified a group responsible for these acts with the masses of Jews and non-Jews who are carrying on this just struggle for Jews in the Soviet Union.

On October 18, 1971, on the David Frost television show, Abba Eban, Foreign Minister of Israel, stated that

(Militant activities) hinder us, because the cause we sustain—both Israel's independence or, in this case, Soviet Jews—have a very powerful appeal. Now, in the United States there is every opportunity for promoting these ideals through peaceful means. When violence is adopted ... I think the cause is, in a sense, corrupted and degraded, and I don't really think that the activities of Mr. Kahane[179] add anything to us at all, and I believe that Soviet Jews would be much better off and so would be Israel's cause without this kind of activity. I believe that some of these people are more interested in their own popularity than in the cause to which they give their devotion.

These activities have been condemned time and time again by American Jewish organizations. I will cite only a few examples:

*　　*　　*

Mr. Chairman, I could continue with innumerable other expressions by Jewish leaders and publications, in the United States, Israel, and elsewhere, on the damage done by anti-Soviet acts of violence perpetrated by extremists.

As for the United States Government's position, let me state again that we consider foreign diplomats and representatives as our invited guests in this country. All decent Americans realize that they must be so treated. Sneak-thief bombings, snipings, and other harassments are repugnant to all of us. The Federal authorities in cooperation with State and local authorities will exert every effort to punish those who engage in such acts.

179 Rabbi Meir Kahane, a leader of the Jewish Defense League.

III
ATLANTIC ALLIANCE
AND DÉTENTE IN EUROPE

[Two major trends contributed in 1971 to a further erosion of the postwar concept of an "Atlantic Community," a group whose power and solidarity had long been regarded as an essential counterweight to the aggressive proclivities of the Soviet Union and the Communist governments of Eastern Europe. The solidarity, if not the power, of the Atlantic nations was increasingly called in question in the early 1970s by new political and economic developments, many of them related to the growing success of the six-nation European Economic Community or "common market," its emergence as a powerful economic competitor of the United States, and its prospective enlargement through the accession of the United Kingdom and other nonmember countries. At the same time, the historic tensions between the North Atlantic Treaty powers and the members of the Soviet-dominated Warsaw Pact were tending to subside with the progress of East–West accommodation, the increase in contacts between the two camps, and the virtual disappearance of any popular expectation of military conflict in Europe. The problems of European security and defense presented themselves in a new light in a period of diminishing East–West tension and of growing distaste for the military and economic burdens involved in maintaining the Western defense system.

A variety of proposals aimed at capitalizing on this new situation engaged the attention of the United States and other interested governments throughout 1971. A group of U.S. senators, headed by Majority Leader Mike Mansfield (Democrat, Montana), maintained its longstanding pressure for a substantial reduction in the military forces the United States had deployed in Europe as part of its contribution to Western defense. The governments composing the North Atlantic Treaty Organization (NATO)—in effect, all of the North Atlantic Treaty powers except France—continued to urge negotiations with the Warsaw group concerning a Mutual and Balanced Reduction of Forces (M.B.F.R.) in Europe. The Soviet Union, while showing more than its

135

previous interest in such a possibility, continued to press the Eastern bloc's proposal for a Conference on Security and Cooperation in Europe (C.S.C.E.) to elaborate new bases for the coexistence of the European states as a group.

Inconclusive discussion of these projects during the earlier part of 1971 (Documents 32-37) was followed in September by the signature of a four-power agreement on Berlin (Documents 38-39) which, as well as promising a further easing of European tensions, in effect removed the chief political obstacle to the proposed Security Conference. At the December 1971 meeting of the North Atlantic Council, the Western governments affirmed their readiness to begin preparatory conversations looking toward a European Security Conference, at the same time voicing the hope that discussions on Mutual and Balanced Force Reduction could also be initiated in the near future (Document 42). The crisis in Western economic and financial relations that had meanwhile developed with the initiation of the United States' "New Economic Policy" in August was eased soon afterward by President Nixon's meeting in the Azores with French President Georges Pompidou (Document 43), the prelude to the so-called Smithsonian Agreement on an international realignment of exchange rates (Document 150). The President's subsequent year-end meetings with the British and German leaders (Documents 44-45) were also instrumental in restoring a degree of inter-allied understanding in both economic and political matters.

Peripheral to the main concerns of the alliance, though hardly less significant to the understanding of American policy in Europe, was the attitude of the United States toward the controversial regimes in power in Greece and Portugal (Documents 46-47), two members of the Atlantic grouping whose policies were frequently at odds with those of the other allies.]

A. The Issues.

[President Nixon devoted many pages of his 1971 report on foreign policy to the problems of Western partnership, alliance defense, and East–West relations in Europe.[1] A briefer analysis of the interplay of political, economic, and military considerations in the European theater is provided in the following address by U. Alexis Johnson, Under Secretary of State for Political Affairs (Document 32).]

[1] Nixon Report, 1971, pp. 24-45.

(32) "The United States, Our NATO Allies, and the Soviet Union in an Era of Changing Foreign Relations": Address by U. Alexis Johnson, Under Secretary of State for Political Affairs, Before the Seventeenth Annual Conference of the Cincinnati World Affairs Council, Cincinnati, Ohio, February 19, 1971. [2]

(Complete Text)

Most of you have spent the day in discussion with a group of distinguished speakers and panelists, who together represent much of the expertise available to us on the subject of this conference, "The United States, Our NATO Allies, and the Soviet Union." I know this is true as a number of them are—or lately have been—my colleagues in dealing professionally with this complex of subjects and the others are well known in this field. This is a hard act to follow, particularly after such a fine dinner.

After sitting all day and after a good meal, it is difficult to ask an audience to sit and listen to abstractions, and I fear that many of us who talk on these subjects, and those who listen, tend to lose sight of the fact that we are not dealing with abstractions but flesh-and-blood people. The State of Ohio is in one sense an abstraction, but in a real sense it is you people sitting here this evening. Similarly NATO [North Atlantic Treaty Organization] is not an abstraction; it is the 200 million of us Americans, you and me, and it is the 325 million Englishmen, Germans, Danes, Icelanders, and so on, who make up the NATO community. On the other side, the Soviet Union is not some vague mechanistic idea; it is made up of flesh-and-blood people. The Soviet Union is not just Brezhnev and Kosygin; it is also [Aleksandr I.] Solzhenitsyn and [Yevgeny] Yevtushenko and the other 240 million with their hopes and fears, their concerns as to how much that apartment or Natasha's shoes are going to cost. Also, in a larger sense, it is made up of those 100 million flesh-and-blood people who, after centuries of troubles, proudly say I am a Pole—or I am a Czech, a Hungarian, a Romanian, or a Bulgarian.

I was reminded of this during this last weekend, when on a brief plane trip in California I met the wife of a close friend of my son. She was a little girl who came out of Hungary with her parents in 1956 at the time I was serving as our Ambassador in Prague. After we landed in Santa Barbara, they were flying over to a little town across the mountains to visit a Hungarian family friend who had been freed from a Budapest prison in 1956. As a result of what this friend had experienced in prison, he subsequently lost both legs above the knees. Yet,

2 *Bulletin*, Mar. 15, 1971, pp. 315-21.

after coming to this country, he had not only made a success as a self-taught jewelry artisan but had become a licensed private pilot, as well as licensed to drive his own car. We Americans owe much to such people.

Yet, when I speak to you this evening, I find of necessity that I must talk to you in broad terms that, of necessity, sound like abstractions. As I do so I only ask that you keep in mind with me that while we do so, we are also talking about people—about real people—about you and me and the other millions in one way or another not very different from you and me.

In doing so I thought that I might first talk about the conceptual framework and some of the present concerns of this administration in developing the European policy of the United States. In hearing me out I am sure you will recognize a good many of the ideas and appraisals voiced by your distinguished panelists earlier today.

Let me first briefly describe the psychological atmosphere in which international relations are now developing in Europe.

A PERIOD OF TRANSITION IN EUROPE

At the outset of this eighth decade of this century the face of Europe is changing. The changes are rapid, pervasive, and—it would seem—profound. No one can forecast with certitude the future pattern of relationships which will emerge among the 30 ancient nations which collectively command so much of the world's resources—military, economic, technological, and intellectual. It is only certain that Europe has passed from a postwar era of rather rapid definition to a period of transition in which relationships are being adjusted to new realities.

We are now 25 years beyond the Second World War. The continent of Europe emerged from that war in a state of material collapse and cruelly divided. The United States resisted the division of Europe. We need not apologize that we offered our cooperation under the Marshall plan to Eastern Europe as well as Western Europe, and it was not our decision that this did not come about. When the Soviet Union thus threw a barrier across the center of Europe, we had no real choice but to look to the security and well-being of the free peoples of Europe. Czechoslovakia in 1948 and Korea in 1950 forced on us the realization that their security was inextricably linked with ours.

Diplomats of my generation have spent much of their professional lives at work in one way or another attempting to remove or reduce the barriers that were made explicit at that time. So far as the achievements of governments are concerned, I must confess that not much has been accomplished.

We in the West have restored the strength—indeed, the affluence—of the nations of Western Europe. We have built a system of collective security which has shielded Western Europe from the Soviet imperial grasp. Moreover, it has made possible an era of peaceful growth and harmony among those nations which is without precedent in the annals of Europe.

These are great accomplishments worthy in themselves of the effort. At the same time we conceded that, up to now, all the vast resources of the West have not availed to end the political and military division of Europe. The challenge and the hope of the 1970's is that we may begin to make some progress. I underline the word "begin."

The soundest basis for that hope is the rising demand of all ordinary Europeans for conditions of life which they consider to be consistent with the needs and dignity of man. That is not, and has not been, a grave problem in the western part of Europe. It is a fair generalization that the governments of Western Europe have been responsive to the will of their citizenry.

This has not been the case in Eastern Europe, as was made painfully evident in the tragedies of 1953 in East Germany,[3] of 1956 in Hungary,[4] and of 1968 in Czechoslovakia.[5] In Poland in these last weeks there has again been exposed the estrangement between the ruling Communist parties and the ordinary citizen,[6] which runs like great fissures through the bodies politic of Eastern Europe. After a generation in power none of the ruling hierarchies in what they call the "Socialist camp" can confidently assert that it governs by consensus.

There are indications that authorities in Eastern Europe are beginning to recognize the gravity of the problem, at the same time awakening to doubt that violent repression can produce long-term solutions. It would appear they are beginning to pay closer attention in their decision-making to the mundane, nonpolitical needs of their populations. One notes a decline of ideological passion among some of the leaders of Eastern Europe, a shift from approaches to problems derived from revealed dogma to approaches based on pragmatic assessments of what might work, be it orthodox Marxist-Leninist doctrine or no.

No doubt economic mismanagement and stagnation occasioned this unacknowledged trend in official thinking, but one consequence has been a stimulation of liberalizing pressures in the so-called "Socialist camp." These forces are clearly troubling to the conservative elements in government. They perceive in them a threat to the permanency of the political structure and social system they imposed on Eastern Europe a generation ago. From the orthodox Communist point of view, a little liberality is a dangerous thing. When I was in Prague in the middle of the 1950's it was clear that the orthodox and conservative

---

[3] *The United States in World Affairs, 1953*, pp. 139-44.
[4] Same, *1956*, pp. 315-19.
[5] *Documents, 1968-69*, pp. 134-42.
[6] Cf. *The United States in World Affairs, 1970*, pp. 57-59.

leadership then in control there looked upon the slight liberalization then taking place with deep suspicion and concern. I thought then, and I think now, they were right. If one is going to run a completely totalitarian regime without regard to the wishes of the people, no compromise is possible or permissible.

Thus this period of transition is marked in Eastern Europe by apparent uncertainty about short-term goals and a notable inconsistency in the sequence of policy decisions. The familiar metaphor of the countries of the Soviet bloc marching to command toward the building of what they call socialism no longer is valid, even if one restricts his view to the governments still oriented to Moscow's leadership.

A particular phenomenon of this transitional period in Europe is a change in the character of relations between East and West. We are witnessing a movement to restore historic ties between the countries of Europe. To move with this tide has become a political imperative in many of the capitals of Europe.

Countries on both sides are searching for accommodations based on mutual advantage. Ordinary citizens, increasingly impatient with arbitrary political barriers, are probably ahead of their governments. President Nixon gave expression to this spirit when he called at the outset of his Presidency for an end to the era of confrontation and pledged his administration to an era of negotiation.[7]

CHANGING ATMOSPHERE IN EUROPE

The changing atmosphere in which international relations are now developing in Europe creates opportunities for peaceful achievements. It also carries the seeds of danger should we become careless of our own vital interest.

It is a matter of satisfaction to us that Western governments of the North Atlantic alliance have proved themselves alert to the challenge of this time of opportunity and risk. NATO's Committee on the Challenges of Modern Society, in which common environmental problems are addressed on an alliancewide basis, is a notable evidence of this responsiveness. In the political-security field, the North Atlantic Council approved in December 1967 a Report on the Future Tasks of the Alliance[8] which set wise guidelines for Western policy in the period we have now entered.

The report defined two main functions of the NATO alliance. The first remains the purpose for which NATO was created 20 years ago— to maintain the military strength and political solidarity necessary to deter aggression and insure the security of the member nations. There is

[7] *Documents, 1968-69*, pp. 41-42.
[8] Same, *1967*, pp. 110-14.

no reason whatever to assume that the insurance policy the NATO nations took out in 1949, and which has remained successful until now, is no longer needed.

The second function of the alliance, as set forth in the 1967 report, is to pursue the search for a more stable relationship between East and West in which the underlying political issues dividing Europe can be resolved. The 15 allies have pledged to work individually or in association with others toward this peaceful goal, bearing in mind the need to preserve a basic harmony within the alliance.

In Brussels last December the Ministerial Council approved another fundamental policy paper[9] which bears a corollary relationship to the 1967 report. On the basis of a searching study of the defense needs of the alliance in the 1970's, the ministers concluded that any relaxation of the defense posture of the alliance was not justified as far as we can see into this decade. On the contrary, they concluded that prospects for success in our striving for peaceful settlements with the East required that the defense posture of the alliance be maintained and indeed improved.

In support of this judgment, the allies undertook at Brussels to bring about qualitative improvements in their defense establishments. The United States, despite budgetary stringency and some political resistance, pledged to maintain in full its present military commitments to the alliance, including those forces now in position in Europe.[10]

The events which gave rise to this vigorous recommitment to the security of the alliance are, I believe, two: the demonstration by the Soviet Union (particularly in Czechoslovakia) that it will not hesitate to resort again to force when it believes its control over an Eastern European country is threatened and the movement toward East-West approaches (particularly the dynamic Eastern policy of the Federal Republic of Germany).[11]

The implications of the Soviet occupation of Czechoslovakia and the regrettable reversion of late to arbitrary harrassment in Berlin are self-evident. Not so obvious but quickly apparent upon reflection is the need for a sound position of strength for those European countries which are reaching out for a new relationship with their Eastern neighbors. It is not by accident that the ally which has lately been most active in Eastern policy, Germany, has also been deeply concerned that the defensive potential of NATO be maintained and that United States forces remain in Europe.

I have referred to Germany's efforts to fulfill the second function of the alliance as defined in the 1967 report. A great deal of political and

---

9 Statement on "Alliance Defense for the Seventies," in same, *1970*, pp. 99-103.
10 Same, pp. 92-93 and 102.
11 *The United States in World Affairs, 1970*, pp. 240-46.

diplomatic activity has been put in train by others of the allies pursuing the search for peaceful settlements.

The United States will soon enter the fourth session of the Strategic Arms Limitations Talks with the Soviet Union.[12] These have been sober discussions, free of polemics, in which a great deal of work has been done to establish a foundation for an agreed limit on the opposing arrays of strategic nuclear weapons systems. We do not yet know whether the talks will result in specific agreements.

The United States, with France and the United Kingdom, has initiated talks with the Soviet Union aimed at improving conditions in and around Berlin. Berlin remains a most sensitive focus of East-West tensions. The Four Power talks there have become linked to the further elaboration of Chancellor [Willy] Brandt's Eastern policy. But there lies the advantage in the fact that the Berlin talks offer the Western nations a useful test of Soviet candor in its protestations of readiness for peaceful agreements working to the disadvantage of no one.[13]

NATO itself has invited the Warsaw Pact powers to explore the possibility of mutual and balanced reduction of the military forces which confront each other in Central Europe.[14] Certainly this massive military confrontation represents a costly symptom of the existing tension and insecurity and a principal element in the continuing division of Europe.

We hope to engage the Soviet Union and its associates in a negotiation which, if successful, would reduce the military burden of European countries and ourselves while preserving the present adequate level of Western security. The Warsaw Pact countries only recently conceded as a possible subject of negotiation the reduction of stationed forces in Europe.[15] In this gesture they acknowledged for the first time that reduction in opposing forces could ease tensions in the center of Europe.

Initiative toward détente has not been solely a Western prerogative. With varying degrees of caution, Eastern European governments have moved toward more active relationships with the West. Their interest has centered, predictably, on intensifying commercial and technological exchange. The past has shown that the works of Marx and Lenin provide few answers to the complex problems of creating a modern industrial society and making it work. In the West, it would appear, at least more of the answers have been found.

In the Communist-ruled countries of Eastern Europe, communication and cooperation with Westerners introduces influences which are not entirely controllable and therefore somewhat risky from the point of

---

[12] Cf. Documents 21-22.
[13] Cf. Documents 38-39.
[14] *Documents, 1968-69*, pp. 133-34; same, *1970*, pp. 89-90.
[15] Memorandum on European security of the Warsaw Pact Foreign Ministers, June 22, 1970, in *Documents on Disarmament, 1970*, p. 247.

view of existing authorities. One notes a determination to limit the undesirable side effects of a freer flow of ideas, goods, and persons between the two parts of Europe. Here we derive some insight into the manner in which the Soviet bloc has developed a détente policy on the political front.

The Warsaw Pact countries have proposed a conference on European security, which is somewhat of a misnomer if one considers the agenda they proposed. It would consist of two principal items: steps to improve economic and cultural relations and conclusion of an agreement to renounce the use of force in resolving issues between European states.[16] This second point constitutes the principal content of treaties which the Soviet Union and Poland have already signed with the Federal Republic of Germany.[17]

Since all member countries of the United Nations have already solemnly renounced the use of force and West Germany—not a member—has done so on its own, one wonders how a conference with such an agenda might improve the existing state of European security.

If one considers the Warsaw Pact proposal in connection with the recently proclaimed doctrine of limited sovereignty—that the integrity of what Moscow calls the "Socialist Commonwealth" transcends any purely national interest of member countries[18]—we come to perhaps a truer definition of European security, as the concept is understood in Moscow.

We are drawn to the conclusion that the real purpose of the authors of the Warsaw Pact security conference proposal is to secure Western acquiescence in the permanent division of Europe along present lines and to proscribe any acts which might tend to weaken the primacy of the parties and the hegemony of the Soviet Union in Eastern Europe, while, of course, preserving its freedom to work through the Communist parties in Western Europe to destroy the governments of Western Europe.

This is not a proposition that recommends itself to the United States or to its European partners. It is offensive to the principles on which relations among free nations are based. Viewed pragmatically, it would tend to perpetuate, not end, the division of Europe. The Foreign Ministers set forth their considered position at the last NATO meeting in Brussels.[19] It is worth quoting:

> Ministers recalled that any genuine and lasting improvement in East-West relations in Europe must be based on the respect of the

[16] Declaration of the Warsaw Pact Foreign Ministers, Prague, Oct. 31, 1969, in *Documents on Disarmament, 1969*, pp. 526-28.
[17] *The United States in World Affairs, 1970*, pp. 244-45; text of the German-Soviet treaty in *Documents, 1970*, pp. 105-6.
[18] Cf. *Documents, 1968-69*, pp. 139n. and 452-53.
[19] Same, *1970*, p. 95.

following principles which should govern relations between states and which would be included among the points to be explored: sovereign equality, political independence and territorial integrity of each European state; non-interference and non-intervention in the internal affairs of any state, regardless of its political or social system; and the right of the people of each European state to shape their own destinies free of external constraint.

The Western allies, nevertheless, agreed to pursue that search for peaceful settlements with patience and tenacity. If the Soviet Union is not prepared to move faster on the fundamental questions, we are prepared to accept progress in limited areas and at a rate of advance that may be painfully slow if, in fact, it is genuine progress.

Despite real and present difficulties, the United States is not pessimistic about possibilities for some progress in the near and medium term. As I stated at the outset, there is a tide running toward more of a reconciliation in Europe. Although authorities in the East have not lost their capacity to make arbitrary decisions, we may hope that they are becoming more responsive to general opinion than heretofore.

In Eastern Europe it is clear that regimes thought by their people to be indifferent to human needs and wants cannot endure, save perhaps by resort to the short-term expedient of armed repression.

Even as we in the United States are encountering some difficulty in reconciling our international obligations with domestic needs, the Soviet Union, with a smaller pool of resources, is having difficulty in ordering its priorities. Tensions with China and the decision to impose a military occupation on Czechoslovakia no doubt have made the problem more acute.

It is not unreasonable to assume that the Soviet Union is interested in achieving a degree of stability and tranquillity on its western flank. Thus we can hope that the Soviet leaders may be moving toward a willingness to enter into serious dialogue with the West on the issues which deprive Europe of genuine security.

IMPACT OF U.S.–U.S.S.R. INTERACTION

In any survey of the Atlantic-European scene one must devote attention to the relationship between the United States and the Soviet Union. These are the two great powers whose interaction unavoidably has impact in every part of the globe. Their influence is of critical significance in Europe, which has been historically the principal arena of contention between the two giants.

Let me first discuss Soviet-American relations in broad context.

There is a specious line of reasoning, often developed by European analysts in moods of resignation, which goes something like this: The

Soviet Union and the United States, by virtue of their vast power potential, are something apart from the rest of the nations of the earth. Nothing is more important to either than the relationship achieved between the two. That relationship takes primacy over any other national interest or foreign policy consideration. Therefore, in the last analysis, United States or Soviet relations with any third country or region are simply a function of their bilateral relations.

Taken to the extreme, this thesis proceeds from the fact that there exists now a balance of terror between the two to the conclusion that each is compelled to strive for some tolerable relationship of coexistence. This will lead in the end to a duumvirate under which the United States and the Soviet Union will by agreement determine the order of the world and the conditions under which other nations live.

This, as I said, is a faulty analysis, the error arising from a misunderstanding of the history of relations between the two countries and of the present situation.

In a recent review, the New Yorker writer Naomi Bliven offered a succinct description of the reality of Soviet-American relations. "We have never had more than one common interest at a time," she said. "Until 1945, it was defeating Hitler; now it is avoiding nuclear war."

The United States has consistently sought to establish other common interests; witness for example our proposals for cooperation in the exploration of space.[20] The problem lies on the other side. For the Soviet Union, while conceding from time to time the necessity for cooperation, as in the defeat of Hitler, regards a basic relationship with the United States of competition and struggle as normal and necessary.

Since 1933, when we established diplomatic relations, the extent of genuine cooperation has been slim and the underlying continuity has been competition, irritation, and trouble. Seen in perspective, troubled relations with the Soviet Union are rather normal. This need not necessarily be so, because viewed purely in national terms there should be no fundamental clash of interests between us. We have no bilateral territorial or boundary disputes, and as two great continental powers, our interests should be largely parallel. Our difficulties arise out of the outmoded and doctrinaire view of the world and themselves taken by the Soviet leadership which leads them to adopt a basically hostile attitude toward all whom they regard as not having the "true faith."

The United States, of course, will continue to bend every effort to reduce the menace of thermonuclear war, which only the Soviet Union can now bring upon us; thus the sober and forbearing attitude we bring to the SALT talks and other negotiations in the area of arms control and limitation.

It does not follow that the United States can or would wish to sub-

20 Cf. note 12 to Document 11

ordinate every other national interest to the formalizing of our strategic relationship with the Soviet Union. We shall maintain our posture of deterrence to nuclear aggression, by national means if necessary, by limitation agreements if possible.

Meanwhile, the national interest demands that we maintain good and constructive relations with the many nations which contribute so vitally to the security and well-being of our own. In this order of priority nothing ranks higher than the Atlantic tie. We have comparable interests in other parts of the world, notably in cooperation with the great, productive nation of Japan. The destiny of the United States is enmeshed in the web of interdependence being spun among the free nations of the world. This web is now such that no nation, including ourselves, can any longer think of itself as being independent of others in either the economic, military, or political sense.

Over the years the American course in its policy toward the Soviet Union has been remarkably steady. We have looked carefully to our security against the potential of a great power which has publicly defined the United States as the great adversary. We shall continue to do so.

We have drawn the unavoidable conclusion from the Soviet assertion that the United States is the principal enemy and impediment to the realization of Soviet aspirations abroad. We have met Soviet expansionism with American steadfastness.

President Nixon seeks to shift the focus of bilateral relations from confrontation to negotiation of issues in dispute. At the same time the President has impressed on the Soviet leaders his intention to stand firm whenever Soviet probes or actions jeopardize United States interests.

In placing emphasis on accommodation, we seek to convey to the Soviet peoples, as well as their leaders, that we do not seek to commit aggression against their country or to harm its legitimate interests. We do seek to preserve a world safe for diversity.

We hope that Soviet policy will evidence a better understanding that they also have more to gain than to lose in accepting a world of diversity. This hope presupposes a gradual change in the outlook of the Soviet leadership. There is clearly enormous resistance to meaningful change within the Soviet establishment. Nevertheless an intellectual case for liberalization of Soviet society has already been made within that country.[21] And the objective problems of internal development argue for wide-ranging reforms.

We have no illusion about the extent to which external influences might participate in the internal evolution of the Soviet Union. The

---

[21] Presumably a reference to Andrei D. Sakharov, "Thoughts on Progress, Peaceful Coexistence and Intellectual Freedom," first reprinted in *New York Times*, July 22, 1968.

West can best play its part in this educational process through patience and firm but sensitive policies.

Soviet-American relations are at present affected by a number of irritants with which you are familiar from a reading of the newspapers. If irritation, as I have said, is something like normalcy in our bilateral dealings, we have perhaps an aggravated condition at the moment.

This tends to divert attention from the fact that we have serious business underway and present opportunities to contribute to peaceful progress toward a stable world order. In certain specific areas we have posed some choices to the Soviet leadership. We hope in the course of the next month or two that we shall have some answers.

An American proposal has been tabled at the SALT talks. The Western Powers have made specific suggestions to the Soviets on ways to improve conditions in and around Berlin. We are looking for the application of constructive Soviet influence toward a peaceful settlement in the Middle East.[22]

None of the Western initiatives threaten Soviet security or interests. We ask of the Soviet Union only to show willingness to make some concessions—in response to our readiness to reach reasonable compromises—and to forsake narrow advantage for the sake of the larger global security.

We believe that these standards constitute a reasonable basis on which to develop relations between the Soviet Union and the United States. If they are accepted by the Soviet leadership as guidelines for forthcoming policy decisions, we shall have entered an era of negotiation. Such an era, I am certain, would bring enduring advantage to the Soviet Union, to the United States, and to all nations of the world.

The European scene which I have sketched this evening does not present a tidy picture. We have entered a period of change, but the decisive changes which will finally close the postwar period have yet to be accomplished.

The ordinary citizen of Europe calls upon his leaders for progress toward ending the division of Europe. We in the West are responsive to that demand. The NATO allies, with prudent concern for preserving their freedom and security, have proposed negotiations on the real issues which divide the continent. It is not yet clear whether the Warsaw Pact group is interested in more than a carefully controlled détente shaped primarily to serve Soviet special interests.

The United States and its allies are willing to take into account the security needs and legitimate interests of the Soviet Union. We are prepared to negotiate with the Soviets on the basis of mutual accommodation, but never at the cost of the vital ties to our allies and friends in the West.

---

[22] Cf. President Nixon's comments in Document 11.

We have put some serious proposals to the East, and we await a response. The nature of that response will tell us much about the prospects for transition to a more constructive era, an era in which the threat of conflict declines and there is an increase in cooperation among all nations in meeting the common problems and challenges faced by all of mankind. This will remain our goal.

B. Reduction of Forces in Europe: Mutual or Unilateral?

[Proposals looking toward a reduction in the military forces that faced each other across the East–West dividing line in Europe[23] were no novelty in 1971. It was in 1966 that Senator Mike Mansfield had first introduced his proposed resolution declaring it to be the sense of the Senate that "a substantial reduction of U.S. forces permanently stationed in Europe can be made without adversely affecting either our resolve or ability to meet our commitments under the North Atlantic Treaty."[24] Reintroduced in 1967 and again in 1969,[25] the Mansfield resolution had gathered the support of more than half the members of the Senate but had been strongly opposed by both the Johnson and the Nixon administrations and had never come to a formal vote. The issue nevertheless had remained alive, and Senator Mansfield stated in February 1971 that he considered the time again ripe for a resolution or an amendment "in an appropriate bill."

An alternative plan, consisting in an invitation to initiate East–West discussions on Mutual and Balanced Force Reductions (M.B.F.R.) in Europe, had been put forward by the North Atlantic allies (other than France) at the Reykjavik meeting of the North Atlantic Council in June 1968[26] and reiterated at the Council's Rome meeting in May 1970.[27] The U.S.S.R. and its Warsaw Pact allies had taken no formal notice of these proposals but had given increasing emphasis to still a third plan, originally advanced by the U.S.S.R. in 1954 and revived by the Warsaw

---

[23] NATO combat and support forces available in peacetime in Northern and Central Europe were estimated by the International Institute for Strategic Studies in 1971 to number 24 divisions or 580,000 men, excluding French forces of some 120,000; Warsaw Pact forces were estimated at 65 divisions or 960,000 men, including 41 Soviet divisions amounting to 588,000 men. (International Institute for Strategic Studies, *The Military Balance 1971-1972* [London: I.I.S.S., 1971], pp. 76-77.) United States forces in Europe approximated 310,000 men, including 200,000 assigned to the Seventh Army in Germany.

[24] Senate Resolution 300, 89th Cong., 2d sess., introduced Aug. 31, 1966.

[25] Senate Resolution 49, 90th Cong., 1st sess., introduced Jan. 19, 1967, and Senate Resolution 292, 91st Cong., 2d sess., introduced Dec. 1, 1969; cf. *The United States in World Affairs, 1967*, pp. 198-99; same, *1970*, p. 250.

[26] *Documents, 1968-69*, pp. 133-34.

[27] Same, *1970*, pp. 89-90.

Pact in 1966, for the convocation of a general Conference on Security and Cooperation in Europe (C.S.C.E.).[28] In addition, General Secretary Brezhnev, addressing the 24th Congress of the Soviet Communist Party on March 30, 1971, hinted for the first time at a possible interest in M.B.F.R. by stating that "...We stand for the reduction of armed forces and armaments in areas where military confrontation is especially dangerous, above all in Central Europe."[29] Commenting on Western uncertainty about the significance of this statement, Brezhnev suggested in a later speech at Tbilisi on May 14, 1971, that the way to find out was to "taste" the Soviet proposals—in other words, to "enter into negotiations."[30]

Brezhnev's Tbilisi speech occurred midway in a renewed debate in the United States over Senator Mansfield's proposal for a unilateral reduction of U.S. forces, which had been reintroduced on May 11, 1971, in the midst of the financial anxieties occasioned by the "floating" of the West German mark two days earlier. Presented in the form of an amendment to a bill amending and extending the Military Selective Service Act of 1967, the Mansfield proposal in its new form (Document 33) sought to bar the use of appropriated funds to maintain a military force exceeding 150,000 in Europe after December 31, 1971. The Nixon administration, alarmed by indications of widespread support for the Mansfield proposal, secured a week's delay in the voting and used the interval to mount a vigorous counteroffensive that included statements by President Nixon (Document 34), Secretary of State Rogers,[31] former Secretary of State Dean Acheson, former Presidents Johnson and Truman, and NATO Secretary-General Manlio Brosio.[32] When voting took place in the Senate on May 19, 1971, the amendment was defeated by a vote of 61-36, though only to be revived by Senator Mansfield in still another context later in the year (Document 41). In the meantime, the administration made known its intention to follow up the recent Brezhnev initiative in a renewed attempt to bring about negotiations on mutual and balanced (as distinguished from unilateral) force reduction (Document 35).]

---

[28] Declaration on Strengthening Peace and Security in Europe, Bucharest, July 6, 1966, in *Documents on Disarmament, 1966*, pp. 407-20; Appeal to All European Countries, Budapest, Mar. 17, 1969, in same, *1969*, pp. 106-9; Declaration of the Warsaw Pact Foreign Ministers, Prague, Oct. 31, 1969, in same, pp. 526-28; Memorandum of the Warsaw Pact Foreign Ministers, Budapest, June 22, 1970, in same, *1970*, pp. 93-94; Communiqué of the Warsaw Pact Foreign Ministers, Bucharest, Feb. 19, 1971, in same, *1971*, pp. 14-16 (excerpt).

[29] Same, p. 196.

[30] Same, p. 293. Further Soviet statements are recorded in *NATO Review*, July–Aug., 1971, p. 29.

[31] Radio-TV interview, May 16, 1971, in *Bulletin*, June 7, 1971, pp. 734-37.

[32] *Public Papers, 1971*, p. 636. Additional statements are recorded in *NATO Review*, July–Aug., 1971, p. 29.

1. Defeat of the Mansfield Amendment.

(33) Address by Senator Mike Mansfield to the Senate, with Proposed Amendment, May 11, 1971.[33]

(Excerpts)

* * *

Mr. MANSFIELD. Mr. President, at the present time there are over 300,000 U.S. military personnel, including 20,000 in the 6th Fleet, stationed in Western Europe. Of this number, 128 are general flag officers, or one general flag officer for every 2,343 men.

That is an introductory statement.

Mr. President, I ask unanimous consent that I may submit an amendment to H.R. 6531, a bill to amend the Military Selective Service Act of 1967; to increase military pay; to authorize military active duty strengths for fiscal year 1972, and for other purposes;[34] and I further ask unanimous consent that, after the reading of the amendment—and I do this with the approval of the authors of the pending amendment— the Senate proceed to its immediate consideration.

* * *

The amendment was read, as follows:

TITLE IV—REDUCTION OF UNITED STATES MILITARY FORCES IN EUROPE

SEC. 401. (a) The Congress hereby finds that the number of United States military personnel stationed in Europe can be significantly reduced without endangering the security of Western Europe, and that such a reduction would have a favorable effect on this Nation's balance-of-payments problem and would help avoid recurring international monetary crises involving the value of the dollar abroad. It is therefore the purpose of this section to provide for such a reduction at the earliest practicable date.

(b) No funds appropriated by the Congress may be used after December 31, 1971, for the purpose of supporting or maintaining in Europe any military personnel of the United States in excess of 150,000.

* * *

Mr. MANSFIELD. Mr. President, the essential purpose of this amend-

---

[33] *Congressional Record* (Daily Edition), May 11, 1971, pp. S 6678-80.
[34] Enacted as Public Law 92-129, the Military Selective Service Act, approved Sept. 28, 1971. (A second Mansfield amendment, included in the legislation as adopted, is printed below as Document 79.)

ment is to bring about a reduction of approximately 150,000 Armed Forces personnel below the number presently stationed in Europe.

In short, the amendment says it is too late for the U.S. Government to keep playing the role of Wilkins Micawber, hoping that something will soon "turn up." Something has indeed turned up; a full-blown monetary crisis created in large part by our failure to deal decisively with our enormous balance-of-payments deficits. These in turn derive mainly from our military expenditures in Vietnam, in Europe, and elsewhere around the world.

Mr. President, for several years now other Senators and I who have long felt that an excessive number of American troops and dependents are stationed in Europe have been strenuously cautioned against precipitous action to reduce those totals. Several times I have introduced resolutions making clear our belief in the need for a substantial reduction in our forces in Europe.[35] Several times I have held off action because I have not wished to disrupt an allegedly delicate situation, or to give any justification to those who might charge that we in the Senate have not given the most mature and informed consideration to the problem.

The cautionary voices urging us to wait and see have raised a variety of reasons for inaction. Again and again we are told there can be no question but that the present level of American troops in Europe in time must be reduced, and reduced substantially. But the cautionary voices keep murmuring that now is not the time.

We have been told that so-called offset agreements with West Germany are going far toward closing the serious U.S. balance-of-payments deficits incurred by our military expenditures in Europe. Yet, on examination we have found that much of the offset payment has turned out to be relatively short-term German loans to the United States. These merely postpone our problem; they do nothing to resolve it.

Then at the NATO ministerial meeting late last year[36] quite a different tack was attempted. In December we were told that our European allies would be making a special effort to strengthen their forces. As part of the supposed bargain the United States would not only maintain its current levels of forces intact, but would also contribute to the projected increased effectiveness of the alliance's military position. Once again, close examination reveals that the much touted special effort over the period of the next 5 years at best will represent rather modest progress.

Over each of the next 5 years the Europeans together plan to spend an additional $100 million toward improving their force levels and readiness, while a similar sum would be invested in infrastructure—that is, the facilities located on European soil for logistical and related purposes. In any one of the next 5 years the combined extra European

---

[35] Cf. above at notes 24 and 25.
[36] *Documents, 1970*, pp. 92-103.

effort would amount to roughly $200 million, or about one-ninth of the annual U.S. balance-of-payments deficit incurred as a result of American military expenditures in Europe. This, to me, is not a very impressive effort when one considers how much energy and time went into arguing for an increase which would encourage Americans to believe that the corner had at last been turned.

When other arguments fail—as indeed they have—the executive branch always seems to fall back on something which we can only call the psychological argument. We have been lectured constantly over the last year on the theme that West German efforts to promote detente, under the heading of "ostpolitik," should not be disrupted or endangered in the slightest by any action which would affect the balance of military forces in Europe. No one is more interested than I in promoting a peaceful dialog between the Soviet Union and the Western allies leading to a permanent and reliable stabilization of the European scene. However, I have never believed that this is a short-term proposition or process. If we are to wait for the full success of ostpolitik before we can change our force levels in Europe, then we may have to be prepared to endure a stalemate which could last for one or two decades, or even longer, because some of the arguments against this proposal to reduce our forces in Europe seem to have a ring of permanency about them, and some of my colleagues feel that U.S. troops should remain in Europe ad infinitum.

The related point is also stressed that we must take no action which could jeopardize the political position of the Brandt government in Germany. There is no question about the depth of the Chancellor's commitment to the West. Yet, it is conjectured that some other German leader in the future might try to work out a unilateral deal with the Soviet Union at the expense of the Alliance if the United States were to jar the supposedly delicate psychological balance of the German people. Frankly, this sort of argument is not flattering to the German people—any more than comparable speculation abroad is to us about the possible faithlessness of the United States. Both countries should resent and reject these hypotheses. Indeed, one could turn the argument around and say that, since the leaders of the two largest German political parties are unquested [sic] advocates of Western European unity, it would be better to scale down the U.S. presence while they are in office and can handle any possible repercussions.

Mr. President, today we are seeing the high cost of postponement of considerations of urgent problems. Time and again Members of this body have taken the floor to discuss our persistent and increasing balance-of-payments deficits, to urge immediate attention to the problem, and to prophesy critical times ahead if matters are left for the most convenient time. The distinguished senior Senator from Missouri (Mr. [Stuart] SYMINGTON) in particular, and also the distinguished

senior Senator from Illinois (Mr. [Charles H.] PERCY), have given us
an excellent lead in warning against just what has come to pass; yet
another international monetary upheaval.

* * *

It seems to me we have been refusing to face up to a paradoxical
European attitude which has persisted for some half dozen years. On
the one hand, many of our European friends constantly urge us to
maintain unchanged our commitments and our military forces. On the
other hand, they argue strenuously for a reduction in our payments
deficits, which are incurred largely from the activities which they say
cannot be altered. As far as Vietnam is concerned, the NATO Allies
offer little advice and less help; at least the French do us the favor of
speaking their minds clearly and forcefully in urging withdrawal.

While a number of palliatives have been proposed and applied, our
payments position in Europe and the world has deteriorated further.
For example, in fiscal year 1968 the amount of U.S. defense expenditures entering the international balance of payments in Western
Europe was about $1.611 billion. In 1969 the figure fell slightly to
$1.586 billion. In fiscal year 1970, however, the figure had risen again
to more than $1.731 billion. This could hardly be termed progress.

* * *

Mr. President, my amendment is designed to bring about early relief
to our pressing payments deficits abroad. It is an amendment which is
necessary and reasonable. It will permit 150,000 American military
personnel still to be stationed in Europe. Further, if these troops that
will be returned are disbanded upon their return to the United States, it
will represent a further gain for our budget, as well as our balance of
payments. The financial savings in that case could well be as high as
$1½ billion.

It may be argued by some that this leaves uncertain the intentions of
the United States with respect to the defense of Western Europe and
with respect to the numbers of American forces for that defense. But if
there is one cardinal foreign policy tenet agreed upon by virtually all
Americans, it is the proposition that Western Europe, for a variety of
reasons, must not be allowed to come under Soviet or other external
domination. I will not go into all the many arguments we have made
publicly over the last few years to support our contention that there is
no compelling military argument for the exact number of forces which
we now maintain in Europe. Instead, I would like to append to this
statement an article on this subject by a recently retired Army officer,

Edward L. King, written for the October 1970 issue of the Forum periodical, published by the Ripon Society. Mr. King makes many of the same arguments, and I ask unanimous consent that the article be printed at the conclusion of my remarks in the Record.

The PRESIDING OFFICER. Without objection, it is so ordered.

(See exhibit 1.)[37]

Mr. MANSFIELD. Mr. President, in closing these remarks, let me stress that I believe my amendment represents a constructive move which will respond not only to the demands of American citizens for greater expenditures at home rather than abroad but also to the demands of our European allies for urgent American measures to get our payments deficits under control. This does not in any way represent a withdrawal from Western Europe or its defense. It is quite simply an illustration of the old French saying that one recoils in order to jump better.

Our forces in Europe have been inflated and musclebound, with far more logistical than combat capability. It is my conviction, and that of many other observers—including experienced military men—that trimming away the fat in the form of excess supplies and headquarters will result in a leaner, more mobile, and more efficient combat force.

(34) Statement by President Nixon, Issued at Key Biscayne, Florida, May 15, 1971. [38]

(Complete Text)

At this point in time, it would be an error of historic dimensions for any of the North Atlantic Treaty allies to reduce unilaterally the military forces maintained in Europe for the common defense.

As the most powerful member of the Alliance, the United States bears a responsibility for leadership.

Let us persevere to carry forward the policy of this Nation under five successive Presidents representing both political parties, confident that our united strength will promote the enduring peace we seek.

---

[37] Not reprinted here.
[38] *Presidential Documents*, May 25, 1971, p. 772. For other statements cf. above at notes 31 and 32.

2. Proposals for Mutual and Balanced Force Reduction (M.B.F.R.).

(35) United States–Soviet Contacts: Statement by Charles W. Bray III, Director, Office of Press Relations, Department of State, May 17, 1971.[39]

(Complete Text)

Since 1968 the United States and its NATO allies have called for the mutual and balanced reduction of forces in Europe.[40] Also, in 1970, the NATO alliance agreed on certain principles which might provide a framework for discussions on such force reductions. At that time, the alliance also invited interested states to begin exploratory talks. As stated in the President's report on U.S. foreign policy (February 25, 1971), the U.S. Government undertook to reinforce the preliminary work done in NATO with an intensive analysis of the issues in an agreement to reduce NATO and Warsaw Pact forces.[41]

On Sunday, May 16, the Secretary of State indicated that he had instructed our Ambassador in Moscow to discuss with the Foreign Minister of the Soviet Union Mr. [Leonid I.] Brezhnev's most recent statement on the question of force reductions in Europe.[42]

On May 17, Ambassador [Jacob D.] Beam saw Foreign Minister [Andrei A.] Gromyko. Mr. Gromyko then confirmed that the Soviet Government was prepared to discuss force reductions and expressed interest in further exchanges on this matter.

Our Ambassador stated that the United States would now consult further with our allies in light of the Soviet response and the U.S. and NATO studies referred to above.

Our U.S. Representative to the North Atlantic Treaty Organization, Ambassador [Robert F.] Ellsworth, has been instructed to consult with our allies on the basis of the Soviet response.

The Secretary of State will continue these consultations with his foreign minister colleagues in the alliance at the ministerial meeting of NATO taking place in Lisbon on June 3-4.[43]

C. The Position of NATO.

[Improving prospects for talks on Mutual and Balanced Force Reduction (M.B.F.R.) were a principal subject of discussion at the semiannual

---

[39] *Bulletin*, June 7, 1971, p. 741.
[40] Cf. above at notes 26 and 27.
[41] Nixon Report, 1971, p. 195.
[42] Cf. above at note 30.
[43] Cf. Document 37.

meetings of responsible NATO ministers in the spring of 1971. The defense ministers of NATO countries other than France, meeting at Brussels on May 28 as the NATO Defense Planning Committee, took special note of this development as it impinged on a broader review of NATO military concerns (Document 36). The spring meeting of the North Atlantic Council, held in Lisbon on June 3-4, afforded the foreign ministers of NATO countries an opportunity to reaffirm their interest in M.B.F.R. as well as their hope that the expected conclusion of a Berlin agreement would clear the way for conversations on a European Security Conference (C.S.C.E.) (Document 37).]

(36) Communiqué of the NATO Defense Planning Committee, Brussels, May 28, 1971.[44]

(Complete Text)

1. The Defence Planning Committee of the North Atlantic Treaty Organization met in Ministerial Session on Friday, 28th May, 1971, for its regular Spring meeting.

2. Ministers discussed the implications for Alliance Defence Policy of the current situation and in particular the latest developments in the East-West dialogue. They noted in this context the recent Soviet reaction to the long standing and repeated allied initiative on mutual and balanced force reductions,[45] which will be the subject of consideration by the North Atlantic Council in Lisbon next week.[46]

3. Ministers reaffirmed that NATO's approach to security will continue to be based on the twin concepts of defence and détente as stated in the 1967 report on the future tasks of the Alliance.[47] They re-stated the vital rôle of a strong capability for the collective defence of the treaty area as a fundamental basis for a confident and successful policy of negotiation for the reinforcement of peace and security. They also confirmed again the principle that the overall military capability of NATO should not be reduced except as part of a pattern of mutual force reductions, balanced in scope and timing.

4. Ministers welcomed the substantial and concrete progress reported in the development and implementation of the European Defence Improvement Programme, which a number of European countries announced in December 1970.[48] They noted that with the help of the infrastructure element of this Programme, NATO would now be able to

---

[44] *NATO Review*, July–Aug. 1971, p. 27.
[45] Cf. above at notes 29 and 30.
[46] Cf. Document 37.
[47] *Documents, 1967*, pp. 110-14.
[48] Cf. same, *1970*, p. 102.

provide an integrated communications system (including space satellite elements) for the mid-1970s, and to execute a greatly-expanded programme of measures to protect their aircraft in case of attack on their bases; and that the European countries concerned had taken steps to secure the earliest possible start on this work. Ministers also welcomed the measures taken to implement the extensive national force improvements and intra-alliance aid which constituted further elements of the European Defence Improvement Programme. They also took note, with great satisfaction, of the reaffirmation by the United States Secretary of Defense of President Nixon's commitment of last December to the effect that, given a similar approach by the other allies, the United States would maintain and improve its own forces in Europe and would not reduce them except in the context of reciprocal East-West action.[49]

5. In reviewing progress in following up the report on Alliance Defence Problems for the 1970s (AD 70 Study),[50] Ministers noted that a starting point had already been established, in that certain measures to improve the defence posture of NATO countries were already in hand; some of these were specifically mentioned by Ministers during their meeting. Ministers agreed on the need for countries to begin implementation of further improvements in accordance with the report before them. A comprehensive report, which would also address further recommendations for specific measures and the question of relative priorities, was called for by Ministers for their meeting next December.

6. Ministers noted the continuing increase in real terms in the allocation of resources to military and military-related programmes by the Soviet Union and other Warsaw Pact countries. In light of this increased capability, Ministers agreed therefore that in order to continue providing modern and sufficient nuclear and conventional forces and to improve the situation in the important areas highlighted in the AD 70 Study, some overall increase in defence outlays was needed. In the light of these considerations, and in keeping with the agreed Conclusions and Recommendations of the AD 70 Report, Ministers provided the NATO Military Authorities with the guidance necessary to enable them to prepare proposals for the size and structure of NATO forces for the planning period 1973-1978.

7. Against the background of the continuing growth of the Soviet military presence in the Mediterranean, Ministers gave special consideration to a report on steps to improve the Alliance's defence posture in that area. They noted that a number of measures to this end had already been taken, particularly for surveillance, while others were in hand or under consideration; and that countries were working both on an individual and on a co-operative basis as well as with the NATO

49 Cf. same, pp. 92-93.
50 Same, pp. 99-103.

Military Authorities to produce the most effective and co-ordinated results. Ministers asked for a further report on the progress made to be submitted to them at their next meeting. In the same context they noted that the Defence Planning Committee in Permanent Session had approved a political directive for unscheduled activities of the Naval On-Call Force for the Mediterranean as an additional mode of activity to regular planned activities for that force, for which authority has existed for some time.

8. Ministers also noted the continuing build-up of Soviet forces in the North-East Atlantic and the need for further planning for external reinforcements and other measures to improve the situation on the Northern flank.

9. Ministers approved a report recommending ways to streamline and generally improve the NATO procedures for collective defence planning. The main aims were to adapt these procedures to conform still more closely to, and thus to provide effective co-ordination with, national systems and timetables; while at the same time keeping them sufficiently flexible to respond to changing circumstances.

10. Finally, Ministers reviewed the status of various on-going Alliance defence planning studies.

11. The next Ministerial Meeting of the Defence Planning Committee will take place in Brussels in December 1971.[51]

(37) Ministerial Session of the North Atlantic Council, Lisbon, June 3-4, 1971: Final Communiqué.[52]

(Complete Text)

The North Atlantic Council met in Ministerial Session in Lisbon on 3rd and 4th June, 1971.

2. The continuing political aim of the Atlantic Alliance is to seek peace through initiatives designed to relax tensions and to establish a just and durable peaceful order in Europe, accompanied by effective security guarantees. The Alliance remains indispensable to peace and stability in Europe and to the security of all its members.

3. Ministers reviewed the international situation, concentrating their attention on Europe and the Mediterranean.

4. They assessed the state of progress of the several initiatives which allied countries had undertaken within the framework of the established policy of the Alliance to intensify contacts, explorations and negotiations with members of the Warsaw Pact and other European states. The purpose of all these initiatives is to seek just solutions to the

[51] Cf. Document 42.
[52] Bulletin, June 28, 1971, pp. 819-21.

fundamental problems of European security and thus to achieve a genuine improvement of East-West relations. They noted with satisfaction the results obtained and expressed the hope that the continuation of these efforts would lead to further progress helping the development of détente. The allies have consulted and will continue to consult closely on these diplomatic activities.

5. Ministers welcomed the continued negotiations between the US and the USSR with the aim of placing limitations on offensive and defensive strategic arms. They noted the useful discussions held in the North Atlantic Council on this subject. Ministers also welcomed the agreement between the US and the USSR announced on 20th May, regarding the framework for further negotiations,[53] and expressed the sincere hope that it would facilitate discussions leading to the early achievement of concrete results enhancing the common security interests of the North Atlantic Alliance and stability in the world.

6. In reviewing the Berlin question, Ministers underlined the necessity of alleviating the causes of insecurity in and around the city. During the past quarter of a century, much of the tension which has characterized East-West relations in Europe has stemmed from the situation in and around Berlin. Thus, the Ministers would regard the successful outcome of the Berlin talks as an encouraging indication of the willingness of the Soviet Union to join in the efforts of the Alliance to achieve a meaningful and lasting improvement of East-West relations in Europe.

7. Ministers therefore reaffirmed their full support for the efforts of the Governments of France, the United Kingdom and the United States to reach an agreement on Berlin. They shared the view of the three Governments that the aim of the negotiations should be to achieve specific improvements based on firm commitments without prejudice to the status of Berlin. In this context, they emphasized the importance of reaching agreement on unhindered movement of persons and goods between the Federal Republic of Germany and Western sectors of Berlin, on improved opportunities for movement by residents of the Western sectors, and on respect for the relationship between the Western sectors and the Federal Republic as it has developed with the approval of the three Governments.

8. Ministers were of the view that progress in the talks between German Authorities on a modus vivendi, taking into account the special situation in Germany, would be an important contribution to a relaxation of tension in Europe.

9. Ministers, having reviewed the prospects for the establishment of multilateral contacts relating to the essential problems of security and co-operation in Europe, again emphasized the importance they attach to the successful conclusion of the negotiations on Berlin. They noted

[53] Document 21.

with satisfaction that these negotiations have entered into a more active phase and have enabled progress to be registered in recent weeks. They hope that before their next meeting the negotiations on Berlin will have reached a successful conclusion[54] and that multilateral conversations intended to lead to a conference on security and co-operation in Europe may then be undertaken. In this spirit they invited the Council in Permanent Session to continue, in the framework of its normal consultations on the international situation, its periodic review of the results achieved in all contacts and talks relative to security and co-operation in Europe so that it could without delay take a position on the opening of multilateral talks.

10. In anticipation of these multilateral contacts, the Council in Permanent Session actively pursued preparations for discussions on the substance and procedures of possible East-West negotiations, and submitted a report to this effect to Ministers. The report stressed that the successful outcome of such negotiations would have to be founded on universal respect for the principles governing relations between states as cited by Ministers in previous Communiqués and Declarations. The various prospects for developing co-operation between East and West in the economic, technical, scientific, cultural and environmental fields were closely examined. The report also reviewed in detail the essential elements on which agreement would be desirable in order to promote the freer movement of people, ideas and information so necessary to the development of international co-operation in all fields.

11. Ministers noted these studies and instructed the Council in Permanent Session to continue them pending the initiation of multilateral contacts between East and West. Ministers stressed that they would press on with their bilateral exploratory conversations with all interested states.

12. Ministers took note of the report on the situation in the Mediterranean prepared by the Council in Permanent Session. While welcoming the efforts currently undertaken to re-establish peace in the Eastern Mediterranean,[55] they observed that developments in the area as a whole continue to give cause for concern. In the light of the conclusions of this report, they instructed the Council in Permanent Session to continue consultations on this situation and to report thereon at their next meeting.

13. The allied Governments which issued the declarations at Reykjavik in 1968[56] and Rome in 1970[57] and which subscribed to paragraphs 15 and 16 of the Brussels Communiqué of 1970[58] have

---

54 Cf. Documents 38-39.
55 Cf. Documents 48-49.
56 *Documents, 1968-69*, pp. 133-34.
57 Same, *1970*, pp. 89-90.
58 Same, 95-96.

consistently urged the Soviet Union and other European countries to discuss mutual and balanced force reductions. They reaffirmed that the reduction of the military confrontation in Europe—at which MBFR is aiming—is essential for increased security and stability.

14. Against this background, Ministers representing these Governments welcomed the response of Soviet leaders indicating possible readiness to consider reductions of armed forces and armaments in Central Europe.[59] These Soviet reactions, which require further clarification, are, together with those [of other][60] states, receiving the closest attention of the Alliance.

15. In an effort to determine whether common ground exists on which to base negotiations on mutual and balanced force reductions, these Ministers expressed the agreement of their Governments to continue and intensify explorations with the Soviet Union and also with other interested Governments on the basis of the considerations outlined in paragraph 3 of the Rome Declaration.[61] They expressed their intention to move as soon as may be practical to negotiations. To this end these Ministers agreed that Deputy Foreign Ministers or High Officials should meet at Brussels at an early date to review the results of the exploratory contacts and to consult on substantive and procedural approaches to mutual and balanced force reductions.

16. These Ministers further announced their willingness to appoint, at the appropriate time, a representative or representatives, who would be responsible to the Council for conducting further exploratory talks with the Soviet Government and the other interested Governments and eventually to work out the time, place, arrangements and agenda for negotiations on mutual and balanced force reductions.[62]

17. Reviewing other developments in the field of arms control and disarmament, these Ministers noted as a significant step forward the conclusion of a treaty banning the emplacement of weapons of mass destruction on the seabed and ocean floor.[63] Allied Ministers noted with satisfaction the work done by the Conference of the Committee on Disarmament with a view to reaching an agreement eliminating bacteriological weapons and toxins.[64] They reaffirmed the importance they attach to effective and adequately verified arms limitation and disarmament measures consistent with the security of all states and invited the Council in Permanent Session to continue to pursue the Alliance efforts and studies related to arms control and disarmament.

---

[59] Cf. above at notes 29 and 30.
[60] Text corrected from Department of State Press Release 124, June 7, 1971.
[61] A footnote to the communiqué which quotes the relevant paragraph is deleted; for text see *Documents, 1970*, pp. 89-90.
[62] Cf. Document 40.
[63] Cf. Documents 13-14.
[64] Cf. Document 17.

18. Ministers expressed satisfaction at the impressive progress achieved by the Committee on the Challenges of Modern Society as reported by the Secretary General. They noted particularly the important contribution made by the Allies to combat the pollution of the seas by oil and to the development of road safety. They welcomed the fact that intensive work was underway on problems relating to coastal and inland water pollution and disaster assistance. They further welcomed the contribution the Committee had made to alerting Governments and public opinion to the problems of modern technology, as well as to the dangers for modern society arising from the deterioration of the environment. They observed that many countries of the Alliance have equipped themselves with new Government structures to cope with such problems. Ministers took special note of the fact that the benefits of allied efforts had not been confined to the countries of the Alliance but were being felt in other countries as well as in broader-based international organizations.

19. Ministers expressed their regret at the impending departure of Mr. Manlio Brosio who had informed them of his intention to resign as Secretary General of the Organization. In their tributes to Mr. Brosio, Ministers dwelt on his outstanding stewardship in often difficult circumstances and stressed the patience and perseverance which have marked his untiring work for both defence and détente. They expressed to him their deep appreciation for the distinguished service he has rendered to the Alliance and to peace in the past seven years.

20. The Council invited Mr. Joseph Luns, Foreign Minister of the Netherlands, to become Secretary General of the Organization as from 1st October, 1971. Mr. Luns informed the Council of his acceptance of this invitation.

21. The next Ministerial Session of the North Atlantic Council will be held in Brussels in December 1971.[65]

22. Ministers requested the Foreign Minister of Italy [Aldo Moro], as President of [the] Council, to transmit this Communiqué on their behalf through diplomatic channels to all other interested parties including neutral and non-aligned Governments.

D. Quadripartite Agreement on Berlin, Signed in Berlin September 3, 1971.

[One of the principal achievements of East–West negotiation in the early 1970s was the Quadripartite Agreement on Berlin which was signed in that city on September 3, 1971. This event marked the culmination of a lengthy diplomatic process whose origins extended back to 1944-45, when the principal Allied powers (the U.S.S.R., United

[65] Cf. Document 42.

Kingdom, United States, and France) had concluded a series of agreements providing for four-power occupation of the former German capital but lacking express provision for freedom of access to the city across the Soviet occupation zone of Germany. A revival of East German pressure against the access routes in 1968 focused Western attention on the desirability of new arrangements to improve the situation in the divided city, and discussion intensified following President Nixon's visit to West Berlin on February 27, 1969.

Responding to an offer by Soviet Foreign Minister Gromyko (July 10, 1969) to "exchange views as to how complications concerning West Berlin can be prevented now and in the future," the three Western powers initiated contacts with the Soviet Government which led on February 10, 1970, to an agreement to hold talks at ambassadorial level in the former Allied Control Council building in West Berlin. Twelve negotiating sessions during 1970 served mainly to illuminate the disparity between Western and Soviet objectives. The Western powers sought assurances of free and unhindered civil access to Berlin, improvement of travel for Berliners and of communication within and around Berlin, and termination of various forms of discrimination against Berlin by the U.S.S.R. and some of its allies. The U.S.S.R., in contrast, appeared primarily interested in securing a redefinition of the status of West Berlin which would serve to eliminate the various political and constitutional ties that had developed between West Berlin and the Federal Republic of Germany.

An important obstacle to agreement was eliminated in May 1971, undoubtedly with Soviet foreknowledge, when Walter Ulbricht, a longtime foe of East-West accommodation in Germany, was succeeded by Erich Honecker as First Secretary of the Central Committee of East Germany's ruling Socialist Unity (Communist) Party. Further negotiations, carried on in close coordination with the two German governments, produced the outlines of a diplomatic bargain whereby the Soviet Union promised unimpeded civilian transit to and from West Berlin, while the Western governments, on their side, confirmed that West Berlin was not a part of the Federal Republic of Germany and would not be governed by it. These and other stipulations were included in the so-called "framework agreement" which was signed by the four ambassadors in Berlin on September 3, 1971—subject, however, to approval by the four governments and the later signature of a Final Protocol bringing the agreement into force.

Among the conditions to be fulfilled before the Final Protocol could be signed was the conclusion of certain implementing agreements by the relevant German authorities, all of which were in fact completed in the course of December 1971.[66] In addition, the Soviet Union took the position during the autumn of 1971 that none of the agreements could

---

[66] Cf. notes 85 and 87 below.

enter into force until the Federal Republic of Germany completed ratification of the bilateral "normalization" treaties it had concluded with the U.S.S.R. and Poland in 1970.[67] Deliberately held up by the West German Government pending the outcome of the Berlin negotiations, these treaties were not submitted to the West German Parliament until December 13, 1971, and did not win final parliamentary approval until May 17–19, 1972. Formally ratified by the President of the Federal Republic of Germany on May 23, 1972, the treaties entered into force June 3, 1972, on which date the foreign ministers of the four powers assembled in Berlin to sign the Final Protocol bringing the entire Berlin arrangement into force.[68]

The following documentation comprises a statement by Secretary of State Rogers on the significance of the Berlin agreement (Document 38), followed by the text of the main body of the agreement itself (Document 39). Annexes to the agreement are described in footnotes, and certain supplementary documents included in the official text are described in a special note at the end.]

(38) Statement by Secretary of State Rogers, Washington, September 3, 1971.[69]

(Complete Text)

Today in Berlin the United States joined with France, the Soviet Union, and the United Kingdom in signing the vital initial element of a Berlin agreement.[70]

This act marks a step forward and is pursuant to President Nixon's desire for reconciliation between East and West. It embraces not only the promise of a better way of life for Berliners but enhances the prospects for greater peace and security in Europe.

The signing brings to a successful close the first phase of a difficult but diligent Allied effort by many dedicated hands. I want to take this opportunity to congratulate the American officials in Germany and in Washington who played a role in these negotiations. It is the product of considered and responsible diplomatic give-and-take.

[67] Cf. note 17 above.
[68] A.F.R., 1972, no. 25.
[69] Department of State Press Release 191, Sept. 3, 1971; text from Bulletin, Sept. 27, 1971, pp. 317-18.
[70] Document 39.

The Western objective was to bring about practical improvements in and around the city without altering the status of Berlin or diminishing our rights and responsibilities there. That objective has been achieved. Among other things—according to the agreement—traffic between Berlin and West Germany by persons and goods on road, rail, and waterways will move unimpeded, West Berliners will be able again to visit East Berlin and East Germany, and ties between the Western sectors of Berlin and the Federal Republic will be maintained and developed.

To be meaningful this first step must be followed by a successful round of inner-German talks. This second step need not be long delayed, given good faith on the part of all the parties.[71]

The third step, the signing of a four-power protocol, will bring the entire Berlin understanding into effect.[72]

Looking beyond Berlin, there are a variety of prospects to be pursued in the search for a more stable and profitable relationship in Europe. The NATO governments, guided by a desire first expressed at their 1968 Reykjavik meeting, are well along in their preparations for intensive diplomatic consultations on mutual balanced force reductions with the Soviet Union and its allies. To that end the NATO deputy foreign ministers will meet in Brussels early next month to discuss the next moves to be made in this critical area.[73]

That is one prospect. Our hope would be that with a successful Berlin accord other efforts toward reconciliation and cooperation can be set in train in Europe.

As President Nixon said in February:[74]

> For 25 years Europe has been divided by opposing national interests and contrary philosophies, which clash over specific issues . . . .
> These issues will not be quickly resolved. To relax tensions means a patient and persistent effort to deal with specific sources and not only with their manifestations.

In my judgment, this first stage of a Berlin accord represents the fruit of just such a "patient and persistent effort."

---

[71] Cf. notes 85 and 87 below.
[72] Cf. above at note 68.
[73] Cf. Document 40.
[74] Nixon Report, 1971, p. 38.

(39) Quadripartite Agreement on Berlin Between the United States of America and Other Governments, Signed at Berlin September 3, 1971.[75]

(Excerpt)

QUADRIPARTITE AGREEMENT

The Governments of the United States of America, the French Republic, the Union of Soviet Socialist Republics and the United Kingdom of Great Britain and Northern Ireland,

Represented by their Ambassadors, who held a series of meetings in the building formerly occupied by the Allied Control Council in the American Sector of Berlin,

Acting on the basis of their quadripartite rights and responsibilities, and of the corresponding wartime and postwar agreements and decisions of the Four Powers, which are not affected,

Taking into account the existing situation in the relevant area,

Guided by the desire to contribute to practical improvements of the situation,

Without prejudice to their legal positions,

Have agreed on the following:

PART I
GENERAL PROVISIONS

1. The four Governments will strive to promote the elimination of tension and the prevention of complications in the relevant area.
2. The four Governments, taking into account their obligations under the Charter of the United Nations, agree that there shall be no use or threat of force in the area and that disputes shall be settled solely by peaceful means.
3. The four Governments will mutually respect their individual and joint rights and responsibilities, which remain unchanged.
4. The four Governments agree that, irrespective of the differences in legal views, the situation which has developed in the area, and as it is defined in this Agreement as well as in the other agreements referred to in this Agreement, shall not be changed unilaterally.

---

[75] TIAS 7551; 24 UST 283. Printed here is the main body of the agreement, minus the Annexes (described in notes 76-79) and the Agreed Minutes and related documents (described in a special note at the end of the text).

PART II
PROVISIONS RELATING TO THE WESTERN SECTORS OF BERLIN

A. The Government of the Union of Soviet Socialist Republics declares that transit traffic by road, rail and waterways through the territory of the German Democratic Republic of civilian persons and goods between the Western Sectors of Berlin and the Federal Republic of Germany will be unimpeded; that such traffic will be facilitated so as to take place in the most simple and expeditious manner; and that it will receive preferential treatment.

Detailed arrangements concerning this civilian traffic, as set forth in Annex I,[76] will be agreed by the competent German authorities.

B. The Governments of the French Republic, the United Kingdom and the United States of America declare that the ties between the Western Sectors of Berlin and the Federal Republic of Germany will be maintained and developed, taking into account that these Sectors continue not to be a constituent part of the Federal Republic of Germany and not to be governed by it.

Detailed arrangements concerning the relationship between the Western Sectors of Berlin and the Federal Republic of Germany are set forth in Annex II.[77]

C. The Government of the Union of Soviet Socialist Republics declares that communications between the Western Sectors of Berlin and areas bordering on these Sectors and those areas of the German Democratic Republic which do not border on these Sectors will be improved. Permanent residents of the Western Sectors of Berlin will be able to travel to and visit such areas for compassionate, family, religious, cultural or commercial reasons, or as tourists, under conditions comparable to those applying to other persons entering these areas.

The problems of the small enclaves, including Steinstuecken, and of other small areas may be solved by exchange of territory.

[76] Annex I (24 UST 290-92), consisting of a communication from the U.S.S.R. to the three Western governments, spells out the treatment to be accorded different forms of transit traffic and provides that implementing arrangements will be agreed by the competent German authorities. See further note 85, below.

[77] Annex II (same, pp. 293-94), consisting of a communication from the three Western governments to the U.S.S.R., declares that (1) constitutional provisions of West Germany and West Berlin which contradict the above declaration have been suspended and continue not to be in effect; (2) West German governmental organs will not perform in the Western Sectors of Berlin constitutional or official acts which contradict the foregoing stipulation; and (3) the West German Government will be represented in West Berlin by a permanent liaison agency. Cf. below at note 83.

Detailed arrangements concerning travel, communications and the exchange of territory, as set forth in Annex III,[78] will be agreed by the competent German authorities.

D. Representation abroad of the interests of the Western Sectors of Berlin and consular activities of the Union of Soviet Socialist Republics in the Western Sectors of Berlin can be exercised as set forth in Annex IV.[79]

PART III
FINAL PROVISIONS

This Quadripartite Agreement will enter into force on the date specified in a Final Quadripartite Protocol[80] to be concluded when the measures envisaged in Part II of this Quadripartite Agreement and in its Annexes have been agreed.

DONE at the building formerly occupied by the Allied Control Council in the American Sector of Berlin this 3rd day of September 1971, in four originals, each in the English, French and Russian languages, all texts being equally authentic.

For the Government of the United States
of America:
    (*Signed*) Kenneth Rush

For the Government of the French Republic:
    (*Signed*) J. Sauvagnargues

For the Governent of the Union of Soviet
Socialist Republics:
    (*Signed*) P. Abrasimov

[78] Annex III (same, pp. 295-96), consisting of a communication from the U.S.S.R. to the three Western governments, repeats the provisions in the text, states that additional crossing points will be opened for West Berlin residents and that external communications of the Western Sectors will be expanded, and provides that implementing arrangements will be agreed by the competent German authorities. See further note 87, below.
[79] Annex IV (same, pp. 297-301), is in two parts. Part A, a communication from the three Western governments to the U.S.S.R., sets forth certain rights reserved to the Federal Republic of Germany having to do with the performance of consular services for West Berlin residents, application of certain international agreements to West Berlin, representation of the interests of the Western Sectors in international organizations and conferences, and joint participation in international exchanges, exhibitions, etc. It also authorizes the establishment of a Soviet Consulate General in West Berlin. Part B, a communication from the U.S.S.R. to the three Western governments, expresses assent to these provisions.

For the Government of the United Kingdom
of Great Britain and Northern Ireland:
(*Signed*) Roger Jackling

* * *

[*Note*: Appended to the Quadripartite Agreement, in addition to the annexes referred to above, are two Agreed Minutes and several related documents, all dated September 3, 1971, except as otherwise noted.

Agreed Minute I[81] prescribes visa requirements for West Berlin residents traveling to the Soviet Union.

Agreed Minute II[82] lays down conditions governing the establishment of a Soviet Consulate General and commercial facilities in West Berlin.

A note from the Western ambassadors to the Soviet Ambassador communicates the text of a letter to the Chancellor of the Federal Republic of Germany setting forth certain clarifications and interpretations of the statements contained in Annex II.[83] A note from the Soviet Ambassador takes cognizance of this communication.[84]

A letter from the Western ambassadors to the Chancellor of the Federal Republic of Germany communicates the text of the Quadripartite Agreement, together with certain interpretations deriving from past correspondence and agreements, and requests the Federal Government to undertake the negotiations envisaged in Annex I.[85]

A letter from the West German Chancellor acknowledges and acquiesces in the communications described in the two preceding paragraphs.[86]

A communication from the Allied Kommandatura to the Governing Mayor of (West) Berlin authorizes and requests the Berlin Senat (Government) to undertake the negotiations envisaged in Annex III.[87]

[80] See below at note 88..

[81] TIAS 7551; 24 UST 302.

[82] Same, pp. 303-5.

[83] Same, pp. 340-41.

[84] Same, p. 343.

[85] Same, pp. 343-44. An agreement between the Federal Republic of Germany and the German Democratic Republic on transit traffic of civilian persons and goods between the Federal Republic of Germany and Berlin (West) was signed in Bonn Dec. 17, 1971, and entered into force June 3, 1972; English text in same, pp. 376-86. Measures for an improvement of postal and telecommunications services for the Western Sectors of Berlin were set forth in a protocol of negotiations between delegations of the Post and Telecommunications Ministries of the two German governments, dated Berlin, Sept. 30, 1971; partial English text in same, p. 392.

[86] English text in same, p. 346.

[87] Same, p. 347. Two arrangements between the West Berlin Senate and the German Democratic Republic, one relating to the facilitation and improvement of travel and visitor traffic and the other to regulation of the enclaves question by exchange of territory, were signed in Berlin on Dec. 20, 1971, and entered into force June 3, 1972; English texts in same, pp. 386-91.

The text of the Final Quadripartite Protocol (signed June 3, 1972)[88] provides for the bringing into force of the Quadripartite Agreement and the agreements and arrangements concluded between the competent German authorities, and for the holding of quadripartite consultations in the event of any difficulties.]

E. Further Discussion of Force Reduction, October–November 1971.

[Hopes for the early commencement of exploratory conversations on Mutual and Balanced Force Reduction (M.B.F.R.) were further stimulated in the wake of NATO's Lisbon meeting (Document 37) by statements of the top Soviet leaders expressing what now began to appear a definite interest in such a project.[89] As had been planned at Lisbon, the North Atlantic Council held a special high-level meeting on October 5-6, 1971, at which former Secretary-General Manlio Brosio was commissioned to sound out the U.S.S.R. and other interested governments in an effort to determine whether a basis for negotiations did in fact exist (Document 40).

The Warsaw Pact governments did not, however, immediately respond to this initiative, and Senator Mansfield in mid-November renewed his campaign in favor of a unilateral reduction of U.S. forces in Europe, this time through an amendment to the pending Defense Department Appropriation Bill—approved by the Senate Committee on Appropriations—which sought to limit U.S. military personnel in Europe to 250,000 as from June 15, 1972 (Document 41a). Like the previous Mansfield amendment in May (Document 33), the new amendment was strongly opposed by President Nixon and other administration spokesmen (Document 41b) and was defeated by a 54-39 vote of the Senate on November 23, 1971.]

(40) High-level Meeting of the North Atlantic Council, Brussels, October 5-6, 1971: Statement by NATO Secretary-General J.M.A.H. Luns.[90]

(Complete Text)

1. On 5 and 6 October, 1971, a meeting of the North Atlantic Coun-

---

[88] Same, pp. 348-51; *A.F.R., 1972*, no. 25b.
[89] Statements by Kosygin (June 9), Podgorny (June 10), and Brezhnev (June 11), quoted in *NATO Review*, July–Aug. 1971, p. 29.
[90] *NATO Review*, Nov.–Dec. 1971, p. 24.

cil was held on the subject of mutual and balanced force reductions, which was attended by Deputy Foreign Ministers, High Officials from capitals and Permanent Representatives. It will be recalled that in paragraph 15 of the final Communiqué of the Lisbon Ministerial Meeting,[91] Ministers representing Allied Governments which issued the Declarations at Reykjavik in 1968 and Rome in 1970 with respect to mutual and balanced force reductions,[92] agreed that such a meeting should take place at Brussels at an early date.

2. The representatives of these Governments, in accordance with paragraph 16 of the Lisbon Communiqué, discussed and approved the mandate of a representative to conduct exploratory talks with the Soviet Government and other interested governments. It was decided that the representative should speak on behalf of the countries appointing him and not for the Alliance as such. His task will be to explore, and to explain the views of Allied countries appointing him on principles for mutual and balanced force reductions and on the question of a forum for eventual negotiations. He should sound out his interlocutors with regard to their intentions on mutual and balanced force reductions and on negotiating fora and seek their reactions to the ideas expressed.

3. Representatives of the countries which issued the Declarations of Reykjavik and Rome invited Mr. [Manlio] Brosio to be the representative. He accepted this invitation.

4. The Government of Belgium was requested to transmit the aforementioned decisions to the countries which were recipients of the Lisbon Communiqué.[93] The Government of Belgium was also asked to make the necessary arrangements so that Mr. Brosio could begin his mission as soon as possible.

5. These decisions constitute a further initiative on the part of the Allied Governments concerned reflecting their belief that the reduction of the danger of military confrontation in Europe could provide for increased security and stability towards which they have been consistently striving. The initiative is proof of their desire to determine, as soon as possible, whether common ground exists for negotiations on mutual and balanced force reductions. These Governments, therefore, hope that their move will meet with a clear, positive and speedy response on the part of other interested governments.[94]

[91] Document 37.
[92] *Documents, 1968-69*, pp. 133-34; same, *1970*, pp. 89-90.
[93] Cf. Document 37, para. 22.
[94] Cf. further Document 42, para. 16.

(41) Mansfield Amendment to the Department of Defense Appropriation Bill.

　(a) Report of the Senate Committee on Appropriations, November 18, 1971.[95]

(Excerpt)

*　　*　　*

SECTION 744: LIMITATION ON U.S. MILITARY PERSONNEL IN EUROPE

The committee recommends the bill be amended to include the following new provision:

Sec. 744. After June 15, 1972, no part of the funds appropriated in this Act shall be available for the support of U.S. military personnel in Europe in excess of 250,000.

It is the view of the committee that the United States should reduce the strength of its military forces stationed in Europe, and recommends the inclusion of the above quoted provision to limit the number of forces stationed there on June 15, 1972, to 250,000. While the number of individuals stationed in Europe varies from day to day, the committee's action is based on approximately 300,000 being currently stationed in Europe, so the committee's recommendation involves a reduction of approximately 50,000.[96]

*　　*　　*

　(b) Letter from President Nixon to Senator John C. Stennis, Chairman of the Senate Committee on Armed Services, November 23, 1971.[97]

(Complete Text)

Dear John:

This week the Senate will once again consider a proposal to make a

[95] U.S. Senate, Committee on Appropriations, 92d Cong., 1st sess., Senate Report 92-498 (on H.R. 11731), pp. 10-11. The pending legislation was enacted—without the Mansfield amendment—as Public Law 92-204, the Department of Defense Appropriations Act, 1972, approved Dec. 18, 1971.

[96] A speech by Senator Mansfield in support of the proposed amendment appears in *Congressional Record* (Daily Edition), Nov. 23, 1971, pp. S 19495-96.

[97] *Presidential Documents*, Nov. 29, 1971, p. 1556. A letter of Nov. 18, 1971, from Defense Secretary Laird to Senator Stennis (Democrat, Mississippi), expressing opposition to the amendment, appears in *Congressional Record* (Daily Edition), Nov. 23, 1971, p. S 19506.

substantial unilateral reduction in United States Armed Forces maintained in Europe for the common defense. I believe passage of such a measure would be a great mistake.

The manifest Congressional concern for a more equitable sharing of defense burdens in Europe and elsewhere has been a significant factor in the formulation of our national policy. We are currently in the final stages of talks to establish improved arrangements for the sharing of the defense burden in Europe, including an agreement with West Germany to offset nearly two billion dollars of United States costs,[98] and the second phase of the European Defense Improvement Program, to be finalized at the NATO meeting beginning December 8.[99]

In the area of East-West relations, we expect that Mr. Brosio will be received in Moscow next week to begin discussions on basic issues in Mutual Balanced Force Reductions.[100] At the same time, the Berlin negotiations have entered the final and most difficult stage.[101] As you know, we are also making significant progress in the SALT negotiations.[102]

Passage of the proposed troop cut would, with one stroke, diminish Western military capability in Europe and signal to friend and adversary alike a disarray and weakness of purpose in the American Government.

We are now preparing to undertake vitally important new initiatives for peace in two great capitals of the world.[103] If these initiatives are to gain positive results in the months and years ahead, I must be able to rely on the firm support and the substantial and creative contribution of a bipartisan Congress. I believe that this ill-timed measure should be rejected, and that our efforts should be directed toward the positive tasks and the great opportunities for achieving a real peace that lie before us.

With best wishes,
Sincerely,

RICHARD NIXON

F. Force Reduction and European Security Before the North Atlantic Council, December 1971.

[The regular semiannual meeting of the North Atlantic Council at ministerial level, held in Brussels on December 9-10, 1971, afforded an

[98] Conclusion of a new offset agreement with the Federal Republic of Germany, covering the period July 1, 1971–June 30, 1973, and providing benefits estimated at $2,304 million at the current rate of exchange, was announced in Brussels on Dec. 10, 1971 (*Bulletin*, Jan. 3, 1972, pp. 9-10).

[99] Cf. Document 42, para. 29.

[100] Cf. Document 42, para. 16

[101] Cf. notes 85 and 87 above.

[102] Cf. Document 25.

[103] Cf. Documents 29 and 91-94.

opportunity to take stock of both the progress of détente in Europe and the state of NATO defenses. Although the U.S.S.R. had not responded to NATO's offer of exploratory talks on Mutual and Balanced Force Reduction (Document 40), prospects for a Conference on Security and Cooperation in Europe had been enhanced by the signature of the Berlin agreement (Documents 38-39), the progress of related negotiations among German authorities, and a proposal by Finland that multilateral preparatory conversations be undertaken by the heads of missions of interested countries in Helsinki.

At a meeting in Warsaw on November 30–December 1, 1971, the foreign ministers of the Warsaw Pact countries took note of the Finnish initiative and urged that preparations for an all-European conference begin immediately (with American and Canadian participation) so as to ensure its convocation in 1972.[104] The NATO Council, in turn, announced at its December meeting (Document 42) that its members were now ready to undertake such conversations "as soon as possible." A further highlight of the NATO meeting was an expression of continuing interest in Mutual and Balanced Force Reduction and a renewal of the United States' promise—given a similar approach by the other Allies—to maintain and improve its forces in Europe and not reduce them "except in the context of reciprocal East–West action."

As a delayed result of these initiatives, multilateral talks on European security were initiated in Helsinki on November 22, 1972, and the Conference on Security and Cooperation in Europe (C.S.C.E.) was formally opened in the Finnish capital on July 3, 1973. Preparatory talks on Mutual and Balanced Force Reduction began in Vienna on January 31, 1973, and a Conference on the Mutual Reduction of Forces and Armaments and Associated Measures in Central Europe opened in that city on October 30, 1973.]

(42) Ministerial Session of the North Atlantic Council, Brussels, December 9-10, 1971: Final Communiqué.[105]

(Complete Text)

The North Atlantic Council met in Ministerial Session in Brussels on 9th and 10th December, 1971. Foreign and Defence Ministers were present.

2. Ministers stressed that their governments would continue to pursue their long-standing objectives of achieving, through a genuine relaxation of tensions, a just and lasting peace and stability in Europe. They recalled that since the creation of the Alliance over twenty years

---

104 *Documents on Disarmament, 1971*, pp. 809-11.
105 *Bulletin*, Jan. 3, 1972, pp. 1-5.

ago the treaty area has been free of armed conflict and that under existing international conditions the North Atlantic Treaty remains indispensable for the security of member States.

3. Ministers examined the international situation and expressed their deep concern over the tragic events in Southern Asia.[106] It is their fervent hope that hostilities between India and Pakistan will give way to an early and peaceful solution of all aspects of the conflict.

4. Turning to developments in and around Europe, including the Mediterranean, Ministers reviewed the status of the various initiatives undertaken or supported by the Allies and assessed the results of the numerous bilateral contacts between the Allies and other European states.

5. Ministers noted the effects which continuing difficulties in trade and monetary policy could have, among other things, on the state of the Alliance. They were encouraged by the various efforts underway in other fora to remedy these difficulties in the economic sphere.[107] The Ministers decided to keep this matter under continuing review.

6. Ministers took note with satisfaction of the signature, on 3rd September, 1971, of the Quadripartite Agreement on Berlin.[108] They also noted that the German arrangements to implement and supplement the Quadripartite Agreement now appear to be nearing completion,[109] and that, once these arrangements have been concluded, the Governments of France, the United Kingdom and the United States would be prepared to sign forthwith the final Quadripartite Protocol which would bring the complete Berlin Agreement into effect. Ministers expressed the hope that this would soon be achieved.

7. Ministers viewed this emerging Agreement as an important and encouraging development. Once completed and in effect, the Agreement should bring about practical improvements, while maintaining the Quadripartite status of Berlin and the rights and responsibilities of France, the United Kingdom, the United States and the Soviet Union with regard to Berlin and Germany as a whole. Specifically, Ministers noted that movement of civilian persons and goods between the Federal Republic of Germany and the Western Sectors of Berlin will then be unimpeded, and that the residents of the Western Sectors will be able to visit East Berlin and the GDR [German Democratic Republic]. Ministers also welcomed the assurance in the Quadripartite Agreement that the ties between the Federal Republic of Germany and the Western Sectors of Berlin will be maintained and developed.

8. Ministers considered that achievement of the Berlin Agreement would also demonstrate that, with a constructive attitude on all sides, it

---

[106] Cf. Documents 56-64.
[107] Documents 145-48.
[108] Document 39.
[109] Cf. notes 85 and 87 above.

should be possible to reach reasonable solutions between the Federal Republic of Germany and the German Democratic Republic which take into account the special situation in Germany.[110] Ministers took the view that this example would encourage progress on other problems in Europe.

9. Ministers recalled that at their meeting in Lisbon they declared their readiness to undertake multilateral conversations intended to lead to a Conference on Security and Co-operation in Europe as soon as the negotiations on Berlin had reached a successful conclusion.[111] In the light of the encouraging developments referred to above they affirmed their readiness to initiate such conversations on this basis as soon as possible.

10. In this perspective, they propose to intensify their preparations and their bilateral contacts with other interested parties.

11. Ministers also took note of the invitation of the Finnish Government to the effect that heads of mission of the countries concerned accredited in Helsinki should undertake multilateral conversations. They stated that their Governments appreciated this initiative and that they will keep in touch with the Finnish Government in order to consult on this matter.

12. Ministers considered that a Conference on Security and Co-operation in Europe should not serve to perpetuate the post-war division of Europe but rather should contribute to reconciliation and co-operation between the participating states by initiating a process of reducing the barriers that still exist. Therefore, Ministers reaffirmed that the Conference should address in a concrete manner the underlying causes of tension in Europe and the basic principles which should govern relations among states irrespective of political and social systems.

13. Ministers took note of the report of the Council in Permanent Session concerning a Conference on Security and Co-operation in Europe. This report examined four areas of discussion at such a conference: (A) Questions of Security, including Principles Governing Relations between States and certain military aspects of security; (B) Freer Movement of People, Information and Ideas, and Cultural Relations; (C) Co-operation in the Fields of Economics, Applied Science and Technology, and Pure Science; and (D) Co-operation to Improve the Human Environment. Ministers requested the Council in Permanent Session to continue these studies with a view to facilitating a constructive discussion of these subjects at the negotiations.

14. Ministers representing countries which participate in the NATO

---

[110] A Treaty on the Bases of Relations Between the Federal Republic of Germany and the German Democratic Republic was signed in East Berlin Dec. 21, 1972, and entered into force June 20-21, 1973.
[111] Document 37, para. 9.

integrated defence programme reaffirmed their long-standing belief that a mutual and balanced reduction of forces in Central Europe which preserves the legitimate security interests of all concerned would maintain security and enhance stability in Europe, make an important contribution to the easing of tension and improve East-West relations generally.

15. These Ministers reviewed the developments with respect to mutual and balanced force reductions since their last meeting in Lisbon.[112] They reaffirmed the decisions taken at the meeting of Deputy Foreign Ministers and High Officials on 5th and 6th October, 1971, to propose exploratory talks with the Soviet Government and other interested governments and to charge Mr. [Manlio] Brosio with this mission on the basis of a substantive mandate.[113] They expressed their thanks to Mr. Brosio for accepting.

16. These Ministers noted with regret that the Soviet Government has so far failed to respond to the Allied initiative in this important area of East-West relations in which that Government had earlier expressed an interest. Noting statements by Soviet leaders to the effect that they hoped East-West talks on force reductions in Europe would begin as soon as possible, these Ministers hope that Mr. Brosio will soon be able to go to Moscow. The interested Allied Governments continue to believe that prior explorations of this question are essential in preparation for eventual multilateral negotiations.

17. These Ministers emphasized the importance they attach to measures which would reduce the dangers of military confrontation and thus enhance security in Europe. They noted that a Conference on Security and Co-operation in Europe should deal with these aspects in a suitable manner.

18. Ministers noted a report on further studies conducted within NATO on mutual and balanced force reductions since the Lisbon Meeting. They instructed the Permanent Representatives to continue this work.

19. Ministers welcomed the fact that the negotiations between the US and USSR on strategic arms limitations have resulted in concrete agreements to reduce the risk of accidental nuclear war and to improve communication arrangements between the two governments.[114] Satisfaction was expressed for the close Alliance consultation which has been conducted throughout the course of the Strategic Arms Limitations talks. Ministers expressed the hope that these negotiations will soon lead to agreements which would curb the competition in strategic arms and strengthen international peace and security.[115]

112 Document 37.
113 Document 40.
114 Documents 26-28.
115 Cf. Chapter II at note 123.

20. Ministers reaffirmed their determination to promote progress in disarmament and arms control and reviewed recent developments in these fields. They expressed satisfaction at the measures envisaged to prohibit the development, production and stockpiling of bacteriological (biological) and toxin weapons and their destruction.[116] They hoped that all States will adopt similar measures. Ministers also expressed the hope that headway could be made towards reaching an agreement on the controlled prohibition of chemical weapons. Ministers representing countries which participate in the NATO integrated defence programme noted with interest the efforts being undertaken to find effective means for the verification of an eventual agreement on a comprehensive test ban.

21. Ministers took note of a report on the situation in the Mediterranean prepared on their instructions by the Council in Permanent Session. They reaffirmed their concern about the course of events in this area, while expressing their hope that a peaceful solution would be found in the Eastern Mediterranean.[117] In the light of the conclusions of the report before them, they instructed the Council in Permanent Session to continue consultations on this subject and to follow the evolution of the various aspects of the situation in order to report thereon at their next meeting.

22. Ministers were pleased by the new achievements of the Committee on the Challenges of Modern Society (CCMS) in its studies, especially in the fields of air and water pollution, and by the initiation of a project on the application of modern technology to health care.

23. The Spring Ministerial Meeting of the Council will be held in Bonn on 30th and 31st May, 1972.[118]

24. Ministers requested the Foreign Minister of Belgium [Pierre Harmel] to transmit the text of the preceding paragraphs on their behalf through diplomatic channels to all other interested parties, including neutral and non-aligned governments.

25. Ministers of the countries participating in NATO's integrated defence programme met as the Defence Planning Committee.

26. In the light of the considerations outlined in the preceding paragraphs, they emphasised that NATO's efforts to achieve sufficient defence capabilities and the striving for détente are not incompatible but

---

[116] Cf. Documents 17-19.

[117] For developments in the Arab–Israeli conflict cf. Documents 48-54. Since the Lisbon meeting, NATO's strategic position in the Mediterranean had been impaired to some extent as the result of political changes in Malta, where a new government headed by Prime Minister Dom Mintoff had insisted upon the removal of NATO's Naval Headquarters for Southern Europe; denounced Malta's 1964 defense agreement with the United Kingdom; and forbidden the use of its naval facilities by the U.S. Sixth Fleet. These actions were thought to raise a possibility that naval facilities in Malta might in future be granted to the Soviet Union.

[118] Communiqué in *A.F.R., 1972*, no. 24.

complementary, and that sufficient and credible defence is a necessary corollary to realistic negotiations on security and co-operation in Europe. In the same context and as a fundamental principle, these Ministers reaffirmed the well-known position of the Alliance that its overall military capability should not be reduced except as part of a pattern of mutual force reductions balanced in scope and timing.

27. These Ministers discussed mutual and balanced force reductions (MBFR) and reaffirmed their intent to continue their close involvement in the development of common allied positions.

28. They noted the growth of Soviet military efforts in recent years and the indications that the Soviet Union continues to strengthen both its strategic nuclear and its conventional forces, especially naval forces. They therefore agreed on the need for continued and systematic improvement of NATO's conventional forces and for the maintenance of adequate and modern tactical and strategic nuclear forces in order to ensure that the deterrent remains effective at all levels, and in order to avoid weakening the basis of NATO's search for détente.

29. They discussed a follow-up report to the Alliance Defence Study for the Seventies (the AD 70 Study).[119] They welcomed the progress being made by members in improving Alliance defences. In particular they noted with satisfaction the further specific and important efforts announced on 7th December by those European member countries which participated in the European Defence Improvement Programme,[120] and recognised the emphasis which these European member countries are placing on modernising the equipment of their forces, land, sea and air, along AD 70 lines. They also welcomed the substantial improvements to their conventional forces planned by the United States, and they noted with satisfaction the enhanced United States contribution to NATO's strategic deterrent which will result from the deployment of the POSEIDON weapon system. They heard with appreciation the reaffirmation by the United States Secretary of Defense [Melvin R. Laird] that, given a similar approach by the other Allies, the United States would maintain and improve their own forces in Europe and would not reduce them except in the context of reciprocal East-West action.

30. They endorsed the priority areas which were proposed to them for the further implementation of the AD 70 recommendations. Within these areas they identified for early action certain fields such as additional antitank weapons and modern tanks; advanced electronic equipment for certain combat aircraft; improved all-weather strike, attack and reconnaissance air forces; improved air defences and aircraft protection; better maritime surveillance and anti-submarine forces; more maritime patrol aircraft and seaborne missile systems; the replace-

[119] *Documents, 1970*, 99-103.
[120] *NATO Review*, Jan.–Feb. 1972, pp. 27-29.

ment of over-age ships; the strengthening and modernisation of local and reinforcement forces on the Northern and South-Eastern Flanks; and larger ammunition stocks for land and air forces.

31. They recognised the global nature of the Soviet maritime capability, and in particular the deployments and activities of the Soviet fleets in the Atlantic and in the Mediterranean. In their discussion they reaffirmed the need for appropriate Allied measures, and reviewed progress.

32. They noted the force commitments undertaken by member nations for the year 1972 and they adopted a five-year NATO Force Plan for the period 1972-1976, including many AD 70 impelementation measures.

33. They concluded that the aim within NATO should be to allocate to defence purposes, where this is within the economic capability of countries, a stable and possibly larger proportion of their growing national wealth, in order to maintain an adequate deterrent and defensive capability.

34. The Defence Ministers comprising the Nuclear Defence Affairs Committee (Belgium, Canada, Denmark, Germany, Greece, Italy, the Netherlands, Norway, Portugal, Turkey, the United Kingdom and the United States) also convened to examine reports on the activity of the Nuclear Planning Group during the past year and on its projected work.

35. The next Ministerial meeting of the Defence Planning Committee will be held in the Spring of 1972.[121]

G. Presidential Meetings with Allied Leaders, December 1971.

[President Nixon's intention to preface his 1972 visits to China and the U.S.S.R. by a series of meetings with leaders of allied and friendly countries was announced in the last week of November 1971.[122] These meetings were expected to provide an opportunity for review of both international and bilateral problems; in addition, the Azores meeting with French President Pompidou was to bring with it a resolution of important differences in the field of international trade and monetary policy, thus paving the way for the general realignment of exchange rates that took place later in December (Document 150). In addition to the meetings with President Pompidou (Document 43), Prime Minister Heath (Document 44), and Chancellor Brandt (Document 45), President Nixon met with Prime Minister Pierre Elliott Trudeau of Canada in Washington on December 6 and with Prime Minister Marcello

---

[121] The Defense Planning Committee met in Brussels May 24, 1972; text of communiqué in *NATO Review*, May–June 1972, pp. 28-29.

[122] *Presidential Documents*, Nov. 29, 1971, pp. 1561, 1563, and 1565; same, Dec. 6, 1971, pp. 1580 and 1582.

Caetano of Portugal in the Azores on December 13.[123] The series was completed by a meeting with Prime Minister Eisaku Sato of Japan at San Clemente, California, on January 6-7, 1972.[124]]

(43) Meeting with President Georges Pompidou of France in the Azores, December 13-14, 1971: Joint Statement.[125]

(Complete Text)

President Nixon and President Pompidou reached a broad area of agreement on measures necessary to achieve a settlement at the earliest possible date of the immediate problems of the international monetary system. In cooperation with other nations concerned, they agreed to work toward a prompt realignment of exchange rates through a devaluation of the dollar and revaluation of some other currencies. This realignment could, in their view, under present circumstances, be accompanied by broader permissible margins of fluctuation around the newly established exchange rates.

Aware of the interest of measures involving trade for a lasting equilibrium of the balance of payments, President Pompidou confirmed that France, together with the governments of the other countries which are members of the European Economic Community, was preparing the mandate which would permit the imminent opening of negotiations with the United States in order to settle the short-term problems currently pending and to establish the agenda for the examination of fundamental questions in the area of trade.

President Nixon underscored the contribution that vigorous implementation by the United States of measures to restore domestic wage-price stability and productivity would make toward international equilibrium and the defense of the new dollar exchange rate.

The Presidents agreed that discussion should be undertaken promptly in appropriate forums to resolve fundamental and interrelated issues of monetary reform.[126]

---

[123] No communiqué was issued on the Trudeau meeting, which was briefly characterized in Rogers Report, 1971, p. 142. On the meeting with Prime Minister Caetano see *Public Papers, 1971*, pp. 1184-89.

[124] *A.F.R., 1972*, no. 62; cf. Chapter VI at note 117. The President also met on Dec. 7, 1971, with President Emílio Garrastazú Médici of Brazil (cf. Chapter VIII at note 101).

[125] *Public Papers, 1971*, pp. 1190-91. The two Presidents met at Angra do Heroísmo, Terceira Island, as guests of the Portuguese Government. In informal remarks at the conclusion of the meeting (same, pp. 1189-90), both Presidents stated that the talks had dealt with a wide range of international and bilateral issues. On the economic significance of the meeting see further Document 149.

[126] Cf. Document 150.

(44) Meeting with Prime Minister Edward Heath of the United King-
dom in Bermuda, December 20-21, 1971: Joint Statement. [127]

(Complete Text)

The President of the United States, the Honorable Richard M. Nixon, and the Prime Minister of the United Kingdom, the Right Honorable Edward Heath, meeting in Government House, Bermuda, on 20 and 21 December 1971, discussed the world situation in all its aspects. They agreed that the period which lies ahead is likely to be one of rapid change, which will offer the free world both opportunity and challenge on an unprecedented scale. This will call for the maintenance of the closest possible degree of understanding and unity of purpose not only between their two countries but also between themselves and their allies and partners. In view of the significance of the natural relationship between the United Kingdom and the United States they resolved to maintain their close and continuing consultation at all levels in their approach to world problems.

They recognized that the fulfillment of their objectives will be promoted by the United Kingdom's forthcoming accession to the European Economic Communities,[128] which will reinforce the strength of the Atlantic Alliance. This Alliance is, and must remain, the cornerstone of the defence of the free world. The President and the Prime Minister agreed that there is no inconsistency between a resolute and determined adherence to the principles which inspire the Alliance and the pursuit of that relaxation of international tension which is necessary to satisfy the natural aspirations of mankind to live in peace and prosperity.

Not the least of the problems confronting the free world is the need to promote conditions for more liberal commercial exchanges. The President and the Prime Minister welcomed the realignment of exchange rates and accompanying measures agreed in Washington on 17 and 18 December[129] and agreed upon the necessity for their two countries, in consultation with their international partners, to intensify their efforts to promote a reformed international monetary system. They noted the importance of reviewing international commercial relations in order to reduce barriers to trade between the major trading countries of the world.

In the same spirit they agreed that one of the most essential tasks of statesmanship today is to lift the sights beyond the problems of immediate urgency to those major political and economic issues, which in the

---

[127] *Presidential Documents*, Dec. 27, 1971, p. 1700. For other developments in connection with the Bermuda meeting cf. Documents 151b and 155.
[128] Cf. note 72 to Document 9.
[129] Cf. Document 150.

longer term will determine the shape of the world in which we all live. They agreed that they would direct all their consultations to this end.

(45) Meeting with Chancellor Willy Brandt of the Federal Republic of Germany, Key Biscayne, Florida, December 28-29, 1971: Joint Statement. [130]

(Complete Text)

The President of the United States and the Chancellor of the Federal Republic of Germany, meeting in Key Biscayne, Florida, on December 28 and 29, reviewed the international developments that have occurred since their last meeting. They agreed that the close partnership between America and Europe has successfully withstood difficult tests and has demonstrated its importance for their common future.

Cooperation on monetary and trade policy, one of the most important conditions and guarantees for close American-European relations, has been successfully adapted to new conditions and now holds out favorable prospects for further development. [131]

The future shape of economic relations between America and Western Europe will be based on close cooperation to be arranged between the United States and the enlarged European community.

Common defense through NATO is an essential component of both U.S. and German policy. In this spirit the progress of joint efforts on the part of the European allies plays a major role.

The President and the Chancellor were in agreement that all members of the alliance must adequately share the defense burden in order to ensure their common security.

The President reaffirmed that no decisions affecting the Alliance will be taken without full consultation with its allies.

The President reiterated that the American commitments in Europe will remain unchanged and that, in particular, no reductions in the American troops stationed in Europe will be made. [132]

Preparations for early East-West talks on Mutual and Balanced Force Reductions should be fully coordinated within the Alliance. Agreed criteria for such reductions must insure that the Alliance's defense capability remains unimpaired. The U.S. will not negotiate its troop levels in Europe on a bilateral basis.

The President and the Chancellor agreed that a conference on European security and cooperation needs to be carefully prepared. In preparing common positions for CSCE and MBFR the United States and

[130] *Presidential Documents*, Jan. 3, 1972, p. 8.
[131] Cf. Document 150.
[132] Cf. Document 42, para. 29.

Western Europe will harmonize their views in the interest of improving East-West relations.

The President and the Chancellor welcomed the solidarity and close coordination between the three Western Powers, the Federal Republic of Germany and the other NATO allies throughout the negotiation of the Quadripartite Agreement on Berlin[133] as well as the implementing agreement between the Federal Republic of Germany and the GDR [German Democratic Republic],[134] which are important elements of the common Western policy.

H. Relations With Greece and Portugal.

[A controversial feature of American foreign policy in 1971 was the warm relationship maintained by the United States with countries whose political regimes and foreign and domestic policies had been widely condemned as undemocratic and/or "colonialist," but whose strategic importance was nevertheless considered in official Washington to outweigh any political shortcomings. Two members of the North Atlantic alliance, Greece and Portugal, were conspicuous representatives of this group.]

1. Greece.

[The reasons for U.S. support of the military-backed regime headed by Prime Minister George Papadopoulos were set forth in some detail during 1971 in State Department testimony before an interested congressional committee (Document 46).]

(46) United States Policy Toward Greece: Statement by Rodger P. Davies, Deputy Assistant Secretary of State for Near Eastern and South Asian Affairs, Before the Subcommittee on Europe of the House Committee on Foreign Affairs, July 12, 1971.[135]

(Complete Text)

I welcome the opportunity to appear before this subcommittee to discuss the administration's policy on Greece. My responsibilities as

---

[133] Documents 38-39.

[134] Cf. notes 85 and 87 above.

[135] *Bulletin*, Aug. 9, 1971, pp. 161-63. Designated as U.S. Ambassador to Cyprus on Apr. 22, 1974, Ambassador Davies was fatally shot in the course of an anti-American demonstration outside the U.S. Embassy in Nicosia on Aug. 19, 1974.

Deputy Assistant Secretary of State for Near Eastern and South Asian Affairs include Greek, Turkish, Iranian, and Cypriot affairs.

The military coup which brought the present Greek Government into power in 1967[136] faced us at once with a problem in our relations with Greece which has persisted to the present day: how to support our mutual interest in free-world security in the Eastern Mediterranean while encouraging a return to representative government which we believe is requisite for Greece's longer term stability and progress. One of our first responses was to suspend temporarily certain deliveries of heavy equipment in our military assistance program, as a practical demonstration of our concern over the military takeover. We could not, of course, lose sight of the fact that Greece is an important NATO ally and has consistently and loyally honored its treaty obligations and its bilateral agreements with the United States through a number of changes of government. Political differences aside, the United States and Greece have mutual security interests that cannot be lightly dismissed. Facilities afforded the United States are important for the Western position in the Eastern Mediterranean. At the same time, we clearly recognized that the interests of the free world and of the Greek people would best be served if Greece were returned to a more normal political order. To help achieve this goal, we felt that our influence in Greece could be used in the most constructive way if we maintained our working relationship with the regime and urged it through continuous quiet exchanges to fulfill its commitment to return the country to democratic norms.

From the beginning, the new Greek regime indicated that it considered its authoritarian rule a temporary expedient, "a parenthesis in the political life of Greece." In accordance with its avowed purpose, the Government took a number of steps toward the establishment of institutions necessary to the foundation of a democratic political order. In 1968 a new constitution was drafted and submitted to plebiscite, and the regime began in the following year to prepare the necessary institutional laws to its implementation. Many persons detained for political reasons were released, and restrictions on the travel of former politicians were relaxed. Press censorship was lifted, although opposition papers remained under the Damocles sword of severe press laws. Martial law was restricted in early 1970 to offenses involving security of the state. Thus through most of 1970 it appeared that a trend toward democratic norms had been established.

In the meantime, it became evident that our partial suspension of military assistance was weakening Greece's ability to meet its NATO obligations and was weakening the credibility of NATO cohesion at a time when the interests of alliance members faced new challenges. This erosion of Greece's position in the critical area of NATO's southern

[136] Cf. *The United States in World Affairs, 1967*, pp. 214-17.

flank came sharply to our attention at the time of the Soviet invasion of Czechoslovakia in 1968, when we found it necessary to deliver to Greece some of the heavy equipment previously embargoed. Although some observers felt that the embargo on military equipment could be used to press the Greek regime to move more rapidly toward constitutional rule, we concluded after careful study that any progress being made was quite independent of our assistance policy. Indeed, we have come to recognize as a general proposition that withholding military or economic assistance is an ineffective tactic in persuading foreign governments to move in directions we consider desirable. When pressures of this kind by this and other governments have been attempted, they have generally not succeeded. Responsible Greek opposition leaders have told us that as Greeks they would resent this form of pressure as would most of the Greek people. It was therefore wise, as former Greek Foreign Minister Evangelos Averoff has pointed out on several occasions, to keep the security aspects of our relationship with Greece separate from the political.

We have shared our views with our other NATO allies, and we were fully aware of their attitudes toward the resumption of our military assistance program. The majority agreed with our view that we should not withhold indefinitely the heavy equipment necessary to allow Greece to meet its NATO commitments, although several countries felt that we should continue the embargo for political reasons. Our NATO allies were informed on an individual basis before our decision to lift the embargo was made public. We also consulted with responsible Greek political leaders outside the present regime, who agreed that military assistance was necessary for the defense of Greece and to support Greece's role in NATO regardless of the nature of the regime.

When we decided after lengthy review to resume normal military shipments,[137] we did so for security reasons alone, and we have made it clear to the Greek regime that our assistance does not imply our support for or endorsement of the form of government now existing in Greece. We have continued to urge the regime at every opportunity to keep moving toward democratic norms. We believe that our ability to influence the outlook of the Government has been enhanced by the resumption of a normal military assistance relationship, which helps to keep open the channels of communication between the two governments.

In December 1970 we were disappointed to learn that the Greek Prime Minister [George Papadopoulos] intended to take no further political steps toward elections during the coming year. Our reaction to this announcement was reflected in statements made by the Secretary

---

[137] Department of State announcement, Sept. 22, 1970, in *Documents, 1970*, pp. 114-15.

of State and by Assistant Secretary Joseph Sisco early this year.[138] In his report on "United States Foreign Policy, 1969-70," the Secretary commented[139] that:

> We believe some progress has been made, but we have been disappointed that more has not been done by the Government of Greece to move toward restoration of representative democracy.

Even though there have been no political steps this year that can be identified as leading to early elections, the situation has by no means been stagnant. There have been some moves since the first of the year in the direction of restoring civil liberties to the Greek people. Detention camps which held some 2,000 persons at the beginning of 1970 were closed in April this year, and the number held without trial was reduced to about 75 persons restricted to remote villages in "administrative exile" status. Martial law was further restricted and is now applicable to only a few specific articles of the Greek penal code. The number of persons tried by courts-martial has been substantially reduced.

On the political side, the Greek regime has set up an advisory committee on legislation, and the Prime Minister has entered into a series of dialogues with former politicians. Although we would not wish to place too much emphasis on these activities, some observers believe the regime may be trying to lay the groundwork for the formation of political parties and for eventual elections.

Our recognition of these improvements in the overall situation does not mean that we are satisfied with the progress being made by the regime. The continuation of martial law, however limited, constitutes an element of intimidation which we believe to be incompatible with the exercise of individual freedoms. We continue to urge the Greek regime to lift the remnants of martial law and to review on humanitarian grounds the cases of some 350-500 persons who were convicted of specific politically motivated offenses and who are now serving sentences some of which seem unduly harsh. Until martial law and other nonjudicial restraints on civil liberties have been removed and until the regime has demonstrated in a convincing way its intention to move toward elections, we must continue to say with regret that we are disappointed with the progress toward the regime's stated objective of full implementation of the 1968 Constitution.

I must emphasize again, however, that the influence the United States Government has in Greece can only be used constructively if it is used with restraint. We agree with the views of a responsible former Greek

---

[138] *Bulletin*, Mar. 29, 1971, p. 447; same, Mar. 8, 1971, p. 295.
[139] Rogers Report, 1969-70, p. 140.

politician who pointed out that public attacks and pressure on the Greek regime are a mistake and that our leverage can best be exercised through continual exercise of quiet persuasion.

While the exercise of our influence in Greece is based on the legitimate interests of the United States and others of Greece's allies, there are practical limits to what we can do.

Thus we have let the Greek regime know in no uncertain terms where we stand on the issues of civil liberties and parliamentary rule, but we have carefully avoided any direct interference in the domestic politics of Greece. Until the Greek people have completed the task of reshaping their governmental institutions, one of the primary goals of our policy in Greece will be the restitution of personal liberties and the reestablishment of the democratic framework within which the people of Greece will be able to decide their own fate.

Our basic policy toward Greece has been to protect our important security interests there and in the broader area of the Eastern Mediterranean and Near East while preserving a working relationship with the regime through which we can exert our influence to encourage a return to representative government.

2. Portugal.

[American friendship for the Portuguese regime of Prime Minister Marcello Caetano, who had been appointed in September 1968 to succeed the late Antonio de Oliveira Salazar, was usually ascribed in a preeminent degree to the desire to ensure continued American use of the Lajes air base in the Azores. A controversial set of agreements that permitted U.S. use of the base for a further 26 months and, in addition, provided major financial aid for Portugal's internal development, was announced December 29, 1971 (Document 47), at the time of the NATO Council meeting and shortly before President Nixon's meeting with Prime Minister Caetano.[140]]

(47) Agreements with Portugal: Department of State Announcement, December 9, 1971.[141]

(Complete Text)

Secretary Rogers and the Minister of Foreign Affairs of Portugal, Rui Patricio, exchanged notes at Brussels on December 9 extending until

---

[140] Cf. note 123 above.
[141] Department of State Press Release 290; text in *Bulletin*, Jan. 3, 1972, pp. 7-8. For comments see Chapter VII at notes 108-9; also *A.F.R., 1972*, no. 21.

February 4, 1974, the arrangement permitting peacetime stationing of U.S. forces at Lajes Field in the Azores.[142]

Since the expiration of the time period of the agreement in 1962, United States forces have been authorized by the Government of Portugal to continue to use the facilities until negotiations could be satisfactorily concluded.

The U.S. Government agreed to the current round of negotiations on February 3, 1969, and the exchange of notes just concluded extends our rights for 5 years from that date without any rental provision.

During the Foreign Minister's visit to Washington in November 1970, negotiations were initiated concerning economic assistance to aid the Portuguese Government in implementing various social and economic development programs.

The United States has agreed[143] to provide a 2-year Public Law 480 program in the amount of $15 million per year. Also, the Export-Import Bank of the United States has declared its willingness to provide, in accordance with its usual loan criteria and practices, the financing for U.S. goods and services for development projects in Portugal, including airport construction, railway modernization, bridge-building, electric power generation, mechanization of agriculture, harbor construction and town planning, and the supplying of equipment for schools and hospitals, valued at approximately $400 million. In direct aid, we are providing one oceanographic vessel on a no-cost lease basis, a grant of $1 million for educational development projects selected by the Government of Portugal, and nonmilitary excess equipment in the amount of $5 million, which amount is to be considered illustrative and not a maximum ceiling so that it may be exceeded if deemed mutually desirable.

[142] Text appears in TIAS 7254; 22 UST 2106; Secretary Rogers' note appears also in *Bulletin*, Jan. 3, 1972, p. 8.
[143] Letters from Secretary Rogers to Foreign Minister Patricio, Dec. 9, 1971, in *Bulletin*, Jan. 3, 1972, pp. 8-9. The Public Law 480 program involved food aid under the terms of the Agricultural Trade Development and Assistance Act of 1954 (Public Law 480, 83d Cong.) as amended.

IV
AMERICAN POLICY IN ASIA:
THE MIDDLE EAST
AND SOUTHERN ASIA

[The aftermath of one war and the outbreak of another were the chief preoccupations of U.S. policy in the Middle East and Southern Asia in 1971. Four years after the Arab-Israeli "June War" of 1967, the situation in the Middle East continued to exhibit the tensions and distortions brought about by Israel's military victory, the fundamental incompatibility of the declared objectives of victors and vanquished, and the far-reaching involvement of the United States and the Soviet Union as friends and sponsors of the respective antagonists. In Southern Asia, meanwhile, the precarious peace of the India-Pakistan Subcontinent was undermined and ultimately destroyed by a secessionist movement in East Pakistan that led before the year's end to a disastrous war between Pakistan and India and the dismemberment of Pakistan together with emergence of the new state of Bangladesh.

In neither of these regional conflicts did U.S. policy accumulate many laurels. In the Middle East, the most American spokesmen could claim was that their efforts continued to play a part in discouraging a renewed resort to arms by either Arabs or Israelis. In the Subcontinent, the United States' declared neutrality was twisted in a pro-Pakistani direction that resulted in strained relations with India and the U.S.S.R., a transitory diplomatic alignment with the People's Republic of China, and widespread bafflement and discontent at home and abroad.

The following documentary selection attempts to illuminate the principal developments of 1971 in both the Middle Eastern and South Asian theaters. In addition to the conflicts between the Arab states and Israel (Documents 48-54) and between India and Pakistan (Documents 56-64), the chapter offers limited coverage of the progress of events in the so-called CENTO or Central Treaty Organization area (Document 55) and of the growing strategic and political importance of the Indian Ocean region (Documents 65-66).]

A. The Arab–Israeli Conflict.

[The importance the United States attached to Middle Eastern developments, both in themselves and as a test of Soviet intentions, was abundantly emphasized in President Nixon's "State of the World" report for 1971[1] and his accompanying broadcast to the nation (Document 1). This was one area in which U.S. attempts to move relations with the U.S.S.R. "from confrontation to negotiation" had thus far yielded little definite result. The catastrophic possibilities inherent in the state of "no war, no peace" that had prevailed in the Middle East since the June War of 1967 were felt in Washington to be gravely aggravated by Moscow's encouragement of the Arab desire for revenge, its shipments of modern armaments to the United Arab Republic (U.A.R.) and Syria, and its operational involvement in the U.A.R. air defense system.

While determined both to ensure the survival of Israel and to furnish it sufficient armaments to maintain a balance of power in the area,[2] the United States continued to urge upon the U.S.S.R. the desirability of joint action to limit arms shipments to Middle Eastern countries in the interests of curbing the regional arms race. More central to its diplomatic efforts during 1971, however, was a continuation of its attempt to encourage movement toward an Arab–Israeli peace settlement consistent with the principles laid down by the United Nations. In addition to supporting the good offices mission of U.N. Special Representative Gunnar V. Jarring (Documents 48-49), the United States devoted special effort during 1971 to trying to promote an agreement between the U.A.R. and Israel that would permit the reopening of the Suez Canal as an initial step toward a wider peace settlement (Documents 50-52).]

1. Implementation of Security Council Resolution 242 (1967).

[International efforts to encourage agreement on terms of a permanent settlement among the belligerents of the 1967 war had developed throughout the past three years within the framework of the U.N. Security Council's basic Resolution 242 of November 22, 1967. That resolution, in addition to conferring a consultative mandate on a Special Representative of the Secretary-General (Ambassador Jarring), had emphasized "the inadmissibility of the acquisition of territory by war" and the obligation of U.N. member states to live up to their Charter commitments. In particular, the resolution affirmed that the establishment of a just and lasting peace in the area should include the

[1] Nixon Report, 1971, pp. 121-34; cf. also Document 11.
[2] Cf. below at note 21.

application of two cardinal principles: "(i) Withdrawal of Israeli armed forces from territories occupied in the recent conflict"; and "(ii) Termination of all claims or states of belligerency and respect for and acknowledgment of the sovereignty, territorial integrity and political independence of every State in the area and their right to live in peace within secure and recognized boundaries free from threats or acts of force." In addition, the resolution had affirmed the necessity for "guaranteeing freedom of navigation through international waterways in the area," "achieving a just settlement of the refugee problem," and "guaranteeing the territorial inviolability and political independence of every State in the area, through measures including the establishment of demilitarized zones."[3]

Although this resolution had been accepted in principle by Israel, Jordan, Lebanon, and the United Arab Republic, it had remained subject to widely varying interpretations. The Arab states, vigorously supported by the U.S.S.R., had insisted upon the need for a commitment by Israel to evacuate all territories occupied in 1967. The United States, too, had taken the position that "any changes in the preexisting lines should be confined to insubstantial alterations required for mutual security," and that "troops must be withdrawn as the resolution provides."[4] Israel, however, had insisted not only that it would not withdraw to the 1967 armistice lines, but that the whole question of withdrawals must await negotiation of and agreement upon "secure and recognized boundaries."

While progress toward a peace settlement remained blocked by these differences, the danger of a resumption of full-scale hostilities had been at least temporarily averted by the conclusion on August 7, 1970, largely on the initiative of the United States,[5] of a cease-fire and standstill agreement between Israel and the U.A.R. as well as the reaffirmation of an existing cease-fire agreement between Israel and Jordan. Indirect peace talks between Israel and the U.A.R. and Jordan had been initiated under Ambassador Jarring's auspices in New York on August 20, 1970, but were interrupted soon afterward by the suspension of Israeli participation pending the removal of Soviet SAM-2 and SAM-3 ground-to-air missiles emplaced by the U.A.R. in the Suez Canal area in violation of the standstill agreement. The cease-fire, initially concluded for a period of 90 days, was renewed November 6, 1970, for a further 90-day period ending February 5, 1971; but U.A.R. President Anwar al-Sadat had given notice that there would be no further renewals in the absence of progress toward implementing Resolution 242. Despite the failure of the U.A.R. to remove the missiles, Israel decided on December 28, 1970, to resume its participation in the Jarring talks in ac-

---

3 *Documents, 1967*, pp. 169-70.
4 Address by Secretary of State Rogers, Dec. 9, 1969, in same, *1968-69*, p. 216.
5 Same, *1970*, pp. 131-35.

cordance with the basic principles already laid down by the Israeli Government.[6]

That the differences regarding the interpretation and application of Resolution 242 persisted without significant abatement is evident from the reports of U Thant, the U.N. Secretary-General, on the new phase of the Jarring talks that opened January 5, 1971 (Document 48). Although the cease-fire was subsequently extended for another 30 days and the U.A.R. for the first time expressed willingness to enter into a peace agreement with Israel provided certain conditions were met, the possibility of fruitful negotiations still appeared blocked by Israel's refusal to commit itself to withdraw to the prewar armistice lines.

Despite this political deadlock, military operations did not immediately resume even after the final expiration of the Israeli–U.A.R. cease-fire and standstill agreement on March 7, 1971. American views on various aspects of a possible settlement were outlined by Secretary of State Rogers in the course of a news conference on March 16, 1971 (Document 49).]

(48) Report on the Jarring Mission: Communications from the Secretary-General of the United Nations to the Security Council, February–March 1971.

(a) Report Dated February 1, 1971.[7]

(Complete Text)

1. On 4 January 1971, in submitting to the Security Council a report on the activities of Ambassador Jarring, my Special Representative to the Middle East,[8] I was able to note that it had been possible to arrange for the resumption of the discussions under his auspices with Israel, Jordan and the United Arab Republic for the purpose of reaching agreement on a just and lasting peace between them.

2. Ambassador Jarring resumed his discussions with the parties at Headquarters on 5 January 1971 and has pursued them actively. He has held a series of meetings with the representatives of Israel (including meetings with the Prime Minister [Golda Meir] and Foreign Minister [Abba Eban] during a brief visit to Israel made from 8 to 10 January 1971 at the request of that Government), of Jordan, and of the United Arab Republic. In addition, he held meetings with the representative of

---

[6] U.N. document S/10070, Jan. 4, 1971, in Security Council, *Official Records: 26th Year, Supplement for Jan., Feb. and Mar. 1971*, pp. 18-28.
[7] U.N. document S/10070/Add. 1, Feb. 1, 1971, in same, p. 28.
[8] Same as note 6.

Lebanon, which is also a State directly concerned with the Middle East settlement.

3. At an early stage in these meetings Israel presented to Ambassador Jarring, for transmission to the Governments concerned, papers containing its views on the "Essentials of Peace". Subsequently, the United Arab Republic and Jordan, having received the respective Israeli views, presented papers containing their own views concerning the implementation of the provisions of Security Council resolution 242 (1967). Papers containing the further reactions of the Governments of Israel and the United Arab Republic have now been received.

4. While recognizing that the resumed discussions are still at an early stage and that much further clarification is required, I find grounds for cautious optimism in the fact that the parties have resumed the talks through Ambassador Jarring in a serious manner and that there has been some progress in the definition of their positions. Furthermore, the parties, who have already indicated their willingness to carry out resolution 242 (1967), are now describing in greater detail their view of their obligations under that resolution. I take this opportunity to appeal to the parties to pursue their role in the discussions in a constructive manner, to co-operate with Ambassador Jarring with a view to the carrying out of resolution 242 (1967) and, in this very difficult and crucial stage of the discussions, to withhold fire, to exercise military restraint, and to maintain the quiet which has prevailed in the area since August 1970.

(b) Report Dated March 5, 1971. [9]

(Complete Text)

1. On 1 February 1971 I submitted to the Security Council a report [S/10070/Add.1] on the activities of Ambassador Jarring, my Special Representative to the Middle East, since the resumption on 5 January 1971 of the discussions under his auspices with the parties to the Middle East conflict for the purpose of reaching agreement on a just and lasting peace between them. In that report,[10] I found grounds for cautious optimism in the fact that there had been some progress in the definition of the position of the parties and I appealed to them to pursue their role in the discussions in a constructive manner, to co-

---

[9] U.N. document S/10070/Add. 2, Mar. 5, 1971, in same, pp. 28-30. The texts of the communications referred to in paras. 8, 9, and 11 are printed as annexes to a subsequent report by the Secretary-General (U.N. document S/10403, Nov. 30, 1971) which appears in Security Council, *Official Records: 26th Year, Supplement for Oct., Nov. and Dec. 1971*, pp. 54-60.

[10] Document 48a.

operate with Ambassador Jarring with a view to the carrying out of Security Council resolution 242 (1967) and, in that very difficult and crucial stage of the discussions, to withhold fire, to exercise military restraint and to maintain the quiet which had prevailed in the area since August 1970.

2. In response to that appeal, the Foreign Ministry of Israel, in a communiqué released in Jerusalem on 2 February, announced that Israel would preserve the cease-fire on a mutual basis; in a speech to the National Assembly on 4 February, the President of the United Arab Republic declared the decision of the United Arab Republic to refrain from opening fire for a period of thirty days ending on 7 March.

3. In pursuing his mandate to promote agreement between the parties, Ambassador Jarring, while sharing my cautious optimism that the parties were seriously defining their positions and wished to move forward to a permanent peace, noted with growing concern that each side was insisting that the other should make certain commitments before being ready to proceed to the stage of formulating the provisions of a final peace settlement.

4. On the Israeli side there was insistence that the United Arab Republic should give specific, direct and reciprocal commitments towards Israel that it would be ready to enter into a peace agreement with Israel and to make towards Israel the various undertakings referred to in paragraph 1 (ii) of Security Council resolution 242 (1967). When agreement was reached on those points, it would be possible to discuss others, including the refugee problem; such items as secure and recognized boundaries, withdrawal and additional arrangements for ensuring security should be discussed in due course.

5. The United Arab Republic continued to regard the Security Council resolution as containing provisions to be implemented by the parties and to express its readiness to carry out its obligations under the resolution in full, provided that Israel did likewise. However it held that Israel persisted in its refusal to implement the Security Council resolution, since it would not commit itself to withdraw from all Arab territories occupied in June 1967. Furthermore in the view of the United Arab Republic Israel had not committed itself to the implementation of the United Nations resolutions relevant to a just settlement to the refugee problem.

6. The papers received by Ambassador Jarring from Israel and Jordan relating to peace between these two countries showed a similar divergence of views. Israel stressed the importance of Jordan's giving an undertaking to enter into a peace agreement with it which would specify the direct and reciprocal obligations undertaken by each of them. Jordan emphasized the inadmissibility of the acquisition of territory by war and expressed the view that the essential first step towards peace lay in an Israeli commitment to evacuate all Arab territories.

7. Ambassador Jarring felt that at this stage of the talks he should make clear his views on what he believed to be the necessary steps to be taken in order to achieve a peaceful and accepted settlement in accordance with the provisions and principles of Security Council resolution 242 (1967), which the parties had agreed to carry out in all its parts. He reached the conclusion, which I shared, that the only possibility to break the imminent deadlock arising from the differing views of Israel and the United Arab Republic as to the priority to be given to commitments and undertakings—which seemed to him to be the real cause for the existing immobility in the talks—was for him to seek from each side the parallel and simultaneous commitments which seemed to be inevitable prerequisites of an eventual peace settlement between them. It should thereafter be possible to proceed at once to formulate the provisions and terms of a peace agreement not only for those topics covered by the commitments, but with equal priority for other topics, and in particular the refugee question.

8. In identical aide-mémoires handed to the representatives of the United Arab Republic and Israel on 8 February 1971 Ambassador Jarring requested those Governments to make to him certain prior commitments. Ambassador Jarring's initiative was on the basis that the commitments should be made simultaneously and reciprocally and subject to the eventual satisfactory determination of all other aspects of a peace settlement, including in particular a just settlement of the refugee problem. Israel would give a commitment to withdraw its forces from occupied United Arab Republic territory to the former international boundary between Egypt and the British Mandate of Palestine. The United Arab Republic would give a commitment to enter into a peace agreement with Israel and to make explicitly therein to Israel, on a reciprocal basis, various undertakings and acknowledgements arising directly or indirectly from paragraph 1 (ii) of Security Council resolution 242 (1967).

9. On 15 February, Ambassador Jarring received from the representative of the United Arab Republic an aide-mémoire in which it was indicated that the United Arab Republic would accept the specific commitments requested of it, as well as other commitments arising directly or indirectly from Security Council resolution 242 (1967). If Israel would give, likewise, commitments covering its own obligations under the Security Council resolution, including commitments for the withdrawal of its armed forces from Sinai and the Gaza Strip and for the achievement of a just settlement for the refugee problem in accordance with United Nations resolutions, the United Arab Republic would be ready to enter into a peace agreement with Israel. Finally the United Arab Republic expressed the view that a just and lasting peace could not be realized without the full and scrupulous implementation of Security Council resolution 242 (1967) and the withdrawal of the Israeli armed forces from all the territories occupied since 5 June 1967.

10. On 17 February, Ambassador Jarring informed the Israeli representative of the contents of the United Arab Republic reply to his aide-mémoire.

11. On 26 February, Ambassador Jarring received a paper from the representative of Israel, in which, without specific reference to the commitment which he had sought from that Government, Israel stated that it viewed favourably "the expression by the United Arab Republic of its readiness to enter into a peace agreement with Israel" and reiterated that it was prepared for meaningful negotiations on all subjects relevant to a peace agreement between the two countries. Israel gave details of the undertakings which in its opinion should be given by the two countries in such a peace agreement, which should be expressed in a binding treaty in accordance with normal international law and precedent. Israel considered that both parties having presented their basic positions should now pursue the negotiations in a detailed and concrete manner without prior conditions.

12. On the crucial question of withdrawal on which Ambassador Jarring had sought a commitment from Israel, the Israel position was that it would give an undertaking covering withdrawal of Israeli armed forces from "the Israeli-United Arab Republic cease-fire line" to the secure, recognized and agreed boundaries to be established in the peace agreement; Israel would not withdraw to the pre-5 June 1967 lines.

13. On 28 February, Ambassador Jarring informed the United Arab Republic representative of the contents of the Israeli paper.

14. Ambassador Jarring has been very active over the past month and some further progress has been made towards a peaceful solution of the Middle East question. The problems to be settled have been more clearly identified and on some there is general agreement. I wish moreover to note with satisfaction the positive reply given by the United Arab Republic to Ambassador Jarring's initiative. However, the Government of Israel has so far not responded to the request of Ambassador Jarring that it should give a commitment on withdrawal to the international boundary of the United Arab Republic.

15. While I still consider that the situation has considerable elements of promise, it is a matter for increasing concern that Ambassador Jarring's attempt to break the deadlock has not so far been successful. I appeal, therefore, to the Government of Israel to give further consideration to this question and to respond favourably to Ambassador Jarring's initiative.

16. To give time for further consideration and in the hope that the way forward may be reopened, I once more appeal to the parties to withhold fire, to exercise military restraint and to maintain the quiet which has prevailed in the area since August 1970.

(49) The Position of the United States: News Conference Statement by Secretary of State Rogers, March 16, 1971. [11]

(Excerpts)

Secretary Rogers: Thank you. Good morning, ladies and gentlemen Mr. Hightower [John Hightower, Associated Press].

Q. Mr. Secretary, will you assess for us where you think the United States and Israel and Egypt and the Soviet Union, the whole complex of powers involved in the Middle East peace search, stand at this point and particularly what contribution international guarantees involving the United States and the Soviet Union might make to a peace settlement?

A. Well, the United States is supporting the Jarring mission because we think that the best prospect for peace is to have the parties negotiate under procedures established by Ambassador Jarring.

At the moment, as you know, because you have read the answers that were given by Israel and Egypt to Ambassador Jarring,[12] there is what seems to be an impasse. We are convinced that that impasse can be overcome. We are going to do what we can to see that it is overcome, and we strongly support the continuation of Ambassador Jarring's mission.

Now, we are going to work behind the scenes; we are going to have discussions with all concerned about what we can do not only to get around this particular impasse but to make substantial progress in the talks.

As far as international guarantees are concerned, we have said that we are willing, as a nation, to play a responsible and appropriate role in a peacekeeping force. Now, we haven't attempted to dictate or lay down any particular ways that that might be done. Obviously a peacekeeping force would have to be supportive of an agreement, and that agreement has to be reached among the parties. On the other hand, the type of peacekeeping force that might be formulated would play an important part in the attitude of the parties when they look toward the final agreement. So, to that extent the two are parallel, and we would hope that the negotiations between the parties would continue under Ambas-

---

11 Department of State Press Release 54, Mar. 16, 1971; text from *Bulletin*, Apr. 5, 1971, pp. 478-81.
12 Document 48b.

sador Jarring's auspices, and at the same time in the four-power talks[13] we will talk about the possibilities of guarantees. ·

Now, an international peacekeeping force would not necessarily be limited to the four powers. It could include forces from other countries, and that is another matter that we are considering at the present time. I am looking forward very much to the meeting that I will have with Foreign Minister Eban on Friday. We will have further opportunities at that time to talk about these negotiations.

Q. Mr. Secretary, I wonder if you could talk a little bit in more detail about these international guarantees that you have talked about and specifically reports that the United States is interested in participating in a peacekeeping force with the Soviet Union and other Big Four powers?

A. Well, as I have said, we are not fixed in our views about how a peacekeeping force would operate. That would have to depend to a large degree on what the parties wanted. But if an agreement is reached, and we hope one can be reached, then we think an international peacekeeping force, properly established—with provision that it would be of a continuing nature, that it could not be removed by any unilateral decision and would be located in areas that were critical—would provide, we believe, possibly the greatest possible security for the parties.

There is a thought that geography is the sole consideration when you are thinking about security. Now, we don't think that geography is solely responsible for security, or even to a large extent responsible for security. Certainly in modern-day world situations, geography is ordinarily not important. What is important is the political arrangement that is made: the agreement itself, whether the parties are belligerent and hostile, or whether they have made an agreement that is understood by the international community, and whether the powers of the world are willing to take part in guaranteeing that the agreement will be kept. And therefore we think that although geographical considerations are important, and certainly Israel is fully justified in considering them, we think an equally important consideration is the political consideration—what is the political climate.

Q. Mr. Secretary, what political arrangements is this Government prepared to make with Israel to assure it that it will not find itself in the same situation it did after 1957, when it also had letters from President

[13] Four-power consultations among France, the U.S.S.R., the United Kingdom, and the United States had taken place intermittently since 1969 and continued during 1971 without positive results. Cf. Rogers Report, 1971, p. 97.

Eisenhower to Ben-Gurion and assurances from John Foster Dulles to Abba Eban?[14]

A. Well, I think it is very incorrect to make an analogy between 1957 and the suggestions that we make today.

In 1957, as you recall, it was a continuation of the armistice. The parties still were in a state of belligerency. The U.N. Force that was established was a very fragile force that could be removed unilaterally.

Now, we are not talking about anything of that kind. We are talking about a contractual agreement entered into by the parties with reciprocally binding commitments, signed, sealed, and delivered; with full agreement of all concerned that belligerency will cease, that they will live in peace with each other, that they will not interfere with each other's internal affairs; with provisions made for security; and with an international force consisting of those nations that are willing to participate and who may participate because the parties are prepared to accept it; with an understanding that that will continue for a definite period of time, probably with options to renew, so that it can't be removed unilaterally—which would mean if the United States participated that the United States would not move its forces except by the agreement.

So, as far as our Government is concerned, we think that that is the most adequate possible guarantee that you can conceive of in modern life. What else can you do?

CLIMATE FOR MIDDLE EAST SETTLEMENT

Q. Well, is there any bilateral thing—

A. Excuse me—go ahead.

Q. I had asked also what bilateral guarantees?

A. Well, we are not thinking of bilateral guarantees at the moment. Of course, we would continue to give support to Israel in terms of economic assistance and other assistance. In other words, that of course would be a very important factor in Israel's attitude toward its security. And we would be prepared to continue to play a supportive role to Israel. But what we are saying is this: that the climate has never been better for a settlement in the Middle East, and if we don't make a settlement now, we are going to plant seeds that will lead to future war.

Now, everyone, it seems to me, is prepared for peace. The difficulties now involve, on the one hand, the question of acquisition of territory,

---

14 *Documents, 1956*, pp. 362-64; same, *1957*, pp. 258-72.

which Egypt says is unacceptable, and which the Security Council resolution[15] says is unacceptable, and security as far as Israel is concerned; and anything that does not provide security to Israel is unacceptable, and unacceptable to us and unacceptable as far as the Security Council resolution is concerned.

Now, we think there is a middle ground. We think those two positions can be negotiated if the parties want to. In other words, the security aspects of it do not necessarily require acquisition of territory. On the other hand, we recognize that Israel has to be satisfied that its security is guaranteed. And the United States is perfectly prepared to play a leading role in that guarantee.

*   *   *

COMPLEX QUESTION OF BOUNDARIES

Q. Mr. Secretary, a few moments ago you said that the security aspects in the Middle East don't necessarily require the acquisition of territory.

A. That is right.

Q. Do you mean that you feel that Israel could be secure if it returned to the pre-1967 borders?

A. Well, let me make it clear, because when you discuss a subject of this kind and this complex, sometimes things can be taken out of context. Our position is very carefully set forth both in the President's state of the world message[16] and in more detail in my December 9, 1969, statement.[17]

We have never said that Israel had to withdraw from all territory. Our position has been that it should not acquire territory, except insubstantial amounts for security purposes.

Now, insofar as the present situation, which primarily deals with Egypt and Israel, we have said that our policy is that the 1967 boundary[18] should be the boundary between Israel and Egypt. Now, that excludes the Gaza Strip. So we are not talking about the Gaza Strip. We also say that that 1967 boundary should be the boundary provided that adequate, satisfactory arrangements are made for demili-

[15] Cf. above at note 3.
[16] Cf. note 1, above.
[17] *Documents, 1968-69*, pp. 212-19; cf. above at note 4.
[18] See map in *The United States in World Affairs, 1967*, p. 90.

tarization of the Sinai—and we say that is a matter that should be negotiated between the parties—and that satisfactory arrangements are made concerning Sharm al-Shaykh. And we say that should be negotiated between the parties.

Now, what I was saying earlier is that it is not necessary to acquire territory to make adequate provisions for security. Acquiring territory is one thing; use of territory is something else again. And one of the uses that might be made of the territory that we are talking about, Sharm al-Shaykh, might be the introduction of a peacekeeping force which would include the permanent members of the Security Council and other nations. And we are not inflexible about it. We just say we think that is a very useful instrumentality for maintaining the peace. And when the United Nations was formed, that was one of the hopes that was then expressed for mankind, that something of this kind might be developed. And we think for that reason that it is a very good prospect if the parties are willing to accept it.

*   *   *

2. Search for an Interim Agreement on the Suez Canal, February–August 1971.

[While the new round of Jarring consultations was running its course, an alternative approach to peacemaking efforts had been suggested by President Sadat, presumably with U.S. encouragement. The U.A.R., the Egyptian leader told the National Assembly on February 4, would be prepared to clear the Suez Canal, which had been blocked since 1967, and to reopen it to international navigation provided that Israel carried out a partial withdrawal from the Canal's east bank as a first step toward a final settlement. Without specifically agreeing to such a withdrawal, Israeli Prime Minister Meir on February 9 voiced Israel's willingness to discuss the reopening of the Canal as a separate issue from other provisions of an overall settlement. Since both parties indicated that they would like the United States to play a role in working out an agreement, the issue was intensively discussed by Secretary of State Rogers on a trip to the Middle East in early May (Document 50), and contacts were subsequently maintained by Assistant Secretary Joseph J. Sisco, whose discussions with Israeli leaders during the summer (Document 51) helped pave the way for the submission of a detailed plan when Secretary Rogers addressed the U.N. General Assembly on October 4, 1971 (Document 52).

These efforts were fated to remain without practical result, however, and the situation involving Israel and the U.A.R. deteriorated in some respects even while the American plan was in gestation. On May 27,

1971, the Cairo government concluded with the Soviet Union a 15-year Treaty of Friendship and Cooperation which, among other things, obligated the U.S.S.R. "to continue to develop cooperation in the military field . . . with a view to strengthening [the U.A.R.'s] capacity to alleviate the consequences of aggression as well as increasing its ability to stand up to aggression in general."[19] President Sadat, who was under considerable internal pressure to adopt a more militant attitude toward Israel, declared on July 23 that the issue of war or peace with that country must be decided one way or the other in 1971, and that the U.A.R. stood ready to sacrifice one million of its people should that be necessary.[20] Such statements, in conjunction with continuing and prospective Soviet arms flows to the U.A.R. (which resumed its historic name of "Egypt" on September 2, 1971), generated considerable sympathy within the United States for Israel's attempts to secure increased deliveries of U.S. military equipment, including F-4 Phantom fighter-bombers and A-4 Skyhawk close-support planes.

In a news conference on September 25, President Nixon attempted to relate the problems of the Middle East arms race to the quest for an overall settlement.

"I have stated over and over again," the President recalled, "that the United States will do what is necessary to see that the balance of power in the region is not altered. That commitment we have kept in the past; that commitment we will keep in the future with regard to Israel. Israel knows it, and Israel's neighbors know it.

"But, on the other hand, while at the same time we keep the commitment, and we will keep it in this general context of seeing that the balance does not shift—and we watch it closely week by week, I can assure you—at the same time we are, of course, trying to influence the negotiations along the line of pointing up that simply maintaining the balance of power is not a policy that can survive; it is not viable because in the end it will blow, and that is why we are pushing for a permanent settlement."[21]]

(50) News Conference Statement by Secretary Rogers on Completion of his Middle East Trip, Rome, May 8, 1971.[22]

(Excerpts)

Q. Your trip to the Middle East seems to have made some progress in

---

[19] Rogers Report, 1971, p. 98.
[20] *New York Times,* July 24, 1971.
[21] *Public Papers, 1971*, pp. 993-94.
[22] *Bulletin,* May 31, 1971, pp. 700-702. After attending the meeting of the

narrowing the differences between the Arabs and the Israelis. What prospects do you now see for reopening the Suez Canal?

A. I think, Mr. Kalb [Marvin Kalb, CBS News], it is difficult to measure the prospects in any numerical way. As you said, we do think that the prospects have been improved to some extent. I think it would be unwise to draw any conclusions from that that the prospect of opening the Suez is bright or that it could be done without a great deal of additional discussion and negotiation, if at all. But in any event, I think there is hope, some hope still alive, I think that there are elements of agreement between Israel and Egypt [the U.A.R.] which would form a basis for an interim agreement if we can resolve the differences that remain. I think the encouraging thing about the discussions in the last few days to me has been a willingness to talk about specifics in a practical way on both sides. And I would hope that Mr. Sisco in his discussions with the officials of Egypt in the next day or two will produce some further narrowing of the gap.

Q. Mr. Secretary, the United States in the past few years has become identified as being the supporter and supplier of Israel in the Arab world, and for that reason there was some skepticism whether the United States still was in a position to play an intermediary role in, for instance, in such a matter as the interim settlement on the canal. Now that you have completed your trip through the Middle East, I was wondering if you could share your thoughts with us on the reaction that you found in the Arab world toward the United States and toward its present diplomatic role.

A. I think that the—I was pleased to find that the Arab nations that I visited were interested in improving relations with the United States. And I found considerable friendship for the United States and for the efforts that we were making. I am sure that those of you who traveled with us noticed that the reception, the public reception in the streets, was favorable almost in every instance; and I experienced the same thing in my discussions with government officials. I believe that there is a realism that is developing about the situation. I think that people are beginning to discuss matters with more practicality than they have in the past, and I believe that although it has been rather difficult for us in the past because we haven't had particularly good relations with Egypt, for example, that our relations are improving, and so we are going to be in a better position, I think, to play a role. Now, when you speak

CENTO Council in Ankara (Document 55), the Secretary of State had visited Saudi Arabia, Jordan, Lebanon, the U.A.R. (May 4-6), and Israel (May 6-8) before proceeding to Rome on his way back to the United States. For documentation on the earlier portions of the trip see *Bulletin*, May 31, 1971, pp. 692-99.

about our acting as mediator, I want to make it clear that we don't intend to act as mediator. We've done what we have done recently with the hope that we could get some momentum going sufficient to help the parties work out an interim agreement, but we are not going to continue to play that active a role. We think the start has been a good one; we think that it's quite clear from all the discussion we've had and from reaction around the world that everyone feels that the trip was useful. And I think it is quite appropriate that I ended the trip here in Italy and had my last meeting with His Holiness Pope Paul [VI], who has dedicated so much of his life and energies to the cause of peace.

* * *

Q. An American paper, the N.Y. [International] Herald Tribune, stated that the Israeli Government should be ready to accept a certain kind of a military Egyptian presence on the Israel side of the canal. Can you tell us if this news is true or untrue?

A. See if I got the question right. The paper reported that the Israeli Government has accepted an Egyptian military presence in the event of an agreement. No, that is not correct.

Q. Mr. Secretary, you were directing yourself earlier to the Suez issue. On the question of a broader settlement, do you believe that as a result of your trip that you are more encouraged that it might be possible?

A. Yes, I would say that I am more encouraged as to a broader settlement, but I would say this: that I am inclined to think that we have to proceed in two ways. First, to achieve a final peace agreement under Ambassador Jarring's auspices. That's the objective that we all have in mind, and that's necessary to achieve if we want a permanent peace. Although I think on the other hand that possibly we have emphasized that almost to the exclusion of anything else; in other words, it may well be that we have thought about solving all the problems and not focused on how we could solve any in the meantime. In other words, for 4 years, as the result of the Security Council resolution[23] and Ambassador Jarring's position, the parties have been talking about a final, binding, total, contractual agreement. Now, we have to maintain that objective; that is the objective, and we have to achieve it. I think in the meantime we should seek ways to take some steps which will improve the climate, develop mutual trust, at least in a limited way, so that the momentum does go on. In other words, if we wait to try to

23 Cf. above at note 3.

solve everything at one time, we neglect any efforts toward solving anything as we go along. That's why I am attracted to the idea of the interim settlement on the Suez Canal. I am particularly attracted because the main considerations, as a matter of principle at least, seem to be agreed upon: (1) that the Suez should be opened; (2) that if opened that it will be run by Egypt; (3) that there will be some withdrawal under conditions that are acceptable to both sides; (4) that the fighting will not be resumed; and (5) that it is not an end in itself, that it will be a step forward in the hope that we can implement Security Council Resolution 242.

Q. Mr. Secretary, in view of the fact that you said that Israel would not accept an Egyptian military presence on the—

A. I didn't say that, Miss Berger [Marilyn Berger, Washington Post]. I said that they had not accepted. The question was did they agree to that now; and I said no, there hasn't been any agreement one way or the other on these things. We've talked over the ideas, but as I understood the paper had reported that they had agreed to this, and I said this was not correct.

Q. Can you tell us whether Egypt has given you the impression that it would not insist on military forces?

A. No, I could not.

(51) Statement by Joseph J. Sisco, Assistant Secretary of State for Near Eastern and South Asian Affairs, Tel Aviv, August 5, 1971. [24]

(Complete Text)

I first want to thank the Israeli Government and the Israeli people for the warm welcome I have received throughout my visit. I have enjoyed this unhurried stay. I leave early tomorrow morning to report to my Government on my talks here on all aspects of Israeli-American relations with your Prime Minister and other officials of the Israeli Government. The talks were practical and concrete in nature and were held in the spirit of openness and friendship.

In particular, I explored with your Government a number of ideas relevant to an interim Suez Canal agreement. This was an in-depth discussion, exploratory in nature. I expected no decisive breakthroughs; none were achieved. We each know more clearly the limits, the possi-

24 *Bulletin*, Sept. 6, 1971, pp. 259-60. Assistant Secretary Sisco was in Israel from July 28 to Aug. 6, 1971.

bilities, the perils, and the opportunities which exist in the present situation in the area. While there are differences between the sides still to be resolved, we believe that a practical basis for future progress on an interim Suez Canal agreement can be achieved.

Saturday, August 7, will mark 1 year of cease-fire resulting from an American initiative last year.[25] In this connection, there is one simple message that I wish to leave with the Israeli Government and with the Israeli people: An interim Suez Canal settlement continues to be the best way to assure that relative quiet will continue and spare people of the area the anguish and heartbreak of loss of lives. The United States will continue its effort to achieve an interim Suez Canal agreement also because it would constitute a practical test of peace that in time could help move matters toward an overall settlement in accordance with the November 1967 resolution of the U.N. Security Council. Thank you very much.

(52) Address by Secretary of State Rogers to the United Nations General Assembly, October 4, 1971.[26]

(Excerpt)

*   *   *

INTERIM SUEZ CANAL AGREEMENT

The other place where progress is urgently required is in the Middle East. Over several years, the United Nations has made determined and persistent efforts to achieve a lasting peace in that critical area. Nonetheless, the opportunities for success and the risks of failure remain in precarious balance.

Security Council Resolution 242,[27] establishing the principles for a durable peace, was the first major step toward reason after 18 years of belligerency and a fragile, often violated armistice.

The cease-fire along the Suez Canal,[28] now nearing its 15th month, was the second major step away from war.

It is time for a third major step toward peace.

---

[25] Cf. note 5 above.
[26] *Bulletin*, Oct. 25, 1971, pp. 442-44. The passage reproduced here was preceded by a discussion of conditions in South Asia which appears below as Document 56. For further comment on the proposed interim agreement see Document 54a.
[27] Cf. above at note 3.
[28] Cf. above at note 5.

For 4 years Ambassador Jarring has worked diligently to secure the agreement called for in Security Council Resolution 242. We support his efforts. We believe his mission remains the best path to an overall settlement and to lasting peace. Our views on such a final peace settlement remain those expressed in President Nixon's foreign policy report earlier this year[29] and in my statement of December 9, 1969.[30]

Both sides to the conflict are committed to the fundamental and reciprocal principles to which the Jarring Mission is dedicated: living in peace with each other and withdrawal from territories occupied in the 1967 conflict as set forth in Security Council Resolution 242. Despite those commitments, a deep gulf of suspicion and distrust remains.

Each side is convinced of the justice of its cause. Each is concerned about its future security. A political settlement based on mutual accommodation could assure both. An attempt to achieve these ends by force will destroy all possibilities for either.

This is why we believe a third major step toward peace is essential:

—A step which can be taken now;
—A step that is practical;
—A step that could help create the confidence and trust which are now lacking;
—A step toward full and complete implementation of Resolution 242.

That step is an interim Suez Canal agreement. That is why the United States has welcomed the interest of both Egypt and Israel in such an agreement. That is why, at the request of the parties, the United States has undertaken to play a constructive role in the process of arriving at an agreement.

In order to explore the positions of each side, we have discussed concrete and specific ideas designed to meet the legitimate needs and concerns of both sides. Those ideas, given willingness and good intentions on both sides, could become the basis for a breakthrough. They require further quiet discussions with the parties, an undertaking we now hope can be expedited along the following lines:

A first point is the relationship between an interim agreement and an overall settlement. A fair approach should be founded on two basic principles:

—That a Suez Canal agreement is merely a step toward complete and full implementation of Resolution 242 within a reasonable period of time and not an end in itself. That has to be clearly established in any agreement.
—That neither side can realistically expect to achieve, as part of an interim agreement, complete agreement on the terms and conditions of

29 Cf. note 1 above.
30 *Documents, 1968-69*, pp. 212-19.

an overall settlement. If it could, there would be no necessity for an interim agreement. Those final terms and conditions will have to be worked out through negotiations under Ambassador Jarring's auspices. And we would hope that if an interim agreement is reached, active negotiations under Ambassador Jarring's auspices could be renewed.

A second point is the matter of the cease-fire. Its maintenance is in the interest of all of us, of everyone concerned, of everyone in this room—in fact, in the interest of the whole world. The ultimate objective, of course, is a permanent end to belligerency as part of a final binding peace agreement. But such a commitment is not realizable in the context of an interim agreement. Neither would a cease-fire of short duration be realistic. With good will on both sides, it should be possible to find common understanding between the parties on this issue.

Third is the zone of withdrawal. There are, of course, very important strategic considerations involved in this key point. However, based on our discussions, we believe it should be possible to meet the principal concerns of both sides. Without going into the details, I would merely say that I believe that in the long run the most significant aspect of an interim agreement might prove to be that it established the principle of withdrawal looking to an overall settlement as a fact rather than as a theory.

Fourth is the nature of the supervisory arrangements. Both sides must have confidence that the agreement will not be violated and that adequate machinery will be provided for prompt detection of any infractions. We are confident that ways reassuring to both Israel and Egypt can be found for altering and strengthening the supervisory mechanisms that have existed in the area for the past two decades.[31]

Fifth is the question of an Egyptian presence east of the Suez Canal. The reopening and operation of the Suez Canal would require Egyptian personnel east of the canal. It is understandable, too, that normal activities should be pursued in as much of the zone evacuated as possible. The question of an Egyptian military presence east of the canal is one on which the parties hold opposite views. But here, too, based on our discussion, we believe that there are possibilities for compromise on this issue.

Sixth is the use of the Suez Canal. The United States has long held that the canal should be open to passage for all nations without discrimination. This principle is clear in the Security Council resolution of November 1967. What is at present at issue in considering an interim agreement is principally the timing at which this right could be exercised. We believe an accommodation on this point is quite possible.

---

[31] The United Nations Truce Supervision Organization (UNTSO) in Palestine had functioned continuously since 1949. The multinational United Nations Emergency Force (UNEF) established in 1956 had been withdrawn in 1967.

With those six points in mind let me say this: Because the parties have asked us, we intend to continue our determined effort to assist them in arriving at an interim agreement. This effort, we believe, is imperative because—and I think it is important to keep this in mind—there is no more realistic and hopeful alternative to pursue.

There are risks to peace; but the greater risk is inaction, unwillingness to face up to the hard decisions.

A practical step now—an interim agreement—would make the next step toward peace less difficult for all the parties to take.

It would restore the use of the Suez Canal as a waterway for international shipping.

It would reestablish Egypt's authority over a major national asset.

It would separate the combatants.

It would produce the first Israeli withdrawal.

It would extend the cease-fire.

It would diminish the risk of major-power involvement.

It would be an important step toward the complete implementation of Security Council Resolution 242.

I submit that the logic for such an agreement is overwhelming. If the leaders of the area would grasp this opportunity, they would give new hope to their peoples for tranquillity, for progress, and for peace.

In all of our efforts, both in the United Nations and elsewhere, we should recall that nothing we do matters so much as the legacy we leave to those who follow, the bridge that we build between the past and the future. There is a tendency, especially when tensions are high and tempers short, to regard the present as the focal point of all of man's history. But ours is only the latest generation, not the last generation; and nothing we leave to future generations will matter so much as a structure of enduring peace.

Peace must be achieved and maintained not by the decree of a few but by accommodation among many.

Each government, in upholding its people's particular interests, must also advance the world interest in a peace which will endure.

To that interest the United Nations, from its creation, has been dedicated.

To that interest the United States pledges anew its best efforts.

3. The Status of Jerusalem.

[That the United States' support for Israel was not unqualified or indiscriminate was emphasized not only by its position on the frontier question (Document 49) but also by its vote in the Security Council on September 25, 1971, in favor of a resolution that deplored Israeli actions affecting the status of occupied East Jerusalem and called urgently for their rescission (Document 53a).

Although Israel had carried out a formal annexation of the Jordanian section of Jerusalem as early as June 27, 1967, Jordan had continued to claim sovereignty over the area and complained to the Security Council on September 13, 1971, that Israel, in addition to ignoring past Security Council resolutions in the matter, was continuing its illegal and unilateral measures and steps to change the Arab character of the city and was contemplating new legislation to extend the borders of Jerusalem to encompass 30 Arab towns and villages with a population exceeding 100,000. The U.S. position was clearly set forth by Ambassador George Bush, U.S. Permanent Representative to the United Nations and U.S. Representative to the Security Council, in a statement following the vote on the resolution (Document 53b).]

(53) Action in the United Nations Security Council, September 25, 1971.

(a) Security Council Resolution 298 (1971), Adopted September 25, 1971.[32]

(Complete Text)

The Security Council,

Recalling its resolutions 252 (1968) of 21 May 1968 and 267 (1969) of 3 July 1969 and the earlier General Assembly resolutions 2253 (ES-V) and 2254 (ES-V) of 4 and 14 July 1967[33] concerning measures and actions by Israel designed to change the status of the Israeli-occupied section of Jerusalem,

Having considered the letter of the Permanent Representative of Jordan on the situation in Jerusalem[34] and the reports of the Secretary-General,[35] and having heard the statements of the parties concerned on the question,

Reaffirming the principle that acquisition of territory by military conquest is inadmissible,

Noting with concern the non-compliance by Israel with the above-mentioned resolutions,

Noting with concern also that since the adoption of the above-mentioned resolutions Israel has taken further measures designed to change the status and character of the occupied section of Jerusalem.

[32] Security Council, *Official Records: 26th Year, Resolutions and Decisions*, p. 6; adopted by a vote of 14-0-1 (Syria).
[33] *Documents, 1967*, pp. 158-59.
[34] U.N. document S/10313.
[35] Footnote in original omitted; see U.N. documents S/10124 and Add. 1 and 2.

1. *Reaffirms* its resolutions 252 (1968) and 267 (1969);

2. *Deplores* the failure of Israel to respect the previous resolutions adopted by the United Nations concerning measures and actions by Israel purporting to affect the status of the City of Jerusalem;

3. *Confirms* in the clearest possible terms that all legislative and administrative actions taken by Israel to change the status of the City of Jerusalem, including expropriation of land and properties, transfer of populations and legislation aimed at the incorporation of the occupied section, are totally invalid and cannot change that status;

4. *Urgently calls upon* Israel to rescind all previous measures and actions and to take no further steps in the occupied section of Jerusalem which may purport to change the status of the City or which would prejudice the rights of the inhabitants and the interest of the international community, or a just and lasting peace;

5. *Requests* the Secretary-General, in consultation with the President of the Security Council and using such instrumentalities as he may choose, including a representative or a mission, to report to the Council as appropriate and in any event within sixty days on the implementation of the present resolution.

(b) Statement by Ambassador Bush to the Security Council, September 25, 1971. [36]

(Complete Text)

Once again we have met to consider Jerusalem, an issue of long standing in this body and other organs of the United Nations. In our view, the ultimate status of Jerusalem should be determined through negotiation and agreement between the Governments of Israel and Jordan in the context of an overall peace settlement, taking into account the interests of its inhabitants, of the international religious communities who hold it sacred, and of other countries in the area.

In December 1969, Secretary Rogers stated: "We have made clear repeatedly in the past 2½ years that we cannot accept unilateral actions by any party to decide the final status of the city." [37] The Secretary then delineated a number of principles which in our view would provide an equitable framework for a final Jerusalem settlement:

1. Jerusalem should be a unified city;

2. There should be open access to the unified city for persons of all faiths and nationalities;

3. Administrative arrangements for the unified city should take into

[36] USUN Press Release 147, Sept. 25, 1971; text from *Bulletin*, Oct. 25, 1971, pp. 469-70.
[37] *Documents, 1968-69*, p. 217.

account the interest[s] of all its inhabitants and of the Christian, Jewish, and Moslem communities; and

4. There should be roles for both Israel and Jordan in the civic, economic, and religious life of the city.

Earlier in 1969 in this hall, my distinguished predecessor Charles [W.] Yost addressed himself more specifically to the kinds of matters which are responsible for our presence here today.[38] He said, and let me just review it briefly: "The expropriation or confiscation of land, the construction of housing on such land, the demolition or confiscation of buildings, including those having historic or religious significance, and the application of Israeli law to occupied portions of the city are detrimental to our common interests in the city." He noted as well that the United States considers that part of Jerusalem which came under Israeli control, like other areas occupied by Israel in the June 1967 war, as occupied territory and thereby subject to the provisions of international law governing the rights and obligations of an occupying power.

We regret Israel's failure to acknowledge its obligations under the Fourth Geneva Convention[39] as well as its actions which are contrary to the letter and spirit of this convention. We are distressed that the actions of Israel in the occupied portion of Jerusalem give rise to understandable concern that the eventual disposition of the occupied section of Jerusalem may be prejudiced. The Report of the Secretary General on the Work of the Organization, 1970-71, reflects the concern of many governments over changes in the face of this city.[40] We have on a number of occasions discussed this matter with the Government of Israel, stressing the need to take more fully into account the sensitivities and concerns of others. Unfortunately, the response of the Government of Israel has been disappointing.

All of us understand, as I indicated earlier in these remarks, that Jerusalem has a very special place in the Judaic tradition, one which has great meaning for Jews throughout the world. At the same time Jerusalem holds a special place in the hearts of many millions of Christians and Moslems throughout the world. In this regard, I want to state clearly that we believe Israel's respect for the holy places has indeed been exemplary. But an Israeli occupation policy made up of unilaterally determined practices cannot help promote a just and lasting peace any more than that cause was served by the status quo in Jerusalem prior to June 1967, which, I want to make clear, we did not like and we do not advocate reestablishing.

[38] Statement of July 1, 1969, in *Bulletin*, July 28, 1969, pp. 76-77.
[39] Convention Relative to the Protection of Civilian Persons in Times of War, signed at Geneva Aug. 12, 1949 (TIAS 3365; 6 UST 3516).
[40] United Nations General Assembly, *Official Records: 26th Session, Supplement No. 1* (A/8401), pp. 16-18.

In conclusion, I would note that the resolution before us today,[41] as in the past, calls for a report on the situation in Jerusalem. We have supported this resolution not because we agree fully with every provision in it; some elements in it in fact, as I mentioned to our distinguished colleague from Somalia [Abdulrahim Abby Farah] gave us difficulty. But we have supported this resolution out of the belief that it was time to reiterate our concern that nothing be done in Jerusalem that can prejudice an ultimate and peaceful solution.

4. Reactivation of the Jarring Mission.

[Discussion of the Middle East situation at the autumn 1971 session of the U.N. General Assembly, though largely overshadowed by the war in the Subcontinent, resulted in a number of resolutions that were unacceptable to Israel and were regarded by the United States as unlikely to advance the cause of peace in the area. In statements to the General Assembly, Ambassador Bush and Ambassador Christopher H. Phillips of the U.S. Delegation detailed the reasons the United States was unable to support a resolution which, in addition to requesting a reactivation of the Jarring mission, expressed approval of the Egyptian stand in the Jarring negotiations and called on Israel to "respond favorably" to Ambassador Jarring's initiative of February 8, 1971 (Document 54). In other actions at its 1971 session, the General Assembly extended the mandate of the United Nations Relief and Works Agency for Palestine Refugees in the Near East (UNRWA) until June 30, 1975, but took exception to various Israeli actions and policies affecting the refugees and (over the negative votes of the United States and others) reiterated an earlier demand for "equal rights and self-determination" for "the people of Palestine."[42] A third resolution, opposed by the United States, was sharply critical of Israeli practices affecting the human rights of the population of the occupied territories.[43]

Despite the approach of President Sadat's deadline for a definite decision on war or peace, an early outbreak of hostilities appeared unlikely as the General Assembly adjourned on December 22, 1971. (President Sadat later explained that his calculations had been thrown off by the Soviet involvement in the India–Pakistan crisis; and the opening of a "fourth round" of hostilities against Israel did not in fact occur until October 1973.) In a news conference on December 23, 1971, Secretary Rogers reported that the United States was encouraging the parties to cooperate in a renewal of Ambassador Jarring's

[41] Document 53a.
[42] Resolution 2792 (XXVI), Dec. 6, 1971. The quoted section (part D) was adopted by a vote of 53-23 (U.S.)-43.
[43] Resolution 2851 (XXVI), Dec. 20, 1971, adopted by a vote of 53-20 (U.S.)-46.

efforts, which were expected to resume in New York in January 1972, and that both Israel and Egypt had been advised of its readiness to continue playing a role in the negotiating process with special reference to an interim agreement on the Suez Canal.[44]]

(54) Action by the General Assembly, December 13, 1971.

(a) Call for a Resumption of Negotiations: Statement by Ambassador Bush to the General Assembly, December 13, 1971.[45]

(Complete Text)

The United Nations has over almost a quarter of a century been intimately concerned with the Arab-Israeli conflict and has agreed upon many constructive principles to guide the parties in its solution. Our support for the efforts of the United Nations and for Security Council Resolution 242,[46] which established the basic principles for a lasting peace in the area, is well known, as is our continuing endorsement of Ambassador Jarring's mission. Our efforts over the years in support of Ambassador Jarring's mission are too familiar to you all to need reiteration here today. Our policy is a consistent one: We favor a peaceful settlement based on agreement among the parties within the framework of the principles and provisions set forth in Resolution 242. The differences over what that resolution means are properly a matter for negotiation, as are the possibilities for interim steps on the road to peace. We believe that all of us should today be focusing on ways of facilitating such negotiations.

Unfortunately, efforts toward an overall peace settlement since 1967 have not produced the results all of us have hoped for. Since February of this year, the most promising avenue for progress has been the possibility of an agreement on measures of an interim nature, involving partial Israeli withdrawal in Sinai and a reopening of the Suez Canal as a step toward a final peace.[47] Both Egypt and Israel on their own initiative expressed an interest in this concept, and both then asked the United States to assist them in pursuing negotiations on this matter. We agreed to undertake this role. We see an interim agreement as being to the potential benefit of all concerned, as a practical step toward an overall peace settlement, as a way to test the intentions of the parties and develop much-needed confidence that a political arrangement could

---

[44] *Bulletin*, Jan. 17, 1972, pp. 53 and 57.
[45] USUN Press Release 214, Dec. 10, 1971; text from *Bulletin*, Jan. 17, 1972, pp. 72-73.
[46] Cf. above at note 3.
[47] Cf. Documents 50-52.

be implemented and observed by the parties, and as a means of promoting a resumption of Ambassador Jarring's mission.

Since February we have undertaken extensive discussions with the parties regarding an interim agreement. We have not laid down any blueprint of our own for an interim agreement. It is our conviction that the detailed terms must be worked out in a genuine negotiating process. Unfortunately, progress on an interim agreement has also run into difficult obstacles. A major difficulty has been that the parties have sought to introduce into the context of an interim agreement concepts which logically belong in an overall settlement. We have maintained that while an interim agreement should be a step toward an overall settlement, there would be no need for an interim agreement at all if it were possible now to arrive at agreement on the many complex issues which remain to be resolved with respect to territory, the shape of the peace, guarantees, and other differences. The merits, in other words, of an interim agreement are precisely that it offers a prospect for practical on-the-ground progress while leaving some of the most difficult issues for further negotiations at a subsequent stage.

Negotiations on an interim agreement are in suspense—we believe only temporarily. We have proposed ways in which negotiations on an interim agreement can be intensified. We will review the prospects for such an agreement once this debate has been concluded. Both sides have put forward positive ideas; both sides hold firmly to key points; both sides will be required to make adjustments in their position if an interim agreement is to be achieved.

It is our hope that all who rise to speak on this agenda item will bear in mind that in the last analysis it is the parties themselves that will have to negotiate the terms of a Middle East peace settlement. Peace cannot be imposed on the area by outsiders. Security Council Resolution 242 of November 22, 1967, recognizes this principle by specifying that a peace settlement must be the result of agreement between the parties. Nothing must be done in this Assembly which seems to reinterpret Security Council Resolution 242 or seems to alter the careful balance of that resolution. We hold to the view that quiet diplomacy is the best format for progress. We hope that all who are genuinely concerned to reach a peace settlement will do their best to see that what is said and done here will not have the effect of stiffening the parties' positions rather than increasing confidence and encouraging flexibility. We hope the parties themselves will exercise care not to narrow or close their political options. Political-diplomatic options will be needed more than ever once the debate here is over.

At this stage, it seems unproductive to engage in polemics as to where the fault lies for the impasse reached in efforts toward an overall settlement. After all, this impasse is not the result of a single diplomatic development. Instead, it is only symptomatic of the bitter and persistent conflict which dates back to 1948 and before. The basic problem, in our view, remains finding ways to help both sides to overcome the deep suspicion and distrust they feel toward each other in this conflict.

One of the promising new developments in the search for a Middle East peace settlement was the recent visit by the mission of the Organization of African Unity (OAU) to the area. The initiative undertaken by the committee of 10 chiefs of state of the Organization of African Unity to promote a narrowing of the differences between the parties is highly commendable.[48] We hope that it will prove to be a constructive element in our present deliberations.

I want to underline that our government intends to pursue vigorously the search for peace in the Middle East by the means which appear most effective and promising of progress. We continue in this spirit to stand ready to assist the parties to the conflict in resolving their differences as long as they desire our assistance.

(b) Shortcomings of the Pending Resolution: Statement by Ambassador Christopher H. Phillips, Deputy United States Representative, to the General Assembly, December 13, 1971.[49]

(Complete Text)

My government is in agreement with much of this resolution.[50] It reflects the central belief of this body and the firm policy of my government that we must continue to give unwavering support to Security Council Resolution 242, which has established the basic principles for a just and lasting peace in the area. It reflects the clear desire of us all that negotiations toward a settlement based on the principles and provisions of that resolution should move forward. It reflects our common support and endorsement of Ambassador Jarring's mission. And it reflects the common conviction that the settlement must be worked out by the parties directly concerned.

---

[48] Following the establishment of a special group on the Middle East by the O.A.U. Assembly of Heads of State and Government in June 1971, the Presidents of Senegal, Nigeria, Cameroon, and Zaïre and the Foreign Minister of Mauritania visited Israel and Egypt during the autumn of 1971 and subsequently formulated a series of recommendations designed to promote a resumption of the Jarring mission. The substance of these recommendations, which did *not* call for an advance Israeli commitment to withdrawal from occupied territories but stated that the terms of withdrawal should be embodied in the peace agreement, was incorporated in proposed amendments to the pending resolution; the amendments, however, were rejected by the General Assembly by a vote of 16 in favor to 65 against, with 42 abstentions (*UN Monthly Chronicle*, Jan. 1972, pp. 92-93).
[49] USUN Press Release 221, Dec. 13, 1971; text from *Bulletin*, Jan. 17, 1972, pp. 73-75.
[50] Document 54c.

My government wishes especially to take note of and commend the efforts of the 10 African heads of government for their constructive initiative. Their designated representatives sought and obtained a deeper understanding of the issues and the prospects for an advance toward peace through their visit to the area and detailed consultations with the Governments of Egypt and Israel. Their efforts reflect a high order of statesmanship, and my government believes that a closer reflection of their viewpoints in the resolution before us might well have obtained a wide endorsement from this body.

My government has given this resolution most careful study. We will abstain in the voting on two counts.

First, we believe the resolution contains language that tends to alter the balance of Security Council Resolution 242, and we attach the greatest importance to a strict and careful adherence to that basic document upon which our hopes for a peaceful settlement in the Middle East are based. This language is contained in the penultimate preambular paragraph and the last clause of operative paragraph 1.

Second, my government is concerned about the practical effect of this resolution. We are all agreed, I believe, that this body should center its attention on what can be done to facilitate and promote the process of negotiations between the parties concerned. We are all disappointed—and none more than my government—that more progress has not been achieved in this direction since the last Assembly. Had we here been able to work out a resolution whose terms were acceptable to the parties directly concerned, we would have made a real contribution toward the restoration of the negotiating process. But this body cannot by itself resolve the differences which Ambassador Jarring has not been able to overcome, and we fear that the present resolution may delay rather than promote the engagement of the parties in productive negotiations.

It is our belief, therefore, that a resolution could have been designed which would have better served the essential purpose of creating the climate for the beginning of serious negotiations. We made a number of suggestions which, in our view, had they been incorporated in the resolution would have contributed to that end. Specifically, we urged that the reference to Ambassador Jarring's initiative last February[51] be taken note of in the preambular section of the resolution and that the operative clauses be more general in order to leave open as many options as possible to Ambassador Jarring in his efforts to resume his mission. This approach, which in our view would parallel that of the OAU Committee of Ten report, would have reflected the reality that Ambassador Jarring's February initiative, commendable as it was, did not then succeed in breaking the deadlock in the negotiations and would be unlikely to do so today.

[51] Cf. below at note 56.

In abstaining on the resolution, I want to stress that nothing in our abstention should be taken as a change in United States policies. We continue to give Security Council Resolution 242 our full support. Our own views on the elements of a peace settlement remain as we have stated them frequently over the past 2 years. We continue to give our full support to Ambassador Jarring's efforts to promote negotiations between the parties.

For our part the United States will continue to do its utmost to get those negotiations underway. This has been our intention and our desire in these past months, and we have exerted our best efforts in that direction, notwithstanding the remarks of the distinguished Representative of the Soviet Union [Yakov A. Malik] to the contrary. We believe that the most promising avenue now available is to continue to explore the possibility of agreement on measures of an interim nature, involving a reopening of the Suez Canal and a partial Israeli withdrawal in Sinai as a step toward a final peace. We will persist in trying to help the parties in pursuing negotiations on this matter so long as they continue to wish us to do so. We regard our endeavors in this respect as supportive of Ambassador Jarring's mission and as directed toward a practical step toward an overall peace settlement in accordance with Security Council Resolution 242.

(c) "The Situation in the Middle East": General Assembly Resolution 2799 (XXVI), Adopted December 13, 1971. [52]

(Complete Text)

The General Assembly,

Deeply concerned at the continuation of the grave situation prevailing in the Middle East, particularly since the conflict of June 1967, which constitutes a serious threat to international peace and security,

Convinced that Security Council resolution 242 (1967) of 22 November 1967 [53] should be implemented immediately in all its parts in order to achieve a just and lasting peace in the Middle East in which every State in the area can live in security,

Determined that the territory of a State shall not be the object of occupation or acquisition by another State resulting from the threat or use of force, which is contrary to the Charter of the United Nations and to the principles enshrined in Security Council resolution 242 (1967) as well as in the Declaration on the Strengthening of International Security adopted by the General Assembly on 16 December 1970, [54]

---

[52] General Assembly, Official Records: 26th Session, Supplement No. 29 (A/8429), pp. 3-4; adopted by a vote of 79-7 (Israel)-36 (U.S.).
[53] Documents, 1967, pp. 169-70; cf. above at note 3.
[54] General Assembly Resolution 2734 (XXV), Dec. 16, 1970.

Expressing its appreciation of the efforts of the Committee of African Heads of State undertaken in pursuance of the resolution adopted on 23 June 1971 by the Assembly of Heads of State and Government of the Organization of African Unity at its eighth ordinary session,[55]

Gravely concerned at the continuation of Israel's occupation of the Arab territories since 5 June 1967,

Having considered the item entitled "The situation in the Middle East",

1. *Reaffirms* that the acquisition of territories by force is inadmissible and that, consequently, territories thus occupied must be restored;

2. *Reaffirms* that the establishment of a just and lasting peace in the Middle East should include the application of both the following principles:

(a) Withdrawal of Israeli armed forces from territories occupied in the recent conflict;

(b) Termination of all claims or states of belligerency, and respect for and acknowledgment of the sovereignty, territorial integrity and political independence of every State in the area and its right to live in peace within secure and recognized boundaries free from threats or acts of force;

3. *Requests* the Secretary-General to take the necessary measures to reactivate the mission of the Special Representative of the Secretary-General to the Middle East in order to promote agreement and assist efforts to reach a peace agreement as envisaged in the Special Representative's aide-mémoire of 8 February 1971;[56]

4. *Expresses its full support* for all the efforts of the Special Representative to implement Security Council resolution 242 (1967);

5. *Notes with appreciation* the positive reply given by Egypt to the Special Representative's initiative for establishing a just and lasting peace in the Middle East;[57]

6. *Calls upon* Israel to respond favourably to the Special Representative's peace initiative;

7. *Further invites* the parties to the Middle East conflict to give their full co-operation to the Special Representative in order to work out practical measures for:

(a) Guaranteeing freedom of navigation through international waterways in the area;

(b) Achieving a just settlement of the refugee problem;

(c) Guaranteeing the territorial inviolability and political independence of every State in the area;

55 Cf. note 48, above.
56 Document 48b, para. 8; text in U.N. document S/10403, Annex I (Security Council, *Official Records: 26th Year, Supplement for Oct., Nov. and Dec. 1971*, p. 58).
57 Doc. 48b, para. 9; texts in U.N. document S/10403, Annex II (*loc. cit.*, pp. 58-9).

8. *Requests* the Secretary-General to report to the Security Council and to the General Assembly, as appropriate, on the progress made by the Special Representative in the implementation of Security Council resolution 242 (1967) and of the present resolution;

9. *Requests* the Security Council to consider, if necessary, making arrangements, under the relevant Articles of the Charter of the United Nations, with regard to the implementation of resolution 242 (1967).

B. The Central Treaty Organization (CENTO).

[Created during the "cold war" era of the 1950s, the Central Treaty Organization (Turkey, Iran, Pakistan, and the United Kingdom, with the United States as a nonmember but an active participant) had entered the 1970s with little if any change apart from a diminution in Pakistan's participation following its war with India in 1965. The new war between Pakistan and India in December 1971 (Documents 56-64) was to affect the easternmost of the CENTO allies in a much more drastic manner. In the meantime, a change in the emphasis of CENTO concerns was already evident at the 1971 session of the alliance's Council of Ministers, held in Ankara on April 30–May 1, 1971, with Secretary of State Rogers heading the U.S. observer delegation (Document 55). While taking minimal public notice of any dangers that might be thought to threaten the CENTO allies from the direction of the Soviet Union, the Council stressed primarily the importance of a "just and lasting peace" in the Middle East and the development of communications and technical assistance activities within the CENTO region.]

(55) Eighteenth Session of the CENTO Council of Ministers, Ankara, April 30–May 1, 1971: Final Communiqué.[58]

(Complete Text)

The Council of Ministers of CENTO held their eighteenth session at the headquarters of the Organization in Ankara April 30 and May 1, 1971. The Heads of the Delegations were:

Ardeshir Zahedi, Minister of Foreign Affairs, Iran
Iftikhar Ali, Ambassador of Pakistan in Turkey
Osman Olcay, Minister of Foreign Affairs, Turkey

[58] Department of State Press Release 93, May 3, 1971; text from *Bulletin*, May 31, 1971, p. 693.

Sir Alec Douglas-Home, Secretary of State for Foreign and Commonwealth Affairs, United Kingdom
William P. Rogers, Secretary of State, United States

The meeting was opened by Mr. Turgut Menemencioğlu, Secretary
General of CENTO.

A message of welcome from Cevdet Sunay, President of the Republic
of Turkey, was read at the Inaugural Session, followed by a speech of
welcome by Nihat Erim, Prime Minister of the Republic of Turkey.

Osman Olcay, Foreign Minister of the Republic of Turkey, as representative of the host government, was President of this session of the
Council.

In their statements at the Inaugural Session, Heads of Delegations and
the Secretary General expressed their thanks for the gracious message
of the President of the Republic of Turkey and the warm hospitality
extended by the Turkish Government.[59]

In their discussions, held in a cordial and friendly atmosphere, the
Council reviewed the international situation in the Middle East. The
Council emphasized the urgent need for establishment of a just and
lasting peace in the Middle East in accordance with the principles and
provisions of the U.N. Security Council Resolution of November 22,
1967.[60] Members of the Council also made statements regarding problems of peace and security which are of special interest to their countries. The subjects covered in these statements included the future of
the Persian Gulf, Cyprus, Southeast Asia, and the deterioration in relations between India and Pakistan.[61] The Council expressed hope that
measures would be taken in all areas of conflict to promote peace and
security, in keeping with the principles and practices of international
law, non-intervention in internal affairs of other countries, equity and
justice.

In approving the Report of the Military Committee, the Council
noted progress made in different fields of cooperation.

Reviewing the report of the Economic Committee, the Council was
pleased to note that major economic projects were in the final phases of
completion. The Iran-Turkey railway, a major engineering achievement,
is scheduled to start operation during the current year.[62] Progress on
the extension of the Iranian railway network up to the Pakistan border
was also noted. Construction of a road system designed to connect
three regional countries also was progressing satisfactorily. Expansion

[59] For statement of Secretary Rogers see *Bulletin*, May 31, 1971, pp. 692-93.
[60] *Documents, 1967*, pp. 169-70; cf. above at note 3.
[61] Cf. Document 56.
[62] A 344-kilometer rail link between Iran and Turkey was formally opened Sept.
27, 1971.

of the port facilities in Iskenderun, on the Mediterranean coast of Turkey, is in final stage.

The CENTO Microwave System is fully in use, and its effectiveness has been enhanced by the establishment in Tehran of a control center managed by technicians from all three regional countries. The CENTO Air Navigational Aid System is also complete, opening a corridor of international standards to airlines operating in the region. These rail, road and air networks have enlarged possibilities of economic cooperation among the peoples of the CENTO region.

Technical cooperation within the framework of CENTO has shown further progress. More funds have been made available for various forms of technical assistance, more training facilities have been provided, and seminars and symposia arranged under the auspices of CENTO have covered a wide variety of subjects valuable for economic development of the region.

The Council expressed deep appreciation for the contribution made to the Alliance by Secretary General Turgut Menemencioğlu during his term of office, and thanked the Government of Turkey for making his services available to the Organization.

As the tenure of Mr. Menemencioğlu will conclude at the end of this year, the Government of Iran agreed to nominate a Secretary General, whose appointment will be announced in due course.[63]

The Council accepted the invitation of the Government of the United Kingdom to hold its next session in May 1972 in London.[64]

C. The Indo–Pakistan Conflict Before the United Nations, October–December 1971.

[The policies and actions of the United States in the most serious new international conflict to develop during the early 1970s have been documented at various levels. President Nixon, in his annual foreign policy report for 1972, devoted several pages to explaining the efforts the United States had made to forestall the threatened outbreak of war between India and Pakistan and, when those efforts failed at the beginning of December 1971, to bring the war to an immediate halt.[65] At the time, the U.S. stand had been widely criticized on the ground that, among other things, it favored a dictatorial government in Pakistan in an attempt to repress a popular revolutionary movement supported by

---

[63] Nassir Assar (Iran) assumed office as Secretary-General on Feb. 1, 1972, for a three-year term ending Jan. 1, 1975.

[64] The nineteenth session met in London June 1-2, 1972; cf. *A.F.R., 1972*, no. 34.

[65] Nixon Report, 1972, pp. 141-52.

India. President Nixon, however, rejected the charge that American action in the crisis had been dictated by bias or by insensitivity to political and humanitarian considerations. The United States, he insisted, had exercised the inescapable responsibility of a great power in a situation in which the alternative course would have entailed unacceptable risks "for the survival of Pakistan, for the stability of many other countries in the world, for the integrity of international processes for keeping the peace, and for relations among the great powers."[66]

A less reflective view of American policy in the December crisis emerges from a group of secret National Security Council documents made public early in 1972 by the columnist Jack Anderson.[67] These documents, the authenticity of which has not been challenged, afford an unusual insight into the workings of the National Security Council system and particularly the Washington Special Actions Group (WSAG), the body charged with developing "options for the implementation of decisions during crises" (Document 3). The impression conveyed is that of a group of distracted senior officials engaged in a frantic attempt to implement a predetermined course of action laid down by an absent and seemingly implacable President. Already historic is the statement ascribed to Dr. Henry A. Kissinger, the President's Assistant for National Security Affairs, at a WSAG meeting on December 3, 1971, when full-scale war was just breaking out but little detailed information was available in Washington: "I am getting hell every half-hour from the President that we are not being tough enough on India. He has just called me again. He does not believe we are carrying out his wishes. He wants to tilt in favor of Pakistan. He feels everything we do comes out otherwise."[68] The accounts of this and subsequent WSAG meetings, as made public by Jack Anderson and preserved in the pages of *The New York Times*,[69] complement the official record and help clarify the background of American policy as set forth in the more formal documentation presented below.]

1. Origins of the Crisis.

[The background of the Indo-Pakistan war—the third major conflict in the Subcontinent in a quarter-century of independent history—has been described in some detail in other publications.[70] Briefly, the Pakistani regime headed by General Mohammad Yahya Khan, having failed to

[66] Same, p. 148.
[67] *New York Times*, Jan. 6, 1972.
[68] Same.
[69] Same.
[70] *The World This Year, 1972*, p. 84; Nixon Report, 1972, pp. 141-47; Rogers Report, 1971, pp. 110-11; Kalb, *Kissinger*, pp. 257-64.

reach a political accommodation with the leaders of a Bengali autonomist movement in the geographically separate province of East Pakistan, embarked in late March 1971 on a campaign of violent repression which led, over the following months, to the flight of millions of refugees to India and the growth of a Bengali resistance movement which was supported by India and operated in the name of an ostensibly independent Bengali state, the "People's Republic of Bangladesh." A sharp deterioration in the relations between Pakistan and India led President Nixon as early as May 28 to warn the leaders of both countries of the need for restraint. Indian–U.S. relations also deteriorated, especially after India concluded a 20-year Treaty of Peace, Friendship, and Cooperation with the U.S.S.R. (its principal arms supplier) on August 9, 1971.

By early October, frontier clashes were becoming more frequent and Secretary of State Rogers gave public expression to American concern in his address to the U.N. General Assembly (Document 56). Proposals for a mutual pull-back of military forces under U.N. auspices were accepted by Pakistan but were rejected by India, which showed little interest in American attempts to promote accommodation and continued to expand its support of the guerrillas as the scale of border hostilities grew (cf. Document 62). By late November, Indian forces were reported crossing the East Pakistan border in direct support of insurgent groups, and the outbreak of full-scale hostilities appeared imminent. (For further details cf. Documents 58, 60, and 62.)]

(56) Conditions in South Asia: Address by Secretary of State Rogers to the General Assembly, October 4, 1971. [71]

(Excerpt)

* * *

In two parts of the world in which the United Nations has been particularly active, South Asia and the Middle East, urgent progress is needed.

In South Asia, renewed and more widespread violence is an ever-present possibility. The events in East Pakistan are internal events with which the Government and people of Pakistan must deal. But their consequences—the flight of refugees into India, the danger of famine, the threat to peace in South Asia—are of grave concern to all nations.

To restore peaceful conditions and to save human lives it is clear that:

---

[71] *Bulletin*, Oct. 25, 1971, pp. 441-42. For the continuation of Secretary Rogers' address see Document 52.

—Restraint must be exercised in the subcontinent;

—The international assistance program must be expanded to avert famine and to create conditions to encourage the return of refugees; and

—Efforts toward an effective political settlement in East Pakistan must be actively pursued.

We are working to those ends.

The United States strongly supports the efforts of the United Nations to organize an effective international relief program. We have made available over $200 million for relief in East Pakistan and for emergency assistance for the refugees in India—well over 50 percent of the total contributions from all foreign contributors, public and private. Last week President Nixon asked Congress to appropriate an additional $250 million to sustain a high level of relief assistance.[72] A much wider response from other countries is clearly required. We urge the major powers and others with substantial financial resources to contribute generously.

*   *   *

2. Action in the Security Council, December 4-6, 1971.

[Full-scale war between India and Pakistan broke out on December 3 as the Pakistani Air Force launched a series of raids on Indian military airfields—ostensibly in response to an Indian ground offensive, though Indian sources denied that such an offensive had taken place.[73] Though each side accused the other of aggression, U.S. officials took the position that India was the "main aggressor," announced the immediate cancellation of outstanding licenses for shipment of military equipment to that country, and, on December 6, suspended $87.6 million in pending economic development loans.[74] A decision to refer the issue to the Security Council (Document 57) was taken on the morning of December 4 at a meeting of the Washington Special Actions Group (WSAG), at which Dr. Kissinger is quoted as expressing the opinion that an appeal to the United Nations would be unlikely to achieve results in view of the probability of a veto by the Soviet Union; that the war was clearly going to end with an Indian occupation of East Pakistan; and that the main purpose of going to the United Nations would be "to make clear our position relative to our greater strategy." It was further agreed at this meeting that the American approach in the United Nations would be "tilted toward the Paks."[75]

[72] For details cf. *Bulletin, passim.*
[73] Keesing's, p. 25053.
[74] *New York Times*, Dec. 7, 1971.
[75] Anderson documents, in same, Jan. 6, 1972.

At the emergency meeting of the Security Council on the evening of December 4, Ambassador Bush outlined the official U.S. view of the situation and introduced a resolution calling for an immediate cease-fire and withdrawal of armed personnel of both sides to their own side of the border (Document 58). Denounced by the U.S.S.R. as one-sided because it equated India and Pakistan and took no account of Pakistani actions that had led up to the fighting, the resolution was supported by China and others but was vetoed by the Soviet Union early on December 5. A second, similar resolution put forward by eight Western and nonaligned countries also incurred a Soviet veto. France and the United Kingdom abstained on both resolutions.

With the Security Council unable to take a stand, proposals to transfer the issue to the General Assembly under the so-called "uniting for peace" procedure were approved by the WSAG on December 6, with the understanding that any resolution introduced in the General Assembly must retain the two key elements of a cease-fire and a withdrawal of forces. Dr. Kissinger, who observed that "it is quite obvious that the President is not inclined to let the Paks be defeated," directed also "that henceforth we show a certain coolness to the Indians; the Indian Ambassador is not to be treated at too high a level."[76] Later on December 6, the proposed procedure was explained to the Security Council by Ambassador Bush and was approved by a vote of 11 to 0, with China voting in favor and the U.S.S.R., Poland, France, and the United Kingdom abstaining (Document 59).]

(57) Request for a Security Council Meeting: Statement by Secretary of State Rogers, December 4, 1971.[77]

(Complete Text)

The United States believes that the deteriorating situation in South Asia poses a threat to international peace and security. Hostilities have intensified in East Pakistan and have involved incursions of Indian troops across the borders of East Pakistan. Recent reports indicate that the forces of both countries are now engaged in military actions along the frontiers between West Pakistan and India.

In view of these developments which the United States views with deep concern and which, in our judgment, increase the risk of even broader hostilities between India and Pakistan, Ambassador Bush has

---

[76] Same.

[77] Department of State Press Release 284, Dec. 4, 1971; text from *Bulletin*, Dec. 27, 1971, p. 729.

been instructed, in concert with other Security Council members,[78] to call for an urgent meeting of the Security Council.

The United States hopes that the Council can take prompt action on steps which could bring about a cease-fire, withdrawal of forces, and an amelioration of the present threat to international peace and security.

(58) Proposals to End Hostilities: Statement by Ambassador Bush to the Security Council, December 4, 1971, with United States Draft Resolution Vetoed by the U.S.S.R. December 5, 1971.[79]

(Complete Text)

From reports we have received today it appears that a state of open hostilities exists between India and Pakistan. There is a grave threat to the peace and stability of Asia. This recourse to war by the nations of South Asia is tragic and unnecessary.

In the months since last March we have all been witness to the unfolding of a major tragedy. Coming on the heels of the cyclone last year,[80] one of the greatest natural disasters of modern times, civil strife in East Pakistan has caused untold suffering to millions of people, has created a new and tragic refugee community in India of unparalleled dimensions, and has brought India and Pakistan to open hostilities. It is time that the United Nations acts to bring the great moral authority of this body effectively and quickly to bear to preserve the peace between two of its largest members.

These events of recent months have been profoundly disturbing to the United States. As the President made clear in his report to the Congress earlier this year, our aim in South Asia has been to build a structure of peace and stability within which the great economic and social problems of the region can be addressed.[81] The effectiveness of our efforts in this task is necessarily determined by the ability of the nations of the area to solve their mutual political problems and to build domestic political and economic systems within which orderly change is feasible. The deteriorating military situation with which we are now confronted makes it increasingly impossible for us to contribute to the economic development and political stability of the area, to which we are committed.

---

[78] Argentina, Belgium, Burundi, Italy, Japan, Nicaragua, Somalia, and the United Kingdom.
[79] USUN Press Release 207, Dec. 4, 1971; text from *Bulletin*, Dec. 27, 1971, pp. 721-23.
[80] Nov. 12-13, 1970; cf. *The United States in World Affairs, 1970*, p. 180.
[81] Nixon Report, 1971, pp. 111-14.

My Government is therefore deeply concerned by the hostilities which are now taking place along the borders of India and East Pakistan. Hostilities have intensified in East Pakistan. There have been admitted incursions of Indian troops across the border of East Pakistan. It is now clear that the forces of both countries are involved in military actions along the frontier between West Pakistan and India. It is of the utmost urgency that there be an end to these hostilities which could escalate into all-out conflict.

We are not oblivious to the complex factors which are at the root of this tragic and dangerous situation. But the United States cannot over-emphasize its conviction that nothing can come out of a resort to force except greater tragedy for the peoples of South Asia.

The United States Government has made a major effort in South Asia to ease the human suffering caused by the present crisis, to prevent war, and to facilitate a political solution to the problem.

The United States early recognized the need to assist refugees in India and to help avert famine in East Pakistan and promptly responded by providing major assistance to United Nations efforts in both countries:[82]

—We have already committed $245 million to these international humanitarian efforts.

—The danger of famine has been averted, but large relief requirements remain in both countries.

—The President therefore has requested the Congress to appropriate an additional $250 million, to which would be added further food shipments if needed.

The United States Government, which values its close relations with both India and Pakistan, has made a vigorous effort to avert war, which would increase human suffering and delay the return of refugees to their homes:

—We have called on both India and Pakistan to avoid actions which would increase military tensions.

—Specifically, the United States Government has proposed that both sides withdraw their military forces from their borders. Pakistan accepted this proposal. Regrettably, India did not. The United States has repeatedly made clear its view that increasing military tensions prevent progress toward resolution of the political problems that caused the refugees to leave their homes and provided the stimulus for guerrilla war.

—The United States Government has sought to facilitate negotiations leading to a political settlement of the East Pakistan problem.

—The United States pointed out to the Indian Government that an increase of military tensions could only stand in the way of necessary

[82] Cf. note 72 above.

progress toward a peaceful political settlement and the return of refugees.

We recognize that a fundamental political accommodation still has not been achieved in East Pakistan. While we continue to feel that the only proper solution is a political one, we do not find justification for the repeated violation of frontiers that has taken place in East Pakistan. The immediate cessation of hostilities and the withdrawal of forces are essential conditions for progress toward a political solution in East Pakistan.

This body cannot accept recourse to force to solve this problem. Indian officials have now announced that regular Indian forces have been instructed to move into East Pakistan in what the Indian Defense Secretary [Jagjivan Ram] is quoted in the press as calling a "no holds barred" operation. The very purpose which draws us together here—building a peaceful world—will be thwarted if a situation is accepted in which a government intervenes across its borders in the affairs of another with military force in violation of the United Nations Charter.

We ask this world body to join us, now, in calling upon the Governments of India and Pakistan to terminate their military confrontation by agreeing to an immediate cease-fire and to the immediate withdrawal of forces from foreign territories. This Council can ask no less.

Mr. President,[83] the Secretary General has endeavored on several occasions to impress upon all of us the gravity of the situation in South Asia. He has offered his personal good offices to assist in a solution of these problems. Regrettably, the Government of India has not welcomed his initiatives. Most recently, on October 20, he warned in letters to Prime Minister [Indira] Gandhi and President Yahya [Khan] that:

> ... this situation could all too easily ... be disastrous to the two countries principally concerned, but might also constitute a major threat to the wider peace.[84]

While both governments have professed a continuing commitment to peace and a determination not to initiate hostilities, the situation has continued to deteriorate until now regular forces are engaged at various points.

It is time that all of us heed the Secretary General's call. It is time that both countries accept an immediate cease-fire and agree on immediate steps to withdraw their forces from foreign territory. It is time that the Government of India join the Government of Pakistan in

[83] Ismael Byne Taylor-Kamara (Sierra Leone), President of the Security Council for Dec. 1971.
[84] U.N. document S/10410, Dec. 3, 1971; Security Council, *Official Records: 26th Year, Supplement for Oct., Nov. and Dec. 1971*, pp. 81-82.

heeding the Secretary General's offer of his good offices to assist in the process of reconciliation that must then begin.

Mr. President, we have all seen too much of war. We have all seen and heard too much of a resort to force to resolve the problems that divide us. The time is past when any of us could justifiably resort to war to bring about change in a neighboring country that might better suit our national interests as we see them. All of us know, certainly the leaders of India and Pakistan know, that the human needs of our people are not met through the terrible cost of war.

Let us then all, and quickly, agree that a cease-fire in this tragic hour is essential and that a withdrawal of forces from foreign territories must take place without delay so that progress can be made in building the conditions in East Pakistan, political and economic and social, in which the refugees will return and in which peace can be assured. The United States is prepared to support appropriate and effective measures by the Council to bring about a cessation of hostilities and a withdrawal of forces so that conditions may be created for progress toward a political solution conducive to a lasting peace in the area.

Mr. President, in an effort to end the bloodshed, to save lives, to reduce the untold suffering, we are introducing a resolution which if promptly enacted offers the world a chance to escape another ghastly war. On behalf of my Government I have the honor to submit this draft resolution[85] which in our view meets the requirements of the situation before us:

> *The Security Council,*
>
> *Having heard* the statements of the representatives of India and Pakistan,
>
> *Convinced that* hostilities along the India-Pakistan border constitute an immediate threat to international peace and security,
>
> 1. *Calls upon* the Governments of India and Pakistan to take all steps required for an immediate cessation of hostilities;
>
> 2. *Calls* for an immediate withdrawal of armed personnel present on the territory of the other to their own sides of the India-Pakistan borders;
>
> 3. *Authorizes* the Secretary-General, at the request of the Government of India or Pakistan, to place observers along the India-Pakistan borders to report on the implementation of the cease-fire and troop withdrawals, drawing as necessary on UNMOGIP [United Nations Military Observer Group for India and Pakistan] personnel;
>
> 4. *Calls upon* the Governments of India and Pakistan and others concerned to exert their best efforts toward the creation of a climate conducive to the voluntary return of refugees to East Pakistan;

[85] U.N. document S/10416.

5. *Calls upon* all States to refrain from any action that would endanger the peace in the area;

6. *Invites* the Governments of India and Pakistan to respond affirmatively to the proposal of the Secretary-General offering good offices to secure and maintain peace in the subcontinent;

7. *Requests* the Secretary-General to report to the Security Council as soon as possible on the implementation of this resolution.

[*Note*: The proposed resolution failed of adoption early on December 5, 1971, by a vote of 11 in favor and 2 opposed (Poland, U.S.S.R.), with 2 abstentions (France, U.K.). A similar draft resolution sponsored by Argentina, Belgium, Burundi, Italy, Japan, Nicaragua, Sierra Leone, and Somalia[86] failed of adoption by an identical vote.]

(59) Referral to the General Assembly.

(a) Statement by Ambassador Bush to the Security Council, December 6, 1971.[87]

(Excerpt)

*   *   *

Now, Mr. President, at our session last night I noted[88] that the Council was meeting because it was faced with a clear and present threat to the peace of the world, because the area and scope of the fighting had broadened and had intensified, and because the Council had a responsibility under the charter to stop the fighting and preserve the territorial integrity of member states.

Eleven members of this Council—a clear majority—signified on two separate occasions their desire to exercise the responsibilities of the Security Council under the charter. They voted in favor of two draft resolutions[89] which called upon the Governments of India and Pakistan to take forthwith measures for an immediate cease-fire and withdrawal

---

86 U.N. document S/10423, in Security Council, *Official Records: 26th Year, Supplement for Oct., Nov. and Dec. 1971*, p. 93.
87 USUN Press Release 209, Dec. 6, 1971; text from *Bulletin*, Dec. 27, 1971, pp. 726-27.
88 Statement of Dec. 5, 1971, in *Bulletin*, Dec. 27, 1971, pp. 724-25.
89 See above at notes 85 and 86.

of their armed forces on the territories of the other to their own side of the borders. And they recognized the need to intensify efforts to bring about speedily, and in accordance with the principles of the charter, conditions necessary for the voluntary return of the East Pakistan refugees to their homeland.

Unfortunately, as our distinguished colleague from Argentina [Carlos Ortiz de Rozos] mentioned and as we touched on last night, one permanent member of this Council [the U.S.S.R.] did not support this approach and exercised under the rules its veto over these two resolutions. In the midst of this grave situation, the action of this member has rendered the Council unable to act in order to restore peace and security in South Asia. We are not able in this crisis even to call for a halt to the fighting and the return of troops to within their own borders.

In these circumstances, we are faced with the prospect that the world will conclude that the United Nations is unable to fulfill its charter obligations to restore international peace and security where they are threatened. This Council must do all within its power to assure this does not happen; it must explore every feasible avenue for action. Judging by the statements made by most other members at our last session, it is also clear that a large majority is agreed that we cannot leave the matter where it is. The status quo is intolerable, and the threat to peace is too real; and the plight of the refugees and the civilian population in general is too urgent for us to engage in further demonstrations of the inability of this Council to carry out its duties under the charter. Fortunately, there are additional steps that we can take to permit the full membership of the United Nations to examine this urgent question and bring their influence to bear in favor of restoring peace in South Asia.

The Uniting for Peace Resolution provides[90] that:

> ... if the Security Council, because of the lack of unanimity of the permanent members, fails to exercise its primary responsibility for the maintenance of international peace and security in any case where there appears to be a threat to the peace, breach of the peace, or act of aggression, the General Assembly shall consider the matter immediately with a view to making appropriate recommendations. ...

Accordingly, Mr. President, the United States joins the representatives of Somalia, Argentina, Burundi [Nsanzé Térence]—hopefully, many more—in supporting the draft resolution which provides for referral of this urgent and important question to the 26th session of the General Assembly for immediate consideration. We fervently hope that the Assembly will prove itself equal to the task so that the United Nations

[90] Resolution 377 (V), Nov. 3, 1950 in *Documents, 1950*, p. 183.

will have fulfilled these grave responsibilities that it bears under the charter.

(b) Security Council Resolution 303 (1971), Adopted December 6, 1971.[91]

(Complete Text)

The Security Council,

Having considered the item on the agenda of its 1606th meeting, as contained in document S/Agenda/1606,

Taking into account that the lack of unanimity of its permanent members at the 1606th and 1607th meetings of the Security Council has prevented it from exercising its primary responsibility for the maintenance of international peace and security,

Decides to refer the question contained in document S/Agenda/1606 to the General Assembly at its twenty-sixth session, as provided for in Assembly resolution 377 A (V) of 3 November 1950.[92]

3. Action in the General Assembly, December 7, 1971.

[The issue presented by the continuing war in the Subcontinent was taken up by the General Assembly on December 7, within hours of its relinquishment by the Security Council the previous day. Following renewed expositions of the positions of the interested parties by Ambassador Bush (Document 60) and other delegates, the Assembly proceeded late on December 7 to adopt a 14-nation draft resolution (Document 61) which, like the resolutions already vetoed by the U.S.S.R. in the Security Council, called for a cease-fire and withdrawal of armed forces—but which, in contrast to a Security Council resolution, would have the force merely of a recommendation rather than a legally binding order. The vote for adoption was 104 to 11, with 10 abstentions. China, Pakistan, and the United States were among those voting for adoption; India and the U.S.S.R. voted against; France and the United Kingdom abstained, as they had done in the Security Council.]

---

[91] Security Council, *Official Records: 26th Year, Resolutions and Decisions*, p. 10; adopted by a vote of 11-0-4 (France, Poland, U.S.S.R., U.K.).

[92] Text in *Documents, 1950*, pp. 183-86.

(60) Urgency of a Cease-fire: Statement by Ambassador Bush to the General Assembly, December 7, 1971. [93]

(Complete Text)

Mr. President, there is no need for me at this time to restate or to summarize the agony which is tearing asunder the Indian subcontinent. While we recoil in horror as this tragedy unfolds before us, none of us can profess to be surprised. As long ago as August 2, the Secretary General called the attention of the world at large to the growing crisis in South Asia. He offered his good offices, and that offer was unfortunately not welcomed by the Indian Government. [94]

In the previous months, in addition to the efforts of the Secretary General to seek a political solution, he organized relief and assistance for the swelling numbers of refugees. [95] Individual member states, my own included, made efforts to avert war.

Let me say just a word here about American policy, the policy of the United States Government. The thrust of our policy has contained four principal elements.

First, before the outbreak of broader hostilities, we counseled restraint on both sides in every conceivable way that we could.

Second, we recognized that the flow of refugees created a great problem for India, a tremendous problem, and the United States therefore has contributed its material resources, not begrudgingly, much more than any other country in the world, but we accept this as our responsibility to care for the refugees.

Third, in seeking to prevent the outbreak of hostilities, the United States made valiant but unfortunately unsuccessful efforts to achieve withdrawal of the forces from both sides of the borders. Pakistan agreed to our proposals. Regrettably, India did not.

And fourth, we recognized that counsels of restraint, material support for the care of refugees that I mentioned earlier, and proposals to withdraw the forces and thereby to defuse the situation, that all of these were not enough, and we felt that a political dialogue to achieve political accommodation was indeed essential.

And to this end, we did suggest directly to President Yahya that he meet with opposition representatives. Pakistan was willing; India was not receptive to this approach.

Mr. President, we attach great value to friendly relations with both countries, just as the speakers who have preceded me to this podium;

---

[93] USUN Press Release 210, Dec. 7, 1971; text in *Bulletin*, Dec. 27, 1971, pp. 727-28.
[94] Texts of Thant statement and Indian reply in *UN Monthly Chronicle*, Aug.-Sept. 1971, pp. 56-62.
[95] Cf. *UN Monthly Chronicle*, July 1971, pp. 26-27.

and we have said, and we repeat, that the beginning of the crisis goes back to the use of force by Pakistan in March of this year. But since the beginning of the crisis it should also be clear that India bears a major responsibility for broadening the crisis by spurning efforts of the United Nations to become involved, even in a humanitarian way in relation to the refugees, spurning the proposals such as the proposal of our Secretary General's offer of good offices which could have helped in defusing the crisis, spurning proposals that could have begun the process of dialogue toward political accommodation.

Mr. President, that having been said, we are not here, any nation, to assess blame. We cannot approach this problem on the basis of rancor or punitive measures. Our task is to bring at this point in history the influence of the United Nations to bear in order to restore conditions of peace which are essential for progress toward a political settlement.

It is upon the civilian population in the areas of conflict that the devastation of war falls most cruelly. The very people, the peaceful farmers of yesterday are indeed the refugees of today. And the emotions of war can be magnified manyfold when they are mixed with longstanding communal and religious differences.

We in this body must be particularly mindful of the need to protect lives and the well-being of all the civilian population in the areas where fighting is going on. And we must remind the parties engaged in the conflict of their duty to observe the basic human rights of those involved.

Mr. President, I am hopeful, and I know others are, that early this afternoon we would hope to vote on and pass overwhelmingly the draft resolution presented so ably by Argentina and the many cosponsors.[96]

Let us act not with recrimination, not out of any desire to assign blame, not out of an effort to make one country look good or one country look bad. Let us act simply to save lives, to reestablish peace, and to get about the important business that is and must be the United Nations itself.

(61) Call for a Cease-fire and Withdrawal: General Assembly Resolution 2793 (XXVI), Adopted December 7, 1971.[97]

(Complete Text)

The General Assembly,
Noting the reports of the Secretary-General of 3 and 4 December

---

[96] Document 61.
[97] General Assembly, *Official Records: 26th Session, Supplement No. 29* (A/8429), p. 3; adopted by a vote of 104-11-10.

1971[98] and the letter from the President of the Security Council[99] transmitting the text of Council resolution 303 (1971) of 6 December 1971,[100]

Gravely concerned that hostilities have broken out between India and Pakistan which constitute an immediate threat to international peace and security,

Recognizing the need to deal appropriately at a subsequent stage, within the framework of the Charter of the United Nations, with the issues which have given rise to the hostilities,

Convinced that an early political solution would be necessary for the restoration of conditions of normalcy in the area of conflict and for the return of the refugees to their homes,

Mindful of the provisions of the Charter, in particular of Article 2, paragraph 4,[101]

Recalling the Declaration on the Strengthening of International Security,[102] particularly paragraphs 4, 5 and 6,

Recognizing further the need to take immediate measures to bring about an immediate cessation of hostilities between India and Pakistan and effect a withdrawal of their armed forces to their own side of the India-Pakistan borders,

Mindful of the purposes and principles of the Charter and of the General Assembly's responsibilities under the relevant provisions of the Charter and of Assembly resolution 377 A (V) of 3 November 1950,[103]

1. *Calls upon* the Governments of India and Pakistan to take forthwith all measures for an immediate cease-fire and withdrawal of their armed forces on the territory of the other to their own side of the India-Pakistan borders;

2. *Urges* that efforts be intensified in order to bring about, speedily and in accordance with the purposes and principles of the Charter of the United Nations, conditions necessary for the voluntary return of the East Pakistan refugees to their homes;

3. *Calls* for the full co-operation of all States with the Secretary-General for rendering assistance to and relieving the distress of those refugees;

4. *Urges* that every effort be made to safeguard the lives and well-being of the civilian population in the area of conflict;

5. *Requests* the Secretary-General to keep the General Assembly and

---

[98] U.N. documents S/10410 and Add. 1 and S/10412, in Security Council, *Official Records: 26th Year, Supplement for Oct., Nov. and Dec. 1971*, pp. 80-86 and 87-88.

[99] U.N. document A/8555, in General Assembly, *Official Records: 26th Session, Annexes*, agenda item 102.

[100] Document 59b.

[101] Obligating all members to refrain from threat or use of force, etc.

[102] Cf. note 54, above.

[103] Cf. above at note 90.

the Security Council promptly and currently informed on the implementation of the present resolution;

6. *Decides* to follow the question closely and to meet again should the situation so demand;

7. *Calls upon* the Security Council to take appropriate action in the light of the present resolution.[104]

4. Action in the Security Council, December 12-21, 1971.

[The General Assembly's call for a cease-fire and withdrawal of armed forces (Document 61) proved no more effective in interrupting the course of military operations than had the vetoed resolutions in the Security Council. Pakistan, whose military position had continued to worsen, announced acceptance of the General Assembly resolution on December 9.[105] But India—which had meanwhile accorded formal recognition to the self-proclaimed state of "Bangladesh"—advised the United Nations on December 12 that its acceptance of a cease-fire and withdrawal would be contingent upon "the rulers of West Pakistan" withdrawing their forces from Bangladesh and reaching a peaceful settlement with the people of that country.[106]

A further source of worry to the United States, according to President Nixon, was the failure of India and its supporters to rebut "convincing evidence that India was seriously contemplating the seizure of Pakistan-held portions of Kashmir and the destruction of Pakistan's military forces in the West." "We had to take action to prevent a wider war," the President later wrote.[107] At an emergency session of the Security Council, convened at the United States' request on December 12, Ambassador Bush presented still another resolution calling for a cease-fire and withdrawal of armed forces (Document 62). This resolution, too, was vetoed by the U.S.S.R. on December 13 in what amounted to a replay of the earlier Soviet vetoes.

Additional tension arose with the disclosure that a task force of the U.S. Seventh Fleet, including the nuclear-powered aircraft carrier *Enterprise*, had left positions off South Vietnam on December 10 and entered the Bay of Bengal on December 15, ostensibly to evacuate U.S. nationals from East Pakistan in case of need. Although India expressed the keenest resentment of what it regarded as U.S. military pressure, its own military success in East Pakistan was by this time virtually complete. Pakistan's military command in the East surrendered uncon-

---

[104] Cf. Documents 62-63.
[105] U.N. document S/10440, Dec. 9, 1971, in Security Council, *Official Records: 26th Year, Supplement for Oct., Nov. and Dec. 1971*, p. 103.
[106] U.N. document S/10445, Dec. 12, 1971, in same, pp. 105-6.
[107] Nixon Report, 1972, p. 147.

ditionally on December 16, and a general cease-fire in both East and West was accepted by President Yahya Khan on December 17.

The Security Council, with a variety of resolutions still pending before it, suspended its discussion with the news of Pakistan's surrender, but met again on December 21 to adopt a compromise resolution calling for strict observance of the cease-fire already in effect and early withdrawal of all armed forces to their respective territories (Document 63). Introduced by six nonpermanent members of the Security Council, this resolution—the first to escape a Soviet veto—was adopted by a vote of 13 to 0, with Poland and the U.S.S.R. abstaining.]

(62) Renewed Call for a Cease-fire: Statement by Ambassador Bush to the Security Council, December 12, 1971, with Draft United States Resolution Vetoed by the U.S.S.R. December 13, 1971.[108]

(Complete Text)

I have asked for the Security Council to reconvene because it is essential that this body promptly and effectively deal with the threat to international peace and security which is continuing in the subcontinent. In asking for this immediate meeting of the Council, the United States today made the following statement:[109]

On December 7 the General Assembly, by vote of 104 to 11, with 10 abstentions, called on India and Pakistan to institute an immediate cease-fire and to withdraw troops from each other's territory.[110] Pakistan has accepted the resolution. India has refused.[111] In view of India's defiance of world opinion expressed by such an overwhelming majority, the United States is now returning the issue to the Security Council. With East Pakistan virtually occupied by Indian troops, a continuation of the war would take on increasingly the character of armed attack on the very existence of a member state of the U.N. All permanent members of the Security Council have an obligation to end this threat to world peace on the most urgent basis. The United States will cooperate fully in this effort.

Mr. President, this is a war that need never have taken place. The opportunity for progress toward a peaceful accommodation was, in our

---

[108] USUN Press Release 220, Dec. 12, 1971; text from *Bulletin*, Jan. 17, 1972, pp. 67-70.
[109] Read to news correspondents by Ronald L. Ziegler, Press Secretary to President Nixon.
[110] Document 61.
[111] See above at notes 105-6.

view, available. It was refused by the Indian Government, just as India has spurned the world organization by not replying to the resolution of the General Assembly.

Let me first focus on events in March of this year. It was on March 25 that the central government of Pakistan decided to use force in East Pakistan. The United States has never supported or condoned that action which was followed by a tragic series of subsequent events. We regretted that action, and we took measures promptly to stop certain military and economic aid that was going into Pakistan. We have always recognized that the events of March 25 had a very important impact on India. We have always recognized that the influx of refugees into India broadened the danger of communal strife. We fully appreciated both the social and economic strain that the influx of refugees imposed on India.

The fact that the use of force in East Pakistan in March can be characterized as a tragic mistake does not justify the actions of India to intervene militarily and place in jeopardy the territorial integrity and political independence of its neighbor Pakistan.

I want to describe to the members of the Council in some detail how we viewed the situation a few weeks before Prime Minister Indira Gandhi came to Washington on November 4[112] and what we did to try to resolve matters peacefully.

We were prepared to take at face value the Indian statements that they preferred a peaceful resolution of the matter to war. We asked ourselves how could we be helpful if in fact India's intentions were peaceful. In the context of that visit, the Indian Government was informed of four things.

First, the small trickle of military spare parts which had remained in the pipeline to Pakistan was terminated. It could no longer be said that this insignificant flow could in any way be considered as a continuing irritant in the relations between the United States and India. We have thereby maintained a climate of confidence in U.S.-Pakistan relations. That climate of confidence in turn helped bring about Pakistan's co-operation with the United Nations relief efforts and with U.S. proposals which could have moved matters to the conference table rather than to the battlefield.

Second, the United States had pledged additional financial and economic assistance for the care of the refugees, making clear that on top of the $90 million already contributed for India in this regard, the President had asked for $250 million additional for relief in the area.[113]

---

112 Prime Minister Gandhi made an official visit to the U.S. on Nov. 3-7 and met with President Nixon and other government officials in Washington on Nov. 4-5, 1971. For documentation see *Public Papers, 1971*, pp. 1079-85.
113 Cf. note 72 above.

Third, we felt that, as important as financial resources were, some practical step was needed to defuse the situation. We knew that the Indian Government some 2 weeks before had already rejected a prior American proposal for mutual withdrawal of forces. We, therefore, after full consultations with President Yahya, were in a position to tell the Indian Government in the context of the visit that the Pakistan Government was willing to make a unilateral step of withdrawal first, provided it could be assured that some subsequent reciprocal step would be taken by India. I repeat that this was a unilateral step of withdrawal about which we had been given assurances. India's response was a public call that the Pakistan Government should pull its forces out of its own territory in East Pakistan.

Fourth, we were particularly concerned that some practical step also be taken toward political accommodation. We accepted the Indian view that a step for military disengagement in and of itself was not enough. Therefore during the visit the Indian Government was informed that after discussions with the United States, the Pakistan Government was prepared to do the following:

a. Its representatives were willing to meet with an appropriate representative of the Awami League from Dacca;[114] alternatively,

b. It was willing to meet with an appropriate so-called "Bangla Desh" representative from Calcutta;[115]

c. It also was willing to consider meeting with a representative designated by [Sheikh] Mujibur Rahman.[116]

Given the extremely difficult nature of the problem, we had some reason to feel after the high-level U.S.-Indian talks in November that while all of the Indian conditions had obviously not been met, these were a series of proposals which could begin to turn the cycle away from violence to a peaceful settlement taking into account the aspirations of the people concerned. These proposals also proved to be an acid test of the intentions of the Government of India.

The Indian response to the first two proposals was rejection. As to the third proposal, while India at first seemed interested, it again took a consistent position that the only step toward political accommodation that was feasible was the release of Mujib and negotiations between him and Yahya. This is the one step President Yahya did not feel able to

[114] The Awami League was the majority party in East Pakistan; Dacca was the provincial capital. The Awami League had been officially outlawed by the Government of Pakistan on Mar. 26, 1971.

[115] Leaders of the Awami League had proclaimed the independence of Bangladesh on Mar. 26, 1971, and had shortly thereafter removed to Calcutta, where they functioned as a government-in-exile.

[116] Sheikh Mujibur Rahman, the most prominent Awami League leader, had been arrested by Pakistani military forces in Mar. 1971 and was under detention in West Pakistan, but had been declared President of Bangladesh on Apr. 11, 1971.

take. We believe that it was much more important for a dialogue to begin without preconditions.

Because India was unresponsive to these diplomatic efforts, I said the following in the General Assembly on December 7:[117]

> ...we have said, and we repeat, that the beginning of the crisis goes back to the use of force by Pakistan in March of this year. But since the beginning of the crisis it should also be clear that India bears a major responsibility for broadening the crisis by spurning efforts of the United Nations to become involved, even in a humanitarian way in relation to the refugees, spurning the proposals such as the proposal of our Secretary General's offer of good offices which could have helped in defusing the crisis, spurning proposals that could have begun the process of dialogue toward political accommodation.

I reaffirm this judgment categorically on behalf of the U.S. Government.

Now India has gone further. With the support of two Soviet vetoes, it has previously prevented the Security Council from adopting resolutions calling for a cease-fire and withdrawal of forces.[118] One hundred and four countries in the General Assembly supported precisely this course of action, but in defiance of this expression of world opinion India again says No.[119] They continue to prefer the use of force to peaceful means. India—which over the years has sought to reflect in and outside of this chamber the moral force of the world, the very precepts for which its great leaders, [Mohandas K.] Gandhi and [Jawaharlal] Nehru, stood—is now disregarding the Charter of the United Nations. And now developments have reached a point in the area where Indian military actions have not only led to virtual occupation of East Pakistan but to a war which is increasingly taking on the earmarks of an attack on the very life of a member state of this organization.

The question now arises as to India's further intentions. For example, does India intend to use the present situation to destroy the Pakistan army in the west? Does India intend to use as a pretext the Pakistan counterattacks in the west to annex territory in West Pakistan? Is its aim to take parts of Pakistan-controlled Kashmir contrary to the Security Council resolutions of 1948, 1949, and 1950?[120] If this is not India's intention, then a prompt disavowal is required. The world has a right to know: What are India's intentions? Pakistan's aims have be-

---

117 Document 60.
118 Cf. above at note 86.
119 Cf. above at note 106.
120 Cf. *Everyman's United Nations* (Eighth ed.), pp. 110-13.

come clear: It has accepted the General Assembly's resolution passed by a vote of 104 to 11.[121] My government has asked this question of the Indian Government several times in the last week. I regret to inform the Council that India's replies have been unsatisfactory and not reassuring.

This Council has a responsibility to demand as a first step immediate compliance of India with the resolutions on cease-fire and withdrawal. It should also insist that India give to the members of this Council a clear and unequivocal assurance that it does not intend to annex Pakistani territory and change the status quo in Kashmir contrary to U.N. resolutions. Otherwise India will be injecting a new and more serious dimension to the risks and hostilities in the subcontinent.

Mr. President, I am submitting the following resolution, which I will read to the Security Council. As the members of the Council will see, it is in substance essentially the same as the resolution adopted in the Assembly with the support of 104 members.[122] Pakistan has accepted the resolution, and we urge India to end its defiance of this overwhelming world opinion and support the resolution and help bring about an immediate end to what the U.N. overwhelmingly feels is a senseless war.

It was in an effort following the instructions of the General Assembly to again try to solve this conflict through peaceful means that we are tabling this resolution[123] that I would like to read at this point:

The Security Council,

Noting the reports of the Secretary-General of 3 and 4 December 1971[124] and Security Council resolution 303 (1971) of 6 December 1971,[125]

Noting General Assembly resolution 2793 (XXVI) of 7 December 1971,[126] adopted by a vote of 104-11-10,

Noting further that the Government of Pakistan has accepted a cease-fire and withdrawal of armed forces as set forth in General Assembly resolution 2793 (XXVI), and India's failure to do so,[127]

Gravely concerned that hostilities continue between India and

---

[121] Cf. note 105 above.
[122] Document 61.
[123] U.N. document S/10446, Dec. 12, 1971.
[124] See note 98 above.
[125] Document 59b.
[126] Document 61.
[127] Cf. above at notes 105 and 106. In the revised draft resolution as voted upon on Dec. 13, the words "and India's failure to do so" were replaced by the words "and the Government of India's letter in U.N. document S/10445." For text of the revised draft resolution (U.N. document S/10446/Rev. 1) see Security Council, *Official Records: 26th Year, Supplement for Oct., Nov. and Dec. 1971*, p. 107.

Pakistan which constitute an immediate threat to international peace and security,

Recognizing the need to deal appropriately at a subsequent stage, within the framework of the Charter of the United Nations, with the issues which have given rise to the hostilities,

Convinced that an early political solution would be necessary for the restoration of conditions of normalcy in the area of conflict and for the return of the refugees to their homes,

Mindful of the provisions of the Charter, in particular of Article 2, paragraph 4,[128]

Recalling the Declaration on the Strengthening of International Security, particularly paragraphs 4, 5 and 6,[129]

Recognizing further the need to take immediate measures to bring about an immediate cessation of hostilities between India and Pakistan and effect a withdrawal of their armed forces to their own side of the India-Pakistan borders,

Mindful of the purposes and principles of the Charter and of the Security Council's responsibilities under the relevant provisions of the Charter,

1. *Calls upon* the Government of India forthwith to accept a cease-fire and withdrawal of armed forces as set forth in General Assembly resolution 2793 (XXVI);

2. *Calls upon* the Governments of India and Pakistan to take forthwith all measures for an immediate cease-fire and withdrawal of their armed forces on the territory of the other to their own side of the India-Pakistan borders;

3. *Urges* that efforts be intensified in order to bring about, speedily and in accordance with the purposes and principles of the Charter of the United Nations, conditions necessary for the voluntary return of the East Pakistan refugees to their homes;

4. *Calls for* the full co-operation of all States with the Secretary-General for rendering assistance to and relieving the distress of those refugees;

5. *Calls upon* all parties concerned to take all possible measures and precautions to safeguard the lives and well-being of the civilian population in the area;

6. *Requests* the Secretary-General to keep the Security Council promptly and currently informed on the implementation of the present resolution;

7. *Decides* to remain seized of the matter and to meet again as circumstances warrant.

---

128 Cf. note 101 above.
129 Cf. note 54 above.

Mr. President, it was almost a week ago that the General Assembly passed a resolution by 104 to 11. Since then the Security Council has been inactive. There have been, I expect, some consultations between some parties, but there have been no intensified consultations. The Security Council indeed has almost not been seized of the matter at all. Before a week has elapsed, it seems to us that the Security Council should now here urgently address itself once again to this question of war and peace, address itself to the question of cease-fire and withdrawal, address itself in the light of a week of destruction and untold loss of lives on both sides, address itself in a statesmanlike fashion to this resolution which we feel—so overwhelmingly adopted by the General Assembly—merits the sincere and urgent consideration of everyone at this table.[130]

(63) Demanding Observance of the Cease-Fire: Security Council Resolution 307 (1971), Adopted December 21, 1971.[131]

(Complete Text)

The Security Council,

Having discussed the grave situation in the subcontinent, which remains a threat to international peace and security,

Noting General Assembly resolution 2793 (XXVI) of 7 December 1971,[132]

Noting the reply of the Government of Pakistan on 9 December 1971,[133]

Noting the reply of the Government of India on 12 December 1971,[134]

Having heard the statements of the Deputy Prime Minister of Pakistan[135] and the Foreign Minister of India,[136]

Noting further the statement made at the 1616th meeting of the Security Council[137] by the Foreign Minister of India containing a unilateral declaration of a cease-fire in the western theatre,

Noting Pakistan's agreement to the cease-fire in the western theatre with effect from 17 December 1971,

---

[130] The revised draft of the U.S. resolution (note 127, above) failed of adoption on Dec. 13, 1971 by a vote of 11-2 (Poland, U.S.S.R.)-2 (France, U.K.).
[131] Security Council, Official Records: 26th Year, Resolutions and Decisions, p. 11; adopted by a vote of 13-0-2 (Poland, U.S.S.R.).
[132] Document 61.
[133] Note 105 above.
[134] Note 106 above.
[135] Zulfiqar Ali Bhutto.
[136] Swaran Singh.
[137] Dec. 16, 1971.

Noting that consequently a cease-fire and a cessation of hostilities prevail,

1. *Demands* that a durable cease-fire and cessation of all hostilities in all areas of conflict be strictly observed and remain in effect until withdrawals take place, as soon as practicable, of all armed forces to their respective territories and to positions which fully respect the cease-fire line in Jammu and Kashmir supervised by the United Nations Military Observer Group in India and Pakistan;

2. *Calls upon* all Member States to refrain from any action which may aggravate the situation in the subcontinent or endanger international peace;

3. *Calls upon* all those concerned to take all measures necessary to preserve human life and for the observance of the Geneva Conventions of 1949[138] and to apply in full their provisions as regards the protection of the wounded and sick, prisoners of war and civilian population;

4. *Calls for* international assistance in the relief of suffering and the rehabilitation of refugees and their return in safety and dignity to their homes, and for full co-operation with the Secretary-General to that effect;

5. *Authorizes* the Secretary-General to appoint if necessary a special representative to lend his good offices for the solution of humanitarian problems;

6. *Requests* the Secretary-General to keep the Council informed without delay on developments relating to the implementation of the present resolution;

7. *Decides* to remain seized of the matter and to keep it under active consideration.

5. Aftermath of the Conflict.

[The surrender of the Pakistani armed forces on December 16-17, 1971, left India in military occupation of the entire territory of East Pakistan (Bangladesh), with roughly 100,000 Pakistani prisoners in Indian hands and with forces of the two countries remaining on both sides of the previous frontier and cease-fire lines. In West Pakistan, President Yahya Khan was removed as head of the national government on December 20 and succeeded by former Foreign Minister and Deputy Prime Minister Zulfiqar Ali Bhutto, West Pakistan's most prominent civilian politician, who showed reluctance to concede the loss of East Pakistan but was quick to adopt a more conciliatory line than that of the previous military regime. Although the new "People's Republic of Bangladesh" had thus far been recognized only by India and Bhutan,

---

[138] Conventions of Aug. 12, 1949 (TIAS 3362-5; 6 UST 3114, 3217, 3316, and 3516).

early recognition by other governments already appeared in prospect. The implications of these developments for the United States were touched upon by Secretary of State Rogers at his year-end news conference (Document 64), in the course of which he also expressed the view that the relationship between the United States and the U.S.S.R. had not been permanently impaired by their diplomatic conflict over the Subcontinent (Document 30).]

(64) Policy Toward India and Pakistan: News Conference Statement by Secretary of State Rogers, December 23, 1971.[139]

(Excerpt)

* * *

Q. Mr. Secretary, the other day President Bhutto said that President Nixon had assured him that the United States was for the unity and integrity of Pakistan, I think his phrasing was. Is it U.S. policy to consider the two wings of Pakistan as one country?

A. Well, U.S. policy is to let the people in that area determine their own future, and we have made that clear to all concerned. We did favor, we do favor, unity as a principle, and we do not favor secession as a principle, because once you start down that road it could be very destabilizing. There are a lot of areas in the world where secession, if it started, if it became a way of life, could be very, very dangerous to the rest of the world.

So we favor, as a matter of principle and as a matter of United States policy, the settlement of international disputes by peaceful means and not by force. And that is the reason that we took the position that we took in the United Nations in connection with the problems in the subcontinent. And that is the reason 104 nations supported the positions the United States took.[140]

Q. Mr. Secretary, can the United States recognize the new state of Bangla Desh, and if so, when?

A. Well, we haven't faced up to that question. We would not anticipate that it would arise for some time. We will just have to watch events, consider it very carefully when the time comes. But certainly

---

[139] Department of State Press Release 303, Dec. 23, 1971; text from *Bulletin*, Jan. 17, 1972, pp. 53-54. For further excerpts from the same news conference see Documents 10, 30, 110, and 116.
[140] Document 61.

there has been no consideration given to that up to this point.[141]

Q. Mr. Secretary, how does the United States intend to reestablish balanced relations in the subcontinent in the wake of the war, particularly in the case of India and in the case of Bangla Desh?

A. Well, as I say, we will watch developments. We will consider our policy very carefully in the light of the events that recently occurred and make our decisions based on those events and on the discussions we have with the parties concerned.

* * *

D. The Indian Ocean

[Increasing international interest in the Indian Ocean region during 1971 was largely though not exclusively attributable to a marked growth in Soviet naval activity in the area since the period of the Arab–Israeli war in 1967. American views on this trend and its possible implications were expounded by the competent State Department expert in an appearance before a subcommittee of the House Foreign Affairs Committee in July 1971 (Document 65).

A plan to safeguard the region from great-power rivalries by keeping it free of military installations and activities, originally advanced by Ceylon at the Third Conference of Nonaligned States in Lusaka (Zambia) in September 1970, was brought before the U.N. General Assembly in October 1971 by Ceylonese Prime Minister Sirimavo Bandaranaike and embodied in a resolution declaring the Indian Ocean to be a "zone of peace" (Document 66). China, however, was the only major power to support this resolution, which was favored mainly by nonaligned countries and adopted by a vote of 61 to 0 with 55 abstentions, including that of the United States. It was the American view, Secretary Rogers later explained, "that the interests of the United States in the Indian Ocean can best be served by normal political, commercial, and military access to the area. At the same time, we seek to avoid military competition with the Soviet Union or other powers in the Indian Ocean."[142]

---

[141] The U.S. established diplomatic relations with Bangladesh on May 18, 1972; cf. *A.F.R., 1972*, nos. 40-42.
[142] Rogers Report, 1971, p. 117.

(65) United States National Security Policy and the Indian Ocean: Statement by Ronald I. Spiers, Director, Bureau of Politico-Military Affairs, Department of State, Before the Subcommittee on National Security Policy and Scientific Developments of the House Committee on Foreign Affairs, July 28, 1971. [143]

(Complete Text)

I am pleased to have this opportunity to contribute to your consideration of our national security policy as it relates to the Indian Ocean area.

The Indian Ocean area, unlike Europe and Asia, is one which has been only on the margins of U.S. attention. Never considered of great importance to the central balance of power, it has been on the edges of great-power rivalry.

Recently, this basic perspective has been challenged and attention has focused anew on the Indian Ocean. The buildup of the Soviet Navy and the more or less regular appearance of Soviet naval vessels in the Indian Ocean, the U.S.-British decision to build an austere communications facility on Diego Garcia [see below], and the controversy in the U.K. on the issue of arms supply to South Africa have all contributed to this renewed interest.

Important issues are raised for U.S. foreign and defense policy which require consideration. Some of the questions are: What are the nature and consequence of the Soviet presence? What are the repercussions of going ahead with Diego Garcia? Is there any way of avoiding an arms competition in the area? What are the attitudes of the littoral states, and how will they affect our course of action? How do we inhibit a Soviet hegemony which might, in time, affect the central balance of power adversely to our interests?

I would like to review the disparate factors which are involved in this problem: our strategic interests, and those of the Soviets and the Chinese, the views of the states in the area, our own political objectives. In doing so, I would like to examine recent developments that bear on U.S. policy toward the Indian Ocean area, including the Red and Arabian Seas, the Persian Gulf, the Bay of Bengal, and the bordering states.

Since the days of the Portuguese navigators, the Indian Ocean area has seen outside power competition and influence. To this day the Portuguese remain a significant regional power through their control of the large and restive territory of Mozambique. French influence is also present, as France controls several islands in the Indian Ocean, including Réunion, and the strategic port of Djibouti in the Gulf of Aden and has maintained access to the large naval base at Diégo-Suarez in the

[143] *Bulletin*, Aug. 23, 1971, pp. 199-203.

Malagasy Republic. However, the basic historic imprint in the region has been British. By the end of World War II, British supremacy in the area was more illusory than real and proved short-lived.

This erosion was one of several factors that caused the gradual emergence of U.S. involvement in the region. Our pre-1945 focus in the area was founded on the treasure trove of oil in the Persian Gulf and by the Persian Gulf Command in Iran, which managed delivery of lend-lease equipment to the Soviet Union. Our close wartime association with Iran survived, in large measure due to the postwar Soviet effort to detach Azerbaijan Province from Iran.

An American military presence was introduced to the area in 1948. This force (COMID-EASTFOR) consists of a small flagship—a converted seaplane tender—home-ported at British facilities in Bahrain and two destroyers assigned on a rotational basis from the Atlantic Fleet.

Under arrangements with the Saudi Government a Strategic Air Command recovery base became operational at Dhahran in 1951, until terminated at Saudi request in the early sixties. Dhahran remains a key Military Airlift Command transit base.

During the 1950's, military advisory and training missions were sent to Iran, Saudi Arabia, and Ethiopia and today remain important assets in the exercising of U.S. influence in the region. Bilateral defense agreements were negotiated with Iran[144] and Pakistan[145] in 1950 and 1954, respectively, which interlocked with the Baghdad Pact of 1955[146] (CENTO after 1958) and, in the case of Pakistan, with SEATO [South-East Asia Treaty Organization]. To underscore and fortify our growing interest in the Indian Ocean area, substantial military and economic aid was initiated in the early 1950's and has continued to this day.

In the sixties, British power and influence continued to decline. Twelve new independent states emerged from former British-controlled territories. The Labor government announced in January 1968 that the British security arrangement with Kuwait would terminate in 1970 and the British military presence in the gulf would be phased out by the end of 1971. The British are still hopeful that their efforts to establish a reasonably viable federation of the Trucial Shaikhdoms, and perhaps Qatar and Bahrain, can serve as a stabilizing factor in the gulf as a substitute for redeployed British forces. This is by no means assured, although we are encouraged by the recent announcement that six of the seven Trucial Shaikhdoms may accede to federation.[147]

During the same period a parallel rise in U.S. activity continued. The

---

[144] Signed May 23, 1950 (TIAS 2071; 1 UST 420); cf. *Documents, 1950*, p. 220.
[145] Signed May 19, 1954 (TIAS 2976; 5 UST 852); cf. same, *1954*, pp. 379-83.
[146] Same, *1955*, pp. 342-44.
[147] Six of the seven former Trucial States formed the United Arab Emirates on Dec. 2, 1971; the seventh (Ras al-Khaima) acceded to membership on Feb. 11, 1972.

Chinese Communist incursion into Indian territory in the North East Frontier Agency and Ladakh in November 1962[148] led to a substantial U.S. military aid program. Our new association with India survived until the Indian-Pakistani 3-week war in September 1965.[149] Meanwhile, our previously close relations with Pakistan had deteriorated rapidly, in part as a result of our post-1962 support of India.

It was during this period of the early 1960's that the Departments of State and Defense began thinking of the longer term strategic requirements of the United States in the Indian Ocean area. This was the actual inception of the British Indian Ocean Territory, or BIOT. The British had parallel interests with ours, which essentially centered on the need for secure communications and transit rights through the Indian Ocean. In 1965 they decided to sequester a number of sparsely populated or unpopulated islands which had been under the administrative jurisdiction of the Seychelles or Mauritius and form a group called the British Indian Ocean Territory. The outcome of the mutuality of U.S.-U.K. interests was the BIOT Agreement, negotiated with the U.K. in December 1966.[150] The agreement provides for the BIOT remaining as U.K. territory, for an agreement in principle on each undertaking, for detailed agreements between designated administrative authorities (i.e., USN and RN [Royal Navy]), and for each government bearing cost of its own sites. The initial period covered by the agreement is 50 years, with a provision for a 20-year extension.

COMPLEX U.S. INTERESTS

An identification of our interests in the Indian Ocean is necessarily complex. It is not in any sense a political unit. In brief our interests are these:

—The oil of the Persian Gulf is vital to our allies and of considerable direct interest to us.

—About 30 of the 127 members of the U.N. belong to the Indian Ocean region, and one-third of the world's population is there. Several of the states—India, Pakistan, Indonesia, Iran, the U.A.R., and, in certain respects, South Africa—play a significant international role. Further, our interests in assisting in the development of these countries have been and continue to be a matter of concern to the United States. We see forward movement in economic development and toward politi-

---

[148] Cf. *The United States in World Affairs, 1962*, pp. 183-89.
[149] Cf. same, *1965*, pp. 215-24.
[150] Agreement relating to the availability of the British Indian Ocean Territory for defense purposes, effected by exchange of notes at London Dec. 30, 1966 (TIAS 6196; 18 UST 28).

cal stability as the best means to promote an environment conducive to our own interests.

—Conversely, the instability and intraregional antagonisms that characterize much of the Indian Ocean area could serve to promote Soviet interests at the expense of ours. We are concerned over the volatile political situation with the attendant growth of Soviet influence in Yemen and Southern Yemen at the mouth of the Red Sea. The Israelis, incidentally, share our unease on this point. We are particularly disquieted by the potential for instability in the Persian Gulf and what this might mean to our and allied oil interests in the event the British are unable to effect some form of federation among the gulf shaikhdoms. Elsewhere, the struggle in Pakistan has already further aggravated the tensions of the subcontinent. We are encouraged, however, that Mrs. Gandhi's impressive success in the recent Indian elections[151] will arrest an earlier drift there toward fragmentation.

—In addition to the BIOT, we have other security interests in the area. The Indian Ocean must remain available to free passage to U.S. commercial and military traffic, if only for contingency purposes. Also, we require secure air routes into and across the region.

—It is to our interest that countries of the area not pass under the control of forces hostile to us. Specifically, we would be concerned if Chinese or Soviet influence in the area extended to control of the water areas or significant parts of the littoral. We do not envisage an immediate threat of this nature, however.

We are quite conscious of the Soviet Union's aspirations to project its power into distant areas. Politically, the Soviets probably view the Indian Ocean as an area where their influence can grow at the expense of Western and, to a lesser degree, Chinese influence by exploiting targets of opportunity among the revolutionary and nationalistic forces in the region.

Now turning to specific military considerations, a naval survey of Diego Garcia in the Chagos Archipelago was undertaken in the summer of 1967. In March 1968 the Joint Chiefs of Staff recommended establishment of a joint U.S.-U.K. military facility on Diego Garcia, which has subsequently evolved into an austere communications facility.

As you may know, Congress funded $5.4 million in the FY '71 military construction bill[152] for the Diego project. The Navy estimates total construction costs at approximately $19 million. Original costs have been reduced by using Navy Seabees and reducing facilities.

I wish to emphasize that construction of this modest communications facility is not a sudden reactive response by the United States to a

---

151 The New Congress party led by Prime Minister Indira Gandhi won a large majority in elections to the House of the People (*Lok Sabha*) on Mar. 1-10, 1971.
152 Public Law 91-544, Dec. 11, 1970.

possible Soviet threat in the Indian Ocean, but rather is the culmination of our efforts to meet a naval communications requirement dating back to the early 1960's.

These requirements are based on the fact that a significant communications gap currently exists in the southern, central, and northeastern Indian Ocean areas. Reliable communications coverage cannot be provided to these areas from any existing U.S. naval communication station. Consequently, an Indian Ocean area facility was required to rectify this situation and provide communications coverage for ships operating in or transiting these areas. An Indian Ocean communications facility will also provide minimum requisite communications for safety of life at sea, safety of flight, weather advisories, and hydrographic and oceanographic research in the area.

U.S. strategic interests in the Indian Ocean include oil requirements. About 60 percent of the oil required by our Western European allies and 90 percent of the oil used by Japan comes from the Middle East. This assumes even greater pertinency when viewed in the light of known oil reserves.

With the U.S.S.R. naval presence in the Indian Ocean now an established fact, we face the prospect of enhanced Soviet politico-military power flanking Africa, South and Southeast Asia, and Australia. This calls attention to the growing Soviet naval capability in reference to the so-called choke points which control ingress and egress to and from the basin. These include Bab el Mandab at the southern entrance to the Red Sea, the Strait of Hormuz at the narrow of the Persian Gulf, and the politically less vulnerable Straits of Malacca and Sunda.

The practical effect of the Soviet presence athwart lines of communication would, of course, be acutely felt in the case of all-out hostilities. A Soviet attempt to block maritime routes in peacetime could, of course, lead to a major world crisis. Nonetheless, with appropriate basing and/or establishment of political preeminence in these funnel areas, Soviet domination of the most critical of these choke points falls within the realm of possibility. The knowledge that in the event of war or great tension the Soviets or their associated states might control traffic in and out of the Indian Ocean at one or more of these points could not but exert some influence on the political orientation of those nations who would be most affected should this contingency come to pass.

In terms of strategic weapons, the Soviets would, of course, make every effort to limit the U.S. use of the Indian Ocean as a launching area for ballistic missile submarines.

SOVIET INTERESTS IN THE AREA

The Soviets, like the czars, have long had an interest in the Indian

Ocean because of the opportunities it offered for trade and for the extension of their political influence and because it lies athwart the ice-free ocean route between ports in the western and far-eastern U.S.S.R. Currently, some 12 percent of the merchant ships transiting the Indian Ocean are Soviet.

There are only a few well-defined shipping routes through the Indian Ocean. Except for those which round the Cape of Good Hope or pass through the Tasman Sea around the south of Australia, the other transoceanic routes converge at the already cited choke points. Ships which desire to avoid these choke points must add many days and, in some cases, thousands of miles to their voyages from European and other North Atlantic ports.

Since the mid-1950's, the Soviets have demonstrated a clear interest in the Indian Ocean area. Since that time, for example, almost two-thirds of their financial and economic aid has been devoted to third-world countries in the Indian Ocean area.

It is, however, in the expansion and classic peacetime employment of their navy in the Indian Ocean area, where they are using seapower to complement ongoing economic and political objectives, that they have made a recent dramatic impact.

It should thus be noted that the Soviets have moved from their traditional land-centered defense-of-the-homeland role to one using their navy worldwide as an instrument of policy.

Soviet naval presence in the Indian Ocean was inaugurated in the spring of 1967 with the deployment of ships with military and civilian crews for oceanographic and space-event support operations. Soviet combatant deployments in the Indian Ocean were initiated in March 1968. Since that date the Soviets have maintained an essentially continuous presence in the Indian Ocean and have increased threefold the number of ship-days in that ocean. This includes naval combatants, naval auxiliaries, and oceanographic ships.

To enhance their staying power, the Soviets are soliciting access to existing support facilities in various locations in the Indian Ocean and on its littoral, which, if their efforts meet with success, could permit them to develop a position of strength in such areas as the Gulf of Aden, the southern gateway to the Red Sea.

The complexities of maintaining the Soviet Indian Ocean squadron would be considerably ameliorated were the Suez Canal to be reopened. Supply lines would be drastically reduced, transit times foreshortened, rotation of units expedited. Similarly, with the canal opened to traffic, the number of Soviet naval deployments into the Indian Ocean could take a quantum jump inasmuch as the assets of their powerful Black Sea Fleet would become available for rapid deployments south and east of Suez. The time required to deploy U.S. naval units to the Indian Ocean would be reduced, but to a lesser extent. The 6th Fleet could be employed on short notice. Access to Persian Gulf oil by our Western allies is of considerable strategic and economic interest to the United States and would be positively affected by the reopening of the Suez Canal. Arrangements associated with the canal's reopening could also act to defuse the Arab-Israeli confrontation.[153]

The Soviets continue to probe for facilities for their growing Indian Ocean fishing fleet, which now accounts for almost one-third of their annual catch. Last year they made a limited support agreement with Mauritius and reportedly are now feeling out other nations for additional assistance.

Unlike the Soviets, the Chinese have no traditional interests in the Indian Ocean. Only since the Communists came to power in 1949 have they made significant diplomatic or economic moves in the area. These efforts, which include both trade and foreign aid to selected countries like Tanzania and Pakistan, are designed to improve the Chinese image to increase Chinese influence.

Militarily, the Chinese have not ventured out of their own coastal waters, although they have a few ships which are capable of such deployments. To date, the Chinese have seen little value in operations of a naval force in the Indian Ocean.

POLICY QUESTIONS FOR THE COMING YEARS

I hope that this review shows that we cannot assign a single value to the totality of our interests in the Indian Ocean. Nevertheless, we do consider that over the next 5 years our interests there will be of a substantially lower order than those in either of the great ocean basins, the Atlantic and the Pacific. We border on the Atlantic and the Pacific, and the states of these areas are for the most part economically, politically, and militarily more important to us than those on the Indian Ocean. Therefore, there appears to be no requirement at this time for us to feel impelled to control, or even decisively influence, any part of the Indian Ocean or its littoral, given the nature of our interests there and the current level of Soviet and Chinese involvement. We consider, on balance, that our present interests are served by normal commercial, political, and military access.

In sustaining our interests in the Indian Ocean region, we should emphasize that there is a real problem for the nonregional powers. A number of the littoral states, among them India, Ceylon, and Tanzania, have on several occasions expressed the desire to see the Indian Ocean kept free of big-power rivalry.[154] While this attitude to some extent may condition the political atmosphere, it does not change the fact that this vast ocean area remains international waters or the fact that the

[153] Cf. Documents 50-52.
[154] Cf. Document 66.

Soviets and the Chinese have not been dissuaded from continuing to augment their presence in the region.

Although the threat to any of our interests in the Indian Ocean is of relatively low order, it nevertheless is an area that merits close and continuing attention, particularly in view of the apparent Soviet and, to a lesser extent, Chinese Communist objective to enlarge their influence and presence in the region. Accordingly, as we look at the region over the period of the next few years, we are faced with three policy dilemmas:

First, how can we best respond to the increased Soviet naval presence in the Indian Ocean area and the extension of Soviet influence? How can we maintain our own ability to exert military influence in that area in case of need without acting in a way that would stimulate a competitive buildup of forces?

Second, how can we encourage economic development, international political responsibilities, and domestic political stability in the countries around the Indian Ocean and have good relations with them as a way of limiting the development of Communist influence hostile to the United States in those countries?

Third, how can we insure maintenance of free transit through the key access points to the Indian Ocean?

We will have to find answers to these questions within the constraints provided by our desire to avoid a great-power competitive buildup in the Indian Ocean. There are factors which favor our objectives. Among them are the efforts of some Indian Ocean countries to restrain Soviet military activity. Nonetheless, the United States must ultimately decide whether or not it will maintain the option to counter an enlarged Soviet military buildup.

(66) "Declaration of the Indian Ocean as a Zone of Peace": United Nations General Assembly Resolution 2832 (XXVI), Adopted December 16, 1971. [155]

(Complete Text)

The General Assembly,

Conscious of the determination of the peoples of the littoral and hinterland States of the Indian Ocean to preserve their independence,

[155] General Assembly, *Official Records: 26th Session, Supplement No. 29* (A/8429), pp. 36-37; adopted by a vote of 61-0-55 (U.S.). For a summary of Ceylon's proposal as outlined to the General Assembly by Prime Minister Sirimavo Bandaranaike on Oct. 12, 1971, cf. *UN Monthly Chronicle*, Nov. 1971, p. 184.

sovereignty and territorial integrity, and to resolve their political, economic and social problems under conditions of peace and tranquillity,

Recalling the Declaration of the Third Conference of Heads of State or Government of Non-Aligned Countries, held at Lusaka from 8 to 10 September 1970, calling upon all States to consider and respect the Indian Ocean as a zone of peace from which great Power rivalries and competition as well as bases conceived in the context of such rivalries and competition should be excluded, and declaring that the area should also be free of nuclear weapons,[156]

Convinced of the desirability of ensuring the maintenance of such conditions in the Indian Ocean area by means other than military alliances, as such alliances entail financial and other obligations that call for the diversion of the limited resources of the States of the area from the more compelling and productive task of economic and social reconstruction and could further involve them in the rivalries of power blocs in a manner prejudicial to their independence and freedom of action, thereby increasing international tensions,

Concerned at recent developments that portend the extension of the arms race into the Indian Ocean area,[157] thereby posing a serious threat to the maintenance of such conditions in the area,

Convinced that the establishment of a zone of peace in the Indian Ocean would contribute towards arresting such developments, relaxing international tensions and strengthening international peace and security,

Convinced further that the establishment of a zone of peace in an extensive geographical area in one region could have a beneficial influence on the establishment of permanent universal peace based on equal rights and justice for all, in accordance with the purposes and principles of the Charter of the United Nations,

1. *Solemnly declares* that the Indian Ocean, within limits to be determined, together with the air space above and the ocean floor subjacent thereto, is hereby designated for all time as a zone of peace;

2. *Calls upon* the great Powers, in conformity with this Declaration, to enter into immediate consultations with the littoral States of the Indian Ocean with a view to:

(*a*) Halting the further escalation and expansion of their military presence in the Indian Ocean;

(*b*) Eliminating from the Indian Ocean all bases, military installations and logistical supply facilities, the disposition of nuclear weapons and weapons of mass destruction and any manifestation of great Power military presence in the Indian Ocean conceived in the context of great Power rivalry;

3. *Calls upon* the littoral and hinterland States of the Indian Ocean,

[156] Text in *International Legal Materials*, Jan. 1971, pp. 215-19.
[157] Cf. Document 65 and note preceding Document 62.

the permanent members of the Security Council and other major maritime users of the Indian Ocean, in pursuit of the objective of establishing a system of universal collective security without military alliances and strengthening international security through regional and other co-operation, to enter into consultations with a view to the implementation of this Declaration and such action as may be necessary to ensure that:

(*a*) Warships and military aircraft may not use the Indian Ocean for any threat or use of force against the sovereignty, territorial integrity and independence of any littoral or hinterland State of the Indian Ocean in contravention of the purposes and principles of the Charter of the United Nations;

(*b*) Subject to the foregoing and to the norms and principles of international law, the right to free and unimpeded use of the zone by the vessels of all nations is unaffected;

(*c*) Appropriate arrangements are made to give effect to any international agreement that may ultimately be reached for the maintenance of the Indian Ocean as a zone of peace;

4. *Requests* the Secretary-General to report to the General Assembly at its twenty-seventh session on the progress that has been made with regard to the implementation of this Declaration;

5. *Decides* to include in the provisional agenda of its twenty-seventh session an item entitled "Declaration of the Indian Ocean as a zone of peace".

V
AMERICAN POLICY IN ASIA:
THE WAR IN INDOCHINA

[The United States completed during 1971 a decade of direct engagement in the long-drawn-out struggle over the political destiny of the Indochinese states that had emerged from French tutelage in the 1950s. Four separate local governments were involved—two of them in Vietnam, which had been divided since 1954 between the northern, Communist-ruled Democratic Republic of Vietnam (D.R.V.) and the U.S.-supported, anti-Communist state which had become the Republic of Vietnam in 1955. In addition, there were the independent Kingdom of Laos and the former monarchical state of Cambodia, which had officially become the Khmer Republic on the overthrow of its traditional regime in 1970.

The earlier years of the American involvement, from 1961 to 1968, had brought a huge increase in the scale and weight of American participation, particularly in helping the existing South Vietnamese regime maintain itself in face of the revolutionary offensive spearheaded, with large-scale North Vietnamese support, by the Communist-led National Liberation Front of South Vietnam (N.L.F.) and its latter-day offshoot, the so-called Provisional Revolutionary Government of the Republic of South Vietnam (P.R.G.). In 1968-69, however, the curve of American involvement had turned downward with President Johnson's suspension of the bombing of North Vietnam, a concurrent limitation of the American troop build-up in South Vietnam, and the commencement of actual troop withdrawals early in President Nixon's administration. From a peak of 543,000 in April 1969, U.S. troop strength in South Vietnam had been reduced in stages to 339,200 in mid-December 1970 and was scheduled to decline still further, to a maximum of 284,000 as of May 1, 1971.

A strategy for bringing the American involvement in Vietnam to a definitive conclusion had been outlined by President Nixon in an address of November 3, 1969, in which the President had spoken of two alternative roads to this objective: (1) negotiation with the enemy, and/or (2) a program of "Vietnamization" involving "the complete withdrawal of all U.S. ground combat forces, and their replacement by

261

South Vietnamese forces on an orderly scheduled timetable."[1] Efforts along both these lines had gone forward through 1969 and 1970, and the President continued during 1971 to speak of "proceeding on two tracks"—active pursuit of "the negotiating channel," combined with continued pursuit of Vietnamization "regardless of what happens on the negotiating front" (Documents 9 and 23).

Experience had demonstrated, however, that the two tracks did not necessarily run parallel or follow an undeviating course. In 1970, the requirements of Vietnamization as seen by President Nixon had led to a large-scale incursion by American and South Vietnamese forces into hitherto neutral Cambodia.[2] Early in 1971, South Vietnamese forces were to undertake a comparable expedition into Laos (Documents 67-68). On the negotiating front, the formal peace negotiations begun in Paris early in 1969 had been supplemented since August of that year by secret contacts between Dr. Kissinger, the President's Assistant for National Security Affairs, and a high-level North Vietnamese representative. Although the public was to remain in ignorance of these contacts until January 1972,[3] it was already aware that President Nixon in an address of October 7, 1970 had broadened the focus of the peace debate by proposing, among other things, a "cease-fire-in-place" for all armed forces throughout Indochina and an Indochina Peace Conference that would deal with the conflict in all three states of Indochina. "The war in Indochina has been proved to be of one piece," he had said; "it cannot be cured by treating only one of its areas of outbreak."[4]

The following documentation, which reflects the projection of these varied tendencies through 1971, falls into five broad divisions. A survey of the military operations and related developments in Laos (Documents 67-70) is followed by a series of reports and documents bearing upon the further progress of the Vietnamization program during the earlier part of the year (Documents 71-73). Important new developments in the peace negotiations reach their climax with the submission of a new and secret American peace plan, which, however, fails to gain the approval of the North Vietnamese (Documents 74-77). A comment by President Nixon on the significance of South Vietnam's presidential election on October 3, 1971 (Document 78) precedes a final series of documents (Documents 79-81) reflecting divergent attitudes in Congress and the White House respecting the tempo of American troop withdrawals, which continued throughout 1971 and would leave the U.S. forces remaining in Vietnam at a level of approximately 157,000 as 1972 began.]

[1] *Documents. 1968-69*, p. 283.
[2] Same, *1970*, pp. 156-79.
[3] Cf. below at note 79.
[4] *Documents, 1970*, pp. 196-97.

A. Military Operations in Laos.

[Though nominally neutralized by the Geneva accords of 1954 and 1962,[5] Laos had long figured as a subsidiary theater of the war in Indochina in consequence of (1) an internal conflict involving the forces of the Royal Laotian Government on one side and some 40,000 Communist-led Pathet Lao troops, backed by North Vietnam, on the other; (2) North Vietnamese use of the so-called Ho Chi Minh Trail in eastern Laos as an infiltration and supply route to Communist-held areas of South Vietnam; and (3) U.S. air operations conducted with Laotian Government consent both against the Trail and against Communist positions in northern Laos. The introduction of American ground combat troops into Laos (and Thailand) had been barred by Congress in 1969, "in line with the expressed intention of the President";[6] but the United States had continued to provide logistical and other assistance to the Laotian Government, using its air power for the purpose of interdicting the flow of North Vietnamese troops and supplies along the Ho Chi Minh Trail, flying so-called "reconnaissance missions" in northern Laos, and flying "combat support missions" for Laotian forces when requested by the Laotian Government.[7]

In spite of increased bombing of the Ho Chi Minh Trail during the latter part of 1970, the military situation in Laos had become increasingly precarious as North Vietnamese forces in the country were built up to an estimated 60,000 and antigovernment troops displayed increased aggressiveness with the approach of the 1970-71 winter dry season (cf. Document 69). The military outlook in Cambodia also remained threatening, despite continued activity in that country by South Vietnamese troops following the large-scale U.S.–South Vietnamese operation against North Vietnamese "sanctuaries" in eastern Cambodia in May–June 1970.

Notwithstanding these unfavorable auguries, Congress late in 1970 had reaffirmed its ban on the introduction of U.S. ground combat troops into Laos or Thailand.[8] In addition, it had for the first time barred the use of appropriated funds to finance the introduction of U.S. ground combat troops into Cambodia, or to provide U.S. advisers to or for Cambodian military forces in Cambodia.[9]

---

[5] Same, *1954*, pp. 302-7 and 311-14; same, *1962*, pp. 284-94.
[6] Section 643, Department of Defense Appropriations Act, 1970 (Public Law 91-171, Dec. 29, 1969).
[7] Nixon statement, Mar. 6, 1970, in *Documents, 1970*, pp. 151-56.
[8] Section 843, Department of Defense Appropriation Act, 1971 (Public Law 91-668, Jan. 11, 1971).
[9] Section 7, Special Foreign Assistance Act of 1971 (Public Law 91-652, Jan. 5, 1971).

Consistent with these restrictions, Secretary of State Rogers made clear at a news conference on January 29, 1971, that the United States had no intention of using ground troops in Cambodia or Laos, but that it nevertheless reserved the right to use its air power in either country to whatever extent might be necessary to protect American troops in South Vietnam as their numbers were reduced under the Vietnamization program. The Secretary of State did not respond directly to an inquiry as to whether any action against a Communist base area in southern Laos was contemplated.[10]

On January 30, 1971, U.S. and South Vietnamese forces launched a major military operation in areas of northern South Vietnam close to the Laotian frontier; and on February 8 it was disclosed that South Vietnamese forces had that day crossed into enemy-occupied territory of Laos. According to the official announcement by the Department of State (Document 67), the purpose of the operation, which would be limited in time and area, was to attack North Vietnamese forces and military supplies assembled in sanctuaries close to the South Vietnamese border, disrupting forces concentrated for use against South Vietnamese and U.S. forces in northern South Vietnam, and inter-cepting or choking off the flow of supplies and men designed for use farther south on the Ho Chi Minh Trail in South Vietnam and Cambodia.

The Royal Laotian Government, in an immediate protest statement, admitted that the primary responsibility for the intrusion rested with North Vietnam in view of its persistent violations of Laotian neutrality and territorial integrity. It nevertheless deplored the entry of foreign troops into Laos, demanded their immediate withdrawal, and called for strict enforcement of the provisions of the Geneva agreement. The incursion was also harshly criticized by U.N. Secretary-General Thant as well as by the People's Republic of China, France, and, more hesitantly, the U.S.S.R.; the British Foreign Office, in contrast, found it "understandable" under the circumstances.[11]

Some information on the background and immediate results of the operation, which was code-named Lam Son 719, was provided by President Nixon at a news conference held on February 17 at a time when the South Vietnamese forces were still advancing into Laos (Document 68). Although the operation did not involve the use of U.S. ground forces, considerable U.S. air and backup support was provided the 24,500 South Vietnamese troops who were ultimately engaged. Tchepone, 25 miles inside Laos, was occupied March 6, but was evac-uated five days later in the face of increasingly powerful North Viet-namese counterattacks which led, over the next two weeks, to a rapid withdrawal of the South Vietnamese forces, the last of which were out

---

[10] *Bulletin*, Feb. 15, 1971, pp. 189-97.
[11] *Keesing's*, p. 24622.

of the country by March 25. In spite of indications that the operation had been terminated prematurely, U.S. and South Vietnamese authorities continued to portray it as a success in terms of its limited objectives and as a vital contribution to the new phase of American troop withdrawals from South Vietnam that President Nixon was to announce on April 7 (Document 71).

Aside from Lam Son 719, the documentation presented below includes authoritative statements on the scale and effects of U.S. air operations in Laos in 1971 (Document 69) and on the activities of foreign, particularly North Vietnamese and Thai, troops in that country (Document 70).]

(67) South Vietnamese Attack on Enemy Sanctuaries in Laos: Statement by Robert J. McCloskey, Department of State Press Spokesman, February 8, 1971. [12]

(Complete Text)

Last evening the Government of the Republic of Viet-Nam announced in Saigon that elements of its armed forces have crossed into enemy-occupied territory of Laos to attack North Vietnamese forces and military supplies which have been assembled in sanctuaries close to the border of South Viet-Nam. [13] These sanctuaries lie between the 16th and 17th parallels and comprise concentrations which are an important part of the Ho Chi Minh Trail system. Our Military Command in Viet-Nam has announced the limits of the U.S. military participation.

The decision of the United States to assist is based on the following policy considerations:

1. No American ground combat forces or advisers will cross into Laos.

2. The operation will be a limited one both as to time and area. The Vietnamese Government has made it clear that its objective will be to disrupt those forces which have been concentrated in this region for use against South Vietnamese and U.S. forces located in the northern military regions of South Viet-Nam and to intercept or choke off the flow of supplies and men during the dry season which are designed for use further south on the Ho Chi Minh Trail in South Viet-Nam and Cambodia.

---

[12] *Bulletin*, Mar. 1, 1971, pp. 256-57.

[13] The operation began Feb. 8, local time (Feb. 7, U.S. time). The announcement by South Vietnamese President Nguyen Van Thieu, released Feb. 7 by the Vietnamese Embassy in Washington, appears in *New York Times*, Feb. 8, 1971.

3. The operation will promote the security and safety of American and allied forces in South Viet-Nam and is consistent with statutory requirements.[14] It will make the enemy less able to mount offensives and strengthen South Viet-Nam's ability to defend itself as U.S. forces are withdrawn from South Viet-Nam. It will protect American lives.

4. This ground operation by the South Vietnamese against the sanctuaries thus will aid in the Vietnamization program. The withdrawal of American forces from Viet-Nam will continue. During the month of April President Nixon will announce further withdrawals.[15]

5. The measures of self-defense being taken by the Republic of Viet-Nam are fully consistent with international law. A report to this effect is being made by the Republic of Viet-Nam to the President of the Security Council of the United Nations,[16] to the Geneva Cochairmen,[17] and to the governments which comprise the International Control Commission.[18]

6. This limited operation is not an enlargement of the war. The territory involved has been the scene of combat since 1965. The principal new factor is that South Viet-Nam forces will move against the enemy on the ground to deny him the sanctuaries and disrupt the main artery of supplies which he has been able to use so effectively against American and South Vietnamese forces in the past.

7. The United States has consistently sought to end the conflict in Indochina through negotiations. President Nixon specifically proposed last October that there be (a) a cease-fire throughout Indochina, (b) a negotiated timetable for the withdrawal of all forces, (c) immediate release of all prisoners of war, (d) an international peace conference for all of Indochina, and (e) a political settlement.[19] This continues to be the policy of the United States.

8. The Royal Lao Government has issued a statement, which, while critical of the current military action, points out that the "primary responsibility for this development rests on the Democratic Republic of Viet-Nam which has violated international law and the 1962 Geneva Agreements. The Democratic Republic of Viet-Nam has violated and is continuing to violate the neutrality and territorial integrity of the Kingdom of Laos."[20] The U.S. Government continues to favor the neutrality of Laos and the restoration of the situation contemplated by the 1962 Geneva accords in which all foreign forces would be withdrawn

[14] Cf. above at note 8.
[15] Cf. Document 71.
[16] U.N. document S/10104, Feb. 8, 1971, in U.N. Security Council, *Official Records: 26th Year, Supplement for Jan., Feb. and Mar. 1971*, p. 61.
[17] The United Kingdom and the U.S.S.R.
[18] Canada, India, and Poland.
[19] *Documents, 1970*, pp. 196-201.
[20] *New York Times*, Feb. 9, 1971.

from Lao territory. A new Indochina conference as proposed by President Nixon could accomplish this objective.

(68) Significance of the Laos Incursion: News Conference Statement by President Nixon, February 17, 1971.[21]

(Excerpt)

*   *   *

SOUTHEAST ASIA

Q. Mr. President, the next logical step in Southeast Asia would seem to be South Vietnamese forces moving into the southern part of North Vietnam for the same reasons that they moved into the Laotian panhandle.

Would our policy rule out support for this type of move, air support for it?

THE PRESIDENT. Well, I won't speculate on what South Vietnam may decide to do with regard to a possible incursion into North Vietnam in order to defend their national security. However, I will restate our policy. I stated that policy on November 3d [1969] and have restated it at least nine different times publicly since that time.

I stated then that at a time we are withdrawing our forces that if I found that the enemy was stepping up its activity through infiltration in a way that would threaten our remaining forces that I would take strong action to deal with the new situation.[22]

On December 10 [1970], as you recall, I reiterated that statement and said that this action would include the use of airpower against the infiltration routes, military complex supply depots.[23]

That is our policy, the policy of the President taking action if he finds that the North Vietnamese are undertaking actions which threaten our remaining forces in South Vietnam.

Q. Mr. President, under that guide, is there any limit to what we might to do protect our forces in South Vietnam?

THE PRESIDENT. We have indicated several limits. For example, we are not going to use ground forces in Laos. We are not going to use advisers in Laos with the South Vietnamese forces. We are not going to use ground forces in Cambodia or advisers in Cambodia as we have previously indicated and we have no intention, of course, of using ground forces in North Vietnam. Those are limitations.[24]

Q. I had reference to our use of airpower.

THE PRESIDENT. I'm not going to place any limitation upon the use of airpower except, of course, to rule out a rather ridiculous suggestion that is made from time to time—I think the latest by [Professor] Hans [J.] Morgenthau—that our airpower might include the use of tactical nuclear weapons.[25]

As you know, Mr. Lisagor,[26] this has been speculated on for a period of 5 years and I have said for a period of 5 years that this is not an area where the use of nuclear weapons, in any form, is either needed or would be wise.

As far as our airpower is concerned, it will be directed against—and I ought to be as precise as I was on December 10—against those military activities which I determine are directed against and thereby threaten our remaining forces in South Vietnam.

Q. Can you tell us, sir—the idea of an incursion into Laos has been under consideration in Saigon on the military level for some years. Why did you decide that now is the time to do it? And second, can you give us some kind of a status report on how it's going and what the prognosis is in terms of the possible enemy resistance, what is it the intelligence suggests?

THE PRESIDENT. Yes. In looking at this situation, I recall, as probably some of you who were there, in 1965, that some of our military people and civilians for that matter, were then saying that the way to stop the North Vietnamese infiltration into South Vietnam was to cut the Ho Chi Minh Trail.

It was not undertaken during the previous administration, as I understand, and, I can speak for this administration, was not undertaken until now for a reason that the South Vietnamese and, for that matter, the United States had enough on our plate in South Vietnam.

Laos would not have been possible had it not been for Cambodia.[27] Cambodia cutting off one vital supply line and thereby practically bringing enemy activity in the southern half of South Vietnam to an end released the South Vietnamese forces, who, by this time, had not only gained confidence in Cambodia but also had additional strength,

[24] For the legal restrictions on the use of U.S. forces in Laos and Cambodia see above at notes 6-9.

[25] Hans J. Morgenthau, "What Price Victory?" *New Republic*, Feb. 20, 1971, pp. 21-23. The author argued that the administration's attempt to win the war by conventional means had failed and that it faced the alternatives of resorting to tactical nuclear weapons, provoking a war with China, or choosing "unconditional disengagement"—which, he added, "has always been the only rational denouement."

[26] Peter Lisagor, *Chicago Daily News.*

[27] Cf. above at note 2.

released them for undertaking what they could not have undertaken even 8 months ago, an incursion on their own into Laos with only U.S. air support.

The decision to do it now or, I think, perhaps, put it this way, the decision not to do it before, is that, one, neither the United States nor the South Vietnamese felt that they apparently had the capability to do it; the second, the decision to do it now was that based on the fact that the South Vietnamese, because of the confidence, the training they gained as a result of their actions in Cambodia, the South Vietnamese felt that they were able to undertake it. Our commanders agreed and, therefore, it was undertaken.

Q. Mr. President, could you discuss with us your evaluation of the possibility of Communist China entering this situation now that it's expanded into Laos or if the South Vietnamese go into North Vietnam?

THE PRESIDENT. Let me refer to the situation as it presently exists rather than the hypothesis of whether the South Vietnamese might go into North Vietnam.

As far as the actions in southern Laos are concerned, they present no threat to Communist China and should not be interpreted by the Communist Chinese as being a threat against them.

As you know, the Communist Chinese have been operating in northern Laos for some time.[28] But this action is not directed against Communist China. It is directed against the North Vietnamese who are pointed toward South Vietnam and toward Cambodia.

Consequently, I do not believe that the Communist Chinese have any reason to interpret this as a threat against them or any reason therefore to react to it.

Q. Mr. President, if I could follow up, could you give us your evaluation of how the Laotian operation is really going militarily and otherwise?

THE PRESIDENT. And incidentally, don't hesitate in this smaller forum to ask for follow-up. To the extent I can cover all the questions, I'll be glad to take them.

As far as the Laotian operation is concerned, the reports that have come from the field I think generally give an accurate picture, except, of course, for the day-to-day tendency to hypo this or that incident into a crisis.

The operation—and I read a complete report from General Abrams[29] this morning—the operation has gone according to plan. The South Vietnamese have already cut three major roads—and we call them "roads," let's say trails—which lead from Tchepone down into Cambodia and, of course, into South Vietnam.

---

[28] On Chinese road-building activity in northern Laos cf. *Keesing's*, p. 24094.
[29] Gen. Creighton W. Abrams, Commander, U.S. Military Assistance Command, Vietnam.

The South Vietnamese have run into very heavy resistance on the road going into Tchepone. We expected that resistance.

Putting it in the context of the earlier reply, the Cambodian action in May and June [1970] cut one lifeline, the lifeline from Sihanoukville [Kompong Som] into the southern half of South Vietnam.

This action would either cut or seriously disrupt the other pipeline or lifeline, the lifeline coming from—down through Laos, the Ho Chi Minh Trail, into the northern half of South Vietnam.

Therefore, we expected the North Vietnamese to fight here. They have to fight here or give up the struggle to conquer South Vietnam, Cambodia, and their influence extending through other parts of Southeast Asia.

Finally, I think it's quite important to note General Abrams' evaluation, which I specifically asked him to give me by cable just a few days ago, his evaluation of how the South Vietnamese are conducting themselves. They are fighting, he said, in a superior way. I use the word that he used. They are proceeding in a way that he believes is in accordance with the plan and holding their own against enemy attack.

And he also pointed up another fact that, of course, has been overridden by the Laotian activity, that the operation in the Chup Plantation [in Cambodia] led by General [Do Cao] Tri is going along in a fashion much better than was expected, with a great number of enemy casualties and, as General Abrams put it, excellent performance on the part of those groups.

Q. Mr. President, it is reported in both the South Vietnamese and, I think, in our statement[30] the operation will be limited in time and scope. Can you define those terms?

THE PRESIDENT. By time, the operation will be limited to the time that is necessary to accomplish the objective. The objective is not to occupy any part of Laos. The South Vietnamese are not there to stay. They are there to disrupt the enemy's lines of communication, their supply lines, their infiltration routes, and then to get out.

Once that is accomplished, if it is accomplished early, they will get out. If it takes a longer time, they will stay in.

There is also another limitation in terms of time. And that is the weather. In the latter part of April or the early part of May, the rains come. And they would have to get out then because then the North Vietnamese also would pose no threat.

In terms of area, space, it is limited to the specific area that you see on the maps here, in terms of cutting across the trails—and it is more than one trail, there are three or four trails—the trails that are the supply lines on which the North Vietnamese operate.

*   *   *

(69) Air Operations and Refugees in Laos: Statement by William H. Sullivan, Deputy Assistant Secretary of State for East Asian and Pacific Affairs, Before the Subcommittee on Refugees and Escapees of the Senate Committee on the Judiciary, April 22, 1971.[31]

(Excerpts)

I have been asked to appear before this subcommittee today to discuss the problems of the refugees in Laos and Cambodia.

*   *   *

With your permission I would like to read a brief prepared statement covering both Laos and Cambodia on behalf of all the witnesses present.[32] We are then prepared to answer questions. I should like to start with a discussion of Laos, where the refugee problem is heavier and where the United States plays a direct role in support of refugee activities. I will end with several paragraphs devoted to the refugee situation as best we know it in Cambodia.

It has often been stated that Laos is a victim of its geography. The assumption is made that Lao territory has been the scene of military activity because North Viet-Nam sends its logistics and its manpower down the Ho Chi Minh Trail in Laos in order to attack South Viet-Nam and Cambodia. This is partly true, and it is a fact that the heaviest concentration of North Vietnamese forces in Laos is located in the southeastern panhandle region of Laos where the Ho Chi Minh Trail runs. This is also the locus of most United States military activity in Laos. About 80 percent of the air sorties flown by United States airpower are concentrated in this area.

However, this is not a populated area of Laos. Even before military activity began there our information indicates that no more than 8,000 or 9,000 hill tribe people lived in the area which is traversed by the Ho Chi Minh Trail and affected by our bombing operations against that trail. Almost all of these original residents have long since left the area; and it is today, for all practical purposes, unpopulated except by the North Vietnamese military forces, their engineering and logistics auxiliaries, and the porters whom they use in the operation of the Ho Chi Minh Trail. Therefore the area of Laos which is subjected to the most intense military activity is not an area which is of direct concern to us in examining the question of refugees.

[31] *Bulletin*, May 17, 1971, pp. 648-52.
[32] The speaker was accompanied by representatives of the Department of Defense, the Agency for International Development, and others. For the discussion of the refugee situation in Cambodia cf. *Bulletin, loc. cit.*, pp. 652-54.

The refugees in Laos are those whose lives have been disrupted by the other war in Laos, which has nothing to do with military operations in South Viet-Nam or Cambodia. This other war is a war which represents the ambitions of the North Vietnamese to extend their control over their peaceful Lao neighbors. The North Vietnamese have fought this war over the years at a pace and priority which is clearly secondary to their principal focus in South Viet-Nam. However, they have committed a significant number of their own forces to this effort and have been aided by tribal people from northern and south-central Laos in association with a very small number of ethnic Lao who are political dissidents. There is very little ideological content to this war; and to most of those who are caught up in it on both sides, it does not represent political or social issues, but rather a continuation of the age-old expansionist tendencies of the North Vietnamese against their Lao neighbors.

This war has been fought through most of its years along the hills and ridgelines of north and northeastern Laos. Until about 3 years ago it had a seasonal seesaw pattern which was governed largely by the monsoons. North Vietnamese units usually entered as shock troops in the dry season, pushing the Lao and Meo defenders westward. The North Vietnamese generally retired back to their own territory during the rains, and much of the terrain they held at the end of the dry season was usually recaptured, mostly by Meo guerrilla activity. In the dry-season fighting, the North Vietnamese forces, who were operating on unfamiliar terrain, usually operated in conventional patterns along the road network and in the valleys, attacking hill outposts from which Meo defenders generally melted away when they were outmanned and outgunned. So long as this pattern obtained and there was a buffer of land between the North Vietnamese and the population, casualties were relatively light and displacements of civilian populations limited.

WESTWARD DISPLACEMENT OF REFUGEES IN LAOS

Nevertheless, as early as 1962 there were approximately 125,000 refugees who had moved southwestward out of the areas of Sam Neua and eastern Xieng Khouang Provinces which were controlled by the North Vietnamese and their Pathet Lao auxiliaries. Depending upon the thrust and parry of military operations in northern Laos over the next 6 years, there were seasonal increases to the refugee population and an inexorable displacement of population gradually westward. However, by the end of the rainy season in 1968 the total number of refugees stood at about 128,000, of whom the largest number were the Meo, whose men formed the forward defense screen in northeast Laos and whose families had to be cared for by the Royal Lao Government and supported by the United States.

Beginning with the dry season in the fall of 1968 the North Vietnamese significantly stepped up their military activities in Laos. They increased sharply the number of shock troops that they sent into the country that year and began a campaign to press all the local population out of eastern Sam Neua Province and northern Xieng Khouang Province. By spring of 1969 they had succeeded in eliminating almost all the Meo outposts north and east of the Plaine des Jarres. They began reinforcing their positions in the Plaine and prepared for an attack across Route 7 to Muong Soui to cut the central highway of Laos which connects the administrative capital of Vientiane and the royal capital of Luang Prabang.

In order to forestall this action and to turn the cutting edge of the North Vietnamese forces, the commander of Laotian Military Region II launched attacks in the late spring of 1969 against the logistics bases and the marshaling grounds of the North Vietnamese forces on the Plaine des Jarres. By fall of 1969 his units had swept over the Plaine and had succeeded in capturing a vast quantity of enemy supplies. Nearly 6 million rounds of ammunition, over 6,000 weapons, 25 tanks, 113 vehicles, and more than 200,000 gallons of fuel were captured in these forays. The net result was to frustrate the North Vietnamese offensive against Route 13.

Another result of this action was, however, to convert the Plaine des Jarres into a battlefield for the first time since 1964. Approximately 20,000 civilians lived in the towns and villages in and around the Plaine des Jarres. Many of them were caught up in the fighting that swirled around them during the last 9 months of 1969.

As the dry season began in the last months of 1969, the North Vietnamese resumed their attacks throughout Laos. Their efforts were not confined merely to northeast Laos but extended also into southern and central Laos, where they laid siege to the provincial capitals of Attopeu and Saravane. In early 1970, the Royal Lao forces were pushed back from the Plaine des Jarres, and approximately 17,000 refugees were moved out with them in February and March of 1970. The North Vietnamese attacks on Attopeu and Saravane reached their climax in April through June, and another 15,000 civilians were displaced in those areas.

By the time the dry season had ended in the early summer of 1970, the North Vietnamese and their Pathet Lao auxiliaries stood in control of a broad new band of territory stretching from the entire Plaine des Jarres in the north to the Bolovens Plateau in the south of Laos. During the course of this military campaign, a total of about 150,000 persons were displaced by this North Vietnamese offensive and moved westward as charges of the Royal Lao Government, supported by the Government of the United States.

In the 1970-71 dry season, North Vietnamese military pressure began again. This year their offensive has been directed not only against Lao Government positions south of the Plaine des Jarres but against the royal capital of Luang Prabang in the north. Once again the North Vietnamese have augmented their forces in Laos. They brought back the 312th Division, and both the 312th and the 316th Divisions are fighting in northern Laos at the present time. They have enhanced their firepower and have kept a steady artillery and rocket pressure on the forward outposts and ridgelines held by the Meo defenders. Once again these actions have caused the westard movement of civilian populations and have created new refugee communities.

In this long, unhappy history of North Vietnamese aggression against Laos from 1962 until the present time, over 700,000 residents of Laos have been displaced at least once and at some time or other have been on the refugee rolls. There are currently approximately 309,000 residents of Laos who receive refugee assistance of one sort or another. Of these 309,000 people, 120,000 are the families of Lao Government forces (most of whom are Meo), 169,000 come from friendly areas from which they were pushed westward by the North Vietnamese, and 20,000 come from areas controlled by the North Vietnamese and Pathet Lao.

It is therefore very clear that the prime cause of these refugee movements to the west has been the constant military pressure of the North Vietnamese. By an examination of the numbers of refugees listed on the rolls at any one time it can be seen that there is a very close correlation between military activity and the generation of refugees. We will submit for the record a map showing the current location of refugee centers, the population in each, and an indication of the areas from which they have been driven. Again the correlation between displacement and North Vietnamese military activity will be clear.

There has been much concern expressed about the exact causes for refugee movements. In some instances the cause is quite clear and quite simple; the North Vietnamese, not trusting the civilian population, drive them out ahead of their forces rather than attempting to capture and control them. This has been particularly true of the Meo population north and east of the Plaine des Jarres. In other instances the civilian population themselves, having experienced or knowing the reputation of life under the North Vietnamese and the Pathet Lao, have chosen to flee rather than submit to that sort of regime. In still other instances the constant pressure and menace of warfare have caused the people to move from their homes and accept refugee status. And finally, in a small number of cases, the Lao Government has moved the civilian population as a result of its own decision, in order to remove them from the path of battle.

U.S. AIR OPERATIONS

I believe I should say something about the role which air attacks have played in this whole tragic picture. It has been suggested that air attacks have been the primary cause of refugee movement or even that air attacks have been deliberately mounted in order to create refugee movement and to deprive the North Vietnamese and the Pathet Lao of human resources represented by the refugees. It has, for example, been suggested that, as a result of the cessation of United States bombing over North Viet-Nam in November 1968, a vast increase of airpower was applied to northern Laos and resulted in the increase of refugee movements in that part of the country.

The facts do not bear this out. There was a significant shift of United States airpower from North Viet-Nam to Laos after the cessation of bombing in November 1968. However, this shift was almost exclusively to the area of the Ho Chi Minh Trail, where sortie rates were very significantly and sharply increased immediately after the cessation in North Viet-Nam. As I have indicated previously, there is no Lao population along the Ho Chi Minh Trail and therefore this augmentation of sorties in that area had no relationship to the generation of refugees. As a matter of fact, in north Laos the sortie level continued almost exactly as it was from November 1968 through February and early March of 1969. It was only in late March of 1969 and subsequently through the military campaigns which rolled over the Plaine des Jarres from then until early 1970 that there was an augmentation of air activity in northern Laos. This air activity was directly associated with the ground operations that had erupted on the Plaine des Jarres. As I previously indicated, this lengthy struggle for the Plaine des Jarres, which eventually resulted in its control by the North Vietnamese, resulted in the westward movement of some 17,000 people out of the total of approximately 150,000 people who were forced to move westward during that North Vietnamese offensive in the same period. These 17,000 were unfortunately caught up in the very center of major military activity, both ground and air. This sort of fighting was an unusual exception to the normal pattern of military activity which has prevailed over the past several years in the north of Laos.

The normal activity in northern Laos, as I have earlier indicated, consists largely of small units sparring for control of logistics routes and terrain features. The function of air activity in this type of warfare has been quite specialized. The greatest number of United States air sorties on a daily basis in north Laos have been flown on route reconnaissance and interdiction missions. They have expended their ordnance either against moving vehicles on the roads or against choke points and known military storage areas. Because these roads run in the valleys away from hill settlements, the greatest proportion of these sorties do not impinge upon areas of civilian population.

Similarly, in the south along the Ho Chi Minh Trail, where the greatest proportion of United States daily sorties are flown, there are no inhabited areas in the zone of operations.

In normal circumstances there are only a few United States aircraft a day that operate in areas of Laos where there is a danger of impinging upon inhabited locations. Whenever there is a request, from whatever source, for sorties of this type, they are carefully examined in advance by the Embassy in Vientiane and the strike has to be personally approved by the Ambassador. These rules of engagement, which are designed to protect the civilian population, have been in effect since 1965 and with respect to this safety feature have not been altered.

I go into this detail not because I am trying to suggest that no civilian casualties have ever resulted from United States air operations but in an effort to demonstrate the care that is taken to minimize the effect of United States air operations upon civilians. It is true that certain civilians have been caught up in military operations in which United States airpower was a component part. We have 17,000 refugees from the fighting in the Plaine des Jarres in 1969 and 1970 as testimony to that fact. They are, however, a decidedly exceptional group in the overall total of 700,000 refugees who have moved westward in the face of North Vietnamese pressure over the past 10 years.

* * *

(70) Position on Foreign Forces in Laos: Department of State Statement, August 9, 1971.[33]

(Complete Text)

The U.S. Government continues to support the 1962 Geneva agreements on Laos and believes that their full implementation would lead to not only the solution of the Lao problem but also to a general reduction in the level of violence on the entire peninsula. Since it is generally held that these agreements are now being violated, the President of the United States in 1970 wrote to the heads of government of all the signatories urging them to support the efforts of the Lao Prime Minister, Prince Souvanna Phouma, to promote consultations among the signatories as is provided for in article 4 of the Declaration on the

[33] Department of State Press Release 171, Aug. 9, 1971; text from *Bulletin,* Aug. 30, 1971, pp. 227-28. The statement was preceded by the release on Aug. 2, 1971, of a Senate Foreign Relations Committee staff report confirming the presence of an estimated 4,800 Thai "volunteers" in Laos as part of an irregular army maintained by the U.S. Central Intelligence Agency (*New York Times,* Aug. 3, 1971).

Neutrality of Laos[34] in cases of violation of the agreements. The response was disappointing: Some governments did not even respond to this appeal. Subsequently in his October 7, 1970, peace proposal, the President urged an Indochina conference which would address the problems of the conflict in Laos and Cambodia as well as in Viet-Nam.[35] To date North Viet-Nam has refused to join us in this effort to bring peace to that troubled peninsula.

The root cause of the current problems in Indochina is the presence beyond the borders of North Viet-Nam of some 250,000 North Vietnamese troops. In the case of Laos, while the United States withdrew its entire military advisory group of 666 men following the signing of the Geneva agreements in 1962, the North Vietnamese withdrew only 40 personnel through the ICC [International Control Commission] checkpoints. Although some of the 10,000 North Vietnamese military then in Laos were apparently withdrawn, many stayed. Over the years the number has grown, and some 80,000 North Vietnamese forces are not only directed against the neutral Government of Laos but also use the territory of Laos, the Ho Chi Minh Trail, to intervene in the internal affairs of a neighboring state, the Republic of Viet-Nam. Such use of Lao territory is in itself also a violation of the 1962 Geneva agreements. It was in response to this continuing threat that the Republic of Viet-Nam mounted an operation in Laos and northern South Viet-Nam in February, March, and April of 1971[36] to disrupt the North Vietnamese use of the trail. The Royal Lao Government, while expressing regret for the South Vietnamese action, noted that ". . . primary responsibility for this development rests on the Democratic Republic of Viet-Nam which has violated international law and the 1962 Geneva agreements. The Democratic Republic of Viet-Nam [DRV] has violated and is continuing to violate the neutrality and territorial integrity of the Kingdom of Laos."

More recently there has been controversy over reports of what have been called "Thai troops" in Laos. Both the Lao and Thai Governments have denied that there are Thai Government troops in Laos. The Thai Government has stated that there are volunteers of Thai nationality in irregular forces in Laos. These volunteers, many of them from areas bordering on Laos and ethnically indistinguishable from the Lao, have enrolled in the Lao military services in response to appeals from the Royal Lao Government [RLG]. These volunteers and the military organizations to which they belong are part of the RLG Armed Forces and are under the command of the Royal Lao Government, through the Lao military region commanders.

[34] *Documents, 1962*, p. 287.
[35] Cf. above at note 4.
[36] Cf. Documents 67-68. The ending of operation Lam Son 719 was officially announced on Apr. 9, 1971.

On June 7 the Department of State spokesman acknowledged that the U.S. Government provided support to these volunteers and to other forces, regular and irregular, in Laos.

The Royal Thai Government has acknowledged that it has provided training for Lao forces, regular and irregular, on Thai soil, acting in response to a request from the Royal Lao Government. The Thai Government's willingness to provide this kind of assistance stems from the extreme importance of Laos to Thai security.

The Royal Lao Government is sensitive to implications with respect to the Geneva agreements created by the presence of volunteers of Thai nationality in Laos. However, in the face of the massive North Vietnamese invasion, the RLG felt constrained to seek reinforcements for the severely depleted Lao forces. It considers that it is fully justified in seeking such assistance. The DRV's violations constitute a material breach of the agreements which entitles—and indeed impels—the RLG to take necessary measures to defend itself. Likewise the U.S. Government, itself a signatory of these agreements, is entitled to withhold complete compliance in light of this failure by the DRV to honor its obligations, and it is justified in responding to requests for assistance from the RLG. The Lao Prime Minister, Prince Souvanna Phouma, has made it clear on many occasions that he is prepared to return to full implementation of the Geneva agreements whenever the DRV is prepared to do likewise, beginning by the withdrawal of all its military forces from Laos. The U.S. Government fully supports this position of the Lao Prime Minister.

B. The Progress of "Vietnamization."

[A definitive evaluation of the South Vietnamese incursion into Laos (Documents 67-68) was offered by President Nixon in a radio-television address on April 7, 1971 (Document 71), in which he announced that the success of the Vietnamization program—as measured by the increased strength of the South Vietnamese and the successful operations in Cambodia and Laos—would permit an increase in the rate of American military withdrawals from South Vietnam. The decision to withdraw 100,000 more troops between May 1 and December 1—in other words, to lower the ceiling on authorized U.S. troop strength from 284,000 to 184,000—demonstrated, the President said, that the American involvement in Vietnam was "coming to an end" and that the goal of a total American withdrawal could be reached through the Vietnamization program even if it unhappily proved not to be attainable by way of the peace negotiations.

An important qualification on the concept of total withdrawal from Vietnam was mentioned by the President at the convention of the

American Society of Newspaper Editors on April 16 when he confirmed reports that the United States intended to leave a "residual force," usually estimated at 50,000-60,000, in South Vietnam until such time as American prisoners of war had been released and the South Vietnamese had gained the capacity to take over full responsibility for the defense of their country (Document 72).

These and other aspects of the Vietnamization program were reviewed at a Washington meeting on April 23 of representatives of the six countries—Australia, the Republic of Korea, New Zealand, Thailand, the United States, and the Republic of Vietnam—that were still participating in the military defense of South Vietnam (Document 73).]

(71) Report on the Situation in Southeast Asia: Radio-Television Address by President Nixon, April 7, 1971.[37]

(Complete Text)

Good evening my fellow Americans. Over the past several weeks you have heard a number of reports on TV, radio, and in your newspapers on the situation in Southeast Asia.

I think the time has come for me as President and as Commander in Chief of our Armed Forces to put these reports in perspective, to lay all the pertinent facts before you and to let you judge for yourselves as to the success or failure of our policy.

I am glad to be able to begin my report tonight by announcing that I have decided to increase the rate of American troop withdrawals for the period from May 1 to December 1. Before going into details, I would like to review briefly what I found when I came into office, the progress we have made to date in reducing American forces, and the reason why I am able to announce a stepped-up withdrawal without jeopardizing our remaining forces in Vietnam and without endangering our ultimate goal of ending American involvement in a way which will increase the chances for a lasting peace in the Pacific and in the world.

When I left Washington in January of 1961, after serving 8 years as Vice President under President Eisenhower, there were no American combat forces in Vietnam. No Americans had died in combat in Vietnam.

When I returned to Washington as President 8 years later, there were 540,000 American troops in Vietnam. Thirty-one thousand had died there. Three hundred Americans were being lost every week and there was no comprehensive plan to end the United States involvement in the war.

[37] *Presidential Documents*, Apr. 12, 1971, pp. 611-16. For further discussion see Document 83.

I implemented a plan to train and equip the South Vietnamese; to withdraw American forces; and to end American involvement in the war just as soon as the South Vietnamese had developed the capacity to defend their country against Communist aggression. On this chart on my right, you can see how our plan has succeeded. In June of 1969, I announced a withdrawal of 25,000 men; in September, 40,000; December, 50,000; April of 1970—150,000.[38] By the first of next month, May 1, we will have brought home more than 265,000 Americans, almost half of the troops in Vietnam when I took office.

Now another indication of the progress we have made is in reducing American casualties. Casualties were five times as great in the first 3 months of 1969 as they were in the first 3 months this year, 1971. South Vietnamese casualties have also dropped significantly in the past 2 years. One American dying in combat is one too many. But our goal is no American fighting man dying anyplace in the world. Every decision I have made in the past and every decision I make in the future will have the purpose of achieving that goal.

Let me review now two decisions I have made which have contributed to the achievements of our goals in Vietnam that you've seen on this chart.

The first was the destruction of enemy bases in Cambodia.[39] You will recall that at the time of that decision, many expressed fears that we had widened the war, that our casualties would increase, that our troop withdrawal program would be delayed. Now I don't question the sincerity of those who expressed these fears. But we can see now they were wrong. American troops were out of Cambodia in 60 days, just as I pledged they would be. American casualties did not rise. They were cut in half. American troop withdrawals were not halted or delayed. They continued at an accelerated pace.

Now let me turn to the Laotian operation.[40] As you know, this was undertaken by South Vietnamese ground forces with American air support against North Vietnamese troops which had been using Laotian territory for 6 years to attack American forces and allied forces in South Vietnam. Since the completion of that operation, there's been a great deal of understandable speculation—just as there was after Cambodia—whether or not it was a success or a failure, a victory or a defeat. But, as in Cambodia, what is important is not the instant analysis of the moment, but what happens in the future.

Did the Laotian operation contribute to the goals we sought? I've just completed my assessment of that operation and here are my conclusions:

[38] *Documents, 1968-69*, pp. 261-63, 275-76, and 288-91; same, *1970*, pp. 181-84.
[39] Same, pp. 156-79.
[40] Documents 67-68.

First, the South Vietnamese demonstrated that without American advisers they could fight effectively against the very best troops North Vietnam could put in the field.

Second, the South Vietnamese suffered heavy casualties, but by every conservative estimate the casualties suffered by the enemy were far heavier.

Third, and most important, the disruption of enemy supply lines, the consumption of ammunition and arms in the battle has been even more damaging to the capability of the North Vietnamese to sustain major offensives in South Vietnam than were the operations in Cambodia 10 months ago.

Consequently, tonight I can report that Vietnamization has succeeded. Because of the increased strength of the South Vietnamese, because of the success of the Cambodian operation, because of the achievements of the South Vietnamese operation in Laos, I am announcing an increase in the rate of American withdrawals. Between May 1 and December 1 of this year, 100,000 more American troops will be brought home from South Vietnam. This will bring the total number of American troops withdrawn from South Vietnam to 365,000. Now that's over two-thirds of the number who were there when I came into office, as you can see from this chart on my left. The Government of South Vietnam fully supports the decision I've just announced.

Now, let's look at the future:

As you can see from the progress we have made to date and by this announcement tonight, the American involvement in Vietnam is coming to an end. The day the South Vietnamese can take over their own defense is in sight. Our goal is a total American withdrawal from Vietnam. We can and we will reach that goal through our program of Vietnamization if necessary.

But we would infinitely prefer to reach it even sooner—through negotiations. I am sure most of you will recall that on October 7 of last year in a national TV broadcast, I proposed an immediate cease-fire throughout Indochina, the immediate release of all prisoners of war in the Indochina area, an all Indochina Peace Conference, the complete withdrawal of all outside forces, and a political settlement.[41] Tonight I again call on Hanoi to engage in serious negotiations to speed the end of this war.[42] I especially call on Hanoi to agree to the immediate and unconditional release of all prisoners of war throughout Indochina. It is time for Hanoi to end the barbaric use of our prisoners as negotiating pawns and to join us in a humane act that will free their men as well as ours.

[41] *Documents, 1970*, pp. 196-201.
[42] Cf. Documents 74-77.

Let me turn now to a proposal which at first glance has a great deal of popular appeal. If our goal is a total withdrawal of all our forces, why don't I announce a date now for ending our involvement?[43] Well, the difficulty in making such an announcement to the American people is that I would also be making that announcement to the enemy. And it would serve the enemy's purpose and not our own.

If the United States should announce that we will quit regardless of what the enemy does, we would have thrown away our principal bargaining counter to win the release of American prisoners of war, we would remove the enemy's strongest incentive to end the war sooner by negotiation, and we will have given enemy commanders the exact information they need to marshal their attacks against our remaining forces at their most vulnerable time.

The issue very simply is: Shall we leave Vietnam in a way that—by our own actions—consciously turns the country over to the Communists? Or shall we leave in a way that gives the South Vietnamese a reasonable chance to survive as a free people? My plan will end American involvement in a way that would provide that chance. And the other plan would end it precipitately and give victory to the Communists.

In a deeper sense, we have the choice of ending our involvement in this war on a note of despair or on a note of hope. I believe as Thomas Jefferson did, that Americans will always choose hope over despair. We have it in our power to leave Vietnam in a way that offers a brave people a realistic hope of freedom. We have it in our power to prove to our friends in the world that America's sense of responsibility remains the world's greatest single hope of peace.

And above all, we have it in our power to close a difficult chapter in American history, not meanly but nobly—so that each one of us can come out of this searing experience with a measure of pride in our Nation, confidence in our own character, and hope for the future of the spirit of America.

I know there are those who honestly believe that I should move to end this war without regard to what happens to South Vietnam. This way would abandon our friends. But even more important, we would abandon ourselves. We would plunge from the anguish of war into a nightmare of recrimination. We would lose respect for this Nation, respect for one another, respect for ourselves.

I understand the deep concerns which have been raised in this country, fanned by reports of brutalities in Vietnam. Let me put this into perspective.

I have visited Vietnam many times, and speaking now from that experience and as Commander in Chief of our Armed Forces, I feel it is

[43] Cf. Documents 79 and 81.

my duty to speak up for the two and a half million fine young Americans who have served in Vietnam. The atrocity charges in individual cases should not and cannot be allowed to reflect on their courage and their self-sacrifice. War is a terrible and cruel experience for a nation and it's particularly terrible and cruel for those who bear the burden of fighting.

But never in history have men fought for less selfish motives—not for conquest, not for glory, but only for the right of a people far away to choose the kind of government they want.

And while we hear and read much of isolated acts of cruelty, we do not hear enough of the tens of thousands of individual American soldiers—I've seen them there—building schools, roads, hospitals, clinics—who, through countless acts of generosity and kindness, have tried to help the people of South Vietnam. We can and we should be very proud of these men. They deserve not our scorn but they deserve our admiration and our deepest appreciation.

The way to express that appreciation is to end America's participation in this conflict, not in failure or in defeat but in achievement of the great goals for which they fought—a South Vietnam free to determine its own future and an America no longer divided by war but united in peace.

That is why it is so important how we end this war. By our decision we will demonstrate the kind of people we are, and the kind of country we will become.

That's why I've charted the course I have laid out tonight: to end this war—but end it in a way that will strengthen trust for America around the world, not undermine it, in a way that will redeem the sacrifices that have been made, not insult them, in a way that will heal this Nation, not tear it apart.

I can assure you tonight with confidence that American involvement in this war is coming to an end.

But can you believe this? I understand why this question is raised by many very honest and sincere people. Because many times in the past in this long and difficult war, actions have been announced from Washington which were supposed to lead to a reduction of American involvement in Vietnam. And over and over these actions resulted in more Americans going to Vietnam and more casualties in Vietnam.

Tonight I do not ask you to take what I say on faith. Look at the record. Look again at this chart on my left. Every action taken by this administration, every decision made, has accomplished what I said it would accomplish. They have reduced American involvement. They have drastically reduced our casualties.

In my campaign for the Presidency, I pledged to end American involvement in this war. I am keeping that pledge. And I expect to be held accountable by the American people if I fail.

I am often asked what I would like to accomplish more than anything else while serving as President of the United States. And I always give the same answer: to bring peace—peace abroad, peace at home for America. The reason I am so deeply committed to peace goes far beyond political considerations or my concern about my place in history, or the other reasons that political scientists usually say are the motivations of Presidents.

Every time I talk to a brave wife of an American POW, every time I write a letter to the mother of a boy who has been killed in Vietnam, I become more deeply committed to end this war, and to end it in a way that we can build lasting peace.

I think the hardest thing that a President has to do is to present posthumously the Nation's highest honor, the Medal of Honor, to mothers or fathers or widows of men who have lost their lives, but in the process have saved the lives of others.

We had an award ceremony in the East Room of the White House just a few weeks ago. And at that ceremony I remember one of the recipients, Mrs. Karl Taylor, from Pennsylvania. Her husband was a Marine sergeant, Sergeant Karl Taylor. He charged an enemy machine gun singlehanded and knocked it out. He lost his life. But in the process the lives of several wounded Marines in the range of that machine gun were saved.

After I presented her the Medal, I shook hands with their two children, Karl, Jr.—he was 8 years old—and Kevin, who was 4. As I was about to move to the next recipient, Kevin suddenly stood at attention and saluted. I found it rather difficult to get my thoughts together for the next presentation.

My fellow Americans, I want to end this war in a way that is worthy of the sacrifice of Karl Taylor, and I think he would want me to end it in a way that would increase the chances that Kevin and Karl, and all those children like them here and around the world, could grow up in a world where none of them would have to die in war; that would increase the chance for America to have what it has not had in this century—a full generation of peace.

We've come a long way in the last 2 years toward that goal. With your continued support, I believe we will achieve that goal. And generations in the future will look back at this difficult, trying time in America's history and they will be proud that we demonstrated that we had the courage and the character of a great people.

Thank you.

(72) Need for a Residual Force in Vietnam: Statement by President Nixon at a Panel Discussion at the Annual Convention of the American Society of Newspaper Editors, April 16, 1971.[44]

(Excerpt)

*   *   *

U.S. INVOLVEMENT IN VIETNAM

EMMETT DEDMON [Vice President and Editorial Director, Chicago Sun-Times and The Chicago Daily News]. Mr. President, you mentioned ending our involvement in the war in Vietnam and, yet, the Secretary of Defense said the other day that our Air Force and naval power would remain in South Vietnam.

How do you reconcile those two statements or is there a conflict there in your opinion?

THE PRESIDENT. No, Mr. Dedmon, there really isn't a conflict between two statements. I said that we would end our involvement in Vietnam. You will recall my speech last Wednesday.[45] I said that our goal is a total American withdrawal from Vietnam.

On October 7 of last year you may recall I said that we not only propose a total American withdrawal but a cease-fire all over Southeast Asia[46] which would, of course, mean no airpower, no American forces there, no use of power in any way.

As far as Mr. Laird's statement was concerned, what he was referring to was that pending the time that we can have a total withdrawal consistent with the principles that I laid down in my speech last week, it will be necessary for the United States to retain air power and to retain some residual forces.

Our goal, however, is a total withdrawal. We do not have as a goal a permanent residual force such as we have in Korea at the present time.

But it will be necessary for us to maintain forces in South Vietnam until two important objectives are achieved; one, the release of the prisoners of war held by North Vietnam in North Vietnam and other parts of Southeast Asia, and two, the ability of the South Vietnamese to develop the capacity to defend themselves against a Communist takeover, not the sure capacity, but at least the chance.

Once those two objectives are achieved, then the total American withdrawal can be undertaken and will be undertaken.

We can achieve them earlier, provided the enemy will negotiate. As

[44] *Presidential Documents*, Apr. 19, 1971, pp. 632-33.
[45] Document 71.
[46] Cf. above at note 4.

you noticed, on October 7 I indicated we will have a total withdrawal in 12 months if they would be willing to mutually withdraw their forces.

And so, in sum, the goal of American policy in Vietnam is a total withdrawal with no residual force. But, as long as the prisoner issue remains unsettled, and as long as they hold prisoners, and as long as the South Vietnamese have not yet developed the capacity of their own country—a capacity that they rapidly are developing—we will have forces there.

MR. DEDMON. Mr. President, may I follow up with one more question?

THE PRESIDENT. Yes, I understand—all follow up if you want to.

TROOP WITHDRAWAL GOALS

MR. DEDMON. I realize that you do not wish to state a date at this time at which we will withdraw, and that there was some confusion in the press about what Senator Scott said following a meeting at the White House.[47] Could I ask this question: Is Senator Scott's use of the date January 1, 1973, in your opinion, a practicable goal?

THE PRESIDENT. Mr. Dedmon, that is a very clever way to get me to answer a question that I won't answer. [*Laughter*] I would expect that from an editor as well as from a reporter.

The date, let me say, cannot and must not be related to an election in the United States. Let's begin with that. I don't want one American to be in Vietnam one day longer than is necessary to achieve the two goals that I have mentioned: the release of our prisoners and the capacity of the South Vietnamese to defend themselves against a Communist takeover.

Now, as far as that date is concerned, it will depend upon the circumstances. I have announced a troop withdrawal which takes us through November (December) 1st.[48] In the middle of October (November), I will make another troop withdrawal announcement.[49]

I will then analyze the training of the South Vietnamese forces and particularly their air force at that time. I will then analyze enemy activity and, also, any progress in negotiation, particularly in negotiation with regard to prisoners.

At that time, I will be able to make a further announcement with regard to what our withdrawal will be. But for me to speculate about a

[47] Senator Hugh Scott (Republican, Pennsylvania), the Senate minority leader, was quoted in the *New York Times* of Apr. 9, 1971, as saying the President had a definite date in mind for ending the war, presumably at about the time of the expiration of his term on Jan. 20, 1973.

[48] Document 71 (parenthetical correction in original).

[49] Document 80 (parenthetical correction in original).

date would not help us; it would only serve the enemy, and I am not going to do that even though it might be politically popular to set a date.

I have to do what is right for the United States, right for our prisoners, and right for our goal of a South Vietnam with a chance to avoid a Communist takeover which will contribute to a lasting peace in the Pacific and the world.

* * *

(73) Conference of Troop-contributing Nations, Washington, April 23, 1971: Final Communiqué.[50]

(Complete Text)

1. The Foreign Minister of Australia, the Honorable Leslie H. Bury; the Minister of Foreign Affairs of the Republic of Korea, H. E. Kyu Hah Choi; the Ambassador of New Zealand, H. E. Frank Corner; the Minister of Foreign Affairs of Thailand, H. E. Thanat Khoman; the Secretary of State of the United States, the Honorable William P. Rogers; and the Minister of Foreign Affairs of the Republic of Viet-Nam, H. E. Tran Van Lam met in Washington on April 23, 1971 at the invitation of the Government of the United States.

2. The representatives agreed that since their last meeting[51] notable progress had been made in the Republic of Viet-Nam toward the goal of bringing an end to the aggression of North Viet-Nam against the people and territory of the Republic of Viet-Nam. They noted the success of the Government of the Republic of Viet-Nam in extending control over and bringing its services to an ever growing percentage of the population. They also noted the increasing participation by the Vietnamese people in the processes of government at all levels. Recognizing the increasing significance of economic problems confronting the Republic of Viet-Nam, the representatives observed with satisfaction the promising measures which had been taken in the last year to promote economic stability. They noted with regret that the considerable progress in all other areas was not accompanied by progress in achieving a negotiated end to the war.[52] The failure so far to reach a negotiated settlement continues to be attributable to the refusal of the North Vietnamese representatives to enter serious negotiations. The representatives reaffirmed their previous agreement that all nations which are

[50] Department of State Press Release 82, Apr. 23, 1971; text from *Bulletin*, May 17, 1971, pp. 635-38. For further discussion of Laos, see Documents 67-70; of Cambodia, Documents 82-83.
[51] *Documents, 1970*, pp. 186-91.
[52] Cf. below at note 71.

making available armed forces to help defend the Republic of Viet-Nam must participate in the settlement of the conflict.

3. The Foreign Minister of the Republic of Viet-Nam reported in detail on the current situation in Viet-Nam. He described the achievements of the operations of the Vietnamese forces, with Allied support, against the sanctuaries and base areas in the Khmer Republic [Cambodia] and in the Kingdom of Laos from which the enemy forces conducted their aggression against the Republic of Viet-Nam. The Minister also cited operations against the few remaining major enemy base areas within the territory of the Republic, notably the dry-season campaign in the U-Minh Forest and other areas in the Mekong Delta. The Minister commented that by reason of vigorous campaigns by Vietnamese forces, the enemy was no longer secure in what had earlier been his sanctuaries. Rural security has been greatly enhanced, because of the increasing ability of the Regional Forces, Popular Forces and the People's Self-Defense Forces to assure the security of their own localities, thereby freeing the regular forces for offensive operations against the enemy's main force. The Foreign Minister discussed the progressive extension of government control and services of all kinds to the population. He noted that over 90% of the Vietnamese people resided in localities under secure or relatively secure government control, whereas only two-tenths of 1% still reside in VC [Viet-Cong] controlled hamlets. The Land-to-the-Tiller program which had been launched just over a year ago will make it possible for large numbers of people, formerly tenants, to become owners of the land which they cultivated. So far 160,000 titles have been issued under this program. The program met its goal for the first year of distributing 200,000 hectares of rice-land.

4. The Foreign Minister of the Republic of Viet-Nam stated that with the decrease in military activity, the enhancement of security of the population, and the extension of government control, economic problems were considered to be the most significant issues confronting his Government. One of the major problems was to obtain through Viet-Nam's own efforts and the assistance of its friends, the resources to defray the increased costs deriving from the assumption by the Republic of Viet-Nam of a larger share of responsibility for its own defense. Another problem was to find means to control inflation arising largely from this increased war effort. Finally, his Government needed to plan for the nation's post-war economic development. To solve these problems the Government had enacted a series of measures to stabilize the economy and increase revenues in October 1970 and again in March 1971. As a result of these reforms, the rate of inflation has been reduced considerably as compared to the earlier rate of inflation which had been about 30% annually in recent years. The Minister cited other indicators of the improving economic situation in the Republic of Viet-Nam, but did not minimize the problems that would continue so long

as the Republic of Viet-Nam was forced to continue to resist North Vietnamese aggression.

5. The representatives noted with satisfaction the description by the Vietnamese Foreign Minister of progress made in the military situation, as well as in the other areas as described by the Foreign Minister. The representatives expressed their earnest hope that the various measures taken by the Government of the Republic of Viet-Nam would help to mitigate the adverse economic and social effects of the war, and to provide the basis for action to promote and facilitate future long-range development of the country. They expressed the hope that the steady improvement in the military situation, accompanied by political and economic stability in the Republic of Viet-Nam might serve to persuade the rulers of North Viet-Nam that they could not reverse this progress by military means; and hence that they must agree to serious nego-tiations. The representatives re-emphasized that all Allied proposals remained fully negotiable, except with regard to the right of self-determination of the Vietnamese people. In this regard they called attention to the proposals made public by the President of the Republic of Viet-Nam on October 8, 1970.[53]

6. The representatives agreed that the progress within the last year had made it possible and desirable for them to re-examine the future combat role of the troop contributing countries. They noted that the steady assumption of responsibility for its self-defense by the Republic of Viet-Nam had made it possible for the troop contributing countries to begin progressive withdrawal of some of their combat forces. They also agreed that as their combat forces were withdrawn at a measured pace, the troop contributing countries should strive to provide for a further period, as desired by the Government of the Republic of Viet-Nam, and according to their respective military and economic capa-bilities, military support forces capable of providing training, engineer construction, medical, advisory, and other forms of assistance. They noted that steps in this direction have already been taken by the Gov-ernment of Australia and the Government of New Zealand (both of which have recently replaced portions of their combat forces with mili-tary training detachments) and that combat force withdrawal planning in conjunction with the Government of the Republic of Viet-Nam is being carried out by all troop contributing countries. Reviewing past accomplishments, the representatives noted that circumstances had al-ready permitted a reduction of 265,000 in the number of US troops in South Viet-Nam by May 1, 1971. It was noted that the United States

---

53 A South Vietnamese Government statement of Oct. 7, 1970 (local time), endorsed President Nixon's five-point proposal of the same date (para. 8, below) and reiterated a 1969 offer by President Thieu (*Documents, 1968-69*, pp. 267-69) to accept the results of free elections supervised by a mixed electoral commission and an international body. For text see *Keesing's*, p. 24276.

Government had just recently announced plans for further withdrawals.[54] The representatives also took note of statements which had been made by the governments of Thailand, Australia and New Zealand regarding withdrawal plans. The Foreign Minister of the Republic of Korea stated that, as the first phase measure of an overall plan for gradual reduction of its troops in the Republic of Viet-Nam, the Government of Korea planned to withdraw one division strength of its troops from Viet-Nam. The period of this withdrawal would be made known through consultations presently under way between the governments of the Republic of Korea and the Republic of Viet-Nam.[55]

7. They agreed that the nations which have assisted the Republic of Viet-Nam militarily should seek to help the Vietnamese people in the equally important endeavors of peace, thus continuing the close coordination and cooperation which had been developed in conducting their common struggle against aggression. In this continuing stage of their cooperation, which would emphasize security and economic measures, the representatives reaffirmed their determination to continue to help the South Vietnamese people to restore their national strength. With its people free from want, as well as enjoying improved security, the Republic of Viet-Nam can better play its role in Southeast Asia. Further, they expressed the hope that other nations will join in this effort.

8. The United States Secretary of State reaffirmed his Government's fundamental policy of continuing to strengthen the forces of the Republic of Viet-Nam while withdrawing United States troops. This policy will result in the continued redeployment of United States forces from the Republic of Viet-Nam. He reported his Government's satisfaction with the growing capabilities of the Vietnamese forces which continue to carry an increasing part of the burden of the defense of the Republic of Viet-Nam. At the same time, the United States has not altered its dedication to the achievement of a negotiated end to the war. The Secretary of State reviewed the initiatives taken by the United States to try to elicit serious negotiations on the part of the other side in the Paris talks. He cited the concrete proposals made by President Nixon on October 7, 1970.[56]

9. The representatives expressed special concern about the enemy's inhumanity with regard to prisoners of war they have captured in North Viet-Nam, South Viet-Nam, the Kingdom of Laos, and the Khmer Republic. They noted that the Governments of the United States and the Republic of Viet-Nam have sought repeatedly for humanitarian reasons

---

[54] Cf. Document 71.

[55] The Republic of Korea, which had about 48,000 troops in South Vietnam as of Dec. 1971, began in that month the withdrawal of 10,000 troops to be completed by June 1972. Thailand withdrew during 1971 the bulk of a force originally totaling about 12,000, and Australia and New Zealand completed the withdrawal of their combat forces during the year. (Rogers Report, 1971, p. 72.)

[56] *Documents, 1970*, pp. 196-201.

to open productive talks on prisoners of war in the Paris meetings, but that the other side had rebuffed all such efforts. They expressed their support for the Republic of Viet-Nam's initiative in undertaking to repatriate sick and wounded prisoners of war to North Viet-Nam. They condemned the enemy's continued refusal to identify all prisoners of war, to allow them all to correspond regularly with their families, and to allow impartial inspection of prisoner of war facilities, as required by the Geneva Prisoner of War Convention of 1949,[57] to which North Viet-Nam is a party. The representatives renewed the undertakings of their governments to ensure full compliance by their forces with the Geneva Conventions.

10. The representatives noted that the North Vietnamese armed forces were continuing their aggression, not only against South Viet-Nam, but that an even larger total number of North Vietnamese troops were deployed also within the sovereign territories of the Kingdom of Laos and the Khmer Republic, inflicting untold death and destruction on the peoples of those neutral nations. They noted the declared intentions of North Viet-Nam to overthrow the legitimate Government of the Khmer Republic. On the other hand the representatives expressed admiration for the courage and determination of the peoples of the Kingdom of Laos and the Khmer Republic in resisting North Vietnamese aggression.

11. The representatives called upon the participants in the 1954 Geneva Agreements to ensure the independence, neutrality and territorial integrity of the Khmer Republic. They also urged that all signatories comply with their obligations to respect the sovereignty, independence, neutrality, unity and territorial integrity of the Kingdom of Laos which they had pledged at Geneva on July 23, 1962.

12. The representatives exchanged their views on the security situation in Asia as a whole. In particular, they noted with concern that a state of tension continued to prevail over the Korean peninsula. The Minister of Foreign Affairs of the Republic of Korea pointed out that the avowed policy of the north Korean communists to bring the whole of Korea under communist rule by all means, including military aggression, and their continuing acts of provocation constituted the main cause of this tension. The representatives welcomed the statement by the President of the Republic of Korea on August 15, 1970 calling upon the north Korean communists to renounce the use of force and to undertake constructive efforts toward a peaceful solution of the Korean question, and noted with regret that it was rejected outright by the north Korean communists. They commended the efforts of the Republic of Korea to defend itself against the aggressive acts of the north Korean communists on the one hand and to develop its economy, at a

[57] TIAS 3364; 6 UST 3316. For review of prisoner-of-war developments during 1971 see Rogers Report, 1971, pp. 74-75, and Nixon Report, 1972, pp. 119-22.

rapid growth rate, on the other. The representatives reaffirmed their support for the Republic of Korea in resisting the aggressive acts of the north Korean communists.[58]

13. It was agreed that the Foreign Ministers would meet again, as required, to coordinate their efforts in the common endeavor, and they received with gratitude an invitation from the Foreign Minister of the Republic of Korea to host the next such meeting. It was also agreed that representatives of the troop contributing countries would meet with the Foreign Minister of the Republic of Viet-Nam in Saigon later in the year.

C. Peace Negotiations in Paris, May–November 1971.

[While pressing forward along the "Vietnamization track" (Documents 71-73), the United States continued its efforts to achieve some progress on the "negotiating track" which President Nixon had identified as the preferred route toward ending the American involvement and securing an Indochina settlement consistent with the American interest in a stable peace.[59] The negotiating track itself, as the President would later reveal in a speech of January 25, 1972,[60] comprised two separate spurs. In addition to the semipublic, two-sided (or four-party) negotiations that had begun in Paris in January 1969, secret contacts between Dr. Kissinger and high-level North Vietnamese representatives were also taking place and providing a separate channel for the more important diplomatic exchanges between the United States and North Vietnam. Although the two sets of negotiations proceeded concurrently through most of 1971, it will be convenient to review developments at the semipublic sessions (Documents 74a and 74b) before examining the record of the secret contacts as subsequently revealed by the two parties (Documents 75-77).]

1. The Two-sided (Four-party) Talks.

[The Paris peace talks between the United States and the Republic of Vietnam on one side and the Democratic Republic of Vietnam (D.R.V.) and the Provisional Revolutionary Government of the Republic of South Vietnam (P.R.G.)[61] on the other entered their third year in January 1971 with few if any signs of progress toward resolving the

---

[58] Cf. Documents 98-100.
[59] Cf. above at note 1.
[60] Cf. below at note 79.
[61] Soon after its establishment in June 1969, the P.R.G. succeeded the National Liberation Front of South Vietnam (N.L.F.) as the political representative of the insurgent forces and their spokesman in the Paris talks.

basic issues over which the war in Vietnam was being fought. The most recent proposals put forward by the two sides remained poles apart with respect to the key question of South Vietnam's political future and the closely related question of a withdrawal of outside military forces from South Vietnam.

The United States, thus far in the talks, had more or less expressly maintained that a cease-fire in Vietnam or Indochina should be followed by a mutual withdrawal of foreign military forces that would include not only the U.S. and allied forces in South Vietnam but also the estimated 250,000 North Vietnamese troops deployed outside the frontiers of North Vietnam in South Vietnam, in Cambodia, and in Laos.[62] In addition, it had insisted that the people of South Vietnam must be given the opportunity "to determine their own political future without outside interference";[63] and it had obviously attached special importance to ensuring the prompt and unconditional release of prisoners of war held by both sides—among them the 1,600 Americans, including some 40 civilians, who were missing or held in North and South Vietnam, Laos, and Cambodia, some of them for as much as six years.[64]

To these objectives, North Vietnam and the "Provisional Revolutionary Government" had opposed a program that called in effect for the withdrawal of U.S. and allied (but not North Vietnamese) troops from South Vietnam and the replacement of the existing Republic of Vietnam Government by a coalition regime under strong Communist influence. The most recent Communist proposal, an eight-point plan put forward on September 17, 1970, by Mrs. Nguyen Thi Binh, the Foreign Minister of the P.R.G. and head of its delegation in Paris, had specifically called for (1) withdrawal of all U.S. and allied forces from South Vietnam by June 30, 1971; (2) resolution of the question of Vietnamese armed forces in South Vietnam by the Vietnamese parties among themselves; (3) the formation in South Vietnam of a new administration without the incumbent President, Vice-President, and Prime Minister; (4) the holding of "really free and democratic general elections"; (5) formation of a provisional coalition government including P.R.G. representatives; (6) reunification of Vietnam in stages by North–South agreement; (7) joint decision by the parties on enforcement and implementation; and (8) implementation of cease-fire modalities following the signature of peace accords.[65] But such a plan, as President Nixon pointed out early in 1971, was basically unacceptable to the United States in that it made no provision regarding the North Viet-

[62] E.g., Nixon speech, May 14, 1969, in *Documents, 1968-69*, p. 256.
[63] Same, pp. 255-56; also Nixon speech, Apr. 20, 1970, in same, *1970*, pp. 183-84.
[64] Nixon Report, 1971, p. 78; cf. note 57 above.
[65] *Documents. 1970*, pp. 192-96.

namese forces in South Vietnam and amounted, in effect, to "a formula for a guaranteed political takeover."[66]

The United States itself, however, had appeared to close observers to be receding from some of the conditions on which it had previously appeared most immovable. The latest American (and South Vietnamese) position was embodied in the five-point plan put forward in President Nixon's broadcast of October 7, 1970, which called for (1) a "cease-fire-in-place" by all armed forces throughout Indochina; (2) convocation of an Indochina Peace Conference; (3) negotiation of an agreed timetable for complete withdrawal of U.S. forces in South Vietnam as part of an agreed overall settlement based on principles stated by the President; (4) joint search for a political settlement reflecting the will of the South Vietnamese people and "the existing relationship of political forces in South Vietnam"; and (5) immediate and unconditional release of prisoners of war held by both sides.[67]

This plan had been denounced by the Communist representatives on the ground that it failed to set a date for the final withdrawal of U.S. troops or to provide for the formation of a broadly based coalition government to organize free and democratic elections.[68] In spite of these objections, however, the U.S. plan of October 7, 1970, appeared to differ from earlier American statements in that it contemplated an eventual withdrawal of all U.S. forces from South Vietnam, but did *not* call specifically for the withdrawal of the estimated 100,000 North Vietnamese troops in the South or the additional North Vietnamese troops in Laos and Cambodia. It is true that the President did not explicitly waive this requirement, which was later stated by his representative in Paris to be still in effect.[69] His decision not to reiterate it at the time can, however, be viewed in retrospect as a step toward the type of peace settlement that was ultimately concluded on January 27, 1973, which likewise called for the withdrawal of U.S. and allied forces from South Vietnam (and of all foreign forces from Cambodia and Laos) but did not require the withdrawal of North Vietnamese forces from South Vietnam.[70]

Discussions at the weekly semipublic sessions in Paris during the first half of 1971 continued to revolve primarily around the elements contained in the two 1970 plans. The North Vietnamese (D.R.V.) and P.R.G. delegations, headed respectively by Xuan Thuy and Mrs. Binh, continued to attach first importance to the withdrawal of U.S. and

[66] Nixon Report, 1971, p. 67.

[67] *Documents, 1970*, pp. 196-201.

[68] *Keesing's*, p. 24276.

[69] Statement by Ambassador David K.E. Bruce, May 6, 1971, in *Bulletin*, May 24, 1971, pp. 666-68.

[70] Agreement on Ending the War and Restoring Peace in Vietnam, signed in Paris Jan. 27, 1973 (TIAS 7542; 24 UST 1); text in *Bulletin*, Feb. 12, 1973, pp. 169-88.

allied troops and the replacement of the existing South Vietnamese leadership headed by President Nguyen Van Thieu, Vice-President Nguyen Cao Ky, and Prime Minister Tran Thien Khiem. Ambassador David K.E. Bruce, the U.S. delegation head, his deputy, Philip C. Habib, and South Vietnamese representative Pham Dang Lam continued to give high priority to the release of prisoners of war and to stress the need for withdrawal from South Vietnam of all external forces, including those of North Vietnam.[71]

The only important new proposal to come before the Paris sessions was put forward by Mrs. Binh on July 1, 1971, in the form of a seven-point plan (Document 74a) that differed in detail from her 1970 submission but, as Ambassador Bruce pointed out the following week, contained numerous ambiguities that would need to be clarified before the United States could take a position on it (Document 74b). But neither Ambassador Bruce, who resigned at the end of July, nor his successor, Ambassador William J. Porter, succeeded in obtaining the necessary clarifications during the balance of the year.]

(74) New "Vietcong" Peace Proposal, July 1, 1971.

    (a) Seven-point Proposal Presented by the Representative of the Provisional Revolutionary Government of the Republic of South Vietnam (P.R.G.) at a Plenary Session on July 1, 1971.[72]

(Complete Text)

[1]

Regarding the deadline for the total withdrawal of U.S. forces.

The U.S. Government must put an end to its war of aggression in Vietnam, stop the policy of "Vietnamization" of the war, withdraw from South Vietnam all troops, military personnel, weapons, and war materials of the United States and of the other foreign countries in the U.S. camp, and dismantle all U.S. bases in South Vietnam, without posing any condition whatsoever.

The U.S. Government must set a terminal date for the withdrawal from South Vietnam of the totality of U.S. forces and those of the other foreign countries in the U.S. camp.

If the U.S. Government sets a terminal date for the withdrawal from

---

[71] Statements by the U.S. representatives are reprinted in the weekly issues of the *Bulletin*.
[72] Reuters dispatch in *New York Times,* July 2, 1971.

South Vietnam in 1971 of the totality of U.S. forces and those of the other foreign countries in the U.S. camp, the parties will at the same time agree on the modalities:

A. Of the withdrawal in safety from South Vietnam of the totality of U.S. forces and those of the other foreign countries in the U.S. camp,

B. Of the release of the totality of military men of all parties and the civilians captured in the war (including American pilots captured in North Vietnam), so that they may all rapidly return to their homes.

These two operations will begin on the same date and will end on the same date.

A cease-fire will be observed between the South Vietnam People's Liberation Armed Forces and the armed forces of the United States and of the other foreign countries in the United States camp, as soon as the parties reach agreement on the withdrawal from South Vietnam of the totality of United States forces and those of the other foreign countries in the United States camp.

[2]

Regarding the question of power in South Vietnam.

The United States Government must really respect the South Vietnam people's right to self-determination, put an end to its interference in the internal affairs of South Vietnam, cease backing the bellicose group headed by Nguyen Van Thieu, at present in office in Saigon, and stop all maneuvers, including tricks on elections,[73] aimed at maintaining the puppet Nguyen Van Thieu.

The political, social and religious forces in South Vietnam aspiring to peace and national concord will use various means to form in Saigon a new administration favoring peace, independence, neutrality and democracy.

The Provisional Revolutionary Government of the Republic of South Vietnam will immediately enter into talks with that administration in order to settle the following questions:

A. To form a broad three-segment government of national concord that will assume its functions during the period between the restoration of peace and the holding of general elections and organize general elections in South Vietnam.

A cease-fire will be observed between the South Vietnam People's Liberation Armed Forces and the armed forces of the Saigon administration as soon as the government of national concord is formed.

B. To take concrete measures with the required guarantees so as to prohibit all acts of terror, reprisal and discrimination against persons

73 Cf. Document 78.

having collaborated with one or the other party, to ensure every democratic liberty to the South Vietnam people, to release all persons jailed for political reasons, to dissolve all concentration camps and to liquidate all forms of constraint and coercion so as to permit the people to return to their native places in complete freedom and to freely engage in their occupations.

C. To see that the people's conditions of living are stabilized and gradually improved, to create conditions allowing everyone to contribute his talents and efforts to heal the war wounds and rebuild the country.

D. To agree on measures to be taken to ensure the holding of genuinely free, democratic, and fair general elections in South Vietnam.

[3]

Regarding the question of Vietnamese armed forces in South Vietnam.

The Vietnamese parties will together settle the question of Vietnamese armed forces in South Vietnam in a spirit of national concord, equality, and mutual respect, without foreign interference, in accordance with the postwar situation and with a view to making lighter the people's contributions.

[4]

Regarding the peaceful reunification of Vietnam and the relations between the North and South zones.

A. The reunification of Vietnam will be achieved step by step by peaceful means, on the basis of discussions and agreements between the two zones, without constraint and annexation from either party, without foreign interference.

Pending the reunification of the country, the North and the South zones will reestablish normal relations, guarantee free movement, free correspondence, free choice of residence, and maintain economic and cultural relations on the principle of mutual interests and mutual assistance.

All questions concerning the two zones will be settled by qualified representatives of the Vietnamese people in the two zones on the basis of negotiations, without foreign interference.

B. In keeping with the provisions of the 1954 Geneva agreements on Vietnam,[74] in the present temporary partition of the country into two zones, the North and the South zones of Vietnam will refrain from

74 *Documents, 1954*, pp. 290-93.

joining any military alliance with foreign countries, from allowing any foreign country to have military bases, troops, and military personnel on their soil, and from recognizing the protection of any country, of any military alliance or bloc.

[5]

Regarding the foreign policy of peace and neutrality of South Vietnam.

South Vietnam will pursue a foreign policy of peace and neutrality, establish relations with all countries regardless of their political and social regime, in accordance with the five principles of peaceful coexistence,[75] maintain economic and cultural relations with all countries, accept the cooperation of foreign countries in the exportation of the resources of South Vietnam, accept from any country economic and technical aid without any political conditions attached, and participate in regional plans of economic cooperation.

On the basis of these principles, after the end of the war, South Vietnam and the United States will establish relations in the political, economic and cultural fields.

[6]

Regarding the damages caused by the United States to the Vietnamese peoples in the two zones.

The U.S. Government must bear full responsibility for the losses and the destructions it has caused to the Vietnamese people in the two zones.

[7]

Regarding the respect and the international guarantee of the accords that will be concluded.

The parties will find agreement on the forms of respect and international guarantee of the accords that will be concluded.

(b) Comment by Ambassador David K.E. Bruce, Head of the United States Delegation, at a Plenary Session on July 8, 1971.[76]

[75] *Documents, 1954,* pp. 279-80.
[76] Department of State Press Release 156, July 8, 1971; text from *Bulletin,* July 26, 1971, pp. 97-98.

(Complete Text)

Ladies and gentlemen: We have examined carefully your remarks of last week and will continue to do so in an attempt to find common areas of agreement. If they mean that you wish at last to enter into serious negotiations, we would welcome such an attitude on your part.

Examination of the various points of your latest proposals[77] makes it evident that questions arising from their contents necessitate serious negotiation between all parties concerned. We will wish to explore them further with you, and in subsequent meetings we will be seeking clarification on specific points. Our analysis thus far, however, indicates that despite some new elements, your proposals do not seem to change your long-asserted basic demands or indicate your intention to end the fighting.

In respect to your deadline for the total withdrawal of U.S. forces, you enumerate certain measures which you demand the United States Government accept "without posing any conditions whatsoever." These demands are so sweeping and categorical in nature that we cannot possibly accept your arbitrary determination that they must be agreed to by us without any discussion or negotiation upon them. This represents an approach which is the very antithesis of what is generally recognized as the process of negotiation.

Your offer to "agree on the modalities" of safe withdrawal and release of prisoners after a date for withdrawal has been named is unclear and may be merely a variation of your previous statement that the parties "will engage at once in discussion on" these questions, not necessarily committing you to the course of action implied. This point, as well as others you have presented, requires clarification.

On the prisoner of war issue itself, we note that you do not deal with the release of those prisoners captured by your forces or forces under your control in Laos and Cambodia. We continue to hold you responsible for the release of these men and for the provision of whatever information you have on all of our men captured and missing in action throughout Indochina.

On the question of political settlement in South Viet-Nam, you continue to insist that the present Government of the Republic of Viet-Nam must be replaced by one which fulfills your own criteria. Our policy on this point has always been perfectly clear and remains so. We will not impose any government on the people of South Viet-Nam, who must be allowed to determine for themselves their own future. This question must be discussed amongst the South Vietnamese themselves, in particular between your side and the Government of the Republic of Viet-Nam. You have always obstructed that process of negotiation despite the fact that this conference was originally convoked with such

[77] Document 74a.

a procedure as one of its principal objectives.

We are especially disappointed that in your proposals you still insist on linking the question of cease-fire to your political demands rather than to the urgent need to stop the killing. If an early end to the fighting throughout all of Indochina could be achieved, this would immediately create a much better atmosphere for fruitful deliberations.

You have asserted that your proposals are intended as a major initiative, and we recognize that they deal with matters requiring serious discussion. You cannot, however, insist that they form the only basis for such discussions. We are ready, as we always have been, to take up with you any points which you have brought or might bring to our attention, and we expect you in turn to adopt the same attitude toward any suggestions made by us. It would be almost unprecedented for a negotiation to take any other course. If real negotiations are to take place, these meetings must stop being used by you simply for propaganda purposes and must be devoted instead to constructive interchanges.

Let us make a fresh start here. I propose that the next meeting be a restricted session at which we could explore further your proposals as well as discuss our own. Such a forum, free from the glare of publicity and without the need to make public statements except to the degree we mutually agree upon, could provide a better atmosphere for productive discussions.[78]

2. Secret United States–North Vietnamese Contacts.

[The history of the secret negotiations between the United States and North Vietnam that took place parallel to the formal discussions in Paris during 1969-71 was first revealed by President Nixon in a radio-television address of January 25, 1972,[79] to be amplified in a news conference held by Dr. Kissinger on the following day[80] and in the President's subsequent foreign policy report for 1972.[81] Some further details were added in a polemical statement issued by the North Vietnamese delegation in Paris on January 31, 1972;[82] and the entire record has since been critically examined by nongovernmental analysts.[83]

[78] The proposal for a restricted session was not accepted. For Ambassador Bruce's remarks at the plenary session on July 15, 1971, see *Bulletin*, Aug. 2, 1971, pp. 136-38.

[79] *A.F.R., 1972*, no. 43.

[80] *Presidential Documents*, Jan. 31, 1972, pp. 126-33.

[81] Nixon Report, 1972, pp. 114-17.

[82] *New York Times*, Feb. 1, 1972.

[83] Tad Szulc, "How Kissinger Did It: Behind the Vietnam Cease-Fire Agreement," *Foreign Policy*, No. 15 (Summer 1974), pp. 21-69; Kalb, *Kissinger*, pp. 174-85.

According to President Nixon's account, it was the lack of progress during the early months of plenary sessions in Paris that determined him to establish in the summer of 1969, "with the full knowledge and approval of President Thieu" of South Vietnam, "a private and secret channel so that both sides could talk frankly, free from the pressures of public debate."[84] Pursuant to this plan, Dr. Kissinger traveled to Paris for secret meetings with the North Vietnamese on twelve separate occasions between August 1969 and September 1971. The first such contact, arranged with French assistance, took place on August 4, 1969, and there were six such meetings in 1969-70 and six more between May and September 1971. Seven of the twelve meetings were held with Le Duc Tho, a member of the North Vietnamese Politburo with the diplomatic rank of Special Adviser, and Xuan Thuy, a North Vietnamese Minister Without Portfolio and head of the D.R.V. delegation to the formal Paris talks; five additional meetings were held with Xuan Thuy in Le Duc Tho's absence.

The first 22 months of the secret contacts would seem to have been as barren of results as the semipublic sessions held during the same period.[85] Almost the first sign of real movement occurred on May 31, 1971, when the United States availed itself of the first secret meeting of the year to table a new proposal which, as has since been pointed out,[86] fell within the same approximate time period as the May 20 "breakthrough" in the SALT negotiations with the U.S.S.R. (Document 21) and the preparations for a presidential visit to the People's Republic of China (Document 91). As with President Nixon's public proposal of October 7, 1970,[87] the still unpublished U.S. proposal of May 31, 1971, appears to have laid considerable emphasis on the release of prisoners of war while giving much less weight than hitherto to the question of a withdrawal of North Vietnamese troops from South Vietnam. According to President Nixon's address of January 25, 1972,[88] "we offered specifically to agree to a deadline for the withdrawal of all American forces in exchange for the release of all prisoners of war and a cease-fire"—or, as stated in his subsequent foreign policy report, "we offered a total U.S. withdrawal in return for a prisoner exchange and an Indochina cease-fire, leaving the other outstanding issues for subsequent resolution among the Indochinese parties themselves."[89] Dr. Kissinger later pointed out that this was the first time the United States had offered to set a date for the withdrawal of U.S. forces, and, moreover,

---

[84] Nixon Report, 1972, pp. 114-15.
[85] Cf. above at notes 61-71.
[86] Szulc, *loc. cit.*, p. 28.
[87] Cf. above at note 67.
[88] Same as note 79.
[89] Nixon Report, 1972, p. 115.

to do so unilaterally, "without an equivalent assurance of withdrawal from the other side."[90]

This U.S. plan was nevertheless rejected by the North Vietnamese at a new secret meeting on June 26, 1971, the reason stated being "that political questions had to be incorporated in any settlement."[91] As an alternative, the North Vietnamese representatives put forward on this occasion a nine-point proposal of their own (Document 75) which provided, among other things, for U.S. and allied—but not North Vietnamese—withdrawals from South Vietnam and the other countries of Indochina, and for abandonment of the South Vietnamese political leadership by the United States so that "a new administration standing for peace, independence, neutrality and democracy" could be set up. Aside from the patently unacceptable character of this proposal from an American viewpoint, the situation was further confused by the public submission on July 1, 1971, of Mrs. Binh's seven-point plan (Document 74a), which, unlike the new North Vietnamese plan, dealt only with Vietnam and not with the other Indochinese countries. Queried about these discrepancies at the next private meeting on July 12, the North Vietnamese stated that the United States should address itself to their nine-point plan rather than to Mrs. Binh's seven-point plan.

While clearly unable to accept the substance of the North Vietnamese proposal as formulated, the United States was now prepared, in President Nixon's words, "in order to speed negotiations, ... to depart from the approach of our May 31 proposal and to deal with the political as well as the military issues." "In effect," the President later reported, "we accepted their nine points as a basis for negotiation; and from that time, every American proposal has followed both the sequence and subject matter of the North Vietnamese plan.... On July 12, and again on July 26, we went through each of the nine points, item by item, seeking to bridge the gap between our positions. We sought to shape an agreement in principle which both sides could sign, and then introduce it into the public talks as the basis for a detailed negotiation of a final agreement."[92]

With this object in view, the United States introduced on August 16 a new proposal in eight points[93] which has remained unpublished, but was later described by President Nixon in the following terms:

—We offered to withdraw all U.S. and allied forces within 9 months of the date of an agreement. We suggested a terminal date

[90] *Presidential Documents*, Jan. 31, 1972, p. 127.
[91] Nixon Report, 1972, p. 115.
[92] Same, pp. 115-16.
[93] The U.S. proposal did not include Point 4 of the North Vietnamese plan, which called for the payment of reparations by the United States to the D.R.V. and the P.R.G.

of August 1, 1972, provided an agreement was signed by November 1, 1971.

—We made specific proposals to ensure a fair political process in South Vietnam based on a number of political principles meeting both North Vietnamese and NLF [National Liberation Front] concerns. These included (1) total U.S. neutrality in Vietnamese elections; (2) acceptance of the outcome of their results; (3) limitations on foreign military aid to South Vietnam if North Vietnam would accept similar restrictions; (4) nonalignment for South Vietnam together with the other countries of Indochina; and (5) reunification on terms for the North and South to work out.

—I also gave my personal undertaking to request from the Congress, immediately after the signing of an agreement in principle, a five-year reconstruction program for Indochina.[94]

This second American proposal was also rejected by the North Vietnamese at a new secret meeting—the last to take place in 1971—on September 13. Their objections, according to Dr. Kissinger, were based essentially on two grounds: "that the withdrawal date was too long, and that we had been unclear about how we defined total withdrawal, that is to say, whether any forces would remain in an individual capacity, and secondly, on the ground that a simple declaration of American political neutrality while the existing government stayed in office would not overcome the advantage of the existing government in running and being in office."[95]

In an attempt to meet these objections, still a third American proposal was drawn up and conveyed to the North Vietnamese on October 11, shortly after the reelection of President Thieu to a new four-year term as South Vietnam's chief executive. There were already signs at this period that North Vietnam might be preparing for the new military offensive in the South that was in fact to commence on March 30, 1972; and the new American proposal was specifically put forward as "one last attempt to negotiate a just settlement before the end of 1971" (Document 76a). As conveyed to the North Vietnamese in Paris by Lieutenant General Vernon A. Walters, U.S. Defense Attaché in the French capital, this third proposal (Document 76b) abbreviated the time that would elapse before a total U.S. withdrawal from nine to seven months after an agreement in principle was signed. In addition, it offered an unprecedented arrangement that would involve the resignation of South Vietnam's President and Vice-President in order to make way for a new presidential election, organized by an independent body

---

94 Nixon Report, 1972, p. 116.
95 Kissinger news conference, Jan. 26, 1972, in *Presidential Documents*, Jan. 31, 1972, pp. 128-29.

and internationally supervised, within six months of a final agreement.

In transmitting this proposal, the United States proposed that a meeting with Le Duc Tho (or some other appropriate official from Hanoi) and Xuan Thuy be scheduled for November 1, 1971 (Document 76a). A North Vietnamese proposal to defer the meeting to November 20 (Document 77a) was accepted by the United States (Document 77b); but on November 17 the North Vietnamese sent word that while Xuan Thuy would be available on the agreed date, Le Duc Tho had suddenly been taken ill and could not attend (Document 77c). The United States, according to Dr. Kissinger, had already learned from experience that "no major change" could occur in Le Duc Tho's absence.[96] It therefore replied on November 19 that under the circumstances "no point would be served" by a meeting, and that it would await a North Vietnamese recommendation as to a suitable date for a meeting with Le Duc Tho, "or any other representative of the North Vietnamese political leadership," together with Xuan Thuy (Document 77d).

No further communication was received from the North Vietnamese during 1971, in spite of various reminders that the channel was still open. "The only reply to our plan," President Nixon stated on January 25, 1972, "has been an increase in troop infiltration from North Vietnam and Communist military offensives in Laos and Cambodia. Our proposal for peace was answered by a step-up in the war on their part."[97]]

(75) Nine-point Proposal Presented by Representatives of the Democratic Republic of Vietnam, June 26, 1971.[98]

(Complete Text)

[1]

The withdrawal of the totality of U.S. forces and those of foreign countries in the U.S. camp from South Vietnam and other Indochinese countries should be completed within 1971.

[2]

The release of all military men and civilians captured in the war

[96] Same, p. 131.
[97] Same as note 79.
[98] North Vietnamese statement, Jan. 31, 1972, in *New York Times*, Feb. 1, 1972.

should be carried out parallel and completed at the same time with the troop withdrawal mentioned in Point 1.

[3]

In South Vietnam, the United States should stop supporting Thieu-Ky-Khiem[99] so that there may be set up in Saigon a new administration standing for peace, independence, neutrality and democracy. The Provisional Revolutionary Government of the Republic of South Vietnam will enter into talks with that administration to settle the internal affairs of South Vietnam and to achieve national concord.

[4]

The U.S. Government must bear full responsibility for the damages caused by the United States to the people of the whole Vietnam. The Government of the Democratic Republic of Vietnam and the Provisional Revolutionary Government of the Republic of South Vietnam demand from the U.S. Government reparations for the damages caused by the United States in the two zones of Vietnam.

[5]

The United States should respect the 1954 Geneva agreements on Indochina and those of 1962 on Laos.[100] It should stop its aggression and intervention in the Indochinese countries and let their peoples settle by themselves their own affairs.

[6]

The problems existing among the Indochinese countries should be settled by the Indochinese parties on the basis of mutual respect for independence, sovereignty and territorial integrity, and noninterference in each other's internal affairs. As far as it is concerned, the Democratic Republic of Vietnam is prepared to join in resolving such problems.

[7]

All the parties should achieve a cease-fire after the signing of the agreements on the above-mentioned problems.

---

[99] Cf. above at note 71.
[100] *Documents, 1954*, pp. 283-314; same, *1962*, pp. 262-94.

[8]

There should be an international supervision.

[9]

There should be an international guarantee for the fundamental national rights of the Indochinese peoples, the neutrality of South Vietnam, Laos and Cambodia, and lasting peace in this region.

The above points form an integrated whole.

(76) Eight-point Proposal Transmitted by the United States to the Representatives of the Democratic Republic of Vietnam, October 11, 1971.

(a) Covering Note. [101]

(Complete Text)

At the September 13th meeting,[102] Minister Xuan Thuy stated that the U.S. side should review the various suggestions made by the North Vietnamese. The North Vietnamese side has also said that it would be forthcoming if a generous proposal is made by the U.S. side. The U.S. believes that this new proposal[103] goes to the limits of possible generosity and fully takes into account North Vietnamese propositions. The United States hopes that the North Vietnamese response will reflect the same attitude. Dr. Kissinger is prepared to meet on November 1st with Mr. Le Duc Tho or some other appropriate official from Hanoi together with Minister Xuan Thuy. He will be prepared at that meeting also to take into account other points that have been discussed in previous meetings in this channel.

In the interim, it is expected that both sides will refrain from bringing pressure from public statements which can only serve to complicate the situation.

The U.S. side is putting forth these proposals as one last attempt to negotiate a just settlement before the end of 1971.

---

[101] Kissinger news conference, Jan. 26, 1972, in *Presidential Documents*, Jan. 31, 1972, p. 126. An almost identical text appears in the North Vietnamese statement of Jan. 31, 1972 (*New York Times*, Feb. 1, 1972).
[102] Cf. above at note 95.
[103] Doc. 76b.

(b) Text of the United States Proposal. [104]

(Complete Text)

1. The United States agrees to the total withdrawal from South Vietnam of all U.S. forces and other foreign forces allied with the government of South Vietnam. This withdrawal will be carried out in the following manner:

—All American and allied forces, except for a small number of personnel needed for technical advice, logistics, and observance of the cease-fire mentioned in point 6, will be withdrawn by July 1, 1972, provided that this statement of principles is signed by December 1, 1971. The terminal date for these withdrawals will in no event be later than seven months after this statement of principles is signed.

—The remaining personnel, in turn, will be progressively withdrawn beginning one month before the Presidential election mentioned in point 3 and simultaneously with the resignations of the incumbent President and Vice President of South Vietnam also provided for in point 3. These withdrawals will be completed by the date of the Presidential election.

2. The release of all military men and innocent civilians captured throughout Indochina will be carried out in parallel with the troop withdrawals mentioned in point 1. Both sides will present a complete list of military men and innocent civilians held throughout Indochina on the day this statement of principles is signed. The release will begin on the same day as the troop withdrawals and will be completed by July 1, 1972, provided this statement is signed by December 1, 1971. The completion of this release will in no event be later than seven months after this statement is signed.

3. The following principles will govern the political future of South Vietnam:

The political future of South Vietnam will be left for the South Vietnamese people to decide for themselves, free from outside interference.

There will be a free and democratic Presidential election in South Vietnam within six months of the signature of the final agreement based on the principles in this statement. This election will be organized and run by an independent body representing all political forces in South Vietnam which will assume its responsibilities on the date of the final agreement. This body will, among other responsibilities, determine

---

104 *Bulletin*, Feb. 21, 1972, pp. 229-30. An identical text appears in the North Vietnamese statement of Jan. 31, 1972 (*New York Times*, Feb. 1, 1972).

the qualification of candidates. All political forces in South Vietnam can participate in the election and present candidates. There will be international supervision of this election.

One month before the Presidential election takes place, the incumbent President and Vice President of South Vietnam[105] will resign. A caretaker Administration, headed by the Chairman of the Senate, will assume administrative responsibilities except for those pertaining to the election, which will remain with the independent election body.

The United States, for its part, declares that it:

—will support no candidate and will remain completely neutral in the election.

—will abide by the outcome of this election and any other political processes shaped by the South Vietnamese people themselves.

—is prepared to define its military and economic assistance relationship with any government that exists in South Vietnam.

Both sides agree that:

—South Vietnam, together with the other countries of Indochina, should adopt a foreign policy of neutrality.

—Reunification of Vietnam should be decided on the basis of discussions and agreements between North and South Vietnam without constraint and annexation from either party, and without foreign interference.

4. Both sides will respect the 1954 Geneva Agreements on Indochina and those of 1962 on Laos.[106] There will be no foreign intervention in the Indochinese countries and the Indochinese peoples will be left to settle by themselves their own affairs.

5. The problems existing among the Indochinese countries will be settled by the Indochinese parties on the basis of mutual respect for independence, sovereignty, territorial integrity and non-interference in each other's affairs. Among the problems that will be settled is the implementation of the principle that all armed forces of the countries of Indochina must remain within their national frontiers.

6. There will be a general ceasefire throughout Indochina, to begin when the final agreement is signed. As part of the ceasefire, there will be no further infiltration of outside forces into any of the countries of Indochina.

7. There will be international supervision of the military aspects of this agreement including the ceasefire and its provisions, the release of prisoners of war and innocent civilians, and the withdrawal of outside forces from Indochina.

[105] In the South Vietnamese presidential election held Oct. 3, 1971, President Thieu was reelected President and Tran Van Huong was elected Vice-President for four-year terms beginning Oct. 31, 1971. See further Document 78.
[106] Same as note 100.

8. There will be an international guarantee for the fundamental national rights of the Indochinese peoples, the neutrality of all the countries in Indochina, and lasting peace in this region.

Both sides express their willingness to participate in an international conference for this and other appropriate purposes.

(77) Postponement of Further Private Meetings, October 25–November 19, 1971. [107]

(a) Democratic Republic of Vietnam Note, October 25, 1971.

(Complete Text)

The DRVN [Democratic Republic of Vietnam] party wishes to answer the U. S. Government's Oct. 11, 1971, proposal of a private meeting to be held on Nov. 1, 1971, between special adviser Le Duc Tho and special adviser Kissinger and Minister Xuan Thuy. [108]

Special adviser Le Duc Tho and Minister Xuan Thuy are prepared to meet with special adviser H.A. Kissinger at the place of the previous meeting, 10:00 hours A.M., Nov. 20, 1971. We propose the above date and time because special adviser Le Duc Tho is being busy with some work in Hanoi. Moreover, Minister Xuan Thuy is under medical treatment for health reason.

(b) United States Note, November 3, 1971.

(Complete Text)

Dr. Kissinger agrees to private meeting with special adviser Le Duc Tho and Minister Xuan Thuy to be held on Nov. 20, 1971, at 11:30 hours A.M. at the usual place.

The U. S. side expects that the other side will make no public proposal for negotiation before the meeting takes place. For its part, the U. S. side will refrain from making any proposal of this kind.

(c) Democratic Republic of Vietnam Note, November 17, 1971.

(Complete Text)

The other day the D.R.V.N. party informed you that Minister Xuan

---

107 The texts of the first three notes (Documents 77a–c) were appended to the North Vietnamese statement of Jan. 31, 1972, as printed in *New York Times*, Feb. 1, 1972. For Document 77d see note 109 below.
108 Document 76a.

Thuy and special adviser Le Duc Tho were prepared to meet with special adviser Henry Kissinger privately on Nov. 20, 1971.

Today I inform you that, to our regret, special adviser Le Duc Tho is suddenly taken ill and cannot attend the proposed meeting. Minister Xuan Thuy is, however, ready to hold a private meeting with special adviser H. Kissinger on Nov. 20, 1971, at 11:30 hours, as agreed upon.

(d) United States Note, November 19, 1971.[109]

(Complete Text)

On October 11, 1971, the U.S. side made a comprehensive proposal[110] designed to bring a rapid end to the war on a basis just for all parties. The United States proposal took fully into account the propositions of the North Vietnamese side, including all the concerns raised at the last private meeting on September 13, 1971.[111]

The U.S. side further indicated that it would be prepared to take account of other points that had been discussed in previous meetings in this channel. The U.S. proposed a meeting on November 1, 1971, between Dr. Kissinger and Special Adviser Le Duc Tho or some other appropriate official from Hanoi, together with Minister Xuan Thuy.[112]

The North Vietnamese, in an October 25, 1971, message said that Special Adviser Le Duc Tho and Minister Xuan Thuy agreed to meet with Dr. Kissinger on November 20, 1971. The U.S. side accepted this date.[113]

On November 17, 1971, the North Vietnamese side informed the U.S. side that Special Adviser Le Duc Tho was now ill and unable to attend the November 20th meeting.[114] The U.S. side regrets his illness. Under these circumstances, no point would be served by a meeting.

The U.S. side stands ready to meet with Special Adviser Le Duc Tho or any other representative of the North Vietnamese political leadership, together with Minister Xuan Thuy, in order to bring a rapid end to the war on a basis just to all parties. It will wait to hear recommendations from the North Vietnamese side as to a suitable date.[115]

---

[109] Kissinger news conference, Jan. 26, 1972, in *Presidential Documents*, Jan. 31, 1972, pp. 126-27. A similar text was appended to the North Vietnamese statement cited in note 107.

[110] Document 76b.

[111] Cf. above at note 71.

[112] Document 76a.

[113] Documents 77a-b.

[114] Document 77c.

[115] Cf. above at note 97.

D. Political Developments in South Vietnam.

[The political processes of the Republic of Vietnam in 1971 afforded only limited encouragement to U.S. hopes for the emergence of a viable democracy that could hold its own against the competition of the Communist-led insurgency and safeguard the South Vietnamese people's right of political self-determination. The institutions established under the South Vietnamese constitution of 1967[116] continued to operate efficiently, with the election of a new Lower House on August 29 and of a President and Vice-President on October 3, 1971. The net effect, however, was to reinforce the political ascendancy already enjoyed by President Nguyen Van Thieu, whose personality and somewhat authoritarian style of government had become a favorite Communist target and had been portrayed by both the "Provisional Revolutionary Government" and the North Vietnamese as one of the main obstacles to a peace agreement (cf. Documents 74a and 75).

While unwilling to withdraw its support from President Thieu and his associates as the Communists demanded, the United States made a point of professing "complete neutrality" in the presidential election and stressed its hope that a contest among two or more candidates would help produce a more open political situation in which the victor would be seen as the product of a popular choice rather than the creation of a political machine. "We believed that a contested election would leave the resulting South Vietnamese Government in a stronger position than an unopposed victory," President Nixon later wrote. " . . . We emphasized our view that there should be more than one candidate, and we worked diligently to encourage opponents of President Thieu to remain in the race."[117]

These hopes were defeated by a series of political maneuvers that resulted in the elimination of rival candidates and in Thieu's reelection without opposition. A new electoral law requiring prospective candidates to prove substantial political backing caused special difficulties for Vice-President Nguyen Cao Ky, a leading presidential aspirant, and ushered in a period of confusion, marked by charges of governmental pressure and trickery, which culminated in the withdrawal of both Ky and General Duong Van ("Big") Minh, an advocate of "national reconciliation" and the favorite of many antigovernment Vietnamese. With both his opponents off the ballot, Thieu was reelected on October 3, 1971, by a 94.3 percent favorable vote, the legality of which was subsequently upheld by the Supreme Court. Thieu and his vice-presidential running mate, former Prime Minister Tran Van Huong, were accord-

---

116 Cf. *Documents, 1967*, pp. 219-20.
117 Nixon Report, 1972, p. 126.

ingly inaugurated October 31, 1971, for a four-year term ending in 1975.

The following comment by President Nixon (Document 78) is one of a series in which the President and Secretary of State Rogers attempted to place these developments in perspective and to parry public and congressional criticism to the effect that the United States was supporting an unpopular puppet regime against the wishes of the South Vietnamese people.[118]]

(78) The South Vietnamese Presidential Election of October 3, 1971: News Conference Observations by President Nixon, September 16, 1971.[119]

(Excerpt)

*   *   *

SOUTH VIETNAMESE ELECTIONS

Q. Mr. President, might the changed political picture in South Vietnam, specifically a one-man race for the presidency there, have any effect on your future plans as far as the level of United States troops and United States activity in that region?

THE PRESIDENT. As far as our plans for ending the American involvement in Vietnam are concerned, we have to keep in mind our major goal, which is to bring the American involvement to an end in a way that will leave South Vietnam in a position to defend itself from a Communist takeover.

Now as far a[s] President Thieu's political situation is concerned, I think it is well to put that subject in perspective. We would have preferred to have had a contested election in South Vietnam. We, however, cannot get people to run when they do not want to run.

It should be pointed out, however, that in fairness to the democratic process and how it is working in South Vietnam, the congressional elections, the elections for the National Assembly should not be overlooked. Eighty percent of the people of South Vietnam voted as compared with, incidentally, 60 percent who voted in our congressional elections in 1970, and one-third of those who were elected opposed

[118] For other comments see Nixon news conferences, Aug. 4, Sept. 25, and Oct. 12, 1971 (*Public Papers, 1971*, pp. 853-54, 994-95, and 1037); Rogers news conferences, Sept. 3 and Oct. 10, 1971 (*Bulletin*, Sept. 27, 1971, pp. 326-27; same, Nov. 1, 1971, pp. 484-85).
[119] *Presidential Documents*, Sept. 20, 1971, pp. 1282-83.

President Thieu, and some of those who were elected to the National Assembly were those that charged that they could not be elected before the election because the election would be rigged.

Now President Thieu has made the election in October for the presidency a vote of confidence. There are criticisms to the effect that this vote of confidence will not be an accurate one, but he has invited foreign observers in to see it and to observe it.

My view is that the United States should continue to keep its eye on the main objective and that is to end the American involvement just as soon as that is consistent with our overall goals, which is a South Vietnam able to defend itself against a Communist takeover and which, of course, includes, from our standpoint, our primary interest in maintaining the release of our POW's.

I note one thing, incidentally, on your question, Mr. Jarriel,[120] that is presently apparently before the Senate or a Senate committee, and that is the recommendation or a resolution to the effect that the United States should cut off aid to South Vietnam unless President Thieu does have a contested election.

Now let's just look at what that means in terms of worldwide policy. We presently provide military and/or economic aid to 91 countries in the world. I checked these various countries as far as their heads of government are concerned, and in only 30 of those countries do they have leaders who are there as a result of a contested election by any standards that we would consider fair. In fact, we would have to cut off aid to two-thirds of the nations in the world—in Africa, in Latin America, in Asia—to whom we are presently giving aid if we applied those standards that some suggest we apply to South Vietnam.

I again say that we would prefer, as far as South Vietnam is concerned, that its democratic processes would grow faster. We believe that considerable headway has been made. We believe that the situation from that standpoint is infinitely better in South Vietnam where they at least have some elections than in North Vietnam where they have none,[121] and we are going to continue to work toward that goal.

Q. Mr. President, may I follow that up, please?

Senator Jackson[122] said that the United States need not feel helpless in this circumstance because it has leverage which could redeem the situation even now. Your answer just now suggested that we don't plan to do anything about it. What would you say to Senator Jackson's statement about it?

---

120 Tom Jarriel, ABC News.

121 North Vietnam's first elections since 1964 were held Apr. 11, 1971, with seven independents and 522 nominees of the Communist-controlled National Fatherland Front contesting the 420 seats in the National Assembly (*The World This Year, 1972*, p. 125).

122 Henry M. Jackson (Democrat, Washington).

THE PRESIDENT. Mr. Lisagor,[123] when we speak of leverage, of course, we have leverage because we do provide military and economic assistance to South Vietnam.

Second, Ambassador Bunker,[124] working diligently, I can assure you, has attempted to, in every way possible, to get people into the race so that there would be a contested election.

And, of course, third, he has, of course, worked toward the end of—once it appeared that others would not run—of getting the election to be one that would at least provide a chance to have a vote of confidence in the President. If what the Senator is suggesting is that the United States should use its leverage now to overthrow Thieu, I would remind all concerned that the way we got into Vietnam was through overthrowing [President Ngo Dinh] Diem[125] and the complicity in the murder of Diem, and the way to get out of Vietnam in my opinion is not to overthrow Thieu with the inevitable consequence or the greatly increased danger, in my opinion, of that being followed by coup after coup and the dreary road to a Communist takeover.

Q. Mr. President, on the South Vietnamese election, once it is completed will you feel then that the American objective of achieving a democratic process in Vietnam, the objective that you stated and before you President Johnson so many times, do you think that with this election that the objective will have been met?

THE PRESIDENT. No, as a matter of fact, that objective will not be met perhaps for several generations. But at least we will be on the road. I think sometimes we forget, as I tried to point out a moment ago in my answer to the question with regard to military and economic assistance to countries around the world, how difficult the process of democracy is.

It took the British 500 years to get to the place where they had what we could really describe as a democratic system under the parliamentary setup, and it didn't spring up full grown in the United States.

I was reading a very interesting account of the battle in 1800 between Jefferson and Adams and I was curious to note how many people were eligible to vote in that great battle of 1800 which changed the whole future of the United States, that brought in the Jeffersonian era. At that time when the United States had 4¼ million people, there were only 150,000 people eligible to vote. And so as we look at our own history we find that it took us time to come where we are.

You cannot expect that American-style democracy, meeting our standards, will apply in other parts of the world. We cannot expect that

123 Peter Lisagor, *Chicago Daily News.*
124 Ellsworth Bunker, U.S. Ambassador to the Republic of Vietnam.
125 Cf. *The United States in World Affairs, 1963,* pp. 192-95.

it will come in a country like South Vietnam which has no tradition whatever, without great difficulty. But we have made progress.

*   *   *

E. Policy on Troop Withdrawals.

[Domestic controversy over South Vietnam's political processes (Document 78) was part of a wider cleavage in American opinion with regard to policy both in Vietnam and in Southeast Asia generally. Despite the rapid reduction of U.S. ground combat forces under the "Vietnamization" program (Documents 71-73), public and congressional pressure for a more rapid pull-out had continued and found expression during 1971 in repeated congressional demands that the administration set a firm date for liquidation of the entire Indochinese venture. Emboldened by the success of its earlier prohibitions on the introduction of ground combat forces into Laos, Thailand, or Cambodia,[126] Congress on two occasions during its 1971 session voiced formal demands for the negotiation of an immediate cease-fire which—subject to the release of American prisoners of war—would permit the withdrawal of remaining U.S. forces in Indochina by a fixed date.

This approach to terminating the American involvement was strongly opposed by President Nixon, who maintained that it "would serve the enemy's purpose and not our own," throw away "our principal counter to win the release of American prisoners of war," "remove the enemy's strongest incentive to end the war sooner by negotiation," and give the enemy commanders "the exact information they need to marshal their attacks against our remaining forces at their most vulnerable time" (Document 71). These caveats did not, however, deter the antiwar forces in Congress from attaching a "final date" amendment to the two-year extension of the Selective Service Act that the President signed in September (Document 79) at the very time the secret negotiations with the North Vietnamese were reaching a climax.[127]

As previously promised (Document 71), the President on November 12 made his own announcement on troop withdrawals under the Vietnamization program, stating that an additional 45,000 men would be withdrawn from Vietnam by February 1, 1972, thus lowering the ceiling on authorized manpower from 184,000 to 139,000 (Document 80). But the congressional preference for a still more rapid rate of

[126] Cf. above at notes 6-9.
[127] Cf. above at note 95.

withdrawal was again made clear by the actions of both houses on the Mansfield amendment, which had originally been attached to the Foreign Assistance Act of 1971 and, after the rejection of that measure by the Senate (Document 154), was shifted to the Military Procurement Authorization Act of 1971.

As introduced by Senator Mansfield and approved by the Senate, this amendment called for a full withdrawal of U.S. forces from Indochina within six months. This language, however, was moderated in Senate-House conference in such a way as to call for the setting of a final date for withdrawal in the same terms as the earlier Selective Service legislation. In signing the procurement measure with the modified Mansfield amendment on November 17 (Document 81a), the President emphasized that this expression of congressional views was without binding force and would in no way alter the policies of his administration (Document 81b).

These discussions took place against a background of increasing military activity in Indochina as Communist forces stepped up their offensives both in Cambodia and in Laos. In the latter country, the northern Plain of Jars and much of the Bolovens Plateau in the south were overrun by North Vietnamese and Pathet Lao troops in the course of December. A concurrent increase in U.S. "protective reaction" air strikes against North Vietnam reached a climax in the last week of December, when the heaviest and most prolonged American bombing of North Vietnamese areas since 1968 underlined the disappointing outcome of recent peace initiatives and offered a foretaste of the still heavier fighting that would occur in 1972 before any agreement on peace terms could be reached.[128]]

(79) An Act to Amend the Military Selective Service Act of 1967: Public Law 92-129, Approved September 28, 1971.[129]

(Excerpt)

*   *   *

TITLE IV—TERMINATION OF HOSTILITIES IN INDOCHINA

SEC. 401. It is hereby declared to be the sense of Congress that the United States terminate at the earliest practicable date all military

---

[128] For the peace agreement signed Jan. 27, 1973, see note 70 above.
[129] Public Law 92-129 (H.R. 6531), Sept. 28, 1971, pp. 13-14.

operations of the United States in Indochina, and provide for the prompt and orderly withdrawal of all United States military forces at a date certain subject to the release of all American prisoners of war held by the Government of North Vietnam and forces allied with such Government, and an accounting for all Americans missing in action who have been held by or known to such Government or such forces. The Congress hereby urges and requests the President to implement the above expressed policy by initiating immediately the following actions:

(1) Negotiate with the Government of North Vietnam for an immediate cease-fire by all parties to the hostilities in Indochina.

(2) Negotiate with the Government of North Vietnam for the establishing of a final date for the withdrawal from Indochina of all military forces of the United States contingent upon the release at a date certain of all American prisoners of war held by the Government of North Vietnam and forces allied with such Government.

(3) Negotiate with the Government of North Vietnam for an agreement which would provide for a series of phased and rapid withdrawals of United States military forces from Indochina subject to a corresponding series of phased releases of American prisoners of war, and for the release of any remaining American prisoners of war concurrently with the withdrawal of all remaining military forces of the United States by not later than the date established pursuant to paragraph (2) hereof.

* * *

(80) Troop Withdrawals from Vietnam: News Conference Announcement by President Nixon, November 12, 1971. [130]

(Complete Text)

Ladies and gentlemen, I have an announcement of a substantially increased troop withdrawal from Vietnam. When I entered office on January 20, 1969, there were 540,000 Americans in Vietnam and our casualties were running as high as 300 a week.

Over the past 3 years, we have made progress on both fronts. Our casualties, for example, for the past 5 weeks have been less than 10, instead of 300, a week, and with regard to withdrawals, 80 percent of those who were there have come home—365,000.

I have now had an opportunity to appraise the situation as it is today. I have consulted with my senior advisers and I have had an up-to-date report from Secretary Laird.

130 *Presidential Documents*, Nov. 15, 1971, p. 1511.

Based on those consultations and consultations with the Government of South Vietnam, I am now able to make this announcement. Over the next 2 months, we will withdraw 45,000 Americans.[131] I will make another announcement before the first of February. As far as that second announcement is concerned, before the first of February, the number to be withdrawn—the rate, that is—as well as the duration of the announcement, will be determined by three factors.

First, by the level of enemy activity and particularly by the infiltration route and its rate because if the level of enemy activity and infiltration substantially increased, it could be very dangerous to our sharply decreased forces in South Vietnam.

Second, the progress of our training program, our Vietnamization program in South Vietnam, and third, any progress that may have been made with regard to two major objectives that we have, obtaining the release of all our POW's wherever they are in Southeast Asia and obtaining a cease-fire for all of Southeast Asia.

Those three criteria will determine the next announcement, both its duration and its rate.[132]

(81) The Military Procurement Authorization Act of 1971: Public Law 92-156, Approved November 17, 1971.

(a) Title VI of the Act: Termination of Hostilities in Indochina.[133]

(Complete Text)

* * *

TITLE VI–TERMINATION OF HOSTILITIES IN INDOCHINA

SEC. 601. (a) It is hereby declared to be the policy of the United States to terminate at the earliest practicable date all military operations of the United States in Indochina, and to provide for the prompt and orderly withdrawal of all United States military forces at a date

[131] In answer to questions, the President explained that it was intended to withdraw 25,000 in Dec. and 20,000 in Jan., and that the total of 45,000 would be subtracted from the Dec. 1 target of 184,000, thus establishing a new ceiling (139,000) as of Feb. 1, 1971. (*Loc. cit.*, pp. 1512 and 1514.)

[132] The President announced on Jan. 13, 1972, that an additional 70,000 troops would be withdrawn from Vietnam over the next three months, thus lowering the troop ceiling to 69,000 by May 1, 1972 (*Presidential Documents*, Jan. 17, 1972, p. 50).

[133] Public Law 92-156 (H.R. 8687), Nov. 17, 1971, pp. 7-8. For a further excerpt from the same act see Document 108b.

certain, subject to the release of all American prisoners of war held by the Government of North Vietnam and forces allied with such Government and an accounting for all Americans missing in action who have been held by or known to such Government or such forces. The Congress hereby urges and requests the President to implement the above-expressed policy by initiating immediately the following actions:

(1) Establishing a final date for the withdrawal from Indochina of all military forces of the United States contingent upon the release of all American prisoners of war held by the Government of North Vietnam and forces allied with such Government and an accounting for all Americans missing in action who have been held by or known to such Government or such forces.

(2) Negotiate with the Government of North Vietnam for an immediate cease-fire by all parties to the hostilities in Indochina.

(3) Negotiate with the Government of North Vietnam for an agreement which would provide for a series of phased and rapid withdrawals of United States military forces from Indochina in exchange for a corresponding series of phased releases of American prisoners of war, and for the release of any remaining American prisoners of war concurrently with the withdrawal of all remaining military forces of the United States by not later than the date established by the President pursuant to paragraph (1) hereof or by such earlier date as may be agreed upon by the negotiating parties.

(b) Statement by President Nixon on Signature of the Act, November 17, 1971. [134]

(Complete Text)

I have today signed H.R. 8687, the Military Procurement Authorization Act of 1971.

To avoid any possible misconceptions, I wish to emphasize that section 601 of this act[135]—the so-called "Mansfield Amendment"—does not represent the policies of this administration. Section 601 urges that the President establish a "final date" for the withdrawal of all U.S. forces from Indochina, subject only to the release of U.S. prisoners of war and an accounting for the missing in action.

Section 601 expresses a judgment about the manner in which the American involvement in the war should be ended. However, it is without binding force or effect, and it does not reflect my judgment about the way in which the war should be brought to a conclusion. My signing of the bill that contains this section, therefore, will not change the

---

[134] *Presidential Documents*, Nov. 22, 1971, p. 1531.
[135] Document 81a.

policies I have pursued and that I shall continue to pursue toward this end.

Let me reiterate what has been and remains United States policy regarding withdrawal of U.S. forces from Indochina.

Our goal—and my hope—is a negotiated settlement providing for the total withdrawal of all foreign forces, including our own; for the release of all prisoners; and for a cease-fire throughout Indochina. In the absence of such a settlement, or until such a settlement is reached, the rate of withdrawal of U.S. forces will be determined by three factors: by the level of enemy activity, by the progress of our program of Vietnamization, and by progress toward obtaining the release of all of our prisoners wherever they are in Southeast Asia, and toward obtaining a cease-fire for all of Southeast Asia.

It is because section 601 of this bill will not in fact alter this policy that I have signed it into law. I would add, regretfully, that legislative actions such as this hinder rather than assist in the search for a negotiated settlement.

VI.
AMERICAN POLICY IN ASIA:
EAST ASIA
AND THE PACIFIC

[An opening to the People's Republic of China and a clouding of established friendships with Japan and other Pacific nations were the highlights of American policy in the East Asian–Pacific region in 1971. Signs of incipient understanding between the United States and mainland China, while generally welcomed in so far as they might portend a lessening danger of international conflict, inevitably caused misgivings on the part of Asian governments whose own relations with the Peking regime had developed within a framework of seemingly permanent U.S.-Chinese antagonism. "The news of my forthcoming trip [to China] had an expectedly galvanic impact and set in motion new currents in international relations," President Nixon wrote in his annual foreign policy report for 1972. "... Regardless of how it was achieved, the change in the U.S.-Chinese relationship after 20 years of animosity was bound to be unsettling."[1]

"No major step in international relations," the President further wrote, "is taken without some painful adjustments and potential costs."[2] The historic breakthrough in relations with Peking did indeed exact its own price in the sense of unease which it evoked, despite American reassurances, throughout much of the Pacific area. In the case of the allied Republic of China on Taiwan, the change in American policy was felt, at least initially, as a mortal threat to an established political and diplomatic position—a threat that seemed to be borne out by the subsequent action of the U.N. General Assembly in ousting Taiwan's accredited representatives from the United Nations in order to seat a delegation from the Communist mainland (Document 125). In the case of Japan, the disorientation occasioned in July by news of the President's intended China visit was aggravated in August by the announcement of a new American economic program that was construed by many Japanese as a direct assault on Japanese commercial and monetary interests. Similar repercussions were felt in greater or less

---

[1] Nixon Report, 1972, p. 33.
[2] Same.

degree in other Asian and Pacific countries, where confidence in the immutability of American purposes had already been shaken by the readjustments in American defense policies associated with the two-year-old "Nixon Doctrine."

These trends, both positive and negative, are clearly evident in the documentation presented below. A review of recent progress under the Nixon Doctrine (Document 82) is followed by the communiqués of the regular annual sessions of the SEATO and ANZUS Councils, the one occurring before and the other after the new departure in Sino-American relations (Documents 83-84). The Chinese-American *rapprochement* itself, with the planning of the President's visit, is documented in some detail from the American side (Documents 85-94). A survey of developments in Japanese-American affairs gives primary emphasis to the long-delayed settlement of the Okinawa problem and to the subsequent evolution of the Japanese-American relationship in the light of the United States' "New Economic Policy" (Documents 95-97). A final group of documents reflects the growing strength and self-reliance of the Republic of Korea and the emergence of what appeared to be new prospects of accommodation with the Communist regime of North Korea (Documents 98-100).]

A. Progress Under the Nixon Doctrine.

[The "doctrine" that President Nixon first enunciated at Guam on July 25, 1969,[3] provides a key to the evolution of U.S. policy under his administration both in the Pacific and, to a large extent, throughout the world. In answer to the Vietnam-induced demand for a reduction in overseas involvements, the President offered a set of formulas purporting to define not only the responsibilities of Asian nations for their own defense but also the limits within which they could in future expect the help of the United States. The essence of the doctrine, as paraphrased by the President himself on one occasion, could be briefly stated: "When you are trying to assist another nation [to] defend its freedom, U.S. policy should be to help them fight the war but not to fight the war for them."[4]

Although the President often spoke of the Nixon Doctrine as having a wider than regional application,[5] it had originally been formulated in Asian terms and it was in Asia that its effectiveness could be most accurately measured. The following statement by the Assistant Secre-

[3] *Public Papers (Nixon), 1969*, pp. 545-49; excerpts in *Documents, 1968-69*, pp. 329-34.
[4] Address of Nov. 3, 1969, in same, p. 282.
[5] E.g., Nixon Report, 1971, pp. 17-21.

tary of State for East Asian and Pacific Affairs (Document 82) offers an authoritative appraisal of the processes of adjustment that had been going forward in Asia in the eighteen months since the President had spoken.]

(82) "The Nixon Doctrine: A Progress Report": Address by Marshall Green, Assistant Secretary of State for East Asian and Pacific Affairs, Before the Far East–America Council, New York, January 19, 1971. [6]

(Complete Text)

After being many times your guest at the Far East–America Council, it is now my pleasure and honor to be your speaker. In casting about for what might be the most appropriate subject to speak on today, I concluded that it might be well to give a progress report on the Nixon doctrine, which the President enunciated at Guam in the summer of 1969. This doctrine is, after all, the key aspect of United States foreign policy today, especially toward East Asia; and it would seem appropriate now, at the start of the new year, to review where we stand in putting this doctrine into effect. The record, I believe, is impressive—far more so than most observers realize. Many of the achievements have been quiet gains attracting little public attention, but these changes have nonetheless had profound importance for East Asia and for our relations with this important region.

The scope of the Nixon doctrine is widely known. Basically this doctrine as applied to East Asia sets a state of mind, a style of diplomacy, a way of conducting our programs abroad, which reduces our direct responsibility and calls upon the nations of the area, individually and collectively, to assume an increasing role in providing for their own internal defense.

Simply stated, the Nixon doctrine contains three basic propositions: [7]

1. The United States will keep its treaty commitments;

2. We will provide a shield if a nuclear power threatens the freedom of a nation allied to us or of a nation whose survival we consider vital to our security or to the security of the region as a whole; and

3. In cases involving other types of aggression, the United States will furnish aid and economic assistance when requested and appropriate. But we shall look to the nation directly threatened to assume the primary responsibility of providing the manpower for its defense.

---

6 Department of State Press Release 16, Jan. 19, 1971; text from *Bulletin*, Feb. 8, 1971, pp. 161-65.
7 This formulation echoes the statement in Nixon Report, 1970, pp. 55-56.

This new approach does not mean in any sense that the United States will cease to be a Pacific power or that we will not continue to play a significant role in East Asia. We can do so and we must. What it seeks is to establish a sound basis upon which we can continue to carry out this role in a manner compatible with Asia's own aspirations and which can command the essential support of the American people.

Having been present at the creation—as Dean Acheson would say—I can vividly recall the immediate circumstances in which the President gave his now-famous backgrounder at the Top of the Mar Hotel in Guam on July 25, 1969.[8] It was an informal affair, called at the last moment by the President, attended by the hundred or more newsmen who accompanied him on his around-the-world trip. The President's backgrounder emphasized the great progress that had taken place in East Asia this past decade or so and stressed that the East Asian countries could now take on a large share of their own defense.

Indeed, the countries of East Asia, though they continued to seek our assistance and to need it, were by 1969 far better able to fend for themselves. Equally important, they were becoming more and more anxious to take their own initiatives and to find "Asian solutions for Asian problems." Likewise, the American people were coming to feel that we had taken on far more than our due share of the burdens of military security and economic assistance abroad. Our people were asking what other developed countries were doing to help East Asia, since those countries also had a stake in the security, stability, and progress of that area.

Meanwhile, of primary importance is the fact that throughout the region there has been steady and, in some cases, spectacular economic growth. The remarkable performance of Japan, Korea, and others is well known. Indonesia, only a few short years ago teetering on the brink of bankruptcy, has now stabliized its currency and is embarked at long last on the road toward economic development. In 1960 the gross national product of free East Asia, excluding Australia and New Zealand, stood at $82 billion. At the end of 1969 it was estimated in constant 1967 dollars at $220 billion. Assuming present growth rates continue, this figure should approach $300 billion by the end of this year.

Coupled with this remarkable economic growth has been a corresponding increase among Asians of a pool of technical skills, managerial competence, and entrepreneurial energy ready to tackle Asia's problems. But in many cases they lack the tools.

With this growth has also come a new sense of confidence and an improved ability to assume a larger share of the burden of their own defense. The sum total of the armed forces of our various East Asian

[8] Cf. note 3, above.

allies has risen from about a million men a decade ago to 2 million today. These forces are better trained and better organized, although much still needs to be done in modernizing their equipment. Growth in effective reserve forces has been equally striking.

Our objective under the Nixon doctrine is to insure U.S. national security and that of our allies while at the same time permitting the reduction of U.S. forces abroad and reducing the likelihood of having to commit combat ground forces in the future.

In January 1969 we had 740,000 U.S. military personnel in East Asia. This figure now stands at 500,000, and it will be reduced on the basis of withdrawals already announced to 420,000 by the end of the current fiscal year. In short, our troop strength in East Asia will have been cut almost in half during the past 2 years, with the nations of Asia them-selves assuming the additional responsibilities. 264,000 of these troops are coming out of Viet-Nam[9]—a dramatic example of the success of the Vietnamization program—but significant cuts are also taking place in Korea, Thailand, Japan, and elsewhere. Meanwhile, South Viet-Nam has increased its own military forces from 800,000 2 years ago to more than 1 million today.

The greatest benefit from our troop withdrawals from South Viet-Nam has been the sharp reduction in U.S. casualties. In 1968 more than 14,000 Americans lost their lives in Viet-Nam; in 1970 the figure was 4,000. In the several months before our actions against the North Viet-namese sanctuaries in Cambodia[10] the monthly rate was 347; now it stands at 149. These figures speak for themselves.

Our troop reductions and our changing role in South Viet-Nam have also produced financial savings for the U.S. taxpayer. The costs of the war have been reduced from $29 billion in fiscal year 1969 to $14.5 billion this fiscal year at current rates of expenditure. I should point out, however, that not all of this represents net savings (though the great bulk of it does). As we reduce our own presence it is essential that we actually step up aid to our friends and allies to enable them to take over missions we have been performing. Thus our withdrawal of a U.S. division from Korea[11] will save us some $500 million per year, but we will have to help modernize the Korean armed forces if there is to be no gap in allied defenses in Korea.

CAMBODIA: A TEST CASE

I suppose many people would agree that the outstanding event in East Asia in 1970 was Cambodia.

[9] Cf. Chapter V at note 38.
[10] *Documents, 1970*, pp. 156-79.
[11] Cf. Documents 98-99.

There are no American ground combat forces in Cambodia, nor are there any American military advisers, nor any large American presence in that country; although some U.S. air activities there are required. All this relates back to a central theme in the Nixon doctrine.

We believe that the Cambodians must have primary responsibility for saving Cambodia. They feel the same way about it and have shown remarkable unity and resolve in the face of North Vietnamese aggression. We believe that if Cambodia is to receive outside assistance in the form of troops, it should come from Cambodia's neighbors, not the United States. That principle is being carried out.

South Viet-Nam has made important contributions to the security of Cambodia through physical involvement in or near the old sanctuary areas, through effectively preventing sea supply to the North Vietnamese-Viet Cong, and through accepting many refugees from Cambodia. South Viet-Nam has also assisted in the training of Cambodian armed forces on South Vietnamese soil, and it has delivered captured equipment to Cambodia for use by the Cambodian armed forces. Similarly, Thailand has helped in the form of repair and overhauling of Cambodian aircraft, the provision of more than a dozen riverine craft, some training of Cambodian forces in Thailand, and the delivery (not yet completed) of tens of thousands of uniforms and field kits manufactured in Thailand.

We thus see for the first time in recent history in Southeast Asia a situation where Cambodia has good, mutually constructive relations with all three of its neighbors—South Viet-Nam, Thailand, and Laos. All this greatly enhances the prospects for future Southeast Asian regional cooperation; for without Cambodia, regional cooperation in continental Southeast Asia would have been greatly complicated. The new configuration resulting from Cambodia's improved relations with its neighbors is therefore most heartening, even though we recognize that it will be some time before traditional animosities are laid to rest.

I should also mention in this connection the diplomatic support extended to Cambodia by virtually all of the free East Asian countries. The Djakarta Conference in May represented an important diplomatic initiative by 11 East Asian nations to try to bring peace to Cambodia.[12] Although those efforts have failed so far in regard to Cambodia, this is the first time in many years that so many East Asian countries got together to speak with one voice on a sensitive political issue; and it is also the first time that the new Japan has involved itself in a prominent role in a political issue of this nature.

Finally, bearing in mind that the principal reason for our operations against the Cambodian sanctuary areas was to promote Vietnamization, which it most certainly has done, I think we can conclude that events in

[12] Cf. *The United States in World Affairs, 1970*, pp. 146-47.

Cambodia in 1970 tested the Nixon doctrine in practice. It was not found wanting.

ECONOMIC AND POLITICAL GAINS

The Nixon doctrine relates not only to military burden-sharing but to economic and political programs as well. These latter developments are less dramatic than what has happened in Viet-Nam or Cambodia, but in the long run they also will make a significant contribution to the objectives we all seek. Several examples indicate what I have in mind.

First, burden-sharing is taking place in the economic as well as the military field. Western Europe, Australia, Japan, and others have stepped up their aid to the developing nations. In 1969, official development aid from Japan rose 22 percent over the previous year to a level of $437 million. If export credits and private flows are included, the total reaches $1.2 billion, or about three-quarters of 1 percent of Japan's GNP [Gross National Product]. The Japanese Government has pledged to raise this to 1 percent of GNP by 1975. Given Japan's growth rate, this would involve a threefold increase in economic aid within the next 4 years. This is very much in line with the principles of the Nixon doctrine.

Indonesia supplies one of the best examples of multilateralism in action. Confronted by enormous economic problems in the wake of Sukarno's regime, Indonesia called upon the World Bank and International Monetary Fund for advice. These international institutions arranged with the Indonesian Government (which was represented by a group of remarkably able economists) a detailed and comprehensive plan of economic action. The Bank then called together a group of nine countries which were prepared to help in Indonesia's economic development. These countries, known as the Inter-Governmental Group on Indonesia [IGGI] meet twice yearly to review Indonesia's economic performance and determine aid requirements for the period ahead. This helps to insure that foreign aid is directly related to top-priority national requirements.

As our share of this multilateral effort, and as an incentive to other donors, we have said we will provide one-third of Indonesia's non-food bilateral aid if other nations and international institutions provide the rest. As the IGGI has matured, this concept has taken hold.

This is one type of cooperation the President had in mind when in his September 15, 1970, message to the Congress, he said that the United States should "channel an increasing share of its development assistance through the multilateral institutions as rapidly as practicable."[13] (I assume the President had the Asian Development Bank Special Fund in

---

13 *Documents, 1970*, p. 430.

mind as a leading example.) Our remaining bilateral assistance, the President added, should be provided largely within a framework established by these international institutions.

All this is attended by growing regional consciousness and cooperation. East Asian nations now see that we mean what we say—we really are reducing our military presence, and we expect them to do more to provide for their internal defense. They are rising to this challenge. For the first time we are seeing the beginnings of widening East Asian cooperation in political and security matters. I am sure that the Nixon doctrine has helped spur this process.

CONTINUING SUPPORT REQUIRED

My emphasis has been on the need for the countries of East Asia to maximize their contributions to their own security and development as well as to support the security and development of their neighbors. I have also stressed the need for other developed countries, notably Japan, to carry more of the burden of economic assistance to the developing countries of East Asia.

But there are at least three areas in which continuing U.S. support is essential:

First, if the reduction of our own military and other presence in East Asia is not to create unacceptable risks, then we must assist those nations in their efforts to strengthen their own defenses. Our economic and military aid may actually have to increase for a few years to achieve this objective. But we will be saving billions of dollars through our troop reductions, while our requirements for new aid will be counted in the millions.

I am convinced that Congress appreciated this point, as demonstrated by the prompt action it took in passing our supplemental aid appropriation last month.[14] Nearly $500 million in that appropriation was earmarked to further these objectives in East Asia. This includes funds to begin the modernization of Korea's armed forces, a move which must go hand in hand with our own troop withdrawals; funds to help equip Cambodia's troops, which have increased fourfold within the past 6 months and which, I might add, show a dedication and a fighting spirit far deeper than many observers originally expected; and funds to further the Vietnamization program, which also is basic to success of the Nixon doctrine.

Secondly, we will need to insure that our policies, particularly in the economic field, do not undercut the ability of these nations to stand on

[14] Public Law 91-652, Jan. 5, 1971; for background cf. *Documents, 1970*, pp. 446-53.

their own feet. In this connection, we have asked the Congress for legislation to make it possible for developing countries to export more to the United States, and we have encouraged other developed countries to provide preferential tariff arrangements for the exports of the developing nations.[15] Care must also be taken in disposing of products from our surplus stockpiles in order that we not adversely affect the foreign exchange earnings of those very countries which we are asking to undertake an increasing share of the burden of their own defense. This is particularly true in the case of nations which rely heavily on earnings from the export of single basic commodities.

Finally, and of particular importance, I wish to emphasize that a reduced official American presence and involvement in East Asia should not, and I hope will not, mean a reduction in the overseas activities of our private sector or the presence of our commercial and investment interests, or indeed of American travelers. On the contrary, the new approach to our assistance and other programs looks toward greater flexibility in the programs that support and stimulate the flow of American investment into developing areas. These investments will play a key role in helping achieve the objectives envisaged under the Nixon doctrine.

To summarize, without reducing the credibility of our East Asian commitment, we are undertaking to assist our friends and allies in this area to develop a better capability to defend themselves individually and collectively. They welcome and accept this challenge, for they, too, want Asian solutions for Asian problems. The basic decisions to improve their lot can only be made by these nations themselves, but the policies we are following under the Nixon doctrine have, I believe, contributed significantly to achieving the objectives which both we and they seek. Much remains to be done, but we have made an encouraging beginning.

B. SEATO and ANZUS.

[The redefinition of U.S. regional policies under the Nixon Doctrine (Document 82) did not directly affect American responsibilities under the mutual security treaties concluded during the 1950s with a number of non-Communist Asian and Pacific states—among them the Tripartite Security Treaty with Australia and New Zealand (ANZUS Pact) of 1951 and the South-East Asia Collective Defense Treaty (Manila Pact) of 1954, the basis of the South-East Asia Treaty Organization (SEATO). As was customary, the councils of both these multilateral

---

15 Cf. *Documents, 1970*, pp. 402-9.

organizations held annual sessions at foreign ministers' level in the course of 1971. The sixteenth meeting of the SEATO Council, held in London on April 27-28 (without the participation of France, which had avoided such meetings since 1967), reviewed developments in the region in terms that tended to minimize the uneasiness induced in some of the members by the Nixon Doctrine and the accelerated withdrawals of U.S. forces from Vietnam (Document 83). The 21st meeting of the ANZUS Council, which took place in New York on October 21 in an interval in the U.N. General Assembly session, provided a first occasion for collective appraisal of East Asian and Pacific trends in the light of President Nixon's impending visit to the China mainland (Document 84).]

(83) Sixteenth Meeting of the Council of the South-East Asia Treaty Organization (SEATO), London, April 27-28, 1971: Final Communiqué. [16]

(Complete Text)

The Council of the South-East Asia Treaty Organization held its sixteenth meeting in London from 27 to 28 April 1971, under the chairmanship of The Right Honourable Sir Alec Douglas-Home, Secretary of State for Foreign and Commonwealth Affairs of the United Kingdom. All member Governments, except France, participated.[17] The Republic of Vietnam, a protocol state, was represented by an observer.

General Observations

The Council discussed developments in South-East Asia during the ten months since it last met. It agreed that the trends in the military situation in Indo-China were encouraging. The Republic of Vietnam had further developed its capability to defend itself effectively, thus enabling its allies to proceed with their troop withdrawals.[18] The Khmer [Cambodian] people and Government continued to show a firm determination to resist North Vietnamese and Viet Cong aggression against them. The Council recognized the necessity for the action taken in southern Laos by forces of the Republic of Vietnam with United States air support[19] in response to the continued abuse of Laotian neutrality, sovereignty and territorial integrity by North Vietnamese

---

[16] Department of State Press Release 86, Apr. 29, 1971; text from *Bulletin*, May 31, 1971, pp. 683-85.
[17] The SEATO member governments were Australia, France, New Zealand, Pakistan (until 1973), Philippines, Thailand, United Kingdom, and United States.
[18] Cf. Document 73.
[19] Cf. Documents 67-68.

forces engaged in prosecuting the war in the Khmer Republic [Cambodia] and South Vietnam.

The Council discussed also covert forms of communist aggression—externally-promoted insurgency, subversion, infiltration and terrorism—which are being employed not only against the three Indo-China states which suffered overt military aggression, but also against other regional countries. Such activities by their disruption of the stability of the economy and society of the countries concerned, threaten vital social and economic development. The Council reaffirmed the importance of SEATO's role in the provision of advice and assistance to threatened countries against these forms of communist aggression, and warmly endorsed the organization's activities in this field.

Economic Assistance

The Council called attention to the great need for external assistance to the programs of economic development in the Republic of Vietnam, Laos and the Khmer Republic as rapidly as decreasing levels of hostilities permit, and expressed the hope that all nations able to make a contribution to meeting this need will do so, either individually or through multilateral assistance programs.

Regional Cooperation

The Council reiterated its support for the principles and objectives expressed in the Pacific Charter.[20] It welcomed the increasing acceptance of the principle of regional cooperation in the South-East Asian area and noted with approval the growing strength of regional organizations concerned with maintaining stability and the pace of economic and social development. It agreed that SEATO's contribution to stability had been helpful to regional cooperation.

The Search for Peace

The Council expressed its sympathy and concern for the suffering endured by those living in the troubled area of Indo-China. It reiterated its support for the continued efforts by the Republic of Vietnam and the United States to negotiate a peaceful solution to the war but regretted that there had been little progress towards a diplomatic settlement. At the Paris Peace Talks North Vietnam and the National Liberation Front had shown no willingness to negotiate but had continued to insist on unrealistic conditions which, if accepted, would amount to a complete capitulation to communist demands.[21] This attitude of North Vietnam and the National Liberation Front prevents a just settlement which would permit the peoples of the area to live in

[20] Signed at Manila Sept. 8, 1954; text in *Documents, 1954*, pp. 318-19.
[21] Cf. Chapter V at note 71.

peace and to choose their way of life without outside interference.

The Council noted with appreciation the interest demonstrated by many Governments and international organizations in making constructive suggestions for diplomatic solutions during the past year, especially the non-aligned Asian countries, and it warmly welcomed the follow-up efforts by the participants in the Djakarta Conference.[22] It regretted that the USSR had refused to join with the other co-chairman, the United Kingdom, in reconvening the Geneva Conference to discuss the situation in Indo-China. The Council restated its conviction that negotiations could be undertaken either through a general conference on Indo-China as a whole or through separate negotiations such as those in Paris on Vietnam.

Vietnam

The Council heard the account given by the observer of the Republic of Vietnam of developments in his country during the year. He emphasized the improved security situation which had enabled the population to lead more normal lives. The Council welcomed the holding of elections there.[23] It noted the progress being made towards even greater self-sufficiency against aggression, both overt and subversive, which has enabled the Republic of Vietnam's forces increasingly to shoulder full ground-combat responsibilities.

The Council noted with approval the continued assistance being given to the Republic of Vietnam in economic and humanitarian as well as military fields both by SEATO member countries and by others outside SEATO, including substantial military assistance from the Republic of Korea.

The Council fully endorsed the desire of the people and Government of the Republic of Vietnam to work for a peaceful solution to the war and for internal stability in accordance with their wish to be left alone to choose their own future. It deplored North Vietnam's failure to show a more realistic and flexible approach to negotiating a settlement. The Council looked forward during the coming year to the further strengthening of democratic processes and improvement in the security and general welfare of the people of the Republic of Vietnam.

Laos

Reviewing the situation in Laos, the Council regretted that the efforts of the Royal Laotian Government to hold direct talks with the Pathet Lao had not so far been successful. It deplored the fact that North Vietnam continues to make use of Laotian territory, in open violation of the 1962 Geneva Agreement, to transport covertly large quantities of

[22] Cf. above at note 12.
[23] Cf. Document 78.

troops and material to the Khmer Republic and South Vietnam, to commit armed attacks on forces of the Royal Lao Government, and to support insurgency in Thailand.

The Council reiterated its call for full implementation by all signatories of the terms of the 1962 Geneva Agreement on Laos, including the withdrawal of all foreign troops. It expressed its support for efforts by the Royal Lao Government to secure peace and to preserve the neutrality of Laos.

Khmer Republic

The Council reiterated its firm support for the sovereignty, independence and territorial integrity of the Khmer Republic [Cambodia], and its determination to honor and respect the desire of the Government of the Khmer Republic to remain neutral. It expressed its admiration for the vigorous response of the Khmer people and Government to aggression during the period under review, and its satisfaction that the support and cooperation are being given to the Khmer people by the Republic of Vietnam and other friendly countries.

The Council condemned North Vietnam's continuing aggression and noted with satisfaction the success of joint Khmer–South Vietnamese military campaigns against communist base areas on Khmer territory. The Council regretted that efforts made by many Asian nations to bring about the end of hostilities had not so far borne fruit, and expressed its readiness and that of its members to lend all possible assistance to diplomatic efforts to achieve an international solution.

Philippines

The Council noted with interest the vigorous work, which continued to meet with success, of the Government of the Philippines against communist subversion and insurgency, especially in Central Luzon. It expressed support for the efforts of the Government of the Philippines to enact a full socio-economic program to raise overall standards of living in the Republic of the Philippines and to eliminate the primary causes of unrest among the people.

Thailand

The Council noted the intensified efforts of the Royal Thai Government and Thai people to further economic and social development in the country, and to counter communist subversive and insurgent activities directed from outside. SEATO as well as its member countries had continued to assist the Royal Thai Government's efforts to counter subversion and insurgency. The Council noted with appreciation the Royal Thai Government's valuable contribution towards the defense of the Republic of Vietnam and its friendly cooperation with other regional countries.

Counter-subversion, Economic, Social, Cultural and Information Activities

The Council reiterated its support for SEATO activities designed to aid regional members to counter externally-promoted subversion and insurgency. It stressed that SEATO economic aid activities should be complementary to these counter-subversion programs. It welcomed the development during the year of the new office for counter-subversion and counter-insurgency at SEATO headquarters.

The Council noted with satisfaction that member countries continue to provide aid to other member countries bilaterally under the general auspices of SEATO. It reaffirmed the importance of SEATO's economic, cultural, social and information programs, while noting that the organization's cultural activities will be reviewed.

Cooperation in the Military Field

The Council noted the report of the military advisers and commended the excellent work done by the military planning office in keeping plans up-to-date and in designing military exercises from which valuable experience was gained. It welcomed the decision of the United Kingdom to continue to make declarations of forces to SEATO and noted that the United Kingdom military adviser to SEATO would in future be the Chief of the Defense Staff.

Five-Power Defense Arrangements

The Council noted the communique issued on 16 April by the Ministerial Meeting in London[24] and the progress made in setting up the Five-Power Defense arrangements.

Seventeenth Meeting of the Council

The Council accepted with pleasure the invitation of the Australian Government to host the Seventeenth Council Meeting in 1972.[25]

Pakistan

The Pakistan Delegate wished it to be recorded that he did not participate in the drafting of the communique.

Expression of Gratitude

The Council expressed its gratitude to the Government and people of the United Kingdom for their generous hospitality and warm welcome

---

[24] Joint arrangements for the defense of Malaysia and Singapore were agreed upon at a meeting of ministerial representatives of Australia, Malaysia, New Zealand, Singapore, and the United Kingdom, held in London on Apr. 15-16, 1971 (*Keesing's*, p. 24596).

[25] The seventeenth meeting of the SEATO Council was held in Canberra on June 27-28, 1972; see *A.F.R., 1972*, no. 64.

and its appreciation for the excellent arrangements made for the meeting.

Leaders of Delegations

The Leaders of the Delegations to the Sixteenth Council Meeting were:

Australia	Hon. Leslie Bury, M.P., Minister for Foreign Affairs.
New Zealand	Right Hon. Sir Keith Holyoake, G.C.M.G., C.H., M.P., Prime Minister and Minister for Foreign Affairs.
Pakistan	H.E. Mr. Salman A. Ali, High Commissioner in the United Kingdom.
Philippines	H.E. General Carlos P. Romulo, Secretary of Foreign Affairs.
Thailand	H.E. Mr. Thanat Khoman, Minister of Foreign Affairs.
United Kingdom	Right Hon. Sir Alec Douglas-Home, K.T., D.L., M.P., Secretary of State for Foreign and Commonwealth Affairs.
United States	Hon. William P. Rogers, Secretary of State.
Republic of Vietnam (observer)	H.E. Mr. Tran Van Lam, Minister of Foreign Affairs.

(84) Twenty-first Meeting of the ANZUS Council, New York, October 2, 1971: Final Communiqué. [26]

(Complete Text)

The ANZUS Council met in New York on October 2, 1971. Australia was represented by the Honorable Nigel H. Bowen, Minister for Foreign Affairs, New Zealand by the Honorable R. D. Muldoon, Minister of Finance, and the United States by the Honorable William P. Rogers, Secretary of State.

The three ANZUS partners concentrated their discussion on the changes which are occurring in Asia and the Pacific, particularly the effects of the Nixon Doctrine, China's growing interest in contacts with other countries and the importance of Japan, both politically and economically, to the stability and welfare of the region.

The Representatives recognized the encouragement and support Japan is giving to economic development and regional understanding and agreed that Japan can make a major contribution to welfare and

[26] Department of State Press Release 225, Oct. 4, 1971; text from *Bulletin*, Oct. 25, 1971, pp. 462-63.

stability in the region. They welcomed the intention which has been expressed by Japan, one of the world's leading industrial nations, to assume a proportionately greater role in international cooperation for development. The Australian and New Zealand Representatives affirmed the importance for the stability of Asia and the Pacific of a continuing close partnership and confidence between the U.S. and Japan, a view which was warmly endorsed by the U.S. Representative.

The Representatives, recognizing the importance of China in East Asia, welcomed the evidence of growing contacts between the People's Republic of China and the ANZUS countries, and they shared the view that improved relations with the People's Republic of China are possible, given flexibility and understanding on both sides.

The Representatives noted their long-standing ties of friendship with the Republic of China. They agreed that it was reasonable and equitable for both the People's Republic of China and the Republic of China, without prejudice to the eventual settlement of the conflicting claims involved, to be represented now in the United Nations with the People's Republic of China seated in the Security Council as one of the five permanent members.[27] The expulsion of the Republic of China would be no more in accord with the realities of the world than would the continued absence of the People's Republic from the U.N. The responsibilities of the organization toward the less powerful demand particular care that their rights should not be ignored or swept away.

The political and military situation in Indochina was reviewed. The Representatives noted with satisfaction that the Republic of Viet-Nam and its armed forces have, during the past year, assumed increasing responsibility for the defense of their country, and have accepted that the gains made in the pacification field must be continued and maintained primarily through their own efforts. The progress made in this regard by the Republic of Viet-Nam had made it possible for the countries contributing troops in Viet-Nam to carry out phased withdrawals of their combat forces while continuing training and economic support.[28]

The Representatives expressed admiration for the resilience displayed by Cambodia in resisting the aggression from the north and indicated the desires of their respective Governments to continue to give effective support to the Cambodians' own efforts.

The Representatives expressed the hope that the continuing contacts between the Laotian parties[29] will lead to a genuine and just peace that

[27] Cf. Documents 122-124.
[28] Cf. Document 73.
[29] For details of the intermittent correspondence between Prince Souvanna Phouma, Prime Minister of the Royal Laotian Government, and Prince Souphanouvong, leader of the Lao Patriotic Front, see *Keesing's*, p. 24959.

will assure the independence, integrity and neutrality of the Kingdom of Laos.

The political and strategic importance of the Indian Ocean was reviewed and the current level of the Soviet naval presence was discussed. The Representatives noted the concerns which had been voiced by a number of States bordering on the Indian Ocean and they expressed the hope that military competition in the area could be avoided.[30] They agreed, however, that a careful watch should be continued in this area.

The ANZUS partners also considered encouraging developments in the Pacific. The New Zealand Representative referred to the progress in regional cooperation made at the recent meeting in Wellington of the South Pacific Forum, composed of independent and self-governing States in the South Pacific.[31] The U.S. Representative reported that within a few days discussions would begin between the U.S. and representatives of the Congress of Micronesia on the future status of the U.S. Trust Territory of the Pacific Islands.[32]

The meeting was the 21st annual consultation among the ANZUS partners. This period has seen striking improvement in the stability and economies of Asia and the Pacific. The three Representatives agreed that, in the new climate which is developing in international relations, continuing close consultations within the Alliance will be of particular value.

C. The People's Republic of China.

[The establishment of high-level contact between the United States and the People's Republic of China undoubtedly ranks among the outstanding diplomatic developments of 1971. A period of intense hostility that extended all the way back to the establishment of the Peking regime in 1949 was virtually concluded in the few short months that preceded the announcement on July 15, 1971, that President Nixon had accepted an invitation to visit the People's Republic at an appropriate date before May 1972 so that leaders on both sides could seek a normalization of relations between the two countries and exchange views on questions of mutual concern.

In his 1972 report on U.S. foreign policy, President Nixon entered

---

[30] Cf. Documents 65-66.
[31] The South Pacific Forum was established at a meeting in Wellington, New Zealand, on Aug. 5-7, 1971, by the heads of government of Fiji, Nauru, Tonga, Western Samoa, and the Cook Islands; the Prime Minister of New Zealand; and the Australian Minister of External Territories (*The World This Year, 1972*, p. 161).
[32] Cf. *The World This Year, 1972*, p. 119.

into some detail concerning the developments that led up to this extraordinary denouement.[33] The need for a new policy toward the People's Republic of China, he pointed out, had been evident to him even before his entry into office; and the direction in which the United States desired to move had been made évident by a series of unilateral gestures on trade and similar matters that had extended throughout 1969 and 1970.[34] The beginnings of a Chinese response in the fall of 1970 had prepared the way for "a series of orchestrated public and private steps" that began with a reaffirmation, in the President's "State of the World" report made public February 25, 1971, of America's readiness for a dialogue and its hope of seeing the People's Republic assume a constructive role in the family of nations.[35]]

1. "Breaking the Ice," March–June 1971.

[The major moves in the complicated shadow play that followed this renewed presidential overture can be traced in the following documentation, in which selected comments by the President himself are interspersed with announcements of concrete measures decided by the American Government. An easing in mid-March of the longstanding restrictions on the use of U.S. passports for travel to mainland China (Document 86) was followed by the sensational visit, on Chinese invitation, of an American table tennis team which was received by Prime Minister Chou En-lai on April 14 and told that it had "opened a new page in the relations of the Chinese and American people." The United States, in the course of the spring, announced additional relaxations of trade and travel restrictions, among them the removal of controls on dollar transactions with China and the ending of a 21-year embargo on trade with that country (Documents 87 and 89). It also initiated studies of the vital question of how China should in future be represented in the United Nations, although a determination on this critical point was not to be announced until later in the year. "I would just summarize it this way," President Nixon remarked on April 29: "What we have done has broken the ice. Now we have to test the water to see how deep it is" (Document 88).]

---

[33] Nixon Report, 1972, pp. 26-33; cf. also Kalb, *Kissinger*, pp. 216-65.
[34] Cf. *The United States in World Affairs, 1970*, pp. 157-59 and 163-64; also Document 86.
[35] Nixon Report, 1971, pp. 105-9; cf. also Document 1.

(85) United States Policy Toward China: News Conference Statements by President Nixon, March 4, 1971. [36]

(Excerpts)

*   *   *

CHINA POLICY

Q. In your foreign policy report, you invited better relations with Communist China,[37] which is being interpreted in Taiwan, I believe, with a little bit of apprehension. Are you actually moving toward a two-China policy?

THE PRESIDENT. I understand the apprehension in Taiwan, but I believe that the apprehension insofar as Taiwan's continued existence and as its continued membership in the United Nations is not justified. You will also have noted that in my foreign policy report I said that we stood by our defense commitments to Taiwan, that Taiwan, which has a larger population than two-thirds of all of the United Nations, could not and would not be expelled from the United Nations as long as we had anything to say about it, and that as far as our attitude toward Communist China was concerned that that would be governed by Communist China's attitude toward us.[38]

In other words, we would like to normalize relations with all nations in the world. There has, however, been no receptivity on the part of Communist China. But under no circumstances will we proceed with a policy of normalizing relations with Communist China if the cost of that policy is to expel Taiwan from the family of nations.

*   *   *

COMMUNIST CHINA AND THE U.N.

Q. May I ask you, sir, when you said earlier about Communist China—at least you were not perfectly clear about your position on Communist China, about seating in the United Nations. Somebody asked you if you would favor a two-China policy, but you were not completely clear about that. Could you say, sir, if Taiwan maintained its position on the Security Council, if it maintained its position in the United Nations, if you would favor seating Communist China.

---

[36] *Presidential Documents*, Mar. 8, 1971, pp. 426-28.
[37] Cf. above at note 35.
[38] Nixon Report, 1971, pp. 107-8.

THE PRESIDENT. That's a moot question at this time, because Communist China or the People's Republic of China, which I understand stirred up people in Taiwan—because that is the official name of the country—but Communist China refuses even to discuss the matter. Therefore, it would not be appropriate for me to suggest what we might agree to when Communist China takes the position that they will have no discussion whatever until Taiwan gets out. And we will not start with that kind of a proposition.[39]

*   *   *

(86) Easing of United States Passport Restrictions: Announcement by Charles W. Bray III, Department of State Press Officer, March 15, 1971.[40]

(Complete Text)

I have an announcement concerning the restriction on the use of American passports for travel to certain areas. With regard to the People's Republic of China, we have decided not to renew the restriction. With regard to the three other areas, North Viet-Nam, North Korea, and Cuba, the restriction remains in effect for another 6 months, at which time the matter will be considered again. Removing a restriction on the use of American passports for travel to the People's Republic of China is consistent with the President's publicly stated desire to improve communication with the mainland.

I could, if you would like, very briefly summarize the unilateral steps we have taken in recent years on the subject of trade and travel.[41]

In July of 1969, we permitted noncommercial tourist purchases of up to $100 of Chinese goods. At the same time, we relaxed restrictions relating to travel to permit almost anyone with a legitimate purpose to travel to mainland China on an American passport. If I recall the figures correctly, we have validated on the order of 1,000 passports, including 270 in 1970.

In December 1969, we permitted unlimited purchases of Chinese goods to enable tourists, collectors, museums, universities, to import Chinese products for their own account. In the same month, that is, December of 1969, we permitted American-controlled subsidiaries abroad to conduct trade in nonstrategic goods with mainland China.

In April of 1970, we announced selective licensing of American-made

---

[39] On the representation of China in the United Nations see Documents 122-128.
[40] *Bulletin*, Apr. 12, 1971, p. 510.
[41] Cf. *The United States in World Affairs, 1970*, pp. 158-59 and 164.

components and related spare parts for nonstrategic foreign goods exported to China.

In August of 1970, we lifted the restriction on American oil companies abroad bunkering free-world ships bearing nonstrategic cargoes to Chinese ports on the mainland.

(87) Further Easing of Trade and Travel Restrictions: Statement by President Nixon, April 14, 1971.[42]

(Complete Text)

In my second annual Foreign Policy Report to the Congress on February 25, 1971, I wrote, "In the coming year, I will carefully examine what further steps we might take to create broader opportunities for contacts between the Chinese and American peoples, and how we might remove needless obstacles to the realization of these opportunities."[43]

I asked the Under Secretaries Committee of the National Security Council[44] to make appropriate recommendations to bring this about.

After reviewing the resulting study and recommendations, I decided on the following actions, none of which requires new legislation or negotiations with the People's Republic of China:

—The United States is prepared to expedite visas for visitors or groups of visitors from the People's Republic of China to the United States,

—U.S. currency controls are to be relaxed to permit the use of dollars by the People's Republic of China.

—Restrictions are to be ended on American oil companies providing fuel to ships or aircraft proceeding to and from China except on Chinese-owned or Chinese-chartered carriers bound to or from North Vietnam, North Korea, or Cuba.

—U.S. vessels or aircraft may now carry Chinese cargoes between non-Chinese ports and U.S.-owned foreign flag carriers may call at Chinese ports.

—I have asked for a list of items of a nonstrategic nature which can be placed under general license for direct export to the People's Republic of China. Following my review and approval of specific items on this list, direct imports of designated items from China will then also be authorized.

After due consideration of the results of these changes in our trade

---

[42] *Presidential Documents*, Apr. 19, 1971, pp. 628-29.
[43] Cf. note 35 above.
[44] Cf. Document 3.

and travel restrictions, I will consider what additional steps might be taken.

Implementing regulations will be announced by the Department of State and other interested agencies.[45]

(88) Appraisal of Current Prospects: News Conference Statement by President Nixon, April 29, 1971.[46]

(Excerpts)

*   *   *

CHINA POLICY

Q. Mr. President, the Commission on the United Nations that you appointed, headed by your 1960 Vice Presidential running mate [Henry Cabot Lodge], has come out rather strongly for a two-China policy.[47] The last time we saw you you weren't prepared to talk about that. I wonder if tonight you could say how you feel about those proposals?

THE PRESIDENT. Well, Mr. Cormier,[48] tnat recommendation by that very distinguished committee, of course, is being given consideration in the high councils of this Government, and I am, of course, considering it along with recommendations which move in the other direction.

I think, however, that your question requires that I put, perhaps, in perspective much of this discussion about our new China policy. I think that some of the speculation that has occurred in recent weeks since the visit of the table tennis team to Peking has not been useful.

I want to set forth exactly what it is and what it is not.

First, as I stated at, I think, one of my first press conferences in this room,[49] the long-range goal of this administration is a normalization of

---

[45] Implementing measures with respect to currency controls, ships, and aircraft were announced by the Departments of State, Treasury, Commerce, and Transportation on May 7, 1971 (Bulletin, May 31, 1971, pp. 702-4). For the subsequent removal of controls over direct trade see Document 90.

[46] Presidential Documents, May 3, 1971, pp. 696-97, 700-701.

[47] The Report of the President's Commission for the Observance of the 25th Anniversary of the United Nations, submitted Apr. 26, 1971, recommended that the United States "under no circumstances agree to the expulsion from the U.N. of the Republic of China on Taiwan, but seek agreement as early as practicable whereby the People's Republic of China might accept the principles of the Charter and be represented in the Organization." (Summary of Recommendations in Bulletin, Aug. 2, 1971, pp. 132-33.)

[48] Frank Cormier, Associated Press.

[49] News conference, Mar. 4, 1969, in Public Papers (Nixon), 1969, p. 181.

our relationships with Mainland China, the People's Republic of China, and the ending of its isolation from the other nations of the world. That is a long-range goal.

Second, we have made some progress toward that goal. We have moved in the field of travel; we have moved in the field of trade. There will be more progress made.

For example, at the present time I am circulating among the departments the items which may be released as possible trade items in the future and I will be making an announcement on that in a very few weeks.[50]

But now when we move from the field of travel and trade to the field of recognition of the Government, to its admission to the United Nations, I am not going to discuss those matters, because it is premature to speculate about that.

We are considering all those problems. When I have an announcement to make, when a decision is made—and I have not made it yet—I will make it.[51]

But up until that time we will consider all of the proposals that are being made. We will proceed on the path that we have been proceeding on. And that is the way to make progress. Progress is not helped in this very sensitive area by speculation that goes beyond what the progress might achieve.

I would just summarize it this way: What we have done has broken the ice. Now we have to test the water to see how deep it is.

I would finally suggest that—I know this question may come up if I don't answer it now—I hope, and, as a matter of fact, I expect to visit Mainland China sometime in some capacity—I don't know what capacity. But that indicates what I hope for the long term. And I hope to contribute to a policy in which we can have a new relationship with Mainland China.

*   *   *

CHINA NEGOTIATIONS AND THE SOVIET UNION

Q. Mr. President, the State Department has said that the legal question of the future of Taiwan and Formosa is an unsettled question. Would you favor direct negotiations between the Nationalist and the Communist Governments to settle their dispute?

THE PRESIDENT. Well, I noted speculation to the effect from various departments and various sources that the way for these two entities to

---

[50] Cf. Document 90.
[51] Cf. Document 122.

settle their differences was to negotiate directly. I think that is a nice legalistic way to approach it, but I think it is completely unrealistic. I am only saying at this point that the United States, is seeking to in a very measured way, while maintaining our treaty commitments to Taiwan—we are seeking a more normal relationship with the People's Republic of China.

There is one other thing I think it's very important to make.

There has been speculation to the effect that the purpose of our, or one purpose of our normalizing our relations or attempting to normalize our relations with Mainland China is to some way irritate the Soviet Union. Nothing could be further from the truth.

We are seeking good relations with the Soviet Union and I am not discouraged by the SALT talk progress.[52] I can only say that we believe that the interests of both countries would be served by an agreement there. We seek good relations with the Soviet Union. We are seeking good relations with Communist China and the interests of world peace require good relations between the Soviet Union and Communist China. It would make no sense for the United States, in the interest of world peace, to try to get the two to get at each other's throats, because we would be embroiled in the controversy ourselves.

VISIT TO MAINLAND CHINA

Q. Mr. President, you spoke of your intention to travel to Mainland China. Is that at the invitation of Chairman Mao?

THE PRESIDENT. I am not referring to any invitation. I am referring only to a hope and an expectation that at some time in my life and in some capacity, which, of course, does not put any deadline on when I would do it, that I would hope to go to Mainland China.

*   *   *

CHINA POLICY ALTERNATIVES

Q. Sir, in your first answer on China, you said that you were considering suggestions for a two-China policy, along with suggestions that move in the other direction. Could you expound a little bit on what you mean by that?

What is the range of alternatives?

THE PRESIDENT. Mr. Bailey,[53] what I meant to convey was that both within the administration and from sources outside the adminis-

---

[52] Cf. Documents 21-22.
[53] Charles W. Bailey 2d, *Minneapolis Tribune, Minneapolis Star.*

tration, there are those who favor a two-China policy; there are those who favor universality in the United Nations; there are those who favor a one-China policy, either Mainland China or Taiwan China.

Now, all of these are positions that are taken. I am not suggesting that they are lively options as far as I am concerned. What I am saying is that this is a very complex problem. I will make the decision after advising with the Secretary of State and my other chief advisers in this field, and when I make it, I will announce it, but I am not going to speculate on it now because I emphasize this is a very sensitive area and too much speculation about it might destroy or seriously imperil what I think is the significant progress we have made, at least in the travel area, and possibly in the trade area, looking to the future.

Reporter: Thank you, Mr. President.

(89) A Further Appraisal: News Conference Statement by President Nixon, June 1, 1971.[54]

(Excerpt)

*   *   *

CHINA POLICY

Q. Mr. President, since April you have been considering policy studies on the China question, easing trade with China, and representation at the United Nations. Can you say where these stand now, please?

THE PRESIDENT. With regard to the United Nations question, a significant change has taken place among the members of the United Nations on the issue of admission of Mainland China. We are now analyzing that situation in consultations with the Republic of China on Taiwan and with third countries.

After we have completed our analysis, which I would imagine would take approximately 6 weeks, we will then decide what position we, the Government of the United States, should take at the next session of the United Nations this fall, and we will have an announcement to make at that time with regard to that particular problem.[55]

A number of various options are open to us.

With regard to trade, the various agencies have now completed their review of the situation and have submitted their recommendations to me. And on June 10th, I will make an announcement releasing a wide

---

[54] *Presidential Documents*, June 7, 1971, p. 849.
[55] Cf. Document 122.

variety of items which previously had been banned.[56] These are all nonstrategic items in which trade can be conducted with Mainland China.

Let me put all of this in context by saying that there are only two areas where we have moved. They are significant, however, in themselves. In the area of opening the door to travel and opening the door to more trade, we have made significant movement. I think what, however, we should realize is that we still have a long way to go.

As I recall, there is a Chinese proverb to the effect that a journey of a thousand miles begins with a single step. We've taken two steps, but the important thing is that we have started the journey toward eventual, a more normal relationship with Mainland China, and eventually, and this is vitally important, ending its isolation and the isolation of 700 million people from the rest of the people of the world. This we think is a goal well worth pursuing.

*   *   *

(90) Lifting of United States Trade Controls: Statement by Ronald L. Ziegler, Press Secretary to the President, June 10, 1971.[57]

(Complete Text)

On April 14, the President announced that he would shortly open the possibility of trade between the United States and the People's Republic of China.[58] That announcement followed a series of moves begun in 1969 to end the strict isolation between the United States and China. Today, President Nixon is announcing the details of the trade controls which he is now lifting.

The United States will permit the free export to China of a range of nonstrategic U.S. products. These include most farm, fish and forestry products; tobacco; fertilizers; coal; selected organic and inorganic chemicals; rubber; textiles; certain metals such as iron, zinc and tin; agricultural, industrial and office equipment; household appliances; electrical apparatus in general industrial or commercial use; certain electronic and communications equipment; certain automotive equipment and consumer goods.

President Nixon has also decided to permit the free export of grains to China as well as to the Soviet Union and Eastern Europe. In the past, these exports have been governed by regulations that have hindered the

[56] Document 90.
[57] *Presidential Documents*, June 14, 1971, pp. 890-91. For the formal White House announcement see same, p. 891.
[58] Document 87.

export of grains to these countries.

The President has also decided that the Government will examine requests for the export of other items to the People's Republic of China, and permit those transactions which are consistent with the requirements of U.S. national security.

The United States will also permit for the first time commercial imports from China, while keeping the possibility of future controls on these imports if necessary.

President Nixon looks upon these measures as a significant step to improve communications with a land of 800 million people after a 20-year freeze in our relations. The President will later consider the possibility of further steps in an effort to reestablish a broader relationship with a country and people having an important role for future peace in Asia.

2. President Nixon's Proposed Visit.

[The idea of a Nixon visit to China, officially described as little more than a vague hope (Document 88), had acquired a topical character with the publication in *Life* magazine of April 30 of an interview by the late Edgar Snow with Chinese Communist Party Chairman Mao Tse-tung[59] that was read in Washington as a confirmation of earlier private signals of Chinese interest in such a project. The subsequent lifting of U.S. trade and currency controls helped consolidate the new trend and paved the way for the celebrated visit to China by Presidential Assistant Kissinger, who sandwiched a secret trip to Peking on July 9-11 between a visit to South Vietnam, Thailand, India, and Pakistan and a meeting with the North Vietnamese in Paris.[60] The announcement of plans for the presidential visit was made by Mr. Nixon himself in a radio-television statement on July 15 (Document 91), and some of the purposes of the trip were expounded in presidential news conferences later in the summer (Document 92).

Preparations for the presidential visit seem not to have been directly influenced by the internal crisis in the People's Republic that accompanied the reported flight and death in an airplane crash of Lin Piao, the second-ranking member of the Communist hierarchy and designated successor of Mao Tse-tung, on the night of September 12-13, 1971. Equally without perceptible effect was the autumn maneuvering over Chinese representation in the United Nations, which reached a climax on October 25 with the decisive defeat of U.S. efforts to make the admission of the People's Republic of China to U.N. representation

---

[59] Edgar Snow, "Conversation with Mao Tse-tung," *Life,* Apr. 30, 1971, pp. 46-48.
[60] Cf. Chapter V at note 92.

contingent on the preservation of a U.N. seat for the Republic of China on Taiwan (Documents 122-128). A second Kissinger trip to Peking on October 20-26 was followed in November by the announcement that the presidential visit would take place on February 21-28, 1972 (Document 93), the experimental nature of the trip being emphasized by Dr. Kissinger in a news conference on November 30 (Document 94). The United States throughout this period made special efforts to assure the Soviet Union that it had no thought of combining with China in opposition to Soviet interests (Documents 29 and 30), notwithstanding the contrary tendency detected by some observers in the support accorded by both China and the United States to Pakistan at a time when the U.S.S.R. was strongly supporting India in its war with Pakistan in the Subcontinent (Documents 57-63).]

(91) Announcement of the Proposed Visit: Radio–Television Statement by President Nixon, July 15, 1971.[61]

(Complete Text)

Good evening:

I have requested this television time tonight to announce a major development in our efforts to build a lasting peace in the world.

As I have pointed out on a number of occasions over the past 3 years, there can be no stable and enduring peace without the participation of the People's Republic of China and its 750 million people. That is why I have undertaken initiatives in several areas to open the door for more normal relations between our two countries.

In pursuance of that goal, I sent Dr. Kissinger, my Assistant for National Security Affairs, to Peking during his recent world tour for the purpose of having talks with Premier Chou En-lai.

The announcement I shall now read is being issued simultaneously in Peking and in the United States:

Premier Chou En-lai and Dr. Henry Kissinger, President Nixon's Assistant for National Security Affairs, held talks in Peking from July 9 to 11, 1971. Knowing of President Nixon's expressed desire to visit the People's Republic of China, Premier Chou En-lai on behalf of the Government of the People's Republic of China has extended an invitation to President Nixon to visit China at an appropriate date before May 1972.

President Nixon has accepted the invitation with pleasure.

The meeting between the leaders of China and the United States is to seek the normalization of relations between the two countries

[61] *Presidential Documents*, July 19, 1971, p. 1058.

and also to exchange views on questions of concern to the two sides.

In anticipation of the inevitable speculation which will follow this announcement, I want to put our policy in the clearest possible context. Our action in seeking a new relationship with the People's Republic of China will not be at the expense of our old friends.

It is not directed against any other nation. We seek friendly relations with all nations. Any nation can be our friend without being any other nation's enemy.

I have taken this action because of my profound conviction that all nations will gain from a reduction of tensions and a better relationship between the United States and the People's Republic of China.

It is in this spirit that I will undertake what I deeply hope will become a journey for peace, peace not just for our generation but for future generations on this earth we share together.

Thank you and good night.

(92) Expectations for the Trip: News Conference Statements by President Nixon, August–September 1971.

(a) Statement of August 4, 1971.[62]

(Excerpt)

* * *

THE PRESIDENT'S TRIP TO CHINA

Q. Mr. President, can you tell us any more about your forthcoming trip to China, when it is likely to occur, and can you give us your assessment of what effect you think this will have on ending the war in Vietnam?

THE PRESIDENT. As far as the timing is concerned, I cannot add to what I said in the original announcement.[63] It will be before May 1 [1972]. The time will be worked out sometime within the next 2 to 3 months, I would assume, and a considerable amount of preparatory activity must take place, setting up the agenda, setting up the numbers in the official party.

These are matters, of course, that must be discussed and worked out before the time of the visit is finally announced.[64]

Second, and I know a number of you are interested in who is going,

---

[62] *Presidential Documents*, Aug. 9, 1971, pp. 1119-20.
[63] Document 91.
[64] Cf. Document 93b.

that is a matter still to be decided. It was raised by Dr. Kissinger and by Premier Chou En-lai in their conversations, and will be worked out by mutual agreement.

As far as our party is concerned, it will be a small working party. The only ones that presently are definitely going are, of course, the Secretary of State and Dr. Kissinger and myself. Beyond that, whatever others will be added will be determined by mutual agreement between the parties concerned.

Now, as to the effect the visit will have and the conversations will have on Vietnam, I will not speculate on that subject. I will only say that as the joint announcement indicated, this will be a wide-ranging discussion of issues concerning both governments. It is not a discussion that is going to lead to instant detente.

What it really is, is moving, as we have moved, I believe, in the situation with regard to the Soviet Union, from an era of confrontation without communication to an era of negotiations with discussion. It does not mean that we go into these meetings on either side with any illusions about the wide differences that we have. Our interests are very different, and both sides recognize this, in the talks that Dr. Kissinger had, very extended talks he had with Premier Chou En-lai. We do not expect that these talks will settle all of those differences.

What is important is that we will have opened communication to see where our differences are irreconcilable to see that they can be settled peacefully, and to find those areas where the United States, which today is the most powerful nation in the world, can find an agreement with the most populous nation in the world which potentially in the future could become the most powerful nation in the world.

As we look at the peace in the world for the balance of this century, and for that matter the next century, we must recognize that there cannot be world peace on which all the peoples in the world can rely, and in which they have such a great stake, unless there is communication between and some negotiation between these two great superpowers, the People's Republic and the United States.

I have put this in general terms because that is the understanding of the People's Republic, Premier Chou En-lai, and it is our understanding that our agenda will be worked out at a later point; before the trip it will be very carefully worked out so that the discussions will deal with the hard problems as well as the easy ones.

We expect to make some progress, but to speculate about what progress will be made on any particular issue, to speculate, for example, as to what effect this might have on Vietnam, would not serve the interests of constructive talks.

ALL-ASIAN CONFERENCE ON VIETNAM?

Q. Can I ask a related policy question on Vietnam?

THE PRESIDENT. Sure

Q. There have been some suggestions, including some indirect hints from China, that a negotiating forum involving an Asian conference to be held in Asia, primarily with Asian participants but the United States as well, might be a better forum for negotiating a settlement in Vietnam. Can you speak to that?

THE PRESIDENT. Mr. Bailey,[65] the question of whether there should be an all-Asian conference, with the Government of the People's Republic participating, as you know, has risen several times over the past few months, and was raised before our announcement was made.

As far as we are concerned, we will consider any proposal that might contribute to a more peaceful situation in the Pacific and in the world. However, at this point there is no understanding between the United States and the People's Republic as to whether or not out of this meeting should come that kind of proposal.

Let me say on that score, there were no conditions asked for on either side, and none accepted. There were no deals made on either side or accepted, none offered and none accepted. This is a discussion which will take place with both sides knowing in advance that there are problems, but with both sides well prepared. This is the secret of any successful summit meeting.

As you know, parenthetically, I have always taken somewhat of a dim view of summitry when it comes in an unprepared form. But both sides will be well prepared, well in advance, on all points of major difference, and we will discuss any points of difference that could affect the peace of the world.

*   *   *

(b) Statement of September 16, 1971.[66]

(Excerpt)

*   *   *

THE PRESIDENT'S TRIP TO CHINA.

Q. A two-part question

THE PRESIDENT. Sure.

Q. Have you decided in your own mind when you are going to China; if not, why not? That's only the first half. Do you want to take that first?

---

[65] Cf. note 53, above.
[66] *Presidential Documents*, Sept. 20, 1971, pp. 1284-85.

THE PRESIDENT. No, no. I want to see what comes later.

Q. The second half is: Can you tell us your plan?

THE PRESIDENT. First, I am going to China.

Second, as far as the date of the trip is concerned, and the agenda, the arrangements, are concerned, all of those will be announced at an appropriate time.[67]

Beyond that, however, I do not think it would be helpful at this point to discuss the date that may be under consideration, the agenda that may be under consideration, and the rest. All I can say is that the plans for the trip are going forward on schedule, and you gentlemen will be the first to know.

Q. Mr. President, have you decided in your own mind when you are going?

THE PRESIDENT. That is a mutual decision, and we are working it out in a satisfactory way. In a case like this, where two governments are involved, one doesn't pick a date and another pick a date. It is not that kind of operation. It is going very well.

Q. Mr. President, on this China trip, Premier Chou En-lai has done quite a bit of talking since you announced your visit was going to take place, particularly in his interview with Mr. [James] Reston of the New York Times.[68] He was quite hard-line and quite firm on a lot of agenda issues or obvious issues that we all assume are going to come up.

I would like to ask you (a) to comment on the fact that he took a hard stand on a number of things, like two Chinas, like entrance into the U.N., like the U.S. commitment in Southeast Asia, your reaction to that hard line; and secondly, did he tell Mr. Reston anything that was a surprise or news to you?

THE PRESIDENT. No, there was nothing in the Reston piece that he had not already told Dr. Kissinger in much greater detail.

Second, for that reason we were not surprised at all at the Reston piece. I think one of the reasons that these talks may be productive is that Premier Chou En-lai, both publicly and privately, doesn't take the usual naive sentimental idea, and neither do I, that, well, if we just get to know each other all of our differences are going to evaporate.

He recognizes and I recognize that there are very great differences between the People's Republic and the United States of America. He recognizes and I recognize that at this point it might serve our mutual interest to discuss those differences.

I reiterate, however, as he has reiterated to us, both privately and then repeated in his interview with Mr. Reston in less detail, that while there are differences, that we must recognize that we have agreed to discuss the differences. That is all that has been agreed. There are no other conditions.

Now that, in my view, is the proper way to begin a conference between two countries that have not had any diplomatic relations.

*   *   *

(93) Preparations for the Visit, October–November 1971.

(a) The Second Kissinger Mission: Announcement Issued Simultaneously in Washington and Peking, October 27, 1971.[69]

(Complete Text)

Premier Chou En-lai and Dr. Henry Kissinger, President Nixon's Assistant for National Security Affairs, held talks in Peking from October 20th to 26th, 1971, in order to make concrete arrangements for President Nixon's visit to China. These arrangements are proceeding well.

It is expected that another announcement concerning President Nixon's visit will be issued in the near future.

(b) Fixing the Date: Joint Statement by the Two Governments, November 29, 1971.[70]

(Complete Text)

The Government of the People's Republic of China and the Government of the United States of America have agreed that President Nixon's visit to China shall begin on February 21, 1972.

(c) Some Further Details: Announcement by White House Press Secretary Ziegler, November 30, 1971.[71]

(Excerpt)

Yesterday in a simultaneous announcement made by the Government of the People's Republic of China and the United States we announced that it had been agreed that President Nixon would visit China beginning on February 21, 1972.

Today I will add a few details to the announcement, but first, I would like to say that Dr. Kissinger, who you have seen, is here to answer your

[69] *Presidential Documents*, Nov. 1, 1971, p. 1453.
[70] Same, Dec. 6, 1971, p. 1580.
[71] Same, p. 1582.

questions today on the President's trip to China,[72] any questions you may have on the meetings the President will hold with the allied leaders which we have announced,[73] prior to his trip to China and to Moscow.

Also, Henry has agreed today to take other questions you may have on the foreign policy subjects. What Dr. Kissinger says will be on the record.

First, the President's trip to China will last 7 days. The President will arrive in Peking on February 21st and leave on February 28th. At the invitation of the Government of the People's Republic of China, Mrs. Nixon will accompany the President on his trip to China.

In addition to Peking, the Government of the People's Republic of China has invited the President to visit Hangchow and Shanghai. Hangchow is about 100 miles south of Shanghai. Most of President Nixon's time in China will be spent in Peking, and the major portion of the President's time will be devoted to conversations with leaders of the People's Republic of China.

President Nixon plans to go directly to and from the People's Republic of China, using American territory for any refueling or rest stops.

And of course, Secretary Rogers and Dr. Kissinger will be accompanying the President. As we have said before, President Nixon will be traveling with a small working group.

*   *   *

(94) Purposes of the Visit: News Conference Statement by Dr. Henry A. Kissinger, Assistant to the President for National Security Affairs, November 30, 1971.[74]

(Excerpt)

*   *   *

Q. Yesterday, Mr. Ziegler, in describing the purpose of the trip,[75] said it was to bring about a new direction in policy and secondary, to

---

[72] Cf. Document 94.

[73] Cf. Documents 43-45.

[74] *Presidential Documents*, Dec. 6, 1971, pp. 1585-86.

[75] Cf. Document 93c. Mr. Ziegler's additional remarks read in part as follows: "As the President has pointed out . . . we shall try in the meetings with the leaders of the People's Republic of China to seek a new direction in our relationship between our two countries and to end the isolation of our two great peoples from each other." (*Presidential Documents*, Dec. 6, 1971, p. 1580.)

end isolation of the two great people—

DR. KISSINGER. From each other.

Q. —from each other. Can you elaborate a little more on that, how you expect to end that isolation? Is this going to mean the opening of more communication, more travel, more trade?

DR. KISSINGER. One of the remarkable aspects of this opening towards China was the difficulty of establishing even rudimentary communication with a country from which one has been cut off for nearly 25 years.

A good part of the first year of this effort which, as you know, started in 1969, was simply to find out how to communicate and with whom to communicate in a reliable way. Our two countries have been cut off from each other, not just in formal diplomatic contact but in all other contacts—cultural, journalistic, academic, and so forth.

Now the minimum we expect to get out of this trip is a better understanding by both sides of each other's positions and a continuing means of remaining informed about these positions, so that one is not so dependent on these very dramatic setpiece encounters.

Secondly, we hope that out of this visit could grow at least a beginning of some exchanges in other than political fields that would permit the two peoples to get to know each other better.

Again, we are not sentimental about this. We recognize that the People's Republic is led by highly principled men whose principles are diametrically opposed to ours. But whatever their purposes, it is in our mutual interest that we understand what we are about; that on those matters that are in our common interest we know how to cooperate; and that on those matters that are not ideologically controversial in the cultural and intellectual field, we can find cooperative means of effort.

This is what the phrase meant.

You did not quote our Press Secretary correctly, and he chooses his words with the greatest care, and he said, "A new direction in our relationship between our two countries," and there was a nuance there somebody missed. [*Laughter*]

Let me make one other general point, and then we will go to this question over there, and to any other questions you may have on the other meetings or on other problems.

The summit in Peking is different from the summit in Moscow.[76] With the Soviet Union we have had diplomatic relations now for nearly 40 years. We have had intense diplomatic exchanges for at least since the Geneva Summit of 1955.[77] We have well-established diplomatic means of communication that function rapidly and, therefore, with the Soviet Union, we have a series of concrete problems that we are attempting to move more rapidly towards a solution or which we are

---

[76] Cf. Document 29.

[77] *Documents, 1955*, pp. 182-232.

attempting to culminate at the summit.

With respect to Peking, we are at the very beginning of a process. We do not impinge on each other as countries on a global basis the way we do with the Soviet Union.

What we are attempting to do with respect to the People's Republic— and I believe they with us—is to set a general philosophical direction or a general direction for the future evolution of our policy and, therefore, you cannot look in Peking to the same type of concreteness that you can in Moscow.

*   *   *

D. The United States and Japan.

[Japanese remember 1971 as the year of the so-called "Nixon shocks" that sent relations with the United States into a tailspin within weeks of an auspicious takeoff marked by final settlement of the decades-old Okinawa problem (Documents 95-96). The "new era" in Japanese-American relations that was supposed to succeed the postwar victor-vanquished relationship was inaugurated by a pair of disagreeable surprises which, President Nixon later wrote, brought both sides "a sharp awareness of the divergence of some of our interests—and in its wake, a better understanding of the need for the mature and equitable management of those divergences."[78]

The change in American policy toward China, reflected in the July 15 announcement of the President's intended visit (Document 85), inevitably proved peculiarly disturbing to a country whose own desire to normalize relations with Peking had been held in check largely out of deference to American wishes. The subsequent suspension of dollar convertibility, the accompanying surcharge on U.S. import duties, and the mounting American pressure for a revaluation of the yen and a revision of Japanese commercial policy admittedly "placed the Japanese Government in a difficult position," even if, in President Nixon's judgment, they constituted "a necessary step in the transformation of our relationship to the more mature and reciprocal partnership required in the 1970's."[79] The impact of these American measures can be judged from the comments of U. Alexis Johnson, Under Secretary of State for Political Affairs and himself a former Ambassador to Japan, at a period midway between the shocks of the summer and the year-end currency realignments that were to provide a basis for restored amity (Document 97).]

[78] Nixon Report, 1972, p. 52.
[79] Same, p. 58.

1. The Okinawa Reversion Agreement.

[The agreement to return to Japanese administration the U.S.-occupied Ryukyu and Daito Islands, including Okinawa with its American military bases, completed the process of "normalization" of the American-Japanese relationship that had begun with the signature of the San Francisco Peace Treaty of 1951. In conformity with Article 3 of that treaty,[80] the Ryukyus and the Daito Islands to the east had continued under U.S. administration and jurisdiction, although the United States recognized Japan's "residual sovereignty"[81] and had gradually come to envisage the eventual return of the islands to Japanese administration under conditions compatible with joint security interests.

A formula for the elimination of what was becoming a serious irritant in U.S.-Japanese relations was worked out by President Nixon and Prime Minister Eisaku Sato at a Washington meeting in November 1969. On that occasion, the two leaders reached general agreement that (1) the Japan-U.S. Mutual Security Treaty of 1960[82] would be kept in force; (2) administrative rights over Okinawa would be returned to Japan during 1972; (3) the United States would retain military facilities and areas in Okinawa under the same conditions as in Japan proper; (4) Japan's remaining restrictions on foreign trade and capital investment would be reduced at an accelerated rate; and (5) Japan's aid programs in Asia would be expanded and improved.[83]

Negotiations pursuant to the Nixon-Sato understanding began in Tokyo in March 1970 and culminated in the agreement and related documents signed in the two capitals on June 17, 1971 (Document 95). In essence, the agreement provided that Japan would assume full responsibility and authority over the islands, but would permit continued American use of designated "facilities and areas" in conformity with the 1960 Security Treaty. This meant, in effect, that American use of the retained facilities and areas would be subject to the same restrictions already applicable to U.S. military installations in Japan proper, which were commonly understood to preclude the introduction of nuclear weapons without Japanese consent or the redeployment of troops for combat purposes without prior consultation.[84] The agreement was to enter into force two months after the exchange of ratifications.

Advice and consent to ratification by the United States was requested by President Nixon in a message to the Senate on September 21 (Docu-

---

[80] *Documents, 1951*, p. 471.
[81] Same, p. 470.
[82] Same, *1960*, pp. 425-28.
[83] Joint statement, Nov. 21, 1969, in *Documents, 1968-69*, pp. 336-41.
[84] For the origin of these restrictions cf. *Documents, 1960*, p. 429 and *The United States in World Affairs, 1960*, pp. 268-69.

ment 96), and was accorded by a Senate vote of 84 to 6 on November 10, 1971. In Japan, the agreement encountered considerable leftist opposition but was approved by the Lower House of the Diet (over a Socialist–Communist boycott) on November 24 and by the Upper House on December 23, 1971. Implementing legislation was completed by the Diet on December 30, 1971, and the agreement was formally ratified by the United States on January 28 and by Japan on March 10, 1972. Ratifications were exchanged in Tokyo on March 15, 1972, and the agreement entered into force May 15, 1972 (Tokyo time),[85] the Ryukyus being incorporated into the Japanese administrative structure as the country's 47th prefecture.]

(95) Agreement Between the United States of America and Japan Concerning the Ryukyu Islands and the Daito Islands, Signed at Washington and Tokyo June 17, 1971.[86]

(Excerpt)

The United States of America and Japan,

Noting that the President of the United States of America and the Prime Minister of Japan reviewed together on November 19, 20 and 21, 1969 the status of the Ryukyu Islands and the Daito Islands, referred to as "Okinawa" in the Joint Communique between the President and the Prime Minister issued on November 21, 1969,[87] and agreed that the Government of the United States of America and the Government of Japan should enter immediately into consultations regarding the specific arrangements for accomplishing the early reversion of these islands to Japan;

Noting that the two Governments have conducted such consultations and have reaffirmed that the reversion of these islands to Japan be carried out on the basis of the said Joint Communique;

Considering that the United States of America desires, with respect to the Ryukyu Islands and the Daito Islands, to relinquish in favor of Japan all rights and interests under Article 3 of the Treaty of Peace with Japan signed at the city of San Francisco on September 8, 1951,[88] and thereby to have relinquished all its rights and interests in all territories under the said Article; and

Considering further that Japan is willing to assume full responsibility

---

[85] *Bulletin*, June 12, 1972, pp. 809-10.
[86] TIAS 7314; 23 UST 447. Printed here is the full text of the agreement minus the Agreed Minutes and related documents, which are described in a special note at the end of the text. For official commentary on the signature see *Bulletin*, July 12, 1971, pp. 33-35.
[87] *Documents, 1968-69*, pp. 336-41.
[88] Same, *1951*, pp. 470-79.

and authority for the exercise of all powers of administration, legislation and jurisdiction over the territory and inhabitants of the Ryukyu Islands and the Daito Islands;

Therefore, have agreed as follows:

ARTICLE I

1. With respect to the Ryukyu Islands and the Daito Islands, as defined in paragraph 2 below, the United States of America relinquishes in favor of Japan all rights and interests under Article 3 of the Treaty of Peace with Japan signed at the city of San Francisco on September 8, 1951, effective as of the date of entry into force of this Agreement. Japan, as of such date, assumes full responsibility and authority for the exercise of all and any powers of administration, legislation and jurisdiction over the territory and inhabitants of the said islands.

2. For the purpose of this Agreement, the term "the Ryukyu Islands and the Daito Islands" means all the territories and their territorial waters with respect to which the right to exercise all and any powers of administration, legislation and jurisdiction was accorded to the United States of America under Article 3 of the Treaty of Peace with Japan other than those with respect to which such right has already been returned to Japan in accordance with the Agreement concerning the Amami Islands[89] and the Agreement concerning Nanpo Shoto and Other Islands[90] signed between the United States of America and Japan, respectively on December 24, 1953 and April 5, 1968.

ARTICLE II

It is confirmed that treaties, conventions and other agreements concluded between the United States of America and Japan, including, but without limitation, the Treaty of Mutual Cooperation and Security between the United States of America and Japan signed at Washington on January 19, 1960 and its related arrangements[91] and the Treaty of Friendship, Commerce and Navigation between the United States of America and Japan signed at Tokyo on April 2, 1953,[92] become applicable to the Ryukyu Islands and the Daito Islands as of the date of entry into force of this Agreement.

ARTICLE III

1. Japan will grant the United States of America on the date of entry

[89] TIAS 2895; 4 UST 2912; cf. *The United States in World Affairs, 1953*, p. 266.
[90] TIAS 6495; 19 UST 4895; cf. *Bulletin*, Apr. 29, 1968, pp. 570-71.
[91] TIAS 4509; 11 UST 1632; text in *Documents, 1960*, pp. 416-31.
[92] TIAS 2863; 4 UST 2063.

into force of this Agreement the use of facilities and areas in the Ryukyu Islands and the Daito Islands in accordance with the Treaty of Mutual Cooperation and Security between the United States of America and Japan signed at Washington on January 19, 1960 and its related arrangements.

2. In the application of Article IV of the Agreement under Article VI of the Treaty of Mutual Cooperation and Security between the United States of America and Japan, regarding Facilities and Areas and the Status of United States Armed Forces in Japan signed on January 19, 1960,[93] to the facilities and areas the use of which will be granted in accordance with paragraph 1 above to the United States of America on the date of entry into force of this Agreement, it is understood that the phrase "the conditions in which they were at the time they became available to the United States armed forces" in paragraph 1 of the said Article IV refers to the condition in which the facilities and areas first came into the use of the United States armed forces, and that the term "improvements" in paragraph 2 of the said Article includes those made prior to the date of entry into force of this Agreement.

ARTICLE IV

1. Japan waives all claims of Japan and its nationals against the United States of America and its nationals and against the local authorities of the Ryukyu Islands and the Daito Islands, arising from the presence, operations or actions of forces or authorities of the United States of America in these islands, or from the presence, operations or actions of forces or authorities of the United States of America having had any effect upon these islands, prior to the date of entry into force of this Agreement.

2. The waiver in paragraph 1 above does not, however, include claims of Japanese nationals specifically recognized in the laws of the United States of America or the local laws of these islands applicable during the period of United States administration of these islands. The Government of the United States of America is authorized to maintain its duly empowered officials in the Ryukyu Islands and the Daito Islands in order to deal with and settle such claims on and after the date of entry into force of this Agreement in accordance with the procedures to be established in consultation with the Government of Japan.

3. The Government of the United States of America will make ex gratia contributions for restoration of lands to the nationals of Japan whose lands in the Ryukyu Islands and the Daito Islands were damaged prior to July 1, 1950, while placed under the use of United States authorities, and were released from their use after June 30, 1961 and before the date of entry into force of this Agreement. Such contributions will be made in an equitable manner in relation to the pay-

[93] TIAS 4510; 11 UST 1652.

ments made under High Commissioner Ordinance Number 60 of 1967 to claims for damages done prior to July 1, 1950 to the lands released prior to July 1, 1961.

4. Japan recognizes the validity of all acts and omissions done during the period of United States administration of the Ryukyu Islands and the Daito Islands under or in consequence of directives of the United States or local authorities, or authorized by existing law during that period, and will take no action subjecting United States nationals or the residents of these islands to civil or criminal liability arising out of such acts or omissions.

ARTICLE V

1. Japan recognizes the validity of, and will continue in full force and effect, final judgments in civil cases rendered by any court in the Ryukyu Islands and the Daito Islands prior to the date of entry into force of this Agreement, provided that such recognition or continuation would not be contrary to public policy.

2. Without in any way adversely affecting the substantive rights and positions of the litigants concerned, Japan will assume jurisdiction over and continue to judgment and execution any civil cases pending as of the date of entry into force of this Agreement in any court in the Ryukyu Islands and the Daito Islands.

3. Without in any way adversely affecting the substantive rights of the accused or suspect concerned, Japan will assume jurisdiction over, and may continue or institute proceedings with respect to, any criminal cases with which any court in the Ryukyu Islands and the Daito Islands is seized as of the date of entry into force of this Agreement or would have been seized had the proceedings been instituted prior to such date.

4. Japan may continue the execution of any final judgments rendered in criminal cases by any court in the Ryukyu Islands and the Daito Islands.

ARTICLE VI

1. The properties of the Ryukyu Electric Power Corporation, the Ryukyu Domestic Water Corporation and the Ryukyu Development Loan Corporation shall be transferred to the Government of Japan on the date of entry into force of this Agreement, and the rights and obligations of the said Corporations shall be assumed by the Government of Japan on that date in conformity with the laws and regulations of Japan.

2. All other properties of the Government of the United States of America, existing in the Ryukyu Islands and the Daito Islands as of the date of entry into force of this Agreement and located outside the

facilities and areas provided on that date in accordance with Article III of this Agreement, shall be transferred to the Government of Japan on that date, except for those that are located on the lands returned to the landowners concerned before the date of entry into force of this Agreement and for those the title to which will be retained by the Government of the United States of America after that date with the consent of the Government of Japan.

3. Such lands in the Ryukyu Islands and the Daito Islands reclaimed by the Government of the United States of America and such other reclaimed lands acquired by it in these islands as are held by the Government of the United States of America as of the date of entry into force of this Agreement become the property of the Government of Japan on that date.

4. The United States of America is not obliged to compensate Japan or its nationals for any alteration made prior to the date of entry into force of this Agreement to the lands upon which the properties transferred to the Government of Japan under paragraphs 1 and 2 above are located.

ARTICLE VII

Considering, inter alia, that United States assets are being transferred to the Government of Japan under Article VI of this Agreement, that the Government of the United States of America is carrying out the return of the Ryukyu Islands and the Daito Islands to Japan in a manner consistent with the policy of the Government of Japan as specified in paragraph 8 of the Joint Communique of November 21, 1969, and that the Government of the United States of America will bear extra costs, particularly in the area of employment after reversion, the Government of Japan will pay to the Government of the United States of America in United States dollars a total amount of three hundred and twenty million United States dollars (U.S. $320,000,000) over a period of five years from the date of entry into force of this Agreement. Of the said amount, the Government of Japan will pay one hundred million United States dollars(U.S. $100,000,000) within one week after the date of entry into force of this Agreement and the remainder in four equal annual installments in June of each calendar year subsequent to the year in which this Agreement enters into force.

ARTICLE VIII

The Government of Japan consents to the continued operation by the Government of the United States of America of the Voice of America relay station on Okinawa Island for a period of five years from the date of entry into force of this Agreement in accordance with the arrangements to be concluded between the two Governments. The two Governments shall enter into consultation two years after the date of entry into force of this Agreement on future operation of the Voice of America on Okinawa Island.

ARTICLE IX

This Agreement shall be ratified and the instruments of ratification shall be exchanged at Tokyo. This Agreement shall enter into force two months after the date of exchange of the instruments of ratification.[94]

IN WITNESS WHEREOF, the undersigned, being duly authorized by their respective Governments, have signed this Agreement.

DONE at Washington and Tokyo, this seventeenth day of June, 1971, in duplicate in the English and Japanese languages, both equally authentic.

For the United States of America: For Japan:

(Signed) William P. Rogers   (Signed) Kiichi Aichi
     [Secretary of State]   [Minister of Foreign Affairs]

[Note: Appended to the official text of the agreement are the following related documents, signed in Tokyo on June 17, 1971, unless otherwise noted:

Agreed Minutes recording certain understandings with regard to definition of territories, claims procedures, jurisdictional matters, transfer of properties, severance pay of Japanese employees, and termination of Voice of America operations.[95]
Memorandum of Understanding listing 88 installations and sites to be retained by the United States and 12 facilities and areas and 34 installations and sites to be returned to Japan.[96]
Exchange of Notes detailing facilities and operations of the Voice of America relay station.[97]
Exchange of Notes concerning disposition of reclaimed lands in the military port of Naha.[98]
Letter from Japanese Foreign Minister Kiichi Aichi to U.S. Ambas-

[94] Cf. above at note 85.
[95] TIAS 7314; 23 UST 475-81.
[96] Same, pp. 493-509.
[97] Same, pp. 536-38.
[98] Same, pp. 538 and 541.

sador Armin H. Meyer defining Japanese policies concerning treatment of foreign nationals and firms in Okinawa after reversion.[99]

Memorandum of Understanding regarding air services to and through Okinawa by U.S. airlines.[100]

Arrangement between the Japan Defense Agency and the U.S. Department of Defense concerning the assumption by Japan of the responsibility for the immediate defense of Okinawa following its reversion to Japan (signed in Tokyo June 29, 1971).[101]]

(96) Request for Advice and Consent to Ratification: Message from President Nixon to the Senate, September 21, 1971.[102]

(Complete Text)

To the Senate of the United States:

I am transmitting for the Senate's advice and consent to ratification the Agreement between the United States of America and Japan concerning the Ryukyu Islands and the Daito Islands, signed at Washington and Tokyo on June 17, 1971.[103] The Agreement was negotiated in accordance with the understandings I reached with Prime Minister [Eisaku] Sato during my meetings with him in November 1969.[104]

I transmit also, for the information of the Senate, the following related documents:[105]

Agreed Minutes,
Memorandum of Understanding concerning Article III,
Exchange of notes concerning the Voice of America facility in Okinawa,
Exchange of notes concerning submerged lands,
Letter from Minister for Foreign Affairs Kiichi Aichi to Ambassador Meyer concerning treatment of foreign nationals and firms,
Memorandum of Understanding on air services to and through Okinawa;
and the Arrangement concerning Assumption by Japan of the Responsibility for the Immediate Defense of Okinawa.

---

[99] Same, pp. 554-63.
[100] Same, pp. 564-65.
[101] Same, pp. 570-74.
[102] *Presidential Documents*, Sept. 27, 1971, pp. 1305-7.
[103] Document 95.
[104] *Documents, 1968-69*, pp. 336-41.
[105] See note following Document 95.

The enclosed report from the Secretary of State[106] describes the Agreement and the related documents.

When Prime Minister Sato arrived in Washington on November 19, 1969, I observed that "whether peace survives in the last third of the century will depend more on what happens in the Pacific than in any other area of the world."[107] I took that particular occasion to emphasize this fact to the American people and to the world because of my strong feelings then, as now, that Japan, as one of the major powers in the Pacific area, will play a central role in determining what happens in that vital region.

Japan's phenomenal economic growth represents a most significant development for us and for the other nations of the Pacific. Japan is now the third largest producer in the world and has developed with us the greatest transoceanic commerce in the history of mankind. The potential for cooperation between our two economies, the world's most productive and the world's most dynamic, is clearly immense. For this among other reasons, Japan and the United States have a strong mutual interest in the peace and security of the Pacific area. This interest is recognized in our Treaty of Mutual Cooperation and Security,[108] which both our countries recognize as a keystone of our security relationships in that part of the world. I think all Americans also realize that a close and friendly relationship between Japan and the United States is vital to building the peaceful and progressive world both of us want for all mankind. The problems involved in strengthening the fabric of peace in Asia and the Pacific will undoubtedly be challenging. But if Japan and the United States go separate ways, then this task would be incomparably more difficult. Whatever differences may arise between our nations on specific policy questions, it is essential that the basic nature of our relationship remain close and cordial.

When Prime Minister Sato came to Washington in 1969, there was still one great unsettled issue between the United States and Japan arising out of World War II: the Okinawan question. Almost one million Japanese on Okinawa were still living under foreign administration nearly 25 years after the end of the Second World War. This situation subjected the entire relationship with our major Asian ally to strain. It was clear that our continued administration of Okinawa was incompatible with the mature relationship which both we and Japan recognized as the only possible basis for lasting cooperation between nations, especially between two great world powers such as the United States and Japan.

[106] S. Ex. J, 92d Cong., 1st sess.; also in *Bulletin*, Oct. 18, 1971, pp. 433-35. For a statement by Secretary Rogers to the Senate Foreign Relations Committee on Oct. 27, 1971, see *Bulletin*, Nov. 15, 1971, pp. 565-68.
[107] *Presidential Papers (Nixon), 1969*, p. 946.
[108] Same as note 91.

The Prime Minister and I therefore agreed that our two Governments would immediately enter into consultations concerning specific arrangements for accomplishing the early reversion of Okinawa to Japan. We determined that it was essential for this to be done without detriment to the security of the Far East, including Japan. We further agreed that the consultations should be concluded as quickly as possible with a view to accomplishing the reversion during 1972, provided that agreement could be reached on the terms and conditions of the reversion and that the necessary legislative support in both countries could be secured.

In undertaking these negotiations, the United States recognized, as a matter of basic principle, that it was consistent with neither our national character nor our national interest to continue to administer a territory which has been historically connected with Japan and whose people desire to rejoin their mother country. Japan recognized that the presence of United States forces in the Far East constituted a mainstay for the stability of the area, and that the security of countries in the Far East was a matter of serious concern for Japan. More specifically, Japan recognized that United States forces in Okinawa played a vital role in the present situation in the Far East and agreed that the United States would retain, under the terms of the Treaty of Mutual Cooperation and Security, such military facilities and areas in Okinawa as required in the mutual security of both countries.

After intensive negotiations, agreement was reached on the terms and conditions for reversion and the Agreement which I now commend to the Senate was signed on June 17, 1971.

This Agreement is founded upon the common security interests which are reflected in the United States-Japan Treaty of Mutual Cooperation and Security signed in 1960 and in the Communique which Prime Minister Sato and I jointly issued on November 21, 1969. The Agreement stipulates that, even after reversion, the Mutual Security Treaty and related arrangements, such as the Status of Forces Agreement of 1960,[109] will apply to Okinawa without modification. The same will be true of the Treaty of Friendship, Commerce and Navigation, signed in 1953.[110]

The new Agreement provides that after reversion Japan will grant the United States the use of facilities and areas in the Ryukyus in accordance with the Mutual Security Treaty of 1960 and its related arrangements, such as the Status of Forces Agreement. This means that the United States will continue to have the use of bases in Okinawa necessary for carrying out our mutual security commitments to Japan and for maintaining peace in the Far East. Under this Agreement, these facilities will be provided to us on the same terms as those now available to us in Japan.[111] After reversion, a sovereign friendly government

[109] Same as note 93.
[110] Same as note 92.
[111] Cf. above at note 84.

will give us permission to maintain these facilities in the Ryukyus, as in Japan, in recognition of mutual security interests. This is the only sound basis for long-term cooperation and I am convinced that it will enable us effectively to protect our own security interests.

The Agreement and related arrangements also deal with other important matters. They provide for appropriate payment to the United States for assets to be transferred to the Government of Japan and for certain costs which will be involved in connection with reversion. They provide protection for United States business and professional interests in Okinawa after reversion. They transfer to Japan responsibility for the immediate defense of the Ryukyus, which will result in substantial savings for the United States, in terms of both budget and foreign exchange.

In summary, then, I am strongly convinced that this Agreement is in the best interests of both countries. It meets United States security needs and it places our relationship with our major Asian ally on a more sound and enduring basis. It fulfills long-held aspirations of the Japanese people, including the people of Okinawa, for the reunification of these islands with Japan.

I believe the return of Okinawa to Japanese administration will be one of the most important accomplishments of our postwar policy in the Far East. It should enhance the prospects for peace and stability in that area, and it is essential to the continuation of friendly and productive relations between the United States and Japan. I therefore urge that the Senate give its early and favorable consideration to this Agreement so that reversion can take place during 1972.[112]

RICHARD NIXON

The White House
September 21, 1971

2. A "New Era" in United States-Japanese Relations.

[Such complacency as might have flowed from the completion of the Okinawa agreement (Document 95) was roughly shattered by the events of July and August with regard to China policy and international economic affairs.[113] The wounds to Japanese *amour-propre* could not be fully assuaged by President Nixon's subsequent journey to Anchorage, Alaska, for a brief meeting with Europe-bound Emperor Hirohito on September 26.[114] Japanese-American economic relations remained a subject of particular sensitivity in view of the unprecedented volume of the two countries' bilateral trade, aggregating over $10 billion in 1970, and a persistent Japanese surplus in trade with the United States which had exceeded $2 billion in 1969 and 1970 and was heading for

112 Cf. above at note 85.
113 Cf. above at notes 78 and 79.
114 *Public Papers, 1971*, pp. 1005-7.

over \$4 billion in 1971. The mutual dissatisfaction of the two govern-ments in regard to numerous trade and monetary matters was voiced with unusual candor at the eighth cabinet-level meeting of the Joint Japan–United States Committee on Trade and Economic Affairs, held in Washington on September 9-10, 1971;[115] and Japanese irritation was maintained at white heat thereafter by U.S. pressure to limit Japanese exports of man-made and woolen textiles to the United States and to revalue the yen in the interest of reducing or eliminating the trade surplus. Although Japan reluctantly agreed on October 15 to a three-year limitation on certain textile exports,[116] it was not until Decem-ber 18 that it acceded to the larger U.S. objective by accepting a 16.88 percent increase in the exchange value of the yen (from 360 to 308 to the dollar) as part of the Smithsonian Agreement on international exchange rates (Document 150).

The following address by Under Secretary of State Johnson (Docu-ment 97) affords an insight into the strains that continued to affect the two countries' relations, notwithstanding Japan's somewhat unenthusi-astic support of the U.S. position in the debate on Chinese representa-tion in the United Nations (Documents 122-126). Prospects for a further clearing of the political atmosphere thus remained in abeyance pending the new meeting between President Nixon and Prime Minister Sato that was scheduled to take place in San Clemente, California, on January 6-7, 1972.[117]]

(97) "Trends in United States–Japan Relations": Address by U. Alexis Johnson, Under Secretary of State for Political Affairs, Before the International Business Outlook Conference, Los Angeles, October 18, 1971.[118]

(Complete Text)

I am very pleased to be here with you today in Los Angeles and am particularly pleased to share with you a few thoughts on U.S.-Japan relations—a subject close to my heart both professionally and person-ally. The title you have suggested for my talk, "Trends in United States-

---

[115] *Bulletin*, Oct. 4, 1971, pp. 346-54.

[116] A memorandum of understanding providing for a three-year limitation on Japanese man-made fiber and wool textile exports to the United States was signed in Tokyo on Oct. 15, 1971 (*Presidential Documents*, Oct. 18, 1971, pp. 1408-9). A formal agreement, retroactive to Oct. 1, 1971, was effected by an exchange of notes in Washington on Jan. 3, 1972 (*Bulletin*, Jan. 31, 1972, p. 140; *New York Times*, Jan. 4, 1972).

[117] *Presidential Documents*, Nov. 29, 1971, p. 1565. For the Nixon–Sato meeting see *A.F.R., 1972*, no. 62.

[118] *Bulletin*, Nov. 8, 1971, pp. 513-17.

Japan Relations," is very timely. Some of the issues and frictions in the relations between our two countries which have arisen lately have tended to be overemphasized in the public media, as compared with those many broad areas, including the U.N., where we are working closely and effectively together. But it is clear that we stand at an important crossroads in U.S.-Japan relations.

Profound changes have been set in motion within Japan as a result of its phenomenal economic achievements. This has also resulted in changing attitudes in this country. We have both entered into a period of transition.

For most of the postwar period the United States and Japan have enjoyed remarkably harmonious relations. Indeed, what some have termed a kind of big brother-little brother relationship grew up. Japan concentrated on economic recovery while leaving the major responsibility for its defense to the United States. This arrangement was not as one-sided or altruistic as it may appear at first glance. It helped us as well as Japan. On our part we felt that an economically prosperous and politically stable Japan with defense ties with us would well serve our interests. The people and leaders of Japan obviously felt it would also be in the interests of Japan, and I think that most people in both countries agreed.

In pursuance of this policy, we concluded a Treaty of Peace[119] and a Security Treaty[120] with Japan in 1951. In 1960 we placed the Security Treaty on a more equitable basis,[121] and last year it made a smooth transition into a so-called automatic extension phase;[122] that is, the treaty continues in effect indefinitely unless renounced by either party.

In those early years we also adopted policies to help strengthen the Japanese economy. To stimulate Japanese production, conserve scarce foreign exchange, and safeguard its balance of payments position we condoned, and in some cases even fostered, economic policies in Japan providing for strict controls over trade and capital flows.

These policies had their intended effect. With the election of Prime Minister [Shigeru] Yoshida in 1949 the mainstream of Japanese leadership down to the present Prime Minister has made close political and economic association with the United States the fundamental tenet of Japan's foreign and domestic policies. As you know, powerful segments in Japanese society often have pressed, sometimes violently, for dissolution of the U.S.-Japan alliance and for a more "independent" foreign policy. Yet the consensus among Japan's ruling elements, and indeed the majority of the populace, has favored alignment with the United States. Public opinion polls have consistently placed the United States first or second among "most liked" nations.

119 *Documents, 1951*, pp. 470-79.
120 Same, pp. 266-67.
121 Same as note 91.
122 *Documents, 1970*, pp. 217-19.

CHANGES IN IMAGE OF JAPAN

In the midsixties, Japan's spectacular economic success began to change both Japan's self-image and the context in which her international economic and political relations were conducted. Public rhetoric, especially after the widely acclaimed 1964 Olympics in Tokyo, moved perceptibly from habitual self-deprecation to pride in national achievements. The rhetoric increasingly included calls for a larger international political role for Japan more commensurate with her newly acquired economic status. Although this role tended to be vaguely defined in terms of greater independence from the United States, few in Japan seemed to have any clear idea of just what this more independent stance would entail.

Similarly, the cultural pendulum swung toward a resurgence of interest in things Japanese after the long period of intense foreign influence. The movement, however, centered characteristically on esthetics, morals, and styles—not political systems. (No evidence has appeared of a popular desire to return to a prewar-style authoritarian government.) Nevertheless, there has been a lag in Japanese understanding of its new position in the world, for many Japanese still tend to think in the same terms as when Japan was a weak economy seeking to recover from the ravages of war.

During approximately this same period of the mid-1960's, the Japanese image in the United States also began to change. To many Americans, Japan appeared to have been transformed from a small and picturesque island to a theatening economic juggernaut. Somehow the Japanese of the Geisha, flower arrangement, and tea ceremony suddenly became 10 feet tall, their economy spewing out goods at an ever-faster rate, their traders single-mindedly engaging in ruthless, not to say unfair, competition—in our own and foreign markets—in such a manner as to threaten our own economy.

Thus, a gap opened in our mutual perceptions of each other—Japanese still tending to think of themselves as a poor and weak country entitled to special treatment from the big and powerful United States, while many here tended to regard Japan as an economic giant against which we had to defend ourselves. The truth obviously lies in between these two extremes. The fact is that Japan is now the second economic power in the free world and must expect to treat and be treated on a basis of equality by the United States, the first economic power. It is my own feeling that our interests in every field, including the economic, coincide to a remarkable degree and that we must not let this gap in our mutual conceptions of each other lead to basic misunderstandings.

For our part, we are seeking to treat Japan on a basis of equality, and it was in part in pursuance of this policy we have signed a treaty to return Okinawa to Japan in 1972[123]—the last piece of Japanese real estate under U.S. administration as a result of World War II. Senate hearings on the ratification of this agreement are scheduled next week.[124]

In turn, in the Nixon-Sato communique of November 1969[125] announcing the opening of negotiations for the return of Okinawa, Japan took cognizance of its vital stake in regional security and agreed to the continued presence of U.S. forces on Okinawa after reversion— subject, of course, to the same provisions that apply to our forces on the home islands.

The understandings embodied in that communique reassured the Japanese people of United States reasonableness and basic friendship and effectively defused a potentially explosive issue ready to be exploited by groups in Japan hostile to the relationship with the United States. It was in large measure due to this wise and statesmanlike agreement that the Mutual Security Treaty continued in effect so smoothly. It was also due in part to the great popularity this historic document enjoyed in Japan that the ruling Liberal Democratic Party achieved an overwhelming victory in the general elections in December 1969, garnering more than 300 of the 467 seats in the lower House of the Diet. Thus, our political and security relationship continues to be soundly based.

POLICIES IN ECONOMIC AREA

It is the economic area to which both countries need to pay increasing attention, for unless this area is properly handled the consequences will be reflected in the political and security areas. A part of the problem is that the growth of the Japanese economy has been so fast. Over the past 10 years, Japan has tripled its GNP [Gross National Product], quadrupled its exports, and tripled its foreign exchange reserves. Its balance of trade shifted firmly from a tenuous deficit to a sustained surplus. That Japan ranks third in the world in GNP is well known. What is less well known is that per capita income now approaches that of the United Kingdom. Our total trade with Japan is now greater than with any country except Canada.

Yet Japan has been slow to change those policies which were appropriate to its previous status of a weak and developing nation. I have often said to my Japanese friends that it seems to me that policies of economic nationalism are no longer compatible with Japan's interests, for such policies can only result in other countries adopting similar policies directed against Japan.

123 Document 95.
124 Cf. note 106, above.
125 *Documents, 1968-69*, pp. 336-41.

In turn, we must be prepared to treat Japan with that consideration and respect that is appropriate to its status as a great power. We ask Japan for equality of treatment of our economic interests, and in turn, we must be prepared to accord equality of treatment to Japan.

Americans obviously like the price and quality of many Japanese products, for when given the opportunity they buy them at a high rate. This is good, for the American consumer is obtaining something he needs and wants. However, the speed and growth of Japanese exports to this country have created two problems. First, the development has in some areas taken place too fast for the American enterprises concerned to make the necessary adjustments without severe dislocations not only to earnings but also to labor. Secondly, there has not been a corresponding growth in American exports to Japan, so that there has been a massive increase in our adverse balance of payments with Japan.

It was due to the recognition by both countries of the first problem that last Friday we entered into an agreement on textiles.[126] It is in recognition of the second problem that Japan has permitted a limited float of the yen, and the two governments are continuing to discuss not only monetary adjustments but also how the Japanese market can be further opened to American goods and investment. We want to solve these problems not by decreasing trade but rather by increasing trade in a manner that is healthy and sound for all parties.

NEW INTERNATIONAL ENVIRONMENT IN EAST ASIA

Dramatic changes in the East Asian international environment are also underway and will, of course, profoundly affect U.S.-Japan bilateral relations. The Nixon doctrine calls for a lower United States profile in Asia and assumes that regional powers will tackle their own problems without extensive United States involvement.[127] The Sino-Soviet split continues to interject new elements in regional affairs. Intensely nationalistic governments among the smaller countries of the region seem to have emerged from the early confusion of the post-colonial period and are acquiring greater maturity and sophistication in their dealings with the major powers. The People's Republic of China has now been responsive to our overtures to establish better communication between us, and as you know, President Nixon will be visiting Peking.[128] In short, a complicated multinational system is taking shape in East Asia, to which many of the old cliches are not applicable.

President Nixon's announced trips to Peking and Moscow[129] and the bold steps he took in the economic sphere have been called by the Japanese press "Nixon shocks." I personally, however, find it difficult to understand why any in Japan would object to steps designed to

126 Cf. note 116, above.
127 Cf. Document 82.
128 Cf. Documents 91-92.
129 Document 29.

lessen the tensions in Asia and diminish the chances of an outbreak of armed conflict. Similarly, the steps we have taken to strengthen our economy and the international monetary and trading system[130] would seem to me to be in Japan's own interest. On this latter subject I note to my Japanese friends that we are not asking our foreign friends to bear the full brunt of our economic adjustments. We are also being very tough on ourselves.

We must recognize, however, that these bold moves have struck at two underpinnings of the world view held by many Japanese: first, that hostility between the United States and mainland China was somehow an unchanging law of nature, and second, that the United States is economically omnipotent. In fact, these so-called "shocks" may be more psychological than substantive. Many nations, and to some extent we ourselves, had come to believe in the postwar era that we are capable of doing virtually anything we wanted to do. It comes as a shock to those holding this view to observe the United States having to ask others for help rather than giving it.

BROAD SPECTRUM OF COOPERATIVE EFFORTS

The dynamic changes taking place both within Japan and in East Asia will have far-reaching effects. But I do not believe they necessarily imply divergent paths for the United States and Japan.

I am firmly convinced that we share the same fundamental goals: peace, prosperity, and an open economy with widening opportunities widely shared. Democratic ideals and institutions have taken firm root in the fabric of Japanese society.

Japan's commitment to private enterprise is equally strong and provides a basis as much for collaboration as for competition. Indeed, in light of the publicity surrounding the frictions, it is well to be reminded of the broad spectrum of our cooperative efforts.

The United States probably has more bilateral governmental and private programs with Japan than with any other country. Among these are the annual U.S.-Japan Conference on Cultural and Educational Interchange, the U.S.-Japan Governors Conference, and the U.S.-Japan Mayors Conference. Last year more Japanese visited the United States than came from any other overseas country.

As first and third ranking nations in GNP, we work together in international agencies such as the IMF, the OECD, and the GATT [International Monetary Fund; Organization for Economic Cooperation and Development; General Agreement on Tariffs and Trade] to insure the effective operation of the international economic system. We are also partners in regional groupings like the Economic Commission for Asia and the Far East. Our current extensive cooperation in space and environment research is the newest in a long series of shared approaches to

[130] Documents 142-143.

technology and science, including medicine, natural resources, and the peaceful uses of atomic energy. By 1975 Japan plans to spend about $10 billion on research and development.

Japan's aid to Asia is second only to our own. The Asian Development Bank and Indonesian Consortium would never have gotten off the ground without Japan's cooperation. In the private field the number of joint ventures, both in Japan and abroad, continues to increase. The possibilities for further fruitful collaboration are good.

NEW ERA OF ADJUSTMENTS

Nevertheless, both sides must fully face up to the fact that a new era is upon us, an era in which we must interact on a basis of equality, mutual respect, and full reciprocity. Japan has outgrown its comfortable position as junior partner of the United States and is groping, however hesitantly and painfully, for a political role commensurate with its economic status.

The adjustments we will have to make in our bilateral relations will be as much in style as in substance. A simple mutual respect for each other's legitimate interests and national sensitivities will go far to keep the economic frictions which inevitably arise between two dynamic and competitive peoples from spilling over into the political arena and undermining the basic relationship. For us this will require an awareness of the deep-seated Japanese sense of vulnerability to events affecting their vital interests over which they have no control. We must also recognize and respect the natural aspirations of the Japanese people for a major part in the conduct of world affairs.

Conversely, Japan must recognize that we no longer can accept a double standard in our economic relations around the world. Japan cannot expect to continue to enjoy unfettered access to world markets and resources, especially in the United States, without according similar treatment to foreign enterprises doing business in and with Japan.

Nevertheless, I cannot help but feel that, barring any gross mismanagement of our relations, the trends in American and Japanese interests will continue to parallel one another and be complementary rather than fractious and mutually destructive.

Thus, I would look forward to an era of expanding trade between the United States and Japan, of greater capital investment in each other's countries, of more and more businessmen who are at ease operating in the other's country.

In the last regard, and in closing, I think it is of critical importance that we train young American businessmen in Japanese language, customs, and business practices. We must have Americans, from trainees to senior executives, who speak and read the language of Japan's highly technological society and who are able, as I say, to operate "comfortably" in the Japanese environment. Our Japanese friends also have much to do in this regard. A trade and financial relationship of the magnitude we have today requires a far deeper mutual understanding than presently exists in the business and financial communities of both countries. Foreign Minister [Takeo] Fukuda is also well aware of the problem and has stated the intention of the Japanese Government to make a major and continuing contribution to the exchange of persons between our two countries.

I hope I have not left you with the impression that our problems overwhelm us. That is not true. But we do have to work hard to continue to enjoy the many real benefits we gain from U.S.-Japan relations. I am convinced it is within our power to do so. To return to the title of my talk, in sum I think the broad trends are good but that with good faith and earnest endeavor on both sides they can be made better.

E. The United States and the Republic of Korea.

[The changing nature of international relations in the Far East was also evident in the affairs of the Korean Peninsula, where the Republic of Korea (R.O.K.) in the South and the Communist-ruled Democratic People's Republic of Korea (D.P.R.K.) in the North still faced each other across the armistice demarcation line and demilitarized zone established in 1953.[131] Satisfaction over South Korea's remarkable economic performance in recent years was tempered during 1971 not only by severe inflation and rising popular unrest but also by uneasiness about the long-term implications of the Nixon Doctrine and the change in U.S. policy toward China. South Korean misgivings about an ongoing reduction of U.S. military forces in the peninsula, whose authorized strength was trimmed from 63,000 to 43,000 as of June 30, 1971, were only partially assuaged by American pledges of solidarity and support in modernizing South Korea's own armed forces (Documents 98 and 99).

In what seemed a direct response to the new situation developing in the Far East, the government of South Korean President Park Chung Hee in August 1971 took the unprecedented step of authorizing the South Korean Red Cross Society to enter into discussions with its North Korean counterpart with a view to setting up a conference on the problems of the numerous families split by Korea's political division. The opening of preliminary North–South contacts at Panmunjom, the seat of the Military Armistice Commission, on August 20, 1971, encouraged the U.N. General Assembly, with the support of the United States, to defer its annual debate on the Korean question until 1972 in

131 *Documents, 1953*, pp. 289-90.

the hope that the talks might prove to be the beginning of a broader process of détente (cf. Document 100).

These hopes were not entirely borne out by subsequent developments in the peninsula. President Park, who had earlier been elected to a third four-year term, accused the D.P.R.K. of using the Panmunjom talks as a smokescreen for invasion and on December 5, 1971, declared a state of national emergency, ostensibly as a means of coping with the fluid state of international politics and the increased aggressiveness of the rival regime. Steps were also taken to begin an initial reduction of 10,000 in South Korea's 48,000-man force in South Vietnam.[132] Secretary of State Rogers, asked at his December 23 news conference whether further U.S. troop withdrawals were in prospect, said that no further withdrawals were currently planned but that additional withdrawals might be considered in due course if tensions were reduced and South Korean military capability increased.[133]]

(98) Agreement on Troop Reduction and Modernization: Joint Statement Issued in Washington and Seoul, February 6, 1971.[134]

(Complete Text)

The Government of the Republic of Korea and the United States Government have completed satisfactory talks on the program for the modernization of the Korean armed forces and arrangements for the reduction of U.S. forces in Korea.

The United States has agreed to assist the Government of the Republic of Korea in its effort to modernize its defense forces, through a long range military assistance program on the basis of joint United States–Republic of Korea military recommendations. The Korean Government notes with satisfaction that the United States Congress has approved $150 million as supplemental funds for the first year portion of the said modernization program.[135]

Consultations between the two governments on the reduction of U.S. troop strength in Korea by 20,000 and on the consequent repositioning of Korean and U.S. troops also have been concluded in a spirit of mutual understanding and close cooperation.

Reductions in the level of United States troops in Korea do not affect in any way the determination of the United States Government to meet armed attack against the Republic of Korea in accordance with the

---

132 Cf. note 55 to Chapter V.
133 *Bulletin*, Jan. 17, 1972, p. 55.
134 *Bulletin*, Mar. 1, 1971, p. 263.
135 Special Foreign Assistance Act, 1971 (Public Law 91-652, Jan. 5, 1971).

Mutual Defense Treaty of 1954 between the Republic of Korea and the United States.[136]

Annual security consultative meetings to be attended by foreign and defense officials of both governments at a high level will be held to assess the nature of the military threat directed against the Republic of Korea. In such discussions, over-all capabilities to defend against the threat will be evaluated.

(99) Progress of the Republic of Korea: Statement by Assistant Secretary of State Green Before the House Committee on Foreign Affairs, May 4, 1971.[137]

(Excerpt)

*　　*　　*

KOREA

In 1950 the armed forces of the Republic of Korea were untrained, poorly equipped, unable to defend their country. Today our military assistance has helped transform the ROK armed forces into highly trained and effective troops able to bear an increasingly large share of the responsibility for their defense. By the end of this fiscal year we will have reduced our forces by 20,000 men by bringing home and deactivating the 7th Division, which had served in Korea since before the Korean conflict. We will also have drawn back the remaining division from the DMZ [demilitarized zone] so that the ROK forces now maintain the defense line all along the 38th parallel from sea to shining sea. I was interested to read a telegram from our Ambassador [William J. Porter] the other day commenting on justifiable Korean pride in this notable achievement. Now the Koreans are beginning to talk in terms of eventual military self-sufficiency. Our present long-range program to modernize their equipment will bring us closer to that day. Meanwhile, the Koreans are contributing to allied forces in South Viet-Nam.

As I comment thus on Korea's improved defenses, I recall that less than two decades ago the Republic of Korea lay in ruins, a poor country made destitute by war. Today Korea has a constructive relationship with Japan and other countries. The vigor and skill of its people have made its economic growth rate about the highest in the world. Our

136 Signed Oct. 1, 1953, and entered into force Nov. 17, 1954 (TIAS 3097; 5 UST 2368); text in *Documents, 1953*, pp. 312-13; ratification document in same, *1954*, pp. 344-45.
137 *Bulletin*, May 31, 1971, pp. 716-17.

economic and technical assistance helped stimulate the economy while at the same time our military assistance served to help protect Korea from outside interference. I say this about a country of strategic importance, where the interests of the four great powers of East Asia converge to the degree they do nowhere else, a nation whose independence is of importance to the United States, Japan, and indeed all of us.

*	*	*

(100) Postponement of Debate in the United Nations: Statement by Ambassador W. Tapley Bennett, Jr., Alternate United States Representative, to the General Assembly, September 25, 1971. [138]

(Complete Text)

The United States wishes to add its voice to those who have supported the recommendations of the General Committee to include the consideration of questions concerning Korea in the provisional agenda of the 27th session next year. Permanent Representatives attending this meeting are only too well aware of how increasingly polemical and sterile the debates on Korea in Committee I have become in recent years. We would have no objection to holding a debate once again this year, but no argument has been advanced to suggest that such a debate would have positive consequences.

My delegation regrets, for instance, that many speakers yesterday and today have chosen to speak in language so reminiscent of cold war dialogue.

Mr. President, we are concerned that the repetition of this polemical and sterile debate could disrupt the hopeful beginnings of a new era on the Korean Peninsula that we see in the Red Cross talks.

The distinguished Representative of the Soviet Union [Yakov A. Malik] has spoken of tension in the Korean Peninsula. We see in Korea today steps being taken by the Korean people themselves to reduce that tension—the first moves toward national reconciliation. We fervently hope that these talks will bear good fruit.

In order to give these talks the best possible chance of success, to act in favor of the reconciliation of the Korean people, we ask all members to support the recommendation of the General Committee. [139]

[138] USUN Press Release 146, Sept. 25, 1971; text from *Bulletin*, Oct. 18, 1971, p. 430.
[139] The recommendation of the General Committee was accepted by the General Assembly on Sept. 25, 1971. For details see *UN Monthly Chronicle*. Oct. 1971, pp. 60-65.

VII.
THE UNITED STATES
AND AFRICA

[The paucity of American policy statements on Africa reflects the somewhat detached position maintained by the United States with respect to many aspects of African affairs in the 1960s and early 1970s. Deeply immersed in the turmoil of the other continents and concerned with Africa primarily from an economic rather than a political standpoint, the United States confined its official participation in African affairs for the most part to the conduct of small-scale aid programs in selected countries and the attempt to exert a moderating influence in those African controversies that had become the concern of the United Nations. Though accompanied by broad professions of support for racial and political justice, the American stand in some of these matters did not escape harsh criticism on the part of those who favored a more vigorous championship of nonwhite aspirations and a less complaisant attitude toward the white-dominated regimes that exercised power in South Africa, Namibia (South West Africa), Southern Rhodesia, and the Portuguese African territories. Particularly deplored in 1971 was the abrogation by action of the U.S. Congress of an embargo on the importation of strategic materials from Southern Rhodesia that had been imposed in 1967 in compliance with the orders of the U.N. Security Council.

The following documentation encompasses a general review of current African questions from an American official viewpoint (Documents 101-102); a more detailed examination of American actions in regard to the critical questions of Namibia and Southern Rhodesia (Documents 103-109); and an attempted answer by the Secretary of State to criticisms of the American position on African affairs as manifested at the 1971 session of the U.N. General Assembly (Document 110).]

A. Basic Policy Considerations.

[Almost the only comprehensive statement on African affairs as they

379

appeared to the U.S. Government in 1971 was the chapter entitled "Africa" in the annual "State of the World" report made public by President Nixon on February 25, 1971. Reprinted here in its entirety (Document 101), it offers a balanced if somewhat general review of the various elements that made up the American interest in Africa as a whole. It is followed by a broad review of African issues at the United Nations (Document 102) that can serve as introduction to the more detailed documentation on Namibia (South West Africa) and Southern Rhodesia presented later in the chapter.]

(101) "Africa": President Nixon's Second Annual Report to the Congress on United States Foreign Policy, February 25, 1971.[1]

(Excerpt)

*   *   *

AFRICA

"Our stake in the Continent will not rest on today's crisis, on political maneuvering for passing advantage, or on the strategic priority we assign it. Our goal is to help sustain the process by which Africa will gradually realize economic progress to match its aspirations."[2]

> U.S. Foreign Policy For the 1970's
> Report to the Congress
> February 18, 1970

Africa is a continental experiment in nation building. The excitement and enthusiasm of national birth have phased into the more sober period of growth.

Our historic ties with Africa are deeply rooted in the cultural heritage of many of our people. Our sympathy for Africa's newly independent states is a natural product of our traditional antipathy for colonialism. Our economic interests in the continent are substantial, and growing. And our responsibilities as a global power inevitably give us an interest in the stability and well-being of so large a part of the world.

Reflecting these close ties, Secretary Rogers last year became the first Secretary of State to visit Africa. His personal observations and experiences in Morocco, Tunisia, Ethiopia, Kenya, Zambia, the Congo,

---

1 Nixon Report, 1971, pp. 114-21; text from *Presidential Documents*, Mar. 1, 1971, pp. 341-43.
2 Nixon Report, 1970, p. 90.

Cameroon, Nigeria, Ghana and Liberia gave a new dimension at the highest level to our knowledge and understanding of Africa. A major result of that visit was the basic policy statement issued with my warm approval in March, 1970.[3] In that statement Secretary Rogers summarized our aim in Africa as a "relationship of constructive cooperation with the nations of Africa—a cooperative and equal relationship with all who wish it."

We recognize that it is not for us to attempt to set the pattern of relationships among the states of Africa. Only the Africans can forge national unity. Those problems having to do with the building of stable national institutions are neither appropriate for, nor amenable to, much of a contribution from us. Only the Africans themselves can do such work.

The promise of the newly independent African nations is great. But they face all the normal problems associated with independence, and some special ones stemming from historic reliance on tribal organizations not always reflected in national boundaries drawn for the administrative convenience of the former colonial powers. Moreover, colonialism and racial injustice in Southern Africa continue to frustrate the African sense of fulfillment.

These facts complicate the essential task of clothing new political institutions with authority. They make more difficult the problem of working out stable relationships among the nations of Africa, and between Africa and the rest of the world. They compound the exigent task of obtaining and applying the resources needed for economic development.

The Nixon Doctrine's encouragement of self-reliance has an immediate and broad applicability in Africa. Africa has depended less than other areas on American leadership and assistance, and its institutions and relationships were created without our providing either the impetus or the concept. In Africa, therefore, the conflict between the application of our new doctrine and the requirements of continuity are minimal. To an unusual degree, our conception of the current realities is unencumbered by the weight of previous undertakings. Our freedom of decision is not constrained by the demands, legal or implicit, of past commitments and actions.

Within the framework of African efforts, however, there are three primary needs of the continent to which we can contribute. Africa seeks peace, economic development, and justice; and she seeks our assistance in reaching those goals. It is in our interest to respond as generously as our resources permit.

3 Text in *Bulletin*, Apr. 20, 1970, pp. 513-21; excerpts in *Documents, 1970*, pp. 229-41.

PEACE

The major contribution we can make to the peace of the continent is to support the African effort to keep free of great power rivalries and conflicts. Africa's unresolved problems should not be used as a pretext for non-Africans to intervene. African needs for assistance should not be manipulated to establish an undue outside influence. The nations of Africa need tranquility and a chance to resolve their own domestic and inter-African problems. Conflict and involvement in Cold War rivalries can only bring harm to Africa and tragic delay in its progress.

For that reason, we seek no positions in Africa which threaten the interests of others. Nor can we condone activities by others which have that effect. Therefore, support for the inviolability of African borders and the integrity of African states is a cardinal point of American policy.

Clearly, our ability to adhere to this posture of restraint is dependent upon a similar posture by others. We believe that the African nations themselves are the best guarantors, as they are certainly the prime beneficiaries, of such restraint.

DEVELOPMENT

The second great African need to which we can contribute is economic development. Africa must obtain material resources and technology from abroad. Multilateral and private investment channels are, we believe, the most efficient means to effect capital development. But external resources can bring real progress only if Africa's own human resources are developed and mobilized for this effort. It is in this area that we believe our bilateral assistance programs can be most effective. We therefore hope to contribute to Africa's economic development in four major ways:

—Our bilateral assistance programs in the years ahead will concentrate on the development of human resources—on education, population problems, and agricultural skills. In the technical assistance field, we intend to send more highly trained technicians. This will be particularly evident in the "New Direction" of the Peace Corps programs in Africa.
—But aid alone is not sufficient. African countries also need new markets. Generalized tariff preferences will help to open new markets for their manufactured goods in the more industrialized countries. I will shortly submit legislation to authorize U.S. participation in this program.[4] We will also continue to participate in inter-

4 Cf. Document 155.

national efforts to maintain and stabilize markets for traditional exports of primary products.

—We intend to use our influence in international lending and development agencies to encourage greater assistance to Africa. In this respect we applaud the decision of the World Bank to increase its assistance to Africa threefold.

—Finally, we will actively encourage private investment in the developing countries of Africa. Private investment is the easiest and most efficient way to transfer both resources and human skills from a developed to a developing society. American investment in Africa now stands at about three billion dollars, of which more than two-thirds is in the developing area. It has been growing annually at over 12%. We expect that a high rate will continue in coming years. In African countries favored with resources and wise leadership, I have no doubt that private investment will play a far more significant role than public aid in speeding their progress.

JUSTICE

The third broad area in which Africans seek our assistance is the search for racial and political justice in southern Africa. There is perhaps no issue which has so pernicious a potential for the well-being of Africa and for American interests there. It is, for many, the sole issue by which our friendship for Africa is measured. I wish to review in all frankness our policy toward this grievous problem.

Both our statements and our actions have, or should have, made it patently clear to all concerned that racism is abhorrent to the American people, to my administration, and to me personally. We cannot be indifferent to apartheid. Nor can we ignore the tensions created in Africa by the denial of political self-determination. We shall do what we can to foster equal opportunity and free political expression instead. We shall do so on both moral and practical grounds, for in our view there is no other solution.

The United States has, therefore, reaffirmed and continued to enforce the embargo on the sale of arms to South Africa.[5] When Southern Rhodesia attempted to sever formal ties with Britain, we closed our Consulate there.[6] We have reaffirmed and continued to enforce the economic sanctions against Rhodesia, and we have sought ways to ensure a more universal compliance with those sanctions.[7]

The United States also has continued its embargo on the sale of arms for use in Portuguese African territories. In support of the United

5 Cf. *Documents, 1970*, pp. 253-56.
6 Same, p. 246 n.28.
7 Cf. Documents 107-109.

Nations effort to terminate South Africa's jurisdiction over South-West Africa, we have adopted a policy of discouraging American investment in that territory.[8] We have sought to provide assistance and encouragement to Botswana, Lesotho, and Swaziland in their efforts to prove the viability of multiracial societies in the heart of southern Africa.

These measures define our policy toward the problems of southern Africa. We intend to continue these efforts, and to do what we can to encourage the white regimes to adopt more generous and more realistic policies toward the needs and aspirations of their black citizens.

However, just as we will not condone the violence to human dignity implicit in apartheid, we cannot associate ourselves with those who call for a violent solution to these problems.

We are convinced that the use of violence holds no promise as the solution to the problems of southern Africa. Neither the military nor the economic strength is available to force change on the white minority regimes. Violence would harden the resistance of the white minorities to evolutionary change. Resort to force would freeze the prejudice and fear which lie at the heart of the problem. Finally, violence would certainly hurt most the very people it would purport to serve.

The interests of the white regimes themselves surely dictate change. The United States believes that the outside world can and should use its contacts with southern Africa to promote and speed that change. We do not, therefore, believe the isolation of the white regimes serves African interests, or our own, or that of ultimate justice. A combination of contact and moral pressure serves all three.

PROGRESS

I have dwelt at length on the problems of Africa because it is to them that our policies are of necessity addressed. But it is necessary also to recognize the progress which is taking place.

The return of peace to Nigeria was the paramount African event of 1970.[9] That event was all the more welcome to us, for the American zeal to help reduce the anguishing human cost of that conflict led to some misunderstanding and strain in our relations with the Nigerian Government. The United States views with admiration the humane and statesmanlike policy of reconciliation which Nigeria has adopted. We ourselves know the suffering and bitterness which a civil war entails. Our country emerged stronger and more united. Nigeria, too, has emerged from the challenge stronger and united, and ready to assume the significant role in Africa which her size, her resources, and her sixty million people dictate. That is a development of the highest significance

8 Cf. below at note 36.
9 Cf. *Documents, 1970*, pp. 242-46.

for the future stability and well-being of Africa. We welcome it.

I should also mention the striking progress which has been made in the Democratic Republic of the Congo [Zaïre]. Five years of peace have transformed that country from perhaps the most tortured of African states to one of the most stable. This development vindicates the faith in a united Congo which the United States displayed in darker days. President [Joseph D.] Mobutu's visit to Washington in August[10] served to recall the support we extended to the Congo at that time, and to reaffirm the strong friendship between our two countries which has resulted.

The Emperor of Ethiopia, unique among world leaders in the length of his reign and his contribution to independent Africa, visited the United States in October. That occasion provided an opportunity for me to review with him the role of the United States in the economic progress of that ancient land, and to reaffirm the close ties of cooperation between our two countries.[11] Ethiopia has been a leader in Africa's creation of regional organizations. Their growing vitality is encouraging, and we hope that activities of this kind will serve increasingly as the focus for economic cooperation between African countries. We believe such a development will both promote and increase the effectiveness of foreign assistance.

THE FUTURE

The potential of Africa is great, but so are its problems. We view Africa with the strongest of goodwill, tempered by the sober recognition of the limits of the contribution which we can make to many of its problems. We look to African leadership to build the framework within which other nations, including the United States, can fully contribute to a bright African future. A peaceful, progressive, and just Africa is an exciting and worthy goal. We hope by our policies to facilitate economic progress in one part of Africa, human and social justice in the other, and peace in both.

*   *   *

---

[10] *Public Papers, 1970*, pp. 644-48. Under a policy enunicated Oct. 27, 1971, the Democratic Republic of the Congo changed its name to the Republic of Zaíre and President Mobutu adopted the name Mobutu Sese Seko.

[11] Emperor Haile Selassie met with the President at the White House on Oct. 25, 1970 (*Presidential Documents*, Nov. 2, 1970, p. 1464).

(102) "A Look at African Issues at the United Nations": Address by David D. Newsom, Assistant Secretary of State for African Affairs, Before the Atlanta Press Club, Atlanta, September 21, 1971. [12]

(Complete Text)

This afternoon the 26th General Assembly of the United Nations opens in New York. One hundred and twenty-seven nations, plus probably three new members, [13] will meet to wrestle with a wide range of political, economic, and social issues. Last year approximately one-fourth of the substantive resolutions in the General Assembly arose out of circumstances in Africa, particularly southern Africa. It is likely to be the same this year.

The United States, as an important member of the United Nations, will be involved. This year, as in past years, we will face the difficult task of reconciling pressing demands for action toward objectives that we generally accept in principle with realities as we see them, with our wider responsibilities, and with our concern for the respect and authority of the United Nations.

You will, I am sure, find frequent references to African issues in New York on your tickers in the weeks to come. I welcome this opportunity today to discuss some of the basic problems which will lie behind the news—as the Africans see them and as we see them.

I speak today for a wider audience, in Africa as well as at home. I think it is particularly fitting that I should do so from Atlanta. Atlanta is well known in Africa. Visitors from that continent remember the warm hospitality you have accorded to them. Many of the Africans who today play important roles in the development of their countries were educated in your universities. The death of two of your great sons, Dr. Martin Luther King, Jr., and Ralph McGill, left a void also in Africa.

The United States response to African issues has a special pertinence this year. In our own country there is an increasing consciousness of Africa and of the hard core of problems of human relations which exist in that continent. At the same time there is more and more questioning in Congress and in the public concerning our international obligations and involvements, including those in the United Nations.

The areas of southern Africa and that smaller region of West Africa which encompasses Portuguese Guinea contain the final and most difficult problems of colonialism. In South Africa, Rhodesia, and South West Africa lie the last vestiges of legalized racial discrimination. As

---

[12] Department of State Press Release 212, Sept. 21, 1971; text from *Bulletin*, Oct. 11, 1971, pp. 373-78.
[13] Bhutan, Bahrain, and Qatar were admitted to U.N. membership on Sept. 21; Oman was admitted Oct. 7, and the United Arab Emirates on Dec. 9, 1971.

such, these problems strike a vibrant emotional chord among Africans—
and Asians—who have over the last three decades sought and achieved,
sometimes with U.N. assistance, their own freedom and independence.

These problems are great in their dimensions. There are no easy or
quick solutions in sight.

At stake, for blacks and whites alike, are basic issues of civil order and
progress, fundamental human rights, and the rule of law.

The issues are legal and political. They also are economic and social.
They concern humanity in the broadest sense of the term. The problems of southern Africa have given rise to much discussion and debate
in our Government and among our people.

These issues present African leaders with some of their most difficult
political problems. When the leaders of Zambia, Tanzania, Senegal,
Guinea—to mention only a few—address these issues, they not only
expound their own strong personal views. They also frequently reflect a
genuine domestic problem: the interplay of pressures for action against
the colonial territories and the possibilities of counteraction by the
Portuguese and Rhodesians. Affected elements of their population and
significant political figures reinforce the demands for action. Prudence
may suggest otherwise.

On the wider scene, other Africans are drawn into these problems by
the pressures of solidarity with their African brothers. Many Africans
look upon the nations along the Zambesi as being in the front lines of
their struggle. These sentiments underlie actions and pressures for
action in the councils of the Organization of African unity—and beyond the OAU, in the United Nations itself.

Admittedly not every black African nation agrees on the more militant approaches often proposed. One can see a growing tendency in
Africa to seek other ways. Nevertheless, the depth of feeling and the
impulses toward solidarity are strong. Even the most conservative members of the Organization of African Unity are reluctant to oppose the
general approaches broadly agreed upon by the OAU. These approaches
are reflected in the recommendations of the OAU African caucus,
which plays a key role in the African issues in New York.

AFRICAN PREOCCUPATIONS AND OBJECTIVES

What are the African preoccupations?

In the Republic of South Africa, the laws and Government policy
seek specifically to maintain the dominance of a white minority.

South West Africa, now known officially in the United Nations as
Namibia, was a former German colony placed under a South African
mandate after World War I. The United Nations, now supported by the
International Court of Justice, has determined that South Africa has
not fulfilled its mandate responsibilities and that the territory is there-

fore under the direct responsibility of the United Nations. The U.N. calls for the withdrawal of South Africa.

In Rhodesia, a white minority of 4 percent of the population dominates the black 96 percent and seeks by its present constitution to prevent the black majority from ever acquiring a decisive voice in their own country.

In Mozambique, Angola, and Portuguese Guinea, the Portuguese hold tenaciously to what they consider integral provinces of Portugal. The Africans regard these as the continent's last significant colonies denied the right to self-determination and independence.

In this situation, the basic African thrust has been and will probably continue to be to isolate South Africa and to manifest support for those seeking radical change in that country. At the outset this fall, there may be a challenge to the South African Government's right to participate in the U.N., on the grounds both of racial policies and refusal to cooperate on South West Africa. There will undoubtedly continue to be demands for the withdrawal of outside investment, for cutting airlinks with South Africa, and for restricting trade. Africans will seek resolutions calling on U.N. members and U.N. specialized agencies to "render moral and material support" to the African liberation movements, targeted not only against South Africa and Namibia but against the Portuguese territories and Rhodesia as well.

The strong pressure by the Africans against any arms sales to South Africa will be highlighted by a continuing special OAU mission mandated to visit NATO nations and other arms suppliers.

Proposals for Namibia will also be laid before the Security Council and the General Assembly by a special OAU mission. These proposals will be based on the advisory opinion handed down by the International Court of Justice, which this June confirmed that South Africa's mandate over this former German colony was terminated and that South Africa's continued presence there is illegal.[14]

The intensity of discussions on Rhodesia will probably depend in part on whether there is any progress in contacts reportedly now going on between the British and the Ian [D.] Smith regime in Rhodesia. The Africans support the United Nations economic sanctions against Rhodesia but remain skeptical of their effectiveness. The African tendency will continue to be to call for the use of military force to oust the Smith regime. It remains their feeling that this should have been the initial reaction of the British in 1965.

African feelings against continuing rule by Portugal in its territories in Africa have undoubtedly been strengthened by the reported Portuguese involvement in an attack on Guinea last year[15] and by complaints

---

[14] Document 104.

[15] Cf. *The United States in World Affairs, 1970*, pp. 217-18, and *Documents, 1970*, pp. 260-62.

brought against Portugal in the Security Council in the intervening months by both Guinea and Senegal. The Africans will probably lose no opportunity to seek U.N. and other support for the liberation movements currently directed against Portuguese rule. The establishment of independent majority governments in these territories remains their objective.

African proposals and speeches on all these issues are likely in the main to reflect an increasing frustration and impatience over what Africans consider a lack of adequate progress on these issues and a lack of genuine support from the major Western nations, including the United States. South Africa to them appears firmly under white minority rule with little indication of immediate change. South African determination to stay in Namibia is clear. The Africans, so far, see little chance for early African rule in Rhodesia. Portugal's determination, both military and political, to retain its territories appears as firm as ever. The more militant Africans see in the new contacts between some black states and South Africa, in the proposals for "dialogue," and in increasing signs of security cooperation among the white-ruled states, a movement away from their objectives. This heightens still further their frustrations.

The Africans stand by no means alone on these issues. In the main they can count on the automatic support of the newly independent countries of Asia and of the Eastern European bloc. Support from us, however, is far less automatic. The issues are frequently posed in simplified terms. Those who vote against a particular resolution often appear to be standing in a small isolated group opposing self-determination and upholding continued racial discrimination.

Each year the U.N. votes are tabulated. The arguments, the explanations, the negotiations, the speeches, are forgotten. What is noted by those in Africa and here at home is whether we have voted yes, or no, or abstained. The issues become simplified; the whys of our vote are forgotten. Depending on points of view, particular votes are seen as good common sense or a denial of fundamental U.S. principles. Some see the votes as reasonable and realistic; others wonder if we're totally ignoring the issue. Still others may see our stance as a refusal to recognize the importance of an anti-Communist ally.

The United States is involved in these issues whether it wishes it or not. We are one of the five permanent members of the Security Council. We strongly desire the continued strength and influence of the U.N. By the example of our own history and in our frequent declarations, we have consistently endorsed the right of self-determination for the people of southern Africa. But it is our very concern for the future of and respect for the U.N. which prevents us from endorsing positions on complex issues posed at the U.N. in simplified or patently unworkable form.

CLEAR U.S. STAND ON AFRICAN ISSUES

The stand we have taken on the African issues is clear. We have demonstrated, as unequivocally as any major nation, our support for the principles involved.

President Nixon said last year in his address to the 25th anniversary session of the General Assembly:[16]

We do hold certain principles to be universal:

—That each nation has a sovereign right to its own independence and to recognition of its own dignity.

—That each individual has a human right to that same recognition of his dignity.

—That we all share a common obligation to demonstrate the mutual respect for the rights and feelings of one another that is the mark of a civil society and also of a true community of nations.

We have maintained conscientiously the arms embargo against South Africa recommended by the United Nations Security Council in 1963,[17] although under the terms of the resolution it is not mandatory.

We have supported fully the U.N.'s determination that continued South African occupation of South West Africa is illegal. We supported the referral of the Namibia case to the International Court of Justice.[18] We discourage U.S. business from going into that territory.

We have been at the forefront in enforcing sanctions against Rhodesia, the only mandatory sanctions ever voted by the United Nations.[19]

We have scrupulously maintained a voluntary arms embargo policy with respect to the Portuguese territories in Africa.

Most African leaders with whom I have spoken recognize and give us credit for what we have done and are doing. They wish only that we would do more.

They recognize, too, that actions in the United Nations are but one part of our total relationship. They know that our manifestation of interest in the causes and concerns of independent Africa occurs in other ways of importance to them. Not the least of these is our contribution to the economic and social development of their countries. Further, the varied currents of opinion in modern independent Africa are not fully manifested in the caucus approach taken by the Africans in the United Nations. The U.N. actions are therefore only a part of the

16 Documents, p. 297
17 Same, *1963*, pp. 355-56.
18 Cf. below at notes 23-25.
19 Cf. Documents 107-109.

picture. This does not diminish, however, the importance of United Nations action on both the world and the African scene.

It is not pessimism, but honesty, to say that we shall undoubtedly fail to achieve full agreement with the African nations on African issues in this General Assembly, just as we have during previous sessions. We hope our African friends and those deeply concerned in this country will recognize that in these issues we are not challenging the principle. The issue is how to achieve the objective.

AFRICAN AND U.S. VIEWPOINTS

The African nations quite understandably approach each issue relating to them from the single viewpoint of Africa. They are honestly and sincerely convinced that what they are calling upon the U.N. to do, sometimes in the way of enforcement actions, is right.

But we, as a major power, need to consider each issue in a wider context. We must look beyond the immediate effect of a United Nations resolution. We have our own congressional and public opinions and the ultimate matter of continuing U.S. support for the United Nations. We must think in terms of the world picture, of how any particular action would affect other problem areas in the world.

We also must consider what effect the resolution will actually have. Experience shows that we must have not only a majority but the votes of those countries whose cooperation is essential to implement a resolution. The United Nations is not a world parliament where it is sufficient to assemble a majority to vote something into law.

Resolutions which express strong sentiments but have no practical effect may have a negative rather than a positive influence on the prestige and authority of the United Nations.

We must consider carefully, for instance, resolutions calling for economic sanctions, since experience has shown that sanctions are most difficult to enforce and will be ineffective if the major countries concerned are not prepared to cooperate. A resolution that will be honored in the breach by a number of countries whose observance is essential to its success helps no one. This isn't good for those who sponsored the resolution, it isn't good for the people who are supposed to benefit from it, and it isn't good for the United Nations.

We may often be in sympathy with the ultimate purpose of a resolution but we cannot support terms which, in our view, detract from the true effectiveness of a resolution. We share with all United Nations members a responsibility to keep U.N. resolutions reasonable and accurate and consistent. Draft resolutions, for example, which take into account the unverified allegations of one side only do not provide an adequate factual basis for the U.N.'s peacemaking processes.

We are particularly sensitive with respect to actions taken pursuant to chapter VII of the United Nations Charter.[20] This is the chapter under which the Security Council has the power to take decisions binding on member nations. We regard that chapter of the charter as a most precious thing. It might someday make the difference between world peace and holocaust. We are most concerned, therefore, that actions voted by the United Nations which in any way involve chapter VII should be clearly related to threats to the peace or breaches of the peace. On this matter we have been especially scrupulous.

Specifically, much as we deplore apartheid in South Africa and other forms of racial discrimination, or the denial of majority rule, we cannot agree that they automatically constitute a "threat to the peace" in the sense of chapter VII, article 39, of the charter, which says that the Security Council shall determine the existence of any threat to the peace, breach of the peace, or act of aggression and shall make recommendations or decide what measures shall be taken to maintain or restore international peace and security.

In our policy and in our actions we cannot be indifferent to our relations with non-African nations involved in these issues.

We have friendly relations, for example, with the Portuguese. We cooperate with them in NATO, but this is a cooperation confined to Europe. We have made clear our basic disagreement with them on their African policy. We believe that the people inhabiting these territories are entitled to the right of self-determination. However, we are not ready automatically, and without clarification of facts, to jump to conclusions regarding the responsibility for incidents between Portugal and African states—as we are often pressed to do.

We have long had relations with South Africa. Although we strongly oppose racial discrimination, we recognize the complexity of the problem South Africa faces. We fully agree that the present situation must change, but we cannot subscribe to oversimplified solutions to complicated and intensely human problems.

Moreover, based on our experience, we cannot agree with the African assumption, often expressed, that we could exert significant influence on these areas if only we wished to do so. Rarely can one nation, any nation, however powerful, affect basic attitudes in another society if that society clings to its vested interests and resists change.

In the broader context, we are also concerned over the impact of these issues on the specialized agencies of the United Nations such as the World Health Organization, the Food and Agriculture Organization, and the Economic Commission for Africa. The constant pressure to inject political considerations into technical bodies and to expel members on political grounds adversely affects their efficiency and the effectiveness both of their administration and of their field work. We do

20 "Action with Respect to Threats to the Peace, Breaches of the Peace, and Acts of Aggression."

not believe it is in the interests of the Africans, who are among the principal benefactors [sic] of U.N. specialized agency work, thus to politicize what began as essentially technical organs.

INEVITABILITY OF CHANGE IN SOUTHERN AFRICA

In conclusion, our differences with the African nations are essentially over how change in southern Africa will be achieved—not whether. It is over how the United Nations can be most effectively used—not whether. In general, the Africans seek support for three broad approaches: isolation of the offenders, economic measures against them, and the use of military force. We have problems with each approach.

We believe change will come in southern Africa. Economic and demographic pressures make this inevitable. In South Africa itself there is a lessening of rigidity. Change is a central theme of discussion; there is psychological and intellectual ferment within the Afrikaner community; there have been isolated instances of acceptance of multiracial activities; there is a growing realism among businessmen that Africans are important to them as skilled workers and as a market. They are beginning to focus on the need for improvement of working conditions for non-whites. We cannot expect change to come quickly or easily. Our hope is that it will come peacefully.

Isolation can breed rigid resistance to change. Open doors can accelerate it. We believe the idea of expelling or suspending South Africa would represent a dangerous precedent, a move toward isolating South Africa's black population, and a move away from that universality of membership which the United Nations is gradually approaching.

Punitive economic measures are unpopular in this country. We have had experience in the problems of enforcement and control. These experiences do not encourage us to believe that such measures are workable against countries which are important economic entities. By their wealth such entities are able to cushion themselves against economic pressures and encourage noncompliance by others to weaken and thwart these pressures.

We have supported the economic sanctions against Rhodesia, but this is a special case. We have supported them as a feasible, if difficult, short-term measure to create pressures for a settlement with the United Kingdom. Despite incomplete compliance by many nations, we feel this boycott is achieving its objective. We do not see it as a precedent for other, different situations.

We can understand the impatience which leads to demands for the use of force. Nevertheless, we see little prospect of its effective use in bringing change in southern Africa, and we cannot favor its use.

The United States is most unlikely to be involved in military intervention on any side in Africa. Moreover, actions of the U.N. itself to support force would not accord with the basic purposes of the organization.

This catalogue of potential differences is long. I have set it forth in order to put our response to the African issues in perspective. I have set it forth, also, as a means of frank communication with our African friends themselves. I have found they appreciate and respond to this type of diplomacy.

We do not expect the Africans to cease pressing their viewpoints on these issues. The United Nations represents one of the few means they have of continually mobilizing world opinion on their behalf. We, further, agree with them that the absence of substantial change in southern Africa will continue to create tensions and ultimately threaten the peace.

We do seek and hope for continuing discussions with the Africans on these issues and continuing cooperation in finding acceptable and effective courses of action. We hope that in this way the substantial influence of the United Nations can be preserved and exercised so as to generate not the appearance of solutions, but fair and workable progress toward human rights and self-determination for all in southern Africa.

B. The Question of Namibia (South West Africa).

[United Nations concern with the former German territory of South West Africa, which had been occupied by South Africa in World War I and was subsequently administered by that country under a League of Nations mandate, goes back to 1946, when the General Assembly declined to approve a South African proposal to annex the territory and recommended instead that it be placed under the U.N. trusteeship system. South Africa's rejection of this solution and its gradual application of policies of racial separation or *apartheid* within the territory gave rise to protracted controversies, culminating on October 27, 1966, in a General Assembly resolution declaring that the mandate was at an end and that South Africa had no other right to administer the territory, which was, accordingly, declared to come "under the direct responsibility of the United Nations" pending arrangements for its people "to exercise the right of self-determination and to achieve independence."[21]

Refusing to concede the legality of this decision, South Africa persisted in its administration of South West Africa despite repeated admonitions by the General Assembly (which formally renamed the territory "Namibia" on December 16, 1968) and by the Security Council, which

21 Resolution 2145 (XXI), Oct. 27, 1966; *Documents, 1966*, pp. 309-11.

called upon South Africa on March 20, 1969, "to withdraw immediately its administration from the territory"[22] and, by Resolution 276 (1970) of January 30, 1970, declared "that the continued presence of the South African authorities in Namibia is illegal and that consequently all acts taken by the Government of South Africa on behalf of or concerning Namibia after the termination of the Mandate are illegal and invalid."[23] South Africa's continued noncompliance with these resolutions led the Security Council on July 29, 1970, to call for what amounted to an international diplomatic and economic boycott of the territory[24] and, at the same time, to ask the International Court of Justice for an advisory opinion on the question, "What are the legal consequences for States of the continued presence of South Africa in Namibia, notwithstanding Security Council resolution 276 (1970)?"[25]

The International Court of Justice, which had previously delivered several advisory opinions in the matter but had declined on technical grounds to rule upon a formal complaint against South African conduct in the territory,[26] accepted written statements pursuant to the Security Council resolution from a dozen interested governments, including the United States, during the autumn of 1970. From February 8 to March 17, 1971, it held 23 public sittings at which it heard oral statements on behalf of the Secretary-General of the United Nations, the Organization of African Unity (O.A.U.), and the governments of Finland, India, the Netherlands, Nigeria, Pakistan, the Republic of Vietnam, South Africa, and the United States (see Document 103). In the course of these proceedings, South Africa proposed that it be permitted to submit additional information about its policies and, in addition, that a plebiscite be held in the territory under joint supervision of the Court and the South African Government in order to determine whether the inhabitants preferred South African or U.N. administration. These requests were rejected by the Court on May 14, the reasons for its rejection being set forth in the advisory opinion it delivered June 21, 1971. In that opinion (Document 104), the Court, by 13 votes to 2, endorsed the proposition that the continued presence of South Africa in Namibia was illegal and that South Africa was under obligation to withdraw its administration immediately and end its occupation of the territory. It further declared, by 11 votes to 4, that U.N. member states were obligated to refrain from any dealings with South Africa implying legal recognition of or support for its presence or administration, and that support of this position was incumbent on nonmember states as well.

22 Resolution 264 (1969), Mar. 20, 1969.
23 Resolution 276 (1970), Jan. 30, 1970.
24 Resolution 283 (1970), July 29, 1970; *Documents, 1970*, pp. 256-59.
25 Resolution 284 (1970), July 29, 1970; *Documents, 1970*, pp. 259-60.
26 *Documents, 1966*, pp. 304-6.

The Court's advisory opinion was immediately rejected by South Africa; and France and the United Kingdom subsequently indicated that they too could not support it fully. The United States, which accepted the Court's conclusions without necessarily endorsing all of its reasoning (Document 105), supported a subsequent resolution in which the Security Council on October 20 (with France and the United Kingdom abstaining) agreed with the Court's opinion, called once again for South African withdrawal, and called upon all states to live up to their responsibilities in the matter (Document 106). The United States did not, however, support a more strongly worded resolution adopted by the General Assembly in December[27] "because of several extreme provisions which had appeared in previous resolutions."[28]]

(103) Namibia Before the International Court of Justice: Oral Statement Presented Before the Court by John R. Stevenson, Legal Adviser of the Department of State, The Hague, March 9, 1971.[29]

(Excerpts)

Mr. President, members of the Court: It is a high personal privilege and honor for me to make this oral statement before you on behalf of my Government. I am pleased to have with me as counsel Louis B. Sohn, Bemis Professor of International Law at Harvard Law School, who is this year serving as State Department Counselor on International Law, and Robert E. Dalton of the Office of the Legal Adviser. My Government appreciates the opportunity of participating in the oral phase of this case.

The written statements submitted by various governments and the remarks of the distinguished representatives who have preceded me in this case have strengthened our opinion as to the importance of the question before the Court.

In accordance with the wishes of the Court, Mr. President, I shall not repeat all the arguments made in the written statement submitted by the United States or reiterate those made by the distinguished representatives who spoke before me. I shall concentrate on a limited number of questions which have been raised in the written and oral statements, and with respect to which, in our view, certain additional considerations should be taken into account.

The first of these issues is the challenge to the jurisdiction of the Court to render an advisory opinion, based on the alleged invalidity of

27 General Assembly Resolution 2871 (XXVI), Dec. 20, 1971; adopted by 111-2-10 (U.S.).
28 Rogers Report, 1971, p. 284.
29 Bulletin, Apr. 26, 1971, pp. 542-49.

the Security Council request for an advisory opinion.[30] My Government believes that the Court has jurisdiction and that the Security Council request was valid.

The second issue is whether the Court should exercise its discretion to accede to or to decline the request of the Security Council for an advisory opinion. My Government believes that the Court should render an opinion.

The third topic which I shall address is the validity of General Assembly Resolution 2145 (XXI).[31] My Government believes that that resolution is valid and that it effectively terminated the administrative authority of South Africa under the mandate of December 17, 1920.

I shall then discuss the Security Council resolutions in the case and the effects of those resolutions for states.

Next, I shall comment briefly on the proposal made by the representative of South Africa to furnish additional information as to conditions in Namibia. My Government would not favor a *de novo* examination of the facts.

Thereafter, I shall discuss the South African Government's proposal that a plebiscite be held in Namibia.

Finally, I shall sum up the conclusions which my Government submits for the consideration of the Court.

*   *   *

VALIDITY OF GENERAL ASSEMBLY RESOLUTION

I turn now to the third question, the validity of General Assembly Resolution 2145 (XXI). Given the possibility that the Court may wish to consider this question, I wish to take a few moments to summarize the attitude of my Government thereon.

The United States and 114 other members of the United Nations voted for Resolution 2145. In the debate on Resolution 2145, the United States Representative stated:[32]

> As the mandatory power, South Africa incurred certain obligations toward the people of the territory—including the promotion of their social progress. It has not fulfilled these obligations.

*   *   *

> As the mandatory power, South Africa incurred certain obligations to the international community, for which the General Assem-

---

30 *Documents, 1970*, pp. 259-60; cf. above at note 25.
31 *Documents, 1966*, pp. 309-11; cf. above at note 21.
32 General Assembly, *Official Records: 21st Session, Plenary Meetings*, 1439th meeting. [Author's reference.]

bly has supervisory responsibilities. Among these are obligations to report annually on its administration of the territory and to transmit petitions from the inhabitants. South Africa has repeatedly refused to carry out these obligations. We are thus confronted with a continuing material breach of obligations incumbent upon the mandatory power.

*   *   *

By virtue of the breach of its obligations and its disavowal of the Mandate, South Africa forfeits all right to continue to administer the Territory of South West Africa. Indeed, it is because of South Africa's own actions that it can no longer assert its right under the Mandate; and apart from the Mandate, South Africa has no right to administer the Territory.

In preparing our written statement in this proceeding we reexamined the premises upon which our Government's 1966 statement was based. We reaffirmed our conclusion that the General Assembly validly terminated South Africa's right to administer the mandate. In particular, we regard the mandate of December 17, 1920, to have been a treaty in force between South Africa and the League of Nations with the United Nations succeeding the League as a party in 1946. Accordingly, we regard the treaty principles relating to *pacta sunt servanda* and to material breach as applicable to the mandate agreement. Under these principles, South Africa's longstanding material breaches of its obligations under the mandate, which it was legally required to carry out in good faith, clearly justified, in my Government's view, the action of the General Assembly in terminating South Africa's rights. In this regard it should be noted that South Africa does not deny that she failed for more than two decades to furnish the General Assembly with the annual report required under the mandate or to transmit petitions as she had been required to do during the League period.

Now, even if the Court were not to accept the argument that termination of South Africa's rights under the mandate by the General Assembly was justified by the treaty doctrine of material breach, it is my Government's view that the General Assembly had the right to terminate South Africa's rights in the General Assembly's capacity as successor to the League of Nations supervisory responsibility. The General Assembly has accepted the 1950 advisory opinion in which this Court stated that the supervisory authority under the mandate of the League of Nations had passed to the United Nations.[33] On the basis of an exhaustive study of the power of the League to terminate rights under a

33 *Everyman's United Nations* (Eighth ed.), pp. 405 and 447; cf. *The United States in World Affairs, 1950*, p. 389.

mandate, my Government has concluded that this supervisory authority which passed to the United Nations clearly included the authority to terminate rights under a mandate.

Given the seriousness of South Africa's failure to carry out its obligations under the mandate and the failure of South Africa to comply with a series of lesser supervisory measures adopted during that period, the United States considered that the Assembly might reasonably resort to termination, the ultimate supervisory measure. While the Assembly might have appointed a member of the United Nations to administer the territory, there was precedent for the United Nations itself to assume direct responsibility for the territory.

*   *   *

It is the view of the United States that the Assembly's action was legally sufficient to terminate the mandate without any action by the Security Council. Should the Court, however, have any doubt as to the sufficiency of the General Assembly's independent authority where the United Nations is acting as successor to the League with respect to the Namibian mandate, this doubt surely must be satisfied when, as is presently the case, the Security Council has expressly affirmed the General Assembly's action.

The Security Council's affirmation of the General Assembly's resolution in any event serves as the point of departure for the Council's further resolutions with respect to Namibia.

EFFECTS OF SECURITY COUNCIL RESOLUTIONS

In its written statement South Africa has contended that none of the relevant provisions of the charter could serve as a basis for the Security Council resolutions with respect to Namibia.

In the view of the United States the Security Council action on the Namibia question could have been taken either under chapter VI[34] or, in the event the Security Council is regarded as sharing with the General Assembly the United Nations responsibility as successor to the League in supervising Namibia, under article 80, paragraph 1, or under both. It is common practice for the Council not to specify that provision of the charter under which it is acting. The United States has taken the view that in the Namibia case the Council was dealing with a situation under chapter VI the continuation of which it believed was "likely to endanger the maintenance of international peace and security." There have been many cases before the Security Council in which the Council has taken action under chapter VI without a finding that the continu-

34 "Pacific Settlement of Disputes."

ance of a dispute or situation is likely to endanger the maintenance of international peace and security.

It is abundantly clear in my Government's view, from the records of the Council, that the measures taken were not based on chapter VII[35] and do not obligate states to take action under that chapter. I would respectfully draw the attention of the Court to the fact that any action under chapter VII as distinguished from chapter VI requires a preliminary finding under article 39 of the charter that a particular situation constitutes a threat to the peace, breach of the peace, or act of aggression. There was no such finding with respect to the situation in Namibia. Consequently, there could have been no action or measures, whether recommendatory or obligatory, under article 40, 41, or 42.

The question presented to the Court relates only to consequences for states of the continued presence of South Africa in Namibia. Care should be taken in defining the legal consequences flowing from the relevant Security Council resolutions so as to protect individual rights of the inhabitants of Namibia or of citizens of other states, leaving these to be determined in the light of the circumstances surrounding each case. In many cases it will be for the courts of member states to determine, in accordance with recognized principles of private and public international law, the effect on private relationships and transactions of acts taken by the Government of South Africa on behalf of, or concerning, Namibia after the adoption of Resolution 2145 (XXI). It would, for example, be a violation of the rights of individuals if a foreign state should refuse to recognize the rights of Namibians to marry in accordance with the laws in force in Namibia, or refuse to accept their marriage certificate on the ground that it was issued by the illegal South African authorities in Namibia, or would consider their children to be illegitimate. A contract for the sale of goods also should not be declared invalid merely because it was entered into in accordance with ordinary commercial laws applied to Namibia by South Africa. These would not be proper consequences of the United Nations actions on Namibia.

On the other hand, as a matter of present and future policy, it would be proper for states to try to limit future investments in Namibia by all legitimate means at their disposal. The United States announced in May 1970 that its policy with respect to Namibia will be as follows:[36]

1. The United States will henceforth officially discourage investment by U.S. nationals in Namibia.

2. Export-Import Bank credit guarantees will not be made available for trade with Namibia.

3. U.S. nationals who invest in Namibia on the basis of rights

35 Same as note 20.
36 *Bulletin*, June 8, 1970, p. 709 [Author's reference.]

acquired through the South African Government since adoption of General Assembly Resolution 2145 (October 27, 1966) will not receive U.S. Government assistance in protection of such investments against claims of a future lawful government of Namibia.

The United States hopes that others will take similar steps and that an accumulation of such measures may cause the South African Government to accept a peaceful resolution of the international issue of Namibia.

SOUTH AFRICA'S OFFER OF INFORMATION

Mr. President, I should like to comment briefly on the offer by the representative of South Africa to furnish additional information as to conditions in Namibia.

Insofar as the present proceedings are concerned, the most relevant information regarding Namibia would be that which established the conduct of the mandatory with regard to the performance of its obligations under the mandate prior to October 27, 1966, the date on which the General Assembly adopted Resolution 2145 (XXI). Two of the elements of material breach referred to in that resolution are failure to submit reports and to transmit petitions. South Africa does not claim performance of either of these obligations.

The third element of breach specified in General Assembly Resolution 2145 (XXI) is failure to insure the moral and material well-being and security of the indigenous inhabitants of the territory. Many states have, in the course of the General Assembly debate, found that failure evidenced by South Africa's application of apartheid to the territory.

Regarding the general question of evidence, my Government would not incline favorably to any *de novo* examination of the facts. We do not believe, Mr. President, that the Court need establish for itself the facts upon which the General Assembly relied.

General Assembly Resolution 2145 recites that before adopting the resolution the Assembly had studied the reports of the various committees which had been established to exercise the supervisory functions of the United Nations over the administration of the territory. At all relevant times those committees had endeavored to obtain the views of South Africa, which consistently refused to participate in the work of the committees or to assist them in establishing the facts.

Should the Court consider it necessary, despite the considerations which I have just described, to confirm the factual basis on which the Assembly's resolutions were grounded, the best contemporaneous evidence would seem to be that presented to the Court in the *South West Africa* cases.[37] Some 2,000 pages of the pleadings in those cases

37 Cf. *Documents, 1966*, p. 309 n.15.

were devoted to factual questions, and much of the information presented to the Court at that time was adduced by South Africa.

In its written statement South Africa has also offered to produce evidence as to the "latest progress" in Namibia. In the view of my Government, such evidence would not be relevant to the question before the Court.

PROPOSAL FOR A PLEBISCITE IN NAMIBIA

In the course of these proceedings, the South African Government has also proposed that a plebiscite be held in Namibia under the joint supervision of the International Court of Justice and the Government of South Africa. The proposal for a plebiscite is not, in the view of the United States Government, material to the question put to the Court by the Security Council. Therefore, we do not believe that this proposal should in any way be viewed as a basis for the Court's postponing the rendering of its opinion.

The United States does believe that the question of holding a fair and proper plebiscite under appropriate auspices and with conditions and arrangements which would insure a free and informed expression of the will of the people of Namibia deserves study. It is a matter which might be properly submitted to the competent political organs of the United Nations, which have consistently manifested their concern that the Namibians achieve self-determination. The Court may wish to so indicate in its opinion to the Security Council. Should these political organs of the United Nations request the Court to play a role in any plebiscite arrangements, the Court could then consider whether it can appropriately participate in such arrangements. It might be recalled that the officers of the Court, though not the Court itself, have appointed observers to attend the plebiscites in Tenda-Briga in 1947 and in the French Settlements in India in 1949.

SOUTH AFRICA'S PRIMARY RESPONSIBILITY

Mr. President, in accordance with the wishes of the Court, I have refrained from repeating the arguments in my Government's written statement. I would like, at this point, to summarize the conclusions which the Government of the United States submitted in that document.

First, the United Nations validly terminated the rights and authority granted to South Africa under the mandate of December 17, 1920.

Second, South Africa no longer has any rights in Namibia under the mandate, and there is no other legal basis for its continued presence in the territory. South Africa is therefore obligated to terminate its occupation of Namibia and to transfer administration of the territory to the United Nations. This is its overriding obligation, and I respectfully urge that this is the most important conclusion that the Court can reach.

Third, a number of important legal consequences flow from South Africa's continued illegal presence in Namibia. These consequences are of two general kinds. South Africa has certain legal duties which, because of its *de facto* occupation, it must observe so long as it remains in Namibia. Other states also have certain duties under international law with respect to Namibia.

Let me turn first to the consequences for other states: They have the duty to respect the direct responsibility of the United Nations for Namibia and to assist it in exercising those responsibilities and to apply certain specified rules to treaties affecting Namibia.

South Africa's duties include obligations to promote the well-being and development of the inhabitants; to act in conformity with chapter XI of the United Nations Charter concerning non-self-governing territories; to act in conformity with chapter IX[38] and certain other provisions of the charter; and under general international law, to adhere to certain standards in the administration of Namibia. However, it should be made clear that compliance with these obligations in no respect relieves South Africa of its primary responsibility—to terminate its illegal presence in Namibia.

Thank you, Mr. President.

(104) "Legal Consequences for States of the Continued Presence of South Africa in Namibia (South West Africa) Notwithstanding Security Council Resolution 276 (1970)": Advisory Opinion of the International Court of Justice, June 21, 1971.[39]

(Excerpt)

*   *   *

128. In its oral statement and in written communications to the Court, the Government of South Africa expressed the desire to supply the Court with further factual information concerning the purposes and

---

38 "International Economic and Social Cooperation."

39 *I.C.J. Reports 1971*, p. 16. The excerpt reproduced here occurs at pp. 44-46 of the English text, which runs to 333 pages and includes a declaration by the President of the Court as well as separate and dissenting opinions. Dissents were filed by Judges Sir Gerald Fitzmaurice (U.K.) and André Gros (France). Judges Sture Petrén (Sweden) and Charles D. Onyeama (Nigeria) stated that they voted for subparagraph (1) of the operative clause but against subparagraphs (2) and (3).

objectives of South Africa's policy of separate development or *apartheid*, contending that to establish a breach of South Africa's substantive international obligations under the Mandate it would be necessary to prove that a particular exercise of South Africa's legislative or administrative powers was not directed in good faith towards the purpose of promoting to the utmost the well-being and progress of the inhabitants. It is claimed by the Government of South Africa that no act or omission on its part would constitute a violation of its international obligations unless it is shown that such act or omission was actuated by a motive, or directed towards a purpose other than one to promote the interests of the inhabitants of the Territory.

129. The Government of South Africa having made this request, the Court finds that no factual evidence is needed for the purpose of determining whether the policy of *apartheid* as applied by South Africa in Namibia is in conformity with the international obligations assumed by South Africa under the Charter of the United Nations. In order to determine whether the laws and decrees applied by South Africa in Namibia, which are a matter of public record, constitute a violation of the purposes and principles of the Charter of the United Nations, the question of intent or governmental discretion is not relevant; nor is it necessary to investigate or determine the effects of those measures upon the welfare of the inhabitants.

130. It is undisputed, and is amply supported by documents annexed to South Africa's written statement in these proceedings, that the official governmental policy pursued by South Africa in Namibia is to achieve a complete physical separation of races and ethnic groups in separate areas within the Territory. The application of this policy has required, as has been conceded by South Africa, restrictive measures of control officially adopted and enforced in the Territory by the coercive power of the former Mandatory. These measures establish limitations, exclusions or restrictions for the members of the indigenous population groups in respect of their participation in certain types of activities, fields of study or of training, labour or employment and also submit them to restrictions or exclusions of residence and movement in large parts of the Territory.

131. Under the Charter of the United Nations, the former Mandatory had pledged itself to observe and respect, in a territory having an international status, human rights and fundamental freedoms for all without distinction as to race. To establish instead, and to enforce, distinctions, exclusions, restrictions and limitations exclusively based on grounds of race, colour, descent or national or ethnic origin which constitute a denial of fundamental human rights is a flagrant violation of the purposes and principles of the Charter.

132. The Government of South Africa also submitted a request that a plebiscite should be held in the Territory of Namibia under the joint supervision of the Court and the Government of South Africa (para. 16

above). This proposal was presented in connection with the request to submit additional factual evidence and as a means of bringing evidence before the Court. The Court having concluded that no further evidence was required, that the Mandate was validly terminated and that in consequence South Africa's presence in Namibia is illegal and its acts on behalf of or concerning Namibia are illegal and invalid, it follows that it cannot entertain this proposal.

133. For these reasons,

THE COURT IS OF OPINION,

in reply to the question:

"What are the legal consequences for States of the continued presence of South Africa in Namibia, notwithstanding Security Council resolution 276 (1970)?"

by 13 votes to 2,

(1) that, the continued presence of South Africa in Namibia being illegal, South Africa is under obligation to withdraw its administration from Namibia immediately and thus put an end to its occupation of the Territory;

by 11 votes to 4,

(2) that States Members of the United Nations are under obligation to recognize the illegality of South Africa's presence in Namibia and the invalidity of its acts on behalf of or concerning Namibia, and to refrain from any acts and in particular any dealings with the Government of South Africa implying recognition of the legality of, or lending support or assistance to, such presence and administration;

(3) that it is incumbent upon States which are not Members of the United Nations to give assistance, within the scope of subparagraph (2) above, in the action which has been taken by the United Nations with regard to Namibia.

Done in English and in French, the English text being authoritative, at the Peace Palace, The Hague, this twenty-first day of June, one thousand nine hundred and seventy-one, in two copies, one of which will be placed in the archives of the Court and the other transmitted to the Secretary-General of the United Nations.

(Signed) ZAFRULLA KHAN,
President.

(Signed) S. AQUARONE,
Registrar.

(105) Support of the Advisory Opinion: Statement to the United Nations Security Council by Ambassador Bennett, Deputy United States Representative, October 20, 1971.[40]

(Complete Text)

My delegation has listened with great interest to the statements that have been made in the Security Council on the question of Namibia. We have paid particular attention to the statement made by His Excellency Moktar Ould Daddah, President of Mauritania, and his colleagues, the distinguished Foreign Ministers from Liberia, Nigeria, Ethiopia, Chad, and the Sudan, who spoke here on behalf of the Organization of African Unity.

Mr. President,[41] the United States supported General Assembly Resolution 2145,[42] and I would like here to reaffirm our support. We supported Security Council Resolution 284, by which the Namibian problem was referred to the International Court of Justice;[43] and when that body deliberated on the legal consequences for states of the continued presence of South Africa in Namibia, the United States made two contributions to its proceedings. In a written statement to the Court in November 1970 and in an oral statement made before the Court in March 1971,[44] the United States stressed the validity of General Assembly Resolution 2145 and the fact that South Africa's continued presence in Namibia is without legal basis.

In the aftermath of the Court's advisory opinion,[45] the Council's ad hoc subcommittee on Namibia began its task of recommending to the Security Council courses of further action to enable the people of Namibia to exercise their right of self-determination. We are pleased with the spirit of cooperation that prevailed in the ad hoc subcommittee. This spirit has carried over into the proceedings of the Security Council and has made possible the draft resolution we now have before us.

The United States will vote for and support the resolution now before us.[46]

The text before us contains references to certain resolutions on which my Government abstained. Our vote for the present resolution should not be construed as constituting any change in position with regard to those earlier resolutions.

40 USUN Press Release 164; text from *Bulletin*, Nov. 22, 1971, pp. 609-10.
41 Guillermo Sevilla-Sacasa (Nicaragua), President of the Security Council for Nov. 1971.
42 Cf. above at note 21.
43 Cf. above at note 25.
44 Document 103.
45 Document 104.
46 Document 106.

The resolution takes note of the advisory opinion of the International Court of Justice, particularly its conclusions. For our part, the United States accepts these conclusions which declare in paragraph 133 that South Africa is under obligation to withdraw its administration from Namibia immediately and thus put an end to its occupation of the territory and which further declare that member states are "under obligation to recognize the illegality of South Africa's presence in Namibia and the invalidity of its acts on behalf of or concerning Namibia, and to refrain from any dealings with the Government of South Africa implying recognition of the legality of, or lending support or assistance to, such presence and administration." In his speech 2 weeks ago in the General Assembly, Secretary of State William P. Rogers stated our acceptance of these conclusions and observed this was consistent with our support of practical and peaceful means to achieve self-determination and end racial discrimination.[47]

Our acceptance also reflects the importance which my Government attaches to the Court. We consider that this advisory opinion adds a significant and authoritative legal element to the effort of the international community to make it possible for the people of the territory to enjoy their right to self-determination. Our acceptance, of course, does not necessarily imply approval of all the Court's reasoning. We note in this connection concerns about charter interpretation which had been mentioned by several Council members.[48]

The resolution reaffirms Resolution 283, which urges member states to take a number of actions vis-a-vis Namibia.[49] Let me recall in this connection that even before the adoption of that resolution, the United States had announced it would officially discourage investment by U.S. nationals in Namibia, would not make available U.S. Export-Import Bank credit guarantees and other facilities, and would not assist U.S. citizens who invest in Namibia on the basis of rights acquired after the adoption of General Assembly Resolution 2145 in protection of such investments against claims of a future lawful government of Namibia.[50] Following this announcement, my Government made sure that in-

47 Addressing the General Assembly on Oct. 4, 1971, Secretary Rogers stated: "In Africa, where the right to a freer existence is still denied to many, we are constant in our support of practical and peaceful means to achieve self-determination and end racial discrimination. . . . Consistent with that objective, we have decided to accept the advisory opinion of the International Court of Justice on the legal consequences for states of South Africa's continuing occupation of Namibia" (*Bulletin*, Oct. 25, 1971, p. 439). For other excerpts from Secretary Rogers' address see Documents 52, 56, and 124.

48 Secretary Rogers later stated that "We especially had in mind certain interpretations of the Court regarding the legally binding nature of Security Council decisions not taken under the Charter provisions for mandatory action" (Rogers Report, 1971, p. 283).

49 Cf. above at note 24.

50 Cf. above at note 36.

vestors were informed of this new policy, and investment has, in fact, been inhibited.

Mr. President, there are a few aspects of the resolution on which my delegation wishes to make specific comments. In preambular paragraph 7, we note that the term "movement" could be subject to several interpretations. I wish to make it clear that we understand this term in a peaceful sense, consistent with our support of practical and peaceful means to achieve self-determination for the people of Namibia. We would further note that use of the term does not connote support for any particular Namibian group to represent the territory.

With respect to operative paragraph 10 of the resolution, I wish to point out that as stated by the United States in July 1970 in relation to Security Council Resolution 283, and in light of the advisory opinion of 1971—especially paragraphs 133, 118, 122, 123, and 125—from which the resolution now before us has [been] drawn, the United States considers states free to take appropriate action to protect their own citizens and to assist the people of Namibia.

Mr. President, we wish to see no doors closed in dealing with the future of Namibia. We hope that South Africa's participation in the discussion of this resolution indicates a willingness to enter into further talks.[51]

(106) Endorsement of the Advisory Opinion: Security Council Resolution 301 (1971), Adopted October 20, 1971.[52]

(Complete Text)

The Security Council,

Reaffirming the inalienable right of the people of Namibia to freedom and independence, as recognized in General Assembly resolution 1514 (XV) of 14 December 1960,[53]

Recognizing that the United Nations has direct responsibility for Namibia, following the adoption of General Assembly resolution 2145 (XXI) of 27 October 1966,[54] and that States should conduct any relations with or involving Namibia in a manner consistent with that responsibility,

---

51 Contacts between the South African Government and the Secretary-General of the United Nations with regard to Namibia were initiated in 1972 within the framework of Security Council Resolution 309 (1972) of Feb. 4, 1972, which invited the Secretary-General to initiate contacts with all parties concerned with a view to establishing conditions for self-determination and independence. Cf. Rogers Report, 1972, pp. 108-9.

52 U.N. Security Council, Official Records: 26th Year, Resolutions and Decisions, pp. 7-8; adopted by a vote of 13-0-2 (France, U.K.).

53 Documents, 1960, pp. 575-77.

54 Same, 1966, pp. 309-11; cf. above at note 21.

Reaffirming its resolutions 264 (1969) of 20 March 1969,[55] 276 (1970) of 30 January 1970[56] and 283 (1970) of 29 July 1970,[57]

Recalling its resolution 284 (1970) of 29 July 1970,[58] in which it requested the International Court of Justice for an advisory opinion on the question:

"What are the legal consequences for States of the continued presence of South Africa in Namibia, notwithstanding Security Council resolution 276 (1970)?",

Gravely concerned at the refusal of the Government of South Africa to comply with the resolutions of the Security Council pertaining to Namibia,

Recalling its resolution 282 (1970) of 23 July 1970[59] on the arms embargo against the Government of South Africa and stressing the significance of that resolution with regard to the Territory of Namibia,

Recognizing the legitimacy of the movement of the people of Namibia against the illegal occupation of their Territory by the South African authorities and their right to self-determination and independence,

Taking note of the statements of the delegation of the Organization of African Unity, led by the President of Mauritania [Moktar Ould Daddah] in his capacity as current Chairman of the Assembly of Heads of State and Government of that organization,

Noting further the statement of the President of the United Nations Council for Namibia [Edwin Ogebe Ogbu of Nigeria],

Having heard the statements of the delegation of the Government of South Africa,

Having considered the report of the *Ad Hoc* Sub-Committee on Namibia,[60]

1. *Reaffirms* that the Territory of Namibia is the direct responsibility of the United Nations and that this responsibility includes the obligation to support and promote the rights of the people of Namibia in accordance with General Assembly resolution 1514 (XV);

2. *Reaffirms* the national unity and territorial integrity of Namibia;

3. *Condemns* all moves by the Government of South Africa designed to destroy that unity and territorial integrity, such as the establishment of Bantustans;[61]

55 Cf. above at note 22.
56 Cf. above at note 23.
57 Cf. above at note 24.
58 Cf. above at note 25.
59 *Documents, 1970*, pp. 251-53.
60 U.N. document S/10330, in Security Council, *Official Records: 26th Year, Special Supplement No. 5.*
61 South Africa was engaged in carrying out a long-range plan to group Namibia's African population in some 11 tribal homelands or "Bantustans" analogous to those being established in South Africa itself.

4. *Declares* that South Africa's continued illegal presence in Namibia constitutes an internationally wrongful act and a breach of international obligations and that South Africa remains accountable to the international community for any violations of its international obligations or the rights of the people of the Territory of Namibia;

5. *Takes note with appreciation* of the advisory opinion of the International Court of Justice of 21 June 1971;[62]

6. *Agrees* with the Court's opinion, as expressed in paragraph 133 of its advisory opinion:

"(1) that, the continued presence of South Africa in Namibia being illegal, South Africa is under obligation to withdraw its administration from Namibia immediately and thus put an end to its occupation of the Territory;

"(2) that States Members of the United Nations are under obligation to recognize the illegality of South Africa's presence in Namibia and the invalidity of its acts on behalf of or concerning Namibia, and to refrain from any acts and in particular any dealings with the Government of South Africa implying recognition of the legality of, or lending support or assistance to, such presence and administration;

"(3) that it is incumbent upon States which are not Members of the United Nations to give assistance, within the scope of subparagraph (2) above, in the action which has been taken by the United Nations with regard to Namibia.";

7. *Declares* that all matters affecting the rights of the people of Namibia are of immediate concern to all Members of the United Nations and, as a result, the latter should take this into account in their dealings with the Government of South Africa, in particular in any dealings implying recognition of the legality of, or lending support or assistance to, such illegal presence and administration;

8. *Calls once again* upon South Africa to withdraw from the Territory of Namibia;

9. *Declares* that any further refusal of the South African Government to withdraw from Namibia could create conditions detrimental to the maintenance of peace and security in the region;

10. *Reaffirms* the provisions of resolution 283 (1970), in particular paragraphs 1 to 8 and 11;

11. *Calls upon* all States, in the discharge of their responsibilities towards the people of Namibia and subject to the exceptions set forth

62 Document 104.

in paragraphs 122 and 125 of the advisory opinion of 21 June 1971:[63]

(*a*) To abstain from entering into treaty relations with South Africa in all cases in which the Government of South Africa purports to act on behalf of or concerning Namibia;

(*b*) To abstain from invoking or applying those treaties or provisions of treaties concluded by South Africa on behalf of or concerning Namibia which involve active intergovernmental co-operation.

(*c*) To review their bilateral treaties with South Africa in order to ensure that they are not inconsistent with paragraphs 5 and 6 above;

(*d*) To abstain from sending diplomatic or special missions to South Africa that include the Territory of Namibia in their jurisdiction;

(*e*) To abstain from sending consular agents to Namibia and to withdraw any such agents already there;

(*f*) To abstain from entering into economic and other forms of relationship or dealings with South Africa on behalf of or concerning Namibia which may entrench its authority over the Territory;

12. *Declares* that franchises, rights, titles or contracts relating to Namibia granted to individuals or companies by South Africa after the adoption of General Assembly resolution 2145 (XXI) are not subject to protection or espousal by their States against claims of a future lawful Government of Namibia;

13. *Requests* the *Ad Hoc* Sub-Committee on Namibia to continue to carry out the tasks entrusted to it under paragraphs 14 and 15 of Security Council resolution 382 (1970) and, in particular, taking into account the need to provide for the effective protection of Namibian interests at the international level, to study appropriate measures for the fulfilment of the responsibility of the United Nations towards Namibia;

14. *Requests* the *Ad Hoc* Sub-Committee on Namibia to review all treaties and agreements which are contrary to the provisions of the present resolution in order to ascertain whether States have entered into agreements which recognize South Africa's authority over Namibia, and to report periodically thereon;

15. *Calls upon* all States to support and promote the rights of the people of Namibia and to this end to implement fully the provisions of the present resolution;

63 Paragraphs 122 and 125 of the advisory opinion state generally that obligations resulting from the illegality of South Africa's presence in Namibia should not be carried out in a manner detrimental to the people of that territory (*I.C.J. Reports 1971*, pp. 55-56).

16. *Requests* the Secretary-General to report periodically on the implementation of the provisions of the present resolution.

C. The Question of Southern Rhodesia.

[Political arrangements in the self-governing British colony of Southern Rhodesia, where effective political power was monopolized by a white minority comprising less than 5 percent of the 1970 population of some 5,400,000, had been a subject of recurrent complaint in the United Nations from 1962 onward, and became a major issue when the colonial government, under pressure from London to initiate constitutional changes that were felt to threaten long-term white predominance, unilaterally declared the colony independent of the United Kingdom on November 11, 1965. This action was opposed and condemned both by the United Kingdom, which promptly invoked a variety of economic and financial sanctions against its breakaway colony, and by the U.N. General Assembly and Security Council.

In a resolution adopted November 20, 1965, the Security Council called upon the United Kingdom "to quell this rebellion of the racist minority" and called upon all states "to refrain from any action which would assist and encourage the illegal régime and, in particular, to desist from providing it with arms, equipment and military material, and to do their utmost in order to break all economic relations with Southern Rhodesia, including an embargo on oil and petroleum products."[64] In implementation of these recommendations (which were voluntary rather than mandatory in character) the United States embargoed the shipment to Southern Rhodesia of all arms, military equipment, and related items; suspended its 1965 and 1966 quotas for Rhodesian sugar; and urged U.S. firms to avoid trade in "commodities of significant importance to the Southern Rhodesian economy, including petroleum, as well as Rhodesian exports of chrome, asbestos, and tobacco."[65] Although the Security Council recommendations were heeded by many governments and none accorded legal recognition to the Rhodesian regime, the latter remained in firm control within the territory and continued to obtain essential imports by way of South Africa and Portuguese-ruled Mozambique.

In 1966, the United Kingdom returned to the Security Council with a proposal for the imposition of "selective mandatory economic sanctions" against Southern Rhodesia under Article 41 of the U.N. Charter, which enumerates measures not involving the use of armed force that

64 Resolution 217 (1965), Nov. 20, 1965; adopted by a vote of 10 (U.K., U.S.)-0-1 (France).
65 White House statement, Jan. 7, 1967, in *Documents, 1967*, p. 308.

may be invoked by the Council in the event of any threat to the peace, breach of the peace, or act of aggression. In a resolution adopted December 16, 1966, the Security Council determined that the situation in Southern Rhodesia constituted a threat to international peace and security and decided that all U.N. member states must prevent "the import into their territories of asbestos, iron ore, chrome, pig-iron, sugar, tobacco, copper, meat and meat products and hides, skins and leather originating in Southern Rhodesia and exported therefrom after the date of this resolution," and must also prevent any activities by their nationals or in their territories, vessels or aircraft that would tend to promote the export of these commodities from Southern Rhodesia or to facilitate the acquisition by Southern Rhodesia of arms and military equipment, aircraft and motor vehicles, or oil or oil products. Member states were reminded that failure or refusal to implement the resolution would constitute a violation of Article 25 of the Charter, under which all U.N. members agree to accept and carry out the decisions of the Security Council.[66] Under authority vested in the President by Section 5 of the United Nations Participation Act of 1945,[67] as amended, President Johnson on January 5, 1967, signed an Executive Order prohibiting the activities proscribed by the Security Council resolution and delegating authority to the appropriate executive departments to promulgate implementing regulations.[68]

These selective mandatory sanctions having likewise proved ineffective in view of their open disregard by South Africa and Portugal, the Security Council on May 29, 1968, adopted still a third resolution, extending the earlier prohibitions on imports and exports to cover all commodities and products except for exports to Southern Rhodesia of publications, news material, and articles needed for medical, educational, and humanitarian purposes. In addition, the resolution obligated U.N. member states to prohibit transfers to Southern Rhodesia of most funds and other economic resources, to prevent their air carriers and aircraft from operating to Southern Rhodesia, and to deny entry to bearers of Rhodesian passports.[69] This resolution, too, was implemented by an Executive Order signed by President Johnson on July 29, 1968.[70]

---

66 Resolution 232 (1966), Dec. 16, 1966, in *Documents, 1966*, pp. 320-22; adopted by a vote of 11 (U.K., U.S.)-0-4 (Bulgaria, France, Mali, U.S.S.R.).
67 Public Law 264, 79th Cong., 1st sess., Dec. 20, 1945; *Documents, 1945-46*, p. 514.
68 Executive Order 11322, Jan. 5, 1967, in *Presidential Documents*, Jan. 9, 1967, pp. 9-10; cf. White House statement, Jan. 7, 1967, in *Documents, 1967*, pp. 307-8.
69 Resolution 253 (1968), May 29, 1968; adopted unanimously.
70 Executive Order 11419, July 29, 1968, in *Presidential Documents*, Aug. 5, 1968, pp. 1170-71; cf. State Department announcement, July 29, 1968, in *Documents, 1968-69*, pp. 370-72.

That there were limits to the pressures the United States would consider appropriate was evidenced by its refusal in June 1969 to support a further proposed Security Council resolution which, if adopted, would have urged the United Kingdom "to take all necessary measures, including the use of force, to bring an end to the rebellion"; required U.N. members to interrupt all communication with Southern Rhodesia; and extended the application of economic sanctions to South Africa and Mozambique as well as Rhodesia itself.[71] In March, 1970, after Rhodesia had declared itself a republic and severed its last remaining ties with the British crown, the United States went so far as to employ its first Security Council veto to help defeat a similar draft resolution which, among other things, sought to condemn the United Kingdom's persistent refusal to resort to force.[72] The United States did, however, close its consulate in Salisbury, the Rhodesian capital, on March 17, 1970; and it supported a compromise Security Council resolution of March 18, 1970, which reaffirmed existing sanctions, called upon member states to take more stringent measures to prevent any circumvention, and urged increased "moral and material assistance to the people of Southern Rhodesia in their legitimate struggle to achieve freedom and independence."[73]

The hitherto exemplary record of the United States in the observance of U.N. sanctions was marred in 1971 by the action of Congress in approving controversial legislation which, in effect, forbade the President to comply beyond the end of the year with that part of the Security Council resolution of 1966 that prohibited the import of chrome ore or other strategic and critical materials from Southern Rhodesia. Originally put forward as an amendment to the United Nations Participation Act, the so-called "Byrd amendment" (named for Democratic Senator Harry F. Byrd of Virginia) was opposed on behalf of the administration by Assistant Secretary of State Newsom (Document 107) but was supported by influential private persons, among them former Secretary of State Dean Acheson. According to an official summary of the Acheson testimony, the former Secretary of State argued "that Rhodesia was a sovereign nation and its racial policies were an internal matter with which the United Nations could not interfere"; that economic sanctions were not only "without effect on Rhodesia, but ... detrimental to U.S. security"; that the "indigenous white cultures" of Southern Africa were "willing to help the welfare of the areas" more than the United Nations or other countries could do; and that, while ending the boycott would "raise a great deal of commotion" among the nations of black Africa, it would not "impair any national interest" of the United States.[74]

71 U.N. document S/9270/Rev. 1; cf. *Documents, 1968-69*, pp. 377-78.
72 U.N. document S/9696/Corr. 1 and 2; cf. *Documents, 1970*, pp. 246-47.
73 Resolution 277 (1970), Mar. 18, 1970, in *Documents, 1970*, pp. 247-51; adopted by a vote of 14 (U.K., U.S.)-0-1 (Spain).
74 Senate Foreign Relations Committee History, p. 126.

Although denied the support of the Senate Foreign Relations Committee, the Byrd amendment was soon afterward adopted by the Armed Services Committee and incorporated into the text of the Military Procurement Authorization Bill, which passed the Senate on October 6, 1971, by a vote of 82 to 4 following the rejection of motions to strike or modify the Byrd provision. Reformulated as an amendment to the Strategic and Critical Materials Stock Piling Act, the amendment was accepted early in November by a Senate–House conference committee (Document 108a) and, in its final form (Document 108b), became an integral part of the Military Procurement Authorization Act of 1971, which was approved by a 251 to 80 vote of the House on November 10 and passed the Senate on November 11 by a vote of 65 to 19. Although President Nixon made no comment on signing the procurement legislation on November 17, 1971, he later cited the amendment as one of several indications of declining congressional support for the United Nations (Document 121).

Reaction to the Byrd amendment at the United Nations was prompt and vigorous. A 23-nation draft expressing "grave concern" was introduced in the competent General Assembly committee even before congressional action was completed, and the United States announced on November 11 that since the matter was still under consideration by the Congress, it would take no part in the vote (Document 109a). Anticipating presidential signature of the legislation, the General Assembly adopted the proposed resolution in slightly modified form on November 16, 1971, by a vote of 106 to 2, with 13 abstentions and with the United States not participating (Document 109b).

The United Nations was further exercised during late 1971 by a new attempt on the part of the United Kingdom to reach a political settlement with the Rhodesian authorities on terms acceptable to "the Rhodesian people as a whole." A series of U.N. resolutions opposing this effort found the United States consistently in a minority position. The disclosure that talks with "the illegal racist minority regime" in Rhodesia were under way evoked a General Assembly resolution of November 22 insisting that "there should be no independence before majority rule" and that any settlement must be worked out with the fullest participation of nationalist leaders and endorsed freely by the people. The United States abstained on the ground that the resolution prejudged the outcome of the talks in progress.[75] Detailed proposals for a settlement, envisaging a very gradual increase in parliamentary representation for Rhodesian Africans, were made public in Salisbury on November 24 by Rhodesian Prime Minister Ian D. Smith and British Foreign Secretary Sir Alec Douglas-Home. These proposals were explicitly rejected by the General Assembly on December 20, with the

[75] Resolution 2769 (XXVI), Nov. 22, 1971; adopted by a vote of 102-3 (U.K.)-9 (U.S.). Cf. Rogers Report, 1971, p. 283.

United States again abstaining.[76] Noting that the people of Rhodesia
had not yet had the opportunity to express their own views, the United
States also abstained on a draft Security Council resolution that likewise rejected the proposals but was vetoed by the United Kingdom on
December 30, 1971.[77] (The proposals themselves were shelved in May
1972 when a British commission headed by Lord Pearce reported that
while acceptable to the great majority of Rhodesia's quarter-million
Europeans, they had been unmistakably rejected by the great majority
of the territory's more than 5 million Africans.) Finally, the United
States voted against an omnibus resolution on Southern Rhodesia (or
"Zimbabwe", as it was beginning to be called) which was adopted by
the General Assembly on December 10, 1971, and, among other things,
deplored the United Kingdom's "intransigent attitude" and called for
broadened sanctions against the Rhodesian regime together with sanctions against South Africa and Portugal.[78]]

**(107) The United States Position on Southern Rhodesia: Statement by
Assistant Secretary of State Newsom Before the Subcommittee
on Africa of the Senate Committee on Foreign Relations, July 7,
1971.[79]**

(Complete Text)

Mr. Chairman:[80] It is a pleasure to be here with you today and to
share with you and members of your subcommittee my thoughts on the
difficult question of Rhodesia. Because this is my first appearance before your subcommittee, I should like to take a few moments to sketch
in the broad outlines of our policy.

I welcome, particularly, this opportunity to present our views to you
on the Southern Rhodesian situation. As in all international problems
in which men differ, there is justifiable concern on both sides. There is
occasionally emotion on both sides. The Southern Rhodesian regime, in
this country as elsewhere, seeks to advance its cause.

I should like, therefore, first to put the problem in perspective. What
we are dealing with here is essentially an international problem, one
involving the highly charged issues of race and colonialism. It is a prob-

76 Resolution 2877 (XXVI), Dec. 20, 1971; adopted by a vote of 94-8 (U.K.)-22
(U.S.).
77 U.N. document S/10489, Dec. 30, 1971, in Security Council, *Official Records:
26th Year, Supplement for Oct., Nov. and Dec., 1971*, pp. 129-30; failed of
adoption by a vote of 9-1 (U.K.)-5 (U.S.). U.S. abstention is explained in Rogers
Report, 1971, pp. 283-84.
78 Resolution 2796 (XXVI), Dec. 10, 1971; adopted by a vote of 91-9 (U.K.,
U.S.)-12.
79 *Bulletin*, July 26, 1971, pp. 111-15.
80 Sen. Gale W. McGee (Democrat, Wyoming).

lem without analogies, either to our history or to other world situations. It is one which must be approached on its merits, with our own national interests in mind but with the objective of preventing a continuing unresolved and provocative situation in the heart of Africa. Such a situation would not be helpful to us or to our friends.

To illustrate what the problem is, let me first touch on the history.

Just as Rhodesia today occupies a pivotal position in south-central Africa, so it earlier occupied the key role in the former Federation of Rhodesia and Nyasaland. The Federation, organized in 1953, represented an effort by the British and the settlers and Africans in the area to link the three territories economically on a multiracial basis. But despite the 1961 Federation Constitution, which provided for procedures which would eventually lead to African majority rule, concern grew on the part of the Africans at the dominant role played in Federation politics by the white Southern Rhodesians. The Federation finally broke up in 1963 at the insistence of the two northern territories and with the reluctant acquiescence of the British, who granted independence to Zambia and Malawi the following year.

The British, while they also contemplated independence for Southern Rhodesia, continued to insist that it could only be granted after establishment of a legitimately multiracial system within which the African population could aspire to eventual majority rule. Negotiations between the British and the Rhodesians on this crucial point continued intermittently for almost 2 years, but the white minority, determined to maintain its economic and political dominance, refused to concede it. Finally, on November 11, 1965, Ian Smith announced Rhodesia's unilateral declaration of independence from the United Kingdom.

In the face of this act of defiance and given the sense of outrage and betrayal expressed by Rhodesian nationalist leaders and independent African nations, there were strong demands for the use of force. The British Government, then and now the legal sovereign authority over Rhodesia, sought U.N. assistance in bringing the rebellion to an end. The British Government decided against the use of military force—a decision which we supported—but sought in sanctions an effective alternative.

U.S. SUPPORT OF U.N. SANCTIONS

Our policy since then, jointly with the British and other United Nations member states, has been to support measures other than the use of force designed to hasten an acceptable solution to this problem. We have actively supported the various U.N. measures to that end. We supported the Security Council resolution of November 12, 1965, condemning the Smith regime.[81] We supported the December 1966 Se-

81 Resolution 216 (1965); cf. *Documents, 1965*, pp. 215-18.

curity Council resolution imposing selective mandatory sanctions[82] and equally strongly supported the resolution of 1968 making the sanctions comprehensive.[83]

The sanctions do not have a punitive intent. They are intended not to cause hardship for actions already taken but it is the hope that the sanctions, combined with other efforts, will influence the regime to change its policies and adopt as a basis for international acceptance the fundamental principle of eventual majority rule for the over 95 percent of the population which is African.

Under the United Nations Participation Act of 1945, which provides authority for domestic enforcement of U.N. sanctions, President Johnson gave effect to these measures with Executive orders in 1967 and 1968.[84] Barring a significant change in the Rhodesian situation, it remains our policy to endorse and support the economic sanctions now in force. The President and the Secretary of State reaffirmed this policy earlier this year.[85]

While we have supported sanctions, enforced them vigorously ourselves, and worked to insure compliance by other nations, we have from the beginning opposed the use of force, either as a solution to the Rhodesian problem or the broader problems which affect southern Africa, of which the Rhodesian problem is an integral part. On March 17 of last year, the same day we closed our consulate general in Salisbury, we vetoed a Security Council resolution which advocated the total isolation of Rhodesia and implied advocacy of the use of force.[86] Measures of this kind which would go further than sanctions, in our judgment, would only exacerbate the problems already existing in that part of the world and would contribute nothing toward their solution. Despite pressures from some quarters, we will continue to oppose such measures.

OVERALL IMPACT OF SANCTIONS UPON RHODESIA

It is a fact that sanctions have been less than fully effective. And they have thus far not brought about their principal objective: a change in policy by the Smith regime and a willingness on the part of that regime to reach a satisfactory negotiated settlement with Great Britain. A major cause has been the outright refusal of Portugal and South Africa to adhere to sanctions. A secondary cause has been the apparent inability of some other governments to enforce sanctions where their own

[82] Cf. above at note 66.
[83] Cf. above at note 69.
[84] Cf. above at notes 67-68 and 70.
[85] Cf. Document 101 and Rogers Report, 1969-70, p. 155.
[86] Cf. above at note 72.

nationals are concerned. We continue to cooperate with the U.N. Sanctions Committee in its efforts to bring about more uniform compliance with sanctions and are currently looking at possible ways of helping the committee perform its difficult job more effectively. For your information, there are now 110 cases of reported sanctions violations now before the Sanctions Committee, including 32 which deal with chrome ore.

Having noted some of the shortcomings of the sanctions program and the fact that it has not yet achieved its goal, it must be quickly added that sanctions continue to impose very serious constraints upon the Salisbury regime, limit its options, and cause it continuing economic difficulties, despite obvious and understandable efforts on the part of the Rhodesians to portray it otherwise. Imports and exports are well below presanctions levels. Foreign exchange is extremely limited, and the authorities announced last September that foreign exchange allocation controls, already tight, would be tightened still further. Deprived of many necessary imports, Rhodesia has had to improvise by setting up costly substitute industries—constituting a major drain on foreign exchange. Lack of foreign exchange has also made it extremely difficult for the Rhodesian regime to obtain spare parts and necessary equipment replacements to support industry, agriculture, and transportation facilities; and this is, of course, one aspect of sanctions which has a cumulative effect over time. As a result, the railways and airline are suffering. Agriculture has also been hurt by sanctions. Overall agricultural production has declined since 1965. Deprived of the traditional British market for tobacco, now largely preempted by American competition, Rhodesia has been forced to subsidize the tobacco industry, to diversify its agricultural sector, and to seek new markets for new crops in violation of sanctions. It has been a costly process.

Rhodesia has had relatively greater success in the mining and minerals sector of the economy, but in assessing the overall impact of sanctions, it is well to remember that exports from this sector accounted in 1965—the last year before sanctions—for only one-fifth of the total value of Rhodesia's exports.

PROPOSED AMENDMENT TO U.N. PARTICIPATION ACT

Mr. Chairman, having reviewed the background to our Rhodesian policy, I would like to turn to the bill now under consideration. This proposed amendment to the United Nations Participation Act,[87] whatever its intent, would have the effect of invalidating the existing embargo on chrome ore imports from Southern Rhodesia so long as such

87 Document 108a.

imports are not prohibited from the Soviet Union or other Communist countries. Other than chrome ore, or chromite, to use the technical term, there is no other product or commodity traditionally supplied us from Rhodesia which would be affected by the proposed amendment.

This proposal is contrary to United States policy interests. It would while providing relief with regard to one commodity—a commodity for which, I might add, relief can be justified not on the basis of national security interests but on the basis of relative price considerations—call into serious question our will to fulfill our international obligations.

We are not unmindful of the national interest which concerns those who propose this legislation. Were the chrome situation indeed critical, we, too, would seek measures of relief. We do not, however, consider it such; for us the overriding considerations are our international obligations and our desire to do nothing which would undermine movement toward an acceptable solution to the Rhodesian problem.

U.S. CHROME ORE SUPPLY

The matter of chrome ore supply is kept under constant review within the executive branch. Our studies indicate that adequate supplies of chrome are available to American industry at the present time. Inventories of American industry increased last year, and imports and domestic consumption were virtually in balance.

Some months prior to the adoption of Rhodesian sanctions, the U.S. Government commenced the disposal of chrome ore and its equivalents from the stockpiles which had been found in excess of U.S. needs. Disposals of 885,000 short dry tons were authorized by the Congress in Public Law 89—415 of May 11, 1966, and are continuing. The Congress is now considering a bill, S. 773, which would authorize the release of an additional 1.3 million tons of chrome ore over the next 3 years. The administration, including the Office of Emergency Preparedness, which is responsible for maintaining and reviewing stockpile requirements, supports this bill on the grounds that our current stockpiles of chrome ore do in fact exceed our national security requirements.

With respect to U.S. imports of Soviet chrome ore, American purchases from the U.S.S.R. long predated Rhodesian sanctions; nor is the Soviet Union the sole supplier now. In the years immediately prior to sanctions, Rhodesia and the U.S.S.R. each accounted for about one-third of U.S. imports of metallurgical grade chromite. In the period 1967-70, the United States has purchased a larger proportion of its supplies from the U.S.S.R. but has also increased purchases from other producers such as Turkey and South Africa.

Soviet and Rhodesian ore prices are not susceptible to comparison. Since Rhodesian chromite is not traded freely, no current Rhodesian price is ascertainable, and it would be misleading to compare 1971

Soviet prices with presanction Rhodesian prices. While prices for Soviet chromite have doubled since 1966, lower quality chromite from other sources has also increased in price more or less proportionately to that for Soviet ore. The overall rise in market prices does reflect to some extent the impact of sanctions, but it also reflects other factors, such as inflation and worldwide demand, which have caused increases in the prices of most raw materials over the same period.

OBLIGATIONS UNDER THE U.N. CHARTER

Were this bill to become law, it would put the United States in clear violation of the international treaty obligations it freely undertook when the U.N. Charter was ratified. Under article 25 of the charter, the United States is obligated to "accept and carry out the decisions of the Security Council." The Security Council has taken such decisions in the form of sanctions against Southern Rhodesia which it is empowered to impose under chapter VII of the charter.[88] The United States participated in and supported the resolutions in question in 1966 and again in 1968.

United States adherence to sanctions, by virtue of the U.N. Participation Act, has the effect of law, and the act itself was designed to cover just such issues as Rhodesian sanctions. Section 5 of the act, as amended, empowers the President to take appropriate action when article 41 of the charter is invoked. It is precisely that provision of the charter that was invoked in 1966 and again in 1968 in the sanctions resolutions.

I might note parenthetically here that the Senate Foreign Relations Committee, in its original reports on the U.N. Participation Act, took specific note of the extent to which authority was thereby granted to the President and approved those provisions as being consistent with our acceptance of the U.N. Charter and in our national interest.

It has been charged that the United Nations, through the Security Council, acted illegally in intervening in the domestic affairs of a sovereign state. Such charges cannot be sustained. Rhodesia is not a state, and this fact is most dramatically reflected in the failure of the Salisbury regime, 5½ years after the illegal declaration of independence from Britain, to have gained diplomatic recognition by a single government in the world. Not only Great Britian, not only the United States, but the international community as a whole continues to regard Rhodesia as a dependent territory of the United Kingdom. It thus involves, in the first instance, the international responsibility of the United Kingdom, which brought the matter to the United Nations to seek that body's assistance in restoring legality and assuring all the citizens of

88 Same as note 20.

Rhodesia their right to self-determination.

The U.N.'s response, in the form of economic sanctions, invoked chapter VII of the U.N. Charter. I would like to note here that while article 2, paragraph 7, of the charter prohibits the United Nations from interfering in the internal affairs of a state—which, as I have explained, Rhodesia is not—article 2 in any case makes it clear that this prohibition would not apply to the adoption of measures under chapter VII.

MINORITY RULE AND RACIAL SEGREGATION

While the legal basis for the U.N. action is clear, I do not wish to stress it at the expense of some of the more fundamental facts of the Rhodesian case. Our policy has from the first been based on our support for eventual majority rule and basic human rights for the 5 million black citizens of Rhodesia who comprise over 95 percent of that territory's population. The present regime, not only by law but by constitutional provision, has excluded the vast majority of its citizens from any meaningful role in the political process for the indefinite future and determined that [the] African majority may never—I stress the word "never"—aspire to a majority role within Rhodesia. The present regime has, by the Land Tenure Act, divided the land on what has been called an "equal" basis—half for the tiny white minority, half for the African majority, with the most desirable lands in the first category. The present regime has introduced a "property owners' protection bill," with the purpose of "protecting" property by a rigid system of legally enforced racial separation, aimed initially at Africans but now directed as well at the approximately 25,000 Asian and Colored residents of Rhodesia. Although education has been called the means whereby all can advance within Rhodesian society, the regime spends about 10 times as much per capita on white students as it does on black ones. Through the constitution promulgated last year and other measures, the regime has strengthened white minority rule and moved toward the kind of rigidly institutionalized system of racial segregation and "separate development" characteristic of South Africa.

IMPLICATIONS FOR PEACE AND SECURITY

Quite apart from our own views about the kind of system now prevailing in Rhodesia, we believe that its denial of self-determination and majority rule, in the present African context, is a legitimate subject for international concern. The course which Rhodesia has followed since 1965 has contributed toward a heightening of the black-white confrontation in southern Africa. The situation there, while it may provide the shortrun illusion of internal stability, is, in our judgment, seriously prejudicial to the longer run stability of Africa and of Rhodesia itself. We do not think it likely that a minority of 230,000 whites can reasonably expect to maintain political domination indefinitely over an African population 21 times as numerous—a population which every 17 months increases by an amount equal to the entire white population. And we are concerned that its efforts to do so, over time, will have serious implications for the peace and security of the entire region.

In this connection, it is our impression that the South African and Portuguese Governments themselves are not happy with the course of Rhodesian developments and would prefer to see a Rhodesian situation more acceptable to the world community. We believe that these misgivings have contributed in part to the refusal of either to recognize the Smith regime.

The British Government and the Rhodesian authorities are now engaged in preliminary discussions which, if a sufficiently broad basis of agreement can be found, could lead to substantive negotiations. We have consistently supported British efforts to obtain a satisfactory settlement, and none are more anxious than I to see such a settlement reached. We are not now in a position to speculate about either the duration or outcome of this current round of talks. But, pending their outcome, it is important that we seek to avoid any action which would lessen their chances of success.[89]

The legislation now under consideration would have exactly this effect. It would encourage the Rhodesian authorities in their determination to maintain a situation which we consider neither practically tenable, except in the short run, nor morally defensible at all. Its enactment would make it clear that the United States, in return for better access to chrome ore at lower prices, is prepared formally and unilaterally to renounce a freely assumed treaty obligation; we would be the first nation to do so over the Rhodesian sanctions issue. We would damage our standing in almost all of Africa and in those other nations of the world that see the Rhodesian issue as a test of our commitment to our international obligations. We would strengthen the arguments of those who maintain that the only possible solution in southern Africa is a violent solution. We would weaken the hand of the British in their efforts to bring about a negotiated settlement. We would undermine the U.N. effort to enforce sanctions, which we have thus far sought to uphold and, wherever possible, to strengthen. And we would open to question the long-term credibility of the United States Government with regard to its treaty obligations and commitments.

89 Cf. above at notes 75-78.

(108) Congressional Abrogation of the Embargo on Imports of Rhodesian Chrome: The Byrd Amendment.

(a) Chrome and the National Stockpile: Conference Report on the Military Procurement Authorization Bill, November 5, 1971.[90]

(Excerpt)

*   *   *

TITLE V–GENERAL PROVISIONS

CHROME AND THE NATIONAL STOCKPILE

Section 503 of the Senate amendment contains language designed to remove the embargo on the importation of chrome ore from Rhodesia.

The language of Section 503, as added by the Senate, would amend the United Nations Participation Act of 1945 (22 U.S.C. 287c(a))[91] by adding the following new language:

On or after January 1, 1972, the President may not prohibit or regulate the importation into the United States pursuant to this section of any material determined to be strategic and critical pursuant to section 2 of the Strategic and Critical Materials Stock Piling Act (50 U.S.C. 98a), which is the product of any foreign country or area not listed as a Communist-dominated country or area in general headnote 3(d) of the Tariff Schedules of the United States (19 U.S.C. 1202), for so long as the importation into the United States of material of that kind which is the product of such Communist-dominated countries or areas is not prohibited by any provision of law.

Stated very simply, the language provides that the President cannot prohibit imports of a strategic material from a free world country if importation of such material is permitted from a Communist-dominated country.

The issue involved in the Senate language is whether the United States need for chrome ore, both from an economic and national security standpoint, should be subordinated to the policy position established by the United Nations in its sanctions against Rhodesia.

The United Nations Security Council, for the first time in the history

---

90 U.S. House of Representatives, 92d Cong., 1st sess., Conference Report 92-618, Nov. 5, 1971 (Washington: G.P.O., 1971), pp. 21-23.
91 Cf. note 67 above.

of the United Nations, on December 16, 1966, imposed mandatory economic sanctions on Rhodesia.[92] The country's primary exports— asbestos, iron ore, *chrome ore*, pig iron, sugar, tobacco, copper, and meat and meat products were placed on the selective sanctions list. The effective date of the sanctions order was January 5, 1967.

On May 29, 1968, the United Nations Security Council voted to broaden the sanctions by imposing a virtual total embargo on all trade.[93] On March 18, 1970, the Security Council reaffirmed existing sanctions and called on member states to enforce them more strictly.[94]

The President of the United States, on January 5, 1967, issued an Executive Order, Number 11322, which effectively implemented the economic embargo adopted by the Security Council of the United Nations.[95]

The United Nations Security Council Sanctions Committee, in a report published in June 1970, reported that it received 21 complaints, all from the United Kingdom, of violations involving chromite and ferrochrome shipments from Rhodesia to France, Japan, Netherlands, Italy, Spain, West Germany and the United States. The U.S.S.R. has identified Red China as another customer for Rhodesian material. Mozambique and the Republic of South Africa did not observe the sanctions from the outset and have helped to facilitate the exportation of Rhodesian chrome.

The principal impact of the economic embargo on imports from Rhodesia is the inability of the United States industry to import chrome ore.

Chromium is a strategic mineral essential to the production of steel. It is not produced in the United States.

There are legitimate and important national security considerations involved in evaluating continuation of our current reliance on the Soviet Union for more than 60 percent of our national needs for a strategic and critical material like chrome. While there is currently a surplus of chrome in the national stockpile of critical materials, the surplus is not large enough to meet U.S. needs for very long and further dissipation of the stockpile would be damaging to the national security. Furthermore, it would defeat the very purpose of the stockpile if the United States were to rely on the stockpile as a major source of chrome in the future as it has in recent years.

As the dominant world supplier of chrome, the Russians have driven the price from a presanction level of about $25 per ton up to present levels of $72 per ton. Thus, the present price is 288 percent of the presanction price, according to U.S. Bureau of Mines figures.

---

92 Cf. above at note 66.
93 Cf. above at note 69.
94 Cf. above at note 73.
95 Cf. above at note 68.

Foreign producers of stainless steel, who may benefit from Rhodesian sanctions (by virtue of a capability of securing lower cost Rhodesian ore in violation of the sanctions) have increased their penetration of U.S. markets. Imports of specialty steels are at an all-time high—22% of the total domestic market in the first quarter of 1971. For some individual specialty steels, the penetration is even greater; 35 percent of stainless cold rolled sheets, 68 percent of the market for stainless wire rods, and 54 percent for stainless wire. The imports have a direct effect on domestic employment and production in the specialty steel and the ferroalloy industries.

Discussion of the Senate position on this matter reflected the general consensus that continued observance of the U.N. imposed embargo against the importation of chrome ore from Rhodesia adversely affects the national interests of the United States in that it—

(a) makes the United States dependent upon the Soviet Union as a major source of a critical defense material,

(b) places U.S. steel producers in a very unfavorable competitive position in both the domestic and international market,

(c) contributes directly to unemployment in the U.S. steel industry, and

(d) substantially increases pressure to reduce the amount of chrome ore maintained in the national stockpile.

In view of these considerations, the House agreed to accept the Senate provision on this subject. However, consistent with the objectives of the House-Senate conferees on this matter, the Senate conferees agreed to accept House language which places this statutory change in the Strategic and Critical Materials Stockpiling Act (50 U.S.C. 98).

*   *   *

(b) The Military Procurement Authorization Act of 1971: Public Law 92-156, Approved November 17, 1971.[96]

(Excerpts)

*   *   *

96 Public Law 92-156, Nov. 17, 1971, p. 4. For a further excerpt from the same act see Document 81a; for presidential comment see Document 121.

TITLE V—GENERAL PROVISIONS

*   *   *

SEC. 503. The Strategic and Critical Materials Stock Piling Act (60 Stat. 596; 50 U.S.C. 98–98h) is amended (1) by redesignating section 10 as section 11, and (2) by inserting after section 9 a new section 10 as follows:

"SEC. 10. Notwithstanding any other provision of law, on and after January 1, 1972, the President may not prohibit or regulate the importation into the United States of any material determined to be strategic and critical pursuant to the provisions of this Act, if such material is the product of any foreign country or area not listed as a Communist-dominated country or area in general headnote 3(d) of the Tariff Schedules of the United States (19 U.S.C. 1202), for so long as the importation into the United States of material of that kind which is the product of such Communist-dominated countries or areas is not prohibited by any provision of law."

*   *   *

(109) Reaction of the United Nations General Assembly.

(a) Statement by Ambassador William E. Schaufele, Jr., to the Fourth Committee of the General Assembly (Trusteeship and Non-Self-Governing Territories), November 11, 1971.[97]

(Complete Text)

I have listened to the statements before the committee yesterday and today. I appreciate the spirit in which most of them were given. Our aims remain the same—the achievement of majority rule in Southern Rhodesia. However, I categorically reject any idea that the United States has been violating the sanctions program.

The matter to which the draft resolution[98] alludes is still under consideration in the U.S. Congress. It would be inappropriate, therefore, for my delegation to take part in the vote.

97 USUN Press Release 183, Nov. 11, 1971; text from *Bulletin*, Dec. 13, 1971, p. 690. Ambassador Schaufele held the position of Senior Adviser to the U.S. Permanent Representative to the U.N.
98 Draft resolution A/C.4/L.988/Rev. 1; adopted by the Fourth Committee Nov. 11, 1971, by a roll-call vote of 93-2-12, with the U.S. not participating.

We recognize the committee's concern in this matter, and the executive branch of the U.S. Government has made known to the Congress its own similar concern and position on this matter.[99] Under these circumstances we believe that the resolution would not serve any useful purpose.

With one exception, which arose from the fulfillment of a contract entered into prior to the imposition of sanctions, the United States has not imported any chrome from Southern Rhodesia since 1965. At the same time estimates in the latest Sanctions Committee report show that more Southern Rhodesian chrome is available and exported than was the case in 1965.

This can only have resulted from violations of the sanctions by other countries. It will not pass unnoticed in my country that no other nation is named in this resolution. Under these circumstances we can hardly consider this an evenhanded resolution.

My Government will continue to adhere to the broad overall sanctions program. Moreover, we will be prepared, at the proper time, to make a report to the Sanctions Committee of the Security Council on this legislation and its possible effects on the sanctions program.

(b) "Question of Southern Rhodesia": General Assembly Resolution 2765 (XXVI), Adopted November 16, 1971.[100]

(Complete Text)

The General Assembly,

Having considered the question of Southern Rhodesia,

Recalling its resolution 1514 (XV) of 14 December 1960, containing the Declaration on the Granting of Independence to Colonial Countries and Peoples,[101] and its resolution 2621 (XXV) of 12 October 1970, containing the programme of action for the full implementation of the Declaration,

Recalling also the relevant resolutions of the Security Council, particularly its resolutions 232 (1966) of 16 December 1966, 253 (1968) of 29 May 1968, 277 (1970) of 18 March 1970[102] and 288 (1970) of 17 November 1970,

Recalling further all previous resolutions concerning the question of Southern Rhodesia adopted by the General Assembly and the Special

99 Cf. Document 107.
100 General Assembly, *Official Records: 26th Session, Supplement No. 29* (A/8429), pp. 97-98; adopted by a vote of 106-2 (Portugal, South Africa)-13, with the U.S. not participating.
101 *Documents, 1960*, pp. 575-77.
102 Cf. above at notes 66, 69, and 73.

Committee on the Situation with regard to the Implementation of the Declaration on the Granting of Independence to Colonial Countries and Peoples, and also the consensus adopted by the Special Committee at its 828th meeting, on 6 October 1971,[103]

Expressing its grave concern at the recent decision taken by the Congress of the United States of America which,[104] if confirmed, would permit the importation of chrome into the United States from Southern Rhodesia and thus would constitute a serious violation of the above-mentioned Security Council resolutions imposing sanctions against the illegal regime in Southern Rhodesia,

1. *Calls upon* the Government of the United States of America to take the necessary measures, in compliance with the relevant provisions of Security Council resolutions 253 (1968), 277 (1970) and 288 (1970) and bearing in mind its obligations under Article 25 of the Charter of the United Nations, to prevent the importation of chrome into the United States from Southern Rhodesia;

2. *Requests* the Government of the United States to inform the General Assembly at its current session of the action taken or envisaged in the implementation of the present resolution;

3. *Requests* the President of the General Assembly to draw the attention of the Government of the United States to the urgent need for the implementation of the present resolution;

4. *Reminds* all Member States of their obligations under the Charter to comply fully with the decisions of the Security Council on mandatory sanctions against the illegal régime in Southern Rhodesia;

5. *Decides* to keep this and other aspects of the question under continuous review.

D. Defense of American Policy.

[Developments concerning Rhodesia during the 1971 session of the U.N. General Assembly[105] afforded a dramatic illustration of the divergence on policy toward Southern Africa that had developed between the United States and a majority of U.N. member nations, partic-

---

103The consensus in question read: "The Special Committee, noting with concern the recent decision of the United States Senate which, if confirmed, would permit the importation of chrome into the United States of America from Southern Rhodesia and thus would violate the sanctions being applied by the Security Council, urges the United States Government to take the necessary measures, in compliance with the relevant provisions of Security Council resolutions ... to prevent the enactment of such legislation" (*UN Monthly Chronicle*, Nov. 1971, p. 85).

104 Document 108b.

105 Cf. above at notes 74-78.

ularly those belonging to the Communist and "third world" groups. The same divergence was apparent both in the Assembly's actions concerning Namibia[106] and in its debates and resolutions on *apartheid* in South Africa and on conditions in the Portuguese-administered African territories. Of the eight resolutions that comprised the basic statement on *apartheid* adopted by the Assembly on November 29, the United States voted for four, abstained on three, and voted "no" on one that called, in the words of Secretary of State Rogers, "for extreme and impracticable measures, including the adoption by the Security Council of enforcement measures against South Africa under chapter VII of the Charter."[107] Similarly with regard to the Portuguese territories, the United States was in the small minority that voted against an Assembly resolution of December 10 which (again quoting Secretary Rogers) "reiterated a number of extreme measures we had opposed in previous years."[108]

The vote on this latter resolution happened to follow by only a day the announcement of a new agreement between the United States and Portugal on American use of the Azores air base and on economic aid for Portuguese development (Document 47). Such a coincidence, in the eyes of anticolonial elements in the United Nations, could only confirm what they regarded as the identification of the United States with Portuguese colonialism in Africa. Such reactions, indeed, were not confined to "third world" or Communist critics but were found even within the United States' own delegation to the General Assembly. Representative Charles J. Diggs, Jr., a Michigan Democrat who was chairman of the Congressional Black Caucus and had been appointed by the President as a delegate to the Assembly session, took the dramatic step of resigning his appointment on December 17 in protest against what he called the "stifling hypocrisy" of the Nixon administration's policy toward black Africa.

Citing an "erosion of our policy here at the United Nations on African questions, beginning in 1969, first to abstaining on important issues on African policy and, finally, to actually voting against such resolutions," Congressman Diggs described the net effect of the American performance during 1971 as a "sub rosa alliance with the forces of racism and repression in southern Africa." "Many people at the mission," he said, "including the Ambassador [George H. Bush], have been frustrated in their desires for a more enlightened policy because of the instructions that have come down. They have fought for a more enlightened position and have lost." The new agreement with Portugal, in

---

[106] Cf. above at notes 27-28.

[107] Resolutions 2775 F (XXVI); adopted by a vote of 86-6 (U.S.)-22. Cf. Rogers Report, 1971, p. 284.

[108] Resolution 2795 (XXVI); adopted by a vote of 105-8 (U.S.)-5. Cf. Rogers Report, 1971, p. 284.

Representative Diggs' opinion, amounted to an "open alliance" with
that country, permitting it to "wage war against the black peoples" in
its African territories; an American "partnership in the subjugation of
the African people."[109]

Some response to these and similar charges was included in a year-end
news conference in which Secretary of State Rogers offered a widely
different appraisal of American policy in Africa (Document 110).]

(110) United States Policy Toward Africa: News Conference Statement by Secretary of State Rogers, December 23, 1971.[110]

(Excerpt)

* * *

Q. Mr. Secretary, Congressman Diggs resigned from the U.N. delegation last week and as part of his resignation statement included a long accusation against the administration's African policy, its decisions on Rhodesian chrome—its aid to Portugal was the watershed, he said.[111] Without repeating that whole thing, I wonder if you have a response to it as to what the administration's policy is toward these states—Portugal, Rhodesia, South Africa—and the question of the black colonies that Portugal has.

A. Well, I don't want to engage in any debate with my friend Congressman Diggs. Our policy in Africa has been set forth, I think, rather fully in our policy statements.[112] We have always supported the idea of self-determination. We oppose racism; we have opposed apartheid; we have taken the leadership over the years in supporting those nations that have become independent. We have good relations with most of the African nations now. We hope to continue that.

Now, our support for Portugal, and with particular reference to the Azores bases,[113] which was one of the complaints of Congressman Diggs, is unrelated to Africa. Portugal is a member of a military alliance. And the Azores, we believe, is an important base for NATO and for our

---

109 *New York Times*, Dec. 18, 1971. The article describes Ambassador Bush as sharply critical of Representative Diggs' action, but does not cite any reply to the latter's substantive charges.
110 Department of State Press Release 303, Dec. 23, 1971; text from *Bulletin*, Jan. 17, 1972, pp. 55-56. For further excerpts from the same news conference see Documents 10, 30, 64, and 116.
111 Cf. above at note 109.
112 Cf. Documents 101-102.
113 Cf. Document 47.

forces. We have put restrictions on any support we have given to Portugal so that it can't be used in connection with any African matters. And we regret the fact that Congressman Diggs feels this way. We think that the policies we are following are in our national interests. And I am particularly pleased that during this administration, I believe, our relations with most African countries have improved. I am particularly pleased that Mrs. Nixon is going to Africa. It is the first time any First Lady has made that visit. She is going to visit three countries.[114]

As you know, I was the first Secretary of State who has ever been there.[115] Our relations continue to be good with African nations.

*   *   *

[114] Mrs. Nixon visited Liberia, Ghana, and the Ivory Coast Jan. 1-8, 1972. For documentation see *Presidential Documents*, Jan. 10, 1972, p. 37; same, Jan. 17, 1972, pp. 44-45.
[115] Cf. above at note 3.

VIII.
INTER-AMERICAN
AFFAIRS

[Concord and harmony were in short supply in the international relations of the American states in 1971. The economic disparities and psychological strains that had long marked the relationship between the United States and its Latin American neighbors had not been healed by President Kennedy's Alliance for Progress,[1] President Johnson's dream of Latin American economic integration,[2] or President Nixon's promise of "a more mature partnership" that would be dedicated to "improving the quality of life in this new world of ours."[3] Economic growth in Latin America, while substantial by any standards, had been largely canceled out by population increases which checked the rise in per capita income and mass living standards. The struggle of revolutionary and antirevolutionary forces in Latin American countries had intensified as hijackings, kidnappings, and other forms of revolutionary violence proliferated, evoking harsh and often cruel repression by defenders of entrenched privilege and/or "guided development." The waning of Fidel Castro's Cuba as a source of revolutionary energy was offset by the emergence of the "Popular Unity" regime of President Salvador Allende Gossens of Chile as a new revolutionary center whose influence extended throughout the Western Hemisphere and even beyond.

In this hemispheric confrontation of leftist and rightist tendencies, the United States was almost automatically aligned with the conservative and military regimes in power in such countries as Brazil and Paraguay—and almost automatically at odds with those governments which, as in Chile, sought to emphasize their socialist and populist character through special efforts to curb the power of foreign, multinational corporations in their countries. With some of these governments, as in Peru, the United States had managed to reach at least a temporary accommodation. With other Latin American countries, such as Ecuador, it was involved in bitter controversies arising less from

[1] *Documents, 1961*, pp. 395-437.
[2] Same, *1967*, pp. 328-60.
[3] Remarks of Oct. 31, 1969, in same, *1968-69*, pp. 429-38.

differences of social philosophy than from specific conflicts of interest with regard to fishing rights and similar matters.

Despite these negative trends, U.S. authorities were able to view the progress of Latin American affairs in 1971 with a measure of reassurance. Secretary of State Rogers, for instance, summed up the year's experience in terms of a continued and even accelerating advance movement "from a relationship of predominance to one of partnership with Latin America." Yet even the Secretary of State did not deny that, while the United States had not swerved from its basic purpose of "helping the Americas help themselves, . . . we were not able to pursue this goal as effectively as we had hoped."[4] The differences between the United States and its American partners had been particularly in evidence during the earlier part of the year at meetings of the principal organs of the newly reconstructed Organization of American States (O.A.S.), the 24-member regional organization in which most independent countries of the hemisphere participated (Documents 111-113). Many of these tensions, moreover, had been aggravated during the second half of 1971 by the enunciation of the United States' "New Economic Policy" on August 15 and the imposition of a temporary surcharge on import duties that bore especially heavily on Latin American countries (Documents 115-116).

The following documentation reflects one positive development of importance in the somewhat tardy ratification by the United States of a protocol of support for the 1967 Treaty for the Prohibition of Nuclear Weapons in Latin America, or Treaty of Tlatelolco (Document 114). In addition, it includes authoritative statements of U.S. policy toward two of the most controversial governments in the Americas—Cuba (Document 117) and Chile (Document 118)—as well as an account of the ongoing negotiations relative to a new status for the Panama Canal and the U.S.-administered Canal Zone (Document 119).]

A. The Organization of American States (O.A.S.).

[Originally established in 1890 and extensively remodeled in 1948[5] and again in 1967,[6] the regional organization of the Americas entered the 1970s with a refurbished institutional structure but with no diminution of the latent opposition between the views and purposes of the

---

[4] Rogers Report, 1971, p. 119.

[5] Charter of the Organization of American States, signed at Bogotá Apr. 30, 1948, and entered into force Dec. 13, 1951 (TIAS 2361; 2 UST 2394); text in *Documents, 1948,* pp. 484-502.

[6] Protocol of Amendment to the Charter of the Organization of American States, signed at Buenos Aires Feb. 27, 1967, and entered into force Feb. 27, 1970 (TIAS 6847; 21 UST 607); summaries in *Documents, 1968-69,* pp. 399-401 and in *The World This Year, 1971,* pp. 149-50.

United States, on one side, and the increasingly self-conscious nationalist aspirations of a number of Latin American countries on the other. Political terrorism, fishing rights, economic policy, and the position of Cuba—excluded from participation in the organization in 1962[7]—were among the issues on which the United States was to clash with various of its hemispheric partners in 1971, and on which serious disagreements also existed among the Latin American countries themselves.[8]

The structural changes in the organization that had taken effect in 1970 centered in the emergence of a new supreme organ, the General Assembly, representing all O.A.S. member states and meeting annually to decide the general action and policy of the organization, determine the structure and function of its organs, and consider any matter relating to friendly relations among the American states. Two special sessions of the new General Assembly had already been held in Washington in 1970,[9] and a Third Special Session was held in the U.S. capital on January 25–February 2, 1971, to deal with the disturbing issue of political terrorism in the Americas (Document 111). The delegates assembled for this purpose were compelled, however, to interrupt their labors on January 30-31 for a special two-day Meeting of Consultation of Ministers of Foreign Affairs which was demanded by Ecuador to consider its fisheries dispute with the United States (Document 112). It was only with the First Regular Session of the General Assembly, held in San José, Costa Rica, on April 14-24, 1971, that this new organ began to exercise its primary function as a forum for broad discussion of inter-American problems and policies (Document 113).]

1. Third Special Session of the General Assembly, Washington, January 25–February 2, 1971.

[The problem of political terrorism in the Americas, especially the recent outbreak of kidnapping of foreign officials and others for the purpose of extorting ransom money, had been the principal subject of discussion at the First Special Session of the O.A.S. General Assembly in June 1970. On that occasion, the participating countries had unanimously voted to condemn such actions as "common crimes" (rather than political offenses) and had charged the Inter-American Juridical Committee with drafting one or more inter-American instruments on

[7] Documents, 1962, pp. 344-46.
[8] For surveys of O.A.S. developments in 1971 see especially The World This Year, 1972, pp. 156-58 and (more fully) Joseph John Jova, "A Review of the Progress and Problems of the Organization of American States," Bulletin, Sept. 13, 1971, pp. 284-93.
[9] For the First Special Session (June 25–July 8, 1970) see Documents, 1970, pp. 263-72. The Second Special Session (Aug. 24-25, 1970) was limited to filling a vacancy in the Inter-American Juridical Committee.

"kidnapping, extortion, and assaults against persons, in cases in which these acts may have repercussions on international relations," for consideration by a further Special Assembly Session.[10] Acting on this mandate, the Juridical Committee had approved in September 1970 a draft convention on terrorism, the kidnapping of diplomats and the hijacking of aircraft. In addition to classifying such acts as common crimes, it stated that persons charged with specified terrorist acts should not be granted the traditional right of political asylum.[11]

In part because it lumped together offenses against both official and unofficial persons, this draft occasioned considerable disagreement when taken up by the Third Special Session of the General Assembly in January 1971. Should the convention in fact attempt to deal with all forms of terrorism, or should it be limited to attacks against foreign government officials and their dependents? "Six countries, led by Brazil and Argentina, argued that no convention would be meaningful in coping with the problem unless it addressed itself to all aspects of terrorism. A larger group felt that such a sweeping approach would endanger the principle of political asylum. The United States, which favored a narrower convention, nevertheless sought to bridge the gap between these two points of view, but our efforts were unsuccessful," reported Ambassador Joseph John Jova, the U.S. Permanent Representative to the O.A.S.[12]

The arguments for prompt agreement on a limited, first-step convention, restricted to offenses against official persons, were put forward by Secretary Rogers in a major statement to the Assembly on January 27[13] but failed to convince those governments, all of them more or less right-wing in character, that favored a broader convention providing for the extradition of all persons charged with political terrorism. Six delegations—those of Argentina, Brazil, Ecuador, Guatemala, Haiti, and Paraguay—actually walked out of the Assembly on February 1 to manifest their dissatisfaction with a convention that, in their view, was far too limited in scope. Of the 17 delegations remaining, 14 approved a watered-down text aimed mainly at assaults against foreign officials and their families; but even this draft was opposed by representatives of the left-wing governments of Bolivia, Chile, and Peru, notwithstanding its explicit affirmation that none of its provisions could be interpreted as impairing the right of asylum. The draft convention thus arrived at (Document 111) was approved by the General Assembly on February 2, 1971, by a mere 13 votes,[14] with Chile opposed, Bolivia and Peru

10 *Documents, 1970*, pp. 270-72.
11 *Keesing's*, p. 24478.
12 Jova, *loc. cit.* (note 8), p. 286.
13 *Bulletin*, Feb. 22, 1971, pp. 228-30.
14 Colombia, Costa Rica, Dominican Republic, El Salvador, Honduras, Jamaica, Mexico, Nicaragua, Panama, Trinidad and Tobago, United States, Uruguay, and Venezuela.

abstaining, and Barbados absent. In a resolution approved the same day, the Assembly instructed the O.A.S. Permanent Council to study those aspects of the problem that the convention failed to deal with.[15]

Transmitting the convention to the Senate on May 11, 1971, with his request for advice and consent to ratification, President Nixon noted that its terms provided for accession by both members and non-members of the O.A.S. and expressed the hope that it would be "ratified promptly by all its signatories and eventually by other states as well." The convention was favorably reported by the Senate Foreign Relations Committee and approved by a 74 to 0 vote of the Senate on June 12, 1972, but ratification was delayed by the administration with the explanation that it awaited the enactment of implementing legislation.[16] In addition, the United States by 1972 had become primarily concerned with seeking United Nations approval of an anti-terrorism convention of worldwide rather than regional scope.]

(111) Convention to Prevent and Punish the Acts of Terrorism Taking the Form of Crimes Against Persons and Related Extortion That Are of International Significance, Approved by the General Assembly of the Organization of American States on February 2, 1971.[17]

(Complete Text)

WHEREAS:

The defense of freedom and justice and respect for the fundamental rights of the individual that are recognized by the American Declaration of the Rights and Duties of Man[18] and the Universal Declaration of Human Rights[19] are primary duties of states;

The General Assembly of the Organization, in Resolution 4, of June 30, 1970, strongly condemned acts of terrorism, especially the kidnapping of persons and extortion in connection with that crime, which it declared to be serious common crimes;[20]

[15] O.A.S. document AG/90, in *Bulletin*, Feb. 22, 1971, pp. 233-34; adopted by a vote of 14 (U.S.)-0-2.

[16] Nixon message in *Bulletin*, July 5, 1971, p. 28; subsequent comment in same, Dec. 4, 1972, p. 648. The treaty was brought into force for ratifying states with the deposit of ratifications by Nicaragua (Mar. 8, 1973) and Costa Rica (Oct. 16, 1973). Ratifications were subsequently deposited by Venezuela on Nov. 7, 1973 and by Mexico on Mar. 17, 1975.

[17] O.A.S. document AG/88 rev. 1; text from *Bulletin*, Feb. 22, 1971, pp. 231-33; approved by a vote of 13 (U.S.)-1-2, with six members not present (cf. above at note 14).

[18] *Documents, 1948*, pp. 528-32.

[19] Same, pp. 430-35.

[20] Same, *1970*, pp. 270-72.

Criminal acts against persons entitled to special protection under international law are occurring frequently, and those acts are of international significance because of the consequences that may flow from them for relations among states;

It is advisable to adopt general standards that will progressively develop international law as regards cooperation in the prevention and punishment of such acts; and

In the application of those standards the institution of asylum should be maintained and, likewise the principle of nonintervention should not be impaired,

THE MEMBER STATES OF THE ORGANIZATION OF AMERICAN STATES HAVE AGREED UPON THE FOLLOWING ARTICLES:

ARTICLE 1

The contracting states undertake to cooperate among themselves by taking all the measures that they may consider effective, under their own laws, and especially those established in this convention, to prevent and punish acts of terrorism, especially kidnapping, murder, and other assaults against the life or physical integrity of those persons to whom the state has the duty according to international law to give special protection, as well as extortion in connection with those crimes.

ARTICLE 2

For the purposes of this convention, kidnapping, murder, and other assaults against the life or personal integrity of those persons to whom the state has the duty to give special protection according to international law, as well as extortion in connection with those crimes, shall be considered common crimes of international significance, regardless of motive.

ARTICLE 3

Persons who have been charged or convicted for any of the crimes referred to in Article 2 of this Convention shall be subject to extradition under the provisions of the extradition treaties in force between the parties or, in the case of states that do not make extradition dependent on the existence of a treaty, in accordance with their own laws.

In any case, it is the exclusive responsibility of the state under whose jurisdiction or protection such persons are located to determine the nature of the acts and decide whether the standards of this convention are applicable.

ARTICLE 4

Any person deprived of his freedom through the application of this convention shall enjoy the legal guarantees of due process.

ARTICLE 5

When extradition requested for one of the crimes specified in Article 2 is not in order because the person sought is a national of the requested state, or because of some other legal or constitutional impediment, that state is obliged to submit the case to its competent authorities for prosecution, as if the act had been committed in its territory. The decision of these authorities shall be communicated to the state that requested extradition. In such proceedings, the obligation established in Article 4 shall be respected.

ARTICLE 6

None of the provisions of this convention shall be interpreted so as to impair the right of asylum.

ARTICLE 7

The contracting states undertake to include the crimes referred to in Article 2 of this convention among the punishable acts giving rise to extradition in any treaty on the subject to which they agree among themselves in the future. The contracting states that do not subject extradition to the existence of a treaty with the requesting state shall consider the crimes referred to in Article 2 of this convention as crimes giving rise to extradition, according to the conditions established by the laws of the requested state.

ARTICLE 8

To cooperate in preventing and punishing the crimes contemplated in Article 2 of this convention, the contracting states accept the following obligations:

a. To take all measures within their power, and in conformity with their own laws, to prevent and impede the preparation in their respective territories of the crimes mentioned in Article 2 that are to be carried out in the territory of another contracting state.

b. To exchange information and consider effective administrative measures for the purpose of protecting the persons to whom Article 2 of this convention refers.

c. To guarantee to every person deprived of his freedom through the application of this convention every right to defend himself.

d. To endeavor to have the criminal acts contemplated in this convention included in their penal laws, if not already so included.

e. To comply most expeditiously with the requests for extradition concerning the criminal acts contemplated in this convention.

ARTICLE 9

This convention shall remain open for signature by the member states of the Organization of American States, as well as by any other state that is a member of the United Nations or any of its specialized agencies, or any state that is a party to the Statute of the International Court of Justice, or any other state that may be invited by the General Assembly of the Organization of American States to sign it.

ARTICLE 10

This convention shall be ratified by the signatory states in accordance with their respective constitutional procedures.

ARTICLE 11

The original instrument of this convention, the English, French, Portuguese, and Spanish texts of which are equally authentic, shall be deposited in the General Secretariat of the Organization of American States, which shall send certified copies to the signatory governments for purposes of ratification. The instruments of ratification shall be deposited in the General Secretariat of the Organization of American States, which shall notify the signatory governments of such deposit.

ARTICLE 12

This convention shall enter into force among the states that ratify it when they deposit their respective instruments of ratification.

ARTICLE 13

This convention shall remain in force indefinitely, but any of the contracting states may denounce it. The denunciation shall be transmitted to the General Secretariat of the Organization of American States, which shall notify the other contracting states thereof. One year following the denunciation, the convention shall cease to be in force for the denouncing state, but shall continue to be in force for the other contracting states.

IN WITNESS WHEREOF, the undersigned plenipotentiaries, having presented their full powers, which have been found to be in due and proper form, sign this convention on behalf of their respective governments, at the city of Washington this second day of February of the year one thousand nine hundred seventy-one.[21]

STATEMENT OF PANAMA

The Delegation of Panama states for the record that nothing in this Convention shall be interpreted to the effect that the right of asylum implies the right to request asylum from the United States authorities in the Panama Canal Zone, or that there is recognition of the right of the United States to grant asylum or political refuge in that part of the territory of the Republic of Panama that constitutes the Canal Zone.

2. Fourteenth Meeting of Consultation of Ministers of Foreign Affairs, Washington, January 30-31, 1971.

[The interruption of the General Assembly session for a Foreign Ministers' meeting took place in accordance with provisions of the revised O.A.S. Charter whereby the Meeting of Consultation of Ministers of Foreign Affairs can be convened to consider problems of an urgent nature and to serve as Organ of Consultation under the Inter-American Treaty of Reciprocal Assistance (Rio Pact) of 1947. Ecuador, which requested the meeting, had (like Peru, Chile, Brazil, and other Latin American states) advanced unilateral claims to jurisdiction over the adjoining ocean to a distance of 200 miles from its coasts, and had made a practice of seizing unlicensed U.S. tuna-fishing boats within this 200-mile zone and fining their captains. The United States, which recognized no Ecuadorean jurisdiction outside of a 12-mile fishing zone

[21] The signatory states are listed in note 14, and ratifying states in note 16.

contiguous to its coast, had responded to this practice on one occasion in 1969 by suspending some $10 million worth of pending military sales to Ecuador. It had also initiated diplomatic talks with Ecuador, Chile, and Peru in an attempt to work out an amicable solution of the problem.

In January 1971, Ecuador embarked on a stepped-up campaign against U.S. fishing within the 200-mile zone and, by the end of the month, had seized a total of 17 vessels and exacted fines amounting to some $800,000. Citing a new amendment to the 1968 Military Sales Act,[22] the United States on January 18 announced a renewed suspension of military sales, credits, and guarantees to Ecuador as well as a review of pending economic assistance to that country.[23] Ecuador, contending that these actions amounted to "coercive measures" in violation of Article 19 of the O.A.S. Charter,[24] lost little time in requesting a special session of the American Foreign Ministers. The United States responded by proposing that the matter be referred to the Inter-American Committee on Peaceful Settlement; however, it did not oppose a decision by the O.A.S. Permanent Council to convene a Foreign Ministers' meeting without reference to "coercive measures."[25]

The U.S. position in the dispute was presented to the Meeting of Foreign Ministers on January 30 by Under Secretary of State John N. Irwin II, who emphasized both the unsettled status of maritime rights throughout the world and the desire of the United States to arrive at a peaceful and practicable solution (Document 112). Although the meeting also heard sharp criticisms of U.S. laws allegedly involving economic sanctions that impinged on other nations' sovereignty, the outcome was a conciliatory resolution worked out by Argentina, Guatemala, and Mexico and supported by both Ecuador and the United States. Noting that "a state of uneasiness" had arisen with respect to the two countries' views on maritime jurisdiction, the resolution urged them to "avoid the aggravation of their differences," "use the negotiations in which they have shown special interest" (i.e., the four-nation negotiations referred to above), and "abstain from the use of any kind

---

[22] Public Law 90-629, Oct. 22, 1968, as amended by Public Law 91-672, Jan. 12, 1971. Section 3 (b) as amended reads in part as follows: "No sales, credits or guaranties shall be made or extended under this Act to any country during a period of one year after such country seizes, or takes into custody, or fines an American fishing vessel for engaging in fishing more than twelve miles from the coast of that country." The President was authorized to waive this provision in specified instances.

[23] *New York Times*, Jan. 19, 1971.

[24] "No State may use or encourage the use of coercive measures of an economic or political character in order to force the sovereign will of another State and obtain from it advantages of any kind."

[25] Jova, *loc. cit.* (note 8), p. 285; same, statement to the Permanent Council, Jan. 27, in *Bulletin*, Feb. 22, 1971, pp. 245-47; *Keesing's*, p. 24598.

of measure that may affect the sovereignty of the States and the tranquility of the Hemisphere."[26] Although Ecuador subsequently requested the withdrawal of the U.S. military mission in Quito, seizures of fishing vessels abated and diplomatic contact on the maritime issue was resumed later in 1971 in an attempt to devise a practical solution in advance of the U.N.-sponsored Conference on the Law of the Sea that was scheduled to convene in 1973.]

(112) Seizure by Ecuador of United States Fishing Vessels: Statement by Under Secretary of State John N. Irwin II to the Meeting of Foreign Ministers, January 30, 1971.[27]

(Complete Text)

I can assure you that there is another side to this unfortunate dispute concerning the seizure of United States fishing vessels by Ecuadorean naval forces, and I wish now to set forth the position of the United States. I characterize this dispute as "unfortunate" advisedly, because the United States cherishes its traditional friendly relations with Ecuador, and we hope that an amicable solution to this problem can be found which is fair to both countries.

The facts are that since January 11, naval forces of the Government of Ecuador have seized 17 United States fishing boats while those vessels were fishing far off the coast of Ecuador in waters which the United States and more than 90 other countries of the world consider to be high seas under established principles of international law. Fines have been imposed on these vessels by Ecuador amounting to over $800,000. But the principle involved is what is important. As a result of these seizures by the Ecuadorean Navy, the United States has, pursuant to its domestic law,[28] suspended its military sales to Ecuador.

The position and views of the United States with respect to the territorial sea and the exercise by the coastal state of rights over the living resources of areas in the seas adjacent to its coast are well known.[29] It is the view of the United States that coastal states, in the absence of broad international agreement, may not make and enforce unilateral territorial sea claims such as the claim under which Ecuador purported to seize fishing boats in the present case. In addition, the

---

[26] O.A.S. document OAS/Ser. F/II.14 Doc. 11, Rev. 1, in *Bulletin*, Feb. 22, 1971, p. 250; approved by a vote of 19 (Ecuador, U.S.)-0-4. Further details in Jova, *loc. cit.* (note 8), p. 287 and *Keesing's*, p. 24598.

[27] Department of State Press Release 24, Feb. 1, 1971; text from *Bulletin*, Feb. 22, 1971, pp. 247-50.

[28] Cf. above at note 22.

[29] Cf. *Documents, 1970*, pp. 287-89 and 331-45; also Document 137.

United States holds the view shared by most other countries of the world that with respect to fisheries a coastal state may exercise jurisdiction in a zone contiguous to its territorial sea but not exceeding 12 miles from its coast. Any changes in the international law governing the territorial sea or coastal state jurisdiction over fisheries must be accomplished through international negotiation and agreement, and not by unilateral action.

The United States recognizes that coastal states have a particular interest in the living resources of the seas adjacent to their coasts. The United States itself has such an interest in the resources off its own coast. The particular problems relating to the use and conservation of offshore living resources can be solved by treaty or bilateral agreement, a course the United States would be happy indeed to follow; but it cannot be solved by unilateral extensions of sovereignty over broad areas traditionally regarded as the high seas. In our view, an attempted solution along these lines benefits neither the coastal state nor noncoastal states which have a concurrent interest in the development of these resources.

For this reason, the United States has been working diligently over the past several years to encourage states to convene an international conference for the purpose of defining precisely the maximum breadth of the territorial sea and preferential rights which a coastal state may exercise in areas of the high seas adjacent to its coast. The United States has circulated several proposals aimed at achieving a mutually beneficial solution. On this issue of high seas fisheries, the United States has suggested the establishment of a new international regime under which the particular interests of coastal states could be recognized and, providing certain criteria are met, special preferences could be granted to meet these interests. At the same time, all fishing nations would cooperate with international organizations, including those of a regional nature, whose aim would be to assure conservation of the living resources of common concern to all states.

In December of 1970 the United Nations General Assembly overwhelmingly adopted a resolution, 2750 C (XXV), which calls for the convening of a conference on the law of the sea in 1973 for the purposes *inter alia* of establishing an equitable international regime for the area and resources of the seabed beyond the limits of national jurisdiction and of reviewing a broad range of related issues, including the breadth of the territorial sea and the regime of the contiguous zone and fishing and conservation of the living resources of the high seas. Both Ecuador and the United States were among the cosponsors of United Nations Resolution 2750 C. The United States intends to employ its best efforts in the intervening years to insure that this conference is a success. Among these efforts will be an attempt to effect a practical solution to the very vexing situation resulting from conflicting claims to territorial sea jurisdiction in this hemisphere.

In this regard, the United States has been negotiating with the countries of Chile, Ecuador, and Peru over the last 2 years with a view toward establishing an arrangement to avoid conflicts in areas where there remains a dispute over jurisdiction. Such a solution would be without prejudice to the respective juridical position of each of the four countries. In the United States view this type of negotiated settlement is the only effective means of ending the longstanding and troublesome dispute which is presently before this Meeting of Consultation of Foreign Ministers.

In these meetings with Ecuador, Peru, and Chile, the United States has advanced several concrete proposals which we believe could serve as practical solutions to the vessel-seizure problem, without prejudice to the juridical positions of any of the parties, and which would also serve to stimulate cooperation among the parties in fishing industry development and the scientific conservation of fishery resources. For example, the United States has proposed establishment of a regional fishery development institute which, among other functions, would regulate the activities of tuna fishing vessels in the waters of the region, using the funds generated thereby for fishery development projects in the coastal countries. Alternately, the United States has proposed an agreement which would set up a joint licensing and enforcement system to regulate the tuna fishery of the region for purposes of conservation and management of the resources, with enforcement activities to be conducted by the coastal states. In connection with this proposed solution the United States has expressed its willingness to assist the coastal countries in fishery research and development including consideration of their trade in fishery products. We feel that the United States has approached the problem with great flexibility and in a true spirit of compromise.

During the last round of these negotiations in September 1970 progress was made toward the establishment of a framework upon which international agreement could be reached. We believe that all four countries have the firm desire to reach a mutually satisfactory solution and that to this end it is important to resume the talks scheduled to be held before July 31, 1971.

It is quite clear, however, that progress toward such a peaceful disposition is made much more difficult by actions such as those during recent weeks when the 17 United States fishing boats were seized by Ecuador in the disputed waters. For its part, the United States remains ready to find a practical solution to this problem through peaceful procedures as required by the Charter of the Organization of American States. We are also prepared to have recourse to the machinery provided by our charter for the peaceful settlement of disputes. We stand ready to resume at once the four-party talks to which I have just referred. Moreover, we have proposed that the fundamental question of the legal status of the waters in question as high seas be submitted for binding determination by the International Court of Justice.

Charges have been made here that the United States suspension of military sales to Ecuador is a violation of article 19 of the OAS Charter.[30] I deny that charge most emphatically.

Underlying this issue is an important consideration—important for all the nations of this hemisphere, increasing numbers of which will become donor nations. This consideration is the basic nature of assistance between nations. In no way can assistance of any kind be considered as obligatory, timeless, and changeless, nor the flow of that assistance a constant. Economic, legal, and administrative factors present in both donor and recipient nations have affected planning for and implementation of assistance and always will. So, to a degree, will politics have an effect, as politics are a vital part of every national existence and are inextricably intermingled with economic, legal, and administrative factors in both donor and recipient nations.

In short, assistance within nations and between nations depends on a high degree of mutuality. The existence of assistance, or its acceptance, cannot be automatic and irrevocable.

In suspending military sales to Ecuador, the United States has in no way adopted coercive measures designed to force the sovereign will of Ecuador and to obtain advantages from it of any kind. The facts show that it is Ecuador which has used economic coercion and force in seizing fishing boats and fining them, thus seeking unilaterally to enforce its claims to territorial seas. Such action by Ecuador is designed to force the sovereign will of the United States into accepting Ecuador's territorial claims and thereby to obtain advantages which Ecuador would not otherwise enjoy under international law. In these circumstances, the United States Government has had no choice but to apply the provisions of *its* law in response to actions of the Government of Ecuador which violate the rights of United States nationals under international law.

But I do not want to belabor the legal arguments regarding the charter. Obviously on this question, as on the underlying issues involved in the dispute between the United States and Ecuador, there are differing views. For our part, we do not wish to get bogged down in juridical arguments. Our objective is to work out a practical solution to the current problem in a way that maintains and solidifies the traditional close relations between Ecuador and the United States. We have made a number of specific proposals here today for the peaceful resolution of

[30] Cf. note 24, above.

this dispute; i.e., resort to machinery for peaceful settlement established in the charter, submission to the International Court of Justice, and resumption of quadripartite negotiations. We hope that the result of this meeting will be to promote a peaceful settlement in accordance with the high principles of our charter rather than to exacerbate the situation with contentious assertions or decisions. We stand ready to cooperate in the spirit of the charter.

3. First Regular Session of the General Assembly, San José, Costa Rica, April 14-24, 1971.

[A somewhat less controversial atmosphere prevailed at the long-awaited formal inaugural of the O.A.S. General Assembly, its first meeting outside the United States. The highlight of the session was an agreement by El Salvador and Honduras to renew their efforts to settle the political differences growing out of their undeclared "soccer war" of June 1969. A full-dress presentation of current U.S. thinking on inter-American affairs by Secretary of State Rogers (Document 113) was primarily noteworthy for its disclaimer of hegemonic ambitions and its profession of respect for the full sovereign equality of the neighboring countries to the south. This conciliatory statement did not, however, prevent the meeting from serving as a sounding board for criticism of U.S. economic policies in the hemisphere, particularly the delays in implementing President Nixon's pledge of October 31, 1969, to promote a system of generalized trade preferences for all developing countries—or, alternatively, for Latin American countries.[31] The United States took little part in the discussion of a proposal by President Misael Pastrana Borrero of Colombia looking toward an arms limitation agreement among Latin American countries, which was referred for study to the O.A.S. Permanent Council.[32]]

(113) "A More Balanced and Reinvigorated Partnership of the Americas": Statement by Secretary of State Rogers to the General Assembly, April 15, 1971.[33]

(Complete Text)

This meeting of the General Assembly is the first one of the Organization's leading body to be held in Central America since regular sessions began 81 years ago. It is time that we met in Central America.

---

[31] *Documents, 1968-69*, p. 433; cf. Documents 115-116.
[32] Jova, *loc. cit.* (note 8), p. 287.
[33] Department of State Press Release 75; text from *Bulletin*, May 10, 1971, pp. 602-7.

This year marks the 150th anniversary of Central America's successful declaration of independence. It is most appropriate that our meeting is in Costa Rica, a country renowned equally for its beauty, the hospitality of its people, and especially for the strength of its democratic institutions.

Since the first inter-American meeting in 1890, support for the inter-American system has continued to broaden. Today we have a newly strengthened and reorganized institution. We who are fortunate enough to represent the member states here today have a special responsibility to contribute to the success of this institution. Today I reaffirm the willingness of the United States to play a useful and constructive role in that endeavor. That is the policy President Nixon stated in 1969 when he reaffirmed our commitment to the inter-American system and to the compacts which bind us in that system.[34] That is the message the President asked me to underscore to this Assembly today.

The work of the Organization of American States contributes importantly to economic and social progress. It also plays a valuable part in resolving political problems in the hemisphere. The peacekeeping role of the OAS in the El Salvador–Honduras conflict[35] demonstrated the continued vitality of our collective security machinery under the Rio Treaty.[36]

Our adoption in February of a convention making terrorism against foreign officials an extraditable crime[37] also aided the cause of a peaceful hemisphere. Just this week I sent to the President the formal papers required for transmitting that convention to the United States Senate.[38] I hope that, in time, all the members of this Organization will sign and ratify it.

OAS meetings are occasionally marked by stresses and disagreements, as the differences we had over the terrorism convention demonstrated. Such dissent, however vigorous, is not a sign of weakness but is a sign of vitality—and, in a sense, of confidence. The hemisphere is not homogeneous. The member states of this Organization are changing and becoming stronger, each in a way compatible with its social and cultural background.

An Organization of American States open to different points of view can help assure that change comes peacefully and with due regard to each other's views.

The involvement of the United States in Latin America—for reasons of history, geography, politics, and economics—has always been close.

---

[34] *Documents, 1968-69*, pp. 429-38; cf, above at note 3.

[35] Cf. *The United States in World Affairs, 1970*, pp. 198-99.

[36] Inter-American Treaty of Reciprocal Assistance, opened for signature at Rio de Janeiro Sept. 2, 1947, and entered into force Dec. 3, 1948 (TIAS 1838); text in *Documents, 1947*, pp. 534-40.

[37] Document 111.

[38] S. Ex. D, 92d Cong., 1st sess.; cf. above at note 16.

In the 1930's with the good-neighbor policy the United States began to turn our close relations into more fully cooperative ones, reversing some of our previous attitudes toward our role in the hemisphere. In the Alliance for Progress[39] we have been seeking together to bring greater substance and closer cooperation to efforts in hemispheric development.

More recently, the United States became convinced that the continuing demand for social change and the growing spirit of nationalism in the hemisphere required still further policy changes. We knew that the countries of the hemisphere wanted to decide for yourselves which road you would follow. We knew that you wanted to direct your own destinies and assume fully your own responsibilities, true to your own cultures, personalities, and social dynamics. It was on this basis, we believed, that the more balanced and reinvigorated partnership urged by President Nixon could be achieved, while still preserving the historically close mutual relationship.

This is the object of the policy the United States is now pursuing.

It is a policy of continued close association. It is also one of support for full sovereign equality.

We want no hegemony. We have no desire for an inward-looking hemisphere. We are therefore seeking to act on four basic principles:

—First, that the problems that affect the hemisphere are the concern of all its states.

—Second, that initiatives in the hemisphere must be the responsibility of all.

—Third, that the interest of other nations in productive and supportive cooperation with Latin America is to be welcomed.

—Fourth, that the growing interest and participation of Latin American countries in global, as well as in hemispheric, affairs gives an important new dimension to this Organization.

We believe these principles are a guide to a new kind of U.S. relationship with Latin America. They are not a prescription for abandonment, or for withdrawal from commitments or obligations. It is in character, rather than in fundamentals, that our association with Latin America is changing. It is a policy merely altered to meet the changing policies of your countries.

A moment ago I said that the United States welcomed the interest of other nations in supportive and constructive cooperation with Latin America. Increased cooperation from West European countries, Canada, and Japan has already been helpful. Each member state of this Organization must, of course, judge carefully, particularly as the problem has been highlighted by recent disclosures, which nations are prepared to

[39] Cf. note 1 above.

play a constructive role in this hemisphere—a role which gives full recognition to sovereign rights—and which nations follow a policy of seeking to undermine and subvert those rights.

How do we intend to implement the four basic principles to which I have referred?

In the economic sphere we support proposals for a larger hemispheric role in setting assistance goals. We favor a greater reliance on multilateral cooperation in development and trade. We welcome the constructive economic interest in the hemisphere of those outside it such as the European states and Japan, just as we welcome Canada's stated intention of drawing closer to the states and institutions of the hemisphere.[40]

During the rest of the century the process of social and economic modernization in this hemisphere will continue to bring with it a stronger sense of nationalism and in some instances disruptive political changes. Some of these developments may well cause short-term problems. But we recognize that in the long run many of these changes will contribute to the constructive and necessary process of social and economic growth.

In the modernization process a certain amount of trial and error will be inevitable. While we naturally expect fair treatment for our interests, we seek to avoid overreaction to short-term problems to the detriment of our long-term relationships and we are ready to engage in cooperative efforts to mitigate the problems which arise in the process.

The decade of the 1970's is already seeing its share of political and social tensions, both in Latin America and in the United States. We hold many social problems in common—the pressures of population, the decay in our cities, the unrest of our young people, and the lack of adequate income levels for sections of our population.

In recent years such stresses in the hemisphere have increasingly produced pressures against representative institutions. The United States has a clear preference for democratic systems and procedures—in this hemisphere as elsewhere. We recognize, nevertheless, that other countries must choose their own political systems, governments, and policies. The Organization of American States now embraces governments with several political systems, governments with differing philosophical orientations, and governments with policies often differing from ours. With all these governments the United States will continue to work as cooperatively as possible.

Thus the policy of the United States is based on our conviction that in the years ahead friendship and confidence within the framework of this Organizaton will consolidate political relationships in the hemisphere to our mutual benefit. As has been pointed out by many of my

[40] Canada became a Permanent Observer to the O.A.S. in 1972 and joined the Inter-American Development Bank on May 3, 1972.

colleagues, our economic relationship in the next few years will be equally vital.

EXPORT TRADE POLICIES

The importance to Latin America of its trade with the United States is obvious. We buy a third of Latin America's exports and supply two-fifths of its imports. This trade is also important to the United States. It is about a seventh of our total international trade.

While Latin America's exports to the United States have continued to grow in quantitative terms, the U.S. share of all Latin American exports has dropped from 42 percent in 1959 to 32 percent in 1969. This reflects in part a healthy growth of new markets for Latin American exports, notably in Japan. Even more significantly, it reflects an increase in trade among Latin American and Caribbean countries themselves. The hemispheric initiatives which created the Latin American and Caribbean Free Trade Areas, the Central American Common Market, and the Andean Group all illustrate this trend.

The Common Market here in Central America, for example, has had notable successes. While there are current differences over the future of regional integration, I am confident that the Central American states will be able to work them out.[41] The United States is ready to continue its assistance to the Common Market, as well as to encourage regional initiatives in Central America and elsewhere in the hemisphere.

Despite the welcome trend toward diversified export markets, Latin America particularly needs an open market in the United States. We remain committed to a policy of freer trade, and we are, as you know, giving special attention in our approach to generalized tariff preferences to products of particular interest to Latin American countries. We are continuing to work for the elimination or reduction of trade barriers in regional as well as international forums.

Perhaps the most important single initiative we have taken in the trade field was our decision to advocate—and urge the other developed countries to accept—a liberal system of generalized tariff preferences.[42] The European Common Market has set a target date of July 1 for implementation of its system. The Japanese Diet has approved implementation for not later than October 1. Most other developed countries have already obtained authority or will seek it soon.

The United States Government has decided, in large part because of the consultations within this Organization, to include in our own preference system some 500 products requested by Latin American coun-

[41] Cf. *The World This Year, 1972*, pp. 137-38.
[42] Cf. *Documents, 1968-69*, pp. 429-38; same, *1970*, pp. 402-9.

tries. The total value of U.S. imports of these items from Latin America in 1969 was $650 million.

Action on generalized preferences will require congressional approval. The President has asked me immediately on my return from this meeting to initiate consultations with Members of Congress with a view to early introduction of legislation to grant to developing countries generalized tariff preferences on a wide range of products, including the 500 items requested by Latin America. The administration will make a concerted effort to secure enactment of this legislation.[43]

While the figure is necessarily rough, we estimate that under this legislation the share by value of Latin American exports entering the United States free of duty would rise from almost 50 percent to over 60 percent. More important, in addition to products currently traded, new opportunities would be created for many other products for which Latin America has, or may develop, an export capacity.

In addition to preferences, other steps will be necessary as well, not all of them concerned with external barriers. As my Government subjects its policies to continuing examination, it will be necessary for the Latin American countries to review their policies and practices with an eye to encouraging export development. The United States is ready to increase our technical and financial assistance to promote this development.

FOREIGN INVESTMENT AND ECONOMIC GROWTH

Economic growth is the product not only of trade and assistance policies but also of judicious investment. The key to higher standards of living is production. The source of production—and the most basic source of development—must inevitably be investment. No matter how much public assistance developed countries make available, long-term economic growth will depend heavily on private investment, domestic and foreign. Foreign investment provides needed capital. It serves to transfer the technology and scientific knowledge critical to the development process. It also increases export earnings.

In his report to the Inter-American Development Bank last year. Raúl Prebisch[44] noted that foreign investment has a unique contribution to make in the development of the exports Latin America needs for acquiring foreign exchange. We believe this is true. In 1968, the most recent year for which we have figures, we estimate that export sales by U.S. affiliates located in Latin America accounted for over a third of Latin America's total exports of manufactures.

[43] Cf. Documents 116 and 155.
[44] Director-General of the U.N. Latin-American Institute for Economic and Social Planning.

It is often claimed that foreign investment, in intent or in fact, deprives developing countries of their wealth. Our own experience is that natural resources, if rationally developed under fair terms, contribute more to a country's development than if left undeveloped. Each country must, of course, determine for itself the pace at which to transform natural resource wealth into other useful forms of property.

In the past, foreign private investment, including that from the United States, tended to be concentrated in extractive industries, but this has changed. The book value of private U.S. direct investment in Latin America amounted at the end of 1969 to $13.8 billion. Of this total, mining and smelting account for less than 15 percent and petroleum for only just over 25 percent. The remaining 60 percent is in manufacturing, trade, and other nonextractive categories. The largest single amount, nearly 33 percent, is in manufacturing—an investment of $4.3 billion which provides about 500,000 jobs.

The allegation that is sometimes made, that foreign investment particularly seeks out weak developing countries, is not correct. Two-thirds of U.S. direct international investment and almost all portfolio investment is in developed, not developing, countries. If there is a problem in the distribution of private capital abroad, it is a problem of encouraging it to go to developing countries where it can help in economic development, not one of keeping it out.

Our belief in the value of private foreign investment for economic growth does not mean an indiscriminate policy of pressing such investment upon other countries. Developing nations must weigh for themselves the relationship between foreign and domestic investment. The decision must be theirs. The United States also shares the Latin American view that foreign investment should be related to development criteria. Indeed, long-term investment is by its very nature developmental.

My Government is sympathetic to new approaches toward a healthy investment relationship. As I said in my recent report on foreign policy:[45]

> ... our own investors, both established and prospective, will need to organize ... their enterprises in ways that are compatible with the legitimate economic and social aspirations and standards of their hosts.

At the same time it must be recognized that a favorable investment climate requires conditions of consistency and stability and that new formulas cannot be applied retroactively to existing enterprises without in many cases damaging future prospects.

[45] Rogers Report, 1969-70, p. 128.

U.S. COMMITMENT TO DEVELOPMENT ASSISTANCE

Development assistance—with trade and investment, the third focus of our economic policy—continues to be required in the hemisphere both for economic purposes and purposes of human betterment. I am aware of expressed concerns that the Alliance for Progress may be dying, that our commitment to assistance for Latin American development may be weakening, that the proposed reorganization of our aid programs may signify decreased assistance.

Reference has been made by the Secretary General [Galo Plaza Lasso, Ecuador] to declining levels of financial cooperation. However, total United States economic flows to the hemisphere remain at substantially the same high levels as over the past 5 years—though we are putting more through multilateral channels. And loan terms are explicitly concessional, averaging well less than half of the cost our own industries and enterprises must pay. The policies which he suggests are policies on which we are seeking to act: a policy of large-scale "multilateral" financial cooperation and "a trade policy that encourages development."

Let me state categorically: The commitment of the United States to assistance for Latin America is undiminished. Our reorganization of foreign assistance,[46] far from lessening that commitment, is intended to make it possible for us to fulfill it more effectively.

As part of that reorganization, we seek to divert larger shares of our assistance into multilateral channels. While our bilateral assistance is somewhat below the peaks of the midsixties, our multilateral commitments have increased and, as I have said, our total U.S. assistance has remained at substantially the same high level. The Inter-American Committee on the Alliance for Progress, in its first review of U.S. economic policy, judged the trend toward the use of multilateral channels as highly beneficial. The Committee also recognized that the United States had complied with the financial assistance and the objectives defined at the beginning of the Alliance for Progress.

Between 1963 and 1970 international institutions increased their lending to Latin America fourfold. Today they account for well over half of all economic assistance to the hemisphere. As a result, total assistance is greater now than ever before. In fiscal 1970 economic assistance allocations to Latin America by the three primary donors— the U.S. bilateral programs, the Inter-American Development Bank, and the World Bank group—reached almost $2.2 billion, more than in any other year. With the addition of bilateral assistance from other countries, plus United Nations and European Economic Community programs, the total assistance to Latin America was about $2.7 billion, also a new high.

[46] Cf. Document 153.

A regional institution, the Inter-American Development Bank, is fast becoming the major source of development funds for Latin America. It has increased its lending commitments from $394 million only 3 years ago to $681 million last year. President Nixon has asked Congress to authorize $1.8 billion as the U.S. share to make possible a further increase in the Bank's lending by 50 percent in the next 3 to 4 years. Part has been authorized; the President has strongly urged approval of the rest this year.[47]

The multilateral framework offers an opportunity for development priorities to be worked out jointly with Latin American countries themselves. In this process the Inter-American Committee on the Alliance for Progress is playing an important role, a role which my Government hopes will become greater. Multilateralism also facilitates the participation of other developed countries, thus increasing the sources of loan funds. In particular, we would like to see the Inter-American Development Bank broaden the financial participation of other developed countries.

The United States will also, of course, continue its bilateral programs. In the last fiscal year these totaled $750 million, about half in AID [Agency for International Development] development assistance and half in agricultural commodities, long-term Export-Import Bank loans, Peace Corps assistance, and educational and cultural exchanges.

I have concentrated today on the broad problems demanding cooperation among us. In concluding I would like to refer to some other developments which should engage our attention.

President Nixon has pledged a new dedication to improving the quality of life in the Americas.[48] Within the Alliance for Progress the United States now hopes to give greater emphasis to areas like education, agriculture, and health—areas which relate directly to the basic concerns of people.

There are other human concerns which the Organization of American States can itself usefully investigate. Unemployment—particularly as it affects young people—the increasing pressures on our cities, and the threats to our environment are problems to which we all must respond. Future meetings of the Inter-American Economic and Social Council should address these important issues.

The limitation of armaments, already suggested by other delegations, is a question which this Assembly will consider. The United States would be glad to cooperate in discussions on this Latin American initiative in any way the other members think appropriate.

I would also like to emphasize the great extent to which our cooperation can be advanced on specific bilateral issues. My Government,

[47] Cf. *Documents, 1970*, p. 265.
[48] Cf. above at note 3.

for example, has been endeavoring to eliminate outdated impediments to its bilateral relations by resolving old problems arising from territorial questions. We have announced that we are prepared to recognize Honduran sovereignty over the Swan Islands.[49] We have agreed with Nicaragua to terminate a 1914 treaty assigning us the right to build a canal across that country.[50] We have negotiated with Mexico a permanent solution to boundary questions which plagued our relations for more than 100 years.[51]

The economic and political policies I have described underline the enduring support by the United States for the inter-American system. They affirm our continuing commitment to the hemisphere's economic development. They embody an approach broad enough to accommodate the political diversity which now characterizes Latin America. They reflect an abiding desire for close and constructive relations with all governments which share the same desire.

In friendship and with respect I will close with these observations:

The challenges facing the members of this Organization are great. Continuous constructive attention to these challenges requires the highest levels of understanding in our inter-American relationships. Effective action to meet these challenges will best be encouraged if all of us emphasize the mutuality, rather than the differences, in our interests.

Last week President Nixon entertained the diplomats of our countries at the White House. He defined our relationship as a governmental and personal one of long standing based on trust and confidence.[52] I believe that we can develop further that "personal" relationship in a way which will contribute to making the rest of the century in our half of the globe a time of peaceful cooperation and effective progress.

B. Treaty for the Prohibition of Nuclear Weapons in Latin America (Treaty of Tlatelolco) of February 14, 1967.

[Ratification by the United States of Additional Protocol II to the

[49] A treaty recognizing Honduran sovereignty over the Swan Islands (TIAS 7453; 23 UST 2630) was signed at San Pedro Sula Nov. 22, 1971, and entered into force Sept. 1, 1972; cf. *Bulletin*, Dec. 13, 1971, p. 691.

[50] A convention terminating the Bryan-Chamorro Treaty of 1914, which granted the United States an exclusive right to construct an interoceanic canal across Nicaragua, was signed at Managua July 14, 1970, and entered into force Apr. 25, 1971 (TIAS 7120; 22 UST 663).

[51] A treaty to resolve pending boundary differences between the U.S. and Mexico was signed in Mexico City Nov. 23, 1970, and entered into force Apr. 18, 1972 (TIAS 7313; 23 UST 371).

[52] Toasts delivered at a dinner honoring Chiefs of Mission of the Americas, in *Public Papers, 1971*, pp. 508-10.

Treaty for the Prohibition of Nuclear Weapons in Latin America (Treaty of Tlatelolco) fulfilled a U.S. commitment of three years' standing and gave some further substance to the "denuclearization" of Latin America effected, at least in theory, by a treaty concluded by a number of Latin American states in 1967. By that treaty,[53] which purported to make Latin America the world's first nuclear-free zone by ensuring that the territories of Latin American countries would remain "forever free from nuclear weapons," the Latin American contracting parties had renounced the acquisition and possession of nuclear weapons and set up a special organization, the Agency for Prohibition of Nuclear Weapons in Latin America (O.P.A.N.A.L.), to help ensure compliance with the obligations assumed. Sixteen Latin American and Caribbean states had become parties to the treaty by the end of 1970, and most of the others had signed it, the principal exceptions being Cuba, which refused to have anything to do with the project, and Guyana, whose eligibility to sign was in doubt for technical reasons. The deposit of ratifications by Panama in 1971 and by Colombia in 1972 increased the number of parties to 18, although Argentina and Chile had not yet ratified and Brazil's ratification was subject to limiting conditions.[54]

Full effectiveness of the nuclear-free zone would obviously require not only the participation of all Latin American states but also the respect of those outside powers that either possessed territories in Latin America or were themselves ranked as nuclear-weapon states. To deal with this situation, the authors of the treaty had drafted two additional protocols for signature by those non-Latin American governments whose support was deemed essential to its success.

Additional Protocol I sought to obligate those countries with territories lying within the treaty zone—viz., France, the Netherlands, the United Kingdom, and the United States—to apply to those territories the status of denuclearization as defined in the treaty. This protocol had been signed by the United Kingdom in 1967 and ratified in 1969; the Netherlands had also signed in 1968 and ratified in 1971. France and the United States had neither signed nor ratified the protocol, and had given no evidence of an intention to do so.

Additional Protocol II[55] sought to obligate nuclear-weapon states—viz., the People's Republic of China, France, the U.S.S.R., the United Kingdom, and the United States—to respect the aims and provisions of the treaty, not to contribute to its violation in the territory to which it applies, and not to use or threaten to use nuclear weapons against

[53] Treaty for the Prohibition of Nuclear Weapons in Latin America (Treaty of Tlatelolco), opened for signature in Mexico City Feb. 14, 1967, and entered into force Apr. 22, 1968 (TIAS 7137; 22 UST 762); text in *Documents on Disarmament, 1967*, pp. 69-83.

[54] Stockholm International Peace Research Institute (SIPRI), *The Implementation of International Disarmament Agreements* (Stockholm, 1973), pp. 20 and 25-62.

[55] TIAS 7137; 22 UST 754; text in *Documents, 1968-69*, pp. 392-94.

parties to the treaty. This protocol, too, had been signed by the United Kingdom in 1967 and ratified in 1969, and had also been signed by the United States on April 1, 1968.[56] Up to 1971 it had not been signed or ratified by China, France, or the U.S.S.R.

In signing Additional Protocol II, the United States had offered a clarifying statement setting forth its view on various points of interpretation with respect to such matters as territories and territorial claims, transit and transport privileges, nonuse of nuclear weapons, and the definition of the term nuclear weapon.[57] A similar, updated statement accompanied the message of August 13, 1970, in which President Nixon requested Senate advice and consent to ratification of the protocol.[58] The delay in signature and submission of the protocol to the Senate, according to administration sources, had been motivated by a desire to see whether the treaty would be widely accepted by the parties, and also by "a desire to test the United States interpretation of the treaty and the protocol in actual practice with the parties over an extended period."[59]

Following a preliminary hearing in September 1970 and a second hearing on February 23, 1971, the protocol was approved by a 13 to 0 vote of the Senate Foreign Relations Committee, subject to certain "understandings and declarations" which embodied the substance of the administration statement and were included in the Resolution of Ratification that was recommended by the committee to the Senate on April 5, 1971.[60] Approved without debate by a 70 to 0 vote of the Senate on April 19, 1971, the protocol, with the understandings and declarations, was ratified by the President on May 8 and became binding on the United States with the deposit of its instrument of ratification on May 12, 1971. The understandings and declarations were repeated once again in President Nixon's formal proclamation of the protocol on June 11, 1971 (Document 114).

The United States' acceptance of Additional Protocol II was noted "with satisfaction" by the U.N. General Assembly on December 16, 1971, in a resolution which deplored the failure of other nuclear-weapon states (except the United Kingdom) to heed its earlier appeals in the matter and urged them once again to sign and ratify the protocol without further delay.[61] France in fact signed the protocol on July 18, 1973, and deposited its ratification on March 22, 1974, while the People's Republic of China signed it on August 21, 1973, and deposited its

56 *Documents*, pp. 396-99.

57 Same, pp. 396-98.

58 Message in *Documents, 1970*, pp. 283-84; statement in *Bulletin*, Sept. 14, 1970, p. 309 and *Documents on Disarmament, 1970*, pp. 317-18.

59 Report of the Senate Foreign Relations Committee (S. Ex. Rept. 92-5, 92d Cong., 1st sess.), Apr. 5, 1971, in *Documents on Disarmament, 1971*, pp. 197-98.

60 Same, pp. 197-201.

61 Resolution 2830 (XXVI), Dec. 16, 1971.

ratification on June 12, 1974.[62] The Soviet position, as stated in 1971, was that the U.S.S.R. would respect the nuclear-free status of any Latin American country that turned its territory into a completely nuclear-free zone, provided the other nuclear powers undertook the same commitment.[63]]

(114) Proclamation by President Nixon on Ratification of Additional Protocol II to the Treaty for the Prohibition of Nuclear Weapons in Latin America, June 11, 1971.[64]

(Excerpts)

BY THE PRESIDENT OF THE UNITED STATES OF AMERICA

A PROCLAMATION

CONSIDERING THAT: :
Additional Protocol II to the Treaty for the Prohibition of Nuclear Weapons in Latin America, done at the City of Mexico on February 14, 1967, was signed on behalf of the United States of America on April 1, 1968, the text of which Protocol is word for word as follows:

[There follows the text of Additional Protocol II]

*   *   *

The Senate of the United States of America by its resolution of April 19, 1971, two-thirds of the Senators present concurring, gave its advice and consent to the ratification of Additional Protocol II,[65] with the following understandings and declarations:

I

That the United States Government understands the reference in Article 3 of the treaty[66] to "its own legislation" to relate only to such

---

[62] *Bulletin*, Sept. 10, 1973, p. 359; same, May 20, 1974, p. 568; same, Aug. 5, 1974, p. 255.
[63] Letter from the Supreme Soviet to the Mexican Senate, Jan. 4, 1971, in *Documents on Disarmament, 1971*, pp. 1-2.
[64] TIAS 7137; 22 UST 754.
[65] Cf. above at note 55.
[66] Article 3 of the Treaty of Tlatelolco reads: "For the purposes of this Treaty, the term 'territory' shall include the territorial sea, air space and any other space over which the State exercises sovereignty in accordance with its own legislation."

legislation as is compatible with the rules of international law and as involves an exercise of sovereignty consistent with those rules, and accordingly that ratification of Additional Protocol II by the United States Government could not be regarded as implying recognition, for the purposes of this treaty and its protocols or for any other purpose, of any legislation which did not, in the view of the United States, comply with the relevant rules of international law.

That the United States Government takes note of the Preparatory Commission's interpretation of the treaty, as set forth in the Final Act,[67] that, governed by the principles and rules of international law, each of the Contracting Parties retains exclusive power and legal competence, unaffected by the terms of the treaty, to grant or deny non-Contracting Parties transit and transport privileges.

That as regards the undertaking in Article 3 of Protocol II not to use or threaten to use nuclear weapons against the Contracting Parties, the United States Government would have to consider that an armed attack by a Contracting Party, in which it was assisted by a nuclear-weapon state, would be incompatible with the Contracting Party's corresponding obligations under Article I of the treaty.[68]

II

That the United States Government considers that the technology of making nuclear explosive devices for peaceful purposes is indistinguishable from the technology of making nuclear weapons, and that nuclear weapons and nuclear explosive devices for peaceful purposes are both capable of releasing nuclear energy in an uncontrolled manner and have the common group of characteristics of large amounts of energy generated instantaneously from a compact source. Therefore the United States Government understands the definition contained in Article 5 of the treaty[69] as necessarily encompassing all nuclear explosive devices. It is also understood that Articles 1 and 5 restrict accordingly the activities of the Contracting Parties under paragraph 1 of Article 18.[70]

That the United States Government understands that paragraph 4 of Article 18 of the treaty[71] permits, and that United States adherence to Protocol II will not prevent, collaboration by the United States with Contracting Parties for the purpose of carrying out explosions of nuclear devices for peaceful purposes in a manner consistent with a policy of not contributing to the proliferation of nuclear weapons capabilities. In this connection, the United States Government notes

---

[67] U.N. document A/6663, Feb. 23, 1967.
[68] Article 1 of the treaty is quoted in *Documents, 1968-69*, p. 393 n.5.
[69] Quoted in same, p. 394 n.8.
[70] Quoted in same, p. 397 n.23.
[71] Same.

Article V of the Treaty on the Non-Proliferation of Nuclear Weapons,[72] under which it joined in an undertaking to take appropriate measures to ensure that potential benefits of peaceful applications of nuclear explosions would be made available to non-nuclear-weapon states party to that treaty, and reaffirms its willingness to extend such undertaking, on the same basis, to states precluded by the present treaty from manufacturing or acquiring any nuclear explosive device.

III

That the United States Government also declares that, although not required by Protocol II, it will act with respect to such territories of Protocol I adherents as are within the geographical area defined in paragraph 2 of Article 4 of the treaty[73] in the same manner as Protocol II requires it to act with respect to the territories of Contracting Parties.

The President ratified Additional Protocol II on May 8, 1971, with the above-recited understandings and declarations, in pursuance of the advice and consent of the Senate.

It is provided in Article 5 of Additional Protocol II that the Protocol shall enter into force, for the States which have ratified it, on the date of the deposit of their respective instruments of ratification.

The instrument of ratification of the United Kingdom of Great Britain and Northern Ireland was deposited on December 11, 1969 with understandings and a declaration, and the instrument of ratification of the United States of America was deposited on May 12, 1971 with the above-recited understandings and declarations.

In accordance with Article 5 of Additional Protocol II, the Protocol entered into force for the United States of America on May 12, 1971, subject to the above-recited understandings and declarations.

NOW, THEREFORE, I, Richard Nixon, President of the United States of America, proclaim and make public Additional Protocol II to the Treaty for the Prohibition of Nuclear Weapons in Latin America to the end that it shall be observed and fulfilled with good faith, subject to the above-recited understandings and declarations, on and after May 12, 1971 by the United States of America and by the citizens of the United States of America and all other persons subject to the jurisdiction thereof.

IN TESTIMONY WHEREOF, I have signed this proclamation and

---

[72] Same, pp. 65-66.

[73] Paragraph 2 of Article 4 of the treaty states in effect that once the treaty and its additional protocols have been fully ratified and entered into force, the zone of application of the treaty will include the entire continents of North and South America and adjacent ocean areas south of 35° north latitude, excluding only the continental United States and its territorial waters.

caused the Seal of the United States of America to be affixed.

DONE at the city of Washington this eleventh day of June in the year of our Lord one thousand nine hundred seventy-one and of [SEAL]	the Independence of the United States of America the one hundred ninety-fifth.

RICHARD NIXON

By the President:
WILLIAM P. ROGERS
Secretary of State

C. Repercussions of the United States' "New Economic Policy."

[Secretary of State Rogers admitted frankly in his annual report on U.S. foreign policy that "U.S. relations with Latin America as a whole suffered some impairment during 1971," primarily for economic reasons. "The principal and immediate problem in Latin American eyes," he wrote, "was U.S. inability to meet some of our commitments and Latin American expectations in the fields of trade and economic assistance. Latin Americans were further distressed by the imposition of a 10 percent import surcharge under the President's new economic policy [Documents 142-143]. The notion grew in Latin America that the United States was uninterested in and neglectful of the hemisphere. Disputes over private investment and fisheries also were troublesome in our relations."[74]

Latin American resentment of U.S. economic moves was voiced with unusual freedom at the seventh annual meeting of the Inter-American Economic and Social Council (IA-ECOSOC), the top O.A.S. organ in the economic and social field, which was held in Panama on September 13-20, 1971, within a few weeks of President Nixon's imposition of the surcharge measure. Although the United States announced that Latin America would be exempted from the 10 percent reduction in foreign aid that also figured in the President's program, discussion at the meeting centered primarily on the import surcharge, which Latin Americans found doubly objectionable in view of the United States' traditional positive balance in trade with their region. Demands for exemption from the surcharge, for the implementation of generalized trade preferences, and for full participation in the planning of international monetary and trade reforms were incorporated in a resolution endorsed by all Latin American delegations.[75]

[74] Rogers Report, 1971, p. 123.
[75] Same, 126-27 and 132-33; details in *OAS Chronicle*, vol. 6, no. 3 (July–Sept. 1971).

The campaign of explanation and justification initiated by U.S. representatives at Panama[76] was continued in October in a remarkable address by Charles A. Meyer, Assistant Secretary of State for Inter-American Affairs, before the Inter American Press Association in Chicago (Document 115). Later Secretary Rogers struck a more optimistic note. "Despite unavoidable delays in implementation," the Secretary pointed out early in 1972, "the President reaffirmed our commitments to Latin America and our determination to move forward as soon as U.S. economic conditions permitted. At year's end the Administration was able to announce significant developments in this connection, including the immediate lifting of the import surcharge. We also intend to submit legislation to Congress establishing generalized tariff preferences for developing countries"[77] (Cf. Document 116).]

(115) "United States Policy Toward Latin America: Where We Stand Today": Address by Charles A. Meyer, Assistant Secretary of State for Inter-American Affairs, Before the Inter American Press Association, Chicago, October 25, 1971.[78]

(Complete Text)

I was truly pleased when your first vice president, John Watkins, invited me to address you tonight. I admit that I was also intrigued by the topic he assigned to me: where we stand today, 2 years after President Nixon's Latin American policy speech.[79]

I was intrigued because having become so sensitive to complaints that this administration has no Latin American policy, I had wondered whether there was a Latin Americanist left who would admit we had a policy to explain.

I cannot remember how many times I have been tempted to put these complaints in the category of a remark made nearly a century and a half ago by the famous English writer Charles Lamb. Lamb was walking along a London street with a friend, and he stopped and pointed. "Do you see that man over there?" he said. "I hate him." "Hate him?" his friend said. "How can you hate him? You don't even know who he is." "Precisely," Lamb said.

Lamb's unreasonable reaction to an unknown might be equated with critical assertions by the uninformed that this administration has no

[76] *Bulletin*, Oct. 11, 1971, pp. 379-84.

[77] Rogers Report, 1971, pp. 123-24. On generalized trade preferences see further Document 155.

[78] Department of State Press Release 244, Oct. 26, 1971; text from *Bulletin*, Nov. 15, 1971, pp. 559-64.

[79] Cf. note 3 above.

Latin American policy or—the common by-product of those complaints—that Latin America ranks so far down our list of priorities that we are "benignly neglecting" our neighbors and partners to the south.

But it was before this group of distinguished publishers and editors of the Inter American Press Association that President Nixon announced his administration's policy toward Latin America 2 years ago, less 1 week.

If any opinion-forming group can be sensitively aware of this administration's Latin American policy, it must be, I have thought, the newspapermen and broadcasters of this hemisphere. I am sure that many of you here tonight were among the President's audience 2 years ago. I am also confident that most of you counted yourselves among the large majority in this hemisphere who applauded the new policy with enthusiasm and with appreciation for its realism. The policy demonstrates the United States is ready to adapt to the changing political, economic, and social environment in Latin America; the policy responds to Latin America's needs and aspirations; and it suggested a series of important actions within the limits of the achievable to follow.

Why in the span of 2 years has such widespread support for the President's Latin American policy slipped to expressed doubt that this administration has a policy?

I believe there are four interlocking factors:

First, there has been an obvious and a serious failure to grasp the far-reaching implications inherent in the President's policy.

Second, the fact that the United States has not yet transformed one of the important policy pledges into policy action has led to the erroneous conclusion that an unfulfilled pledge equals no policy or no commitment at all.

Third, the fact that the President has taken a series of decisions within his executive powers in behalf of the hemisphere has been overlooked or even taken for granted.

Fourth, the fact that even the most sophisticated among us interchange bilateral problems with regional objectives and vice versa, depending often on whether we want to accentuate the negative or the positive—and far too often it is the negative—tends to distort relationships between the United States and any one or all of the nations of the Americas.

MUTUALITY AND SHARED RESPONSIBILITY

Let's begin with item one.

The fact is that the President has kept his promise. He has changed our policy radically. The problem is that today's policy is still being measured by yesterday's yardstick.

The essence of the President's new policy was captured in the term "mature partnership," which he used in his address to this association. The term has been repeated so often that it has attained the status of a slogan. Unfortunately, as is so often the case in this era of instant global communications, the slogan overpowered and obscured the message it conveyed and has been negatively interpreted from disengagement through disinterest to abandonment.

The positive message is clear and simple: The United States is dedicated to bringing about a new equilibrium in our relations with Latin America by loosening our long-held paternal grip on the other nations of the hemisphere. Tutelary leadership would be, and has been, replaced by a balanced relationship, including discreet leadership, that respects the sovereign rights of our Latin American partners.

This policy is confirmed by our continuing support to Latin America's drive for economic and social development, but increasingly only in response to Latin America's initiatives. The shift of emphasis from bilateral to multilateral assistance and the arduous but still unfinished business of expanding Latin America's trade opportunities are concrete developments that reflect this policy change.

The new policy also foresaw change in Latin America as a continuing force and the need to live with diversity as one of its outgrowths. We now deal with governments as they are—which is what Latin America wants. We are shaping our relations with governments around the contours of the actions they take affecting us and the inter-American system.

The policy of mature partnership does and should and must emphasize constant progress toward reciprocal understanding. It, in short, strives to develop a true two-way street in bilateral, subregional, and regional relationships. It just may be that Latin America has felt itself at the end of a one-way street for so long that its response to reciprocity or mutuality is initially one of a 180-degree reverse in the one-way street. In such a reverse of direction the interests of the United States would be considered expendable, principally because we are the richest and most powerful nation and therefore should be the givers in a relationship of "give-and-take," not "take-it-or-leave-it," to quote from the President's October 1969 speech.

However, the broad aspect of our policy is one which embodies increased recognition of mutuality and shared responsibility, acceptance of diversity, while pledging continued support for development.

DEVELOPMENTS IN TRADE POLICY

The broad policy concept obviously leads to specifics and again to negative interpretation to the degree that any one or more unimplemented specifics can be represented as no policy or no commitment.

Therefore, to present a complete picture I must now turn to both inaction and action in the broad field of trade, in which field some negative developments have adversely affected our relations with Latin America in the past year. I believe these "non-developments" (if I may coin a word) are responsible in part for the simplistic preachment: "U.S. relations with Latin America have reached their lowest point since . . . ."

We have not fulfilled our commitment to implement a system of generalized tariff preferences for the developing countries, which preferences represent Latin America's highest priority objective in its economic relations with the United States. The United States and Latin America agree they are important to development, for as you know, generalized preferences would eliminate tariffs of all major developed countries on a large number of manufactured and semimanufactured products from all LDC's [less developed countries]. Therefore they would stimulate developing countries to diversify their exports and reduce their traditional dependence for foreign exchange earnings on raw materials and commodities and would reduce the high cost of import substitution.

Trade—with good reason—is now considered the unwritten Magna Carta of Latin America's economic development. It offers potential for transferring resources indispensable to development and growth without the real or imagined infringing on national sovereignty that so often conditions bilateral and even multilateral loans and investment, private and public.

In 1969 and early 1970, the United States took the lead in urging the European Common Market countries and Japan to establish with us a system that would benefit the developing countries. The Common Market countries and Japan have since put their generalized preference systems into effect.[80] We have delayed submission of legislation because, concurrent with our negotiations with Latin America, the United States trade and balance of payments position was deteriorating rapidly. This deterioration, coupled with a sluggish economy, created not only an unreceptive mood but a strong protectionist sentiment in Congress. In this unfavorable climate, the administration considered that not only was passage of a preference bill unlikely but that submission of a bill by the executive branch might be unwise.

Our inability to meet a commitment of such importance to Latin America has disappointed and dismayed many Latin American leaders and cast doubt on our sincerity.

I, for one, have tried to explain to our Latin neighbors in these past 2 years that readjustments in global claims on the U.S.A. have become a reality. Our commitments remain firm, but the timing of their implementation is not necessarily determined unilaterally. In today's

---

[80] Cf. above at note 42.

world, every event everywhere has a ripple effect all over the world, and timing is affected by those ripples.

On August 15, President Nixon announced his new economic policy aimed at reversing the deficit in our worldwide trade account and reviving our economy.[81]

The further dismay expressed by Latin America in the aftermath of the announcement reached its peak at the Inter-American Economic and Social Council meeting in Panama last month.[82] The Latin Americans demanded removal of the 10-percent surcharge on dutiable exports to the United States. They protested that the United States has had a large favorable balance of trade with Latin America for years and that they should not suffer from a program of global readjustment insofar as they were not contributors to the problem.

The United States has stressed that the surcharge is only a temporary measure, that its real impact in Latin America may be slight, and that a robust United States economy—which is the goal of the new program—is in the long-range benefit of all developing countries. Nevertheless, the Latin Americans have not been placated. In addition to its economic impact, the sudden and sweeping nature of the new program along with our inability to consult with the Latin Americans in advance took its toll politically and psychologically. They saw it as dramatic evidence of their impotence and lack of influence on decisions that can crucially affect their own economic planning. In the train of the indefinite timing of the generalized preference legislation, there is no doubt that even if the economic effect is undetermined, the psychological and political shock of the August 15 measures are real, despite their temporary nature and despite the fact that the administration remains wedded to generalized tariff preferences.

CONCRETE ACHIEVEMENTS

The third facet which we must consider is what has been undertaken.

Our policy, as the President has said, is one of give-and-take, not take-it-or-leave-it. Our relationship is a two-way relationship that, in fact, transcends official policy to include ties that have been developed government to government, industry to industry, school to school, scientist to scientist, and volunteer to volunteer. There are so many ties that no one has at hand even a partial catalogue.

And I hasten to add—in the event these remarks are interpreted by some as setting the stage for cutbacks in our official economic commitment to Latin America—that President Nixon has repeatedly reaffirmed our partnership in the development challenge. And he has

[81] Document 142.
[82] Cf. above at notes 75-76.

backed that partnership with resources. Contrary to a popular misconception, economic assistance levels continue to match the annual average during the first 10 years of the Alliance for Progress. The difference is: bilateral aid levels have fallen and multilateral aid contributions have risen, largely in response to Latin American desires.

That leads me to other concrete achievements, not only of this administration's policy but also of the inter-American system which that policy supports. A monetary value can be placed on some. Others can be priced only in terms of the value each of us places on cooperation among the nations of this hemisphere.

We have eased restrictions so that our neighbors may now spend aid dollars elsewhere in Latin America or the developing world. We have submitted U.S. economic policies for annual review to the Inter-American Committee on the Alliance for Progress, an unprecedented step for a donor nation. We have consulted whenever possible with Latin America prior to taking actions that affect their economies. We have participated enthusiastically and generously in inter-American organizations that in the last 2 years have launched programs to develop capital markets, tourism, and export promotion, a vital program regardless of trade preferences. We are studying how best to transfer technology for the hemisphere's social and economic development.

We signed agreements with Colombia and Panama covering the U.S. financing of its share of completion of construction on the Darien Gap, the last unfinished link of the Pan American Highway.[83] The OAS approved a convention on kidnaping and other crimes against foreign officials.[84] We have achieved closer cooperation with Latin American countries in the control of illicit traffic in narcotics and dangerous drugs. Congress passed new sugar legislation[85] which, on the whole, favored Latin American suppliers. And President Nixon exempted Latin America from the 10-percent reduction in foreign economic assistance expenditures called for under the new economic policy.[86]

Regionally, our interlacing of mutual objectives has produced results. Subregionally and bilaterally this is also true, perhaps even more evident.

Subregionally, we have continued our support of the Central American Bank for Economic Integration, formalized our financial support of the Caribbean Development Bank, held available up to $10 million to assist in loans to the Andean Development Corporation as it develops.

Bilaterally, in the purest sense of a mature partnership, we have

[83] TIAS 7111 and 7112; 22 UST 602 and 617; cf. Nixon statement, May 6, 1971, in *Public Papers, 1971*, pp. 622-23.
[84] Document 111.
[85] Public Law 92-138, Oct. 14, 1971.
[86] Statement by Deputy Under Secretary of State Nathaniel Samuels, Panama, Sept. 13, 1971, in *Bulletin*, Oct. 11, 1971, p. 382.

abrogated the Bryan-Chamorro Treaty,[87] reformalized bilateral negotiations to modernize the 1903 treaty between the United States and
Panama,[88] negotiated a border settlement agreement with Mexico
which once and for all settles disputes over the changing course of the
Rio Grande.[89] Traditional recurring trade agreements—textiles, meats,
fruits, and vegetables—have been successfully negotiated, although
obviously in a buyer-seller negotiation neither side reaches its maximum
aspirations.

In short, respected friends, neither are our policy objectives stagnant,
nor are our relationships sterile.

This, however, leads to the fourth factor—that even the most sophisticated among us interchange bilateral problems with regional objectives
and vice versa, usually with negative distortion.

BILATERAL PROBLEMS AND REGIONAL OBJECTIVES

Inherent in President Nixon's policy concept was and is the recognition that differences of priorities, differences of interest, are
to be expected but that in the spirit of negotiation not confrontation,
differences can be manageable.

There are two significant differences of interest which require this
spirit to the fullest. The first of these is what is broadly described as the
territorial sea. The second of these is the role of foreign private investment. These differences are not new, are unresolved, and adversely
color our total relationship in the minds of all too many of us at home
and abroad who, on the one hand, evaluate all of Latin America in the
light of the actions of one or more individual nations or who, on the
other hand, sadly and inaccurately and negatively evaluate all U.S.
interests as "imperialistic" or "exploitative."

I suspect that everyone here tonight has an opinion on the subject of
distant fishing in traditional fishing grounds preempted by unilateral
claims of maritime sovereignty. And I further suspect that the majority
of opinion would be that the interested parties should find a practical
solution to the fishing conflict instead of escalating punitive measures,
recognizing that the complicated question of the sea and its seabed are
both subjects of a U.N. conference scheduled for 1973.[90] Such a practical solution has been sought and is being sought, and it does require
give-and-take without compromising the fundamental differences in
legal concepts that are involved. What is transcendentally important is
that none of us in South or North America allow this specific problem

---

[87] Cf. note 50 above.
[88] Cf. Document 119.
[89] Cf. note 51 above.
[90] Cf. above at note 26.

negatively to influence the basic relationships between us nor to spill over into unrelated retribution.

The second important difference which is disruptive to a wholly unnecessary degree is a difference in concept relative to foreign private investment—and to be wholly honest, one would qualify "foreign" as "U.S." private investment.

As many of you will recall, the Presidential address 2 years ago placed balanced emphasis on the importance of the private sector in the total development picture, said private sector to include private foreign investment. And President Nixon urged that the Americas write the rules of the game, rules by which all investors would be governed without the risk of constant change and certainly without the unbelievable risk of retroactivity in the application of whatever rules.

This balanced emphasis reflected and reflects our conviction that development, both economic and social, depends on transfer of resources. This transfer is effected by bilateral and unilateral development loans and grants, by trade, and by direct foreign investment, which may be the one most effective method of transferring the savings of the developed world to the developing world—which is short of savings—at a negligible real cost to the developed world.

This conviction is neither imperialist nor exploitative. It is an honest reflection of the importance of the entrepreneurial instinct and the profit motive in development and an honest evaluation of the mobility of private capital as contrasted with government funds. Yet my Government recognizes the right of a sovereign state to nationalize a foreign-owned property—even though the wisdom, short- and long-range, of some nationalization we would question. The vital point is compensation, prompt, adequate, and effective, for any part or all of a property that is nationalized.

Here is where we of the Americas need the fullest application of mutual understanding, of give-and-take, of negotiation not confrontation, of third-party adjudication when necessary. For no one can overlook the fact that it is difficult for the American taxpayer to support development assistance or adopt an attitude of "business as usual" with any nation when that very same taxpayer may have lost an important part of his or her savings through uncompensated or inadequately compensated nationalization by that nation.[91]

This is not a "hard-line" reaction nor a "get-tough" reaction; it is merely human—once burned, twice shy.

It is these two areas of difference that develop or that have developed most of the public heat between the United States and Latin America even though these are not regional differences common to all, nor are these differences identical nation by nation where they exist.

[91] Cf. Document 118.

So, to restate the fourth aspect in evaluation of this administration's policy and our inter-American relationships, the sad fact is that all of us, north and south, still unconsciously confuse a living, growing, maturing hemispheric relationship with bilateral differences.

Distinguished ladies and gentlemen, the Nixon policy is a living policy. It has been incompletely understood because it is not a pyrotechnic policy conceived for instant impact but a sound policy for now and the future responsive to the nations of Latin America.

The implementation of the trade portion of this policy has been deferred, and this presents a criticism of U.S. policy toward Latin America.

The implementation of scores of initiatives within the authority of the executive branch has proceeded and may, as I have said, have been unnoticed or taken for granted.

Bilateral problems emerging from a subregional concept of maritime jurisdiction and from nationalism as this affects the past, present, and future investment of private capital have been interpreted by some as evidence of deterioration in our inter-American relationships. If my task were to pass around blame, I could suggest that these latter two areas of difference require a better understanding of the U.S.A. on the part of the Latin nations involved.

But to evenly distribute blame or to unevenly distribute blame is not and must not be the basic underpinning of our inter-American convictions, of the U.S. policy for Latin America, nor of the Latin American policy for the United States.

During the balance of this century we simply must build on the concept of mature partnership. All of us face similar problems. No nation among us is developed if one accepts the fact that development is a career, not a destination. It never ends. Our community of interests will not prevent the emergence of differences. The give-and-take, the mutuality, the reciprocity, which we apply to solution of these differences will continue the tradition of the Americas.

In your honor I am proud to close with a message:

"My very best wishes go to the members of the Inter American Press Association as I welcome its delegates to our country.

"I have pleasant memories of the evening 2 years ago when I had the privilege of addressing your last meeting on U.S. soil.

"In the policy statement I made to you then, I told you that the United States hoped to achieve a more mature partnership in which all voices are heard and none predominates. I also expressed our desire to maintain our basic commitment to the hemisphere's social [and] economic development.

"I wish to assure you today that the destiny of every nation within our inter-American system remains of foremost concern to the United

States. But I also believe that only through the shared responsibility I called for 2 years ago can we ultimately achieve the equality in our relations that we all seek as partners in the Americas.

"I also want to take this opportunity to say that once the problems to which our new economic program in the United States has been addressed are alleviated, we shall again move forward in many of the basic areas I discussed with you in 1969.[92]

"Meanwhile, I ask for the patience and understanding of our Latin American neighbors during this hopefully brief period in which the imbalances in the U.S. economy are corrected.

"As you are among the most distinguished journalists in our hemisphere, your members have gained the respect, esteem, and trust of countless men and women. You have an awesome responsibility toward them and a role in their continuing well-being. I wholeheartedly applaud your staunch defense of freedom of expression and look forward with the leaders of the countries you represent to your important assistance in bringing into focus the needs of our people and in marshaling the best resources for the sustained progress of our societies."

RICHARD NIXON

(116) Economic Cooperation with Latin America: News Conference Statement by Secretary of State Rogers, December 23, 1971.[93]

(Excerpt)

I would like to start this press conference by reference to Latin America, and I have a prepared statement I would like to read:

I would like to take this opportunity to express my gratification on the measures we have been able to take this past week which will benefit the developing nations, especially those of Latin America.

I refer to the lifting of the 10-percent surcharge[94] and to the President's decision to present legislation to the next Congress establishing generalized trade preferences.[95] These two measures will be of particular benefit to our friends in Latin America.

Had we not been able to lift the 10-percent surcharge globally fol-

---

[92] Cf. Document 116.
[93] Department of State Press Release 303, Dec. 23, 1971; text from *Bulletin*, Jan. 17, 1972, p. 49. For further excerpts from this news conference cf. Documents 10, 30, 64, and 110.
[94] Document 151.
[95] Document 155.

lowing the Group of Ten talks,[96] I think you should know, and I particularly want the Latin American countries to know, that the President was prepared to lift the surcharge on a product-by-product basis with special attention to those items important to the developing nations in general and to Latin American countries specifically.

The adjustments in our monetary policy will also bring benefits to many Latin American countries by improving their balance of payments positions and thereby enhancing their own ability to develop.

The well-being of the peoples and nations of Latin America continues to be of major interest and concern to President Nixon. To that end, this administration will press for the full replenishment of funds required by the Inter-American Development Bank when Congress reconvenes.[97] We also anticipate that the International Coffee Agreement will be addressed favorably by the next session of the Senate as our contribution to stabilizing the price of a product so vital to so many economies of Latin America and the world.[98]

We have never swerved from our basic purposes of seeking to help the Americas help themselves. We have not been able to pursue these in the past as rapidly as we desired and as I had hoped when I met with the Foreign Ministers from Latin America in Costa Rica last April.[99] However, I am pleased to be able to report on this optimistic note as this year draws to a close. As we move forward to meet the challenges of peaceful cooperation and effective progress in the hemisphere, I expect to engage in close consultation with our friends in Latin America during the coming year regarding other cooperative measures we may take.

In this connection, the Foreign Ministers will be here in the spring for a meeting of the OAS,[100] and I hope at that time to have the opportunity to consult fully with them about further measures that we might take in a cooperative effort with our Latin American friends.

D. Relations With Particular Countries.

[Some of the most significant manifestations of U.S. policy toward

[96] Document 150.

[97] By Public Law 92-246, Mar. 10, 1972, Congress authorized additional U.S. contributions of $900 million toward the replenishment of the Fund for Special Operations of the Inter-American Development Bank. Cf. Nixon signature statement in *Presidential Documents*, Mar. 13, 1972, pp. 554-55.

[98] Continued participation in the International Coffee Agreement until Oct. 1, 1973, was authorized by Public Law 92-262, Mar. 24, 1972.

[99] Cf. above at notes 31-33.

[100] The O.A.S. General Assembly held its Second Regular Session in Washington on Apr. 11-21, 1972. The address delivered by Secretary Rogers on that occasion appears in *A.F.R., 1972*, no. 75.

Latin America in 1971 occurred in its relationships with individual countries whose role in hemisphere affairs was viewed in Washington with special interest or, in some cases, mistrust. Prominent in the former category was the Federative Republic of Brazil; indeed, one of the celebrated remarks of the year was President Nixon's statement, in connection with a laudatory evaluation of Brazilian progress during a visit from President Emílio Garrastazú Médici, that " as Brazil goes, so will go the rest of the Latin American Continent."[101] The observation sent shock waves throughout South America and led Brazil to issue a series of statements aimed at reassuring anxious neighbors that it harbored no aspirations toward continental hegemony.

Two governments that were regarded with less benevolence in official Washington were those of Cuba and Chile, the former because of its close ties with the U.S.S.R. and continuing commitment to the support of revolutionary movements in Latin America, the latter primarily because of the actions of the new Allende administration in expropriating foreign-owned property without making satisfactory provision for compensation of the owners. Likewise of special concern to the United States was the attitude of the Panamanian Government led by Brigadier General Omar Torrijos, with whose representatives it was attempting to negotiate a revision of the treaty arrangements governing the Panama Canal and the Canal Zone.]

1. Cuba.

[A statement to the Senate Foreign Relations Committee by the Deputy Assistant Secretary of State for Inter-American Affairs (Document 117) provided confirmation of the stability of U.S. views on policy toward the Castro regime at a time when several Latin American states were beginning to show a disinclination to maintain the economic and diplomatic ostracism of Cuba decreed by the O.A.S. in the early 1960s.]

(117) United States Policy Toward Cuba: Statement by Robert A. Hurwitch, Deputy Assistant Secretary of State for Inter-American Affairs, Before the Senate Committee on Foreign Relations, September 16, 1971. [102]

[101] Toast to President Médici, Dec. 7, 1971, in *Public Papers, 1971*, p. 1167.
[102] *Bulletin*, Oct. 11, 1971, pp. 391-95. The statement was made in the course of a one-day hearing on three pending resolutions, two of which called for repeal of the 1962 Cuba resolution (note 103) while the third favored a review of policy toward Cuba. No action was taken on the resolutions during the 92d Congress.

(Complete Text)

I am very pleased to have this opportunity to testify before the Committee on Foreign Relations on Senate Joint Resolution 146, a joint resolution to repeal Public Law 87-733,[103] and upon Senate Resolution 160, expressing the sense of the U.S. Senate with respect to U.S. policy toward Cuba.

With regard to Senate Joint Resolution 146, as the Department has stated before—in letters of March 12 and June 3, 1970—it neither advocates nor opposes repeal of Public Law 87-733 since the executive branch does not depend on it as legal or constitutional authority for our policy toward Cuba. However, the Department would not wish this position to be misinterpreted. The joint resolution was expressive of a common understanding of the legislative and executive branches at that time of the threat to the peace and security of the Western Hemisphere nations posed by the Cuban Government's policy of interference in the internal affairs of these nations through support of subversive activities and by its military ties with the Soviet Union. The history of the actions undertaken by the Organization of American States (OAS) in response to this threat is well known to the committee.[104]

In the Department's view, there has been no significant change in the basic conditions upon which U.S. Cuban policy has been based in the years since 1962 that would warrant a change in U.S. policy. Therefore, the Cuban resolution of 1962 still reflects U.S. policy toward Cuba.

The essential elements of our policy toward Cuba were described as follows by President Nixon in his report to the Congress of February 25, 1971:[105]

Cuba continued to exclude itself from the inter-American system by its encouragement and support of revolution and its military ties to the Soviet Union. The latter meanwhile attempted to expand its influence and its military presence.

We do not seek confrontations with any government. But those which display unremitting hostility cannot expect our assistance. And those which violate the principles of the inter-American system, by intervening in the affairs of their neighbors or by facilitating the intervention of non-hemispheric powers, cannot expect to share the benefits of inter-American cooperation. We will work

---

[103] Joint resolution expressing the determination of the United States with respect to the situation in Cuba, approved Oct. 3, 1962; text in *Documents, 1962*, pp. 372-73.
[104] Cf. *Documents, 1962*, pp. 344-46 and 380-83; same, *1964*, pp. 290-301; same, *1967*, pp. 370-83.
[105] Nixon Report, 1971, p. 54.

constructively with other members of the community to reduce the disruptive effect of such actions.

United States policy, therefore, derives from these principal considerations: our national interest; our obligations as a member of the Organization of American States; our concern over Cuba's export of its revolution; and Cuba's military ties to the Soviet Union.

With regard to the last, the crisis of October 1962 as well as the more recent developments last year at Cienfuegos[106] are illustrative of our concern about Cuba's present military ties with the Soviet Union. You will recall, Mr. Chairman [J. William Fulbright], that at Cienfuegos, Cuba permitted the Soviet Union to take new steps which could have afforded the Soviets the ability to again operate offensive weapons systems from this hemisphere. President Nixon stated on February 25, 1971, that this would have been contrary to the earlier undertaking between the Soviet Union and the United States following the missile crisis. Only after a period of discussion with the Soviet Union did we reaffirm our understanding and amplify it to make clear that the agreement included activities related to sea-based systems.[107]

Cuba's open pursuit of a policy of attempting to subvert existing governments in the hemisphere, as well as its cooperation with Soviet military purposes, continues to constitute, in our view, a threat to the peace and security of this hemisphere. I wish to invite the committee's attention to the fact that, consistent with the above-described policy statement by the President, our concern is based upon external, not internal, policies and activities of the Cuban Government.

By refraining from steps that might assist Cuba and by strongly supporting the measures adopted by the OAS, the United States has not sought the overthrow of the present Cuban regime but rather sought the reduction of Cuba's capability to export armed revolution and the discouragement of Soviet adventures in this hemisphere. As a result, Cuba has been deprived of substantial sums of hard currency which would otherwise be available to promote Cuban goals in Latin America, and some of the energy, money, and manpower now required to keep the Cuban economy functioning would otherwise be available for support of subversive activities. Cuba today (due also in part to Prime Minister [Fidel] Castro's mismanagement) is not an attractive model likely to stimulate emulation elsewhere in the hemisphere. Moreover, Cuba is a financial burden for the Soviet Union, costing the U.S.S.R. more than $1 million per day.

[106] Cf. *The United States in World Affairs, 1970*, p. 197.
[107] Cf. Nixon statements of Jan. 4 and Feb. 17, 1971, in *Public Papers, 1971*, pp. 17-18 and 163. For the correspondence exchanged by President Kennedy and N.S. Khrushchev during the 1962 Cuban missile crisis, see *Bulletin*, Nov. 19, 1973, pp. 635-55.

The Department wishes to assure the committee, however, that the above-described U.S. policy toward Cuba is under constant review to determine whether such policy toward Cuba continues to serve the complex of U.S. national interests involved or whether some other policies might not serve better. Any such review would, of course, take into account our commitments in the OAS.

We recognize, Mr. Chairman, that there is great ferment in Latin America. We know that modernization brings extensive and frequently unsettling change. We are not opposed to change.

I would recall that President Nixon in his toast at a dinner honoring President [Rafael] Caldera [Rodríguez] of Venezuela on June 2, 1970, said:[108]

> ... all of us come from and were born to this world, our nations, through violent revolution. Now our charge and our task is to provide the means and the method through which those great changes that need to be made in the world, in our own countries and in the world, can be made through peaceful change.

Nor are we bent upon a policy that insists that others forgo their histories and traditions and arrange their societies to conform to ours. We firmly believe that our Nation which values a pluralistic society at home should in equal measure respect diversity abroad.

In this connection, I would also recall that President Nixon has stated that while we hope that governments will evolve toward constitutional procedures, we deal with governments as they are. Our relations depend not on their internal structures or social systems but on actions which affect us and the inter-American system.

The Government of Cuba advocates change, however, through violent means. Cuba's policies encourage polarization within the many fragile societies of Latin America and tend to lead to repressive regimes of the right or dictatorships of the left when successful. Cuba's policies have also forced other nations of the hemisphere to divert a portion of the scarce resources they have available for development to improve their internal security capability, including the purchase of arms, in order to counter Cuban influence. Illustratively, the then President of Colombia, Dr. Carlos Lleras Restrepo, a well-known liberal statesman, replied to a reporter's question in February 1970 as to whether his country should follow Chile's example in seeking a normalization of relations with Cuba:

> Chile is in the south and we are in the Caribbean. Colombia and Venezuela are countries which have been lashed by guerrilla movements, by urban interventions in our domestic matters. That is the

108 *Public Papers, 1970*, p. 471.

source of Cuba's sanction. I do not believe Chile's position is the position of the continent and I consider it is Cuba that must change toward us and not the reverse. We have had to invest major sums to maintain public order because of the Cubans.

Mr. Chairman, our consultations with our Latin American neighbors in the hemisphere suggest that the view of former President Lleras reflects prevailing sentiment.

In its continuing review of policy toward Cuba, the Department sees no evidence of any developments that materially affect the twin foundations of U.S. policy. On the contrary, the most recent evidence confirms the validity of continuing this policy. Cuba continues to interfere in the internal affairs of other hemispheric nations by providing training in Cuba for urban and rural terrorists, by providing monetary and other material support to subversive groups, and occasional direct participation by Cubans in insurgencies. On July 26 Prime Minister Castro openly took sides in the pending Uruguayan elections and drew a stiff rejoinder from the Uruguayan Government. His publicly expressed disappointment over the turn of events in Bolivia[109] drew the reminder from the Bolivian Government that Cubans in 1967[110] and again in 1970 had blatantly interfered in the internal affairs of Bolivia, a nation that had experienced one of the most fundamental socioeconomic revolutions in the hemisphere in 1952, 7 years before he came to power. Last month, on August 27, Prime Minister Castro vigorously reaffirmed that he would not abandon his support for violent change in other nations of the hemisphere and spoke of Cuba's intention to give material support to Bolivian guerrillas.

Despite Prime Minister Castro's renewed effort to project himself as a Latin American revolutionary leader, it is fair to say that in the period 1968-71 there seems to have been some falling off in the material support which Cuba provided to subversive movements in other countries. As has been previously testified before this committee, Cuban support has become more selective, and there has been a shift from rural guerrilla warfare to urban terrorism. Cuban adoption of new tactics on subversion, however, does not mean that it has renounced support of violent revolution; neither does it represent an abandonment of other forms of subversion, which we believe Cuba continues to regard as useful political tools.

An important factor accounting for some reduction in Cuban support is the fact that the measures adopted by the OAS to counter Cuban interference in the internal affairs of other countries have succeeded in

[109] The left-wing military regime of Gen. Juan José Torres González was supplanted Aug. 22, 1971, by a more conservative military regime led by Col. Hugo Banzer Suárez.

[110] Cf. *The United States in World Affairs, 1967*, pp. 304-6, 321-22, and 327.

weakening Cuba's capability to commit such interference. Cuba's long series of disastrous foreign adventures, culminating in the "Ché" Guevara 1967 fiasco in Bolivia, had its effect as well. Finally, economic mismanagement at home matched the failure abroad. Prime Minister Castro said in August 1970 that if Cuba had not given full support to revolutionary movements in Latin America, it was in part because "we have not been able to." To abandon now these policies which hinder the Cuban Government's capability to achieve its objectives would therefore be neither prudent nor justified.

With regard to Senate Resolution 160, the Department of State notes that the proposed resolution is in two sections. I shall address comments to each.

The first section proposes that it be the sense of the Senate that the President take steps to review U.S. policy toward Cuba with the objective of beginning a process which would lead to the reestablishment of normal relations between the United States and Cuba. It appears to assume that a process leading to the reestablishment of normal relations between the United States and Cuba would serve U.S. interests and that such a process would meet with Cuban agreement. We do not believe this to be true. We believe that the resolution might be misinterpreted to imply that we are no longer concerned over Prime Minister Castro's policies of demonstrating hostility toward the United States, of exporting his revolution, and of seeking ever closer military ties with the U.S.S.R. It could well enhance his prestige and lend him the stature on the international scene he seeks but does not enjoy. I believe it would also give an aura of legitimacy to the extremist movements supported by Cuba that seek violent overthrow of governments in Latin America. These are some of the pertinent political considerations.

From the economic standpoint, the United States has little, if anything, to gain. Arrangements have been made with a number of friendly nations to assure a reliable supply of sugar for the United States domestic market; therefore Cuban sugar is not essential as long as the present government remains in power. The absence of Cuban tobacco or the few other Cuban export products has also not had significant effect upon our economy.

Thus, from the standpoint of U.S. interests, unless the Cuban Government were to abandon its policies and actions which constitute a threat to the peace and security of the hemisphere, the benefits to be derived from normalization of relations with Cuba are not readily apparent, whereas the costs are clear.

U.S. policy toward Cuba is not, as I have stated at the outset, inflexible. Should the Government of Cuba abandon the policies by which it excluded itself from the family of American nations, the United States would, in consultation with the other members, review existing policies in the light of such new circumstances. The President said as much

publicly on April 16 of this year;[111] on April 19, Fidel Castro, in direct
reply to the President's statement, declared that he scorned normalized
relations with the United States. Several days later, on April 21, the
New York Times editorialized:

> His (Castro's) stance implies that continued hostility is in the
> interests of the Cuban people.
> Castro's verbal supermilitancy can only be interpreted as a public
> attack upon and repudiation of the more conciliatory lines now
> being followed in Moscow and Peking. His words guarantee, unfor-
> tunately, that Cuban-American antagonism will continue. But he
> himself must now bear the responsibility.

We know of no basis for believing that Cuba, which forced the break
in relations with the United States, would now welcome their
reestablishment.

With regard to the second section of the proposed resolution, hemispheric policy toward Cuba, including that of the United States, derives
from a series of resolutions adopted by the Organization of American
States at meetings convoked at Latin American initiative. These resolutions excluded the present Government of Cuba from participation in
the OAS. They condemned Cuba for acts of intervention and aggression
against various countries of the hemisphere and imposed sanctions suspending all trade and shipping as well as diplomatic relations between
member countries and Cuba until the OAS decided by a two-thirds vote
that Cuba has ceased to be a threat to the peace and security of the
hemisphere.[112]

The Department notes that the proposed Senate resolution envisages
a reexamination by the OAS of its Cuban policy and concurs that
should circumstances so warrant, review of policy toward Cuba should
properly take place within the OAS, but only when a change in circumstances warrants such a review. Unilateral change of policy toward Cuba
by any of the OAS member nations violates binding obligations taken
under the terms of the Rio Treaty,[113] derogates from the prestige and
authority of the OAS, and consequently weakens the ties that bind
the nations of the Americas. For this reason, it is not the intention of
the United States to take unilateral steps, much less without prior
consultation with the other OAS members, that would lead toward
normalizing relations with Cuba. For this reason we have deplored
Chile's action.[114]

---

[111] News conference statement, Apr. 16, 1971, in *Public Papers, 1971*, pp.
544-45.
[112] Cf. note 104 above.
[113] Cf. note 36 above.
[114] Chile reestablished diplomatic relations with Cuba shortly after the inauguration of President Allende on Nov. 3, 1970.

Although the United States is, of course, prepared to participate in the discussion of items placed upon the OAS agenda, the Department does not believe that the considerations which led to the substance of the OAS resolutions affecting Cuba has changed in any significant way; therefore no change in these resolutions is warranted. Nor would the Department urge that the OAS, which Prime Minister Castro as recently as a few weeks ago characterized as "that cesspool, that filth, that cadaver," should dignify Cuba by allocating any of its valuable time to taking note of it.

For these multiple reasons, the Department of State would oppose the adoption of Resolution 160 by the United States Senate.

2. Chile.

[The even more controversial subject of U.S. relations with Chile, where the leftist "Popular Unity" coalition government headed by Salvador Allende Gossens had taken office November 3, 1970, was imperfectly illuminated on the public record during 1971. Still widely unrecognized at that time was the antipathy toward the new regime that existed not only in the management of a giant U.S. corporation like the International Telephone and Telegraph Corporation but even at those governmental echelons concerned with the operations of the U.S. Central Intelligence Agency (CIA). Not until September 1974 would it be disclosed, for example, that the Nixon administration had authorized CIA expenditures exceeding $8 million between 1970 and 1973 for covert activities designed to "destabilize" the Allende regime—or at least, in President Ford's words at a news conference on September 16, 1974, to influence Chilean internal developments in such a way as "to help and assist the preservation of opposition newspapers and electronic media and to preserve opposition political parties."[115]

So far as the public record was concerned, U.S. policy toward Chile under its new government had been fully defined in President Nixon's "State of the World" report made public February 25, 1971:

". . . We deal with governments as they are. Our relations depend not on their internal structures or social systems, but on actions which affect us and the inter-American system.

"The new Government of Chile is a clear case in point. The 1970 election of a Socialist President may have profound implications not only for its people but for the inter-American system as well. The government's legitimacy is not in question, but its ideology is likely

[115] *Presidential Documents*, Sept. 23, 1974, p. 1159.

to influence its actions. Chile's decision to establish ties with Communist Cuba, contrary to the collective policy of the OAS, was a challenge to the inter-American system. We and our partners in the OAS will therefore observe closely the evolution of Chilean foreign policy.

"Our bilateral policy is to keep open lines of communication. We will not be the ones to upset traditional relations. We assume that international rights and obligations will be observed. We also recognize that the Chilean Government's actions will be determined primarily by its own purposes, and that these will not be deflected simply by the tone of our policy. In short, we are prepared to have the kind of relationship with the Chilean government that it is prepared to have with us."[116]

This definition sufficed to place on Chile the responsibility for any further deterioration in the relations between the two countries, and Chilean actions in the following months undoubtedly hit the United States at sensitive points. This was particularly true of its treatment of the U.S.-owned copper companies which had only recently accommodated themselves to the policy of "Chileanization" (joint ownership) instituted by the previous Chilean government under President Eduardo Frei Montalva. On June 11, 1971, the Chilean Congress unanimously approved the full nationalization of the Chilean copper industry, at the same time stipulating that the expropriated U.S. companies should be paid compensation over a 30-year period. But on October 11, 1971, the Chilean Comptroller General announced that compensation due the Anaconda Copper Company and the Kennecott Copper Corporation was offset by "excessive profits" and other items, with the result that the two companies allegedly owed to Chile the equivalent of $378 million.

The U.S. reaction to this move, which signaled a hardening of attitudes on both sides, was set forth in a public statement by Secretary of State Rogers and a lengthier comment by Assistant Secretary of State Meyer before a subcommittee of the House Committee on Foreign Affairs (Document 118).]

(118) United States Policy Toward Chile: Statement by Assistant Secretary of State Meyer Before the Subcommittee on Inter-American Affairs of the House Committee on Foreign Affairs, October 15, 1971.[117]

[116] Nixon Report, 1971, pp. 53-54.
[117] *Bulletin*, Nov. 1, 1971, pp. 498-500.

(Complete Text)

I would like to preface my remarks on our overall policies toward Chile and the specific issue of compensation for expropriated U.S. copper holdings in that country by reading the statement issued on October 13 by Secretary Rogers on the compensation question.[118]

"The Controller General [Héctor Humeres Magnan] of Chile announced his findings on October 11 that no compensation would be paid for the U.S. copper mining investments expropriated on July 16 except for modest amounts in the cases of two smaller properties.[119]

"The United States Government is deeply disappointed and disturbed at this serious departure from accepted standards of international law. Under established principles of international law, the expropriation must be accompanied by reasonable provision for payment of just compensation. The United States had made clear to the Government of Chile its hope that a solution could be found on a reasonable and pragmatic basis consistent with international law.

"It appears that the major factor in the Controller General's decision with respect to the larger producers was the determination on September 28 of alleged "excess profits."[120] The unprecedented retroactive application of the excess profits concept, which was not obligatory under the expropriation legislation adopted by the Chilean Congress, is particularly disquieting. The U.S. companies which are affected by this determination of the Chilean Government earned their profits in Chile in accordance with Chilean law and under specific contractual agreements made directly with the Government of Chile. The excess profits deductions punish the companies today for acts that were legal and approved by the Government of Chile at the time. No claim is being made that these excess profits deductions are based on violations of Chilean law. This retroactive determination has serious implications for the rule of law.

"Should Chile fail to meet its international obligations, it could jeopardize flows of private funds and erode the base of support for foreign assistance, with possible adverse effects on other developing countries. The course of action which the Chilean Government appears to have chosen, therefore, could have an adverse effect on the international development process.

[118] Read to news correspondents by Robert J. McCloskey, Deputy Assistant Secretary of State for Press Relations, and issued as Department of State Press Release 234; text from *Bulletin*, Nov. 1, 1971, p. 478.
[119] Text in *International Legal Materials*, Nov. 1971, pp. 1240-53.
[120] Text in same, pp. 1235-40.

"The United States hopes that the Government of Chile, in accordance with its obligations under international law, will give further careful consideration to this matter."

News analysts and Chile analysts and foreign policy analysts have already commented on the "moderation" or "hardness" of Secretary Rogers' statement, and the Foreign Minister of Chile [Clodomiro Almeyda Medina] has, in his turn, speculated as to the pressure intent of the next to last paragraph.

The statement contains no threat. It is purely factual, and the next to last paragraph alludes to the "ripple effect" that Chile's ultimate action in the compensation process, which has not terminated, could have.

I am sure that the fact that Chile has expropriated U.S.-owned copper interests comes as no surprise to anyone on the subcommittee. The nationalization of copper and other natural resources was a well-advertised part of Dr. Allende's electoral campaign.[121] However, repeated public and private statements were made that expropriated properties would be accorded just compensation.

None of the content of Secretary Rogers' statement can constitute a surprise to the Government of Chile. Through diplomatic channels our serious concern with the expropriation legislation and our valid interest in effective, adequate, and prompt compensation have been expressed continuously, and we have gone to great and sincere lengths to advocate a pragmatic solution to the question of compensation for the copper companies. One of our purposes in this persistent effort has been precisely to avoid the "ripple effect," which by my definition is in its ultimate the growth of public and congressional opinion adverse to authorizing or appropriating or allocating sufficient funds, public and private, for development assistance because of negation of generally accepted rules of international law and equity.

We have no reason or desire to seek or welcome a confrontation with the Government of Chile. The entire thrust of our policy in the past year has been to try our level best to minimize the chances of a confrontation. Nor do we question Chile's right to self-determination. We cannot be expected, however, to be indifferent or to remain silent when established international norms applicable to our nationals are in jeopardy. We believe the acknowledged right of any sovereign state to expropriate property on a nondiscriminatory basis cannot be disassociated from the equally valid right of the expropriated to receive prompt, adequate, and effective compensation. Otherwise, expropriation becomes simple confiscation.

As the Secretary's statement indicates, we regard the retroactive application of the "excess profits" concept as a particularly disturbing

121 Cf. *The United States in World Affairs, 1970*, pp. 194-96.

departure from legal norms. In effect, the U.S. companies which earned their profits in Chile in accordance with Chilean law and under specific contractual agreements with the Chilean Government are now told after the fact that they will be penalized for making such profits. The deduction of these so-called "excess profits" from the Controller General's valuation of the companies' properties punishes the companies today for actions that were legal and approved by the Chilean Government yesterday. Significantly, no claim is being made that these "excess profits" are being deducted because they resulted from violations of Chilean law. Obviously the deduction of $774 million in "excess profits" from a "book value" of $629 million—in itself a dubious measure of true worth—for three of the five mines involved means there will be no effective compensation at all for these properties unless modifications are made before the compensation process is completed.

In addition to the basic question of compensation, there is considerable ambiguity and uncertainty regarding the Government of Chile's intentions to repay debts owed to the expropriated U.S. copper interests and third parties. These debts are normal obligations of the Chilean Government. We do not have, however, a clear indication of what the Chilean Government intends to do about them.

I wish to make it clear that any differences we may have with Chile are neither political nor ideological in their origin. President Nixon has stated clearly that the United States is prepared to have the kind of relationship with the Chilean Government that it is prepared to have with us.[122] We deal with governments as they are. Our relations depend not on their internal structures or social systems, but on actions which affect us and the inter-American system. In pursuit of this policy we have maintained a correct and positive attitude toward the present Government of Chile since its inception.

We would like to believe that the Chilean Government shares our desire for normal relations, but we cannot ignore the fact that there are some important elements among the political forces within the present Chilean Government which have appeared to welcome a confrontation with the United States for ideological as well as for internal political reasons.

Despite these discouraging signs, we have persisted in our efforts to maintain normality in our relations with Chile and have sought to exhaust every possibility for reaching practical solutions to problems as they have arisen. We have continued bilateral economic and military assistance programs. While these levels are lower than for previous years, the decline reflects the absorption of $500 million of AID [Agency for International Development] loans over recent years and also reflects the internal and external income which accrued to Chile

[122] Cf. above at note 116.

from the very copper operations which Chile now is attacking.

Our positive stance has been further evidenced by the prompt and effective disaster relief assistance totaling approximately $260,000 which we recently extended to Chile. In this connection we also supported project reallocations by the Inter-American Development Bank (IDB) for earthquake rehabilitation totaling more than $16 million. We have maintained our ongoing cooperative efforts on Antarctic research, satellite tracking, Peace Corps, Food for Peace programs, and cultural exchange activities.

In the multilateral field we have considered Chilean loan applications to the IDB and the World Bank on their merits. Following President Allende's inauguration, we supported IDB loans to two Chilean universities totaling $11.6 million. Despite allegations to the contrary, we have maintained an open position with respect to pending Chilean loan applications before the Eximbank. I would add that this includes the LAN-Chile request for commercial aircraft, which was subject to the normal criteria for such projects.

We have, in short, sought by all available means to make known our genuine desire to maintain normal relations and to resolve bilateral problems pragmatically. To this end, we offered our good offices to aid the search for acceptable solutions to the compensation issue while the basic discussions on nationalized and expropriated U.S. properties were conducted between the Chilean Government and the private companies involved. To date, the results of our efforts can hardly be described as encouraging. We are aware that no amount of reason or good will on our part can by itself create the objective conditions required for an acceptable solution.

As matters stand, the compensation proceedings thus far do not provide for just compensation for the expropriated properties. There is still pending the appeals procedure to a special tribunal, and we will reserve our final judgment until the entire compensation process has been completed.[123] We sincerely hope that the Chilean Government, in accordance with Chilean tradition, will honor its obligations under international law.

3. Panama.

[Another issue of special importance to the United States, the progress of negotiations with Panama relating to the status of the existing Panama Canal and Canal Zone and the possible construction of a second waterway, was elaborated in a congressional appearance by

[123] The decision of the Special Copper Tribunal on Aug. 11, 1972, appears in *International Legal Materials*, Sept. 1972, pp. 1013-61.

Ambassador John C. Mundt, Special U.S. Representative for Panama treaty negotiations (Document 119).]

(119) Panama Canal Treaty Negotiations: Statement by Ambassador John C. Mundt, Special Representative of the United States for Panama Treaty Negotiations, Before the Subcommittee on the Panama Canal of the House Committee on Merchant Marine and Fisheries, November 29, 1971. [124]

(Complete Text)

I welcome this opportunity to appear before you to discuss the Panama treaty negotiations. As you may be aware, I have been working for 5 months on this matter as deputy to Ambassador Robert B. Anderson. Both of us consider the counsel and support of the Merchant Marine Committee very important to the creation of a mutually satisfactory new treaty relationship between the United States and Panama. Ambassador Anderson has the flu, and he asked me to express his regrets at not being here today.

Public declarations by negotiators concerning controversial treaty issues currently in negotiation could make agreement more difficult. For this reason we have requested this hearing in executive session. However, we have attempted to draft this opening statement for release by this committee so there can be public assurance that while we seek an improved treaty relationship with Panama, U.S. interests are being given the most careful attention in the negotiations.

Before dealing with the specific questions raised by Chairman Murphy [Representative John M. Murphy], it might be useful to review the background of the negotiations and the developments since the United States entered into them in 1964.

Panama has been discontented with the treaty of 1903 [125] since its inception and has pressed for more favorable terms with increasing intensity in recent years. The United States acknowledged as early as 1905 that under the 1903 treaty, Panama retained titular sovereignty over the Canal Zone. Treaty revisions were made in 1936 [126] and 1955. [127] However, the most objectionable feature from Panama's viewpoint—United States exercise of rights as if sovereign in the Canal

[124] *Bulletin*, Dec. 27, 1971, pp. 731-35.
[125] Signed at Washington Nov. 18, 1903, and in force Feb. 26, 1904; text in Department of State *Treaty Series*, No. 431.
[126] Signed at Washington Mar. 2, 1936, and in force July 27, 1939; text in *Treaty Series*, No. 945.
[127] Signed at Panama Jan. 25, 1955, and in force Aug. 23, 1955 (TIAS 3297; 6 UST 2273).

Zone in perpetuity—remained unchanged. Neither did the increases in payments and other economic benefits for Panama in the two revisions provide what Panama considered a fair sharing of the benefits of the canal. Panama's discontent led to destructive riots along the Canal Zone border in 1958 and 1964.[128]

Following discussion of the Panama situation in the OAS,[129] the U.N., and in other international forums, President Johnson agreed in 1964 to begin negotiations for a new treaty relationship. On December 18, 1964, he announced:[130]

> Today we have informed the Government of Panama that we are ready to negotiate a new treaty. In such a treaty we must retain the rights which are necessary for the effective operation and the protection of the canal and the administration of the areas that are necessary for these purposes. Such a treaty would replace the treaty of 1903 and its amendments. It should recognize the sovereignty of Panama. It should provide for its own termination when a sea-level canal comes into operation. It should provide for effective discharge of our common responsibilities for hemispheric defense. Until a new agreement is reached, of course, the present treaties will remain in effect.

In reaching this decision, President Johnson had consulted with and obtained the support of Presidents Hoover, Truman, and Eisenhower.

Three draft treaties were negotiated by the United States and Panama between 1964 and 1967 but were never ratified. They contained the following major provisions:

—The first treaty, relating to the present canal, would have abrogated the treaty of 1903 and provided for: (a) recognition of Panamanian sovereignty and sharing of jurisdiction in the canal area, (b) operation of the canal by a joint U.S.-Panamanian authority with U.S. majority membership, and (c) ultimate possession of the existing canal by Panama.

—The second treaty, for a sea-level canal, would have granted the United States an option for 20 years to start constructing a sea-level canal in Panama and U.S. majority membership in the controlling authority for 60 years after its opening.

—The third treaty would have provided for continued U.S. defense of the existing canal and, subsequently, U.S. defense of the sea-level canal, if built.

The President of Panama did not act to have these treaties ratified.

[128] Cf. *The United States in World Affairs, 1964*, pp. 226-34.
[129] *Documents, 1964*, pp. 304-12.
[130] Same, p. 314.

Consequently, no action was taken on them by the United States.

The Government of Panama has changed twice since 1967,[131] and the Government now in power is entering upon its fourth year. It is recognized by the United States. President Nixon agreed more than 1 year ago to renew treaty negotiations and has established negotiating objectives similar to those set by President Johnson in 1964, modified by developments since that time. United States objectives and positions thus reflect a bipartisan approach toward treaty negotiations with Panama. As a citizen, I have been favorably impressed by the continuity in our foreign policy between the two major parties.

The United States has three essential objectives:

1. That the United States control canal operations for a very long period to insure that the canal remains available to our and the world's vessels on a nondiscriminatory basis at reasonable tolls.

2. That the United States have unimpaired rights to defend the canal from any threat and to maintain its uninterrupted operation in peace or war.

3. That the United States have the right to expand canal capacity, either by adding an additional lane of locks to the existing canal or by building a sea-level canal.

The Government of Panama has indicated that it is willing to grant these rights to the United States in a new treaty but wishes to eliminate the causes of conflict with the United States in Panama. What are these causes of conflict from Panama's standpoint? The answer includes a spectrum of economic, political, and psychological reasons.

Let us take an objective look at some aspects of the situation that rankle Panamanians most:

—The United States maintains a strip 10 miles wide across the heart of Panama in which 40,000 U.S. citizens live to too large an extent outside the jurisdiction and economy of Panama. This is a legal arrangement, authorized by treaty. Nevertheless, it exists today against the wishes of Panama, although, of course, the power of the United States can maintain the status quo.

—The U.S. policy of support of the free enterprise system is not consistent with U.S. Government operation of almost all commercial-type enterprises throughout the Canal Zone, despite the fact that private enterprise in Panama is potentially capable of providing most of them satisfactorily.

—The United States Government controls all the deepwater ports serving the Republic of Panama.

---

131 President Marco A. Robles was constitutionally succeeded Oct. 1, 1968, by President Arnulfo Arias; the latter was overthrown on Oct. 11-12, 1968, in a coup directed by Col. (later Brig. Gen.) Omar Torrijos Herrera, Commander-in-Chief of the National Guard and subsequent "Leader of the Revolution."

—The United States maintains a police force, courts, and jails in the Canal Zone to enforce U.S. law on U.S. and Panamanian citizens alike. Many of the actions of the police and courts involve traffic offenses and minor crimes by Panamanians living in or passing through the zone. Surely most of this law enforcement on Panamanians could be carried out by the Government of Panama, relieving the United States of a source of unnecessary friction.

—The United States has not increased the $1.93 million annuity to Panama since 1955. This payment could be adjusted upward. Incidentally, canal tolls have not been increased since the canal opened 57 years ago. Recent studies have indicated that tolls could be increased modestly without serious impact on canal users, if Congress decides that more revenues should be raised in this manner to support the increased payment to Panama. We negotiators will not decide whether to increase tolls, however. This will be a decision for the Congress.

—The United States conducts some activities in the Canal Zone that Panama maintains were not authorized by the treaty of 1903. This is a matter of argument, but a point of conflict.

—The Canal Zone is a haven for refugees from Panamanian jurisdiction. A Panamanian fleeing Panamanian police needs only to step across the streets of Panama City or Colón that mark the division between Panama and the zone and the entire legal process of international extradition must be undertaken to recover him. This is a situation the United States neither needs nor desires, but it exists and can be changed only by treaty revision.

There are many other things that I could cite that are irritants to our relations with Panama: U.S. occupation of land needed by Panama (that we do not need), the presence of a U.S. Canal Zone Government in Panama, and the contrast in living standards between the zone and nearby Panamanian communities. Suffice it to say that Panamanian resentments are sufficient that they have boiled over in destructive and bloody riots twice in recent years. It is in our interest to develop in place of this a relationship that is based upon mutual needs and benefits and that is adhered to willingly on both sides.

Now let me respond to the questions in your invitation to appear before you. Some of them can best be answered by the representatives of the Department of State, who will follow me today,[132] and by representatives of other agencies of the executive, scheduled to appear before you later. However, I will give you my own views to the extent that they bear upon my conduct of the treaty negotiations.

I believe that there is a great bond of friendship and respect for the United States in Panama. The presence of the canal on Panamanian territory—so important to the national security of the United States—

132 Cf. *Bulletin*, Dec. 27, 1971, pp. 735-41.

makes Panama and the United States de facto allies. This association has been and continues to be highly beneficial to both nations. Let me cite a few current facts to illustrate the importance of the canal to Panama:

—Of Panama's gross national product in 1970 of approximately $992 million, nearly one-third is directly and indirectly attributable to the canal and its military bases.

—Of Panama's total foreign exchange earnings from export of goods and services in 1970 of $367 million, $162 million, or 45 percent, comprises direct payments from the canal and its military bases.

—Of Panama's employment nationwide, nearly one-third is directly or indirectly due to the presence of the canal. Within 30 miles of the Canal Zone more than two-thirds is canal oriented.

—Panama's per capita income of $693 is the highest in Central America and more than twice the average. It is the fourth highest in Latin America as a whole, exceeded only by that of Argentina, Venezuela, and Uruguay.

As I have already mentioned, a primary United States objective is the right to administer, operate, and defend the canal for an extended period of time. We are confident this can be negotiated.

The United States seeks clear provisions which would permit the expansion of canal capacity to meet world shipping needs by the construction of either a sea-level canal or third locks for the present canal. The Atlantic-Pacific Interoceanic Canal Study Commission reported that greater canal capacity will probably be needed before the end of the century. A new treaty is needed to permit the construction of a sea-level canal and to insure Panamanian acceptance of a United States decision to expand the existing lock canal by addition of a third set of locks. No decision has yet been made as to which alternative will be adopted, and a decision is not likely until well after a new treaty has been ratified. It is estimated that a sea-level canal, which would be less vulnerable to attack or sabotage, would cost about $2.8 billion to build and that a third set of locks would cost about $1.5 billion.

I will defer to others more expert than I your question about the legal aspects of ceding U.S.-controlled territory to Panama. We plan only to release certain land and water areas in the Canal Zone not needed for canal operation and defense but useful in the agricultural, industrial, and urban development of Panama. The areas being considered have been selected with the concurrence of the Department of Defense and the Panama Canal Company.

Panama seeks the application of its laws to various activities in the present Canal Zone. Certain jurisdictional rights and activities, including commercial operations, not necessary for the administration, operation, and defense of the canal, can be transferred to Panama without adversely affecting the United States interests. Panama today can provide nearly all the commercial services essential to the health and welfare of the personnel who operate the canal. Right now some 5,000 U.S. citizens live in the Republic of Panama. Some are engaged in a wide variety of private business activities, and others commute daily to jobs in the Canal Zone. They are fully subject to Panamanian law and police jurisdiction and have experienced no significant difficulties. Throughout the world tens of thousands of U.S. Government employees live and work satisfactorily under the legal jurisdiction of foreign governments. The United States will continue to have adequate protection of the rights of its canal employees under a new treaty, and I assure you that we will not negotiate away legal rights essential to the operation and protection of the canal. Our military personnel will be protected by a status of forces agreement comparable with other such agreements elsewhere in the world.

Commercial activities currently conducted by the Panama Canal Company will gradually be phased into private operation as arrangements can be worked out for their satisfactory conduct under Panamanian law. The United States will reserve the right to continue to conduct essential commercial services where satisfactory private operation cannot be arranged. Military commissaries and post exchanges will not be affected by the proposed changes. Some piers we plan to turn over to Panama outright as proposed in 1967, inasmuch as the United States now controls all deepwater port capacity in the Republic of Panama and the U.S. needs for such capacity will be greatly reduced with the termination of Canal Company commercial activities. Pier capacity for military and canal administration requirements will be retained under U.S. control.

I will leave to my State Department colleagues the definitive answers to your question about the impact of the current Panama treaty negotiations on other Latin American countries. However, in the course of the recently completed Sea-Level Canal Study Commission investigation, we did conduct an informal survey of Latin American attitudes toward the U.S. operation and defense of the Panama Canal and found general approval and general acceptance of the necessity for its continuation. The economies of many Central and South American countries are closely tied to the uninterrupted operation of the Panama Canal at reasonable tolls. There is considerable fear among canal users in Latin America and worldwide that without continued U.S. control, the canal might be operated to produce maximum revenues rather than as a utility serving world trade at reasonable tolls. On the other hand, there is widespread support in Latin America for Panama's efforts to obtain greater practical exercise of its sovereignty and to terminate the objectionable aspects of the U.S. presence in the Canal Zone, which is exactly one of the U.S. objectives in the current negotiations.

State [Department] representatives will deal with your questions about U.S. Canal Zone activities that Panama alleges to go beyond the authorizations of the treaty of 1903. I would like to say that in the current negotiations the Panamanians have indicated that they are willing to negotiate for continuation of the disputed activities. Their position is that the authority for the United States to conduct them must be clearly established in our new treaty relationship.

The Panama Canal is of great importance to world trade. The United States has always regarded its responsibility for its operation and defense as a responsibility to all canal users. Although 70 percent of canal cargoes in recent years has either originated in or been destined for the United States, these cargoes represented only 16 percent of the total U.S. ocean trade. On a relative basis, the canal is far more important to 10 other countries which have larger portions of their ocean trade passing through the canal. For the record, I have a table from the Canal Commission's report showing the use of the canal by each of the world's nations in terms of total tonnages passing through the canal to and from each country and the percentage of each country's total ocean trade that these canal tonnages represent.

U.S. control and defense of a canal in Panama well into the next century is not at stake in the current negotiations. We are seeking a treaty arrangement with Panama that will insure the continuation of the U.S. presence in tranquillity. This means that this presence must not be imposed on an unwilling partner. It must be established on a mutually acceptable basis. We can afford to make adjustments in our treaty relations with Panama. At present the most serious threat to U.S. interests in Panama is the unrest generated by treaty arrangements that in certain respects have become outmoded.

There should be no reason for Panama not to adhere to a new treaty far more beneficial to Panama than the current treaty. Panama's economic well-being is tied to efficient operation of the canal and the expenditures associated with the U.S. presence. Panama has not caused one act of sabotage against the canal in the 68 years since 1903. The canal is largely run by Panamanian citizens; 11,000 of the 15,000 employees are Panamanian citizens, and the proportion will grow greater with the passage of time. Our military forces will remain on the scene. It is hard to conceive of future developments in Panama under the contemplated new treaty arrangements that could truly threaten the U.S. capability to control and defend the canal. It is far easier to foresee difficulties if we refuse to meet reasonable Panamanian demands in a new treaty relationship.

IX.

THE UNITED NATIONS AND INTERNATIONAL COOPERATION

[Changes in the organization and character of the United Nations outweighed the substantive actions of the Security Council, the General Assembly, and other U.N. and U.N.-related bodies during 1971. The record of U.N. activity with regard to the limitation of armaments, the Middle East conflict, the war in the Subcontinent, the status of the Indian Ocean, and the issues of colonialism and racial discrimination in southern Africa has been reviewed in earlier chapters of this collection. The present chapter focuses more sharply on the processes of internal transformation that had long been apparent in the life of the United Nations and seemed to be accelerating as the organization emerged from its 25th anniversary observance in 1970[1] and commenced its second quarter-century.

The most sensational of these developments was the change in the representation of China that took place on October 25, 1971, when the General Assembly decided not only to admit the mainland, Communist government of the People's Republic of China to U.N. representation but also to terminate the representation of the Taiwan-based, U.S.-supported government of the Republic of China, a founding member of the United Nations and one that still claimed jurisdiction over the 750,000,000 mainland Chinese as well as the 14,000,000 inhabitants of Taiwan. This action amounted to an unprecedented defeat not only for Taiwan but for the United States, which had spared no effort to promote a dual form of Chinese representation that would have given preferential status to the mainland government while preserving a seat for Taiwan as well (Documents 122-128).

In addition to the change in the representation of China, the United Nations during 1971 increased its membership from 127 to 132 with the admission of Bhutan, Bahrain, Qatar, Oman, and the United Arab Emirates; decided to double the size of the 27-member Economic and Social Council (Document 132); and chose Kurt Waldheim of Austria to succeed U Thant of Burma in the exacting post of Secretary-General (Documents 133-135).

[1] Cf. *Documents, 1970*, pp. 290-304.

In part related to these organizational changes—which were briefly reviewed by President Nixon in transmitting his annual report to Congress on United States participation in the United Nations (Document 120)—was a perceptible falling-off in American enthusiasm for the United Nations and in the cordiality of the relationship between the organization and the host country. Evidences of declining congressional support for the United Nations, among them the flouting of the U.N.-imposed embargo on the import of Rhodesian chrome ore (Documents 107-109), claimed special notice in the President's annual survey of U.S. foreign policy developments (Document 121). Additional strains arose from the United States' announced determination to reduce its proportionate contribution to the U.N. budget (Document 129), and from incidents of harassment and violence experienced by the Soviet and other foreign missions to the United Nations (Documents 130-131).

Paradoxically, these negative trends were gaining increased prominence at the very time when governmental authorities in the United States and elsewhere were becoming more keenly aware of the need for increased international cooperation in dealing with issues that had previously been dealt with, if at all, at governmental or subgovernmental levels. These "new dimensions of diplomacy," which far transcended the existing capabilities of the United Nations and other international institutions, were reviewed by President Nixon in a special chapter of his annual foreign policy report (Document 136). His comments serve as introduction to a number of key 1971 documents relating to the law of the sea, the protection of civil aviation, and the peaceful uses of outer space (Documents 137-140).]

A. Review of United Nations Affairs in 1971.

[The many-sided operations of the United Nations and its related agencies in 1971 have been reviewed in varying detail in a number of official and unofficial publications.[2] Highlights of the year's experience as seen from an official American point of view were presented by President Nixon in two official papers: a message accompanying his annual report on U.S. participation in the United Nations (Document 120), and an excerpt from his general report on U.S. foreign policy developments, made public early in 1972 (Document 121).]

[2] Among the most detailed compendiums are the *Yearbook of the United Nations, 1971* and *U.S. Participation in the UN: Report by the President to the Congress for the Year 1971*. Briefer surveys appear in *The World This Year, 1972*, which contains separate articles on the United Nations (pp. 162-64), the International Court of Justice (p. 149), and each of the specialized and related agencies.

(120) United States Participation in the United Nations, 1971: Message from President Nixon to the Congress Transmitting the 26th Annual Report on United Nations Participation, September 8, 1972.[3]

(Complete Text)

To the Congress of the United States:

It is a pleasure to transmit to the Congress the 26th annual report on United States participation in the work of the United Nations.[4] This report covers the calendar year 1971.

During the period under review there were many developments within the UN framework of importance to the United States and to other member states. Some of these events were favorable; others were not. Among the former:

— The General Assembly decided to seat the representatives of the Peoples Republic of China,[5] and this was followed by corresponding action in the Security Council.

— The United Nations established a Fund for Drug Abuse Control that will finance a concerted worldwide action program to assist member states in reducing both the demand for and the supply of dangerous drugs.[6]

— At a plenipotentiary conference in Vienna sponsored by the United Nations, a Convention on Psychotropic Substances was adopted, designed to curb the misuse of such substances as the hallucinogens, amphetamines, barbiturates, and tranquilizers.[7]

— The 26th General Assembly endorsed two treaties, both sponsored by the United States, and expressed its hope for the widest possible adherence to them. The first was the Convention on International Liability for Damage Caused by Space Objects;[8] the second was the Convention on the Prohibition of Development, Production and Stockpiling of Bacteriological (Biological) and Toxin Weapons and on Their Destruction.[9]

— In December the United Nations elected a new Secretary General, Ambassador Kurt Waldheim of Austria.[10]

— At an international conference in Montreal sponsored by the Inter-

[3] H. Doc. 92-81, 92d Cong., 1st sess.; text from *Presidential Documents, 1971,* pp. 1351-52.
[4] *U.S. Participation in the UN: Report by the President to the Congress for the Year 1971.*
[5] Documents 122-127.
[6] Cf. below at notes 103-104.
[7] Cf. below at notes 108-109.
[8] Document 139.
[9] Document 19.
[10] Documents 133-135.

national Civil Aviation Organization, a Convention for the Suppression of Unlawful Acts Against the Safety of Civil Aviation[11] was adopted.

—The UN Economic and Social Council was strengthened by the Assembly's decision to adopt and submit to member states for ratification an amendment to the Charter that will double the Council's membership to 54, thereby making it a more representative body.[12] In addition the Council created two new standing committees, one concerned with review and appraisal of the progress toward the goals of the Second UN Development Decade,[13] and the other concerned with problems of science and technology.[14]

—The United Nations created the position of Disaster Relief Coordinator within the UN Secretariat to assist countries stricken by disasters.[15]

In addition to these favorable developments there were others that were disappointing.

—The Republic of China, a member in good standing for many years, was deprived of representation by the same resolution that gave representation to the Peoples Republic of China.[16] This action was extremely regrettable and was strongly opposed by the United States.

—Despite determined efforts by the United States and others, the war between India and Pakistan demonstrated again the severe limitations on the organization's ability to carry out its primary function, the maintenance of international peace and security.[17]

—No progress was made toward resolving the differences among UN members on the organization and conduct of peace-keeping missions.

—The General Assembly's effort to rationalize its organization and procedures fell far short of our hopes.

—The United Nations made no great progress toward resolving its difficult financial problems.[18]

During 1971 the United States Government announced its intention to negotiate a reduction in the rate of its UN assessment to a level no higher than 25 percent. This decision is in line with a recommendation by the Commission for the Observance of the 25th Anniversary of the

---

11 Document 138.
12 Document 132.
13 Resolution 2801 (XXVI), Dec. 14, 1971; adopted without objection.
14 Resolution 2804 (XXVI), Dec. 14, 1971; adopted without objection.
15 Resolution 2816 (XXVI), Dec. 14, 1971; adopted by a vote of 86 (U.S.)-0-10.
16 Document 125.
17 Cf. Documents 57-63.
18 Cf. Document 129.

United Nations, chaired by Ambassador Henry Cabot Lodge, and is consonant with our belief that an organization of almost universal membership should not be overly dependent upon a single member for its financial support.[19]

This proposed reduction in our rate of assessment does not affect our voluntary contributions to various UN programs. Indeed, the Lodge Commission recommended increases of at least corresponding size in voluntary contributions whose size depends on each nation's judgment of its own interests and capabilities.

These and many other topics are covered in the report. I commend to the Congress this record of our participation in the United Nations during 1971.

RICHARD NIXON

The White House
September 8, 1972

*(121) "The Decline in Congressional Support for the United Nations":
President Nixon's Third Annual Report to the Congress on
United States Foreign Policy, February 9, 1972.*[20]

(Excerpt)

During the past year, the United States Congress took four actions which require mention in this report:

- —The House of Representatives, although the action is not final, for the first time refused to provide a voluntary contribution to the UN Development Program (UNDP).
- —For the second year in a row, the Congress refused to pay the United States assessed dues to the International Labor Organization [ILO].
- —The Congress failed to provide the U.S. contribution to the expansion of the UN Headquarters facilities in New York City.
- —The Congress exempted strategic and critical materials, notably chrome, from the U.S. implementation of the mandatory UN sanctions on imports from Rhodesia.[21]

It would be a mistake to conclude that these actions were motivated by Congressional hostility to the United Nations. These were not con-

[19] Cf. below at notes 61-62.
[20] Nixon Report, 1972, pp. 191-92; text from *Presidential Documents*, Feb. 14, 1972, pp. 394-95.
[21] Document 108b.

certed actions, and they took place for a variety of reasons. But it would also be a mistake not to recognize the implications of these actions. They could hardly have taken place if the UN, as an entity, enjoyed stronger support in the Congress and among the American people. That fact is, I believe, far more significant than the individual arguments upon which the Congress based its decisions.

A reduction of U.S. support for the UNDP would be particularly unfortunate. The UN system has gradually become a major instrument for encouraging economic and social progress in the developing countries, and the UNDP is the primary instrument by which the UN fills this role. The United States has been the major contributor of funds to the UNDP, and since its inception the UNDP has been headed by a distinguished American, Paul [G.] Hoffman.

Last year there were several developments which should reconfirm the American attachment to this program. Progress continued in making the UNDP's machinery more efficient. The contributions to the UNDP from other countries were significantly increased. And when Paul Hoffman retired at the end of the year, the UN chose another outstanding American, Rudolph [A.] Peterson, as his successor. The UNDP deserves our continuing support.

During its current session, the Congress must also face the problem of American participation in the ILO. The United States is now almost two years in arrears, and therefore on the verge of losing its vote under the ILO rules. There were cogent reasons behind the Congressional dissatisfaction with the ILO. During the past two years, however, the ILO has responded to our efforts to revitalize its tripartite structure and procedures. It is simply not consistent with our national dignity to attempt to maintain influence and membership in the ILO if we are not prepared to pay our dues. This Administration will, therefore, have no choice but to give notice of withdrawal from the ILO unless the Congress sees fit to provide our assessed contributions to that organization.[22]

*   *   *

B. The Representation of China in the United Nations.

[The historic decision of the General Assembly to substitute the Communist-ruled People's Republic of China for the (Nationalist) Republic of China as the only lawful representative of China in the

---

[22] For details see Rogers Report, 1969-70, pp. 238-39; same, 1971, p. 333; same, 1972, pp. 167-68; similarly *The World This Year, 1971*, p. 142; same, *1972*, pp. 149-50; same, *1973*, p. 156. Appropriations by Congress during 1972 sufficed to wipe out arrears of over $11 million in the U.S. assessed contributions to the ILO for 1970 and 1971 and to provide an initial payment against the 1972 assessment.

United Nations resolved—albeit in a manner highly unsatisfactory to the United States and some other member governments—a problem that had troubled the United Nations since the establishment of the People's Republic on the Chinese mainland in 1949. Earlier moves to seat the representatives of mainland China and expel "the representatives of Chiang Kai-shek," the Nationalist President, had been warded off by the United States in strict conformity with the provisions of Article 18 of the U.N. Charter, which stipulates that decisions of the General Assembly on important questions—including the suspension of the rights and privileges of membership and the expulsion of members— shall be made by a two-thirds majority of the members present and voting. By getting the Assembly to reaffirm each year that any proposal to change the representation of China was an "important question"—a declaration that could be carried by a simple majority—the United States had maintained an effective barrier against a movement which, while gaining in force from year to year, had not thus far been able to muster the two-thirds majority required for an actual change in representation.

The situation nevertheless had altered with the gradual increase in the number of countries favoring a change, and, still more, with the realization that the United States itself had modified its attitude toward the People's Republic and by early 1971 was actively engaged in seeking closer contact with the mainland government. Admittedly, a change in the U.S. attitude regarding bilateral relations with the mainland regime did not in itself portend a change with respect to the separate question of Chinese representation in the United Nations; and President Nixon stated more than once during the spring of 1971 that the American position in this latter regard had not been determined but was under continuing study and would be announced at the proper time (Documents 88-89). In taking this stand, Mr. Nixon neither endorsed nor disapproved a recommendation by the President's Commission for the Observance of the 25th Anniversary of the United Nations—a panel of distinguished citizens headed by Ambassador Henry Cabot Lodge—that the United States espouse a "two-China" policy involving concurrent representation in the United Nations for both Chinese governments.[23] Thus far, neither Peking nor Taiwan had appeared to favor such a solution; Peking, indeed, had strenuously insisted that it would not itself accept U.N. representation unless Taiwan's representatives were expelled.

In spite of these unfavorable auguries, it was announced by Secretary of State Rogers on August 2, 1971, that the United States would seek U.N. acceptance of a "two-China" solution involving both the seating of the People's Republic of China and continued representation for the Republic of China. The decision as to which of the two governments

[23] Cf. note 47 to Chapter VI.

should occupy China's seat in the Security Council, Secretary Rogers added, should be left to the members of the United Nations (Document 122). Further consultation with "about 90 other governments" having revealed "a good deal of support for having the Security Council seat go to the People's Republic of China,"[24] President Nixon on September 16, 1971, offered a modified statement of the U.S. position in the following terms:

". . . We favor the admission and will vote for the admission of the People's Republic to the United Nations and that will mean, of course [sic], obtaining a Security Council seat.

"We will vote against the expulsion of the Republic of China, and we will work as effectively as we can to accomplish that goal."[25]

Although the United States professed to have found widespread support for this "dual representation" concept,[26] those countries that had previously favored both the admission of Peking and the expulsion of Taiwan prepared to renew their effort as the 26th Regular Session of the General Assembly got under way on September 21, 1971. Led by Albania, Peking's most faithful ally in the United Nations, a total of 23 nonaligned and Communist countries submitted a draft resolution that called in no uncertain terms for the seating of the People's Republic of China and the expulsion "forthwith" of "the representatives of Chiang Kai-shek" (Document 123a). Adherents of the opposing U.S.-supported position submitted two draft resolutions: a 22-nation draft declaring that any proposal which would deprive the Republic of China of U.N. representation was an "important question" under Article 18 of the Charter (Document 123b); and a 19-nation "dual representation" resolution that called for representation for the People's Republic, recommended that it be seated as a permanent member of the Security Council, but affirmed at the same time "the continued right of representation of the Republic of China" (Document 123c).

The case for dual representation was vigorously argued by Secretary Rogers in his October 4 address to the Assembly (Document 124) and by Ambassador Bush, the U.S. Permanent Representative and head of the U.S. delegation, in later plenary sessions.[27] But though the United States undoubtedly made an "all-out effort" to sway the Assembly to its point of view, the effort ultimately failed because a majority of the members were no longer willing to be bound by the two-thirds rule imposed by Article 18 of the Charter. In the first of two crucial votes taken on October 25, 1971, the U.S.-supported "important question" resolution was defeated by a vote of 55 in favor, 59 opposed, and 15

24 Rogers news conference, Sept. 3, 1971, in *Bulletin*, Sept. 27, 1971, p. 327.
25 News conference, Sept. 16, 1971, in *Public Papers, 1971*, p. 950.
26 Rogers, *loc. cit.* (note 24), p. 328.
27 *Bulletin*, Nov. 15, 1971, pp. 548-55.

abstentions, among those voting for rejection being Canada, France, the U.S.S.R., and the United Kingdom. Having thus decided that the two-thirds rule did not apply in this particular instance, the Assembly then proceeded to adopt the Albanian resolution by a vote of 76 in favor, 35 opposed, and 17 abstentions. In voting for this second resolution, Canada, France, the United Kingdom, and other U.S. allies (as well as the U.S.S.R. and other members of the Soviet bloc) again took a position directly contrary to that of the United States. The fact that even now the Albanian resolution was carried by less than a two-thirds majority was irrelevant in view of the prior defeat of the "important question" resolution. The issue of Chinese representation having been settled with the adoption of the Albanian resolution, no vote was taken on the U.S.-supported "dual representation" resolution.

By the terms of the Albanian resolution as adopted (Document 125), the General Assembly found in effect that the representatives of the People's Republic of China were "the only lawful representatives of China to the United Nations" and that the People's Republic of China was one of the five permanent members of the Security Council. It therefore decided not only to recognize the representatives of the People's Republic as "the only legitimate representatives of China to the United Nations," but also "to expel forthwith the representatives of Chiang Kai-shek from the place which they unlawfully occupy at the United Nations and in all the organizations related to it." This sweeping expulsion order was obviously intended to apply not only to the Security Council and all other U.N. organs, but also to the 13 U.N. specialized and related agencies of which China was a member. Most of the latter in fact took action during the following months to follow the General Assembly's lead, the principal exceptions being the International Bank and Monetary Fund.

While not contesting the will of a majority of U.N. members, both Ambassador Bush in New York[28] and Secretary Rogers in Washington were quick to express the belief that the Assembly had made "a mistake of major proportion" (Document 126). At the White House, Press Secretary Ron Ziegler emerged from a discussion with the President to condemn the cheering, handclapping, and dancing with which some delegates had greeted the vote. Such a "shocking demonstration" of "undisguised glee" and of "personal animosity" toward American policy, Mr. Ziegler intimated, "could very seriously impair support for the United Nations in the country and in the Congress" and might also "affect foreign aid allocations"—although, he added, the United States did not intend to retaliate against the nations involved.[29] In fact, the Senate on October 29 departed from all precedent in voting 41 to 27 to

---

[28] Bush statement, Oct. 25, 1971, in *Bulletin*, Nov. 15, 1971, pp. 555-56.
[29] *New York Times*, Oct. 28, 1971; for comment by Secretary Rogers see *Bulletin*, Nov. 22, 1971, p. 585.

kill the pending foreign aid authorization bill, which carried a total of $143 million for the U.N. Development Program (UNDP), the U.N. Children's Fund (UNICEF), and other U.N. voluntary programs (cf. Document 154). Not long afterward came the final votes in Congress on the abrogation of U.N. sanctions against the import of Rhodesian chrome ore (Document 108).

In spite of widespread uneasiness about the long-term impact on U.S.–U.N. relations, Ambassador Bush accorded a courteous welcome to the mainland Chinese delegation which made its appearance at the United Nations on November 15 under the leadership of Deputy Foreign Minister Chiao Kuan-hua and Ambassador Huang Hua (Document 127); and the United States soon found itself operating on parallel lines with the People's Republic in the December crisis over the war in the Subcontinent (Documents 57-63). Secretary Rogers, at a news conference on December 1, coupled a declaration of continued support for the United Nations with an admission of some disappointment over the organization's past accomplishments. In addition, he emphasized that the United States would persevere in the attempt to reduce its budgetary contribution and intended to keep close watch on the expenditures of the U.N. specialized agencies (Document 128).]

(122) The Position of the United States: Policy Statement by Secretary of State Rogers, August 2, 1971.[30]

(Complete Text)

The world is approaching the midpoint between the end of World War II and the end of the 20th century. The United Nations, founded in the aftermath of the war, has passed its 25th anniversary.

President Nixon has been adapting American foreign policy with these facts in mind—forging policies directed to the future while taking fully into account the legacies of the past.

From its inception the United Nations was designed above all else to keep the peace shattered by two world wars within a generation. The first words of the United Nations Charter, adopted at San Francisco in 1945, express a common determination to "save succeeding generations from the scourge of war."

In October 1969 President Nixon said with regard to Latin America that "we must deal realistically with governments . . . as they are."[31] Both in Asia and elsewhere in the world we are seeking to accommodate our role to the realities of the world today. Our objective is to

---

[30] Department of State Press Release 166, Aug. 2, 1971; text from *Bulletin*, Aug. 23, 1971, pp. 193-94.
[31] *Documents, 1968-69*, p. 437.

contribute in practical terms to the building of a framework for a stable peace.

No question of Asian policy has so perplexed the world in the last 20 years as the China question—and the related question of representation in the United Nations. Basic to that question is the fact that each of two governments claims to be the sole government of China and representative of all of the people of China.

Representation in an international organization need not prejudice the claims or views of either government. Participation of both in the United Nations need not require that result.

Rather, it would provide governments with increased opportunities for contact and communication. It would also help promote cooperation on common problems which affect all of the member nations regardless of political differences.

The United States accordingly will support action at the General Assembly this fall calling for seating the People's Republic of China. At the same time the United States will oppose any action to expel the Republic of China or otherwise deprive it of representation in the United Nations.

Our consultations, which began several months ago, have indicated that the question of China's seat in the Security Council is a matter which many nations will wish to address. In the final analysis, of course, under the charter provision, the Security Council will make this decision. We, for our part, are prepared to have this question resolved on the basis of a decision of members of the United Nations.[32]

Our consultations have also shown that any action to deprive the Republic of China of its representation would meet with strong opposition in the General Assembly. Certainly, as I have said, the United States will oppose it.

The Republic of China has played a loyal and conscientious role in the U.N. since the organization was founded. It has lived up to all of its charter obligations. Having made remarkable progress in developing its own economy, it has cooperated internationally by providing valuable technical assistance to a number of less developed countries, particularly in Africa.

The position of the United States is that if the United Nations is to succeed in its peacekeeping role, it must deal with the realities of the world in which we live. Thus, the United States will cooperate with those who, whatever their views on the status of the relationship of the two governments, wish to continue to have the Republic of China represented in the United Nations.

The outcome, of course, will be decided by 127 members of the United Nations.[33] For our part we believe that the decision we have

32 Cf. above at notes 24-25.
33 With the admission to membership of Bhutan, Bahrain, Qatar, and Oman, 131 nations were eligible to vote on Oct. 25, 1971; cf. below at notes 35 and 49.

taken is fully in accord with President Nixon's desire to normalize relations with the People's Republic of China in the interests of world peace and in accord with our conviction that the continued representation in the United Nations of the Republic of China will contribute to peace and stability in the world.

(123) Draft Resolutions Before the General Assembly.

(a) The "Albanian" Resolution. [34]

(Complete Text)

Albania, Algeria, Burma, Ceylon, Cuba, Equatorial Guinea, Guinea, Iraq, Mali, Mauritania, Nepal, Pakistan, People's Democratic Republic of Yemen, People's Republic of the Congo, Romania, Sierra Leone, Somalia, Sudan, Syrian Arab Republic, United Republic of Tanzania, Yemen, Yugoslavia and Zambia: draft resolution

[Original: French]
[25 September 1971]

The General Assembly,

Recalling the principles of the Charter of the United Nations,

Considering that the restoration of the lawful rights of the People's Republic of China is essential both for the protection of the Charter of the United Nations and for the cause that the United Nations must serve under the Charter,

Recognizing that the representatives of the Government of the People's Republic of China are the only lawful representatives of China to the United Nations and that the People's Republic of China is one of the five permanent members of the Security Council,

Decides to restore all its rights to the People's Republic of China and to recognize the representatives of its Government as the only legitimate representatives of China to the United Nations, and to expel forthwith the representatives of Chiang Kai-shek from the place which they unlawfully occupy at the United Nations and in all the organizations related to it.

---

[34] U.N. document A/L.630 and Add. 1 and 2; texts of this and the two following draft resolutions from General Assembly, *Official Records: 26th Session, Annexes,* Agenda Item 93, pp. 3-4. Burma and Sierra Leone became sponsors of the Albanian resolution on Sept. 29 and Oct. 19, respectively. The text as printed is identical with that of Document 125.

(b) The "Important Question" Resolution.[35]

(Complete Text)

Australia, Bolivia, Colombia, Costa Rica, Dominican Republic, El Salvador, Fiji, Gambia, Guatemala, Haiti, Honduras, Japan, Lesotho, Liberia, Mauritius, New Zealand, Nicaragua, Philippines, Swaziland, Thailand, United States of America and Uruguay: draft resolution

[Original: English]
[29 September 1971]

The General Assembly,
Recalling the provisions of the Charter of the United Nations,
Decides that any proposal in the General Assembly which would result in depriving the Republic of China of representation in the United Nations is an important question under Article 18 of the Charter.[36]

(c) The "Dual Representation" Resolution.[37]

(Complete Text)

Australia, Bolivia, Chad, Costa Rica, Dominican Republic, Fiji, Gambia, Haiti, Honduras, Japan, Lesotho, Liberia, Mauritius, New Zealand, Philippines, Swaziland, Thailand, United States of America and Uruguay: draft resolution

[Original: English]
[29 September 1971]

The General Assembly,
Noting that since the founding of the United Nations fundamental changes have occurred in China,
Having regard for the existing factual situation,

[35] U.N. document A/L.632 and Add. 1 and 2; text as in note 34. Mauritius and Bolivia became sponsors respectively on Oct. 7 and Oct. 12, 1971. The resolution was rejected Oct. 25, 1971, by a roll-call vote of 59-55(U.S.)-15, with Maldives and Oman recorded as absent.
[36] Article 18 of the Charter provides that decisions of the General Assembly on important quesions, including the suspension of the rights and privileges of membership and the expulsion of members, shall be made by a two-thirds majority of the members present and voting.
[37] U.N. document A/L.633 and Add. 1 and 2; text as in note 34. Mauritius and Bolivia became sponsors respectively on Oct. 7 and Oct. 12, 1971. The resolution was not put to a vote.

Noting that the Republic of China has been continuously represented as a Member of the United Nations since 1945,

Believing that the People's Republic of China should be represented in the United Nations,

Recalling that Article 1, paragraph 4, of the Charter of the United Nations establishes the United Nations as a centre for harmonizing the actions of nations,

Believing that an equitable resolution of this problem should be sought in the light of the above-mentioned considerations and without prejudice to the eventual settlement of the conflicting claims involved,

1. *Hereby affirms* the right of representation of the People's Republic of China and recommends that it be seated as one of the five permanent members of the Security Council;

2. *Affirms* the continued right of representation of the Republic of China;

3. *Recommends* that all United Nations bodies and the specialized agencies take into account the provisions of this resolution in deciding the question of Chinese representation.

(124) Address by Secretary of State Rogers to the General Assembly, October 4, 1971.[38]

(Excerpt)

*   *   *

REPRESENTATION OF CHINA IN THE U.N.

This organization, during this session, faces a decision on the China question—a decision with major consequences for the United Nations.

In our interdependent world, no significant segment of the world's population and of the world's power should be isolated. It was this consideration which led President Nixon to alter the China policy of the United States.[39] To pursue a policy which did not respond to present realities would risk the future for the sake of the past. On the other hand, to seek to improve relations with the People's Republic of China, and to contribute to its greater contact with the international community, could foster prospects for a stable peace in years to come.

[38] Department of State Press Release 227; text from *Bulletin*, Oct. 25, 1971, pp. 439-41. For other excerpts from this address see note to Document 52.
[39] Cf. Documents 85-90.

Thus, President Nixon began over 2 years ago, unilaterally and at first without response, to improve bilateral relations. Recently he resolved to move decisively into a new era of relations by accepting an invitation to visit Peking before May 1, 1972.[40] And he decided to support the seating of the People's Republic of China in the General Assembly and as a permanent member of the Security Council.[41]

The United States wants to see the People's Republic of China come to this Assembly, take its seat, and participate. We want to see it assume as a permanent member of the Security Council the rights and responsibilities which go with that status. On the seating of the People's Republic of China there is widespread agreement in this body.

This Assembly does, however, face a related and momentous issue. It could become the first Assembly in United Nations history to take action to expel a member, an action which would have the effect of expelling 14 million people from its councils. The path of expulsion is perilous. To open it for one would be to open it for many.

So the United States and 16 other countries have introduced a draft resolution which would seat the People's Republic of China as a permanent member of the Security Council while providing representation both for it and for the Republic of China in the General Assembly.[42] That resolution is based on political reality and on basic equity:

—It is only realistic to recognize a factual situation which has persisted for more than 20 years: that two governments now exercise authority over territory and over people who were given representation in the United Nations when China ratified the charter in 1945 as an original member.

—It is only realistic that *all* the Chinese people who were once represented here should again be represented, and represented by those who actually govern them.

—It is only realistic that the Security Council seat should be filled by the People's Republic of China, which exercises control over the largest number of people of all the world's governments.

—It would be unrealistic to expel from this body the Republic of China, which governs a population on Taiwan larger than the populations of two-thirds of the 130 United Nations members.

—Further, it would be unjust to expel a member which has participated for over 25 years in the work of this organization with unfailing devotion to the principles set forth in the charter.

—The proposal that both the People's Republic of China and the Republic of China should be represented in the United Nations should commend itself to member states of varying national policies.

—It would assure that the long-prevailing de facto situation in China is

---

40 Document 91.
41 Cf. above at note 25.
42 Document 123c.

reflected in United Nations representation, but it does not ask member states to alter their recognition policies or their bilateral relations.

—It would provide representation for the people concerned by those who actually govern them, but it does not divide China into two separate states; after all, we all know Byelorussia and the Ukraine are not separate states.[43]

—The dual representation resolution is founded on the reality of the current situation; but it does not seek to freeze that situation for the future, expressly providing that the present decision is without prejudice to a future settlement.

In short, the dual representation resolution asks simply, and only, that the United Nations take account of the situation as it exists today and give all the people of China representation in this organization. As the charter has accommodated practical solutions of other unusual situations in the past, so it is flexible enough to accommodate the realities of this one.

The other proposal before this Assembly, the draft resolution advanced by Albania and others,[44] is punitive in substance and in intent. It does not seek to deal with facts, but to excoriate and condemn. Its essence is not to admit the People's Republic of China, but to expel the Republic of China and to expel it "forthwith."

That resolution would exacerbate, not harmonize, relations in Asia, and it would weaken, not strengthen, the moral and political fiber of this organization.

The issue, then, before this body is the issue of expulsion. That is why we have proposed a draft resolution which we refer to as the "important question resolution"[45] but which more properly should be referred to as the "non-expulsion resolution." This draft resolution requires a two-thirds vote to expel a present member of the United Nations. It is consistent with the letter and the spirit of the charter.

Some members have argued that whatever the equities and realism of our proposal to maintain the representation of the Republic of China, it should not be supported because they feel that the People's Republic of China would refuse to take its seat. Such predictions are hazardous. Certainly the People's Republic of China may be expected to oppose the proposal so long as there is any possibility for a resolution that meets its maximum demands. But just as certainly, after a General Assembly decision providing the People's Republic of China with the status of a permanent member and a seat on the Security Council but not expelling the Republic of China, a new situation would exist. In

[43] As constituent Republics of the U.S.S.R., Byelorussia and the Ukraine were granted separate membership in the U.N. in 1945.
[44] Document 123a.
[45] Document 123b.

any event, I submit, in deciding how to vote on this question we should look more to what the United Nations should do.

It is ironic that just as the sentiment for universality in the Assembly is growing, many of those who have long extolled it now seek to violate it. If the United Nations is to embrace universality, as some have suggested, then surely the admission of one member should not be accompanied by the expulsion of another.

Our task here, it seems to me, must be to make a decision that is reasonable, that accepts the realities of the existing situation, that does not prejudice the ultimate outcome, and that provides for representation of all the people concerned. Thereafter our efforts should be to convince those directly involved to take advantage of the decision we have made. The cause of peace has been greatly benefited in recent years by greater pragmatism in many capitals; it would be served by the same pragmatism on this issue.

As the United Nations becomes a more universal body it will be better able to deal with the lengthening list of global issues confronting it—in conciliating political differences, in reducing the world's armaments, in curbing the epidemic spread of narcotics addiction, in protecting the environment, in assuring the exploitation of the oceans for the benefit of mankind.

In meeting those responsibilities, the United Nations must during this session deal with two important matters:

It must choose an outstanding successor to our most able and distinguished Secretary General U Thant,[46] to whose dedication and idealism we all pay tribute. And as I pay respects to the Secretary General, I am sure my colleagues will understand if I also single out for special attention two American citizens who are now retiring: Paul Hoffman, who has devoted himself so effectively to the economic welfare of the developing countries, and Ralph Bunche, a Nobel Prize winner, who has contributed so markedly to the cause of peace.[47]

The Assembly must also arrest the continuing deterioration of the United Nations financial position, which, as the Secretary General has pointed out, has eroded its fiscal credit and undermined confidence in its potential.

Responsibility for halting this decline rests primarily on those who fail to pay their share. Given assurances of adequate contributions by others, the United States will be prepared to assist toward an overall solution. Meanwhile we find it hard to understand why the membership should continue to recommend and approve budget increases beyond

---

[46] Cf. Documents 133-135.
[47] Paul G. Hoffman retired as Administrator of the U.N. Development Program on Jan. 15, 1972. Ralph J. Bunche, Under-Secretary for Special Political Affairs, died Dec. 9, 1971; for a tribute by Ambassador Bush see *Bulletin*, Jan. 17, 1972, p. 71.

those necessary to meet inescapable cost increases.[48]

*   *   *

(125) "Restoration of the Lawful Rights of the People's Republic of China in the United Nations": General Assembly Resolution 2758 (XXVI), Adopted October 25, 1971.[49]

(Complete Text)

The General Assembly,

Recalling the principles of the Charter of the United Nations,

Considering that the restoration of the lawful rights of the People's Republic of China is essential both for the protection of the Charter of the United Nations and for the cause that the United Nations must serve under the Charter,

Recognizing that the representatives of the Government of the People's Republic of China are the only lawful representatives of China to the United Nations and that the People's Republic of China is one of the five permanent members of the Security Council,

Decides to restore all its rights to the People's Republic of China and to recognize the representatives of its Government as the only legitimate representatives of China to the United Nations, and to expel forthwith the representatives of Chiang Kai-shek from the place which they unlawfully occupy at the United Nations and in all the organizations related to it.[50]

(126) Implications of the Assembly's Action: News Conference Statement by Secretary of State Rogers, October 26, 1971.[51]

(Excerpt)

*   *   *

Last night's decision to admit the People's Republic of China as a

[48] Cf. Document 129.

[49] General Assembly, *Official Records: 26th Session, Supplement No. 29* (A/8429), p. 2; adopted by a vote of 76-35(U.S.)-17, with three absences (China, Maldives, Oman). The text is identical to Document 123a.

[50] A U.S. motion for a separate vote on the final clause of the resolution was rejected by a recorded vote of 51 (U.S.)-61-16. Following this vote, the representative of the Republic of China stated that his delegation would not take part in any further proceedings of the General Assembly. (*UN Monthly Chronicle*, Nov. 1971, p. 34.)

[51] Department of State Press Release 246, Oct. 26, 1971; text from *Bulletin*, Nov. 15, 1971, p. 541. For further comment cf. above at notes 28-29.

member of the United Nations, of course, is consistent with the policy of the United States. President Nixon hopes that this action, which will bring into the United Nations representatives of more than 700 million people, will result in a reduction of tensions in the Pacific area.

At the same time, the United States deeply regrets the action taken by the United Nations to deprive the Republic of China of representation in that organization. We think that this precedent, which has the effect of expelling 14 million people on Taiwan from representation in the United Nations, is a most unfortunate one which will have many adverse effects in the future.

We and the cosponsors of our resolution[52] made an all-out effort to prevent the expulsion of the Republic of China. We are particularly grateful to all of our cosponsors for the very dedicated and determined effort that was made to retain a place for the Republic of China in the United Nations.

The Republic of China, of course, continues to be a respected and valued member of the international community, and the ties between us remain unaffected by the action of the United Nations.

Although we believe that a mistake of major proportion has been made in expelling the Republic of China from the United Nations, the United States recognizes that the will of a majority of the members has been expressed. We, of course, accept that decision.

We hope that the United Nations will not have been weakened by what it has done. We continue to believe in its principles and purposes and hope that ways can be found to make it more effective in the pursuit of peace in the future.

*   *   *

(127) Seating of Delegates from the People's Republic of China: Statement by Ambassador Bush to the General Assembly, November 15, 1971.[53]

(Complete Text)

The United States joins in welcoming to the United Nations the representatives of the People's Republic of China, Vice Foreign Minister Chiao [Kuan-hua], Ambassador Huang [Hua], and their colleagues.

Their presence here makes the United Nations more reflective of the world as it now exists, and we hope that it will contribute to the organization's potential for harmonizing the actions of nations. The issues of principle that divided the General Assembly in recent weeks were deeply felt and hard fought. Those differences should not obscure

52 Document 123c.
53 USUN Press Release 187; text from *Bulletin*, Dec. 20, 1971, pp. 715-16.

the proposition on which nearly all of us, including the United States, agreed: that the moment in history has arrived for the People's Republic of China to be in the United Nations.

The United States, whose people are linked by long ties of friendship with the great Chinese people, is confident that with renewed dedication to the principles of the charter we can move toward peace and justice in the world. We shall not cease to work here with all who share that hope and who wish to cooperate in its realization.

(128) United States Support for the United Nations: News Conference Statement by Secretary of State Rogers, December 1, 1971.[54]

(Excerpt)

*   *   *

Q. Mr. Secretary, two questions in one, sir. One, the United Nations is out to appoint a new Secretary General. I would like to know the U.S. position as far as we are concerned about who that Secretary General might be. And two, there has been a lot of comment recently at the U.N. that we, the United States, are not very much for the United Nations. What is our position basically on the United Nations— the Secretary General and the U.N., sir?

Secretary Rogers: Well, on the first one, there has been some hope on the part of some nations that the present Secretary General would continue in office. We have satisfied ourselves that that is not the case. He has told us repeatedly he is not willing to continue to serve, and as you know, he has had a health problem recently. So we assume that there will be a vacancy in that office. We have had some discussions with the other permanent members of the Security Council. We have not come to any conclusion. We don't have any candidate as such. Several names have been mentioned of well-qualified persons, and we are going to consult with the permanent members of the Security Council because, as you know, they have to be unanimous before the Security Council can recommend a successor to the present Secretary General.[55]

As to the second question, I think I have answered that before. We think the United Nations should have our support, and we are going to continue to support the United Nations. We think the United Nations

54 Department of State Press Release 279, Dec. 1, 1971; text from *Bulletin*, Dec. 20, 1971, p. 701.
55 Cf. Document 133.

has not lived up to its expectations. I think all Americans have been somewhat disappointed in its accomplishments. But we still hold out hope for its future success.

We think we have probably contributed too much financially, and, as you know, Ambassador Lodge's committee recommended that we go down from roughly 32-percent contribution to the annual budget to about 25 percent, and we are going to attempt to accomplish that.[56] We are not going to diminish our support to the specialized agencies, but we are going to look very carefully to see if we are getting our money's worth, if the results are worth the money that is being spent.

But generally speaking, we are going to continue to support the United Nations, because we think it is a very important institution.

*　　*　　*

C. United Nations Organization and Finances.

[A number of crucial organizational and financial questions confronted the United Nations in 1971. Among matters of special interest to the United States—some of which were touched upon by Secretary Rogers in the preceding document (Document 128)—were the precarious financial position of the organization and the prospective measure of U.S. financial support (Document 129); the security of U.N. delegates and their families in the politically turbulent atmosphere of New York City (Documents 130-131); a plan to double the membership of the Economic and Social Council (Document 132); and the necessity of appointing a new Secretary-General to succeed U Thant of Burma, who had announced his intention to retire on the expiration of his current term at the end of the year (Documents 133-135).]

1. United Nations Financial Problems.

[The congenitally strained condition of U.N. finances, originating mainly in the refusal of the U.S.S.R., France, and certain other states to pay their assessed share of the costs of U.N. operations in the Congo during the early 1960s, had been aggravated of late years both by the general impact of inflation and by a proliferation of new programs and activities that had helped to swell the regular budget of the organization from $154,915,250 for 1969 to $168,420,000 for 1970 and $192,149,300 for 1971. By the middle of the latter year, unpaid assessments owed by member countries amounted to $176,700,000 and the organization's current debt was estimated at some $70,000,000,

---

56 Cf. Document 129.

over and above its long-term obligation to repay a total of $119,000,000 outstanding from the special U.N. bond issue authorized in 1961.[57]

Although the United States had met its own obligations and advertised its readiness to assist toward an overall solution—"given assurances of adequate contributions by others"[58]—no definite progress toward such a solution was achieved in 1971 despite renewed urging by Ambassador Bush[59] and others.

A relatively new factor in the budgetary outlook was the growing pressure within the United States for a curtailment of the scale of U.S. financial support of the organization, which currently amounted to 31.52 percent of the U.N. regular budget and also included comparable or larger contributions to the budgets of the specialized agencies and to a wide variety of U.N.-sponsored peacekeeping, economic, social, and humanitarian programs. Preliminary figures for the calendar year 1971 would show a grand total of $461,931,000 in U.S. contributions to the activities of the U.N. system as a whole, representing 37.78 percent of the amounts contributed by all states during that year. Included in the total were $56,312,000 for the U.N. regular budget and bond issue, $55,437,000 for the specialized agencies, $4,800,000 for the U.N. peacekeeping force in Cyprus (UNFICYP), $201,587,000 for U.N. voluntary programs, and $52,920,000 for South Asian humanitarian assistance.[60]

Concerned at what seemed the disproportionate scale of U.S. financial support for an organization established a full quarter-century earlier, the President's Commission on the Observance of the 25th Anniversary of the United Nations, headed by Ambassador Henry Cabot Lodge, recommended in April 1971 that the United States "affirm its intention to maintain and increase its total contributions to the UN, but that, as part of a redistribution of responsibilities, it will seek over a period of years to reduce its current contribution of 31.52 percent to the assessed regular budget of the Organization so that eventually its share will not exceed 25 percent."[61] The intention of the United States to act on this advice was made known in the course of the 26th Regular Session of the General Assembly in 1971[62] and was to be accepted by that body—though only after prolonged and bitter debate—at its 27th Regular Session in 1972.[63] In the meantime, the

57 Rogers Report, 1971, pp. 293-94.
58 Cf. above at note 48.
59 Cf. Bush statement, Oct. 15, 1971, in *Bulletin*, Nov. 15, 1971, pp. 556-58.
60 Rogers Report, 1971, pp. 296-99.
61 *Bulletin*, Aug. 2, 1971, p. 134. On the report of the Lodge Commission cf. note 47 to Chapter VI.
62 Documents 128-129.
63 Resolution 2961 B (XXVII), Dec. 13, 1972; adopted by a vote of 81 (U.S.)-27-22.

United States found itself unable to support a further large increase in U.N. expenditures and therefore abstained from voting on the $213,124,410 expenditure budget for 1972, which was approved by the Assembly on December 22, 1971 (Document 129).]

(129) Abstention on the 1972 Budget: Statement by Congressman Edward J. Derwinski, United States Representative, to the General Assembly, December 22, 1971.[64]

(Complete Text)

I wish to explain the vote which the United States delegation will cast on the United Nations budget estimates for 1972.[65]

First, I wish to comment on a matter related to the budget about which many delegates have addressed questions to the United States delegation. This is the announced intention of the United States to seek a reduction at the earliest possible opportunity of its assessed contribution percentage from its present level to 25 percent.

A Presidential Commission headed by Ambassador Henry Cabot Lodge reported last April that as new member states are admitted to the United Nations, their assessed contributions to the regular budget would call for a redistribution of the financial burdens reflected in the scale of assessments. It recommended that the United States, while maintaining its overall commitment of resources to the United Nations system, should seek over a period of years to reduce its current assessment percentage so that eventually its share would not exceed 25 percent.[66] We have decided that the recommendation of the Lodge Commission is an appropriate goal for the United States to pursue as rapidly as possible and, hopefully, in connection with the admission of new members.

Mr. President, we believe that a reduction of the United States assessment percentage to 25 percent would be beneficial to the United Nations because the organization ought not to be overly dependent on the contribution of a single member. We do not believe it is politically advisable for an organization of sovereign and juridically equal states, which is approaching universality of membership, to perpetuate the existing extreme disparity between voting power on the one hand and financial contributions on the other.

[64] USUN Press Release 226; text from *Bulletin*, Feb. 7, 1972, pp. 175-78. Congressman Derwinski (Republican, Illinois) was a public member of the U.S. delegation to the 26th General Assembly.
[65] Resolution 2899 A (XXVI), Dec. 22, 1971; adopted by a vote of 106-9-7 (U.S.).
[66] Cf. above at note 61.

Let me turn now to the budget estimates. The proposed expenditure level for 1972 of about $213.1 million represents an increase of about $21 million over the original appropriation level for 1971. We note, however, that the magnitude of the increase (about 11 percent) is not as great as it was last year (about 14.3 percent). We believe that this cutback in the rate of increase reflects an effort by the Secretary General, and particularly by the Controller and his staff, to limit budgetary requests for 1972 to what they consider essential for high-priority activities. Our delegation cannot say that we are satisfied with the success of the effort made, but it was a move in the right direction.

Mr. President, we feel that in voting on United Nations budgets, governments tend to give too much weight to the dollar level of these budgets and to ignore other important aspects of the problem. The budget level is less important than what the budget discloses about the manner in which this organization is administered and managed.

For example, section 3 of the budget, which deals with salaries and wages,[67] discloses several important facts. First of all, it provides not only for a sizable increase in established posts but also for very significant increases in the use of temporary assistance, consultants, and experts. It may well be that the organization should have greater recourse today than in the past to temporary assistance, consultants, and experts than to established posts. However, we cannot accept such a substantial increase in all of these elements at the same time, particularly when the United Nations is experiencing a financial crisis. In the Fifth [Administrative and Budgetary] Committee the United States delegation proposed a substantial decrease of about $900,000 in funds provided for temporary assistance, consultants, and experts. We regret that this was not accepted by the committee.

Section 3, with its provisions for increased manpower for the Secretariat in 1972, also focuses attention on several other points. There is the question of whether all of the many programs initiated by the United Nations years ago are today of sufficient importance to warrant the continued utilization of the organization's resources. We believe the Secretary General should review each and every ongoing program and, where appropriate, suggest to governments which activities no longer retain high-priority status in relation to new and more important ones.

There is also the question of the productivity and effectiveness of the present staff. We all know that a substantial portion of the United Nations staff members are highly qualified. However, it is unfortunately true that a number of individuals employed by the United Nations do not have the requisite ability of [sic] training to perform at a very high level, and this leads to the recruitment of extra staff to get the job done. A number of governments which have been critical of the size of

[67] Budgeted at $96,189,160.

the Secretariat would perform a greater service if they made certain that the candidates they propose for Secretariat service were fully qualified. It is of critical importance that the United Nations obtain from all member states the services of only highly competent individuals who serve the interests of the United Nations and are not improperly influenced by their own or other governments.

Section 7 of the budget[68] represents an area in which there is room for improvement. At the present time the United Nations is engaged or about to be engaged in the construction of new buildings in Geneva, Santiago, Addis Ababa, and Bangkok. As a result of building simultaneously in a number of locations, there has been a substantial increase in section 7, which has had an abnormal impact on the budget. We find it particularly difficult to accept a building program of this magnitude when the organization is virtually bankrupt.

Part VI of the budget[69] is a cause of serious concern, and here the responsibility must fall squarely upon governments. This year an amount of $1.8 million was added arbitrarily to part VI. We continue to oppose strongly such increases in part VI, particularly because of the difficulties which have arisen in connection with the financing of that part and the need to avoid such difficulties if further erosion of the organization's financial stability is to be avoided. We believe a solution might be to remove part VI from the budget and redistribute its components elsewhere, both within and without the budget.

Mr. President, we hope that other delegations realize how seriously we view the increase in part VI of the budget for 1972. As we have stated for many years, we believe that the U.N. technical assistance programs should be financed by voluntary contributions. I am sure that the General Assembly will realize that the United States cannot accept indefinitely a situation in which it pays increased dollar contributions while the Soviet Union and a few other states continue to derive a one-sided advantage by offering payments in nonconvertible currencies.

My final comments concerning the budget itself relate to the substantial provisions contained therein for meetings and documentation. We believe that too many meetings are scheduled at times of the year when the meeting program is already overloaded rather than in the slack periods. The attempt appears to be to insure the convenience of delegates rather than economy. We also find that a number of committees are wandering about the world holding meetings here and there and spending substantial sums of money with very little to show for their efforts. Discipline must be developed in this regard.

For many years governments have wept bitterly about the unmanage-

68 Construction, alteration, improvement and major maintenance of premises, budgeted at $9,614,000.
69 United Nations Conference on Trade and Development, budgeted at $12,525,000.

able amount of documentation which is produced each year, but they have done almost nothing to limit or control it. Last year the United States delegation proposed an overall budgetary decrease of $1 million in documentation in an attempt to force some reduction in volume, but that proposal was rejected. We are pleased that this year the Fifth Committee decided to make an overall reduction in the budget of $1.25 million to reflect a reduction which it called for in the volume of documentation.

My remarks demonstrate, Mr. President, why we have serious reservations both about the level and about the content of the 1972 budget estimates. We are very concerned about the budget because of its relationship to the financial deficit facing the organization and the attitude which it reflects with respect to that deficit.

A review of the United Nations balance sheet reveals that at the end of last month assessed contributions outstanding amounted to about $219 million. For the regular budget alone, unpaid assessments were in excess of $87 million. The Controller has informed the Fifth Committee that by the end of this year about $65.2 million in unpaid budget assessments will remain on the books with no assurance that more than $13.4 million will eventually be paid. He has stated that by December 31, 1972, it is estimated that arrears will have reached about $70 million with no more than $14 million likely to be collected. The magnitude of these amounts should dispel any lingering thoughts about the seriousness of the United Nations financial plight.

What are the causes of this untenable situation? One of the contributing causes is the failure of many governments to pay their annual assessments in the year in which they fall due. In my opinion, this cause should not be too difficult to remove, and all governments should make a serious effort to pay their contributions as early as possible.

The primary cause of the critical financial situation is the refusal of some governments to pay certain assessments which have been levied on them by the General Assembly. Several countries, principally members of the Soviet bloc and France, have refused to pay assessments relating to peacekeeping operations levied against them for the Congo and UNEF [United Nations Emergency Force] operations. They have refused also to pay their share of certain other items included annually in the regular budget, such as the amortization of U.N. bonds. These longstanding nonpayments amount to more than $140 million, or about two-thirds of the total of unpaid assessments.

Obviously, if all of the sums owed were paid, the liquidity of the United Nations would be stabilized and the mounting deficit problem would be eliminated. The heart of the deficit problem, past and future, lies in its causes. My delegation believes that ways must be found to deal effectively with these root causes.

Some members states have already made sizable voluntary contributions in an effort to maintain the solvency of the organization. However, it has long been clear that if we are to be successful in keeping the United Nations from bankruptcy, other member states must pitch in and help. A particularly heavy responsibility falls upon those who have caused the deficit problem to arise.

Turning now to the relationship of the deficit to the 1972 budget level, it is, of course, true that a reduction in the budget level will not directly solve the deficit problem. However, we fail to understand how, when the organization is faced with a situation in which it forecasts the impossibility of meeting its payroll next year, governments can take a business-as-usual attitude with respect to the 1972 budget estimates just as if no financial problem existed. We have found it frustrating to sit through this year's session of the Fifth Committee and listen to long debates on matters such as proposed budgetary increases for public information activities when absolutely nothing was being done to provide the organization with the necessary cash to carry on its activities next year. It is true that Ambassador Hambro [Edvard Hambro, of Norway] made a gallant effort to enlist the support of all member states in an endeavor to find a complete solution to the deficit problem.[70] However, although there were some meetings of the major contributors in an attempt to find a formula for solution, there was no indication until the last week that they intended to come to grips with the problem.

Late last week the U.N. Controller came before the Fifth Committee and spelled out once more the desperate nature of the financial situation. He proposed that in an attempt to meet in 1972 the shortfall of $3.9 million expected to result from the withholdings of contributions by certain governments: (a) The Assembly should decide to credit to the Working Capital Fund the amount of $1.8 million available in surplus account for the financial year 1970, and (b) the Secretary General should make savings of $2.1 million in administering the appropriation for 1972. We considered this to be a first step by the Secretary General to deal with the matter, but in all honesty, we viewed it as merely a gesture which could not possibly achieve its objective. Further, the proposal for the use of the 1970 surplus meant transferring to all member states the burden resulting from the failure of a few governments to

---

[70] Proposals by Ambassador Hambro, who had served as President of the 25th Regular Session of the General Assembly, included among other things waivers of certain debts owed by the United Nations to member states, set-offs of certain amounts of interest and principal due on the U.N. bond issue, and voluntary cash contributions. Up to Dec. 1971, a $3.9 million voluntary contribution by France represented the only positive response to the Hambro proposals by "major delinquents." (Rogers Report, 1971, p. 294.)

pay what they owe, and we were not surprised that it received no support in the Fifth Committee. In our view, unless and until this deficit problem is solved with the necessary cooperation by states which have not paid their assessments, the only proper method of dealing with the matter is to limit expenditures by the organization to the level of contributions actually received.

Mr. President, we support your proposal based on the suggestion of Ambassador Hambro to establish a working group to meet during the coming year in an effort to find the solution to this problem. We will, of course, participate and cooperate fully in that effort.[71]

Mr. President, for the foregoing reasons the United States delegation cannot support the expenditure budget proposed for 1972 and will abstain in the vote on Parts A and C of Resolution XI, dealing with the appropriation for 1972 and its financing.[72]

2. Security of Missions to the United Nations.

[The act of an unidentified assailant who fired four bullets into the Soviet Mission to the United Nations in New York on the evening of October 20, 1971, highlighted a problem that had caused increasing concern to the United States and many other U.N. member countries. While the Soviet Mission and its personnel had been a frequent target of Jewish activist groups protesting the disabilities experienced by members of the Jewish community in the U.S.S.R., various other delegations had also experienced instances of harassment by persons who disapproved their governments' policies. Such incidents had given rise to recurrent suggestions that the U.N. Headquarters itself should be removed to a more peaceful environment outside the United States.

Condemnation of the October 20 attack on the Soviet Mission by Ambassador Bush (Document 130) and other U.S. spokesmen (Document 31) was followed on December 15, 1971, by the unanimous adoption of a resolution in which the General Assembly expressed "extreme concern" at such acts and decided to set up a Committee on Relations with the Host Country to work with the United States in trying to provide better security for U.N. missions and personnel (Document 131). The 15-member committee[73] appointed by the President

---

[71] The quest for a solution was continued by a 15-member working group whose membership paralleled the composition of the Security Council.

[72] For part A of Resolution 2899 (XXVI), see note 65 above. Part C of the resolution, adopted by a vote of 110-0-13 (U.S.), provided for the financing of the appropriation for 1972 together with supplementary appropriations of $2,478,500 for 1971.

[73] The members appointed to the committee were Argentina, Bulgaria, Canada, China, Cyprus, France, Guyana, Iraq, Ivory Coast, Mali, Spain, Tanzania, the U.S.S.R., the United Kingdom, the United States. Zenon Rossides (Cyprus) was named Chairman.

of the General Assembly (Adam Malik of Indonesia) held its first meeting on December 28, 1971, and requested the United States to provide effective protection to the Syrian Mission following a forcible entry by two persons who had defaced the interior of that mission with red and black paint.[74]]

(130) Shooting Incident at the Soviet Mission: Statement by Ambassador Bush, October 21, 1971.[75]

(Complete Text)

I strongly condemn the cowardly and hostile action of the extremists who fired four bullets into the U.S.S.R. Mission Wednesday evening [October 20].

This outrageous, cowardly, and hostile act represents the very worst in the fanatical fringe of our society.

This incident works against everything we are trying to do in seeking improved relations between our country and the Soviet Union.

There were four little children in the room where the bullets hit. Any one of them could have been killed. Naturally they were terrified.

Today I have expressed my regrets to the Permanent Representative of the U.S.S.R. [Yakov A. Malik]. Last night, on the scene, I expressed my deep concern to the parents of the four little terrified children.

I have been assured by the New York police of the highest level of attention being devoted to this matter. The FBI will cooperate, too.

I would appeal to those who threaten, those who attack and violate the law, those who cower and shoot from rooftops: You are damaging this country—and whatever end it is you seek to achieve will not be achieved by barbaric acts such as this shooting incident.

The New York Police Department is doing its level best to protect the U.S.S.R. Mission against hostile acts, but all would agree that the hidden coward is tough to protect against.

We are making no accusations as to what particular individual group or members of a group are involved and responsible for this crime. We simply appeal to decency and common sense that those who perpetrated this incident and other similar incidents will stop acting the part of madmen.

We cannot afford to do less. There is too much at stake.

---

[74] UN Monthly Chronicle, Jan. 1972, p. 203.
[75] USUN Press Release 165, Oct. 21, 1971; text from Bulletin, Nov. 22, 1971, pp. 598-99. For further comment see Document 31.

(131) "Security of Missions Accredited to the United Nations and Safety of Their Personnel and Establishment of the Committee on Relations with the Host Country": General Assembly Resolution 2819 (XXVI), Adopted December 15, 1971.[76]

(Complete Text)

The General Assembly,

Having considered the item entitled "Security of missions accredited to the United Nations and safety of their personnel" and the report of the Secretary-General on the work of the Informal Joint Committee on Host Country Relations,[77]

Drawing attention to its resolution 2747 (XXV) of 17 December 1970, in which it urges the Government of the host country to make certain that the measures taken to ensure the protection and security of diplomatic missions and their diplomatic personnel are adequate to enable permanent missions to the United Nations to perform properly the functions entrusted to them by their Governments,

Expressing its gratitude to the Secretary-General for his valuable contribution to the work of the Informal Joint Committee on Host Country Relations,

Noting with extreme concern the illegal acts of individuals or groups against the inviolability of various missions accredited to the United Nations involving the commission and the repetition of violent and other criminal acts, including in some cases the use of bombs or firearms, against their premises and the residences of their personnel and also the assaults, the uttering of threats and insults against such personnel, and picketing accompanied by violence,

Expressing its deep sympathy with the missions and their personnel that have become the victims of such acts,

Recalling the responsibilities of the Government of the host country with respect to the United Nations and missions accredited to it and their personnel under the Agreement between the United Nations and the United States of America regarding the Headquarters of the United Nations,[78] the Convention on the Privileges and Immunities of the United Nations[79] and general international law,

Taking into account the profound concern expressed by representatives of States at the twenty-sixth session of the General Assembly over the perpetration and repetition of violent and increasingly dan-

---

[76] General Assembly, *Official Records: 26th Session, Supplement No. 29* (A/8429), pp. 138-39; adopted unanimously.

[77] U.N. document A/8474.

[78] Signed at Lake Success June 26, 1947, and entered into force Nov. 21, 1947 (TIAS 1676); text in *Documents, 1947*, pp. 304-14.

[79] Done at New York Feb. 13, 1946, and entered into force for the U.S. Apr. 29, 1970 (TIAS 6900; 21 UST 1418); cf. *Documents, 1968-69*, pp. 495-97.

gerous attacks against the premises of certain missions accredited to the United Nations, and also over the repeated threats and the hostile and intimidating acts against the personnel of these missions, which indicates a deterioration in the security of missions and the safety of their personnel,

Considering that the problems related to the privileges and immunities of the United Nations and to the status of the diplomatic missions accredited to it are of mutual concern to Member States, including the host country, as well as to the Secretary-General,

1. *Strongly condemns* the acts of violence and other criminal acts against the premises of certain missions accredited to the United Nations and against their personnel as being flagrantly incompatible with their status under international law;

2. *Urges* that the Government of the United States of America, the host country of the United Nations, should take all requisite measures to ensure, in conformity with its international obligations, the protection and security of the United Nations Headquarters, of the missions accredited to it and of their personnel, thereby ensuring normal conditions for the performance of their functions;

3. *Calls upon* the Government of the United States of America, in consultation with the Secretary-General, to take all possible measures, including the use of information and publicity, to ensure a favourable atmosphere for the normal functioning of the United Nations and the missions accredited to it;

4. *Notes with appreciation* the assurances given by the representative of the host country that it will intensify in a diligent and energetic manner its efforts to strengthen the protection and safety of the missions accredited to the United Nations and their personnel;

5. *Decides* to establish a Committee on Relations with the Host Country, composed of the host country and fourteen Member States to be chosen by the President of the General Assembly in consultation with regional groups and taking into consideration equitable geographic representation thereon;[80]

6. *Requests* the Secretary-General to participate actively in the work of the Committee on Relations with the Host Country with a view to ensuring the representation of the interests concerned;

7. *Instructs* the Committee on Relations with the Host Country to deal with the question of the security of missions and the safety of their personnel, as well as all the categories of issues previously considered by the Informal Joint Committee on Host Country Relations; the Committee is authorized to study the Convention on the Privileges and Immunities of the United Nations and shall consider, and advise the host country on, issues arising in connexion with the implementation of

[80] Cf. note 73 above.

the Agreement between the United Nations and the United States of America regarding the Headquarters of the United Nations;

8. *Authorizes* the Committee on Relations with the Host Country to have summary records of its meetings and to convene on a periodic basis and whenever it is convoked by its Chairman at the request of any State Member of the United Nations or the Secretary-General;

9. *Requests* the Secretary-General to solicit the views of Member States with respect to the measures needed to ensure the future security of missions and the safety of their personnel and to transmit such replies to the Committee on Relations with the Host Country;

10. *Requests* the Secretary-General to bring to the attention of the Committee on Relations with the Host Country, if so requested by missions accredited to the United Nations, cases involving infringements of their status;

11. *Requests* the Secretary-General to furnish all appropriate assistance to the Committee on Relations with the Host Country and to bring to its attention issues of mutual concern relating to the implementation of the Agreement between the United Nations and the United States of America regarding the Headquarters of the United Nations and the Convention on the Privileges and Immunities of the United Nations;

12. *Requests* the Committee on Relations with the Host Country to submit to the General Assembly at its twenty-seventh session a report on the progress of its work and to make, if it deems it necessary, appropriate recommendations;

13. *Decides* to include in the provisional agenda of its twenty-seventh session an item entitled "Report of the Committee on Relations with the Host Country".

3. Enlargement of the Economic and Social Council (ECOSOC).

[Originally composed of 18 members, the Economic and Social Council—the body charged with general responsibility for the economic and social activities of the United Nations—had already been expanded in 1966 to a membership of 27 in recognition of the increase that had taken place in the number of U.N. member states, especially in Asia and Africa. This increase, however, had been found insufficient to give the developing countries an adequate sense of representation, and the United States assumed the initiative in 1971 in trying to revitalize the Council through a further increase in its membership and an improvement in its capacity for appraising the progress of the U.N. Second Development Decade and providing guidance and recommendations concerning the application of science and technology to development.[81] Approved by the Economic and Social Council in the sum-

81 Rogers Report, 1971, p. 295; cf. above at notes 13-14.

mer of 1971, a proposal to increase the membership to 54 through an appropriate amendment of the U.N. Charter was brought before the General Assembly at its autumn session and approved on December 20, 1971, by a vote of 105 to 2 (France and the United Kingdom) with 15 abstentions, including those of the U.S.S.R. and most of its allies. The Charter amendment as adopted by the General Assembly (Document 132) was approved by an 80-7 vote of the U.S. Senate on September 5, 1973, ratified by the President on September 13, 1973, and entered into force with the deposit of the U.S. ratification on September 24, 1973.[82]]

(132) "Enlargement of the Economic and Social Council": General Assembly Resolution 2847 (XXVI), Adopted December 20, 1971.[83]

(Complete Text)

The General Assembly,

Recognizing that an enlargement of the Economic and Social Council will provide broad representation of the United Nations membership as a whole and make the Council a more effective organ for carrying out its functions under Chapters IX and X of the Charter of the United Nations,

Having considered the report of the Economic and Social Council,[84]

1. *Takes note* of Economic and Social Council resolution 1621 (LI) of 30 July 1971;

2. *Decides* to adopt, in accordance with Article 108 of the Charter of the United Nations, the following amendment to the Charter and to submit it for ratification by the States Members of the United Nations:

"Article 61

"1. The Economic and Social Council shall consist of fifty-four Members of the United Nations elected by the General Assembly.

"2. Subject to the provisions of paragraph 3, eighteen members of the Economic and Social Council shall be elected each year for a term of three years. A retiring member shall be eligible for immediate re-election.

"3. At the first election after the increase in the membership of the Economic and Social Council from twenty-seven to fifty-four members, in addition to the members elected in place of the nine

---

[82] TIAS 7739; text identical with Document 132 except as noted in note 87, below.

[83] General Assembly, *Official Records: 26th Session, Supplement No. 29* (A/8429), pp. 67-68; adopted bv a vote of 105 (U.S.)-2-15.

[84] General Assembly, *Official Records: 26th Session, Supplement No. 3* (A/8403).

members whose term of office expires at the end of that year, twenty-seven additional members shall be elected. Of these twenty-seven additional members, the term of office of nine members so elected shall expire at the end of one year, and of nine other members at the end of two years, in accordance with arrangements made by the General Assembly.

"4. Each member of the Economic and Social Council shall have one representative.";

3. *Urges* all Member States to ratify the above amendment in accordance with their respective constitutional processes as soon as possible and to deposit their instruments of ratification with the Secretary-General;[85]

4. *Further decides* that the members of the Economic and Social Council shall be elected according to the following pattern:

(*a*) Fourteen members from African States;
(*b*) Eleven members from Asian States;
(*c*) Ten members from Latin American States;
(*d*) Thirteen members from Western European and other States;
(*e*) Six members from socialist States of Eastern Europe;

5. *Welcomes* the decision of the Economic and Social Council, pending the receipt of the necessary ratifications, to enlarge its sessional committees to fifty-four members;

6. *Invites* the Economic and Social Council, as soon as possible and not later than the organizational meetings of its fifty-second session,[86] to elect the twenty-seven additional members from States Members of the United Nations to serve on the enlarged sessional committees; such elections should be in accordance with paragraph 4 above and should be held each year pending the coming into force of the enlargement of the Council;

7. *Decides* that, as of the date of the entry into force of the above amendments, rule 147 of the rules of procedure of the General Assembly[87] shall be amended to read:

"Rule 147

"The General Assembly shall each year, in the course of its regular session, elect eighteen members of the Economic and Social Council for a term of three years."

[85] Cf. above at note 82.
[86] Held at U.N. Headquarters on Jan. 5-7, 1972.
[87] As originally adopted, the resolution referred to rule 146, and this numbering was retained in the official U.S. text of the resolution (note 82, above). Rule 146 was subsequently renumbered 147 pursuant to Resolution 2837 (XXVI) of Dec. 17, 1971, and the new number 147 appears in the official U.N. text as reproduced here.

4. Appointment of a New Secretary-General.

[Agreement on the choice of a Secretary-General to succeed U Thant at the beginning of 1972 was achieved with an absence of friction all the more remarkable in light of the difficulties that had preceded the designation of U Thant himself as successor to the late Dag Hammarskjold of Sweden in 1961. Originally appointed in an acting capacity, the Burmese statesman had been formally appointed Secretary-General in 1962 and reappointed in 1966 for a term of office expiring December 31, 1971. The likelihood that he could be persuaded to serve beyond that date had been thought minimal, as Secretary Rogers noted at his news conference on December 1 (Document 128), and alternative candidates for the post included H.S. Amerasinghe of Ceylon, Endalkachew Makonnen of Ethiopia, Felipe Herrera of Chile, Max Jacobson of Finland, and Kurt Waldheim of Austria, a former Permanent Representative to the United Nations and a defeated candidate in the Austrian presidential election of June 9, 1971. The range of possible choice was narrowed by the Security Council in the course of three closed meetings held December 17, 20, and 21, at the conclusion of which the Council announced unanimous agreement to recommend the appointment of Dr. Waldheim (Document 133). Acting in accordance with this recommendation, the General Assembly on December 22, 1971, approved by acclamation Mr. Waldheim's appointment as Secretary-General for a term of office beginning January 1, 1972, and ending December 31, 1976 (Document 134). This action was followed by an expression of good wishes to both the outgoing and the incoming Secretaries-General by Ambassador Bush as Permanent Representative of the host country (Document 135).]

(133) Recommendation of the Security Council: Security Council Resolution 306 (1971), Adopted at a Private Meeting on December 21, 1971.[88]

(Complete Text)

The Security Council,

Having considered the question of the recommendation for the appointment of the Secretary-General of the United Nations,

Recommends to the General Assembly that Mr. Kurt Waldheim be appointed Secretary-General of the United Nations.

---

[88] Security Council, *Official Records: 26th Year, Resolutions and Decisions*, p. 13; adopted unanimously.

(134) "Appointment of the Secretary-General of the United Nations":
General Assembly Resolution 2903 (XXVI), Adopted December
22, 1971.[89]

(Complete Text)

The General Assembly,

Acting in accordance with the recommendation contained in Security
Council resolution 306 (1971) of 21 December 1971,[90]

Appoints Mr. Kurt Waldheim Secretary-General of the United Nations
for a term of office beginning on 1 January 1972 and ending on 31
December 1976.

(135) Statement by Ambassador Bush to the General Assembly,
December 22, 1971.[91]

(Complete Text)

As host country representative, let me add just a few brief remarks.

First, we pay tribute, we pay our deepest respect to you, Mr. Secretary General. We salute U Thant as a man of peace; we salute him as a world leader; we salute him, as each of us has come to know him, as a great individual. Sometimes we might have disagreed with a decision; much more often we have been in total agreement. But never, never did we have cause to question his motive, to question his character, to question his fundamental dedication, his total commitment to a world at peace.

U Thant, Your Excellency, we salute you. You have taught us all—all 133 [132] of us—and you have taught us well. We know that you will never stop in your efforts to make this a better world, but as you leave this office you leave us all a legacy of challenge and honor.

And now, with regard to our Secretary-General-elect, Mr. Waldheim, some say that even though it is Christmastime we should be offering him condolences rather than congratulations. True, the job is awesome in its magnitude. It is hard to quantify its difficulty. Its frustrations are unimaginable. But somehow, in spite of the magnitude of his undertaking, there is in this hall, sir, an unmistakable air of optimism, and clearly it stems from our common certain knowledge of the fact that we have elected a man of great experience, great diplomatic experience

---

[89] General Assembly, *Official Records: 26th Session, Supplement No. 29*
(A/8429), p. 18; adopted by acclamation.
[90] Document 133.
[91] USUN Press Release 228, Dec. 22, 1971; text from *Bulletin*, Feb. 7, 1972, pp.
178-79.

leavened with enough political experience to guarantee a deep concern for people, for all the people of this world.

We wish you Godspeed, Secretary-General-elect Waldheim. We pledge to you our support. To you as a friend and as an ex-colleague, to your wonderful family, our warmest congratulations. To you as Secretary General, our prayers will go with you. We have abiding confidence that you will do this job well.

D. New Dimensions of Diplomacy.

[The expanding scope of international relations in a technological age was one of the important themes in President Nixon's comprehensive report to Congress and the public on the foreign policy developments of 1971. The relevant chapter of the President's "State of the World" message, made public early in 1972, is reproduced in its entirety (Document 136) as a balanced and informative survey of the "new dimensions of diplomacy" that challenged the imagination as well as the skill of American policy-makers.

The status of the oceans, the control of drug abuse, aircraft hijacking and sabotage, population growth, protection of the environment, the peaceful uses of outer space, and disaster relief were among the varied topics that engaged the attention of the international community in 1971, producing, in each case, a mass of documentation at once too specialized and too voluminous for reproduction in a single annual volume.

Four documents in this area are nevertheless included in the present collection because of their special importance as landmarks in the evolution of an international approach to the solution of new global problems. The draft articles on the territorial sea, straits, and fisheries elaborated by the United States in preparation for the 1973 Conference on the Law of the Sea (Document 137) reflect important adjustments in the United States' historic position on one of the most controversial issues of contemporary international affairs. The Montreal Convention for the Suppression of Unlawful Acts Against the Safety of Civil Aircraft (Document 138) signaled a further step in the international effort to contain a growing threat to peaceful use of the world's airways. The Convention on International Liability for Damage Caused by Space Objects (Document 139) marked the completion of a protracted effort to fill a gap in the existing international law of outer space. Finally, the Agreement on Establishment of the International Telecommunications Satellite Organization "Intelsat" (Document 140) provided a definitive legal and organizational framework for the further development of an important new mode of international communication made possible by the evolution of space technology.]

(136) "New Dimensions of Diplomacy": President Nixon's Third Annual Report to the Congress on United States Foreign Policy, February 9, 1972. [92]

(Excerpt)

*   *   *

"Thus there has come into being a new dimension in the foreign policy of the United States, not as a matter of choice and deliberate action on our part, but as a reflection of the demanding realities of the world in which we live." [93]

> U.S. Foreign Policy for 1970's
> Report to the Congress
> February 25, 1971

The rise of modern science and the technological revolution it has brought in train have been monuments to the creativity of man and powerful catalysts to a betterment of the human condition. Yet man cannot escape the irony of history—solutions to old problems spawn new ones.

—In our time, man has mastered distance as it is measured on this planet. But modern transport and communications can lead to poisoned air, polluted water, the dissemination of corrupting and dangerous drugs, and air piracy for personal or political advantage.
—Man is rapidly developing the ability to exploit the new twin frontiers of the ocean and outer space. However, being rich in potential benefits, these frontiers are also potential sources of international dispute.
—Man is on the threshold of ending his vulnerability to pestilence and famine. But one of the results of this boon is a new specter of uncontrollable population growth.

We have no choice but to cope with the new problems of technological civilization. Individual governments must do what they can,

---

[92] Nixon Report, 1972, pp. 195-205; text from *Presidential Documents, 1972,* Feb. 14, 1972, pp. 396-406.
[93] Nixon Report, 1971, p. 208.

but in a world grown small, these issues must be recognized for what they are—problems of the human species to be addressed on a global scale.

This is one of the great challenges of our time. Human rationality enables us to see the need clearly, but it is sobering to reflect that in the past it has always been more effective when applied to nature than when directed to the intractable difficulties of getting man to cooperate with man.

I have in the past called on the international community to focus attention and energy on these problems.[94] I am happy to say that the response has, in general, been vigorous. The global challenge has been accepted and the new tasks for diplomacy are being addressed.

THE OCEANS

Future generations may well look back upon the 1970's as the decade in which the nations of the world made the fundamental decisions regulating the use of over two-thirds of our planet.

The task is urgent. Technological advances have made all nations increasingly aware of the new benefits which the ocean can yield. Competition among nations for control of the ocean's resources, and the growing divergence of national claims, could constitute serious threats to world peace.

The United States relies upon the seas to meet its global responsibilities. Our security, and that of our friends, depends upon freedom of navigation and overflight of the high seas, and on free movement through and over international straits. A significant portion of our strategic deterrent is seaborne. The trend to more extensive territorial sea claims by other nations thus threatens very directly our national security.

Shortly after taking office, this Administration began what is probably the most comprehensive review of U.S. oceans policy in our history. Several conclusions emerged.

First, multilateral agreement is essential. Nations have interests in the seas which differ widely and result in different national priorities. Unilateral claims to the sea or its resources force other nations to make a stark choice between confrontation and acquiescence in situations prejudicial to their interests.[95] Neither result contributes to stable world peace.

Second, freedom of navigation and overflight must be protected. Any significant diminution of such freedoms beyond a narrow territorial sea would fundamentally affect international security and trade. The basic

94 Same, pp. 207-24.
95 Cf. Document 112.

political decision, made centuries ago, that nations would not interfere with each other's rights to communicate by sea must be preserved. We need, however, to reconcile traditional uses of the seas with their new potential.

Third, an equitable system must be established for regulating the exploitation of the resources of the ocean and seabeds beyond national jurisdiction. The value of the resources ensures that exploitation will follow promptly the development of the necessary technology. Therefore, it is essential to set up a system under which the exploitation will contribute to, rather than endanger, peace among nations. No state should be permitted to treat these resources as an exclusive national property or to exploit them in a manner harmful to the interests of other states or the global environment. Moreover, the smaller and poorer nations of the world should be given a fair share of the benefits from these resources, which are the common heritage of mankind. While nations with long coastlines can acquire this share from resources solely off their own coasts, others with short coastlines or none at all must look to a reasonable international system if they are to receive a fair portion of the ocean's wealth. A system which permits a just allocation of ocean resources is, therefore, an important ingredient of a stable arrangement which all nations will support because all have a stake in its preservation.

Fourth, it is not possible for any nation, acting unilaterally, to ensure adequate protection of the marine environment. Unless there are firm minimum international standards, the search for relative economic advantage will preclude effective environmental protection.

These principles underlie the new U.S. oceans policy which I announced in May 1970[96] and the detailed proposals we have made to the world community since then.

Our initiatives have received a ready response. Following considerable discussion in the fall of 1970, the UN General Assembly called for a comprehensive international conference for 1973. A multination UN Seabed Committee was given the job of drafting, in the interim, the agreement required to assure the success of that conference.[97]

The U.S. has put forward four detailed proposals—on the seabeds, the breadth of the territorial sea, transit through straits, and living resources. The first of these proposals was given to the UN in August 1970 in the form of a draft United Nations convention on the international seabed area.[98] I described its essentials in last year's Report to the Congress.[99]

On August 3, 1971 we supplemented this initiative by putting for-

[96] *Documents, 1970*, pp. 331-33.
[97] Resolution 2750 (XXV), Dec. 17, 1970; cf. *Documents, 1970*, pp. 342-45.
[98] Same, pp. 334-41.
[99] Nixon Report, 1971, pp. 211-12.

ward proposals on the breadth of the territorial sea, on free transit through and over international straits, and on carefully defined preferential rights over fisheries.[100]

Breadth of Territorial Sea

The U.S. has adhered to a three-mile territorial sea for almost two centuries. The claims of other states vary widely, ranging to a maximum of 200 miles. There is a clear need for a uniform territorial sea and a general sentiment in the international community that it should be somewhat broader than three miles. We therefore proposed that the maximum breadth of the territorial sea be set at 12 miles.

Straits

Since many straits used for international navigation, however, are less than 24 miles wide, and thus would be completely overlapped by a 12-mile sea, the U.S. put forward, as a condition to our agreement to a 12-mile territorial sea, a provision for a new right of "free transit."

That provision is essential because the ambiguous doctrine of "innocent passage" would otherwise apply, and states bordering straits would be required to decide which ships and planes should, and which should not, pass. Domestic and international pressures could be brought to bear on every decision. The oceans are too vital a highway of communication, and guaranteed passage through straits is too essential to our security, to be subject to such uncertainty. At the same time, the U.S. recognizes that adjacent coastal states do have legitimate concerns about traffic safety regulations and pollution, and has indicated its willingness to accommodate these concerns in a manner not prejudicing the basic right of free transit.

Living Resources

The question of fisheries management and conservation is intimately associated with the world's food needs. Fish are a primary source of protein for nations with low nutritional levels, and they make the difference between starvation and survival for millions of human beings. Modern fishing methods and careless conservation practices have now made it painfully clear that international and regional cooperation is urgently needed to maintain the productivity of this valuable, self-replenishing resource. There is, however, an inherent conflict between the interests of those who fish off the coasts of other countries, and the coastal states themselves. The former seek to protect what they consider traditional rights. The latter seek recognition of their priority interest in the resources off their own coasts.

The U.S. proposal on fisheries offered a pragmatic solution based on

[100] Document 137.

sound conservation practices. Appropriate worldwide or regional fisheries organizations would be established to regulate the harvest of the living resources of the high seas. Coastal states would be recognized as having a priority interest based on their actual fishing capacity. Traditional fishing rights would be a matter of negotiation between the coastal and distant-water fishing states most concerned. All states would be eligible to fish for the remainder of the allowable catch. Special provisions would be made for highly migratory stocks and anadromous species, for enforcement procedures, and for compulsory dispute settlement.

In summary, the U.S. is deeply engaged in an international effort to write a new law of the sea. We have put forth comprehensive proposals designed to harmonize the multiple uses of the oceans. There is no inherent incompatibility between proper utilization of ocean resources and traditional freedoms of the sea. But territorial concepts such as absolute sovereignty cannot be applied either to seabed resources beyond the limits of national jurisdiction or to international navigation rights. Modified maritime doctrines and rules are needed to accommodate the diverse interests involved. The time has arrived for monumental decisions on the law of the sea, and the U.S. has acted forthrightly to meet the challenge.

CONTROL OF DRUG ABUSE

Narcotics addiction continues to spread at an alarming rate, in the United States and elsewhere. In my message to the Congress on June 17, 1971[101] I said that the problem had assumed the proportions of a national emergency, and I committed this Administration to the leadership of an intense international attack on the supply, demand, and illicit traffic in narcotics and other dangerous drugs.

In August, I established a Cabinet Committee on International Narcotics Control under the chairmanship of the Secretary of State.[102] This committee is charged with the formulation and coordination of all policies of the Federal Government relating to the goal of curtailing the flow of narcotics and other dangerous drugs into the United States.

Turkey has been the single most important source of the opium which is converted to heroin marketed in the U.S. Therefore, it was a signal achievement when, on June 30, 1971 the Prime Minister of Turkey [Nihat Erim] announced that Turkey will ban all production of opium after the 1972 crop is harvested. We must now be particularly vigilant against others stepping in to replace the illicit heroin supplies which formerly originated in the Turkish poppy fields.

Southeast Asia is another major source of illicit drugs, and during the

101 *Public Papers, 1971*, pp. 739-49.
102 Same, pp. 937-38.

past year important steps were taken to tighten controls in that area. In September, the United States agreed to support Thailand's efforts to suppress the supply and trafficking in illicit narcotics and dangerous drugs. In November, the Government of Laos put into effect a tough new narcotics law banning the manufacture, trading, and transportation of opium and its derivatives, including heroin. Subsequently Laos placed strict controls on the importation and distribution of acetic anhydride, a key ingredient in the production of heroin. In addition, President [Nguyen Van] Thieu has sent an anti-narcotics law to the Vietnamese National Assembly. During November the Government of Australia sponsored a meeting of regional narcotics officials to discuss and develop regional approaches to the drug problem in Asia.

These actions will contribute positively to combating the drug problem in Southeast Asia, and, in particular, to reducing the flow of heroin to American servicemen in the area.

On February 26, 1971 the Attorney General [John N. Mitchell] and the French Minister of the Interior [Raymond Marcellin] signed an agreement for the detailed coordination of our two governments' attack on the illicit drug traffic. The primary objective of this joint effort is the discovery and destruction of heroin conversion laboratories in southern France, and the interception of the illicit heroin traffic from France to North America. The Canadian authorities have also joined in this endeavor. Seizures and destruction of illegal narcotics shipments in the France-North America channel increased during the past year in the wake of this combined effort.

The Governments of the United States and Mexico have been cooperating closely in narcotics control since 1969. That effort has resulted in the seizure by Mexican authorities of hundreds of pounds of crude opium, heroin, and cocaine and the destruction of over 12,000 fields of marijuana and opium poppy. Mexican officials have also intercepted large quantities of psychotropic substances intended for illegal sale in the United States.

At United States initiative, a United Nations Fund for Drug Abuse Control was established in March to finance a concerted worldwide action program.[103] We made the initial pledge to the fund of $2 million,[104] which has been augmented by pledges from several other countries including substantial amounts from Canada, Germany, and France. We are encouraging more countries to contribute, and we will seek additional U.S. contributions from the Congress when required. The fund will assist UN members to reduce both the illegal demand for and supply of dangerous drugs.

In March 1971, we also proposed amendments to increase the effec-

---

[103] The U.N. Fund for Drug Abuse Control was formally established Apr. 1, 1971 (*Yearbook of the United Nations, 1971*, p. 382).
[104] *Bulletin*, May 3, 1971, pp. 574-75.

tiveness of the 1961 Single Convention on Narcotic Drugs.[105] Under the Convention's present terms, parties are committed to restrict the production, manufacture, export and import of narcotic drugs so that they will be used exclusively for legitimate medical and scientific purposes. Compliance with these undertakings, however, is essentially voluntary. Our amendments[106] are designed to tighten compliance, and we are conducting extensive diplomatic consultations throughout the world to support this objective. An international conference will be held in Geneva in March 1972 to consider these and other proposals to amend the Convention.[107]

Cooperation in control of dangerous drugs works both ways. While the sources of our chief narcotics problem are foreign, the United States is a source of illegal psychotropic drugs—such as LSD and other hallucinogens, the amphetamines, barbiturates, and tranquilizers—which afflict other nations. If we expect other governments to help stop the flow of heroin to our shores, we must act with equal vigor to prevent equally dangerous substances from going into their nations from our own. Accordingly, following the signature last year by the United States and 22 other nations in Vienna of a Convention on Psychotropic Substances,[108] I sent it to the Senate for its early advice and consent to ratification.[109] This is the first international agreement to combat the abuse of psychotropic substances. It will bring these drugs under rigorous controls similar to those envisaged for narcotic drugs under a strengthened Single Convention.

In summary, during the past year our Government has made an intense effort to widen and strengthen controls over narcotic and other dangerous drugs, both domestically and internationally. It is gratifying to report that these efforts are enlisting increasing international support.

AIRCRAFT HIJACKING AND SABOTAGE

The growth of air transportation has brought the people of the world

[105] Done at New York Mar. 30, 1961, and entered into force for the U.S. June 24, 1967 (TIAS 6298; 18 UST 1407).
[106] U.N. documents E/4971 and Add. 1, Mar. 18, 1971, and E/4985, Mar. 26, 1971.
[107] The U.N. Conference to Consider Amendments to the 1961 Single Convention on Narcotic Drugs, held at Geneva on Mar. 6-24, 1972, adopted a Protocol Amending the Single Convention on Narcotic Drugs. Opened for signature Mar. 25, 1972, the protocol was ratified by the United States Oct. 24, 1972, and entered into force Aug. 8, 1975. For details see *UN Monthly Chronicle*, Apr. 1972, pp. 52-53, and *Bulletin*, Apr. 17, 1972, pp. 569-70.
[108] Signed in Vienna Feb. 21, 1971, but not yet in force as of the fall of 1975; details in *Bulletin*, Aug. 2, 1971, pp. 141-42.
[109] Transmitted June 29, 1971 (*Public Papers, 1971*, p. 784). A public hearing on the convention was held by the Senate Foreign Relations Committee on Feb. 4. 1972, but no further action was taken during that year.

in closer contact with each other. Perhaps it was inevitable that some would find the means of preying upon this bounty. If so, it is equally inevitable that the world must protect itself against air hijacking and sabotage. It is doing so.

The aircraft hijacking convention, negotiated in The Hague in December 1970,[110] requires contracting states to extradite or prosecute hijackers apprehended on their territory. More than 80 states have signed the convention thus far. In September a companion convention was concluded at Montreal on suppression of other unlawful acts against civil aviation, notably sabotage.[111] This agreement, too, provides for the prosecution or extradition of offenders.

These two conventions will increase the likelihood that hijackers, saboteurs, and persons committing other attacks against civil aircraft will be punished—regardless of the motive, where the act took place, or where the criminal is found. Universal ratification would ensure that air pirates could find no place to hide.

We intend to press for wide adherence to these agreements and for continued international cooperation, including exchanges of information on security measures. We will also continue to urge international agreement to suspend air services to countries which refuse to cooperate in the release of hijacked aircraft and in the punishment of hijackers.

POPULATION GROWTH

The worldwide population growth rate is still explosive. It implies vastly larger numbers of people in each future decade—numbers far beyond the capacities of most countries to educate, employ, house decently, or even feed adequately. This is a problem of the greatest urgency. The international community must give priority to the task of preventing these potential tragedies from becoming realities.

Last year, we continued to encourage and support United Nations leadership in this field. We pledged to match the contributions of other countries to the United Nations Fund for Population Activities,[112] which has grown with a speed which demonstrates that the world community realizes the exigent nature of the problem. In only its second year of existence, the fund was able to provide $31.6 million to the population control activities of UN agencies and 58 countries. At the same time, our Agency for International Development contributed

110 Convention for the Suppression of Unlawful Seizure of Aircraft, done at The Hague Dec. 16, 1970, and entered into force Oct. 14, 1971 (TIAS 7192; 22 UST 1641); text in *Documents, 1970*, pp. 350-55. Following approval by the Senate on Sept. 8, 1971, the convention entered into force with the deposit of the U.S. instrument of ratification on Oct. 14, 1971; for details see *Bulletin*, Oct. 4, 1971, p. 371.
111 Document 130.
112 *Bulletin*, Mar. 1, 1971, p. 259.

funds, training and technical support to the population control programs of 33 countries. AID also provided support for several lines of research which hold considerable promise for greatly improved means of fertility control.

PROTECTION OF THE ENVIRONMENT

The earth's resources of air and water are not—as we used to think— unlimited. There is a common requirement of mankind for fresh air, clean water, and uncontaminated soil. This interest is threatened, and the international community must respond to the challenge. Discussions were held in a variety of forums last year, and we should expect soon to see results beginning to emerge.

Preparations are well underway for the UN Conference on the Human Environment to be held in Stockholm this June. We expect the Conference to encourage global monitoring of the oceans, the atmosphere, and the ecological systems. The Conference will also focus attention on such immediate practical problems as managing urban areas, providing potable water, and disposing of solid waste.

As a contribution toward specific accomplishment, the United States has introduced a draft convention on ocean dumping and is participating in the development of a World Heritage Trust Convention, both for possible completion at Stockholm. We hope the Stockholm Conference will also bring greater support for an international agreement to protect endangered species.[113]

Cooperation on the pressing problems of modern society has become an important third dimension of the Atlantic Alliance. NATO's Committee on the Challenges of Modern Society (CCMS), established at our

---

[113] The U.N. Conference on the Human Environment was held in Stockholm on June 5-16, 1972, and, among other actions, endorsed completion of a convention on ocean dumping and proposals for a world heritage trust convention and an endangered species convention (*Bulletin*, Sept. 18, 1972, pp. 313-14; additional documentation in same, July 24, 1972, pp. 105-18, and in *A.F.R., 1972*, nos. 83-85).

A Convention on the Prevention of Marine Pollution by Dumping Wastes and Other Matter ("Ocean Dumping Convention") was opened for signature in London, Mexico City, and Moscow on Dec. 29, 1972; U.S. instruments of ratification were deposited Apr. 29 and May 6, 1974 (details in *Bulletin*, Jan. 22, 1973, pp. 95-96; same, Mar. 26, 1973, p. 369; same, May 20, 1974, pp. 567-68).

A Convention Concerning the Protection of the World Cultural and Natural Heritage was concluded at Paris on Nov. 23, 1972; the U.S. ratification was deposited Dec. 7, 1973 (details in *Bulletin*, May 14, 1973, pp. 629-31).

A Convention on International Trade in Endangered Species of Wild Fauna and Flora was signed in Washington on Mar. 3, 1973; the U.S. ratification was deposited Jan. 14, 1974 (details in *Bulletin*, May 14, 1973, pp. 608-29).

The Ocean Dumping Convention entered into force Sept. 27, 1975, and the Endangered Species Convention July 1, 1975.

suggestion in 1969,[114] continues to develop new initiatives in such fields as advanced health care services, waste treatment, and urban problems. As a result of a CCMS road safety project, all major automobile producing countries are now developing experimental safety vehicles designed to reduce auto injury rates worldwide. Agreement has been reached on a systems approach to air pollution problems, including jointly developed air quality criteria based on health factors, and the CCMS initiative to eliminate oil spills has stimulated broader international attention to that problem.

An Environmental Committee of the Organization of Economic Cooperation and Development was established in 1970.[115] The United States has taken the lead in seeking guidelines that would avoid trade problems that could result from national measures to abate pollution. The Committee has also arranged for systematic consultation on government action to control the use of chemicals, including pesticides, and is now considering general guidelines for government policies in this field.

The Economic Commission for Europe held a symposium on the environment in Prague last May, and took steps to promote East-West cooperation to deal with common environmental problems.

Significant progress was made last year to combat the oil pollution of the world's oceans and shorelines. In October, the major maritime nations adopted regulations on the size of tanks in oil tankers, which will reduce the spillage of oil as a result of accidents. We are negotiating actively on a new convention to ban all intentional discharges from vessels. And we have successfully concluded two conventions which will provide rapid and certain compensation, on a strict liability basis, to victims damaged by oil spills.[116]

In addition to these multilateral efforts, the U.S. has broadened bilateral discussions with our immediate neighbors, Canada and Mexico, and with Japan, Argentina, Italy, and others, to solve certain basic environmental problems of particular concern to us.[117]

We are, therefore, rapidly overcoming the initial lack of recognition of the need for international cooperation to protect the environment. However, the world community now faces a more difficult problem, that of determining how the cost of remedial action is to be assigned. We believe that a keystone in the effort to develop compatible national approaches should be the principle that the polluter pays for the economic costs of environmental control. It is the objective of this Administration that the costs of pollution control be allocated in a uniform

114 Cf. *Documents, 1968-69*, pp. 167-68.
115 Cf. same, *1970*, p. 413.
116 Cf. Rogers Report, 1971, pp. 223-24.
117 Cf. same, 222-23.

manner among different countries. Otherwise, international trade patterns would be distorted, and we do not think economic disadvantages should accrue to nations because of efforts made in a common cause.

OUTER SPACE

As our astronauts have seen, the unity of the Earth is experienced most vividly from outer space. And conversely, seen from our planet, space itself is a frontier to mankind as a whole, not merely to individual nations. Space is, therefore, an unparalleled field for cooperation among nations.

As we move into the second decade of space exploration, the U.S. is committed to work with others in space for the benefit of all mankind. We are taking whatever steps can reasonably and properly be taken to work with other countries in the development of their space skills.

Specifically, we have assured the European Space Conference that its member countries may obtain our assistance in launching satellites which are for peaceful purposes[118] and which are consistent with international obligations embodied in such agreements as the Outer Space Treaty[119] and the arrangements for the International Telecommunication Satellite Consortium (INTELSAT).[120] We are prepared to consider such assistance to other interested countries. In addition, we are working closely with the Europeans on the concepts and design of a reusable space transportation system.

Over the past year, NASA [National Aeronautics and Space Administration] has agreed with the Soviet Academy of Sciences to significant cooperation in specific space tasks, and in the exchange of information and plans concerning our respective space programs.[121] We have exchanged samples of lunar soil. We are examining together the means to enable Soviet manned spacecraft and our own to rendezvous and dock in space. Joint expert groups have been meeting to arrange details of further collaboration in space meteorology, biology, and medicine, in the study of the natural environment, and in exploration of the moon and planets.

In 1971, after years of negotiation in which the United States has played a leading role, the United Nations General Assembly approved an Outer Space Liability Convention.[122] The Convention, when it enters into force, will provide for the payment of compensation for damage caused by space activities.

Last year also brought a new definitive charter for the operation of INTELSAT.[123] When ratified and signed by two-thirds of the 80 mem-

---

[118] Cf. *Bulletin*, Nov. 29, 1971, pp. 624-27.
[119] *Documents, 1966*, pp. 391-98; cf. note 39 to Chapter II.
[120] Document 140.
[121] Cf. note 12 to Chapter II.
[122] Document 139.
[123] Cf. Document 140.

ber countries, sometime this year, this will replace the interim arrangements under which INTELSAT has been operating since 1964.

DISASTER RELIEF

Each year, the sudden, savage violence of natural and man-made disasters strikes at millions of our fellowmen. Despite the certainty that disasters will continue to occur, the world community has been very slow in establishing a central mechanism to plan for and coordinate disaster relief.

We have encouraged the United Nations to meet this need. Last year, the General Assembly voted to create a coordinator for disaster relief.[124] He will have a small staff—rapidly expandable in emergencies—to undertake his vital task. I applaud this development.

Even before it accepted the new role of coordinating disaster relief, the UN last year showed its ability to mount a very impressive large-scale relief effort to assist the refugees and to avert famine during the crisis in South Asia. The job was effectively done—although interrupted by the India-Pakistan war—and our Government supported it with large financial contributions.[125]

These, then, are beginnings the international community has made in addressing the new tasks for diplomacy. Our country is in the forefront of these efforts, and we will continue to be. But these are world challenges, and nothing less than a global response can suffice. Thus far, the response is heartening.

(137) Draft Articles on the Territorial Sea, Straits, and Fisheries, Submitted by the United States to Subcommittee II of the United Nations Committee on the Peaceful Uses of the Sea-bed and the Ocean Floor Beyond the Limits of National Jurisdiction, Geneva, August 3, 1971.[126]

(Complete Text)

ARTICLE I

1. Each State shall have the right, subject to the provisions of Article II, to establish the breadth of its territorial sea within limits of no more

---

[124] Resolution 2816 (XXVI), Dec. 14, 1971; adopted by a vote of 86-0-10.
[125] Cf. above at note 60.
[126] U.N. document A/AC.138/SC.II/L.4, Aug. 3, 1971; text from *Bulletin*, Sept. 6, 1971, pp. 266-68. For an explanatory statement by John R. Stevenson, Legal Adviser of the Department of State, see same, pp. 261-66; a briefer comment by President Nixon appears above at note 100.

than 12 nautical miles, measured in accordance with the provisions of the 1958 Geneva Convention on the Territorial Sea and Contiguous Zone.[127]

2. In instances where the breadth of the territorial sea of a State is less than 12 nautical miles, such State may establish a fisheries zone contiguous to its territorial sea provided, however, that the total breadth of the territorial sea and fisheries zone shall not exceed 12 nautical miles. Such State may exercise within such a zone the same rights in respect to fisheries as it has in its territorial sea.

ARTICLE II

1. In straits used for international navigation between one part of the high seas and another part of the high seas or the territorial sea of a foreign State, all ships and aircraft in transit shall enjoy the same freedom of navigation and overflight, for the purpose of transit through and over such straits, as they have on the high seas. Coastal States may designate corridors suitable for transit by all ships and aircraft through and over such straits. In the case of straits where particular channels of navigation are customarily employed by ships in transit, the corridors, so far as ships are concerned, shall include such channels.

2. The provisions of this Article shall not affect conventions or other international agreements already in force specifically relating to particular straits.

ARTICLE III

1. The fisheries and other living resources of the high seas shall be regulated by appropriate international (including regional) fisheries organizations established or to be established for this purpose in which the coastal State and any other State whose nationals or vessels exploit or desire to exploit a regulated species have an equal right to participate without discrimination. No State Party whose nationals or vessels exploit a regulated species may refuse to cooperate with such organizations. Regulations of such organizations pursuant to the principles set forth in paragraph 2 of this Article shall apply to all vessels fishing the regulated species regardless of their nationality.

2. In order to assure the conservation and equitable allocation of the fisheries and other living resources of the high seas, the following principles shall be applied by the organizations referred to in paragraph 1:

A. Conservation measures shall be adopted that do not discriminate in form or in fact against any fishermen. For this purpose, the allowable

[127] Done at Geneva Apr. 29, 1958, and entered into force for the U.S. Sept. 10, 1964 (TIAS 5639; 15 UST 1606).

catch shall be determined on the basis of the best evidence available, at a level which is designed to maintain the maximum sustainable yield or restore it as soon as practicable, taking into account relevant environmental and economic factors.

B. Scientific information, catch and effort statistics, and other relevant data shall be contributed and exchanged on a regular basis.

C. The percentage of the allowable catch of a stock in any area of the high seas adjacent to a coastal State that can be harvested by that State shall be allocated annually to it. The provisions of this sub-paragraph shall not apply to a highly migratory oceanic stock identified in Appendix A.[128]

D. The percentage of the allowable catch of an anadromous stock that can be harvested by the State in whose fresh waters it spawns shall be allocated annually to that State.

E. With respect to sub-paragraphs C and D above:

(1) [The percentage of the allowable catch of a stock traditionally taken by the fishermen of other States shall not be allocated to the coastal State. This provision does not apply to any new fishing or expansion of existing fishing by other States that occurs after this Convention enters into force for the coastal State.] [129]

(2) The allocation to the coastal State shall not be implemented in a manner that discriminates in form or in fact between the fishermen of other States.

(3) When more than one coastal State qualifies for an allocation of a percentage of a stock, the total amount which may be allocated shall be equitably divided in accordance with principles of this Article.

F. All States including the coastal State may fish on the high seas for that percentage of the allowable catch not allocated in accordance with this Article.

3. The provisions of paragraph 1 shall not apply in the event that States directly concerned, including the coastal State, are unable or deem it unnecessary to establish an international or regional organization in accordance with that paragraph for the time being. In that event:

A. In the case of a highly migratory oceanic stock identified in Appendix A, such stock shall be regulated pursuant to agreement or consultation among the States concerned with the conservation and harvesting of the stock.

---

[128] Appendix A is not attached. [Footnote in original.]
[129] It is the view of the U.S. Government that an appropriate text with respect to traditional fishing should be negotiated between coastal and distant water fishing states. [Footnote in original.]

B. In the case of any other stock, a coastal State may implement the principles of paragraph 2 provided:

(1) The coastal State has submitted to all affected States its proposal for the establishment pursuant to paragraph 1 of an international or regional fisheries organization applying the principles of paragraph 2;

(2) Negotiations with other States affected have failed to produce, within four months, agreement on measures to be taken either with respect to the establishment of an organization or with respect to the fisheries problems involved;

(3) The coastal State has submitted to all affected States the available data supporting its measures and the reasons for its actions.

The implementing regulations of the coastal State may apply in any area of the high seas adjacent to its coast or, with respect to an anadromous stock that spawns in its fresh waters, throughout its migratory range.

4. Enforcement of the fisheries regulations adopted pursuant to this Article shall be effected as follows:

A. Each State Party shall make it an offense for its nationals and vessels to violate the fishery regulations adopted pursuant to this Article.

B. Officials of the appropriate fisheries organization, or of any State so authorized by the organization, may enforce the fishery regulations adopted pursuant to this Article with respect to any vessel fishing a regulated stock. In the event an organization has not been established in accordance with this Article, properly authorized officials of the coastal State may so enforce these regulations. Actions under this subparagraph shall be limited to inspection and arrest of vessels and shall be taken in such a way as to minimize interference with fishing activities and other activities in the marine environment.

C. An arrested vessel shall be delivered promptly to the duly authorized officials of the State of nationality. Only the State of nationality of the offending vessel shall have jurisdiction to try any case or impose any penalties regarding the violation of fishery regulations adopted pursuant to this Article. Such State has the responsibility of notifying the enforcing organization or State within a period of six months of the disposition of the case.

5. The international or regional fisheries organizations referred to in this Article shall, *inter alia*, promote:

A. Cooperation with the United Nations, its specialized agencies and other international organizations concerned with the marine environment;

B. Scientific research regarding fisheries and other living resources of the high seas;

C. Development of coastal and distant water fishing industries in developing countries.

6. Exploitation of the living resources of the high seas shall be conducted with reasonable regard for other activities in the marine environment.

7. Any dispute which may arise between States under this Article shall, at the request of any of the parties, be submitted to a special commission of five members, unless the parties agree to seek a solution by another method of peaceful settlement, as provided for in Article 33 of the Charter of the United Nations. The commission shall proceed in accordance with the following provisions:

A. The members of the commission, one of whom shall be designated as chairman, shall be named by agreement between the States in dispute within two months of the request for settlement in accordance with the provisions of this Article. Failing agreement they shall, upon the request of any State Party, be named by the Secretary-General of the United Nations, within a further two month period, in consultation with the States in dispute and with the President of the International Court of Justice and the Director-General of the Food and Agriculture Organization of the United Nations, from amongst well-qualified persons being nationals of States not involved in the dispute and specializing in legal, administrative or scientific questions relating to fisheries, depending upon the nature of the dispute to be settled. Any vacancy arising after the original appointment shall be filled in the same manner as provided for the initial selection.

B. Any State Party to proceedings under these Articles shall have the right to name one of its nationals to sit with the special commission, with the right to participate fully in the proceedings on the same footing as a member of the commission but without the right to vote or to take part in the writing of the commission's decision.

C. The commission shall determine its own procedure, assuring each party to the proceedings a full opportunity to be heard and to present its case. It shall also determine how the costs and expenses shall be divided between the parties to the dispute, failing agreement by the parties on this matter.

D. The special commission may decide that pending its award, the measures in dispute shall not be applied.

E. The special commission shall render its decision, which shall be binding upon the parties, within a period of five months from the time it is appointed unless it decides, in case of necessity, to extend the time limit for a period not exceeding two months.

F. The special commission shall, in reaching its decisions, adhere to this Article and to any agreements between the disputing parties implementing this Article.

G. Decisions of the commission shall be by majority vote.

8. The provisions of this Article shall not affect conventions or other international agreements already in force specifically relating to particular fisheries.

(138) Convention for the Suppression of Unlawful Acts Against the Safety of Civil Aircraft, Done at Montreal September 23, 1971.[130]

(Complete Text)

The States Parties to this convention

CONSIDERING that unlawful acts against the safety of civil aviation jeopardize the safety of persons and property, seriously affect the operation of air services, and undermine the confidence of the peoples of the world in the safety of civil aviation;

CONSIDERING that the occurrence of such acts is a matter of grave concern;

CONSIDERING that, for the purpose of deterring-such acts, there is an urgent need to provide appropriate measures for punishment of offenders;

Have agreed as follows:

ARTICLE 1

1. Any person commits an offence if he unlawfully and intentionally:

   (a) performs an act of violence against a person on board an aircraft in flight if that act is likely to endanger the safety of that aircraft; or

   (b) destroys an aircraft in service or causes damage to such an aircraft which renders it incapable of flight or which is likely to endanger its safety in flight; or

   (c) places or causes to be placed on an aircraft in service, by any

---

[130] TIAS 7570; 24 UST 564. Adopted by a Conference on International Air Law which met at Montreal on Sept. 8-23, 1971, under the auspices of the International Civil Aviation Organization (ICAO), the so-called "sabotage convention" was transmitted to the U.S. Senate Sept. 15, 1972 (*Public Papers, 1972*, p. 870), approved by that body Oct. 3, 1972, and ratified by the President Nov. 1, 1972, on which date the U.S. ratification was deposited in Washington. The convention entered into force for the U.S. Jan. 26, 1973.

means whatsoever, a device or substance which is likely to destroy that aircraft, or to cause damage to it which renders it incapable of flight, or to cause damage to it which is likely to endanger its safety in flight; or

(d) destroys or damages air navigation facilities or interferes with their operation, if any such act is likely to endanger the safety of aircraft in flight; or

(e) communicates information which he knows to be false, thereby endangering the safety of an aircraft in flight.

2. Any person also commits an offence if he:

(a) attempts to commit any of the offences mentioned in paragraph 1 of this Article; or

(b) is an accomplice of a person who commits or attempts to commit any such offence.

ARTICLE 2

For the purposes of this Convention:

(a) an aircraft is considered to be in flight at any time from the moment when all its external doors are closed following embarkation until the moment when any such door is opened for disembarkation; in the case of a forced landing, the flight shall be deemed to continue until the competent authorities take over the responsibility for the aircraft and for persons and property on board;

(b) an aircraft is considered to be in service from the beginning of the preflight preparation of the aircraft by ground personnel or by the crew for a specific flight until twenty-four hours after any landing; the period of service shall, in any event, extend for the entire period during which the aircraft is in flight as defined in paragraph (a) of this Article.

ARTICLE 3

Each Contracting State undertakes to make the offences mentioned in Article 1 punishable by severe penalties.

ARTICLE 4

1. This Convention shall not apply to aircraft used in military, customs or police services.

2. In the cases contemplated in subparagraphs (a), (b), (c) and (e) of paragraph 1 of Article 1, this Convention shall apply, irrespective of whether the aircraft is engaged in an international or domestic flight, only if:

(a) the place of take-off or landing, actual or intended, of the aircraft is situated outside the territory of the State of registration of that aircraft; or
(b) the offence is committed in the territory of a State other than the State of registration of the aircraft.

3. Notwithstanding paragraph 2 of this Article, in the cases contemplated in subparagraphs (a), (b), (c) and (e) of paragraph 1 of Article 1, this Convention shall also apply if the offender or the alleged offender is found in the territory of a State other than the State of registration of the aircraft.

4. With respect to the States mentioned in Article 9 and in the cases mentioned in subparagraphs (a), (b), (c) and (e) of paragraph 1 of Article 1, this Convention shall not apply if the places referred to in subparagraph (a) of paragraph 2 of this Article are situated within the territory of the same State where that State is one of those referred to in Article 9, unless the offence is committed or the offender or alleged offender is found in the territory of a State other than that State.

5. In the cases contemplated in subparagraph (d) of paragraph 1 of Article 1, this Convention shall apply only if the air navigation facilities are used in international air navigation.

6. The provisions of paragraphs 2, 3, 4 and 5 of this Article shall also apply in the cases contemplated in paragraph 2 of Article 1.

ARTICLE 5

1. Each Contracting State shall take such measures as may be necessary to establish its jurisdiction over the offences in the following cases:

(a) when the offence is committed in the territory of that State;
(b) when the offence is committed against or on board an aircraft registered in that State;
(c) when the aircraft on board which the offence is committed lands in its territory with the alleged offender still on board;
(d) when the offence is committed against or on board an aircraft leased without crew to a lessee who has his principal place of business or, if the lessee has no such place of business, his permanent residence, in that State.

2. Each Contracting State shall likewise take such measures as may be necessary to establish its jurisdiction over the offences mentioned in Article 1, paragraph 1 (a), (b) and (c), and in Article 1, paragraph 2, in so far as that paragraph relates to those offences, in the case where the alleged offender is present in its territory and it does not extradite him pursuant to Article 8 to any of the States mentioned in paragraph 1 of this Article.

3. This Convention does not exclude any criminal jurisdiction exercised in accordance with national law.

ARTICLE 6

1. Upon being satisfied that the circumstances so warrant, any Contracting State in the territory of which the offender or the alleged offender is present, shall take him into custody or take other measures to ensure his presence. The custody and other measures shall be as provided in the law of that State but may only be continued for such time as is necessary to enable any criminal or extradition proceedings to be instituted.

2. Such State shall immediately make a preliminary enquiry into the facts.

3. Any person in custody pursuant to paragraph 1 of this Article shall be assisted in communicating immediately with the nearest appropriate representative of the State of which he is a national.

4. When a State, pursuant to this Article, has taken a person into custody, it shall immediately notify the States mentioned in Article 5, paragraph 1, the State of nationality of the detained person and, if it considers it advisable, any other interested States of the fact that such person is in custody and of the circumstances which warrant his detention. The State which makes the preliminary enquiry contemplated in paragraph 2 of this Article shall promptly report its findings to the said States and shall indicate whether it intends to exercise jurisdiction.

ARTICLE 7

The Contracting State in the territory of which the alleged offender is found shall, if it does not extradite him, be obliged, without exception whatsoever and whether or not the offence was committed in its territory, to submit the case to its competent authorities for the purpose of prosecution. Those authorities shall take their decision in the same manner as in the case of any ordinary offence of a serious nature under the law of that State.

ARTICLE 8

1. The offences shall be deemed to be included as extraditable offences in any extradition treaty existing between Contracting States. Contracting States undertake to include the offences as extraditable offences in every extradition treaty to be concluded between them.

2. If a Contracting State which makes extradition conditional on the existence of a treaty receives a request for extradition from another Contracting State with which it has no extradition treaty, it may at its option consider this Convention as the legal basis for extradition in respect of the offences. Extradition shall be subject to the other conditions provided by the law of the requested State.

3. Contracting States which do not make extradition conditional on the existence of a treaty shall recognize the offences as extraditable offences between themselves subject to the conditions provided by the law of the requested State.

4. Each of the offences shall be treated, for the purpose of extradition between Contracting States, as if it had been committed not only in the place in which it occurred but also in the territories of the States required to establish their jurisdiction in accordance with Article 5, paragraph 1 (b), (c) and (d).

ARTICLE 9

The Contracting States which establish joint air transport operating organizations or international operating agencies, which operate aircraft which are subject to joint or international registration shall, by appropriate means, designate for each aircraft the State among them which shall exercise the jurisdiction and have the attributes of the State of registration for the purpose of this Convention and shall give notice thereof to the International Civil Aviation Organization which shall communicate the notice to all States Parties to this Convention.

ARTICLE 10

1. Contracting States shall, in accordance with international and national law, endeavor to take all practicable measures for the purpose of preventing the offences mentioned in Article 1.

2. When, due to the commission of one of the offences mentioned in Article 1, a flight has been delayed or interrupted, any Contracting State in whose territory the aircraft or passengers or crew are present shall facilitate the continuation of the journey of the passengers and crew as soon as practicable, and shall without delay return the aircraft

and its cargo to the persons lawfully entitled to possession.

ARTICLE 11

1. Contracting States shall afford one another the greatest measure of assistance in connection with criminal proceedings brought in respect of the offences. The law of the State requested shall apply in all cases.
2. The provisions of paragraph 1 of this Article shall not affect obligations under any other treaty, bilateral or multilateral, which governs or will govern, in whole or in part, mutual assistance in criminal matters.

ARTICLE 12

Any Contracting State having reason to believe that one of the offences mentioned in Article 1 will be committed shall, in accordance with its national law, furnish any relevant information in its possession to those States which it believes would be the States mentioned in Article 5, paragraph 1.

ARTICLE 13

Each Contracting State shall in accordance with its national law report to the Council of the International Civil Aviation Organization as promptly as possible any relevant information in its possession concerning:

(a) the circumstances of the offence;
(b) the action taken pursuant to Article 10, paragraph 2;
(c) the measures taken in relation to the offender or the alleged offender and, in particular, the results of any extradition proceedings or other legal proceedings.

ARTICLE 14

1. Any dispute between two or more Contracting States concerning the interpretation or application of this Convention which cannot be settled through negotiation, shall, at the request of one of them, be submitted to arbitration. If within six months from the date of the request for arbitration the Parties are unable to agree on the organization of the arbitration, any one of those Parties may refer the dispute to the International Court of Justice by request in conformity with the Statute of the Court.
2. Each State may at the time of signature or ratification of this Con-

vention or accession thereto, declare that it does not consider itself bound by the preceding paragraph. The other Contracting States shall not be bound by the preceding paragraph with respect to any Contracting State having made such a reservation.

3. Any Contracting State having made a reservation in accordance with the preceding paragraph may at any time withdraw this reservation by notification to the Depositary Governments.

ARTICLE 15

1. This Convention shall be open for signature at Montreal on 23 September 1971, by States participating in the International Conference on Air Law held at Montreal from 8 to 23 September 1971 (hereinafter referred to as the Montreal Conference). After 10 October 1971, the Convention shall be open to all States for signature in Moscow, London and Washington. Any State which does not sign this Convention before its entry into force in accordance with paragraph 3 of this Article may accede to it at any time.

2. This Convention shall be subject to ratification by the signatory States. Instruments of ratification and instruments of accession shall be deposited with the Governments of the Union of Soviet Socialist Republics, the United Kingdom of Great Britain and Northern Ireland, and the United States of America, which are hereby designated the Depositary Governments.

3. This Convention shall enter into force thirty days following the date of the deposit of instruments of ratification by ten States signatory to this Convention which participated in the Montreal Conference.

4. For other States, this Convention shall enter into force on the date of entry into force of this Convention in accordance with paragraph 3 of this Article, or thirty days following the date of deposit of their instruments of ratification or accession, whichever is later.

5. The Depositary Governments shall promptly inform all signatory and acceding States of the date of each signature, the date of deposit of each instrument of ratification or accession, the date of entry into force of this Convention, and other notices.

6. As soon as this Convention comes into force, it shall be registered by the Depositary Governments pursuant to Article 102 of the Charter of the United Nations and pursuant to Article 83 of the Convention on International Civil Aviation (Chicago, 1944).[131]

ARTICLE 16

1. Any Contracting State may denounce this Convention by written notification to the Depositary Governments.

[131] TIAS 1591; *Documents, 1944-45*, p. 604.

2. Denunciation shall take effect six months following the date on which notification is received by the Depositary Governments.

IN WITNESS WHEREOF the undersigned Plenipotentiaries, being duly authorized thereto by their Governments, have signed this Convention.

DONE at Montreal, this twenty-third day of September, one thousand nine hundred and seventy-one, in three originals, each being drawn up in four authentic texts in the English, French, Russian and Spanish languages.

(139) *Convention on International Liability for Damage Caused by Space Objects, Approved by the United Nations General Assembly November 29, 1971.* [132]

(Complete Text)

The States Parties to this Convention,

Recognizing the common interest of all mankind in furthering the exploration and use of outer space for peaceful purposes,

Recalling the Treaty on Principles Governing the Activities of States in the Exploration and Use of Outer Space, including the Moon and Other Celestial Bodies,[133]

Taking into consideration that, notwithstanding the precautionary measures to be taken by States and international intergovernmental organizations involved in the launching of space objects, damage may on occasion be caused by such objects,

Recognizing the need to elaborate effective international rules and procedures concerning liability for damage caused by space objects and to ensure, in particular, the prompt payment under the terms of this Convention of a full and equitable measure of compensation to victims of such damage,

---

[132] TIAS 7762 (24 UST 2839). Negotiated at length in the Committee on the Peaceful Uses of Outer Space, the finished text of the "Space Liability Convention" was commended to prospective signatory and ratifying states by the U.N. General Assembly in Resolution 2777 (XXVI), adopted Nov. 29, 1971, by a vote of 93 (U.S.)-0-4 (Canada, Iran, Japan, and Sweden). The convention was subsequently opened for signature at Washington, London, and Moscow on Mar. 29, 1972, and entered into force Sept. 1, 1972, for those governments that had deposited instruments of ratification. In the case of the United States, the convention was submitted to the Senate on June 15, 1972, approved by that body Oct. 6, 1972, ratified by the President May 18, 1973, and entered into force with deposit of the U.S. instruments of ratification on Oct. 9, 1973.
[133] Same as note 119.

Believing that the establishment of such rules and procedures will contribute to the strengthening of international cooperation in the field of the exploration and use of outer space for peaceful purposes,

Have agreed on the following:

ARTICLE I

For the purposes of this Convention:

(a) The term "damage" means loss of life, personal injury or other impairment of health; or loss of or damage to property of States or of persons, natural or juridical, or property of international inter-governmental organizations;

(b) The term "launching" includes attempted launching;

(c) The term "launching State" means:

(i) A State which launches or procures the launching of a space object;

(ii) A State from whose territory or facility a space object is launched;

(d) The term "space object" includes component parts of a space object as well as its launch vehicle and parts thereof.

ARTICLE II

A launching State shall be absolutely liable to pay compensation for damage caused by its space object on the surface of the earth or to aircraft in flight.

ARTICLE III

In the event of damage being caused elsewhere than on the surface of the earth to a space object of one launching State or to persons or property on board such a space object by a space object of another launching State, the latter shall be liable only if the damage is due to its fault or the fault of persons for whom it is responsible.

ARTICLE IV

1. In the event of damage being caused elsewhere than on the surface of the earth to a space object of one launching State or to persons or property on board such a space object by a space object of another launching State, and of damage thereby being caused to a third State or to its natural or juridical persons, the first two States shall be jointly

and severally liable to the third State, to the extent indicated by the following:

(a) If the damage has been caused to the third State on the surface of the earth or to aircraft in flight, their liability to the third State shall be absolute;

(b) If the damage has been caused to a space object of the third State or to persons or property on board that space object elsewhere than on the surface of the earth, their liability to the third State shall be based on the fault of either of the first two States or on the fault of persons for whom either is responsible.

2. In all cases of joint and several liability referred to in paragraph 1 of this article, the burden of compensation for the damage shall be apportioned between the first two States in accordance with the extent to which they were at fault; if the extent of the fault of each of these States cannot be established, the burden of compensation shall be apportioned equally between them. Such apportionment shall be without prejudice to the right of the third State to seek the entire compensation due under this Convention from any or all of the launching States which are jointly and severally liable.

ARTICLE V

1. Whenever two or more States jointly launch a space object, they shall be jointly and severally liable for any damage caused.

2. A launching State which has paid compensation for damage shall have the right to present a claim for indemnification to other participants in the joint launching. The participants in a joint launching may conclude agreements regarding the apportioning among themselves of the financial obligation in respect of which they are jointly and severally liable. Such agreements shall be without prejudice to the right of a State sustaining damage to seek the entire compensation due under this Convention from any or all of the launching States which are jointly and severally liable.

3. A State from whose territory or facility a space object is launched shall be regarded as a participant in a joint launching.

ARTICLE VI

1. Subject to the provisions of paragraph 2 of this article, exoneration from absolute liability shall be granted to the extent that a launching State establishes that the damage has resulted either wholly or partially from gross negligence or from an act or omission done with intent to cause damage on the part of a claimant State or of natural or

juridical persons it represents.

2. No exoneration whatever shall be granted in cases where the damage has resulted from activities conducted by a launching State which are not in conformity with international law including, in particular, the Charter of the United Nations and the Treaty on Principles Governing the Activities of States in the Exploration and Use of Outer Space, including the Moon and Other Celestial Bodies.

ARTICLE VII

The provisions of this Convention shall not apply to damage caused by a space object of a launching State to:

(a) Nationals of that launching State;

(b) Foreign nationals during such time as they are participating in the operation of that space object from the time of its launching or at any stage thereafter until its descent, or during such time as they are in the immediate vicinity of a planned launching or recovery area as the result of an invitation by that launching State.

ARTICLE VIII

1. A State which suffers damage, or whose natural or juridical persons suffer damage, may present to a launching State a claim for compensation for such damage.

2. If the State of nationality has not presented a claim, another State may, in respect of damage sustained in its territory by any natural or juridical person, present a claim to a launching State.

3. If neither the State of nationality nor the State in whose territory the damage was sustained has presented a claim or notified its intention of presenting a claim, another State may, in respect of damage sustained by its permanent residents, present a claim to a launching State.

ARTICLE IX

A claim for compensation for damage shall be presented to a launching State through diplomatic channels. If a State does not maintain diplomatic relations with the launching State concerned, it may request another State to present its claim to that launching State or otherwise represent its interests under this Convention. It may also present its claim through the Secretary-General of the United Nations, provided the claimant State and the launching State are both Members of the United Nations.

ARTICLE X

1. A claim for compensation for damage may be presented to a launching State not later than one year following the date of the occurrence of the damage or the identification of the launching State which is liable.

2. If, however, a State does not know of the occurrence of the damage or has not been able to identify the launching State which is liable, it may present a claim within one year following the date on which it learned of the aforementioned facts; however, this period shall in no event exceed one year following the date on which the State could reasonably be expected to have learned of the facts through the exercise of due diligence.

3. The time-limits specified in paragraphs 1 and 2 of this article shall apply even if the full extent of the damage may not be known. In this event, however, the claimant State shall be entitled to revise the claim and submit additional documentation after the expiration of such time-limits until one year after the full extent of the damage is known.

ARTICLE XI

1. Presentation of a claim to a launching State for compensation for damage under this Convention shall not require the prior exhaustion of any local remedies which may be available to a claimant State or to natural or juridical persons it represents.

2. Nothing in this Convention shall prevent a State, or natural or juridical persons it might represent, from pursuing a claim in the courts or administrative tribunals or agencies of a launching State. A State shall not, however, be entitled to present a claim under this Convention in respect of the same damage for which a claim is being pursued in the courts or administrative tribunals or agencies of a launching State or under another international agreement which is binding on the States concerned.

ARTICLE XII

The compensation which the launching State shall be liable to pay for damage under this Convention shall be determined in accordance with international law and the principles of justice and equity, in order to provide such reparation in respect of the damage as will restore the person, natural or juridical, State or international organization on whose behalf the claim is presented to the condition which would have existed if the damage had not occurred.

ARTICLE XIII

Unless the claimant State and the State from which compensation is due under this Convention agree on another form of compensation, the compensation shall be paid in the currency of the claimant State or, if that State so requests, in the currency of the State from which compensation is due.

ARTICLE XIV

If no settlement of a claim is arrived at through diplomatic negotiations as provided for in article IX, within one year from the date on which the claimant State notifies the launching State that it has submitted the documentation of its claim, the parties concerned shall establish a Claims Commission at the request of either party.

ARTICLE XV

1. The Claims Commission shall be composed of three members: one appointed by the claimant State, one appointed by the launching State and the third member, the Chairman, to be chosen by both parties jointly. Each party shall make its appointment within two months of the request for the establishment of the Claims Commission.

2. If no agreement is reached on the choice of the Chairman within four months of the request for the establishment of the Commission, either party may request the Secretary-General of the United Nations to appoint the Chairman within a further period of two months.

ARTICLE XVI

1. If one of the parties does not make its appointment within the stipulated period, the Chairman shall, at the request of the other party, constitute a single-member Claims Commission.

2. Any vacancy which may arise in the Commission for whatever reason shall be filled by the same procedure adopted for the original appointment.

3. The Commission shall determine its own procedure.

4. The Commission shall determine the place or places where it shall sit and all other administrative matters.

5. Except in the case of decisions and awards by a single-member Commission, all decisions and awards of the Commission shall be by majority vote.

ARTICLE XVII

No increase in the membership of the Claims Commission shall take place by reason of two or more claimant States or launching States being joined in any one proceeding before the Commission. The claimant States so joined shall collectively appoint one member of the Commission in the same manner and subject to the same conditions as would be the case for a single claimant State. When two or more launching States are so joined, they shall collectively appoint one member of the Commission in the same way. If the claimant States or the launching States do not make the appointment within the stipulated period, the Chairman shall constitute a single-member Commission.

ARTICLE XVIII

The Claims Commission shall decide the merits of the claim for compensation and determine the amount of compensation payable, if any.

ARTICLE XIX

1. The Claims Commission shall act in accordance with the provisions of article XII.
2. The decision of the Commission shall be final and binding if the parties have so agreed; otherwise the Commission shall render a final and recommendatory award, which the parties shall consider in good faith. The Commission shall state the reasons for its decision or award.
3. The Commission shall give its decision or award as promptly as possible and no later than one year from the date of its establishment, unless an extension of this period is found necessary by the Commission.
4. The Commission shall make its decision or award public. It shall deliver a certified copy of its decision or award to each of the parties and to the Secretary-General of the United Nations.

ARTICLE XX

The expenses in regard to the Claims Commission shall be borne equally by the parties, unless otherwise decided by the Commission.

ARTICLE XXI

If the damage caused by a space object presents a large-scale danger to human life or seriously interferes with the living conditions of the population or the functioning of vital centers, the States Parties, and in particular the launching State, shall examine the possibility of rendering appropriate and rapid assistance to the State which has suffered the damage, when it so requests. However, nothing in this article shall affect the rights or obligations of the States Parties under this Convention.

ARTICLE XXII

1. In this Convention, with the exception of articles XXIV to XXVII, references to States shall be deemed to apply to any international inter-governmental organization which conducts space activities if the organization declares its acceptance of the rights and obligations provided for in this Convention and if a majority of the States members of the organization are States Parties to this Convention and to the Treaty on Principles Governing the Activities of States in the Exploration and Use of Outer Space, including the Moon and Other Celestial Bodies.

2. States members of any such organizaton which are States Parties to this Convention shall take all appropriate steps to ensure that the organization makes a declaration in accordance with the preceding paragraph.

3. If an international intergovernmental organization is liable for damage by virtue of the provisions of this Convention, that organizaton and those of its members which are States Parties to this Convention shall be jointly and severally liable; provided, however, that:

(a) Any claim for compensation in respect of such damage shall be first presented to the organization;

(b) Only where the organization has not paid, within a period of six months, any sum agreed or determined to be due as compensation for such damage, may the claimant State invoke the liability of the members which are States Parties to this Convention for the payment of that sum.

4. Any claim, pursuant to the provisions of this Convention, for compensation in respect of damage caused to an organization which has made a declaration in accordance with paragraph 1 of this article shall be presented by a State member of the organization which is a State Party to this Convention.

ARTICLE XXIII

1. The provisions of this Convention shall not affect other international agreements in force in so far as relations between the States

Parties to such agreements are concerned.

2. No provision of this Convention shall prevent States from concluding international agreements reaffirming, supplementing or extending its provisions.

ARTICLE XXIV

1. This Convention shall be open to all States for signature. Any State which does not sign this Convention before its entry into force in accordance with paragraph 3 of this article may accede to it at any time.

2. This Convention shall be subject to ratification by signatory States. Instruments of ratification and instruments of accession shall be deposited with the Governments of the United States of America, the United Kingdom of Great Britain and Northern Ireland and the Union of Soviet Socialist Republics, which are hereby designated the Depositary Governments.

3. This Convention shall enter into force on the deposit of the fifth instrument of ratification.[134]

4. For States whose instruments of ratification or accession are deposited subsequent to the entry into force of this Convention, it shall enter into force on the date of the deposit of their instruments of ratification or accession.

5. The Depositary Governments shall promptly inform all signatory and acceding States of the date of each signature, the date of deposit of each instrument of ratification of and accession to this Convention, the date of its entry into force and other notices.

6. This Convention shall be registered by the Depositary Governments pursuant to Article 102 of the Charter of the United Nations.

ARTICLE XXV

Any State Party to this Convention may propose amendments to this Convention. Amendments shall enter into force for each State Party to the Convention accepting the amendments upon their acceptance by a majority of the States Parties to the Convention and thereafter for each remaining State Party to the Convention on the date of acceptance by it.

ARTICLE XXVI

Ten years after the entry into force of this Convention, the question

[134] Cf. note 132 above.

of the review of this Convention shall be included in the provisional agenda of the United Nations General Assembly in order to consider, in the light of past application of the Convention, whether it requires revision. However, at any time after the Convention has been in force for five years, and at the request of one third of the States Parties to the Convention, and with the concurrence of the majority of the States Parties, a conference of the States Parties shall be convened to review this Convention.

ARTICLE XXVII

Any State Party to this Convention may give notice of its withdrawal from the Convention one year after its entry into force by written notification to the Depositary Governments. Such withdrawal shall take effect one year from the date of receipt of this notification.

ARTICLE XXVIII

This Convention, of which the English, Russian, French, Spanish and Chinese texts are equally authentic, shall be deposited in the archives of the Depositary Governments. Duly certified copies of this Convention shall be transmitted by the Depositary Governments to the Governments of the signatory and acceding States.

IN WITNESS WHEREOF the undersigned, duly authorized, have signed this Convention.

DONE in triplicate, at the cities of Washington, London and Moscow, this twenty-ninth day of March, one thousand nine hundred and seventy-two.

(140) Agreement on Establishment of the International Telecommunications Satellite Organization "Intelsat": Department of State Announcement, August 18, 1971.[135]

(Complete Text)

The United States and (53) other countries on August 20 signed new

[135] Department of State Press Release 180, Aug. 18, 1971; text from *Bulletin*, Sept. 20, 1971, p. 303. Definitive arrangements for the organization and operation of a global commercial communications satellite system, superseding the provisional International Telecommunications Satellite Consortium (INTELSAT) established under an interim agreement concluded in 1964, were worked out by a Plenipotentiary Conference of INTELSAT member states which met intermittently in Washington between Feb. 24, 1969, and May 21, 1971, and approved

agreements that next year will bring into being a new permanent organization for worldwide satellite communications. Once the new Intelsat [International Telecommunications Satellite Organization] agreements have been ratified and signed by two-thirds of the 80 member states—54 countries—the permanent organization will come into being. The agreements were the result of 2 years of painstaking negotiation which ended in accord here last May 21.

Intelsat was established in 1964 under interim arrangements, with the Communications Satellite Corporation, Comsat, as overall manager on behalf of the partners. Its membership has increased from 11 partner countries in August 1964 to the present 80. Its first satellite, Early Bird, was launched in 1965. Today there are satellites in operation over the Atlantic, Pacific, and Indian Oceans providing complete global coverage. These make possible the "live-via-satellite" TV broadcasts from abroad, as well as overseas telephone and telegraph service between all countries with access to 50 earth stations around the world.

The signing took place exactly 7 years after the opening for signature of the interim arrangements on August 20, 1964.

The accords consist of two agreements, one between governments and one between telecommunications organizations. Secretary Rogers signed the intergovernmental agreement on behalf of the United States, and Dr. Joseph V. Charyk, President of Comsat, signed the operating agreement.[136]

U.S. Ambassador Abbott Washburn, chairman of the 79-nation conference which negotiated the agreements, predicted early ratification and signature by the necessary 54 countries: "The overwhelming vote in favor of the texts last May—and now this large number of signatures on opening day—virtually assures that the new setup will come into existence next spring, probably in May or June."

Under the definitive Intelsat arrangements a Secretary General and international staff will be installed in headquarters at Washington to handle administrative, financial, and support services. Comsat will continue as operating and technical manager for 6 years under contract to the Board of Governors.

two agreements opened for signature on Aug. 20, 1971: an intergovernmental Agreement Relating to the International Telecommunications Satellite Organization "Intelsat," and an Operating Agreement to be signed either by governments or by their "designated communications entities" (operating agencies). The official texts of both agreements appear in TIAS 7532 (23 UST 3813); their main provisions are summarized in *The World This Year, 1972*, pp. 152-53. Although the agreements had been signed by approximately 64 countries as of the end of 1971, their entry into force was delayed until Feb. 12, 1973.

[136] For remarks by Secretary Rogers see *Bulletin*, Sept. 20, 1971, pp. 303-4.

X.
INTERNATIONAL ECONOMIC
AND FINANCIAL AFFAIRS

[Economic and financial matters have rarely claimed the central position in American foreign policy that they occupied during much of 1971. The sequence of events that began with the announcement of President Nixon's "New Economic Policy" on August 15, culminating in mid-December in a far-reaching international agreement on the realignment of world currencies, impinged on nearly every aspect of international affairs and ranks in importance with the breakthrough in American–Chinese relations (Documents 85-94) and the progress of American–Soviet détente (Documents 21-30).

At the root of these developments was the continued unsatisfactory performance of the U.S. economy in a post-recession year that was marked by limited economic growth, rising inflation, persistent unemployment, and a deteriorating balance of payments that threatened to play havoc not only with the nation's international economic relationships but with its entire global position—a point convincingly argued by the President in his informal briefing of news media executives in Kansas City on July 6, 1971 (Document 9). In contrast to the complete lack of economic growth in 1970, preliminary figures for 1971 would indicate a gain of something like 2.7 percent in real terms as the economy began to regain momentum and piled up a gross national product of some $1,047 billion.[1] Alarmingly, however, the normal surplus of exports over imports gave way to a deficit in excess of $2 billion, the first since 1888. All balance-of-payments measures registered record deficits, and reserve assets declined to under $12.2 billion, the lowest year-end figure since World War II.

These difficulties, in the view of official Washington, were attributable not merely to the activities of "international money speculators" but also, in a considerable measure, to the absence of a more cooperative attitude on the part of such major trading partners as the European Economic Community and Japan. Disagreement with the E.E.C., which was preparing to increase its membership from six to ten with

---

[1] Later corrected to $1,054.9 billion.

the expected entry of Denmark, Ireland, Norway, and the United Kingdom at the beginning of 1973,[2] were particularly intense throughout most of 1971 as the existing membership, led by France, resisted U.S. pressure for a revaluation of European currencies and for the initiation of trade negotiations looking toward a far-reaching liberalization of E.E.C. commercial policies. Japan, too, had incurred U.S. displeasure by its restrictions on foreign investment and its reluctance to take measures aimed at reducing its strongly positive balance in trade with the United States.

A determination to arrest and, if possible, reverse the negative tendencies in the U.S. economic position was the primary inspiration of the startling measures announced by President Nixon on August 15, 1971, which included a 90-day freeze on domestic wages and prices, suspension of the convertibility of the dollar into gold, addition of a 10 percent temporary surcharge to the duties on imported goods, and a 10 percent reduction in foreign aid (Document 142). Aside from their immediate economic effect, these measures were consciously designed to increase the pressure on the United States' main trading partners to readjust their own commercial and monetary policies in a direction more favorable to U.S. interests. The immediate effect, however, was a further heightening of economic tensions, particularly with the E.E.C., with Japan (Document 97), and with Latin American countries (Document 115).

Although the resultant problems were not resolved at the September 1971 meeting of the Boards of Governors of the International Bank and Monetary Fund (Documents 146-148), the outlines of a solution began to emerge when President Nixon, at his meeting with French President Pompidou in the Azores on December 13-14, agreed for the first time to a devaluation of the dollar as the price of early negotiations on a broad range of trade matters (Documents 43 and 149). As part of the general realignment of exchange rates embodied in the "Smithsonian Agreement" of December 18, 1971 (Document 150), the United States agreed to devalue the dollar by 8.57 percent and to lift the 10 percent import surcharge in consideration of the revaluation of numerous other currencies and the promise that trade negotiations would begin promptly. Domestic inflation, meanwhile, was to be held in check by a "Phase Two" program of selective wage and price controls that had been instituted November 14, 1971, and was intended to limit inflation to an annual rate of 2 to 3 percent.

The following documentation traces the evolution of these problems from the June ministerial meeting of the Organization for Economic

[2] An agreement on the terms of British entry into the E.E.C., announced June 23, 1971, paved the way for the signature in Brussels on Jan. 22, 1972, of a Treaty of Accession and related documents whereby Denmark, Ireland, Norway, and the United Kingdom would formally enter the European Communities on January 1, 1973. The treaty was later rejected by Norway pursuant to a national referendum held on Sept. 24-25, 1972.

Cooperation and Development (Document 141) through the initiation and immediate aftermath of the "New Economic Policy" (Documents 142-145) and the inconclusive meeting of the International Bank and Monetary Fund (Documents 146-148) to the Azores and Smithsonian meetings (Documents 149-150) and the termination of the import surcharge (Document 151). Also documented are the conclusion early in 1971 of a new International Wheat Agreement (Document 152); the rejection by Congress of the President's foreign aid program (Documents 153-154); and the renewal late in the year of a longstanding U.S. pledge to institute a system of generalized trade preferences for developing countries (Document 155).]

A. The Organization for Economic Cooperation and Development (O.E.C.D.).

[This 23-member organization of the leading non-Communist industrial powers had served for nearly a decade as one of the principal forums for the discussion of both "Western" and global economic problems. The tenth anniversary meeting of the O.E.C.D. Council at ministerial level, held in Paris on June 7-8, 1971, under the chairmanship of Secretary of State Rogers—the first American Secretary of State to attend such a meeting—afforded a particularly timely opportunity for discussion of the pervasive problems of inflation, balance-of-payments disequilibriums, and the need to maintain and increase the liberalization of international trade despite the emergence of strong protectionist tendencies in many member countries. These were the underlying concerns both of Secretary Rogers' opening statement (Document 141a) and of the final communiqué of the meeting (Document 141b), which reported the Council's decision to set up a small high-level group on trade and related problems. Its chairman would be Jean Rey of Belgium, formerly President of the Commission of the European Communities.]

(141) Tenth Meeting at Ministerial Level of the O.E.C.D. Council, Paris, June 7-8, 1971.

(a) Opening Statement by Secretary of State Rogers, June 7, 1971. [3]

(Complete Text)

It is a great honor for me to call to order the 10th meeting of the

---

[3] Department of State Press Release 155, June 7, 1971; text from *Bulletin*, July 5, 1971, 11-13. For statements by other U.S. representatives see same, pp. 13-19.

Ministerial Council of the Organization for Economic Cooperation and Development.

This meeting comes at a critical time in the evolution of international cooperation in economic matters. When I was asked to accept the position of your chairman for this meeting I responded affirmatively because the administration I represent here today believes many of our common problems can be solved only through the most active cooperation among the free-world industrial powers. The OECD is the appropriate place to begin that cooperation. Because we face profound changes in the conduct of international economic relations, this meeting can help to determine the international economic climate for years to come.

To refer to the history of this Organization and its predecessor is to recall a remarkable economic success story of two decades. The decade of the 1950's—the decade in which Marshall plan aid was implemented through the Organization for European Economic Cooperation—saw a determined Europe, with our help, achieve recovery from the war's devastation. It saw the advent of economic prosperity, marked by a return to full convertibility of currencies and the end of the dollar shortage in Europe. During the decade of the 1960's we built on those solid foundations. The creation of the OECD in 1961 was designed to promote economic growth and stability, to further the expansion of world trade on a nondiscriminatory basis, and to contribute to the economic expansion of developing countries. Membership in this Organization of the United States and Canada, and later of Japan, has made the OECD the principal organ of economic consultation and cooperation in the developed world.

Today, at the start of the 1970's, further changes of considerable magnitude are in process.

1. The movement toward wider European unity, which the United States has consistently encouraged, is quickening. The European Community is on the point of enlargement. The United States applauds the creative statesmanship which is giving new impetus to this great undertaking. The governments directly engaged in it have our full support. We in turn will expect our interests to be taken fully into account.

2. Across the globe, Japan's continued unprecedented growth has made it the third pillar of the structure represented by the OECD. We welcome that fact and look to Japan to contribute to the liberalization of world trade.

3. The relative economic roles of the United States and other industrialized countries are changing. There is not sufficient appreciation of the costs of the role the United States plays today in the security of the free world and how that role relates to economic conditions. For example, the deficit in our balance of payments—which we strenuously seek

to correct—helps to purchase security for the free world. The fact is that our international obligations, in particular our $5 billion balance of payments costs for military expenditures overseas, consistently have exceeded the size of our basic payment deficits, even when foreign military expenditures in the United States are subtracted. Our overseas expenditures provide security benefits for our allies as well as for us. They must be taken into account in the OECD when our economic and balance of payments position is examined. And they must also be taken into account by our allies when allocations of defense responsibilities are under consideration.

4. Within the developing world there is a growing need, and desire, for a fuller economic relationship with industrialized countries. The countries represented here not only have responsibilities to each other, we also have responsibilities to cooperate with the two-thirds of the world's population living in underdeveloped countries.

These changes offer significant opportunities to increase the well-being of the peoples of both developed and developing countries. And yet, because the policies of one country or of a group of countries affect economic conditions in all, changes can also bring problems.

Our growth and prosperity are due in large measure to the openness of our economies to the flow of goods, services, and capital across our borders. To attack our problems by re-erecting barriers whose removal has brought us such benefit would be a tragic mistake. It would prevent us from maximizing the welfare of our citizens through the most efficient international allocation of resources.

We must instead build on the liberal policies of economic openness which have created the remarkable progress of the last two decades. Intensified cooperation through the OECD should be a central part of this effort.

Each of us has a responsibility to the world economy. As the keeper of the reserve currency and as the largest trader, the United States has fully recognized its own obligations. But other countries and groupings are beginning to match our position. We hope they realize the responsibilities that go with their new roles.

To solve the short-term monetary problems which have caused recent concern, OECD members need better methods for the international adjustment of fiscal and monetary policies. We are ready to join our OECD partners in reducing incentives to short-term money flows seeking higher interest rates.

Through tight money, high interest rates, and substantial tax rates, the Nixon administration has successfully worked to reduce inflation. While we would like to reduce it still further, OECD studies confirm that we have held inflation rates below those of our major European partners. Obviously, we have also had to direct our policies to stimulating greater employment, output, and productivity; no responsible government could do otherwise. These policies, together with a continuing effort to lower inflation, should enhance our trading position, and they should to some extent reduce the balance of payments deficit we have sustained in recent years—in large measure because of our international obligations.

Trade issues, like monetary issues, will receive close attention at this meeting. With the enlargement of the European Community and the burgeoning of Japan's trade, new partners of world trade are emerging, bringing with them the possibility of unprecedented trade expansion.

It is 4 years since the conclusion of the last round of tariff negotiations.[4] While none of our countries is ready for a new round of trade liberalization negotiations at present, it is time to reaffirm our determination to maintain and expand a liberal and nondiscriminatory world trade system. The United States is committed to such a system. We are convinced that it is in our own interest and in the interest of the world as a whole. But we must be able to show that everyone is applying the international rules fairly. Many in the United States are not convinced this is the case.

The governments here today represent most of the world's leading trading nations. It is up to us to lead the way in assuring the continued growth of international trade. To help do so, the United States strongly endorses the suggestion put forward by the Secretary General [Emile van Lennep] to establish an OECD special group. This group could examine current and prospective trade issues—including tariffs and tariff discrimination, nontariff barriers, and agricultural policies—and develop action program guidelines for dealing with them. Sober thought and careful preparation now can prevent a cycle of restrictions which, in the end, would benefit none of us. On trade, as on the other economic issues we will examine here, let us take the open approach which our own national experiences have shown will best advance the welfare of our people.

It is a part of our heritage from Rome that we take special note of 10-year periods. At this 10th meeting of the Ministerial Council we shall reaffirm our common commitment to the objectives of the Organization. In truth, of course, what we do after this meeting—in the 11th and 12th and later years of the OECD—will determine the usefulness of our deliberations today and tomorrow. If as a result of this meeting we can extend and deepen the habits of consultation and cooperation, and if we can agree on courses of mutual action, then the 10th session of this Council will have been a historic one.

[4] *Documents, 1967*, pp. 451-57.

(b) Final Communiqué, June 8, 1971.[5]

(Complete Text)

The Council of the O.E.C.D. met at ministerial level in Paris on 8th June, 1971, under the Chairmanship of the Honourable William P. Rogers, Secretary of State of the United States of America.

Ministers expressed their pleasure that the Australian Government, having fulfilled the terms and conditions of membership, had accepted the Council's invitation to join OECD and had become a Member on 7th June.

THE INTERNATIONAL ECONOMIC SITUATION

Ministers discussed the prospects for economic activity and prices. The growth of output in the OECD area as a whole is likely to pick up in the course of 1971. On the other hand, in the OECD area as a whole, the price rise may not yet be slowing down sufficiently to enable the Organisation's growth objectives for the 1970s to be achieved in the non-inflationary climate essential to its wider economic and social aims.

Ministers re-affirmed that their Governments continue to give high priority to a substantial reduction in the rate of inflation. Excessive demand, where it still exists, needs to be eliminated; where this has been achieved, renewed expansion should be so designed as to avoid a return to excessive demand conditions. In designing stabilisation policies close attention will continue to be paid both to their effect on employment and to the social repercussions of rising prices.

The work of the Organisation during the past year on the problem of inflation was noted with appreciation. Ministers agreed that, in addition to demand-management, there were many fields in which national policies should be applied to the task of damping down inflation, and that further analysis in the Organisation of the dynamics of inflation could help Governments better to formulate their stabilisation policies.

Ministers called for closer international co-operation in the OECD to combat inflation and expressed the view that, when Member countries work out their strategies for this purpose, they should adopt a combination of policies which takes into account both their own situation and the interests of other countries.

Ministers discussed underlying trends in the balance of payments and recent developments in the international monetary situation. They recognised that the balances of some countries on current and long-term capital account still diverge from what is appropriate over the longer run. They noted the position of certain Member countries con-

[5] *OECD Observer*, July 1971, pp. 3ff.

cerning the special factors affecting their balances of payments. They also recognised that massive undesirable short-term capital movements raise serious and recurrent problems from the point of view of domestic and international stability.

Ministers welcomed the resolve expressed by Member countries to make further progress towards better balance on current and long-term capital account. They also instructed the Organisation to give special attention to the factors leading to undesirably large short-term capital flows. Ministers agreed that solutions to these problems would require more effective international co-operative action concerning economic policies in general in which the OECD has an important role to play.

QUALITY OF LIFE AND ENVIRONMENT POLICIES

Ministers recalled that growth should be considered in the wide context of economic and social development which includes both qualitative and quantitative aspects. In this connection, they noted with satisfaction the new direction given to OECD work on environment policies, which aims at taking into consideration a wide range of relevant factors, especially those affecting international economic relations, and at proposing constructive solutions to the most urgent problems facing Member countries. The recently-established procedure for notification and consultation among Member countries on measures for the control of substances affecting man or his environment is a welcome contribution in this field.

PERSPECTIVES FOR INTERNATIONAL TRADE

Ministers expressed the resolve of their Governments to maintain the high degree of liberalisation of international trade which has been achieved through continuous multilateral co-operation and through negotiations in the last twenty-five years. They noted the progress made in a number of current OECD activities and lent their support to efforts towards the general aim of freer trade on a non-discriminatory basis and under fair conditions of competition in both industrial and agricultural products.

Ministers furthermore affirmed that their Governments will pursue policies aiming at greater liberalisation of international trade. Having in mind the changing nature of trade and related problems, and the particular responsibilities which OECD Member countries will continue to carry in world economic affairs, Ministers agreed that broader opportunities for progress towards this general aim should be explored. To this end they decided to set up within the Organisation a small high-level group whose members would be chosen by reason of their wide competence and experience from among high officials or other personalities designated by Governments. This group will analyse the trade and related problems which arise in a longer-term perspective, i.e. it will define the problems and assess their relative urgency, consider how these problems might be dealt with, and set out options for their solution.[6] Ministers stressed that this study should take account of the work being undertaken in the GATT [General Agreement on Tariffs and Trade] by virtue of its responsibilities and prerogatives under the General Agreement.

DEVELOPMENT CO-OPERATION

Ministers expressed the determination of their Governments to pursue policies which combine domestic economic and social objectives with the objectives of development co-operation. The OECD work on a coherent approach to development co-operation will contribute to strengthening the efforts of Member countries to attain the goals and objectives of the International Development Strategy for the Second Development Decade.[7]

Ministers noted that provisional figures of net financial flows from members of the Development Assistance Committee (DAC)[8] to developing countries in 1970 showed some increase over the preceding year, owing to the growth of export credits and private investment; expressed as a percentage of GNP [Gross National Product], however, these flows remained in 1970 about the same as in 1969. Within the total, official development assistance hardly changed between 1969 and 1970 in absolute value, and, as a percentage of GNP, continued to decline. The trend varied from country to country and the figures of several DAC members showed substantial progress. Ministers agreed that Member countries would pursue their efforts to increase the volume of financial resources transferred to developing countries, in particular official development assistance, and to provide such assistance on terms adjusted to the development requirements and the repayment capacity of recipient countries. Ministers emphasised that aid policies should be aimed at both an increase in volume and an improvement in the quality of assistance.

Among the means of improving the quality of aid, Ministers considered the state of discussion within the DAC on untying.[9] They noted that substantial progress had been made in drawing up a draft agree-

[6] The report of the High-level Trade Group chaired by Jean Rey of Belgium was published Sept. 5, 1972, under the title *Policy Perspectives for International Trade and Economic Relations* (Paris: O.E.C.D., 1972).
[7] U.N. General Assembly Resolution 2626 (XXV), Oct. 24, 1970; excerpts in *Documents, 1970*, pp. 324-31.
[8] Composed of 16 O.E.C.D. member countries and the Commission of the European Communities.
[9] I.e., the freeing of development assistance from the requirement that use of aid funds be limited to the acquisition of goods and services from the donor country. Cf. *Documents, 1970*, pp. 444-46.

ment on aid untying to be proposed to Governments who would be invited to indicate whether they wish to participate. There is unanimous agreement in principle on the untying of multilateral contributions as well as a wide area of agreement for the untying of bilateral loans. Ministers agreed that work on aid untying should be actively pursued in the DAC and expressed the hope that co-ordinated action with respect to untying could be taken at an early date.

Ministers noted the progress made towards the introduction in the near future of the generalised system of tariff preferences in favour of developing countries[10] and discussed questions of trade and development of special concern to developing Member countries in the light of the OECD Convention.

Ministers urged that every effort be made to ensure that the generalised system of tariff preferences is brought into effect as soon as possible in 1971. They agreed that the Organisation should pursue its work with the view to enabling the developing countries to draw full advantage from the preference system.

Moreover, Ministers instructed the Organisation to examine other means which might help to improve export earnings by the developing countries, particularly for goods which in general are not directly affected by the introduction of the preference system.

ECONOMIC POLICY CO-OPERATION

Recognising the ever-closer economic relationships between Member countries, Ministers resolved to use the OECD to concert more closely their short- and medium-term economic policies so as to ensure that the policies of each country shall be more compatible with the interests of all and with the responsibilities of OECD countries to the developing countries as set forth in the OECD Convention.

Ministers took note of the proposals put forward to this end by the Secretary-General, agreed with the general principles of these proposals, and requested the Council to take the necessary action to implement these principles.

B. The United States' "New Economic Policy."

[The background, character, and hoped-for effects of the drastic economic measures invoked by the United States on August 15, 1971, were detailed by President Nixon in a celebrated broadcast whose text is here printed under its official title of "The Challenge of Peace"

10 Cf. Document 155.

(Document 142). Aside from the unexpectedness and somewhat nationalistic tone of the President's pronouncement, the United States' trading partners were upset by a number of the specific steps he announced, particularly the imposition of a 10 percent supplemental import duty admittedly aimed at helping the U.S. balance of payments by curbing the import of their products (Document 143). American spokesmen were kept busy over the next few weeks in explaining the new measures to the Europeans,[11] the Latin Americans,[12] the Japanese,[13] the General Agreement on Tariffs and Trade (Document 144), the Congress,[14] and the press (Document 145). These measures, they insisted, were temporary in character, had been imposed only through sheer necessity, and betokened no real retreat from America's traditionally internationalist stance.]

(142) "The Challenge of Peace": Radio-Television Address by President Nixon Outlining a New Economic Policy for the United States, August 15, 1971.[15]

(Complete Text)

Good evening:

I have addressed the Nation a number of times over the past 2 years on the problems of ending a war. Because of the progress we have made toward achieving that goal,[16] this Sunday evening is an appropriate time for us to turn our attention to the challenges of peace.

America today has the best opportunity in this century to achieve two of its greatest ideals: to bring about a full generation of peace, and to create a new prosperity without war.

This not only requires bold leadership ready to take bold action—it calls forth the greatness in a great people.

Prosperity without war requires action on three fronts: We must create more and better jobs; we must stop the rise in the cost of living; we must protect the dollar from the attacks of international money speculators.

We are going to take that action—not timidly, not half-heartedly, and not in piecemeal fashion. We are going to move forward to the new

[11] *Bulletin*, Sept. 27, 1971, p. 333.
[12] Same, Sept. 13, 1971, pp. 278-79 and Oct. 11, 1971, pp. 378-84; cf. Chapter VIII at notes 74-76.
[13] Same, Sept. 27, 1971, p. 333, and Oct. 4, 1971, pp. 346-53; cf. Chapter VI at notes 114-16.
[14] Nixon address to the Congress, Sept. 9, 1971, in *Public Papers, 1971*, pp. 938-44.
[15] *Presidential Documents*, Aug. 23, 1971, pp. 1168-71.
[16] Cf. Documents 71-75.

prosperity without war as befits a great people—all together, and along a broad front.

The time has come for a new economic policy for the United States. Its targets are unemployment, inflation, and international speculation. And this is how we are going to attack those targets.

First, on the subject of jobs. We all know why we have an unemployment problem. Two million workers have been released from the Armed Forces and defense plants because of our success in winding down the war in Vietnam. Putting those people back to work is one of the challenges of peace, and we have begun to make progress. Our unemployment rate today is below the average of the 4 peacetime years of the 1960's.

But we can and we must do better than that.

The time has come for American industry, which has produced more jobs at higher real wages than any other industrial system in history, to embark on a bold program of new investment in production for peace.

To give that system a powerful new stimulus, I shall ask the Congress, when it reconvenes after its summer recess, to consider as its first priority the enactment of the Job Development Act of 1971.

I will propose to provide the strongest short term incentive in our history to invest in new machinery and equipment that will create new jobs for Americans: a 10 percent Job Development Credit for 1 year, effective as of today, with a 5 percent credit after August 15, 1972. This tax credit for investment in new equipment will not only generate new jobs; it will raise productivity; it will make our goods more competitive in the years ahead.

Second, I will propose to repeal the 7 percent excise tax on automobiles, effective today. This will mean a reduction in price of about $200 per car. I shall insist that the American auto industry pass this tax reduction on to the nearly 8 million customers who are buying automobiles this year. Lower prices will mean that more people will be able to afford new cars, and every additional 100,000 cars sold means 25,000 new jobs.

Third, I propose to speed up the personal income tax exemptions scheduled for January 1, 1973, to January 1, 1972—so that taxpayers can deduct an extra $50 for each exemption 1 year earlier than planned. This increase in consumer spending power will provide a strong boost to the economy in general and to employment in particular.

The tax reductions I am recommending, together with this broad upturn of the economy which has taken place in the first half of this year, will move us strongly forward toward a goal this Nation has not reached since 1956, 15 years ago—prosperity with full employment in peacetime.

Looking to the future, I have directed the Secretary of the Treasury to recommend to the Congress in January new tax proposals for stimulating research and development of new industries and new techniques to help provide the 20 million new jobs that America needs for the young people who will be coming into the job market in the next decade.

To offset the loss of revenue from these tax cuts which directly stimulate new jobs, I have ordered today a $4.7 billion cut in Federal spending.

Tax cuts to stimulate employment must be matched by spending cuts to restrain inflation. To check the rise in the cost of Government, I have ordered a postponement of pay raises and a 5 percent cut in Government personnel.

I have ordered a 10 percent cut in foreign economic aid.

In addition, since the Congress has already delayed action on two of the great initiatives of this administration, I will ask Congress to amend my proposals to postpone the implementation of revenue sharing for 3 months and welfare reform for 1 year.

In this way, I am reordering our budget priorities so as to concentrate more on achieving our goal of full employment.

The second indispensable element of the new prosperity is to stop the rise in the cost of living.

One of the cruelest legacies of the artificial prosperity produced by war is inflation. Inflation robs every American, every one of you. The 20 million who are retired and living on fixed incomes—they are particularly hard hit. Homemakers find it harder than ever to balance the family budget. And 80 million American wage earners have been on a treadmill. For example, in the 4 war years between 1965 and 1969, your wage increases were completely eaten up by price increases. Your paychecks were higher, but you were no better off.

We have made progress against the rise in the cost of living. From the high point of 6 percent a year in 1969, the rise in consumer prices has been cut to 4 percent in the first half of 1971. But just as is the case in our fight against unemployment, we can and we must do better than that.

The time has come for decisive action—action that will break the vicious circle of spiraling prices and costs.

I am today ordering a freeze on all prices and wages throughout the United States for a period of 90 days. In addition, I call upon corporations to extend the wage-price freeze to all dividends.

I have today appointed a Cost of Living Council within the Government. I have directed this Council to work with leaders of labor and business to set up the proper mechanism for achieving continued price and wage stability after the 90-day freeze is over.

Let me emphasize two characteristics of this action: First, it is temporary. To put the strong, vigorous American economy into a permanent straitjacket would lock in unfairness; it would stifle the expansion of our free enterprise system. And second, while the wage-price freeze will be backed by Government sanctions, if necessary, it will not be accompanied by the establishment of a huge price control bureaucracy. I am relying on the voluntary cooperation of all Americans—each one of you—workers, employers, consumers—to make this freeze work.

Working together, we will break the back of inflation, and we will do it without the mandatory wage and price controls that crush economic and personal freedom.

The third indispensable element in building the new prosperity is closely related to creating new jobs and halting inflation. We must protect the position of the American dollar as a pillar of monetary stability around the world.

In the past 7 years, there has been an average of one international monetary crisis every year. Now who gains from these crises? Not the workingman; not the investor; not the real producers of wealth. The gainers are the international money speculators. Because they thrive on crises, they help to create them.

In recent weeks, the speculators have been waging an all-out war on the American dollar. The strength of a nation's currency is based on the strength of that nation's economy—and the American economy is by far the strongest in the world. Accordingly, I have directed the Secretary of the Treasury to take the action necessary to defend the dollar against the speculators.

I have directed Secretary [of the Treasury John B.] Connally to suspend temporarily the convertibility of the dollar into gold or other reserve assets, except in amounts and conditions determined to be in the interest of monetary stability and in the best interests of the United States.

Now, what is this action—which is very technical—what does it mean for you?

Let me lay to rest the bugaboo of what is called devaluation.

If you want to buy a foreign car or take a trip abroad, market conditions may cause your dollar to buy slightly less. But if you are among the overwhelming majority of Americans who buy American-made products in America, your dollar will be worth just as much tomorrow as it is today.

The effect of this action, in other words, will be to stabilize the dollar.

Now, this action will not win us any friends among the international money traders. But our primary concern is with the American workers, and with fair competition around the world.

To our friends abroad, including the many responsible members of the international banking community who are dedicated to stability and the flow of trade, I give this assurance: The United States has always been, and will continue to be, a forward-looking and trust-worthy trading partner. In full cooperation with the International Monetary Fund and those who trade with us, we will press for the necessary reforms to set up an urgently needed new international monetary system. Stability and equal treatment is in everybody's best interest. I am determined that the American dollar must never again be a hostage in the hands of international speculators.

I am taking one further step to protect the dollar, to improve our balance of payments, and to increase jobs for Americans. As a temporary measure, I am today imposing an additional tax of 10 percent on goods imported into the United States.[17] This is a better solution for international trade than direct controls on the amount of imports.

This import tax is a temporary action. It isn't directed against any other country. It's an action to make certain that American products will not be at a disadvantage because of unfair exchange rates. When the unfair treatment is ended, the import tax will end as well.

As a result of these actions, the product of American labor will be more competitive, and the unfair edge that some of our foreign competition has will be removed. This is a major reason why our trade balance has eroded over the past 15 years.

At the end of World War II the economies of the major industrial nations of Europe and Asia were shattered. To help them get on their feet and to protect their freedom, the United States has provided over the past 25 years $143 billion in foreign aid. That was the right thing for us to do.

Today, largely with our help, they have regained their vitality. They have become our strong competitors, and we welcome their success. But now that other nations are economically strong, the time has come for them to bear their fair share of the burden of defending freedom around the world. The time has come for exchange rates to be set straight and for the major nations to compete as equals. There is no longer any need for the United States to compete with one hand tied behind her back.

The range of actions I have taken and proposed tonight—on the job front, on the inflation front, on the monetary front—is the most comprehensive new economic policy to be undertaken in this Nation in four decades.

We are fortunate to live in a nation with an economic system capable of producing for its people the highest standard of living in the world; a system flexible enough to change its ways dramatically when circumstances call for change; and, most important, a system resourceful enough to produce prosperity with freedom and opportunity unmatched in the history of nations.

[17] Document 143.

The purposes of the Government actions I have announced tonight are to lay the basis for renewed confidence, to make it possible for us to compete fairly with the rest of the world, to open the door to new prosperity.

But government, with all of its powers, does not hold the key to the success of a people. That key, my fellow Americans, is in your hands.

A nation, like a person, has to have a certain inner drive in order to succeed. In economic affairs, that inner drive is called the competitive spirit.

Every action I have taken tonight is designed to nurture and stimulate that competitive spirit; to help us snap out of the self-doubt, the self-disparagement that saps our energy and erodes our confidence in ourselves.

Whether this Nation stays number one in the world's economy or resigns itself to second, third, or fourth place; whether we as a people have faith in ourselves, or lose that faith; whether we hold fast to the strength that makes peace and freedom possible in this world, or lose our grip—all that depends on you, on your competitive spirit, your sense of personal destiny, your pride in your country and in yourself.

We can be certain of this: As the threat of war recedes, the challenge of peaceful competition in the world will greatly increase.

And we welcome competition, because America is at her greatest when she is called on to compete.

As there always have been in our history, there will be voices urging us to shrink from that challenge of competition, to build a protective wall around ourselves, to crawl into a shell as the rest of the world moves ahead.

Two hundred years ago a man wrote in his diary these words: "Many thinking people believe America has seen its best days." That was written in 1775, just before the American Revolution, the dawn of the most exciting era in the history of man. And today we hear the echo of those voices, preaching a gospel of gloom and defeat, saying the same thing: "We have seen our best days."

I say, let Americans reply: "Our best days lie ahead."

As we move into a generation of peace, as we blaze the trail toward the new prosperity, I say to every American: Let us raise our spirits. Let us raise our sights. Let all of us contribute all we can to this great and good country that has contributed so much to the progress of mankind.

Let us invest in our Nation's future; and let us revitalize that faith in ourselves that built a great nation in the past and that will shape the world of the future.

Thank you, and good evening.

(143) Imposition of Supplemental Duty for Balance-of-Payments Purposes: Proclamation by the President, August 15, 1971. [18]

(Excerpts)

By the President of the United States of America
a Proclamation

WHEREAS, there has been a prolonged decline in the international monetary reserves of the United States, and our trade and international competitive position is seriously threatened and, as a result, our continued ability to assure our security could be impaired;

WHEREAS, the balance of payments position of the United States requires the imposition of a surcharge on dutiable imports;

WHEREAS, pursuant to the authority vested in him by the Constitution and the statutes, including, but not limited to, the Tariff Act of 1930, as amended (hereinafter referred to as "the Tariff Act"), and the Trade Expansion Act of 1962[19] (hereinafter referred to as "the TEA"), the President entered into, and proclaimed tariff rates under, trade agreements with foreign countries;

WHEREAS, under the Tariff Act, the TEA, and other provisions of law, the President may, at any time, modify or terminate, in whole or in part, any proclamation made under his authority;

NOW, THEREFORE, I, RICHARD NIXON, President of the United States of America, acting under the authority vested in me by the Constitution and the statutes, including, but not limited to, the Tariff Act, and the TEA, respectively, do proclaim as follows:

A. I hereby declare a national emergency during which I call upon the public and private sector to make the efforts necessary to strengthen the international economic position of the United States.

B. (1) I hereby terminate in part for such a period as may be necessary and modify prior Presidential Proclamations which carry out trade agreements insofar as such proclamations are inconsistent with, or proclaim duties different from, those made effective pursuant to the terms of this Proclamation.

(2) Such proclamations are suspended only insofar as is required to assess a surcharge in the form of a supplemental duty amounting to 10

[18] Proclamation 4074, Aug. 15, 1971; text from *Presidential Documents*, Aug. 23, 1971, p. 1174. For an explanation of the surcharge, cf. below at note 24; for its termination, see Document 151.

[19] Public Law 87-794, Oct. 11, 1962; summary in *Documents, 1962*, pp. 496-508, especially p. 504.

percent ad valorem. Such supplemental duty shall be imposed on all dutiable articles imported into the customs territory of the United States from outside thereof, which are entered, or withdrawn from warehouse, for consumption after 12:01 a.m., August 16, 1971, provided, however, that if the imposition of an additional duty of 10 percent ad valorem would cause the total duty or charge payable to exceed the total duty or charge payable at the rate prescribed in column 2 of the Tariff Schedules of the United States, then the column 2 rate shall apply.

*   *   *

IN WITNESS THEREOF, I have therunto set my hand this fifteenth day of August in the year of our Lord nineteen hundred and seventy-one, and of the Independence of the United States of America the one hundred and ninety-sixth.

RICHARD NIXON

(144) Explanation to GATT: Statement by Nathaniel Samuels, Deputy Under Secretary of State for Economic Affairs, Before the Council of the General Agreement on Tariffs and Trade, Geneva, August 24, 1971. [20]

(Complete Text)

I welcome the opportunity to be here today to discuss the aims of the new economic program announced by President Nixon on August 15.[21] In so doing, I shall also discuss the relationship of the actions taken in pursuance of this program to the General Agreement on Tariffs and Trade. At the same time, and most importantly, I welcome the opportunity today to express the earnest desire of the Government of the United States that all the members of GATT will recognize the need to deal promptly and effectively with the underlying problems which made the program a necessity.

We are grateful to Director General [Olivier] Long for his constructive leadership and are keenly aware and deeply appreciative of the important role which the GATT has played and will continue to play in dealing with international trade.

The problems are of common concern to all of us, each country's policies and practices playing a part. A quarter of a century of enormous progress now fortifies our advance to the future, in which the General Agreement on Tariffs and Trade, the International Monetary Fund, and the International Bank for Reconstruction and Development have provided the framework for orderly trade, monetary, and development relationships. The United States has played a key role in providing the essential economic energy and motive power of the system. Great benefits have flowed from the operation of the system. But there have been high costs as well, and stresses and strains have become visible. The system needs a new equilibrium, and it is incumbent upon all of us to help alleviate the stresses and ease the strains so that this may be accomplished.

THE BACKGROUND

Lest anyone believes that the President's action exceeded the requirements of the situation, let me describe the dimensions of the problem. Throughout the 1960's, from 1960 to 1969, the United States was in continuous deficit on its liquidity balance, averaging $3 billion per year. Our deficit on current account and long-term capital account—in other words, our basic balance—has averaged $1.5 billion per year. While these deficits were manageable in any particular year, and were not without great benefits to the rest of the world, cumulatively they have created severe distortions for us and for you.

In 1970 and 1971 these persistent balance of payments deficits turned sharply worse. In all probability there were special factors at work during the first half of 1971 which contributed to the magnitude of the deficit, but we were facing the stark possibility of a liquidity deficit that was running at the staggering annual rate of $17 billion and an official settlements deficit at an annual rate of $23 billion. It would have required an impossible current and long-term capital surplus in the second half of 1971 to diminish the deficits of the first half at all significantly.[22] Can anyone have doubted the need for decisive action in such a situation?

In parallel with these payments deficits, the United States reserve position has been severely and persistently eroded. Although declines in reserves during the early postwar years reflected conscious U.S. policy to achieve better distribution of world reserves to assist recovery, our gold stock now has fallen from a postwar high of approximately $23 billion to the present level of approximately $10 billion. It may be of interest to bear in mind that while U.S. reserves declined by about $7 billion since 1960, the rest of the world's reserves increased during the same period by some $40 billion. Our gross reserves now stand at about

[22] For the full year 1971, the United States incurred a "basic" balance-of-payments deficit of $10.559 billion and a "liquidity" deficit of $21.965 billion.

26 percent of 1971 imports, which means that relative to trade our level of reserves is well below the world average. Meanwhile our liquid liabilities have risen sharply, from $21 billion in 1960 to $57 billion now.

While the very persistence of our balance of payments deficits and the erosion of our reserves have tended to breed tolerance in some quarters of an unsatisfactory situation, the appearance of a trade deficit this year in place of our long-standing trade surplus has jolted us, if not all others, into recognition of the fact that the time for change had arrived. Our trade balance deteriorated by more than $8 billion in 7 years. In 1964, we had a comfortable trade surplus of $6½ billion. For 1971, a deficit of about $2 billion was forecast before the President's new program was announced. This, incidentally, would be the first year of merchandise trade deficit by the United States since 1893.

In mid-August 1971, not only was the U.S. balance of payments and external financial position highly unsatisfactory, but there was little prospect for improvement. Further deterioration in the trade and current accounts in the latter part of 1971 and in 1972 appeared inevitable as we came out of our economic slowdown and as our economy gathered an anticipated upward momentum. We could no longer afford the luxury of an academic exercise on the desired trade and payments position of the United States but had to grasp the nettle of necessity and exercise the responsibilities of leadership.

I would like to make clear here today that the difficulties we are encountering in the world's trade and payments system grow out of both internal and external causes. Our costs of production have risen sharply over the years, our productivity gains have not been as large as required, and protracted unemployment and inflation, side by side, have bedeviled us. Although our total employment continues to rise steadily and we have succeeded in slowing down the rate of consumer price increases in the first half of 1971, the depth of the unemployment (5 million workers, or nearly 6 percent of the work force) and the inflationary pressures against which we have undertaken to battle have required relentless effort on our part. But our ability to deal with these problems is circumscribed by our key role in the international monetary and payments system, by the defense burdens we carry for ourselves and our allies and trading partners, and by certain trade policies which we accepted in a postwar effort to enable other countries to rebuild their economies and to revitalize their political systems.

THE PROGRAM

On August 15, President Nixon declared a national emergency due to the deterioration of the balance of payments position of the United

States.[23] The program he announced to deal with this situation mounted an interrelated attack on both domestic and foreign problems; namely, unemployment, inflation, and disequilibrium in the international economy. It is intended to accelerate the upward momentum of the domestic economy by putting idle resources of capital and labor to productive use, to stanch the hemorrhage in our balance of payments and trade position, and to restore equilibrium and bring about fundamental reform in the international monetary system. I lay stress on the interrelated and integrated nature of the program. The sacrifices necessary to achieve it will bear heavily on our own citizens. The overriding imperative, however, for the United States, its trading partners throughout the world, and the international trade and payments system is a sound and strong and expanding U.S. economy. From time to time there is a tendency to forget how fundamental the American economy is to the health of the whole free world. By preserving this health we can contribute most effectively to the free, strong, and expanding world economy that we seek.

Let me summarize the program:

Domestic

1. A 90-day freeze on all prices and wages.

2. Creation of a Cost of Living Council to effect a transition from the temporary freeze to continued price and wage stability.

3. Recommendation that Congress enact an accelerated tax credit on investment at the rate of 10 percent for 1 year, to be followed by a permanent credit at the rate of 5 percent.

4. Recommendation that Congress repeal the 7-percent excise tax on automobiles.

5. Recommendation that Congress advance by 1 year to January 1, 1972, the scheduled January 1, 1973, increase of $50 for each exemption on personal income taxes.

6. Reduction of Federal expenditures in fiscal year 1972 by $4.7 billion.

7. Postponement of revenue sharing and welfare reform proposals.

International

1. The temporary suspension of full convertibility of dollars into gold or other reserve assets for governments and central banks.

2. The imposition (not without interest to those of us assembled here today) of a temporary surcharge on imports into the United States, generally at a rate of 10 percent.

3. A 10-percent reduction in foreign economic aid.

---

[23] Document 142.

THE SURCHARGE

Let us turn to the surcharge. The import surcharge is a temporary measure imposed by Presidential proclamation, effective August 16, 1971.[24] It levies a 10-percent ad valorem surcharge on nonexempt imports into the United States. It is being applied on a most-favored-nation (MFN) basis. The 10 percent is calculated on the same basis as normal tariffs; that is, generally on the f.o.b. price of the product. The surcharge does not apply to items which are not the subject of a trade concession by the United States. The surcharge is not applicable to duty-free imports and goods subject to quantitative restrictions pursuant to U.S. law. The goods subject to quotas which are exempt include cotton textiles, petroleum, petroleum products, sugar, certain meats, and various other agricultural products, principally dairy products. The surcharge will be less than 10 percent on those items where its application, in addition to the effective most-favored-nation rate, would exceed the U.S. statutory rate of duty. In the case of automobiles, for example, where the MFN rate is currently 3½ percent and the statutory rate is 10 percent, the surcharge will be 6½ percent.

The surcharge is intended to achieve a relatively rapid benefit for our balance of trade and payments while more fundamental measures take effect. Of the several types of action which might have been taken under the circumstances, a surcharge on imports appeared to offer certain advantages or, shall we say, fewer disadvantages. It seemed more easily dismantled than other possible actions, more compatible with a competitive approach and efficient resource allocation, would not require an elaborate administrative structure, would be less discriminatory than quota restrictions, and was most rapidly applicable under existing U.S. legal authority. The sum of these reasons added up to an action less severe on our trading partners than that envisaged in the GATT articles[25] in similar circumstances. As the President's address indicated, it was a temporary action, taken reluctantly.

We recognize that the surcharge will pose problems for others, as it does for us. Our trading partners will be faced with dislocations of varying degrees. But the surcharge will be costly to our own citizens also, particularly our importers and consumers.

In notifying the surcharge, my Government has not invoked a particular article of the General Agreement. The trade and monetary situation to which we address ourselves, and in which every country has a fundamental stake, transcends any particular article. My Government considers that it is entitled under the provision of article XII to insti-

---

[24] Document 143.
[25] Signed at Geneva Oct. 30, 1947 (TIAS 1700).

tute quantitative restrictions. However, the need for prompt action and the desire to avoid the administrative complications and the greater restrictiveness of import quotas led the United States Government to adopt the import surcharge. There is, of course, precedent in the GATT for adopting import surcharges rather than quotas for alleviating balance of payments problems. The duration of the surcharge will be related, obviously, to the speed and the effectiveness with which collectively we can deal with the circumstances that dictated its use.[26]

My Government stands ready to consult with the Contracting Parties on all aspects of the surcharge, and I propose that consultations start promptly. The United States Government expects that the Contracting Parties will wish to establish a working party to consider this issue in depth. We shall, of course, support the establishment of such a working party.[27]

I would like to bring this statement to a close by stressing the intention of my Government to seek such prompt, fundamental, and effective adjustments as will bring our trade and monetary relationships into healthy balance. Our action was taken on the basis of a clearly established balance of payments need. That is beyond challenge. We have run deficits for too many years, and it is high time that we run surpluses. The contributing causes of our balance of payments disequilibrium, which has developed over more than a decade, are to be found in certain international trading practices and other international policies, in certain deficiencies in the monetary system, and in certain stresses and strains which have cumulatively developed in our domestic economy. We are ready to grapple with all of these.

We are not interested in piecemeal repairs and patchwork mending. We seek lasting improvements in the trade and payments system. There is a time for debate and a time for action. Great opportunities and deep dangers are equally before us; if we are to overcome the latter we must move vigorously to seize the former. Recognition of this choice in our deliberations here today will contribute materially to the environment in which all trading nations can meet their responsibilities constructively.

---

[26] Cf. Document 151.
[27] For the agreement on the establishment of a working party by the Council on Aug. 25, 1971, see *Bulletin*, Sept. 20, 1971, p. 908.

(145) International Aspects of the New Economic Program: News Conference Statement by President Nixon, September 16, 1971.[28]

(Excerpt)

*   *   *

INTERNATIONAL ASPECTS OF ECONOMIC PROGRAM

Q. Mr. President, the international aspects of your economic program seem to have shaken up our friends more than our enemies. I'm thinking of Europe particularly, and Japan. What is your feeling about that? Isn't this going to be a worry for us, aren't we hurting some very good and important friends in the process?

THE PRESIDENT. It is inevitable that those policies would shake up our friends rather than our potential enemies—I should say, rather than our opponents—because it is our friends with whom we primarily have trade and monetary dealings. And, of course, our international policies dealt with trade and monetary policy. On the other hand, what we have to realize is that the structure of international monetary affairs that had been built 25 years ago and then patched up from time to time over the years had simply become obsolete. It was essential that the United States move as it did to protect its interests and also to get a solution to that problem.

Now, one question that I know is often asked by our friends, by the Japanese, for example, in Asia and by the Europeans in Europe, is: How long is "temporary"—the temporary surcharge? My answer to that is that if all we were seeking was a temporary solution, "temporary" would be very brief, but we are not seeking a temporary solution.

A temporary solution is one that I would say would be going back to the old system and patching it up a bit. What we are seeking is a permanent solution and that is why the length of the temporary surcharge will be somewhat longer, because we need to address ourselves not only to the matter of monetary policy and exchange rates, we have to address ourselves to burden-sharing, we have to address ourselves also to trade restraints, including non-tariff barriers.[29]

This is a time for our friends around the world—and we are all competitors—to build a new system with which we can live so that we don't have another crisis in a year. With regard to the Japanese, incidentally, I think I can best summarize our dilemma in this way: After the Japanese were here, I found that, both from the information they gave and the information we had ourselves, that Japan is our biggest customer in the

---

[28] *Presidential Documents*, Sept. 20, 1971, pp. 1285-86.
[29] Cf. Document 151.

world and we are their biggest customer in the world.[30]

Also I found that Japan at the present time produces more than all the rest of East Asia combined, including the People's Republic of China. Now that shows you the problem.

It means that the United States and Japan inevitably are going to be competitors because we are both strong economies. On the other hand, it means that friendship and alliance between the United States and Japan is indispensable. So what we are trying to do—and this was why these discussions were helpful—what we are trying to do is to work out a new system that will recognize the realities so that we can reduce these tensions that have developed, the number of crises that have come up over and over again in the international monetary field in the future.

The other point that I would make with regard to the United States: I know that some have raised the question as to whether in my message to the Congress[31] I was really announcing to the world that we were—by looking to our own interests—we were going to now be isolationists. On the contrary, a weak America will inevitably be isolationist. An America that is unable to maintain its military strength—and, incidentally, in the whole free world the United States pays two-thirds of the military bill today—a weak America that is unable to have its economic policies abroad, our economic, our foreign aid programs, the rest, inevitably will withdraw into itself.

We have to have a strong America, strong economically and strong in the sense of its competitive spirit if the United States is to continue to play a vigorous, activist role in the world. That is why I addressed myself to that problem and that is why we moved as drastically, as we had to, at home and abroad to deal with the basic problems that hurt America today economically.

* * *

C. The International Bank for Reconstruction and Development (I.B.R.D.) and the International Monetary Fund (I.M.F.).

[The "New Economic Policy" and its implications overshadowed other topics at the annual meetings of the Boards of Governors of the International Bank and Fund, which were held concurrently in Washington on September 27–October 1, 1971. The International Monetary Fund (I.M.F.), as custodian of the international monetary system established at the Bretton Woods Conference of 1944, was particularly distraught by the uncertainty and disorder that had developed in recent

[30] For the Japanese visit cf. Chapter VI at note 115. President Nixon publicly corrected his statement about the magnitude of U.S.-Japanese trade while on a visit to Canada in 1972 (*A.F.R., 1972*, Chapter X, note 85a).
[31] Cf. note 14 above.

months with the floating of the West German mark and other European currencies on May 9 and the suspension by the United States on August 15 of what had been the very basis of the system, the convertibility of the dollar into gold at the fixed rate of $35 per ounce. Japan, too, had floated its currency on August 27, and relationships among the principal world currencies were currently being determined by day-to-day market conditions while ministers of the leading financial powers groped for a means of stabilizing the monetary system on some new basis.

The American conception of what was needed, implicit in the remarks of President Nixon at a White House reception (Document 146) and in the formal statement of Secretary of the Treasury John B. Connally (Document 147), had been set forth with even greater clarity in meetings of the so-called Group of Ten, an informal committee of leading financial powers originally set up in 1962 to provide the I.M.F. with additional financial backing when required.[32] What the United States was asking, in addition to a substantial measure of trade liberalization, was an upward revaluation of other currencies on a scale sufficient to produce a $13 billion "turnaround" in the balance of payments by converting an estimated "basic" deficit of $9 billion on current account and long-term capital into a $4 billion surplus. But U.S. intimations that the import surcharge could be lifted if tangible progress were made on trade liberalization, and if exchange rates were allowed to float "cleanly"—i.e., without interference by national monetary authorities—failed to elicit a favorable reaction on the part of most delegates to the I.M.F. meeting, and the Board of Governors in its formal resolution (Document 148) confined itself to stressing the importance of prompt agreement that would permit an orderly resumption of Fund operations.]

(146) Remarks by President Nixon at a White House Reception for Officials Attending the Annual Meetings of the Boards of Governors of the International Monetary Fund and the International Bank for Reconstruction and Development, September 29, 1971.[33]

(Complete Text)

Mr. Secretary [of the Treasury] and ladies and gentlemen:
I hope you will not allow these microphones to frighten you into

---

[32] For the origins of the Group of Ten cf. *Documents, 1962*, pp. 516-18. Its members were Belgium, Canada, France, West Germany, Italy, Japan, the Netherlands, Sweden, the United Kingdom, and the United States.
[33] *Presidential Documents*, Oct. 4, 1971, pp. 1359-60.

thinking that after all the speeches you have been hearing, you are going to hear a long one as you are standing here in the East Room of the White House.

But I did want this opportunity to welcome you officially as those who have come to this historic meeting, before having the chance to greet each of you personally on this occasion.

I have just been reading some notes with regard to meetings of the Fund that have taken place over the years. It is always, perhaps, difficult to try to compare one year with another. I think, however, that in terms of the great issues that are involved, it might well be said that this meeting, in terms of what follows, in terms of what is built for the future, could well prove to be the most important meeting that has occurred since over 25 years ago, or approximately 25 years ago.

The reasons for that, I think, are quite obvious to all of you as world statesmen: the fact that the world has changed so much in the past 25 years. I was just thinking, for example, when I was greeting the Emperor of Japan in Anchorage the other day,[34] that over half of the world's people, approximately 60 percent, had been born since World War II. Half of all the people in the world now living were born since World War II. Over half of the nations in existence in the world today have come into being since World War II.

I think we should also, perhaps, agree that, as we look at the situation now, compared to what it was then, and even 10, 15 years ago, that today the dangers of war on a world scale are significantly less than they have been. The challenges of peace, therefore, have significantly increased. They have increased in ways that we should all be very happy about, in many ways at least: the fact that nations that were devastated by war now are strong and vigorous competitors of other nations in the world; the fact that new nations are beginning to develop economic strength with cooperation and assistance from older ones.

All of this means that the situation that the world confronts today is totally different than the one it was confronted with 25 years ago when the United States had over half of the world's production, with only 7 percent of the world's people.

Now, turning to the role of the United States today, and without just indulging in the glittering generalities that you expect on such occasions, let me simply say with all of the sincerity at my command that as one who came to Congress 25 years ago, who supported the Marshall Plan, who has supported reciprocal trade, who believes in the world role of the United States, who has traveled to more countries in the world than anyone who has ever served in this office, that I believe that the United States, for its own interest as well as for the world interest, must play a forthcoming and constructive role in international affairs.

[34] Cf. Chapter VI at note 114.

I would be less than candid if I were not to say that there is a growing and disturbing isolationism developing in our country because of the burden that America has carried, because of two wars that we have fought since World War II, because of other developments in world affairs. But whatever you may read about what the attitudes of people may be with regard to the desire to build new barriers for trade, with regard to the desire for the United States to lay down the burden or lay down at least a great part of the burden that we bear militarily and in terms of foreign assistance around the world, with regard to the idea that the United States should turn its attention almost exclusively to the problems within and forget the problems without, those are not views that I share. They are not views that are shared by the Secretary. They are not views that are shared, I trust, by the leaders of both major parties in this country.

We believe in the international role. We believe that one of the reasons we have come so far in the world in the past 25 years is because the United States has been willing to play a role. We trust that we can continue to play it.

Now, of course, we come to the present situation. You wonder, after these words, how was it possible that we have taken the actions that we have on the international front.[35] The reason that we have taken those actions I do not and should not try to go into in detail before such a sophisticated group, except very simply to say that we have taken those actions because if the United States is to play a world role and not turn inward, the United States must be strong and sound economically.

A weak United States will be isolationist without question. A strong United States will continue to play a role that is responsible in the world. That is the reason that I had to take some of these actions, actions that I know were distressing to some of you, but actions that we felt were essential to strengthen the position of the United States so that we could continue to be as forthcoming in world affairs in the future as we have in the past.

Looking to the future, you can be assured of our cooperation in reducing barriers of trade, rather than raising them; our cooperation in sharing the burden, and sharing it fairly with others, of free world defense; our cooperation, also, in the area in which you, of course, are so expert, in the area of international monetary affairs.

On that score, I can only add one perhaps interesting anecdote. Perhaps most Americans' favorite humorist, at least that was as far as the 19th century was concerned, was Mark Twain. And he had something, usually, to say about virtually everybody in our society, something that was quite appropriate about lawyers, politicians, and also about bankers. This was his description of a banker:

[35] Documents 142-143.

He said, "A banker is someone who will loan you his umbrella when the sun is shining and ask for it back when it's raining."

Now, let me say, we understand that at this particular period there will be hard bargaining between bankers representing other countries and our own. And that is all to the good. I think a banker does no favor to a borrower by making a bad loan. It appears that it is a favor, but in the end the banker is right in insisting on responsibility and the ability to pay.

It certainly does not mean that we are going to have a sound structure for the future if it is based on simply going back to one that has broken down from time to time. The measures we have taken are temporary. How long temporary is depends upon what we want to come up with. If we want to go to another temporary system, it would be very, very short; but if we want to build permanently for the future and build well, then we must have that kind of discussion in which all sides bargain hard in their own interest—we expect you to, we expect to—and then have an understanding which is in all of our mutual interest. It can be done and it will be done.

One final thought: I just concluded a meeting with the Foreign Secretary of the Soviet Union.[35] And it was a very constructive meeting—however, a meeting which as we both recognize, still discussed many differences that we have and will continue to have. But as I thought of that meeting, I thought back to the time when so many in this world immediately after World War II talked about one world politically. That is something that is not going to happen, not in our time and probably it should not happen because of the differences that people have and will inevitably have in their political systems, their economic systems, what they want, what kind of government they want.

But while that may not happen, certainly, as we look at the free world today, as we look at Europe, as we look at Latin America, we look at Africa, we look at the rim of nations around Asia, the mainland of Asia, we can think of the possibility of one world economically. And as we move toward one world economically, one world which is highly competitive, but with rules of the game which are fair to all, this means that those political differences that otherwise would divide us can be substantially reduced.

What has happened in Europe—free Europe—over the past 25 years has eloquently demonstrated that. So, I say to you: I greet you today as bankers, as great experts in this field. I know that you will build well for the next 25 years as you have built well for the past 25. I can assure you, as you help to develop this new monetary system, you are not only doing something which is good for international finance, but you are making an immeasurable contribution to world peace.

Thank you.

[36] Cf. note 155 to Chapter II.

(147) Statement to the Annual Meeting of the Boards of Governors by Secretary of the Treasury John B. Connally, September 30, 1971.[37]

(Complete Text)

After a remarkable quarter century of stability and development nurtured by close collaboration within the International Monetary Fund and the World Bank, events have challenged the underlying premises and functioning of the system devised at Bretton Woods. Some of those basic premises are now invalid.

Those at Bretton Woods planned for the transition from a war-torn world to a world of reconstruction and peaceful prosperity. The founders could assume, without challenge, a world in which the United States, for a time, possessed the dominant economic and financial power. The challenging goal was to rebuild the strength of others, in a context of flourishing trade, freedom for payments, and rapid development.

Now our very success has produced new problems. Trade has grown enormously, but the patterns have not been in sustainable balance. International transactions have been substantially freed and investment accelerated, but we have not learned to maintain an equilibrium in underlying payments or in exchange markets. And after 25 years, international monetary stability can no longer depend so heavily on a single nation.

The announcements by President Nixon on August 15[38] recognized these long-building realities. In doing so, his intention was to launch the United States into a new economic era—and to assure more balanced and sustainable economic relationships with the rest of the world. His actions accept, as a basic point of departure, the links already emphasized here by several Governors between effective domestic performance, a secure balance of payments, and international financial stability.

We are committed to curbing inflation and revitalizing the American economy—not just this year or next, but for the longer pull. We are committed to ending the persistent deficit in our external payments; indeed, at this point in time, the only choice can be the means to that end, not the end itself. Finally, in taking the difficult decision to suspend the convertibility of the dollar into reserve assets, we are committed to negotiating with our friends for a monetary order responsive to the needs and conditions of this generation.

The United States has not been alone among the countries represented here in grappling with the problem of achieving vigorous growth

[37] *Bulletin*, Oct. 25, 1971, pp. 453-57.
[38] Document 142.

and productivity while dealing with the destructive forces of domestic inflation.

To cope with this situation, President Nixon moved boldly to apply a 90-day wage-price freeze to make a simple point as forcibly and directly as he could: Cooperation in the elimination of inflation is a prime national priority.

We are now deeply engaged in a broad effort, involving all elements in our economy, to develop an effective, forceful follow-on program to the freeze. In a matter of weeks, that program will be announced. At the same time, we will be implementing other parts of the President's domestic program to assure both near-term growth and lasting gains in efficiency, productivity, and technology.

In its entirety, this program is designed to fulfill our first obligation both to ourselves and to the international monetary system: a stable, prosperous domestic economy.

Nevertheless, crucial as they are, I believe it is now fully understood that domestic measures alone cannot deal with the present and prospective imbalance in the external payments of the United States. The specific monetary and trade measures which we introduced on August 15, including the imposition of a temporary import surcharge,[39] will not in themselves solve the problem. They were, however, the necessary first steps to arrest an intolerable deterioration in the balance of payments position of the United States. The deterioration in our position has, of course, had its counterpart in improvement abroad, and only by working together can we find solutions conducive to expanding trade and monetary stability.

LONG-RANGE REFORMS REQUIRED

I would like to emphasize the connection we see between the balance of payments adjustment now required, on the one hand, and the long-range evolution and improvement of the monetary system on the other.

First, without a full and lasting turnaround in the balance of payments position of the United States, any new monetary arrangements inevitably would break down.

Secondly, such a turnaround cannot be fully assured and lasting unless necessary exchange rate changes are accompanied by trading arrangements that assure fair access to world markets for U.S. products.

Thirdly, a more balanced sharing of responsibilities for the security of the free world can and must be a part of a balanced economic order.

These adjustments are both entirely feasible and eminently desirable in the light of the impressive economic growth and strength of other leading trading nations. Indeed, we believe our objectives are shared by

[39] Document 143.

all nations with a fundamental interest in a stable and balanced world trading and monetary system. We also share a common concern in seeing our deficit eliminated by means consistent with open economies and expanding trade.

We do not underestimate the difficulties of the process. But I am in no way disheartened or surprised by the absence of instant solutions in the 6 weeks since the President's action. The simple fact is that progress is being made. In contrast to early August, I believe there is explicit and general recognition that:

—We face together an adjustment problem of substantial magnitude.

—There is a need for a broad realignment of relative currency values.

—Measures outside of the exchange rate field are a factor in restoring lasting strength in the U.S. balance of payments.

—For the longer run, the international monetary system requires far-reaching reform, including a lesser role, at the least, for gold.

Indeed, we are now launched into an agreed program of work toward a solution in all these areas as soon as feasible.

Much can be done in bilateral and multilateral negotiations in the weeks ahead.

We are all gratified, I believe, that we have progressed this far. But none of us—at least I don't—make progress in understanding and agreement on procedures for the hard policy decisions necessary for a satisfactory solution. Much difficult work remains, both of an urgent and of a painstaking nature.

As you know, the United States has made explicit its own analysis of the needed turnaround in our own balance of payments position. It reflects the hard fact of a substantial underlying adverse trend in our trade position.

Some have urged that the adjustment sought by the United States is too large. We are told time is of the essence. It is said we must be satisfied with an admittedly partial solution, lest restrictions and even retaliation begin and recessionary forces take hold. At the same time, we are told that the quick and partial solution must entail a change in the official dollar price of gold and that our surcharge must be removed as a prelude to negotiations.

We can fully appreciate the expressed concerns. We also fully understand that our surcharge—while applied across the board in a nondiscriminatory way—as a practical matter affects products and countries unevenly. We are conscious of the political sensitivities of decisions on exchange rates. Yet, in the interest of frankly discussing the issues, I must say plainly that we find a certain inconsistency between the expressed concerns and the proposed remedies.

A change in the gold price is of no economic significance and would be patently a retrogressive step in terms of our objective to reduce, if not eliminate, the role of gold in any new monetary system. Removal of the surcharge, prior to making substantial progress toward our objectives, would accomplish nothing toward correcting the balance of payments deficit. Nor can measures by others to resist exchange rate realignment or other adjustment measures by controls, restraints, or subsidies help the process of resolving the situation promptly and effectively.

We must find more timely and constructive ways to meet these economic and negotiating problems—to avoid the contentious issue of the gold price, to achieve the earliest possible removal of the surcharge, and to help determine the size and distribution of the needed exchange rate realignment. Faced with these difficulties, I believe we should welcome the help that the market itself can provide in reaching crucial decisions.

Many nations already are allowing their currencies temporarily to float, but they have done so with widely varying degrees of intervention and controls. As a result, some adjustments clearly needed are being delayed or thwarted, the process of multilateral decisionmaking impeded, and political questions multiplied. In this respect, our surcharge and restrictions on capital flows could, like those applied by other countries, themselves be a disturbing influence.

If other governments will make tangible progress toward dismantling specific barriers to trade over coming weeks and will be prepared to allow market realities freely to determine exchange rates for their currencies for a transitional period, we for our part would be prepared to remove the surcharge.

This would provide one possible path for moving expeditiously, reversing any tendency to maintain and extend restrictive trade and exchange practices, and for providing more satisfactory arrangements for settling individual transactions, consistent with the resolution that has been proposed to the Governors.[40]

I recognize that floating rates will not necessarily, over any short time period, indicate a true equilibrium. I also know full well from experience that the present fixed rate system has failed to maintain an equilibrium, and we need assistance, during this difficult transitional period, from the objective, impersonal forces of the marketplace in making decisions.

In any event, we will continue to work in detailed and frank negotiations, bilaterally and multilaterally, to seek agreement on appropriate measures which may most fruitfully achieve and maintain the needed adjustments. This will lay the foundation for constructive consideration of the longer term problems of our trading and monetary arrangements.

DEVELOPMENT OF NEW MONETARY SYSTEM

I am following with great interest the suggestions of other Governors

[40] Document 148.

concerning the shape of the future world monetary system. These comments bear out what President Nixon said on August 15 regarding the need for a new monetary system. Chairman Schiller [Karl Schiller, Minister for Economics and Finance, Federal Republic of Germany] forcefully pointed out at the start: We cannot expect or wish simply to go back to the old and familiar.

In contrast to the world that faced the architects at Bretton Woods, there is a far greater balance of strength, particularly among the North American, the European, and Japanese economies. This development—so welcome in its own right—in turn calls for a different and more symmetrical balance of opportunities and responsibilities.

We and the world had grown accustomed to U.S. deficits. The counterpart of those deficits was rather persistent surpluses for others, and those surpluses helped satisfy the individual goals of other countries. But a monetary system dependent on U.S. deficits is no longer tolerable, economically, financially, or politically, for you or for us.

The implications are fundamental. A return to specified parities without United States deficits will require ample alternative sources of official liquidity, internationally managed and controlled. There must be arrangements for adequate exchange rate flexibility, available to all countries, to help maintain a reasonable payments balance. There must be means—more effective than those incorporated in the Fund agreement[41] at present—of encouraging timely and appropriate action by surplus countries which escape the financial pressures forcing adjustment on deficit countries.

There is another area in which we are, in a sense, victims of our own progress. As economies have become more closely intertwined, as international capital markets become more effective and efficient, and as controls and restrictions are reduced, the potential for volatile and disturbing capital flows expands enormously. This had already been a matter for international consideration before August 15 and for considerable comment at this meeting.

If not yet unanimously acceptable, substantially wider margins are already viewed as a necessary part of any establishment of new parities. Other difficult questions concern the mix of national fiscal and monetary policies, joint or coordinated action in international money markets, and the proper role, if any, for limited restrictions on financial intermediaries—always keeping in the forefront the fundamental need of free and competitive markets to serve the needs of traders and investors.

A number of speakers have already emphasized that whatever the particulars of new monetary arrangements, a fundamental need will remain for fair, widely understood, and enforceable international codes

[41] Opened for signature at Washington Dec. 27, 1945 (TIAS 1501).

of conduct in trade and monetary matters. I share that emphasis. The further corollary is that the International Monetary Fund itself should play a central role in developing and monitoring such codes.

Discussions of these matters have now been launched not only in the Executive Board but in the Group of Ten.[42] In emphasizing the need for these discussions, I also note these matters are of direct interest not only to large and highly developed countries but to that wider spectrum of Fund membership ready and able to assume a share of the responsibility for maintaining an effective monetary system.

While dealing with the monetary system as a whole, we shall, for our part, also proceed with the associated task of dismantling unfair barriers to trade and impediments, including our own, to the free flow of long-term capital.

MULTILATERAL DEVELOPMENT ASSISTANCE

We will also need to deal with many questions bearing more specifically upon the economic well-being of developing countries. My Government particularly welcomes the discussion at this meeting and elsewhere of the pressing problems posed by population trends in much of the world, the new emphasis on nutritional and environmental concerns, and the more careful consideration of the implications of external debt burdens.

We are impressed by the growing scope of the traditional activities of the World Bank and its affiliates under the able leadership of President [Robert S.] McNamara. President Nixon has called for an increase in the emphasis that we ourselves give to multilateral institutions in our development assistance effort,[43] and we plan to continue that process.

The high levels of lending by the World Bank Group are supported for the most part by Bank borrowing in the developed countries. Twenty-five years of activity has encouraged increased direct financial support by all developed countries, and I hope other nations will continue to open their capital markets to the Bank.

As the level of activity expands, the Bank must take even more care with the efficiency and effectiveness of its operations and must question old premises. It is in this light that I welcome the evaluation of efforts being undertaken by the Bank. It is important not only that we insure that the Bank Group processes projects quickly and efficiently but also that its funds have their planned impact—including assurance that these resources are reaching all the people of the developing countries.

As the World Bank Group further develops its ambitious plans, I must

[42] Cf. above at note 32.
[43] Cf. Document 153.

also speak frankly of our own situation and intentions. I can do so explicitly with respect to the pending replenishment of the International Development Association (IDA), without which the plans for the years ahead will be gravely impaired.[44]

We firmly support that replenishment. In reducing our total of assistance by some 10 percent over the current fiscal year, we mean to avoid any reduction in that major commitment. Within our constitutional system, however, IDA replenishment requires, but has not yet received, congressional approval. The fundamental sympathy and support of the Congress for IDA over the years has, I believe, been amply demonstrated. Nevertheless, Congress will have to be convinced, as never before, that: First, this development assistance efficiently serves to promote growth in the developing world; and second, that our own situation will strengthen to the point where this and other burdens on our payments can be safely assumed.

All these official efforts must be supplemented by flows of private capital. I am disturbed when I see instances of developing countries treating private investment in a manner not accepted by international law. In a world already short of capital to meet pressing demands, the adverse effects on the investment climate of such practices are bound, in a very tangible sense, to deny real benefits to the people. The damage in reducing the flow of capital can extend beyond the parties immediately involved to other potential investors or recipients of funds.

It is in this context that the United States firmly supports the creation of the proposed International Investment Insurance Agency. The maintenance of a healthy climate for private investment in those countries which recognize the important role such investment can play has become a matter of concern for all such nations. The interest in this proposal at last year's meeting has not yet produced a result. I am hopeful that a new resolve and firmer commitment to this idea by both developed and developing countries will produce agreement in the coming year.

A logical complementary development would be more active reliance on the Centre for the Settlement of Investment Disputes. Of course, the policies of the World Bank itself, in situations when existing foreign investments are unfairly treated, will importantly affect the future climate for the flow of public development assistance as well as for foreign private investment.

In conclusion, I would only reiterate we have a large agenda before us. We all know the present situation has both risk and opportunity.

We should not fear the one nor fail the other.

With the same vision that motivated those at Bretton Woods, we can build a better monetary and trading world.

---

[44] Cf. *The World This Year, 1972*, p. 147.

With wisdom, we can devise monetary arrangements that combine an essential stability with the capacity to adapt.

With courage, we can move together to reduce restrictions on trade and payments, in recognition of our mutual dependence.

With patience, we can work together, finding a balance of opportunity and responsibility for rich and poor alike that fits the imperatives of today's world.

These qualities are present in the men who have come to Washington this week and in the governments they represent. You can be sure the United States will join you in the vanguard of the effort. In this sure knowledge, I look ahead with confidence.

(148) Resolution on the International Monetary System, Adopted by the Board of Governors of the International Monetary Fund, October 1, 1971.[45]

(Complete Text)

INTERNATIONAL MONETARY SYSTEM

WHEREAS the present international monetary situation contains the dangers of instability and disorder in currency and trade relationships but also offers the opportunity for constructive changes in the international monetary system; and

WHEREAS it is of the utmost importance to avoid the aforesaid dangers and assure continuance of the progress made in national and international wellbeing in the past quarter of a century; and

WHEREAS prompt action is necessary to resume the movement toward a free and multilateral system in which trade and capital flows can contribute to the integration of the world economy and the rational allocation of resources throughout the world; and

WHEREAS consideration should be given to the improvement of the international monetary system and the adjustment process; and

WHEREAS the orderly conduct of the operations of the International Monetary Fund should be resumed as promptly as possible in the interest of all members; and

WHEREAS all members of the Fund should participate in seeking solutions of the aforesaid problems;

[45] Resolution No. 26-9, adopted by the Board of Governors of the I.M.F. in joint session with the Boards of Governors of the I.B.R.D. and affiliated institutions; text from International Monetary Fund, *Summary Proceedings of the Twenty-sixth Annual Meeting of the Board of Governors, September 27–October 1, 1971* (Washington: I.M.F., n.d.), pp. 331-32.

NOW, THEREFORE, the Board of Governors hereby RESOLVES that:

I. Members of the Fund are called upon to collaborate with the Fund and with each other in order, as promptly as possible, to

(a) establish a satisfactory structure of exchange rates, maintained within appropriate margins, for the currencies of members, together with the reduction of restrictive trade and exchange practices, and

(b) facilitate resumption of the orderly conduct of the operations of the Fund.

II. Members are called upon to collaborate with the Fund and with each other in efforts to bring about

(a) a reversal of the tendency in present circumstances to maintain and extend restrictive trade and exchange practices, and

(b) satisfactory arrangements for the settlement of international transactions which will contribute to the solution of the problems involved in the present international monetary situation.

III. The Executive Directors are requested:

(a) to make reports to the Board of Governors without delay on the measures that are necessary or desirable for the improvement or reform of the international monetary system; and

(b) for the purpose of (a), to study all aspects of the international monetary system, including the role of reserve currencies, gold, and special drawing rights, convertibility, the provisions of the Articles with respect to exchange rates, and the problems caused by destabilizing capital movements; and

(c) when reporting, to include, if possible, the texts of any amendments of the Articles of Agreement which they consider necessary to give effect to their recommendations.

D. The Azores Meeting and the Smithsonian Agreement.

[In the course of further discussion centering in the Group of Ten, the United States reduced somewhat its demands for currency revaluation by others and intimated that a "turnaround" of $9 billion in the U.S. balance of payments—rather than the $13 billion previously called for—would be acceptable if combined with the opening of negotiations

looking toward far-reaching modifications of trade policy by the
E.E.C., Japan, and others. In the absence of such steps, however, the
U.S. declined either to lift the 10 percent surcharge or to contemplate
the small, *pro forma* devaluation of the dollar that was favored by some
governments as a counterpart to any upward revaluation of their own
currencies.

This impasse was broken on December 13-14, 1971, when President
Nixon met in the Azores with President Pompidou, obtained the latter's
consent to the "imminent" opening of trade negotiations between the
United States and the E.E.C., and agreed that the two countries would
"work toward a prompt realignment of exchange rates through a devaluation of the dollar and revaluation of some other currencies" (Document 43). The significance of this agreement was spelled out by
Secretary Connally on his return to the United States (Document 149),
and the outlines of the new exchange rate structure were agreed upon
at a Washington meeting of the Group of Ten on December 17-18
(Document 150) and approved the following day by the Executive
Directors of the I.M.F.

The heart of the Smithsonian Agreement was a commitment by the
United States to suppress the import surcharge and related measures—as
was done on December 20 (Document 151)—and to seek congressional
approval of a devaluation of the dollar in terms of gold, to be effected
by means of an increase in the official gold price from the historic $35
per ounce established in 1934 to $38 per ounce. This change, which
was subsequently approved by Congress,[46] involved a percentage devaluation of the dollar that was variously stated at 7.89 percent or 8.57
percent, depending on the calculation used. Convertibility of the dollar
into gold, suspended August 15, 1971, was not restored.

Among other leading currencies affected by the Smithsonian Agreement,[47] the British pound sterling and the French franc remained unchanged in terms of gold but appreciated against the dollar. The West
German mark was revalued upward against the dollar by 13.58 percent,
the Swiss franc by 13.86 percent, and the Japanese yen by an extraordinary 16.88 percent. Some countries devalued their currencies, in
parallel with the dollar or by an even larger amount. Canada maintained
the floating rate it had instituted in May 1970. Under a policy decision
announced by the I.M.F. Executive Directors,[48] countries that preferred to do so were permitted to establish temporary "central rates" in
lieu of par values, and to allow their currencies to fluctuate within the
"wider margins" of 2¼ percent—instead of the previous 1 percent—

---

[46] Public Law 92-268, Mar. 31, 1972. A second, 10 percent devaluation of the
dollar, effected Feb. 12, 1973 by increasing the official gold price to $42.22 per
ounce, was validated by Public Law 93-110, Sept. 21, 1973.
[47] For details see *The World This Year, 1972*, pp. 172-74.
[48] Text in *New York Times*, Dec. 20, 1971.

above or below their par value or central rate.

The negotiations on trade matters which were supposed to form the counterpart of this arrangement were to remain in a preliminary stage through most of 1972. In November of that year, agreement was reached by the contracting parties to the General Agreement on Tariffs and Trade (GATT) that a new round of multilateral trade negotiations would be formally launched at a ministerial meeting to be held in Tokyo in September 1973. In the meantime, proposals for reform of the international monetary system were again discussed by the I.M.F. Board of Governors at their annual meeting on September 25-29, 1972, and the task of drawing up an outline of a monetary reform plan was entrusted to a Committee of Twenty which held its first meeting September 28, 1972. All such plans, however, were to be thrown into renewed uncertainty by the crisis in international trade and financial relations that followed the reopening of hostilities between the Arab states and Israel in October 1973 and the adoption of new distribution and pricing policies by leading petroleum exporting countries.]

(149) Significance of the Nixon-Pompidou Agreement: Remarks by Secretary of the Treasury Connally, Andrews Air Force Base, Maryland, December 14, 1971.[49]

(Complete Text)

Thank you. With respect to the international monetary affairs, I would simply like to say that the communiqué that was issued by the two Presidents[50] was not specific in its treatment of the many items that were discussed. This was partially, deliberately so designed for the simple reason that our international monetary problems encompass the actions and the reactions of a great many more countries than just the United States and France. Consequently, we are not in a position to divulge all of the details of the discussion. I think it is fair to say that the meeting between the two Presidents resulted in a very significant step forward—looking toward the settlement of the international monetary problems that exist. The Group of Ten meeting which will occur here this weekend hopefully will bring us even closer to a solution.[51] I would not now predict that we will finally settle it this weekend because I can't prejudice the actions of other nations. I will say that, beyond any question, the very significant step that results from the meeting of the two Presidents will contribute enormously toward an alternate solution and an early solution.

Q. Mr. Secretary, could you tell us anything about the timetable for

49 *Public Papers, 1971*, pp. 1191-92.
50 Document 43.
51 Cf. Document 150.

devaluation and any idea of what the devaluation will be?

SECRETARY CONNALLY. No, we don't know the timetable, again, simply because this is going to depend entirely upon the actions of the Group of Ten and all the nations. And this is the thing that we want to emphasize, that this is not a two-nation affair. It is a package of actions that have to be taken by the Group of Ten. Trade issues have to be included. So, I can't give you a timetable, but we are certainly looking in the very short range for a solution to all these problems.

Q. One other question, Mr. Secretary. Do you feel assured that other nations will revalue their currencies forthwith to accommodate us?

SECRETARY CONNALLY. Well, certainly anticipated in any solution to the problem is a revaluation of some of the currencies around the world, yes.

(150) Meeting of the "Group of Ten" at the Smithsonian Institution, Washington, December 17-18, 1971.

(a) Final Communiqué, December 18, 1971.[52]

(Complete Text)

1. The Ministers and Central Bank Governors of the ten countries participating in the General Arrangements to Borrow[53] met at the Smithsonian Institution in Washington on 17th–18th December, 1971, in executive session under the Chairmanship of Mr. J. B. Connally, Secretary of the Treasury of the United States. Mr. P.-P. Schweitzer, the Managing Director of the International Monetary Fund, took part in the meeting, which was also attended by the President of the Swiss National Bank, Mr. E. Stopper, and in part by the Secretary-General of the O.E.C.D. [Organization for Economic Cooperation and Development], Jonkheer E. van Lennep, the General Manager of the Bank for International Settlements, Mr. R. Larre, and the Vice-President of the Commission of the E.E.C. [European Economic Community], Mr. R. Barre. The Ministers and Governors welcomed a report from the Managing Director of the Fund on a meeting held between their Deputies and the Executive Directors of the Fund.

2. The Ministers and Governors agreed on an inter-related set of measures designed to restore stability to international monetary arrangements and to provide for expanding international trade. These measures will be communicated promptly to other governments. It is the hope of the Ministers and Governors that all governments will coop-

[52] *Bulletin*, Jan. 10, 1972, pp. 32-34.
[53] Cf. note 32 above.

erate through the International Monetary Fund to permit implementation of these measures in an orderly fashion.

3. The Ministers and Governors reached agreement on a pattern of exchange rate relationships among their currencies. These decisions will be announced by individual governments, in the form of par values or central rates as they desire. Most of the countries plan to close their exchange markets on Monday [December 20]. The Canadian Minister informed the Group that Canada intends temporarily to maintain a floating exchange rate and intends to permit fundamental market forces to establish the exchange rate without intervention except as required to maintain orderly conditions.

4. It was also agreed that, pending agreement on longer-term monetary reforms, provision will be made for 2¼ percent margins of exchange rate fluctuation above and below the new exchange rates. The Ministers and Governors recognized that all members of the International Monetary Fund not attending the present discussions will need urgently to reach decisions, in consultation with the International Monetary Fund, with respect to their own exchange rates. It was the view of the Ministers and Governors that it is particularly important at this time that no country seek improper competitive advantage through its exchange rate policies. Changes in parities can only be justified by an objective appraisal which establishes a position of disequilibrium.

5. Questions of trade arrangements were recognized by the Ministers and Governors as a relevant factor in assuring a new and lasting equilibrium in the international economy. Urgent negotiations are now under way between the United States and the Commission of the European Community, Japan, and Canada to resolve pending short-term issues at the earliest possible date and with the European Community to establish an appropriate agenda for considering more basic issues in a framework of mutual cooperation in the course of 1972 and beyond. The United States agreed to propose to Congress a suitable means for devaluing the dollar in terms of gold to $38.00 per ounce as soon as the related set of short-term measures is available for Congressional scrutiny. Upon passage of required legislative authority in this framework,[54] the United States will propose the corresponding new par value of the dollar to the International Monetary Fund.

6. In consideration of the agreed immediate realignment of exchange rates, the United States agreed that it will immediately suppress the recently imposed 10 percent import surcharge and related provisions of the Job Development Credit.[55]

7. The Ministers and Governors agreed that discussions should be promptly undertaken, particularly in the framework of the IMF, to

[54] Cf. above at note 46.
[55] Cf. Document 151.

consider reform of the international monetary system over the longer term. It was agreed that attention should be directed to the appropriate monetary means and division of responsibilities for defending stable exchange rates and for insuring a proper degree of convertibility of the system; to the proper role of gold, of reserve currencies, and of Special Drawing Rights in the operation of the system; to the appropriate volume of liquidity; to re-examination of the permissible margins of fluctuation around established exchange rates and other means of establishing a suitable degree of flexibility; and to other measures dealing with movements of liquid capital. It is recognized that decisions in each of these areas are closely linked.

(b) Remarks by President Nixon During an Informal Visit After the Meeting, December 18, 1971.[56]

(Complete Text)

Ladies and gentlemen:

It is my very great privilege to announce on behalf of the Finance Ministers and the other representatives of the ten countries involved, the conclusion of the most significant monetary agreement in the history of the world. I know that may seem to be an overstatement, but when we compare this agreement with Bretton Woods, which, of course, was the last very significant agreement of this kind,[57] we can see how enormous this achievement has been.

Bretton Woods came at a time when the United States, immediately after World War II, was predominant in economic affairs in the world and the decision of the United States was, perhaps, the most important one to be made at that time.

Now we have a new world, fortunately a much better world economically, where instead of just one strong economic nation, the nations of Europe, Japan and Asia, Canada and North America, all of these nations are strong economically, strong competitors, and, as a result, it was necessary in these meetings for a negotiation to take place between equally strong nations insofar as their currencies were concerned. And the fact that these gentlemen, over a period of weeks, finally culminating in the last 2 days, have reached agreement on the realignment of exchange rates is, indeed, the most significant event that has occurred in world financial history.

I express appreciation to them for the work they have done and I would say finally this. The question will inevitably be asked when each returns to his country, as it will be asked of Secretary Connally and me when we refer to the Congress: Who won, who lost?

[56] *Public Papers, 1971*, pp. 1195-96. The President spoke at the Smithsonian Institution.
[57] Cf. note 41 above.

The answer is: When agreements are reached in which all parties bargain hard and fight hard for their positions, when that agreement is mutually reached, then it is an agreement which is to the mutual benefit of both. What has happened here is that the whole free world has won, because as a result of this agreement, we will have, from a financial and monetary standpoint, a more stable world. We will have a world in which competition can be more fair. We will have a world in which we can have more true prosperity than would be the case if we continue to have an alignment which was inevitably doomed to fail because of the instability.

And so congratulations, in this historic room, to these men for their achievement, for their service to the cause of financial stability in the world, for progress economically in the world, and, of course, in the long run, to a more peaceful world.

Thank you.

(151) Termination of the Import Surcharge, December 20, 1971.

(a) Termination of Additional Duty for Balance-of-Payments Purposes: Proclamation by the President, December 20, 1971.[58]

(Complete Text)

By the President of the United States of America
a Proclamation

WHEREAS, in order to impose a surcharge required by the balance of payments position of the United States, Proclamation 4074, dated August 15, 1971,[59] terminated in part for such period as necessary prior Presidential Proclamations insofar as such proclamations were inconsistent with, or proclaimed duties different from, those made effective pursuant to the terms of Proclamation 4074;

WHEREAS, a multilateral agreement has been reached among the Group of Ten major industrial nations[60] which permits removal of the surcharge;

WHEREAS, under section 350(a) (6) of the Tariff Act of 1930, as amended (hereinafter referred to as "the Tariff Act"), and section 255(b) of the Trade Expansion Act of 1962[61] (hereinafter referred to as "the TEA"), and other authority, the President may, at any time,

---

[58] Proclamation 4098, Dec. 20, 1971; text from *Presidential Documents*, Dec. 27, 1971, p. 1693.
[59] Document 143.
[60] Document 150a.
[61] Cf. note 19 above.

terminate, in whole or in part, for such period as may be necessary, any proclamation, issued pursuant to section 350 of the Tariff Act or Title II of the TEA;

WHEREAS, under section 350(a) (1) (b) of the Tariff Act and section 201(a) (2) of the TEA, the President may proclaim modifications of any existing duty as he determines to be required or appropriate to carry out trade agreements entered into under the authority of those Acts; and

WHEREAS, I hereby determine that modification of existing duties to restore the rates of duty applicable on August 15, 1971, terminated in part for such period as necessary by Proclamation 4074, is required or appropriate to carry out such trade agreements;

NOW, THEREFORE, I, RICHARD, NIXON, President of the United States of America, acting under the authority vested in me by the Constitution and the statutes, including, but not limited to, the Tariff Act, and the TEA, respectively, do proclaim as follows:

A. I hereby terminate paragraphs B and C of Proclamation 4074.

B. I hereby proclaim such modification of duties as is necessary to restore the rates of duty in effect on August 15, 1971.

C. To implement this Proclamation, the subpart inserted after subpart B of part 2 of the Appendix to the Tariff Schedules of the United States, entitled "SUBPART C–TEMPORARY MODIFICATIONS FOR BALANCE OF PAYMENTS PURPOSES" is deleted therefrom.

D. This Proclamation shall be effective with respect to merchandise entered, or withdrawn from warehouse, for consumption on or after December 20, 1971.

IN WITNESS WHEREOF, I have hereunto set my hand this twentieth day of December in the year of our Lord nineteen hundred and seventy-one, and of the Independence of the United States of America the one hundred and ninety-sixth.

RICHARD NIXON

(b) Remarks by the President in Bermuda, December 20, 1971.[62]

(Complete Text)

Ladies and gentlemen, I have just had my first meeting with the Prime Minister. He felt that it would be well that I make this announcement prior to the time that we go into our more extended meetings this afternoon.

I have today made the first decision implementing the agreement that was reached over the weekend by the Group of Ten in their meetings in

[62] *Presidential Documents*, Dec. 27, 1971, p. 1693. For the President's Bermuda meeting with Prime Minister Heath see Document 44.

Washington.[63] After consultation with the Secretary of the Treasury and the Secretary of State today, I have signed a proclamation removing the 10 percent surcharge.[64]

This first step having been taken, we can now move on to the trade areas and the monetary areas in which agreement was also reached over the weekend.

Later today, on the American side, Secretary Connally and Secretary Rogers will brief the press,[65] and on the British side I know arrangements will probably be made for proper briefings also.

Thank you very much.

E. The International Wheat Agreement, 1971.

[The object of the International Wheat Agreement, 1971, was to provide for a continuation of the three-year International Grains Arrangement concluded in 1967 as an outgrowth of the Kennedy Round of international trade negotiations. The 1967 Arrangement had consisted of two parts: a Wheat Trade Convention—the latest in a series of international wheat agreements to which the United States had been a party since 1949—that was designed to help stabilize wheat prices at remunerative levels; and a Food Aid Convention that provided for annual shipments by the United States and others of 4.5 million metric tons of wheat and other grains to developing countries. Opened for signature in Washington in the fall of 1967, the International Grains Arrangement[66] had entered into force July 1, 1968, for the three-year period expiring June 30, 1971.

The International Wheat Agreement, 1971,[67] drafted early in 1971 at a United Nations Wheat Conference in Geneva, was open for signature in Washington on March 29–May 3 and signed by the United States on April 14, 1971. Like the 1967 Arrangement, it was concluded for a three-year period and consisted of two parts linked by a common preamble. The Wheat Trade Convention, 1971, signed by 33 governments and the European Economic Community, provided for cooperation and consultation on supply and prices, but, unlike its predecessor, did not embody any agreement on maximum and minimum prices or purchase and supply obligations. The new Food Aid Convention, 1971, signed by

---

[63] Document 150a.

[64] Document 151a.

[65] Rogers' remarks in *Bulletin*, Jan. 17, 1972, pp. 64-66, reproduced in part in Document 155; Connally remarks in *Presidential Documents*, Dec. 20, 1971, pp. 1695-98.

[66] TIAS 6537 (19 UST 5499); details in *bulletin*, May 6, 1968, pp. 590-94.

[67] TIAS 7144; 22 UST 820.

13 countries and the E.E.C., resembled the 1967 convention except for the withdrawal of three of the former donors (Denmark, Norway, and the United Kingdom); a reduction from 4,500,000 to 3,974,000 in the total minimum annual contribution; and a broadening of the terms under which contributions could be made. Of the nine donors under the new agreement, the United States would contribute 1,890,000 metric tons a year or 47.56 percent of the total, an increase from 42 percent under the earlier agreement. The E.E.C. would contribute 1,035,000 tons per year; Canada, 495,000; Japan and Australia, 225,000 each. Smaller amounts in grain or cash would be contributed by Argentina, Finland, Sweden, and Switzerland.

Although the texts of the conventions called for the deposit of ratifications not later than June 17, 1971, the agreement was not transmitted to the U.S. Senate until June 2 (Document 152), and the State Department deposited a declaration of provisional application and requested an extension of time while awaiting Senate action. Approved by the Foreign Relations Committee on June 30, the agreement was endorsed by a 78 to 0 vote of the Senate on July 12 and ratified by the President on July 24, 1971, on which date the agreement definitively entered into force for the United States.]

(152) Message from President Nixon to the Senate Requesting Its Advice and Consent to Ratification, June 2, 1971.[68]

(Complete Text)

To the Senate of the United States:

With a view to receiving the advice and consent of the Senate to ratification, I transmit herewith a copy of the International Wheat Agreement, 1971,[69] which was open for signature in Washington from March 29 through May 3, 1971. The Agreement was formulated at the United Nations Wheat Conference, 1971, held in Geneva.

I transmit also, for the information of the Senate, the report of the Secretary of State and the memorandum enclosed therewith concerning this Agreement.[70]

The Agreement is in two parts, the Wheat Trade Convention and the Food Aid Convention, covered by a common preamble. Both Conventions were signed in behalf of the Government of the United States of America. The Wheat Trade Convention was signed also for the European Economic Community and its six member States and for the governments of 26 other countries. The Food Aid Convention was

---

[68] *Presidential Documents*, June 7, 1971, pp. 852-53.
[69] Cf. note 67 above.
[70] S. Ex. F, 92d Cong., 1st sess.

signed also for the European Economic Community and its six member States and for the governments of six other countries.

The International Wheat Agreement, 1971, is intended to succeed the International Grains Arrangement, 1967,[71] which will terminate by its own terms on June 30, 1971.

The new Wheat Trade Convention continues international cooperation in wheat trade, maintaining the International Wheat Council and most of its functions and establishing a new Advisory Sub-Committee on Market Conditions charged with the task of continuously reviewing current market conditions and making prompt reports to the Executive Committee of the Council concerning the existence or threat of market instability. On the basis of such reports, the Executive Committee is to meet, review the situation, and consider the possibility of mutually acceptable solutions. The Council may also be convened to review such situations.

In contrast to previous wheat agreements, the 1971 Convention does not contain price provisions and purchase and supply obligations, principally because the exporting countries were unable to agree on the reference wheat or wheats to be used for setting minimum and maximum prices. Major changes in the Canadian grading system made uncertain the trading relationships among the several top quality wheats that were being considered as reference wheats. The negotiating conference decided that progress on establishing minimum and maximum prices and the related supply and purchase provisions must await the establishment and the testing in trade of the new Canadian grading system.

The Food Aid Convention continues the commitment initiated under the 1967 Food Aid Convention whereby parties contribute specified amounts of wheat, coarse grains, or products derived therefrom, or the cash equivalent, to developing countries. The principal changes in the new Convention are a reduction in the number of donors from 12 to 9, a slight reduction in the total minimum annual contribution, and a broadening of the terms under which contributions can be made.

Both Conventions provide that instruments of ratification shall be deposited no later than June 17, 1971. The Wheat Council may, however, grant an extension of time to any signatory government that had not deposited an instrument of ratification by that date.

It is my hope that the Senate will give early and favorable consideration of the two Conventions of the 1971 Agreement so that ratification by the United States can be effected and an instrument of ratification can be deposited without undue delay.

RICHARD NIXON

The White House
June 2, 1971

[71] Cf. note 66 above.

F. Foreign Aid and Economic Development.

[Debates about the U.S. program of economic and military aid to other nations reached a climax in 1971 with the submission in April of detailed proposals by the President for reform of the entire program (Document 153); the President's action on August 15 in ordering a 10 percent reduction in current foreign aid allocations (Document 142);[72] and the Senate vote of October 29 which killed the foreign aid authorization for the ongoing fiscal period (Document 154). This negative action was offset in some slight measure by a renewal of the administration's promise to seek congressional approval of a system of generalized trade preferences for developing countries (Document 155)—a pledge which, however, was not followed by any positive action.

The principal innovation suggested in President Nixon's April 21 message on the foreign aid program (Document 153) was the enactment of separate legislation for military and economic development and humanitarian assistance, hitherto dealt with in the same annual authorization and appropriation bills. Military aid or security assistance would be the subject of an International Security Assistance Act that would authorize a total of $1,993 million for the fiscal year 1972; economic aid would be covered by an International Development and Humanitarian Assistance Act authorizing $3,023 million for bilateral and $1,960 million for multilateral assistance programs over a period of two to three fiscal years.[73]

Although the Senate initially acquiesced in this two-bill concept, the House of Representatives chose once again to combine both military and economic assistance in a single bill that authorized continuation of the two programs for a further two-year period encompassing the fiscal years 1972 and 1973. Passed by the House on August 3, the bill was examined by the Senate Foreign Relations Committee and, after extensive amendment, reported to the Senate on October 21, 1971. As it left the Foreign Relations Committee, the bill provided a two-year authorization for economic and a one-year authorization for military aid; it also included the Mansfield amendment on withdrawal from Indochina that was later to be appended to the Military Procurement Authorization Act (Document 81).

The Senate's foreign aid debate on October 26-29 was strongly influenced by the recent U.N. General Assembly action in admitting Communist China to U.N. representation and expelling the U.S.-allied Republic of China on Taiwan (Document 125). After considering vari-

---

72 Aid to Latin America was subsequently exempted from the 10 percent reduction; cf. Chapter VIII at note 75.
73 Details, as presented to the Senate Foreign Relations Committee by Under Secretary of State Irwin on June 11, in *Bulletin*, July 5, 1971, pp. 23-27. For the detailed legislative history see Senate Foreign Relations Committee History, pp. 40-56.

ous proposals to restrict the U.S. contribution to U.N. programs or reduce the scale of U.S. aid to developing countries, the Senate on October 29 rejected the entire bill by a vote of 41 opposed to 27 in favor. This was a shattering development from the standpoint of its potential impact on the developing countries, whose difficult plight had been stressed in the President's foreign aid message and had evoked innumerable expressions of concern on the part of the O.E.C.D. (Document 141b) and other international institutions.

Although the dismayed reaction of the President and the Secretary of State (Document 154) failed to bring about a reversal of the Senate's action, attempts to repair the damage by other means were promptly initiated in that body. While the aid program was kept in being by emergency authorizations, the Senate in November passed a pair of interim authorization bills, the Special Foreign Military and Related Assistance Act of 1971 and the Special Foreign Economic and Humanitarian Assistance Act of 1971. These were later combined into a single bill, the Foreign Assistance Act of 1971, which, like the defeated Senate bill, authorized two years of economic aid and a single year of military aid. As signed by the President on February 7, 1972,[74] it authorized for the fiscal year 1972 a total of $2.7 billion for both military and economic aid programs. This amount was further reduced to $2.6 billion in the appropriation bill for fiscal 1972 that was finally signed March 8, 1972.[75]

A more positive development was the decision of the U.S. administration, in the wake of the December 18 Smithsonian Agreement (Document 150), to initiate action on President Nixon's 26-month-old pledge to seek legislation providing special trade preferences that would give the products of developing countries easier access to the U.S. market. The delay in implementing this promise, originally put forward in President Nixon's address of October 31, 1969, to the Inter American Press Association,[76] had been officially ascribed to the United States' deteriorating trade balance, a sluggish economy, and an unreceptive mood in Congress (Document 115). Although the European Economic Community and Japan had meanwhile elaborated their own trade preference systems and the President had foreshadowed similar U.S. action in his April 21 foreign aid message (Document 153), any such plans had once again been thrust aside by the new balance-of-payments crisis that developed in August 1971. Thus it was only on December 20, after the Smithsonian Agreement on currency realignments, that Secretary Rogers was able to announce the President's decision—as "a natural follow-up to the decisions taken in the monetary field"—to introduce

[74] Public Law 92-226, Feb. 7, 1972; cf. Nixon signature statement in *Public Papers, 1972*, pp. 176-77.
[75] Public Law 92-242, Mar. 8, 1972.
[76] *Documents, 1968-69*, p. 433.

appropriate legislation "after the Congress reconvenes in January" (Document 155).

No such proposal was actually presented to the Congress during 1972, although the United States participated actively in O.E.C.D. discussions regarding the form and structure of a system of "generalized nonreciprocal preferences." "Action on generalized preferences by the United States," Secretary Rogers reported in the spring of 1973, "was delayed in 1972 by the unsatisfactory state of our balance of payments. The realignment of exchange parities, however, should facilitate U.S. action ... in the near future."[77] A provision for preferential treatment of certain products of developing countries over a temporary ten-year period was in fact included in the proposed Trade Reform Act which President Nixon sent to Congress on April 10, 1973.[78] As enacted by Congress in December 1974 and signed by President Ford on January 3, 1975, the Trade Act of 1974[78a] authorized the President to institute a system of generalized preferences for developing countries but excluded certain groups of countries, notably those belonging to the Organization of Petroleum Exporting Countries (OPEC).]

(153) Proposals for Foreign Aid Reform: Message from President Nixon to the Congress, April 21, 1971.[79]

(Excerpts)

To the Congress of the United States:

On September 15, 1970 I proposed a major transformation in the foreign assistance program of the United States.[80] My purpose was to renew and revitalize the commitment of this Nation to support the security and development objectives of the lower income countries, and thereby to promote some of the most fundamental objectives of U.S. foreign policy.

Today, I report to you on the progress of the last seven months in effecting that transformation and ask the Congress to join me in taking the next creative step in our new approach—the reform of the United States bilateral assistance program.

To achieve such reform, I am transmitting two bills—the proposed International Security Assistance Act and International Development and Humanitarian Assistance Act—and announcing a number of actions which I intend to take administratively. Taken together, they would:

—Distinguish clearly between our security, development and human-

---

77 Rogers Report, 1972, p. 19.

78 *Presidential Documents*, Apr. 16, 1973, p. 351.

78a Public Law 93-618, Jan. 3, 1975.

79 *Presidential Documents*, Apr. 26, 1971, pp. 661-69.

80 *Documents, 1970*, pp. 429-44.

itarian assistance programs and create separate organizational structures for each. This would enable us to define our own objectives more clearly, fix responsibility for each program, and assess the progress of each in meeting its particular objectives.

—Combine our various security assistance efforts (except for those in Southeast Asia which are now funded in the Defense budget) into one coherent program, under the policy direction of the Department of State. This would enable security assistance to play more effectively its critical role in supporting the Nixon Doctrine and overall U.S. national security and foreign policy in the 1970's.

—Create a U.S. International Development Corporation and a U.S. International Development Institute to replace the Agency for International Development. They would enable us to reform our bilateral development assistance program to meet the changed conditions of the 1970's.

—Provide adequate funding for these new programs to support essential U.S. foreign policy objectives in the years ahead.

THE IMPORTANCE OF FOREIGN ASSISTANCE

U.S. foreign assistance is central to U.S. foreign policy in the 1970's in three ways:

First, we must help to strengthen the defense capabilities and economies of our friends and allies. This is necessary so that they can increasingly shoulder their own responsibilities, so that we can reduce our direct involvement abroad, and so that together we can create a workable structure for world peace. This is an essential feature of the Nixon Doctrine.

Second, we must assist the lower income countries in their efforts to achieve economic and social development. Such development is the overriding objective of these countries themselves and essential to the peaceful world order which we seek. The prospects for a peaceful world will be greatly enhanced if the two-thirds of humanity who live in these countries see hope for adequate food, shelter, education and employment in peaceful progress rather than in revolution.

Third, we must be able to provide prompt and effective assistance to countries struck by natural disaster or the human consequences of political upheaval. Our humanitarian concerns for mankind require that we be prepared to help in times of acute human distress.

THE NEED FOR REFORM

We cannot effectively pursue these objectives in the 1970's with programs devised for an earlier period. The world has changed dramatically. Our foreign assistance programs—like our overall foreign policy—must change to meet these new conditions.

In my September special message to the Congress I spelled out the major changes in the world which require new responses. Let me summarize them here:

—Today the lower income countries are increasingly able to shoulder the major responsibility for their own security and development and they clearly wish to do so. We share their belief that they must take the lead in charting their own security and development. Our new foreign assistance programs must therefore encourage the lower income countries to set their own priorities and develop their own programs, and enable us to respond as our talents and resources permit.

—Today the United States is but one of many industrialized nations which contribute to the security and development of the lower income countries. We used to furnish the bulk of international development assistance; we now provide less than half. The aid programs of other countries have grown because they recognize that they too have a major stake in the orderly progress which foreign assistance promotes, and because their capabilities to provide such assistance have grown enormously since the earlier postwar period.

—Today the international institutions can effectively mesh the initiatives and efforts of the lower income countries and the aid efforts of all of the industrialized countries. We can thus place greater reliance on such institutions and encourage them to play an increasing leadership role in the world development process.

Our ideas on the reforms needed in the world of the 1970's have evolved significantly since I received the Report of my Task Force on International Development, chaired by Mr. Rudolph Peterson,[81] and since my special message of last September, as the result of our own deliberations and our further consultations with the Congress, the business community and many other sectors of the American public, and our friends abroad. Before spelling out a new blueprint for our bilateral assistance program, however, I wish to report to you on the gratifying progress achieved since last September in reorienting our assistance policies.

PROGRESS TOWARD REFORM

First, the Congress in December passed supplemental assistance legislation for FY [Fiscal Year] 1971[82] which represented a major step in implementing the security assistance component of the Nixon Doctrine. This legislation authorized additional funds for military assistance and

[81] Excerpt in *Documents, 1970*, pp. 417-22.
[82] Special Foreign Assistance Act of 1971 (Public Law 91-652, Jan. 5, 1971).

supporting economic assistance for countries in which the U.S. has major interests and which have convincingly demonstrated the will and ability to help themselves—including Israel and Jordan in the Middle East and Cambodia, Vietnam and Korea in East Asia.

Such support is necessary to carry out one of the central thrusts of the Nixon Doctrine—moving us from bearing the major responsibility for the defense of our friends and allies to helping them achieve an increasing capability to maintain their own defense. This increase in security assistance enables us to continue to reduce our direct presence abroad, and helps to reduce the likelihood of direct U.S. military involvement in the future.

Second, the international development institutions have continued their progress toward leadership in the international development process. For example:

—*The World Bank* continues to increase the size and improve the effectiveness of its operations. It also has decided to broaden the scope of its lending beyond the traditional financing of projects to the provision of funds to support overall development programs in appropriate circumstances, and it is developing an improved internal evaluation and audit system.

—*The United Nations Development Program* has initiated a reorganization to improve its administration. In time this will enable it to assume a leading role in coordinating the international technical assistance effort.

—*The World Health Organization* has effectively guided and coordinated the worldwide effort to cope with the present cholera epidemic in Africa.

Third, the industrialized countries have now agreed on comparable systems of tariff preferences for imports from the lower income countries. The preferences plan is a major step in the crucial international effort to expand the export earnings of these countries, and hence to reduce their reliance on external aid. The European Community has indicated that it plans to put its tariff preferences into effect on July 1, and Japan has announced that it will do so before October 1.

Fourth, there has been satisfying progress toward achieving the untying[83] of bilateral development loans on a fully reciprocal basis. This action will enhance the value of economic assistance to recipient countries, and eliminate the political frictions which tied aid now causes. Virtually all of the industrialized countries have agreed to the principle of untying. Details of a system offering suppliers of all participating countries a fair and equitable basis for competition are now being worked out in the Organization for Economic Cooperation and Development.

[83] Cf. note 9 above.

Fifth, I have established a Council on International Economic Policy, which I chair, to coordinate all aspects of U.S. foreign economic policy, including development assistance.[84] It will provide top-level focus for our policies in this area, and accord them the high priority which they require in our foreign policy for the 1970's.

I am heartened by this progress, but much more remains to be done:

—I again urge the Congress to vote the additional funds which I have requested for the Inter-American Development Bank and the Asian Development Bank.

—We will shortly transmit legislation to authorize the U.S. contribution to the doubling of the resources of the International Development Association, the soft-loan affiliate of the World Bank, which stands at the center of the network of international financial institutions, and I urge the Congress to approve it.

—We are working with others to help establish a soft-loan window for the African Development Bank.

—We will shortly transmit legislation to authorize U.S. participation in the system of generalized tariff preferences for developing countries, and I urge Congress to approve it.

THE NEW U.S. BILATERAL ASSISTANCE PROGRAM

The next major step is the reform of the U.S. bilateral assistance program, incorporated in the proposed International Security Assistance Act and International Development and Humanitarian Assistance Act.

Our new bilateral assistance program must achieve several objectives. It must:

—Clearly identify our distinct aid objectives: security assistance, development assistance and humanitarian assistance.

—Be truly responsive to the initiatives of the lower income countries themselves and encourage them to play the central role in solving their own security and development problems. In the area of development assistance, this means working within a framework set by the international institutions to the maximum extent possible.

—Be concentrated in countries of special interest to the United States, and in projects and programs in which the United States has a special ability to be of help.

—Recognize the improved economic capacity of many of the lower income countries in establishing the terms of our assistance.

—Assure improved management.

—Reduce substantially the number of U.S. Government officials operating our assistance program overseas.

84 Cf. Document 5.

Let me now spell out the details of our new approach, based on these principles.

Security Assistance

I have repeatedly stressed the essential role played by our military and related forms of assistance in supporting the foreign policy of the United States and our own security interests. The primary purposes of this assistance have been, and will continue to be, the preservation of peace through the deterrence of war, and the support of efforts by allied and friendly countries to move toward self-sustaining economic growth and social progress. To abandon our responsibilities would risk magnifying the world's instability in the short run, and impairing its peaceful development for the longer run, and therefore increase the threat to our own security both now and in the future.

The new course on which we are set, however, encourages others to take on greater responsibilities themselves. Our new security assistance program will seek to strengthen local defense capabilities by providing that mix of military and supporting economic assistance which is needed to permit friendly foreign countries to assume additional defense burdens themselves without causing them undue political or economic costs. If we are to move toward reducing our own physical presence, the effectiveness of our security assistance program will become of ever more crucial importance.

In Asia, this new strategy has already encouraged the nations of the area to assume greater responsibility for their own defense and provided a basis for a major reduction in our military presence. The funds which have been provided to assist the Government of South Vietnam have been essential to the progress of Vietnamization, and helped insure continued U.S. troop withdrawals. We have helped Cambodia to mobilize its manpower and other resources in defense of its independence and neutrality. We are providing Korea with equipment to improve and modernize its defenses and we are withdrawing some of our own troops.[85]

Our friends and allies know that it is no longer possible nor desirable for the United States to bear the principal burden of their defense. A clear lesson of the 1960's is that deterrence against local aggression, or against subversion supported from outside a country's borders, cannot be achieved without a strong contribution by the threatened country itself. We can meet our security assistance objectives effectively only if we link our efforts closely with those of our friends and thereby build the foundations for peace in partnership with them.

To help do so, and also in recognition of the improved economic capability of many of the countries receiving security assistance, I pro-

[85] Cf. Document 98.

pose today significant changes in our authorities to provide military assistance to our friends and allies.

Our military assistance programs have suffered from undesirable rigidity. The only choice has been between grant assistance and sales on hard credit terms. Many of those nations that need our assistance are unable to meet the hard credit terms—so grant assistance has been the only course open for us to help meet their essential security needs. But as the lower income nations begin to develop an ability to shoulder the costs of their defense, we need to be able to assist them in doing so even though they cannot immediately assume the entire burden. Sales on concessional credit terms would permit earlier participation by some recipient countries in the financing of their essential defense needs and would thus engage their own assessment of priorities for the allocation of their resources at an earlier stage of development than is now possible.

To fill the existing gap between grant assistance and sales on relatively firm commercial terms, the International Security Assistance Act that I propose today includes authorization to finance sales of military equipment on concessional terms. Grant assistance will remain necessary for some nations whose financial resources are simply not adequate to meet their defense needs. But our objective is to move countries, as quickly as possible within the context of international security requirements and their own economic capabilities, along the spectrum from grants to concessional sales to the harder terms we have required for sales under the present act and finally to outright cash arrangements. We will also stress the transition from Government sales to those made directly by private industry to the extent feasible. By making these changes we would help countries move from dependence on the United States to independence in the creation and financing of their own security programs. We would not intend to provide concessional credits to countries able to meet the terms of the present program.

I am also asking, under the new act, greater flexibility to transfer funds among the various security assistance programs. Such flexibility is particularly important, for example, in this period of transition in Southeast Asia, where our troop withdrawals are freeing up substantial amounts of military equipment formerly used by our troops. I am asking that the ceiling on the amount of surplus equipment which can be granted to our friends and allies be increased; this will save us money as well as permit us to better help those of our friends who need it. In the long run, sound management of security assistance demands that there be enough flexibility to transfer funds among various programs in order to insure that the proper mix is used to meet our specific objectives in each instance.

For these international security assistance programs, I request authorization of $1,993 million for FY 1972: $778 million for supporting economic assistance, $705 million for grant military assistance, and

$510 million for military credit sales.

These security assistance programs are at the core of our relations with certain key friendly countries. They critically affect our ability to meet our bilateral and collective security commitments. They are central to the achievement of major objectives of U.S. national security and foreign policy.

I therefore intend to direct by administrative action a reorganization of our security assistance program to meet more effectively the objectives of the Nixon Doctrine. Various components of security assistance—military assistance, military credit sales, grants of excess military stocks, supporting economic assistance, and the public safety program—have been fragmented in different pieces of legislation and managed through a series of different administrative arrangements. My proposals would bring these programs under one legislative act to assure that each is viewed as part of a coherent overall program. Military assistance for Vietnam, Laos and Thailand will continue to be funded in the Defense budget because these country programs are subject to the uncertainties of active hostilities and are intimately linked to the logistical support systems of our own forces in Southeast Asia.

To assure effective policy control and management of this new security assistance effort, I would direct that a Coordinator for Security Assistance be established at a high level in the Department of State. I would also direct that the supporting economic assistance program be administered by the Department of State. The Department of Defense will continue to have primary responsibility for administering our military assistance and sales programs, and for relating these programs to overall U.S. national defense planning.

These new arrangements would be a significant step in the direction of improving the management of our security assistance program. They would therefore represent a significant step toward achieving greater accountability to the Congress and the public as well.

This new security assistance program would, I am confident, serve our national interest in the 1970's in a number of important ways. It would:

- —enable us to meet U.S. commitments more effectively and at lower cost;
- —strengthen the self-defense capabilities of nations to whose security the U.S. is committed by treaty, by special political ties, or by essential U.S. interests;
- —help to reduce the need for, and likelihood of, U.S. military involvement overseas;
- —foster increased local initiative and self-sufficiency;
- —promote constructive political relations with foreign governments;
- —support U.N. peacekeeping operations;
- —reduce potential frictions by lowering the U.S. profile abroad.

I am also requesting in the International Security Assistance Act authority for $100 million for the President's Foreign Assistance Contingency Fund for FY 1972. This would permit the administration, with due notification to the Congress, to meet worldwide contingencies—in the security, development and humanitarian areas—in ways compatible with our national interests. It is particularly important to have available uncommitted funds which can be used on short notice, when sudden crises in the international community require us to act promptly and decisively.

Development Assistance

The United States continues to have special national interests in particular lower income countries. We continue to have special capabilities in particular functional areas. We continue to need an effective bilateral development assistance program.

In order to advance such a program, I therefore propose legislation which would authorize the creation of two new development assistance institutions. Together with the two created by the last Congress, they would replace the Agency for International Development and enable us to develop a new approach based on the principles outlined above.

The two I now propose to create are:

—An International Development Corporation (IDC) to provide loans to finance development projects and programs in the lower income countries.

—An International Development Institute (IDI) to seek research breakthroughs on the key problems of development and to administer our technical assistance programs.

These would join two created by the last Congress:[86]

—The Overseas Private Investment Corporation (OPIC) to promote the role of private investment in the development process.

—The Inter-American Social Development Institute (ISDI) to provide special attention to the social development needs of Latin America.

The U.S. International Development Corporation

The new IDC would administer our bilateral lending program. The authorities which I seek for it, and the operating style which I would direct it to pursue, would mark a major change in the U.S. approach to development assistance.

*   *   *

---

[86] Foreign Assistance Act of 1969 (Public Law 91-175, Dec. 30, 1969); cf. *Documents, 1970*, pp. 282-83 and 439-40.

The U.S. International Development Institute

The new IDI would administer a reformed bilateral technical assistance program and enable us to focus U.S. scientific, technological and managerial know-how on the problems of development.

*   *   *

Humanitarian Assistance

U.S. humanitarian assistance programs cover a wide spectrum of human needs; disaster relief and rehabilitation; famine; refugee and migration relief and assistance. They aim to help people around the world recover from unfortunate situations by which they have been victimized. In the past year alone, such help has been extended to refugees from civil war in Nigeria and Jordan, earthquake victims in Peru, flood victims in Romania and Tunisia, and cyclone victims in Pakistan.

These activities rely heavily for program implementation on private voluntary agencies. In the past year alone, U.S. voluntary agencies registered with the Advisory Committee on Voluntary Foreign Aid contributed $370 million of their own resources in over 100 countries.

At present, humanitarian assistance programs are carried out through numerous offices in the U.S. Government. I propose to centralize the responsibility for coordinating all humanitarian assistance programs under a new Assistant Secretary of State. We would thereby assure a coherent effort to carry out this vital and literally life-saving aspect of our foreign assistance policy. This new approach would also improve our capability to respond quickly and effectively through better contingency planning, additional stockpiling and training, and the maintenance of closer and better coordinated relationships with the United Nations, other donor countries, and the private voluntary agencies.

COORDINATION

I have outlined the overriding need to separate our overall foreign assistance program into its three component parts: security assistance, development assistance, and humanitarian assistance. I have indicated that we would pull together all parts of our security assistance and humanitarian assistance under central management, so that each can function effectively as a total program within the context of U.S. foreign policy. And I have also proposed the creation of two new institutions, to go along with the two created by the last Congress, to carry forward our development assistance program in the 1970's.

There is thus a need for new mechanisms to assure effective coordination of our new foreign assistance program.

First, there must be effective coordination among the several components of the new development assistance program. This would be done through my appointing a single Coordinator of Development Assistance, responsible directly to the President, as Chairman of the Boards of the IDC, IDI, and OPIC.

The Coordinator would also chair an executive coordinating committee composed of the chief executive officers of each of these institutions and ISDI. He would be available for congressional testimony on our overall bilateral development assistance policy and the operations of the several institutions. Both the Congress and I could look to him as the administration's chief spokesman on bilateral development assistance policy and programs.

Second, the Secretary of State will provide foreign policy guidance for all components of our new foreign assistance program. His representatives would be members of the boards of each of the development institutions, and he would have direct responsibility for both security and humanitarian assistance. In each country our Ambassador, as my personal representative, will of course be responsible for coordination of all of our assistance programs.

Third, foreign assistance issues which raise broader questions of foreign economic policy will be handled through my new Council on International Economic Policy.

Finally, coordination among the three major components of our assistance program, and between them and our overall national security policy, would be handled through the National Security Council. We will thus establish strong management, coordination, and policy guidance over all of our foreign assistance programs.

CONCLUSION

This Nation can no more ignore poverty, hunger and disease in other nations of the world than a man can ignore the suffering of his neighbors. The great challenge to Americans of this decade, be they private citizens or national leaders, is to work to improve the quality of life of our fellow men at home and abroad.

We have a unique and unprecedented opportunity. We do not have all the answers to the questions of poverty, nor adequate resources to meet the needs of all mankind. We do possess the greatest scientific and technological capacity, and the most prosperous and dynamic economy, of any nation in history. More importantly, we have, as a vital element of the American character, a humanitarian zeal to help improve the lives of our fellow men.

We are therefore a nation uniquely capable of assisting other peoples in preserving their security and promoting their development. By doing so, we accomplish three major objectives:

—We strengthen international cooperation for a peaceful world.

—We help to relieve the poverty and misery of others less fortunate than ourselves.

—We help to build firm foundations of friendship between this Nation and the peoples of other nations.

I have seen for myself just how important is our aid in helping nations preserve their independence, and in helping men achieve the dignity of productive labor instead of languishing on crowded streets. I have seen its importance to children whose chances for a rewarding life have been increased because they have adequate nutrition, schools and books. It is right that we, the richest nation in the world, should provide our share of such assistance.

And such help, in addition to being right for its own sake, also creates strong bonds.

I recognize that whenever an American firm is nationalized without prompt, fair, and effective compensation; whenever an anti-American demonstration takes place; or whenever a leader of a developing country criticizes the United States, many question the effectiveness of our aid.

But the headline reporting the occasional anti-American act overlooks the many countries which do thank us for providing them the means to preserve their own security; and it also overlooks the countless number of villages where farmers do appreciate our helping provide the know-how and the tools necessary to grow larger crops, the school children who cherish the education our assistance makes possible, and the people everywhere who recognize our help in eliminating disease.

For these people, our aid is a source of encouragement. And they, not those who demonstrate or destroy, are the real revolutionaries—for they, in quietly attempting to preserve their independence and improve their lives, are bringing about a quiet revolution of peaceful change and progress. They are working hard to build the foundations for a better tomorrow and they recognize that we have helped provide them with the tools to do the job.

But while such appreciation is gratifying, foreign assistance has a more basic purpose. Foreign assistance is quite clearly in our interest as a nation. We are a people whose sons have died, and whose great statesmen have worked, to build a world order which insures peace and prosperity for ourselves and for other nations. We are aware that this world order cannot be sustained if our friends cannot defend themselves against aggression, and if two-thirds of the world's people see the richer third as indifferent to their needs and insensitive to their aspirations for a better life. To these people it is critical that this be a generation of peace, and our foreign policy is directed at helping to make it so; and for the impoverished it is equally important that it be a generation in which their aspirations for a better life, improved health conditions, and adequate food supply can be realized—a generation of development, a generation of hope.

Foreign policy is not a one-way street. It requires that other nations understand our problems and concerns, but it also requires that we understand theirs. We cannot ask the lower income countries of the world to cooperate with us to solve the problems which affect our vital interests unless we cooperate with them to help solve the problems critical to their vital interests—the problems affecting their security and development, and thus affecting the quality of life of their people.

The legislation I propose today, along with the corollary administrative actions which I will take, will permit this Nation to carry out the major reforms which are necessary to improve the effectiveness of our foreign assistance program and to fit it to our new approach.

I believe that this new approach is of major importance in promoting the national security and foreign policy interests of the United States in this decade and beyond. I believe that it is sound, and will blend as effectively as possible our special strengths with those of other nations and institutions. It is an approach through which we can focus the energies and resources of this great Nation on the security and development problems of those peoples living in poorer nations who wish to improve their lives, but lack the resources and the expertise to do so. I believe that this program is worthy of your support.

I therefore reaffirm my commitment, and the commitment of this administration, to seek an effective U.S. foreign assistance program for the 1970's. It is our objective to work for peace, not only in our time but for future generations, and we can make no better investment toward that end than to participate fully in an international effort to build prosperity and hope for a better tomorrow among all nations. I urge the Congress to join with me in making the reforms I propose today so that together we can achieve these great goals.

RICHARD NIXON

The White House
April 21, 1971

(154) Rejection of the Foreign Aid Bill by the Senate, October 29, 1971.

   (a) Views of President Nixon: Statement by White House Press Secretary Ziegler, October 30, 1971. [87]

(Complete Text)

President Nixon feels this vote by the Senate is a highly irresponsible

[87] *Presidential Documents*, Nov. 1, 1971, p. 1457.

action which undoes 25 years of constructive bipartisan foreign policy and produces unacceptable risks to the national security of the United States.

President Nixon urges immediate restoration of the absolutely vital foreign assistance program so that we can continue the efforts to construct a more peaceful world.

It is up to the Congress to act immediately to restore a coordinated foreign aid program. Foreign assistance has been the fundamental framework of a bipartisan foreign policy for over a quarter of a century, and it is vital to the United States interest that it continue.

A piecemeal or patchwork restoration of foreign aid is not an alternative. A carefully planned foreign aid program is essential in order to continue assisting underdeveloped countries and providing urgently needed humanitarian, economic, and other assistance to friendly nations.

(b) News Conference Statement by Secretary of State Rogers, November 2, 1971.[88]

(Excerpt)

*   *   *

We talked a good deal this morning about the action of the Senate in defeating foreign aid legislation. Let me say that the action of Congress in defeating this legislation has been a very serious blow to the foreign policy of the United States. Tomorrow morning I will appear before the Senate Foreign Relations Committee to convey this message to that committee and to express the hope that action will be taken quickly to repair the damage that has been done.

As you know, there is now general support, I believe, for the idea that a continuing resolution will be enacted which will enable us to continue the foreign aid programs during the life of that continuing resolution. We think it is essential that Congress now act to pass a foreign aid bill which will be coordinated and balanced and which will permit us to carry on the very successful foreign policies of President Nixon.

I think any action of the kind that the Senate has taken, unless remedied, will seriously affect our foreign policy in a number of ways.

First, it will be a damaging blow to the Nixon doctrine, because the Nixon doctrine, as you know, provides that we will gradually reduce our troop strength in some of the Asian countries and at the same time

[88] White House Press Release, Nov. 2, 1971; text from *Bulletin*, Nov. 22, 1971, pp. 583-84. Secretary Rogers spoke at the White House following a conference with the President.

support them financially and in military ways so they can take up the slack. And if our foreign aid program is defeated, of course, this would not be possible.

Secondly, it makes it impossible or at least difficult to maintain the security commitments that we have with the Asian nations. They have relied on the United States over the years to carry out these treaty obligations, and we have given them our assurance that as we end the war in Viet-Nam, and as we reduce our troop strength in Korea and other Asian nations, that we will provide assistance to help them to make the adjustments that are necessary as a result of this policy.

Thirdly, I think it weakens the President's power in negotiations which we are conducting throughout the world.

Consequently, we will make a very stern and strong appeal to the Members of Congress to act responsibly to correct this damage that has been done.

I might say in conclusion that I have been, I am sure, as you have been, impressed by the fact that Congress does act responsibly when the occasion arises, and I am confident they will in this case. As you know, this bill was defeated at a time when there were 32 absentees in the Senate. It was defeated probably as a result of conflicting irritations and emotions and frustrations. But the fact is that the foreign policy of this country has, over the years, been bipartisan.

Congress has acted responsibly in every occasion when they were called upon by the President, and we are convinced they will act responsibly in this.[89]

Thank you.

*   *   *

(155) Generalized Trade Preferences for Developing Countries: Statement by Secretary of State Rogers, Hamilton, Bermuda, December 20, 1971.[90]

(Excerpts)

*   *   *

Secretary Rogers: Ladies and gentlemen, I think I should say that at the luncheon meeting the Finance Ministers also attended, and we had a general discussion about the effect of the decision of the Group of Ten on Saturday in Washington.[91] There is no question that this was a

[89] Cf. above at note 74.
[90] *Bulletin*, Jan. 17, 1972, pp. 64 and 66. On the Bermuda meeting cf. Documents 44 and 151b.
[91] Document 150a.

decision which will have tremendous benefits for the free world and will be helpful to the United States in foreign affairs generally.

In this connection, the President decided on the way over, and I notified the British that he had made the decision, after the Congress reconvenes in January to introduce legislation to authorize him to extend the general preferences to the developing countries of the world.

This subject has been under discussion between the United States and the Common Market for more than a year, and the Common Market, as you know, has already taken action to introduce its own system of preferences to such countries. We all know the need which the developing countries have, if they are to progress economically, of access to the markets of the more developed countries. We hope by next year to be in a position to contribute our share in this connection.

Of course, this decision by the President of the United States to send legislation to provide generalized preferences to the less developed countries is a natural followup to the decisions taken in the monetary field.

*   *   *

Q. Will you take questions?

Secretary Rogers: What was the question? I really don't want a press conference.

On generalized preferences, let me say what it does is open some of the United States markets to less developed nations. It gives them preferential treatment in our markets. So what it means is that these countries, and I refer particularly to Latin America,[92] will be greatly benefited by this legislation.

Now, we had indicated earlier that we would take this action, but because of the problems in the monetary field the President did not send this legislation to the Congress. Now that the President has decided to send this legislation to the Congress at the beginning of the year, it will be of tremendous importance to less developed countries, and especially Latin America, which depends so heavily on American markets.

Q. Can you tell us factually how much the Common Market has already done in this connection?

Secretary Rogers: They have taken action. I cannot tell you precisely what the action has been, but they have taken action to provide the same kind of treatment for less developed countries, which means that

[92] Cf. Document 116.

they have opened their markets and given preferential treatment to less developed countries, and they did that in part because we encouraged them to.

Because of the difficulty we had in the monetary field, we did not send the legislation to the Congress this fall, but the President will do it in the first of the year.[93]

Q. You mean independent of this action, the Common Market and the United States?

Secretary Rogers: Yes.

[93] Cf. above at notes 77-78.

APPENDIX:
PRINCIPAL SOURCES

"A.F.R.": *American Foreign Relations: A Documentary Record* (annual vols., 1971-   ). Continues the *"Documents"* series listed below. Volumes for 1971 and 1972 published for the Council on Foreign Relations by New York University Press (New York).

American Foreign Policy: Current Documents (Washington: G.P.O.;* 2 vols. for 1950-55, and annual vols. for 1956-67). The official documentary publication of the Department of State, now discontinued.

"Bulletin": *The Department of State Bulletin* (Washington: G.P.O., weekly). The official source for material of State Department origin appearing in this volume; contains also numerous documents originated by the White House and other governmental and international bodies.

"Documents": *Documents on American Foreign Relations* (annual vols., 1939-70). Volumes in this series were published prior to 1952 by Princeton University Press (Princeton, N.J.) for the World Peace Foundation; subsequent volumes published for the Council on Foreign Relations by Harper & Brothers/Harper & Row (New York and Evanston) for 1952-66 and by Simon and Schuster (New York) for 1967-70. For subsequent volumes see *A.F.R.*, above.

Documents on Disarmament (Washington: G.P.O.; annual vols. for 1960-72). The most comprehensive collection of documents on disarmament and related topics, published annually by the U.S. Arms Control and Disarmament Agency.

Everyman's United Nations (New York: United Nations; eighth ed., 1968). A detailed account of the evolution of the U.N. system, brought up to date by occasional supplements.

International Legal Materials: Current Documents (Washington: American Society of International Law, bimonthly). Includes numerous documents of non-U.S. origin.

Kalb, Marvin and Bernard, *Kissinger* (Boston: Little, Brown and Company, 1974). A detailed account of the diplomacy of the Nixon administration from 1969 until early 1974.

*The abbreviation G.P.O. as used throughout this volume refers to the U.S. Government Printing Office.

Keesing's Contemporary Archives (Bristol: Keesing's Publications, Ltd., weekly). A detailed review of current developments throughout the world.

NATO Letter/NATO Review (Brussels: NATO Information Service, bimonthly). The official informational and documentary publication of the North Atlantic Treaty Organization.

The New York Times (New York: The New York Times Co., daily). Contains unofficial texts of numerous documents of international interest.

"Nixon Report, 1970": *U.S. Foreign Policy for the 1970's: A New Strategy for Peace—A Report to the Congress by Richard Nixon, President of the United States, February 18, 1970* (Washington: G.P.O., 1970, 160 p.). Text appears also in *Presidential Documents,* Feb. 23, 1970, pp. 194-239; *Public Papers, 1970*, pp. 116-190; and *Bulletin*, Mar. 9, 1970, pp. 273-332. Excerpts are printed in *Documents, 1970*, pp. 6-15.

"Nixon Report, 1971": *U.S. Foreign Policy for the 1970's: Building for Peace—A Report to the Congress by Richard Nixon, President of the United States, February 25, 1971* (Washington: G.P.O., 1971, 235 p.). Text appears also in *Presidential Documents*, Mar. 1, 1971, pp. 305-77; *Public Papers, 1971*, pp. 219-345; and *Bulletin*, Mar. 22, 1971, pp. 341-432. Excerpts appear in the present volume as Documents 3, 11, and 101.

"Nixon Report, 1972": *U.S. Foreign Policy for the 1970's: The Emerging Structure of Peace—A Report to the Congress by Richard Nixon, President of the United States, February 9, 1972* (Washington: G.P.O., 1972, 215 p.). Text appears also in *Presidential Documents*, Feb. 14, 1972, pp. 235-411; *Public Papers, 1972*, pp. 194-346; and *Bulletin*, Mar. 13, 1972, pp. 311-418. Excerpts appear in the present volume as Documents 121 and 136.

"Nixon Report, 1973": *U.S. Foreign Policy for the 1970's: Shaping a Durable Peace—A Report to the Congress by Richard Nixon, President of the United States, May 3, 1973* (Washington: G.P.O., 1973, 234 p.). Text appears also in *Presidential Documents*, May 14, 1973, pp. 455-653; and *Bulletin*, June 4, 1973, pp. 717-834.

"OAS Chronicle": *Chronicle of the OAS* (Washington: Secretariat of the Organization of American States, quarterly).

OECD Observer (Paris: OECD Information Service, bimonthly). The official review of the Organization for Economic Cooperation and Development.

"Presidential Documents": *Weekly Compilation of Presidential Documents* (Washington: G.P.O., weekly). The official source for White House materials reproduced in this volume. Much of the contents is republished in *Public Papers*, and many texts relating to foreign affairs appear also in the Department of State *Bulletin*.

Public Laws of the United States, cited in this volume by serial number and date of approval (e.g., Public Law 92-156, Nov. 17, 1971), are issued by the G.P.O. in leaflet form and subsequently collected in the *United States Statutes at Large (Stat.)*.

"Public Papers": Public Papers of the Presidents of the United States (Washington: G.P.O., annual). Contains definitive texts of most presidential statements and some other material of White House origin, most of it previously published in *Presidential Documents*. Available volumes for the administration of Richard Nixon cover the years 1969, 1970, 1971, and 1972.

"Rogers Report, 1969-70": *United States Foreign Policy 1969-1970: A Report of the Secretary of State* (Department of State Publication 8575; Washington: G.P.O., 1971, 617 p.).

"Rogers Report, 1971": *United States Foreign Policy 1971: A Report of the Secretary of State* (Department of State Publication 8634; Washington: G.P.O., 1972, 604 p.).

"Rogers Report, 1972": *United States Foreign Policy 1972: A Report of the Secretary of State* (Department of State Publication 8699; Washington: G.P.O., 1973, 743 p.).

"Senate Foreign Relations Committee History": U.S. Senate, 92d Cong., *Legislative History of the Committee on Foreign Relations . . . January 21, 1971–October 18, 1972* (Committee print; Washington: G.P.O., 1973, 160 p.). Records congressional action on treaties and legislation considered by the Foreign Relations Committee.

Soviet News (London: Press Department of the Soviet Embassy, weekly). Includes unofficial texts or condensations of numerous documents of Soviet origin.

TIAS: *Treaties and Other International Acts Series* (Washington: G.P.O.). The definitive texts of treaties and agreements to which the United States is a party, as authenticated by the Department of State. Issued in leaflet form under their individual serial numbers items in this series are later republished with consecutive pagination in the official *United States Treaties and Other International Agreements* (UST) series. Treaties and agreements that entered into force in 1971 (TIAS Nos. 7035-7264) are collected in vol. 22, parts 1 and 2 (Washington: G.P.O., 1972); those that entered into force in 1972 (TIAS Nos. 7265ff.) are collected in vol. 23, parts 1-4 (Washington: G.P.O., 1973), and vol. 24, part 1 (Washington: G.P.O., 1974).

United Nations General Assembly, *Official Records* (New York: United Nations). The *Official Records* of each session of the General Assembly include texts of all resolutions adopted during the session together with much related material.

United Nations Security Council, *Official Records* (New York: United Nations). Includes texts of all resolutions adopted by the Security Council, with much related material.

UN Monthly Chronicle (New York: United Nations Office of Public Information, monthly). The official account of current U.N. activities, with texts of major resolutions and other documents.

The United States in World Affairs (annual vols., 1931-40, 1945-67, and 1970). The annual survey of U.S. foreign policy developments, published for the Council on Foreign Relations by Harper & Brothers/Harper and Row (New York and Evanston) from 1931 through 1966 and by Simon and Schuster (New York) for 1967 and 1970.

U.S. Participation in the UN: Report by the President to the Congress for the Year 1971 (Washington: G.P.O., 1972, 238 p.). The official record of U.S. participation in the United Nations, issued annually.

"USUN Press Releases": Press releases of the U.S. Mission to the United Nations, as reprinted in the Department of State *Bulletin.*

The World This Year: Supplement to the Political Handbook and Atlas of the World (annual vols., 1971, 1972, and 1973). Condensed accounts of the organization and activities of governments and intergovernmental organizations, published for the Council on Foreign Relations by Simon and Schuster (New York).

Yearbook of the United Nations, 1971 (New York: United Nations Office of Public Information, 1974). A comprehensive review of U.N. activities, issued annually.

INDEX

The following pages provide a detailed listing of the documents and editorial notes that make up the present volume. As in the *Documents on American Foreign Relations* series, each document is listed under (1) its official name, if any; (2) its main subject and principal subordinate subjects; (3) the name of the originating country, organization, or individual, and the addressee or recipient where appropriate; and (4) its place of origin when this is deemed historically significant. *Not* listed are names and subjects appearing in the body of the text but falling into none of the above categories. Acts and resolutions of the U.S. Congress will be found under the heading "Congress (U.S.)," where they are listed by subject and, where appropriate, by Public Law or Resolution number. Resolutions of the U.N. General Assembly and Security Council are also listed by subject and by resolution number.

A

Africa, discussion and documentation, 379-432; Nixon report (Feb. 25, excerpt), 380-85; Newsom address on UN issues (Sept. 21), 386-96; question of Namibia (South West Africa), 396-412; criticism of US policy, 429-31; Rogers rebuttal (Dec. 23, excerpt), 431-32

Aircraft Sabotage Convention (Convention for the Suppression of Unlawful Acts Against the Safety of Civil Aviation, signed Montreal Sept. 23, 1971), background, 538-39; text 548-55

"Albanian" Resolution, *see* China, U.N. Representation

American Foreign Ministers, *see* Organization of American States (O.A.S.)

American Society of Newspaper Editors, Nixon address (Apr. 16, excerpt), 285-87

American-Soviet relations, *see* East-West relations

ANZUS Pact, Council meeting (New York, Oct. 2): communiqué, 335-37

Arab-Israeli conflict, discussion and documentation, 191-222; report on Jarring mission (Feb. 1), 194-5; same (Mar. 5), 195-8; Rogers statement (Mar. 16, excerpts), 199-203; Rogers statement on interim

Canal agreement (Rome, May 8, excerpts), 204-7; Sisco statement (Tel Aviv, Aug. 5), 207-8; Rogers address (Oct. 4, excerpt), 208-11; UNSC resolution on Jerusalem (Sept. 25), 212-13; Bush statement (same), 213-15; Bush statement to UNGA (Dec. 13), 216-18; Phillips statement (same), 218-220; UNGA resolution (same, 220-22

Asia, American policy in, 191-378; Middle East and Southern Asia, 191-259; the war in Indochina, 261-320; East Asia and the Pacific, 321-78; see also regional and country entries

Asia, Green address, 323-29; Johnson address, 368-75; see also regional and country entries

Atlanta Press Club, Newsom address on Africa, 386-96

Atlantic Community, see Europe, Western, and country and organizational entries

Australia, see ANZUS Pact

Aviation, see Aircraft Sabotage Convention

Azores, Nixon-Pompidou meeting (Dec. 13-14): joint statement, 181; Connally statement, 606-7

B

Bacteriological (Biological) Weapons Convention (Convention on the Prohibition of the Development and Stockpiling of Bacteriological [Biological] and Toxin Weapons and on Their Destruction, approved Dec. 16, 1971): Bush statement (Nov. 11), 84-88; UNGA resolution (Dec. 16), 88-90; text, 90-95

Balance of payments (U.S.), Nixon address (Aug. 15), 577-82; Nixon Proclamation (Aug. 15, excerpts), 583-4; Samuels statement (Geneva, Aug. 24), 584-9; Nixon Proclamation (Dec. 20), 610-11; Nixon remarks (Bermuda, Dec. 20), 611-12

Bennett, W. Tapley, Jr., statements on Korea, 378; on Namibia, 406-8

Berlin, Quadripartite Agreement on (signed Berlin, Sept. 3, 1971): Rogers statement (Sept. 3), 164-65; text (excerpt), 166-68

Brandt, Willy, statement with Nixon (Key Biscayne, Dec. 29), 183-84

Bray, Charles W., III, statement on U.S.-Soviet contacts (May 17), 155; on passports for China (Mar. 15), 340-41

Bruce, David K.E., statement on Vietnam (Paris, July 8), 298-300

Bush, George H., statement on bacteriological weapons convention (Nov. 11, excerpt), 84-88; on disarmament (same, excerpt), 96-101; on Middle East (Sept. 25), 213-15; same (Dec. 13), 216-18; on Indo-Pakistan conflict (Dec. 4), 229-33; same (Dec. 6, excerpt), 233-5; same (Dec. 7), 236-7; same (Dec. 12), 240-46; on China (Nov. 15), 513-14; on security of UN missions (Oct. 21), 523; on appointment of new UN Secretary-General (Dec. 22), 530-31

Byrd amendment, see Southern Rhodesia

C

Cambodia, *see* Khmer Republic

CCD, *see* Conference of the Committee on Disarmament

CENTO, *see* Central Treaty Organization

Central Treaty Organization (CENTO), Council meeting (Ankara, Apr. 30-May 1): communiqué, 222-24

Chile, discussion and documentation, 481-86; Nixon report (Feb. 25, excerpt), 481-82; Meyer statement (Oct. 15), 482-86; Rogers statement (Oct. 13), 483-4

China, People's Republic of (P.R.C.), discussion and documentation, 337-56; Nixon statement (Mar. 4, excerpts), 339-40; Bray announcement (Mar. 15), 340-41; Nixon statement (Apr. 14), 341-2; same (Apr. 29, excerpts), 342-5; same (June 1, excerpt), 345-6; Ziegler statement (June 10), 346-7; Nixon statement on proposed visit (July 15), 348-9; same (Aug. 4, excerpt), 349-51; same (Sept. 16, excerpt), 351-3; announcement of Kissinger mission (Oct. 27), 353; US-PRC joint statement (Nov. 29, excerpt), 353; Ziegler statement (Nov. 30, excerpt), 353-4; Kissinger statement (same), 354-6; *see also* China, UN representation

China, Republic of (Taiwan), *see* China, U.N. representation

China, U.N. representation, background discussion, 500-14; Rogers statement (Aug. 2), 504-6; "Albanian" draft resolution (Sept. 25), 506; "Important Question" resolution (Sept. 29), 507; "Dual Representation" resolution (same), 507; Rogers address (Oct. 4, excerpt), 508-11; UNGA resolution (Oct. 25), 512; Rogers statement (Oct. 26, excerpt), 512-13; Bush statement (Nov. 15), 513-14; Rogers statement (Dec. 1, excerpt), 514

Cincinnati World Affairs Council, Johnson address, 137-48

Conference of the Committee on Disarmament (CCD), Nixon message (Feb. 23), 67-69; review of activities (Bush statement, Nov. 11), 84-88; *see also* Disarmament

Congress (U.S.)

Legislation (92d Cong., 1st sess.):

P.L. 92-129, Sept. 28, Amending the Military Selective Service Act of 1967: Mansfield address (May 11, excerpts), 150-54; text (excerpt on Indochina), 316-17

P.L. 92-156, Nov. 17, Military Procurement Authorization Act of 1971: Title VI (on Indochina), 318-19; Nixon signature statement, 319-20; Newsom statement (July 7), 416-23; House-Senate report (Nov. 5, excerpt), 424-26; Title V (on Rhodesian chrome), 426-27

P.L. 92-204, Dec. 18, Department of Defense Appropriation Act, 1972: S. Rept. 92-498 (Nov. 18, excerpt on US force reduction in Europe), 172; Nixon letter to Stennis (Nov. 23), 172-73

H.J. Res. 1, Aug. 2, on war powers of the President: H. Rept. 92-383

(July 17, excerpt), 28-30; text, 30-31

S. 731, Feb. 10, on war powers of the President: Javits statement (Feb. 10, excerpts), 32-34; text, 34-35; Rogers statement (May 14, excerpts), 35-41

H. Con. Res. 8, on status of Soviet Jews: Davies statement (Nov. 9, excerpts), 125-33

Treaty actions:

Seabed arms control treaty (signed Feb. 11, 1971): Rogers remarks, 69-70; Nixon remarks, 70-71; Nixon message (July 21), 71-72

Geneva Protocol (signed June 17, 1925): Rogers statement (Mar. 5), 74-80; Fulbright letter to Nixon (Apr. 15), 80-93

Okinawa reversion agreement (signed June 17, 1971): text (excerpt), 358-64; Nixon message (Sept. 21), 364-67

International Wheat Agreement (signed Apr. 14, 1971): Nixon message (June 2), 613-14

Decline in support for UN: Nixon message (Feb. 9, 1972), 499-500; rejection of foreign aid legislation, 615-17, 630-31

Connally, John B., statement to IBRD/IMF meeting (Sept. 30), 596-603; remarks on Nixon-Pompidou meeting (Dec. 14), 606-7

Convention for the Suppression of Unlawful Acts Against the Safety of Civil Aircraft (signed Montreal Sept. 23, 1971), *see* Aircraft Sabotage Convention

Council on International Economic Policy, White House announcement, 25-26

Convention on International Liability for Damage Caused by Space Objects (approved Nov. 29, 1971), *see* Space Liability Convention

Convention on the Prohibition of the Development, Production and Stockpiling of Bacteriological (Biological) and Toxin Weapons and on Their Destruction (approved Dec. 16, 1971), *see* Bacteriological (Biological) Weapons Convention

Convention to Prevent and Punish Acts of Terrorism Taking the Form of Crimes Against Persons and Related Extortion That Are of International Significance (approved by the O.A.S. Feb. 2, 1971), *see* Terrorism, O.A.S. Convention on

Cuba, Hurwitch statement, 474-81

D

Davies, Richard T., statement on Soviet Jews, 125-33

Davies, Rodger P., statement on Greece, 184-88

Defense (U.S.), Laird statement (Mar. 9, excerpt), 12-19

Defense Department, Senate report on appropriations (Nov. 18, excerpt), 172

Derwinski, Edward J., statement on UN budget, 517-22

Diggs, Charles J., on African policy, 430-32

Disarmament, discussion and documentation, 60-114; Nixon report (Feb. 25, excerpt), 60-65;

Multilateral disarmament efforts: seabed arms control treaty, 69-72; Geneva Protocol of 1925, 74-83; prohibition of bacteriological (biological) weapons, 83-95; unresolved questions, 95-101

CCD meeting (Feb. 23-May 13; June 29-Sept. 30): Nixon message (Feb. 23), 67-69; Bush review (Nov. 11, excerpts), 84-88, 96-100

UNGA meeting (26th session, Sept. 21-Dec. 22): Bush statement on prohibition of bacteriological (biological) weapons (Nov. 11, excerpt), 84-88; resolution on same (Dec. 16), 88-90; text of convention, 90-95; Bush statement on disarmament agenda (Nov. 11, excerpt), 96-101

SALT meetings (Fourth session, Vienna, Mar. 15-May 28): Nixon statement (May 20), 103-4; US-Soviet communiqué (May 28), 104-5; (Fifth session, Helsinki, July 8-Sept. 24): US-Soviet communiqué (Sept. 24), 105-6; Nixon comments (Portland, Sept. 25, excerpt), 106-8; (Sixth session, Vienna, Nov. 15, 1971-Feb. 4, 1972): Nixon statement (Nov. 12), 108-9; White House announcement on US-Soviet agreements (Sept. 24), 109-10; agreement to reduce nuclear war risks (signed Washington Sept. 30), 110-12; agreement to improve "hot line" (same), 113-14

See also Mutual and Balanced Force Reductions; Tlatelolco Treaty
Disaster relief, Nixon report (Feb. 9, 1972, excerpt), 543

E

East Asia and the Pacific, discussion and documentation, 321-78; progress under the Nixon Doctrine, 323-9; SEATO and ANZUS, 329-37; the People's Republic of China, 337-56; the US and Japan, 356-75; the Republic of Korea, 375-78; see also regional and country entries
East-West relations, discussion and documentation, 59-133; Nixon message (Feb. 25, excerpt), 60-65; progress in multilateral arms control, 65-101; Strategic Arms Limitation Talks (SALT), 101-9; agreements to reduce the risk of nuclear war, 109-14; projected Nixon visit to the USSR, 115-24; status of Jews in USSR, 124-33; see also Berlin; Disarmament; Europe, détente in; USSR
Economic and financial affairs, discussion and documentation, 567-633; Organization for Economic Cooperation and Development, 569-76; the US "New Economic Policy," 576-91; International Bank for Reconstruction and Development and International Monetary Fund, 591-604; the Azores meeting and Smithsonian Agreement, 604-12; International Wheat Agreement, 1971, 612-14; foreign aid and economic development, 614-33
Ecuador, statement by Irwin, 443-47
Environment, Nixon report (Feb. 9, 1972, excerpt), 540-42

Europe, détente in, discussion and documentation, 135-84; the issues, 135-48; question of reduction of forces, 148-56; position of NATO, 156-62; quadripartite agreement on Berlin, 162-70; further discussion of force reduction and European security, 170-80

Europe, Eastern, Johnson address, 137-48

Europe, Western, Johnson address, 137-48; *see also* country, topical and organizational entries

F

Far East-America Council, Green address, 323-29

Foreign aid program (U.S.), background, 615-17; Nixon message on reforms (Apr. 21, excerpts), 617-29; Ziegler statement on rejection of foreign aid bill (Oct. 30), 629-30; Rogers statement on same (Nov. 2), 630-31

France, Nixon-Pompidou statement (Azores, Dec. 14), 181; Connally statement (same), 606-7

Fulbright, J. William, letter to Nixon (Apr. 15), 80-83

G

GATT, *see* General Agreement on Tariffs and Trade

General Agreement on Tariffs and Trade, statement by Samuels (Geneva, Aug. 24), 584-89

Geneva Protocol (signed June 17, 1925): Rogers statement (Mar. 5), 74-80; Fulbright letter to Nixon (Apr. 15), 80-83

Germany, Democratic Republic of, and Berlin, 162-70

Germany, East-West relations in, 162-70

Germany, Federal Republic of, and Berlin problem, 162-70; Brandt-Nixon statement (Key Biscayne, Florida, Dec. 29), 183-84

Great Britain, *see* United Kingdom

Greece, statement by Davies, 184-88

Green, Marshall, address on Nixon Doctrine, 323-29; statement on Korea, 377-78

"Group of Ten" meeting (Washington, Dec. 17-18, 1971): communiqué, 607-9; Nixon remarks, 609-10

H

Heath, Edward, statement with Nixon (Bermuda, Dec. 21), 182-83

Hijacking, *see* Aircraft Sabotage Convention

"Hot Line" Agreement, *see* Measures to improve the USA-USSR direct communcations link, US-Soviet agreement on

House of Representatives, *see* Congress (U.S.)

Hurwitch, Robert A., statement on Cuba, 474-81

I

I.B.R.D., *see* International Bank for Reconstruction and Development

I.C.J., *see* International Court of Justice

I.M.F., *see* International Monetary Fund

India, *see* Indo-Pakistan conflict

Indian Ocean, background, 249; Spiers statement, 250-57; UNGA resolution, 257-59; ANZUS communiqué, 337

Indochina, discussion and documentation, 261-320; background, 261-2; military operations in Laos, 263-78; progress of Vietnamization, 278-92; peace negotiations in Paris, 292-310; political developments in South Vietnam, 310-15; policy on troop withdrawals, 315-20

Indo-Pakistan conflict, discussion and documentation, 224-49; Rogers address (Oct. 4, excerpt), 226-7; Rogers statement (Dec. 4), 228-9; Bush statement to UNSC (Dec. 4), 229-33; US draft resolution (Dec. 5), 232-3; Bush statement (Dec. 6, excerpt), 233-5; UNSC resolution (same), 235; Bush statement (Dec. 7), 236-7; UNGA resolution (same), 237-9; Bush statement (Dec. 12), 240-46; US draft resolution (Dec. 13), 244-5; UNSC resolution (Dec. 21), 246-7; Rogers statement (Dec. 23, excerpts), 122-4, 248-9

Intelsat Agreement (Agreement on Establishment of the International Telecommunications Satellite Organization "Intelsat," signed Aug. 20, 1971): Nixon report (Feb. 9, 1972, excerpt), 542-43; State Department announcement, 564-65

Inter-American Affairs, *see* Latin America

Inter-American Development Bank (I.D.B.), Rogers address (San José, Apr. 15, excerpts), 452, 454-55

Inter-American Committee on the Alliance for Progress, Rogers address (San José, Apr. 15, excerpts), 454, 455

Inter-American Economic and Social Council (IA-ECOSOC), discussion, 462

Inter American Press Association, Meyer address (Chicago, Oct. 25), 463-71; Nixon message (same), 471-72

International Bank for Reconstruction and Development (I.B.R.D.), Nixon remarks (Sept. 29), 592-95; Connally statement (Sept. 30), 596-603

International Business Outlook Conference, Johnson address, 368-75

International Court of Justice (I.C.J.), Stevenson statement on Namibia (The Hague, Mar. 9, excerpts), 396-403; I.C.J. advisory opinion (June 21, excerpt), 403-5; Bennett statement to UNSC (Oct. 20), 406-8; UNSC resolution (Oct. 20), 408-12

International economic and financial affairs, *see* economic and financial affairs

International Labor Organization (ILO), Nixon report (Feb. 9, 1972, excerpt), 499-500

International monetary affairs, Nixon-Pompidou statement (Azores, Dec. 14), 181; Nixon remarks (Sept. 29), 592-95; Connally statement (Sept. 30), 596-603; I.M.F. resolution (Oct. 1), 603-4; Connally statement (Dec. 14), 606-7; "Group of Ten" communiqué (Dec. 18), 607-9; Nixon remarks (Dec. 18), 609-10

International Monetary Fund (I.M.F.), Nixon remarks (Sept. 29), 592-95; Connally statement (Sept. 30), 596-603; resolution of Board of Governors (Oct. 1), 603-4

International Telecommunications Satellite Organization, agreement on (Aug. 20, 1971), see Intelsat Agreement

International Wheat Agreement (open for signature in Washington Mar. 29-May 3, 1971), background, 612-13; Nixon message (June 2), 613-14

Irwin, John N., II, statement on Ecuador, 443-47

J

Japan, discussion and documentation, 356-75; background, 357-8; Okinawa reversion agreement (signed Washington and Tokyo June 17): text (excerpt), 358-64; Nixon message (Sept. 21), 364-67; reaction to US moves, 367-8; Johnson address (Oct. 18), 368-75

Jarring, Gunnar V., UN Secretary-General's report on mission (Feb. 1), 194-5; same (Mar. 5), 195-98; Rogers statement (Mar. 16, excerpts), 199-203; Bush statement (Dec. 13), 216-18; Phillips statement (Dec. 13), 218-20; UNGA resolution (Dec. 13), 220-22

Javits, Jacob K., statement on war powers bill (Feb. 10, excerpts), 32-34; text of bill (Feb. 10), 34-35

Jerusalem, status of, 211-15

Johnson, U. Alexis, address on Europe, 137-48; on Japan, 368-75

K

Kansas City (Missouri), Nixon remarks (July 6), 41-53

Khmer Republic (Cambodia), Green address (Jan. 19, excerpt), 325-7; SEATO communiqué (Apr. 28, excerpt), 333; ANZUS communiqué (Oct. 2, excerpt), 336

Kissinger, Henry A., and Indo-Pakistan conflict 225, 227-8; negotiations on Vietnam, 300-10; mission to P.R.C.: announcement (Washington and Peking, Oct. 27), 353; statement (Nov. 30, excerpt), 354-6

Korea, Democratic People's Republic of, see Korean problem

Korean problem, Bennett UN statement (Sept. 25), 378

Korea, Republic of, discussion and documentation, 375-78; joint statement with US on troop reduction (Feb. 6), 376-77; Green statement (May 4, excerpt), 377-78

L

Laird, Melvin R., statement on defense (Mar. 9, excerpt), 12-19

Laos, discussion and documentation, 263-78; McCloskey statement on military operations (Feb. 8), 265-7; Nixon statement (Feb. 17, excerpt), 267-70; Sullivan statement on air operations and refugees (Apr. 22, excerpts), 271-76; State Department statement on foreign forces (Aug. 9), 276-78

Latin America, discussion and documentation, 433-93; the Organization of American States (O.A.S.), 447-56; Treaty for the Prohibition of Nuclear Weapons in Latin America (Treaty of Tlatelolco), 456-62; repercussions of US "New Economic Policy," 462-73; US relations with Cuba, 474-81; with Chile, 481-6; the Panama Canal question, 486-93; see also O.A.S., Inter-American and country entries

Luns, J.M.A.H., statement on NATO Council (Brussels, Oct. 5-6), 170-71

M

Mansfield amendments, proposed force reductions in Europe: Mansfield address (May 11, excerpts), 150-54; text (same), 150; Nixon statement (Key Biscayne, May 15), 154; amendment to Defense Appropriation bill: report (Nov. 18, excerpt), 172; Nixon letter to Stennis (Nov. 23), 172-73; amendment to Military Procurement Authorization Act on withdrawal from Indochina: background, 315-16; text (Nov. 17), 318-19; Nixon signature statement (same), 319-20.

Mansfield, Mike, address on proposed force reductions in Europe (May 11, excerpts), 150-54; see also Mansfield amendments

M.B.F.R., see Mutual and Balanced Force Reductions

McCloskey, Robert J., statement on Laos, 265-67

Measures to improve the USA-USSR direct communications link, US-Soviet agreement on (signed Washington, Sept. 30, 1971): background, 109-10; text (excerpt), 113-14

Measures to reduce risk of outbreak of nuclear war, US-Soviet agreement on (signed Washington, Sept. 30, 1971): background, 109-10; text (excerpt), 110-12

Meyer, Charles A., address on Latin America, 463-72; statement on Chile, 482-86

Middle East, discussion and documentation, 191-222; for details see Arab-Israeli conflict; Central Treaty Organization; country names

Military Procurement Authorization Act of 1971, see Congress (U.S.)

Military Selective Service Act of 1967, see Congress (U.S.)

Montreal Convention, see Aircraft Sabotage Convention

Mundt, John C., statement on Panama Canal, 487-93

Mutual and Balanced Force Reductions (M.B.F.R.), background, 148-49; Bray statement (May 17), 155; NATO communiqués (June 4, Dec. 10), 160-61, 176-77

N

Namibia (South West Africa), background discussion, 394-96; Newsom address, 387-88, 389-90; Stevenson statement to I.C.J. (excerpts), 396-403; I.C.J. advisory opinion (June 21, excerpt), 403-5; Bennett statement to UNSC (Oct. 20), 406-8; UNSC resolution (same), 408-12

Narcotics, Nixon report (Feb. 9, 1972, excerpt), 536-38

National Security Council (N.S.C.), Nixon report (Feb. 25, excerpt), 19-22

NATO, see North Atlantic Treaty Organization

"New Economic Policy," Nixon address (Aug. 15), 577-82; Nixon proclamation (same, excerpts), 583-84; Samuels statement to GATT (Aug. 24), 584-89; Nixon statement (Sept. 16), 590-92; see also economic and financial affairs

Newsom, David D., address on Africa, 386-96; statement on Southern Rhodesia, 416-23

New Zealand, see ANZUS Pact

Nixon Doctrine, Green address, 323-29

Nixon, Richard M., messages and communications to Congress: 2nd annual foreign policy report (Feb. 25), excerpts on National Security Council system, 19-22; on USSR, 60-65; on Africa, 380-85; radio-TV address, 3-11; message on seabed treaty (July 21), 71-72; on Okinawa reversion agreement (Sept. 21), 364-67; on UN (Sept. 8, 1972), 497-99; same (Feb. 9, 1972), 499-500, 532-43; on International Wheat Agreement (June 2), 613-14; on foreign aid (Apr. 21, excerpts), 617-19

Addresses and remarks: on 2nd annual foreign policy report (Feb. 25), 3-11; on US world problems (Kansas City, Mo., July 6), 41-53; on seabed treaty (Feb. 11), 70-71; on SALT agreement (May 20), 103-4; on SALT (Portland, Sept. 25, excerpt), 106-8; same (Nov. 12, excerpt), 108-9; on proposed USSR visit (Oct. 12, excerpts), 115-22; on Mansfield amendment (Key Biscayne, May 15), 154; on Laos (Feb. 15, excerpt), 267-70; on Vietnam (Apr. 7), 279-84; same (Apr. 16, excerpt), 285-87; same (Sept. 16, excerpt), 312-16; same (Nov. 12), 317-18; same (Nov. 17), 319-20; on relations with China (Mar. 4, excerpts), 339-40; same (Apr. 14), 341-42; same (Apr. 29, excerpts), 342-45; same (June 1, excerpt), 345-46; on proposed China visit (July 15), 384-89; same (Aug. 4, excerpt), 349-51; same (Sept. 16, excerpt), 351-53; on "New Economic Policy" (Aug. 15), 577-82; same

(Sept. 16, excerpt), 590-91; to IBRD/IMF (Sept. 29), 592-95; on Smithsonian agreement (Dec. 18), 609-10; on import surcharge (Dec. 20), 611-12; on foreign aid bill (Oct. 30), 629-30
Joint statements: with Pompidou (Azores, Dec. 14), 181; with Heath (Bermuda, Dec. 21), 182-83; with Brandt (Key Biscayne, Dec. 29), 183-85
Other communications and exchanges: to CCD (Feb. 23), 67-69; from Fulbright (Apr. 15), 80-83; to Stennis (Nov. 23), 172-73; on Tlatelolco treaty (June 11), 459-62; to Inter American Press Association (Chicago, Oct. 25), 471-72; on balance of payments (Aug. 15, excerpts), 583-84; same (Dec. 20), 610-11
North Atlantic Treaty Organization (NATO), Johnson address (Cincinnati, Feb. 19), 137-38; communiqué of Defense Planning Committee (Brussels, May 28), 156-58; Council meeting (Lisbon, June 3-4): communiqué, 158-62; Council meeting (Brussels, Oct. 5-6): Luns statement, 170-71; Council meeting (Brussels, Dec. 9-10): communiqué, 174-80; see also Mansfield amendments; Mutual and Balanced Force Reductions
North Korea, see Korea, Democratic People's Republic of
N.S.C., see National Security Council

O

O.A.S., see Organization of American States
Oceans, Nixon report (Feb. 9, 1972, excerpt), 533-36; see also Sea, law of the; Seabed
O.E.C.D., see Organization for Economic Cooperation and Development
Okinawa Reversion Agreement (signed June 17, 1971), text (excerpt), 358-64; Nixon message (Sept. 21), 364-67
Organization for Economic Cooperation and Development (O.E.C.D.), Council meeting (Paris, June 7-8): Rogers statement, 569-72; communiqué, 573-76
Organization of American States (O.A.S.), discussion and documentation, 434-56; Third Special Session of the General Assembly (Washington, Jan. 25-Feb. 2): background, 435-37; resolution on terrorism convention (Feb. 2), 437-41
First Regular Session of the General Assembly (San José, Costa Rica, Apr. 14-24): Rogers statement (Apr. 15), 447-56
Fourteenth Meeting of Consultation of Ministers of Foreign Affairs (Washington, Jan. 30-31): background, 441-43; Irwin statement on seizure by Ecuador of US fishing vessels (Jan. 30), 443-47; see also Inter-American entries
Outer space, see Space

P

Pacific, Green address, 323-29
  See also Asia; country and organizational entries
Pakistan, *see* Indo-Pakistan conflict
Panama, background, 486-7; Mundt statement on treaty negotiations, 487-93
Paris peace talks, *see* Vietnam conflict
Phillips, Christopher H., statement on Middle East, 218-20
Pompidou, Georges, meeting with Nixon (Azores, Dec. 13-14): joint statement, 181; Connally remarks (Dec. 14), 606-7
Population problem, Nixon report (Feb. 9, 1972), 539-40
Portugal, State Department announcement on agreements, 188-89; *see also* Portuguese African Territories
Portuguese African territories, Newsom address, 380-85 *passim*; 430-31
Presidential war powers, *see* War powers of the President
Provisional Revolutionary Government of the Republic of South Vietnam (P.R.G.), seven-point peace plan (Paris, July 1), 295-98; Bruce comment (same, July 8), 298-300; *see also* Vietnam conflict
Public Laws (U.S.), *see* Congress (U.S.)

Q

Quadripartite Agreement on Berlin, *see* Berlin Agreement

R

Rhodesia, *see* Southern Rhodesia (Zimbabwe)
Rogers, William P., statement on State Department reorganization (July 6), 22-25; on war powers (May 14, excerpts), 35-41; on foreign policy accomplishments and disapointments (Dec. 23, excerpts), 53-57; remarks on signing seabed treaty (Feb. 11), 69-70; statement on Geneva Protocol of 1925 (Mar. 5), 74-80; on India-Pakistan hostilities (Dec. 23, excerpt), 122-24; on Berlin agrement (Sept. 3), 164-65; on Middle East (Mar. 16, excerpts), 199-203; same (Rome, May 8, excerpts) 204-7; address on Middle East (Oct. 4, excerpts), 208-11; on South Asia (Oct. 4, excerpt), 226-27; statement on South Asia (Dec. 4), 228-29; same (Dec. 23, excerpt), 248-49; on Africa (Dec. 23, excerpt), 431-32; on Latin America (Apr. 15), 447-56; same (Dec. 23, excerpt), 472-73; on Chile (Oct. 13), 483-84; on China representation (Aug. 2), 504-6; address on same (Oct. 4, excerpt), 508-11; statement on same (Oct. 26, excerpt), 512-13; same (Dec. 1, excerpt), 514; statement to O.E.C.D. (Paris, June 7), 569-72; on foreign aid bill (Nov. 2, excerpt), 630-31; on generalized trade preferences (Bermuda, Dec. 20, excerpts), 631-33
Ryukyu Islands, *see* Okinawa Reversion Agreement

S

SALT, *see* Strategic Arms Limitation Talks

Samuels, Nathaniel, statement to GATT, 584-89

San José, meeting of the O.A.S. General Assembly (San José, Costa Rica, Apr. 14-24, 1971), *see* Organization of American States

Schaufele, William E., Jr. statement on Southern Rhodesia, 427-28

Seabed Arms Control Treaty (Treaty on the Prohibition of the Emplacement of Nuclear Weapons and other Weapons of Mass Destruction on the Seabed and the Ocean Floor and in the Subsoil Thereof, signed Washington Feb. 11, 1971): Rogers remarks, 69-70; Nixon remarks, 70-71; Nixon message (July 21), 71-72

Sea, law of the, Nixon report (Feb. 9, 1972, excerpt), 533-36; draft articles on the territorial sea, straits and fisheries (Aug. 3), 543-48; *see also* Seabed Arms Control Treaty

SEATO, *see* South-East Asia Treaty Organization

Senate, *see* Congress (U.S.)

Sisco, Joseph J., statement on Middle East, 207-8

Smithsonian Agreement, Connally statement (Dec. 14), 606-7; "Group of Ten" meeting (Smithsonian Institution, Dec. 17-18): communiqué (Dec. 18), 607-9; Nixon remarks (same), 609-10

South Africa, Republic of, 380-85 *passim*; 431-32; *see also* Namibia

Southeast Asia, Nixon report (Apr. 7), 279-84; *see also* Indochina; SEATO; Vietnam conflict; country and organizational entries

South-East Asia Treaty Organization (SEATO), Council meeting (London, Apr. 27-28): communiqué, 330-35

Southern Rhodesia (Zimbabwe), background, 412-16; Newsom statement (July 7), 416-23; Congressional action on chrome imports (Byrd amendment): conference report (Nov. 5, excerpt), 424-26; text of Byrd amendment (approved Nov. 17, excerpt), 426-27; Schaufele statement to UNGA (Nov. 11), 427-28; UNGA resolution (Nov. 16), 428-29

South Vietnam, Provisional Revolutionary Government of, *see* Provisional Revolutionary Government of the Republic of South Vietnam

South West Africa, *see* Namibia

Space, Nixon report (Feb. 9, 1972, excerpt), 542-43; *see also* Intelsat Agreement; Space Liability Convention

Space Liability Convention (Convention on International Liability for Damage Caused by Space Objects, approved Nov. 29, 1971), text, 555-64

Spiers, Ronald I., statement on Indian Ocean, 250-57

State Department (U.S.), Rogers announcement on reorganization, 22-25; announcement on Portugal, 188-89; statement on Laos, 276-78; announcement on Intelsat, 564-65

Stennis, John C., letter from Nixon (Nov. 23), 172-73

Stevenson, John R., statement on Namibia (excerpts), 396-403
Strategic Arms Limitation Talks (SALT), *see* Disarmament
Suez Canal, *see* Arab-Israeli conflict
Sullivan, William H., statement on Laos (excerpts), 271-76

T

Taiwan, *see* China, Republic of
Terrorism, O.A.S. Convention on (Convention to Prevent and Punish
Acts of Terrorism Taking the Form of Crimes Against Persons and
Related Extortion That Are of International Significance, approved
Feb. 2, 1971), background, 435-37; text, 437-41
Thailand, 333
Thant, U, *see* U.N. Secretary-General
Tlatelolco Treaty (Treaty for the Prohibition of Nuclear Weapons in
Latin America, Feb. 14, 1967), background, 456-59; Nixon procla-
mation on ratification of Additional Protocol II (June 11), 459-62
Treaty for the Prohibition of Nuclear Weapons in Latin America, *see*
Tlatelolco Treaty
Treaty of Tlatelolco (Feb. 14, 1967), background, 456-59; Nixon pro-
clamation on ratification of Additional Protocol II, 459-62
Treaty on the Prohibition of the Emplacement of Nuclear Weapons and
Other Weapons of Mass Destruction on the Seabed and the Ocean
Floor and in the Subsoil Thereof (signed Washington Feb. 11, 1971),
see Seabed Arms Control Treaty

U

Union of Soviet Socialist Republics (U.S.S.R.), Nixon foreign policy
report (Feb. 25, excerpt), 60-65; Nixon statement on proposed visit
(Oct. 12, excerpts), 115-22; Davies statement on status of Jews, 125-
33; attack on mission to UN, 132, 523; *see also* Berlin; Disarmament;
East-West relations
United Arab Republic, *see* Arab-Israeli conflict
United Kingdom, Nixon-Heath joint statement (Hamilton, Bermuda,
Dec. 21), 182-83
United Nations and International Cooperation, discussion and documentation, 495-565; Africa issues in UN (Newsom address, Sept. 21),
386-96; review of UN affairs in 1971, 495-96; Nixon message on US
participation (Sept. 8, 1972), 496-99; Nixon comment on decline in
congressional support (Feb. 9, 1972, excerpt), 499-500; representa-
tion of China in UN, 500-14; Rogers comment on US support for UN
(Dec. 1), 514-15; UN organization and finances, 515-31; background
on financial problems, 515-17; Derwinski statement on UN budget
(Dec. 22), 517-22; security of missions to UN, 522-26; enlargement

of Economic and Social Council (ECOSOC), 526-28; appointment of new Secretary-General, 529-31; "new dimensions of diplomacy," 531-43; Nixon third annual report (Feb. 9, 1972, excerpt), 532-43; *see also* Sea, law of; Aircraft Sabotage Convention; Space

U.N. Committee on the Peaceful Uses of the Sea-bed and the Ocean Floor Beyond the Limits of National Jurisdiction, text of US draft articles (Geneva, Aug. 3), 543-48

UNDP, *see* U.N. Development Program

U.N. Development Program (U.N.D.P.), Nixon report (Feb. 9, 1972, excerpt), 499-500

U.N. Economic and Social Council, UNGA resolution on enlargement, 526-28

UNGA, *see* U.N. General Assembly

U.N. General Assembly (26th session, Sept. 21-Dec. 22, 1971), Rogers address (Oct. 4), 208-11, 226-27, 508-12

Resolutions and statements: on bacteriological weapons, 84-95; on disarmament, 96-101; on Middle East, 208-11, 216-20; on South Asia, 226-27, 236-39; on Indian Ocean, 257-59; on Korea, 378; on Southern Rhodesia, 427-29; on China representation, 506-12, 513-14; on budget, 517-22; on security of missions, 522-26; on ECOSOC enlargement, 526-28; on new Secretary-General, 530-31

Resolutions by number:

2758 (XXVI), Oct. 25, on China representation, 512

2765 (XXVI), Nov. 16, on Southern Rhodesia, 428-29

2793 (XXVI), Dec. 7, on South Asia, 237-39

2799 (XXVI), Dec. 13, on Middle East, 220-22

2819 (XXVI), Dec. 15, on security of missions 524-26

2826 (XXVI), Dec. 16, on bacteriological weapons, 88-90

2832 (XXVI), Dec. 16, on Indian Ocean, 257-59

2847 (XXVI), Dec. 20, on ECOSOC enlargement, 527-28

2903 (XXVI), Dec. 22, on appointment of new Secretary-General, 530

UNSC, *see* U.N. Security Council

U.N. Secretary-General, report on Jarring mission (Feb. 1), 194-95; same (Mar. 5), 195-98; UNSC resolution recommending Waldheim (Dec. 21), 529; UNGA resolution appointing Waldheim (Dec. 22), 530; Bush statement (Dec. 22), 530-31

U.N. Security Council (UNSC), statements and resolutions, other communications: on Jarring mission, 194-98; on status of Jerusalem, 212-15; on South Asia, 228-35; on Namibia, 406-12; recommending new Secretary-General, 529

Resolutions by number:

298 (1971), Sept. 25, on status of Jerusalem, 212-13

301 (1971), Oct. 20, on Namibia, 408-12

303 (1971), Dec. 6, on South Asia, 235

306 (1971), Dec. 21, recommending new Secretary-General, 529

307 (1971), Dec. 21, on observance of cease-fire in South Asia, 246-47

United States, discussion and documentation, 1-57; Nixon address on 2nd annual foreign affairs report (Feb. 25), 3-11; Laird statement on national security policy (Mar. 9, excerpt), 12-19; Nixon report on National Security Council system (Feb. 25, excerpt), 19-22; Rogers announcement on State Department reorganization (July 6), 22-25; establishment of Council on International Economic Policy (Jan. 19), 25-26; discussions of presidential war powers, 26-41; Nixon background briefing on America's world position (Kansas City, July 6), 41-53; Rogers comments on 1971 accomplishments and disappointments (Dec. 23), 53-57; "New Economic Policy" (Aug. 15), 577-82; repercussions on Latin America, 462-73; foreign aid program, 615-31; and generalized trade preferences, 631-33; *see also* appropriate topical, organizational and geographic entries

V

Vietnam conflict, discussion and documentation 261-320; Nixon foreign policy report (Feb. 25, excerpt), 4-5; Nixon remarks (Kansas City, Mo., excerpt), 42-43; Rogers remarks (Dec. 23, excerpts), 54, 55; Nixon address (Apr. 7), 279-84; Nixon statement (Apr. 16, excerpt), 285-87; conference of troop-contributing nations (Apr. 23), 287-92; "Vietcong" peace proposal (Paris, July 1), 295-98; Bruce comment (Paris, July 8), 298-300; North Vietnamese proposal (June 26), 304-6; US note (Oct. 11), 306; US proposal (same), 307-9; North Vietnamese note (Oct. 25), 309; US note (Nov. 3), 309; North Vietnamese note (Nov. 17), 309-10; US note (Nov. 19), 310; policy on troop withdrawals: P.L. 92-129 (Sept. 28, excerpt), 316-17; Nixon statement (Nov. 12), 317-18; P.L. 92-156 on termination of hostilities (Nov. 17), 318-19; Nixon signature statement (Nov. 17), 319-20; SEATO communiqué (Apr. 28), 330-31; ANZUS communiqué (Oct. 2), 336-37

Vietnam, Democratic Republic of, nine-point peace proposal (June 26), 304-6; exchange of notes with US (Oct. 25-Nov. 19), 309-11

Vietnam, Republic of, operations in Laos, 263-78; McCloskey statement (Feb. 8), 265-67; political developments, 311-12; Nixon statement on elections (Sept. 16, excerpt), 312-15

W

Waldheim, Kurt, *see* U.N. Secretary-General

War powers of the President, discussion, 26-27; Zablocki resolution: report (July 27, excerpt), 27-30; text (Aug. 2), 30-31; Javits bill:

Javits statement (Feb. 10, excerpts), 32-34; text (same), 34-35; Rogers statement (May 14, excerpts), 35-41

Western Hemisphere, *see* Latin America

White House, announcement on Council on International Economic Policy, 25-26; on US-USSR arms agreements, 109-10

Z

Zablocki, Clement, *see* Zablocki resolution

Zablocki resolution, report on presidential war powers (July 27, excerpt), 27-30; text (Aug. 2), 30-31

Ziegler, Ronald L., statement on China (June 10), 346-47; on proposed Nixon visit to China (Nov. 30, excerpt), 353-54; on foreign aid bill (Oct. 30), 629-30

Zimbabwe, *see* Southern Rhodesia